THE LECTIONARY COMMENTARY

THE LECTIONARY COMMENTARY

Edited by

Roger E. Van Harn

Consulting Editors

Richard Burridge
Thomas Gillespie
Colin Gunton
Robert Jenson
James F. Kay
Hughes Oliphant Old
Fleming Rutledge
Marguerite Shuster

THE LECTIONARY COMMENTARY

Theological Exegesis for Sunday's Texts

THE THIRD READINGS

The Gospels

Edited by

Roger E. Van Harn

WILLIAM B. EERDMANS PUBLISHING COMPANY
GRAND RAPIDS, MICHIGAN / CAMBRIDGE, U.K.

CONTINUUM
LONDON · NEW YORK

Published 2001 in the United States of America by
Wm. B. Eerdmans Publishing Co.
255 Jefferson Ave. S.E., Grand Rapids, Michigan 49503 /
P.O. Box 163, Cambridge CB3 9PU U.K.
www.eerdmans.com
and in Great Britain by
Continuum
The Tower Building, 11 York Road,
London SE1 7NX
www.continuumbooks.com

Printed in the United States of America

06 05 04 03 02 01   7 6 5 4 3 2 1

Library of Congress Cataloging-in-Publication Data

The lectionary commentary: theological exegesis for Sunday's texts /
edited by Roger Van Harn.
p.   cm.
Contents: v. 1. The Old Testament and Acts (the first readings) —
v. 2. Acts and the Epistles (the second readings) —
v. 3. The Gospels (the third readings).
ISBN 0-8028-4751-X (v. 1: cloth: alk. paper);
ISBN 0-8028-4752-8 (v. 2: cloth: alk. paper);
ISBN 0-8028-4753-6 (v. 3: cloth: alk. paper)
1. Bible — Homiletical use. 2. Bible — Criticism, interpretation, etc.
3. Common lectionary (1992) 4. Lectionary preaching.
I. Van Harn, Roger, 1932- II. Common lectionary (1992)

BS534.5.L43 2001
251'.6 — dc21

2001040531

British Library Cataloguing-in-Publication Data

A catalogue for this book is available from the British Library.

ISBN 0-8264-5681-2 (Vol. 1)   ISBN 0-8264-5751-7 (Vol. 2)
ISBN 0-8264-5752-5 (Vol. 3)   ISBN 0-8264-5867-X (Set of 3)

Contents

CONTENTS

CONTENTS

CONTENTS

CONTENTS

CONTENTS

Preface

Preaching pastors, ministers, and priests know how rapidly Sundays come and go in the pressures of parish life. Protecting time for study and theological reflection is an art not easily mastered once and for all. Flyby Sundays tend to collide with that steady resolve harbored since theological college and seminary to ground preaching in careful exegesis and extensive dialogue with biblical texts. The result is that sermon preparation suffers.

These volumes will not slow the pace of the weekly calendar, but they will provide tastes of theological exegesis for Sunday's texts that will stimulate reflection. These are not books of sermons. They leave homiletical work to the preachers, who are called to contextualize the gospel from biblical texts. Exegetes who have contributed to these volumes have come to name their work affectionately as exegetical "jump starts" for preaching. As such, they provide a place to stand in the text for starting a sermon.

The lections are all derived from the Revised Common Lectionary, Years A, B, and C. All the Sundays of the three-year cycle are included, as well as the texts for the Nativity of the Lord (Christmas Day), the Epiphany of the Lord, and the Ascension of the Lord. The pericope for each entry is identified in bold type in the heading and is accompanied by a listing of the other lections for the day. Although the responsorial psalm is not exegeted, it is listed following the first lesson and may be read or sung for liturgical purposes or used as a preaching resource. The applicable day(s) for each lection is indicated with each heading. Worded titles such as "Water into Wine," "Blind from Birth," or "The Prodigal Son" have been intentionally omitted. Such identifications may get ahead of the exegesis and may block the preacher's dialogue with and exploration of the text. When these happen, the preacher is prevented from seeing and hearing fresh possibilities for the sermon.

With seventy-eight exegetes representing a variety of traditions contributing to these volumes, the reader can expect a wide variety of styles and insights. No attempt has been made on the part of the editors to homogenize these styles. Exegetes have been asked to answer this question concerning their assignments: What does the preacher need to know about this lesson in order to preach a faithful sermon from it? The resulting literary and theological variety, therefore, is similar to the variety in the biblical genres themselves. The resulting unity derives from the story of what God has done for the salvation of the world in the history of Israel and in the person of Jesus Christ. Faithful preaching is not about Bible texts; rather, it proclaims the good news of God to which the texts witness.

Each exegetical essay includes some combination of three elements: engagement with the biblical text, theological reflection, and awareness of the context in which the sermon will be spoken and heard. While the reader will find these elements present in differing degrees, they suggest and stimulate the concerns the preacher brings to sermon preparation. The preacher will also bring the specific congregational context into dialogue with the text in order to discover and express the pastoral and evangelical purposes of the gospel. Wherever the exegesis illumines events of our history, features of our culture, or characteristics of the church that call for celebration or judgment, these may be indicated by the exegete or discovered by the preacher for possible inclusion in the sermon.

The three volumes are organized according to the first, second, and Gospel lections for each day. The lections are arranged in their canonical order in each volume. Each volume appends an essay for preaching: "Preaching as Worship," by Hughes Oliphant Old (vol. 1); "Preaching from the Letters," by Colin Gunton (vol. 2); and "Augustinian Preaching and the Nurture of Christians," by C. Clifton Black (vol. 3). Two indexes provide a ready reference for the lections of the three-year cycle and the contributors to the three volumes.

Through the long months of preparation, the publishers are indebted to the consultants whose guidance gave shape and direction to the project: Richard Burridge, Thomas Gillespie, Colin Gunton, Robert Jenson, James F. Kay, Hughes Oliphant Old, Fleming Rutledge, and Marguerite Shuster. Their wisdom contributed to whatever value these volumes offer; lapses of good judgment and faithful insight are solely the responsibility of the editor.

Preachers who follow the Revised Common Lectionary will find these volumes useful. The organization and content will also serve other preaching patterns and possibilities such as a modified *lectio continua* or a thematically arranged series. However they are used, they are hereby offered as an aid to those commissioned to preach the gospel from biblical texts for the congregations they serve.

Roger E. Van Harn,
Editor

Fourth Sunday of Advent, Year A

First Lesson: Isaiah 7:10-16
(Psalm 80:1-7, 17-19)
Second Lesson: Romans 1:1-7
Gospel Lesson: Matthew 1:18-25

Although Luke and John start elsewhere, Matthew's genealogy introduces Jesus' background by affirming that he is an heir to and the climax of Israel's history. Whereas other genealogies of the period normally emphasized the purity of one's Jewish or priestly ancestry, Matthew's genealogy specifically highlights the mixed nature of Jesus' ancestry (1:3, 5-6), preparing the way for his theme of reaching even the Gentiles with God's good news (e.g., 2:1; 28:19). Having established Jesus' origin in Israel's history, Matthew now introduces his background from a different angle: in the story of Jesus' godly stepfather, he introduces the miraculous and moral character of Jesus' birth.

Ancient writers liked to emphasize the special circumstances of a hero's birth when possible, and it is not surprising that the two Gospels which recount Jesus' birth (Matthew and Luke) would do so. Of course, ancient stories about gods seducing and raping women are quite different from the biblical story of a virgin birth; although more dramatic, it is closer in kind to the miraculous births of the Hebrew Bible, in which God enabled Sarah, Rebekah, and Rachel to conceive after they had proved unable to do so. But few ancient Jewish hearers would have questioned the power of Israel's God to accomplish such a feat.

Unlike ancient hearers, many modern hearers, especially those shaped by the radical Enlightenment, have problems believing in a virgin birth. For those of us who believe, however, that God began the universe and is responsible for our existence, a virgin birth is hardly a philosophical problem. From a historical standpoint, the idea is not Matthew's invention; his account is independent of Luke's, indicating that both drew on earlier information. Luke in fact claims to have investigated; he probably interviewed eyewitnesses (Luke 1:1-4), and probably one of the close relatives of Jesus and Mary (Acts 21:18).

While Christians need not doubt the virgin birth, later debates about its nature may miss Matthew's primary point. Although Matthew emphasizes the supernatural character of our Lord's birth, he is interested in teaching ethics (28:20) and here focuses on several moral lessons which later Gospel teachings will reinforce. Matthew provides us lessons about the importance of Scripture, about commitment, mercy, obedience, and self-control.

Matthew in fact gives only one reason for the virgin birth: that Scripture might be fulfilled (1:22). From this we learn that Matthew valued Scripture very highly, a point reinforced repeatedly in his Gospel (e.g., 2:15, 17, 23; 5:17-20); following Matthew's example, we can also stress the importance of trusting Scripture. Exactly how Matthew is interpreting the text he quotes from Isaiah is more complicated. In Isaiah's immediate context the son that would be born would still be a child when the two kings then challenging Judah's king would falter, ultimately leading to their destruction within a generation (Isa. 7:1-25, esp. 7:8-16); this could be Isaiah's own son, whose name signaled the imminent end of Judah's enemies (Isa. 8:3-4). But Matthew was more biblically literate than some of his modern critics recognize; indeed, he presupposes that his hearers will think of a broader context of surrounding chapters. Recognizing that Isaiah's children pointed beyond themselves to God's actions in history (Isa. 8:18), Matthew could emphasize the consistent patterns of God's acts and look to Isaiah's mention of a child who really would be "God with us" sitting on David's throne (Isa. 9:6-7). This context remains fresh in Matthew's mind as his Gospel proceeds (see Matt. 4:15-16, using Isa. 9:1-2).

This narrative not only reinforces Matthew's consistent emphasis on the importance of Scripture but also teaches us, as narratives often do, through the examples of characters. Matthew teaches through the example of Joseph (we hear Mary's voice more in Luke), who is explicitly called a "righteous," hence positive, model (1:19). What can we learn from the behavior of the couple God chose to raise Jesus? This passage provides lessons about commitment, compassion, consecration, and control.

First, we learn something about the nature of marital commitment. In ancient Judaism betrothals (unlike our modern engagements) were as binding as marriage; an economic transaction had united the couple. Even though they had not yet consummated the marriage (indeed, traditional Galilean couples might not even have had time alone together), their betrothal could be ended only by divorce or by the death of one party. Unfaithfulness, however, was universally regarded as grounds for divorce, and Jewish law, like Roman law and all ancient Mediterranean custom, would have expected Joseph to divorce Mary.

That Joseph is about to divorce Mary, yet is called a "righteous" man, challenges some of our assumptions today. Whereas later in this Gospel Jesus condemns unfaithfulness to one's marriage covenant by divorce, he does make an exception for a party wronged by a spouse's unfaithfulness

2

(5:32; 19:9). There are some churches today, however, who condemn anyone who has experienced divorce, never asking the circumstances, which sometimes include the spouse's continued unfaithfulness, abandonment, or abuse; sometimes one is divorced against one's will. Indeed, many churches will treat adultery more lightly than divorce; repentance is often accepted as more efficacious for the former. Clearly Matthew demands that we forgive our spouse and do our very best to make our marriage strong. But he also recognizes that in some very exceptional circumstances it is possible for a person to divorce yet be a "righteous" person (1:19). Adultery, of which Joseph wrongly supposes Mary guilty, was a terrible breach of commitment to marriage. (Although Joseph's culture was harder on women, biblical stories like Genesis 38–39, which contrasts an earlier Joseph's behavior with Judah's, show that *God* expects both genders to be faithful.)

Second, Joseph illustrates compassion. Matthew's primary point, in fact, is not that Joseph was righteous "even though" he was preparing to divorce Mary; rather, Joseph was righteous "because" he was going to divorce her *privately,* to reduce her shame (1:19). In his society, such behavior would have cost Joseph something significant. If he had paid a bride-price, it may have represented several years of savings; by taking her to court, he could guarantee the return of the full bride-price and also impound any dowry her father might have given her for the marriage. More importantly, he could make public his repudiation of her alleged misdeed, making it clear that he was not the child's father. In his culture her act would shame him in any case, but by publicly shaming her his own shame would be reduced.

Yet Joseph was more concerned to guard what remained of Mary's honor than to increase his own. By granting her a certificate of divorce in front of two witnesses instead of in a court, he could reduce the attention drawn to her pregnancy — though in small towns like Nazareth or even Bethlehem, word would travel quickly. Joseph probably had had little or no time alone with Mary; further, many young men of his day would have chosen to avenge their honor. But Matthew tells us that righteousness includes mercy (1:19; cf. 9:13; 12:7). A few churches even today expose unwed mothers and others to shame to punish sin; Joseph would not have done so because he was righteous.

Third, Joseph models consecration. Although most ancient Mediterranean peoples did affirm that dreams often revealed divine purposes, Joseph's obedience to the angel's appearance in his dream (1:20) is noteworthy. In view of small-town gossip and the critical centrality of values like honor and shame in his culture, Joseph was making a big commitment by embracing Mary; people would assume that Joseph himself had gotten

3

Mary pregnant before the wedding. This offense would not be viewed as severely as adultery, but it would still leave them both as objects of gossip for years to come. Luke tells us that Mary had already valued God's will more highly than her own honor (Luke 1:38); Matthew tells us that Joseph embraced shame for the same reason (Matt. 1:24).

Fourth, Joseph and Mary model control. If Joseph was the average age for Jewish grooms, he may have been eighteen to twenty, Mary likely being a few years younger; whatever their ages, conservative Jewish culture mistrusted a man and woman left alone together for even an hour or two. As a young married couple, Joseph and Mary likely shared the same small bed in a small space; newlyweds often roomed in a makeshift chamber on top of the home of the groom's parents. Yet in contrast to the expectations of their culture or ours, they were able to restrain themselves at least until Mary brought forth her son (1:25). Their self-control challenges the claims of many people today that sexual temptation is too great to resist.

Yet they were married; why did they refrain? Possibly to fulfill the language of the verse quoted in 1:23: not only would a virgin conceive, but a virgin would bear. This self-control would have cost them honor, however. It meant that Joseph and Mary did not have intercourse on their wedding night, hence gave up the opportunity to prove, as virgins often did on their wedding nights, that Mary was, after all, a virgin. They were more concerned with God's honor than with the opinions of their society.

Sometimes when I have preached from this text about betrayal, commitment, intimacy, and self-control, I have found that many of my hearers experience a deep sense of remorse for past or current sexual sins. That is why I have always been happy to point them, at the end, to another character in this narrative: Jesus, who came to save his people from their sins (1:21). He befriended sinners and put up with faltering disciples elsewhere in this Gospel; he came to us the way we were to make something better of us. The examples of righteous behavior are not pure moralism; they are examples of what we can be as we follow the God who is with us (1:23), the real hero of Matthew's Gospel who promises to be with us today as well (18:20; 28:20).

Craig S. Keener

Epiphany of the Lord, Years A, B, C

First Lesson: Isaiah 60:1-6
(Psalm 72:1-7, 10-14)
Second Lesson: Ephesians 3:1-12
Gospel Lesson: Matthew 2:1-12

In common parlance, if someone says she has just had an "epiphany," what she means is a new insight or revelation that came from out of a clear blue sky. Technically, of course, "epiphany" means "appearing" or "appearance," which is how it is used in the New Testament in terms of Christ's "appearing" in judgment at the end of history (indeed, this usage of the Greek word is found primarily in the Pastoral Epistles). The Savior who has been invisible since his ascension into heaven will one day be made manifest once again. In terms of the liturgical year, Epiphany in the Western Church tradition refers to the appearance of the star in the east, leading the Magi to the cradle of the Christ child.

But for Matthew's original readers/hearers, the story of Matthew 2 must surely have been something of an epiphany in the sense of a shocking revelation that came from out of nowhere. Modern churchgoers largely miss the scandal of this text. Because of the Magi's routine (and largely erroneous) inclusion in Christmas pageants next to the shepherds and angels, we have come to expect and even welcome the presence of these Magi, or wise men, or three kings of the Orient. They add a dash of color to the spectacle with their royal blue garments embroidered with gold foil. They provide a whiff of the exotic through their Persian ways as hints of spices fill the air. Above all, perhaps, they sound just the right note of royalty for the child-king in the manger.

No such thoughts were intended by Matthew, however, and his original reading audience sensed this acutely. The Magi were almost certainly not royalty — at best they may have been associated with the royal courts of Persia, though even that much is uncertain. Further, we don't really know how many there were. The long tradition of "three wise men" is mostly based on the slender piece of evidence that they gave young Jesus three gifts. (Though that proves virtually nothing. If you tell me you received a bathrobe, a watch, and a bottle of cologne for Christmas, I will not necessarily infer that you received these items from three different people.) The notion of three kings was furthered in the eighth century when Saint Bede the Venerable strangely supplied the names of Melchior, Gaspar, and Baltasar for the

Magi. Some centuries after this, Empress Helena made her own contribution to Magi mythology by claiming to have had a vision which led her to the burial site of these three kings. She had the remains exhumed, and the ostensible skulls of the three kings remain on display in Cologne, Germany.

It's all fantasy, of course, on a par with Steven Spielberg's fast-and-loose fiddling with the legend of the Holy Grail or the ark of the covenant in the Indiana Jones films. The biblical record is the only evidence which interpreters should take into account, and this evidence is rather slim. What can be said with some certainty is that these *magoi* were the ancient equivalent of "magicians" — they were astrologers and stargazers who tried to get the hang of present and future events by what was in the stars. These were the Jeane Dixons of old Persia, writing the daily horoscopes for the *Baghdad Gazette* based on the movements of the heavens. The Magi were what many today would call quacks and maybe even charlatans. The Old Testament actually provides even choicer language for such persons: the Bible condemns Magi types as idolatrous deceivers to be avoided by godly folk. Indeed, a Jewish rabbi wrote not long before the birth of Jesus: "He who learns from a magi is worthy of death."

Oddly, however, in Matthew's Gospel these Magi managed to get at least one thing right: something cosmic had happened in Bethlehem of Judea. By their lights they somehow correctly sensed from the heavens that something important had happened on the earth. They were so sure of this, in fact, that they undertook a long and dangerous journey to investigate the matter. Thus Matthew presents them at the side of the Messiah.

Unlike modern congregations observing the Magi next to Christ in a Christmas pageant, few in Matthew's largely Jewish reading audience would have welcomed these Magi. For one thing they were the same bumblers who tipped off Herod, leading to the slaughter of the innocents. Though modern scholarship has suggested the actual number of children killed in Herod's pogrom may have been as small as twenty or thirty, the memory of such a mini-holocaust surely lingered. Had the Magi not queried Herod, that bloody episode may have been prevented. Any fool who had even the slightest inkling of Herod's raging paranoia would know that coming to him with news of a new king in the area was like tossing a match into a gas can.

But it's not primarily that mistake that would have appalled most of the original readers of Matthew 2. Instead it would very simply have been the scandal of having astrologers from a foreign land mingling so freely with the one Matthew claims to be God's Christ. How could the likes of these magicians, condemned by Scripture, be a welcome presence next to the Messiah?

In reality, however, Matthew has been presenting similar scandals from the very outset of his Gospel. He is intent on opening up the circle of salvation to include all people and all nations in fulfillment of what God had promised to Abraham millennia before ("You will be a blessing to all nations").

That's why in his opening genealogy Matthew broke with genealogical convention by including not only four women, but four women each of whom had something foreign or scandalous attached to her. Tamar played prostitute in order to get impregnated by her father-in-law, Judah. Rahab *was* a prostitute, and from Jericho at that. Ruth brings Moab into the picture, and though Bathsheba is not specifically named in Matthew 1, Matthew actually finds a way to twist the knife more painfully by referring to Solomon's mother as "Uriah's wife" (and everyone remembers what David did to Uriah!).

Apparently, Matthew is trying to strike a universal tone in his Gospel. He wants not just men but women included; not just Israelites but people from all nations; not just those whose lives conform to the standard shape of orthodoxy but even Magi who could not have seemed less likely candidates for God's love. Matthew 2, of course, does not vindicate astrology or deny the Bible's earlier warnings about diviners and quacks such as these Magi. What Matthew may be trying to convey, however, is the reach of grace. Matthew is giving a Gospel sneak preview: the Christ child who attracted these odd Magi to his cradle will later have the same magnetic effect on Samaritan adulterers, immoral prostitutes, greasy tax collectors on the take, despised Roman soldiers, and ostracized lepers.

Matthew 2 truly is an epiphany for any and all who tend to think that salvation is a members-only club the adherents of which are easily recognizable to those in the know. As such, this Epiphany passage, which launches us into that time of the church year when we follow the prepassion ministry of Jesus, is at once the shoe that fits and the shoe that pinches. The Epiphany question brought out in bold relief by Matthew 2 is: Who are today's Magi? What people or types of people make us uncomfortable or upset when they try to come to the Christ?

Coming as it always does near the head of a new year, Epiphany is a good chance for congregations to ponder what kind of church they want to be in the new year and beyond. How wide open is the front door? How wide open are the hearts of the people already inside? What will outsiders sense if they themselves come inside?

During the Advent and the Christmas season it is easy to look at manger scenes and crèches of all kinds and find them lovely and maybe even moving. It is so easy to view that hodgepodge of shepherds, Magi, animals, new parents, angels, and the infant in the middle of it all and not bat an eye at the spectacle of all those wildly diverse people and creatures dwelling under one little roof. But then the season ends, and by the time Epiphany rolls around the manger scenes have been packed away for another year. Epiphany, however, returns us to the reality of the church as a place likewise filled with a motley hodgepodge of all kinds of different people, all standing together around the Christ under one roof, and all called together by the one singular grace of God. How challenging it is, however, to view the real church with its real mishmash of divergent people with the same unalloyed joy we so often capture during Christmas. Perhaps sustaining that joy of grace is one of Epiphany's challenges.

Scott Hoezee

First Sunday after Christmas, Year A

First Lesson: Isaiah 63:7-9
(Psalm 148)
Second Lesson: Hebrews 2:10-18
Gospel Lesson: Matthew 2:13-23

The lection is comprised of three episodes, each delineated by a closing reference to the Old Testament. Matthew sets forth a Jesus who is grounded in the experience of Israel in terms of parallels to the lives of great figures of the past, and of connections to important experiences and geographic locations in Israelite history. The figures of Joseph and Herod are at the center of the narrative, and offer a significant contrast between the godly and ungodly response to the presence of God. The horrifying slaughter of the innocent male infants of Bethlehem puts an end to overly sentimental understandings of Jesus' birth, disconnected from the dire realities of the world into which he was born and in which the reader also dwells.

The departure of the Magi by a road other than that which leads back to Herod is followed by an angelic appearance in Joseph's dream (cf. 1:20; 2:19;

2:22). Like his namesake of long before (Gen. 37–50), Joseph is an astute listener to dreams and also on the verge of a sojourn in Egypt. His righteousness consists not only of a moral commitment to virtue, but even more in his responsiveness to the leading of God (Thomas G. Long, *Matthew* [Louisville: Westminster John Knox, 1997], p. 20). The angel informs Joseph that Herod (no longer King Herod in the text since the true King of the Jews has now been born and worshiped by the Magi) will soon seek the baby's life. That very night Joseph gathers his threatened family and flees Bethlehem, the city of David by which Jesus' connection to Israel's great king is established, to go to Egypt. Like the patriarchs Abraham and Jacob and indeed the whole people Israel, Jesus leaves the Promised Land to dwell in Egypt for a time. The famine of justice drives him there. The formula "this was to fulfill what was spoken through the prophet" is a favorite of Matthew, and here links the initial episode specifically to Hosea 11:1 and more generally to the central formative event of the Old Testament, the exodus.

The Magi's departure triggers not only the flight of the holy family; it also puts Herod into a murderous rage. Like Pharaoh before him, and many a tyrant even unto contemporary history, Herod slaughters innocent children in an attempt not only to kill Jesus but also to intimidate any of the local population who might have heard of the birth and whose messianic hopes might thereby have been aroused. Jesus is thus linked to Moses as the object of deadly monarchial insecurity. A man like Herod, who killed some of his own sons, would not hesitate at all to kill the sons of others. Matthew concludes this episode with a reference to Jeremiah 31:15, but does so with a significant modification of his fulfillment formula. The usual "this was to fulfill" becomes here "then was fulfilled," lest it appear God is responsible for the massacre (Long, p. 22). The Jeremiah text refers to Rachel's weeping in Ramah as her children's children head into exile. She is a beloved mother of Israel who weeps for her children, in all times and places, when they suffer at the hands of the cruel and violent. Jesus is part of the community for whom Rachel forever weeps.

With little fanfare Herod dies. Again an angel appears and tells Joseph it is time to return to Israel since "those who were seeking the child's life are dead" (cf. similar words to Moses in Exod. 4:19). Joseph obeys, but upon learning Herod's son Archelaus is in power, decides not to live in Judea. Yet again he is warned of the danger in a dream, and goes to an obscure village named Nazareth to live and raise Jesus. And again the fulfillment formula is used to end the episode, yet here problematically because the phrase "He will be called a Nazorean" does not appear in the Old Testament. Scholarly consensus suggests a pun on the word "Nazareth." A Nazirite was a person set apart to be holy (see Num. 6 for laws concerning such, and the story of Samson in Judg. 13, particularly vv. 5 and 7, and 16:17). Nazareth may also be a subtle allusion to the Hebrew word *neṣer*, meaning branch, used as a reference to the Messiah in Isaiah 11:1. A third option is the use of the Hebrew verb *naṣar*, meaning "kept," as in Isaiah 42:6 and 49:6. Matthew's intention may well be to emphasize God's power to raise up the Anointed One from obscurity (cf. Nazareth's reputation in John 1:46 and 7:41). In any event, the reader now knows how Jesus, born in Bethlehem, came to be raised in Nazareth (Frederick Dale Bruner, *The Christbook: A Historical/Theological Commentary* [Waco, Tex.: Word, 1987], p. 61).

In only ten verses Matthew has drawn parallels between Jesus and Moses, Abraham, and Jacob. He has connected Jesus with places of historical significance in Israel's history: Bethlehem, Egypt, and Ramah. He has tied events — flight, massacre, return — to prophetic texts. With this last device and through the angel's guidance, the protective hand of God is made clear and is understood to be at work protecting the holy family as events whirl around them. Jesus' reenactment of Israel's sacred history marks him as the fulfillment of that history in Matthew's vision (Long, p. 19).

For all his scheming and violence, it is ironically Herod who grasps what is at stake in the birth of Jesus. Where the Magi have been drawn to Jesus by wonder and where Joseph acts in faithful trust and obedience, Herod understands that if Jesus is Lord, then he is not. Infants are not usually thought of as threatening (although in their demands they can exert considerable control over the lives of those around them!). But Herod grasps, if not the cosmic significance of this birth, the potential political implications for his own power and authority. He will brook no rivals, as his murderous behavior in his own family made clear. He stands in a long tradition of despotism that will not hesitate to eliminate any perceived threat, innocent or not, to his power. Herod fails to kill the King of the Jews, but others like him will succeed in doing so, and with the same label applied to the slain and innocent one.

Jesus' birth evokes hostility in those seeking to remain enthroned and will not bow down to anything other than themselves. Not all the world, then or now, welcomes God's presence in human affairs. This struggle between Herod and the Christ is waged outwardly in the world and inwardly in every person. Who shall rule? To whom shall allegiance be given? Although Herod and his ilk are the extreme manifestation of resistance to God's rule, they are not to be dismissed merely because they are a logical extension of mild forms of resistance to the sovereignty of God. "Those who begin by hating the Child will end by hurting children. Hating revelation leads to hurting people. If people will be ungodly, they will be inhumane. Herod is the gospel's earliest evidence of this fact" (Bruner, p. 53).

Someone has to carry out Herod's murderous orders: his soldiers. They stand as those who, although perhaps not instrumental in conceiving evil, are essential for its actualization. Their "only following orders" behavior is deadly and serves as an implicit call to examine where we collude with evil by not intentionally standing against it. From what evil do children of our time need protection? Terrorists whose victims include children, dictators who use hunger as a political weapon, enslavers of Third World children for sexual abuse by the affluent of the First World, and exploiters of street children are but a few to whom the church's strongest "No" must be proclaimed.

Throughout the lection Joseph stands as one who submits to God, who serves the Child by protecting him. He is a human counterpoint to Herod's refusal of God's rule. Making lengthy journeys, living patiently in exile, and finding a new home are costs of faithfulness he willingly bears. He is attentive to the leading of God, and relies on his gift of listening to dreams to find the path he is to walk. His task of protecting the Child and his mother now completed, Joseph quietly exits as Matthew's introductory section concludes, an account in which he has been the key, if underplayed, character since its beginning.

Finally, Jesus' participation in all manner of human suffering in these verses confirms that in his incarnation he is to be part of even the most desperate aspects of the human condition. In these few verses Jesus is displaced and homeless. He is an exile and refugee. He is pursued by a violent oppressor, part of a world stalked by injustice and death. He is most certainly to be counted among the poor. In rapid and dramatic contrast to "the glory all around" of Christmas, he takes his place where so many of his children live. And there should the church, his body, always be. Though death attends his birth, his own death will declare that death is never the answer in spite of every Herod's belief. His presence amidst life's direst need and his triumph over life's adversary are the birth of hope for his followers in all times, places, and circumstances.

Lawrence W. Farris

Second Sunday of Advent, Year A

First Lesson: Isaiah 11:1-10
(Psalm 72:1-7, 18-19)
Second Lesson: Romans 15:4-13
Gospel Lesson: Matthew 3:1-12

The lifestyle and message of the prophet John provide a relevant challenge to most Christians today. John's lifestyle challenges our addiction to comfort and material prosperity, inviting us to count more highly what matters to God than what our culture values (cf. Matt. 16:23). Like the merchant who sold all he owned for a more precious pearl, or the tenant farmer who sold all he owned for incomparably greater treasures (13:44-46), John sacrificed what people normally value in life to fulfill his mission.

We learn of John's lifestyle through his place of residence, his wardrobe, and his diet. John lived in the wilderness, which can be significant for a number of reasons. The prophets had promised a new exodus in the wilderness (Hos. 2:14-15); included in them is the passage the Gospels apply directly to John's ministry (Isa. 40:3). This was so important that various people claiming to be prophets sought to gather followers in the wilderness (e.g., Acts 21:38); of course, practical considerations restricted them from gathering too close to urban centers, where Romans or their agents might have obstructed their activities. Many members of a group that wrote many of the Dead Sea Scrolls lived in the wilderness and even used the same text (Isa. 40:3) to justify this location.

But the wilderness was also an uncomfortable place to live. One living alone there could not depend on others for his food or for the sorts of conveniences most of us today take for granted. John's residence there prefigures a greater prophet who would soon appear there (Matt. 4:1).

John's wardrobe (3:4) has special prophetic significance: it resembles the apparel of Elijah (2 Kings 1:8), who was promised to return before the coming of the Lord himself (Mal. 4:5). If John was the promised Elijah, no one could doubt that Jesus, whose coming he announced (Matt. 3:11), was the promised final deliverer. But like his location in the wilderness, John's apparel also tells us something about the cost of this call. John wore the garments of the poor, not those of the rich (11:8).

Finally, John's diet reveals his commitment as well. That he ate locusts sweetened with natural honey is not itself remarkable. Many people ate locusts, and they were readily available in the wilderness; the Dead Sea Scrolls actually include instructions for kosher preparation of locusts. Someone who lived in the wilderness could acquire natural honey the way beekeepers acquired honey from domestic hives: after smoking out the bees, one would break open the honeycomb.

What is remarkable is that sweetened locusts constituted John's entire diet. Even most of the poor in the land subsisted on grains (wheat and barley) and, depending on their location, would usually have access to fish and perhaps some fruit like figs; locusts were at most a supplement in the seasons when they were most common. Yet these locusts constitute John's entire diet! Although we should be responsible stewards of our health, John's location limited his options to the sorts of foods available in the wilderness, a dilemma the small number of wilderness pietists of his era faced at other times as well.

John's call thus required sacrifice. Although not all callings require the same kind of sacrifice (11:18-19), Jesus when in the wilderness fasted completely (4:2). John's sacrifice challenges us to consider what we are willing to sacrifice for God's work in today's world. We should contemplate the different, practical ways God seeks for each of us to discover how to implement this in our lives today.

While John's lifestyle challenges us, his message also challenges us. John announced that God's kingdom was coming, the time when God would reign unchallenged and establish perfect justice and peace. Only those who were already submitting to God's rule in the present, however, would be ready for the fullness of God's reign. Therefore John not only announced what God was going to do; he summoned his hearers to prepare for it by repenting (3:2). With such language he echoed the earlier prophets who often called Israel to "turn" or to "return" to the Lord.

Whom John addressed is important. Matthew specifies that John addressed the religious elite of his day (3:7); they are the recipients of his harshest critique. Merely being religious is no guarantee of being right with God; the rest of Matthew's Gospel critiques the religious establishment of his day no less forthrightly (see esp. chap. 23). John calls the religious leaders "offspring of vipers" (3:7). In his day people commonly believed that vipers hatched inside their mothers' wombs, then gnawed their way out to freedom, killing their mothers in the process; and parent murder was the most reprehensible of sins. While calling someone a viper today would no doubt be construed negatively, calling his hearers "offspring of vipers" in the first-century Mediterranean world was worse. It was equivalent to calling them parent murderers! Such language would hardly endear the prophet to the religious elite.

That John is baptizing Jewish people in the Jordan to symbolize their repentance is noteworthy (3:6). Jewish people normally baptized Gentiles who were converting to Judaism, to wash away the impurities which accrued to their former Gentile state. To baptize Jewish people in the same way as Jewish people baptized Gentiles required John's hearers to humble themselves. They could not depend on their ancestry in Abraham (3:9). Many people of faith today depend on inherited faith or religion without ever committing themselves personally to Christ. They stand to learn much from John's message to his first hearers.

John's message about the coming kingdom, for which his hearers needed to repent (3:2), was in part a message of judgment. God would set matters straight with his justice, and those whose lives did not accord with his justice would be banished. He spoke of the kingdom time as "coming wrath" (3:7). He compared his hearers with trees, and noted that those among them who did not repent would be cut down and thrown into the fire (3:10) — most small trees in the region were useless except as fuel.

John also employs another agricultural metaphor, relevant since many or most of those who came to hear him would have been rural peasants: God would separate the wheat from the chaff (3:12). When farmers harvested wheat, they needed to separate the inedible chaff from it. So they "winnowed" it — throwing the wheat into the air and letting the lighter chaff blow out. The farmer would gather the wheat to the storehouse, but the chaff was useless except as fuel, and not even good fuel at that — it burned quickly. The Bible had already compared the wicked with chaff (Pss. 1:4; 35:5; 83:13; Isa. 17:13; 29:5; Dan. 2:35; Hos. 13:3; Mal. 4:1), so there was no mistaking John's point: the wicked would be burned with fire. But unlike normal chaff, this human chaff would burn with "unquenchable" fire; that is, it would burn forever. In John's day Jewish teachers differed on the nature of hell (Gehinnom): some said God would burn the wicked up at once, annihilating them; others said the torment would be only temporary. Only a minority said hell would burn forever; by articulating this, the most horrifying image of hell in his day, John drives home the point of God's displeasure quite forcefully.

But not everyone would remain wicked; even among his hearers, John expected that some would repent. Thus he speaks of some trees that might bear good fruit (3:8, 10), of wheat as well as chaff (3:12), and of baptism in the Spirit as well as baptism in fire (3:11). When John announces that the one coming after him will baptize "you" (plural) in the Holy Spirit and in fire, he speaks of Jesus' end-time baptism for his hearers as a group, but some within that group would receive the Spirit whereas others would receive the fire. In this context (as usually, but not always, in the Bible), the "fire" must mean judgment.

John's message also tells us about Jesus' identity. John says he is not worthy to remove the coming one's sandals (3:11); in short, he is claiming to be unworthy to be the coming one's slave. Of menial chores in the ancient world, those most commonly associated with slaves in particular involved the slaveholder's feet: washing them, carrying the sandals or latching or removing them. It was said that a disciple could perform for a teacher any activity a slave normally would except the most menial task of dealing with the teacher's sandals. Biblical prophets had called themselves "slaves of the Lord" (e.g., Jer. 7:25; 29:19), but John says he is not worthy even to be the coming one's slave. Clearly John recognizes that the coming one is God himself!

Further, John announces that the coming one will baptize in the Holy Spirit and fire. Biblical prophets had announced that God would judge the wicked with fire and pour out his Spirit on the righteous (e.g., Isa. 44:3; 66:15-16; Joel 2:28-29); indeed, no one but God could be thought to pour out God's own Spirit! Again, John recognizes that the one whose way he prepares is God himself; the biblically informed reader might have already guessed this from the quotation in Matthew 3:3: Isaiah had announced that John would prepare the way for "the LORD" — in Hebrew, for God himself. Thus the Christian reader is not surprised by John's reaction when Jesus arrives to be baptized: John himself needs Jesus' greater baptism in the Holy Spirit (3:14). To borrow the language early Christians later adopted to summarize the biblical data, Jesus is "God the Son," God in the flesh.

This passage thus challenges the way we live, summons us to readiness for the coming of God's justice, and teaches us about the Lord Jesus whom we worship.

Craig S. Keener

First Sunday after the Epiphany (Baptism of the Lord), Year A

First Lesson: Isaiah 42:1-9
(Psalm 29)
Second Lesson: Acts 10:34-43
Gospel Lesson: Matthew 3:13-17

The baptism of Jesus is recorded in all three synoptic Gospels, but only in Matthew are we given the highly significant words exchanged between John the Baptist and Jesus. As our Lord counters John's reluctance to baptize him (his first recorded words in Matthew), a phrase is given which holds the key to his mission to the world: "It is proper for us in this way to fulfill all righteousness."

By declaring his baptism by John "proper" ("fitting," RSV; "becometh," KJV; *prepon* in the Greek text), Jesus leaves John still puzzling over what manner of Messiah this one is, so suddenly arrived from Nazareth. Jesus, however, is opening a new horizon of meaning. It is proper, fitting, *prepon* that in his baptism he unites himself with a humankind that stands under God's wrath and judgment. It is proper, fitting, *prepon* that in this solidarity with humankind he points to its goal, "to fulfill all righteousness." Against the background of John's proclamation of the coming wrath of God, righteousness takes on its distinctive meaning. Righteousness is not a human accomplishment of heroic merit; it is the redeeming righteousness which comes as a gift. It is the very core of the gospel itself, the power of God for salvation.

Jesus announces himself as the *fulfiller* of the grace which gives sinners who have no standing before God a place to stand in a new relationship to God. He himself *is* that place. He takes his baptismal commission from the hand of the greatest of all the prophets before him. He is both the continuity of that prophetic line as well as its fulfillment.

Righteousness fulfilled, then, means salvation has come. Deliverance, long hoped for in the Psalms (22:31; 40:10; 98:2-3) and the Prophets (Isa. 11:4-5; 61:10-11; Mic. 6:5), is now under way in Jesus, the Christ of God. His baptism is the decisive opening event that further unfolds that for which he came, to lay his healing hands upon a broken, alienated world to make it right with God again. In only a few verses Matthew lays out the basis which connects baptism with righteousness. The relationship binds together Christ's doing the will of the Father with the power that makes alienated sinners into sons and daughters in the household of God, that is, "righ-

16

teous" through him. Here at the outset of Jesus' public ministry, his baptism is the beginning step on the way that will lead to his cross and resurrection as the cost of such righteousness.

"Just as he was coming up from the water, suddenly the heavens were opened to him and he saw the Spirit of God descending like a dove and alighting on him." The Evangelist stresses the immediacy of the baptismal event and the divine witness to its profound meaning. Heaven and earth, once parted through sin, are united in a new way in the person of Jesus. The kingdom of God for which Jesus taught his followers to pray (6:10) is already coming in Christ himself. The ancient cry of the prophet: "O that thou wouldst rend the heavens and come down" (Isa. 64:1), is heard. Ezekiel's vision of the heavens opened to reveal the God who never abandons his people is fulfilled. John called the multitudes to the Judean desert to warn of the cracking open and breaking up of the old order. Now that time has come. It is at once a contradiction of John's vision of a fiery denouement and a confirmation of John's portrayal of the Messiah as one whose sandals he was not worthy to untie.

The descent of the dove as a symbol of the Spirit is exactly that, a symbol. The dove, above all other creatures, is associated with gentleness, beauty, purity. Instead of revealing a thunderclap, a whirlwind, or a devastating lightning strike, the open heavens reveal a dove in descent, resting upon Jesus.

Much has been made of this descent of the dove upon Jesus. In the fourth-century doctrinal struggles over the relationship of the Son to the Father, some saw the baptism of Jesus as his assuming a divine nature in which he did not previously share. Arius and Arianism did not end with the doctrinal assertions of the orthodox fathers at Nicaea in 325. This diversion from orthodoxy continued, appearing and reappearing in history in varied forms, and still is with us today, as popularized versions of Jesus as a model of moral virtue — but no more — would indicate. The interpretation of the baptism of the Lord, if noted at all, reveals much about the theological presuppositions of the interpreter. The apostolic tradition handed down to us lays a firm foundation for the church which heeds this biblical grounding for faith and is determinative for how the Matthew 3:13-17 text is preached. "This is my beloved Son" sets the stage for those towering phrases of the creed: "the only begotten Son of the Father, begotten from all eternity, God from God, light from light, true God from true God, begotten not made. . . ." Such affirmations of the core truth of Jesus Christ, truly God and truly human, echo the witness of the Father to his Son in his baptism in the Jordan.

It is well to hear the text also as a theological reflection on Psalm 2 (an encouragement to king and people in a time of crisis) and the first of the four great servant songs of Isaiah (42:1-4). Deeply embedded in Israel's memory was the vision of the coming one whose might is inseparable from tender care, who will not snap a bruised reed or quench a smoldering wick, who will not grow faint or be crushed until he has made many righteous. Jesus, coming up from the waters of baptism, is declared the Son in whom the Father is pleased, rather than the Sovereign humans might expect. He is the beloved Son, marked by meekness and singleness of mind and purpose, passionate for the righteousness of God as the transforming power and guiding force in life. Though mocked, he is yet trusting of the Father whose good pleasure rests upon him in dovelike grace. Though despised and afflicted, he is yet uncomplaining and obedient. Matthew draws again on this powerful imagery in documenting Jesus' ministry in healing the multitudes (12:15-21). It is an expansive unfolding of the meaning of his baptism: the descent of the dove, the empowering of the Spirit, the trinitarian benediction upon him.

The full range of the meaning of Jesus' baptism is needed as today's preacher takes this text to today's hearers. It surely calls for connections of Jesus' baptism to our own. Baptism can be overlooked altogether. It can be trivialized as a name giving, a rite of passage. It can be lost in the wrangling over the manner of its administering: immersion or sprinkling. In all of these distortions, baptism is worlds away from Paul's Romans 6 depiction of it as a dying with Christ to sin, that a wholly new life of righteousness and renewal might emerge — "living wet," as the baptized life has been called. And even as the baptism of our Lord was not private but public, so the problem of isolating baptism from the community of the baptized must be addressed. The key lies in preaching the baptism of Jesus as good news for anxious, isolated hearts, the gracious offer of the baptized Lord to call, gather, enlighten, and sanctify all whose lives are open to him in repentance. In a world beset by paralyzing fears, the connecting of Christ's baptism to our baptism can be for anxious souls today what it was for an anxious Martin Luther as he struggled through the lonely months of his safekeeping in the Wartburg Castle. "I am baptized," he would scribble on his desktop, and remember his baptism as he battled back despair. Salvation by faith alone is vividly proclaimed in every baptism administered as the sign and seal of the unmerited grace of Jesus Christ.

Wherever baptism is tamed down to a cultural rite with no consequences for costly discipleship, lessons can be learned from Christians whose baptismal unity with Christ puts them at odds with their surroundings. Though Communism appeared to have collapsed in a heap in eastern Europe in 1989, its leftovers still darken the lives of a whole generation lost to baptismal nurture and the life of covenantal discipline. In Sudan, in the Gulf States, in mainland China, in sections of India and Indonesia, in North Korea, persecution of the baptized is a harsh reality. Perhaps because of those very pressures, those whose identity is forged by their baptism know the power of costly grace. What forces undermine the full meaning of Christ's baptism and our identity with him in our part of the world? How can the congregation better prepare candidates for living the baptized life in ways which still reveal the Father's good pleasure at work? How can grievous divisions in the human family catch a glimpse of their welcome into the community of believers who are discovering ever deeper levels of reconciliation through their baptismal unity?

Matthew places Jesus' baptism back-to-back with his temptation in the wilderness. The order is significant. His baptism was not insurance against conflict, but his arming for meeting it and mastering it. Preaching this Gospel text today is best done with a view toward the perils and the promise which lie just ahead for faithful hearers. Now that Jesus has come forth from the waters of the Jordan, bearing the Father's good pleasure into the world, nothing is the same. Let pastor and people celebrate this public anointing and commissioning of Jesus and cherish it as the opening of the new age, brimming with unimagined blessing, and as bread for the journey through every wilderness of temptation.

F. Dean Lueking

First Sunday in Lent, Year A

First Lesson: Genesis 2:15-17; 3:1-7
(Psalm 32)
Second Lesson: Romans 5:12-19
Gospel Lesson: Matthew 4:1-11

No sooner is Jesus baptized than he is "led up by the Spirit into the wilderness to be tempted by the devil." Though he is tempted by the devil, he is "led up" by the Spirit to this encounter with so much at stake. Mark's account is even stronger; the Spirit "drove" (*ekballei* — the verb used for Jesus' own driving out demons; Matt. 8:31; 12:27) Jesus into the wilderness.

Jesus' identity as the beloved Son in whom the Father is well pleased has been revealed in his baptism. Now he, like Israel before him, must struggle in the wilderness, where it will become clearer what the deeper meaning of his messianic calling is. His temptation covers forty days in the desert. Israel journeyed forty years in the desert. There is a connection established by the number forty. Jesus is led, even driven, by the Spirit of God to the wilderness, the place where his people Israel came to know their destiny under God, the place where they also went wrong. Jesus now faces that demonic tempter who lured his Israel into idolatry and injustice. In order to forge a different outcome, he must confront the past. The temptation of Jesus sets the stage for the radical encounter with evil. Nothing less than that will get at the root causes of what bedevils the human race in the world.

The role of the Holy Spirit is basic in the narrative. Matthew uses the shorthand term here, "the Spirit," for the Spirit of God (3:16) and the Holy Spirit (1:18, 20; 3:11). These longer titles are to remind the reader that not all spirits are holy or of God, but that evil has its spirit status as well.

From early on, and certainly in our own day, Christians who are troubled by struggles with temptation are drawn to Jesus' temptation. The power of the account begins not with Jesus' victory but with the reality of his vulnerability and his humanity. The temptation is not shadowboxing. The wider testimony of sacred Scripture speaks to the full humanity of Jesus in the light of sharply real, terrifying temptation (Heb. 2:18; 4:15; 5:7). The temptation account is notable in that it does not attempt to explain evil or cast temptation only in the light of bodily, especially sexual, disobedience. Notice the absence of deliberating the fine points of balancing divine sovereignty with human freedom. We have no biography of Satan offered either, or any clue to Satan as the once and former member of the heavenly court (Job). Nor does Matthew distinguish between God's testing and Satan's tempting.

Matthew simply tells how Jesus wrestled with Satan and conquered in each of the three temptations. The point Matthew is making has to do with Jesus as the *Christus Victor*, the Savior from Satan's realm of darkness (1:21; 12:28) who can provide rescue to struggling mortals because he has faced what we face and defeated what would otherwise defeat us.

Theologically, the temptation of Jesus is rich in meaning. The whole point of temptation by the tempter (the descriptive term for Satan used only in Matt. 4:3 and 1 Thess. 3:5) is to drive a wedge between Jesus and God. The heart of sin, as the three temptation episodes make clear, is to draw Jesus away from holy reliance upon the Father to an unholy independence. Our Lord expanded upon that truth in the warning discourses to the disciples (Matt. 24:10-12, 24). Furthermore, temptation does not limit its range to obvious evils, but invades the good creation ("turn these stones into bread"), the holy place ("leap from the temple pinnacle"), and worship itself ("all these I will give you if you will fall down and worship me"). The common association of temptation with the Seven Deadly Sins has its place, for those sins are indeed deadly. But the real essence of temptation attacks where humans expect the best: daily bread, sacred spaces, the devotion of the heart. Learning this from the text of Matthew 4:1-11 brings an end to prideful finger-pointing at others whose transgressions are headline news and brings about a reflective examining of the inner places of the soul, where the real and daily struggle becomes absolutely personal.

As people who live in the most affluent time of the most affluent nation on earth, the first temptation cries out for understanding and response. The tempter shifts the focus to bread and all bread symbolizes for what is essential to the good life. In assaulting Jesus at the very point of his deepest vulnerability following a forty-day fast, the tempter raises the stakes of the encounter by invoking the name "Son of God" with a question mark after it. It is the "if-then" ploy. If Son of God, then prove it by producing bread from stones. The assumption is subtly thrown in with the proposal; surely the first need of life is to eat. What is more elemental than the nourishing of a body famished by hunger? And the thoughtful hearer must extrapolate from that subtle question all the rest that has come to be taken for granted as essential for daily existence in our time and place — the astonishing array of possessions that feed, clothe, shelter, sustain, transport, amuse, and distract us from giving first place in the heart to God. But Jesus, obedient to the certainty that life is more than bread and all that goes with it (6:25), speaks not only for himself but for all in using the generic "One ['Man,' RSV] does not live by bread alone. . . ." Every being worthy of the name "human" cannot be reduced to what is visible and edible, tangible and collectible, bankable and investable. The core of being human rests upon response to the speaking of God, who first spoke human life and all things into existence. In this direct reply Jesus does not even flatter the enemy by cleverness or originality. He simply quotes Scripture (Deut. 8:3) in the spirit of submission and trust. Notice that each of the responses to each temptation Jesus draws from the eighth and sixth chapters of Deuteronomy, which describes how Israel was taught how to withstand temptation.

The second temptation shifts the scene to the holy city, a name Matthew interestingly applies to Jerusalem (repeated in 27:53), since that city had more than its share of unholy plots and trumped-up charges and was the very center of opposition to Jesus by those who were in charge of the city's most holy place — the temple. The temple architecture is not the main thing. Rather, "the pinnacle of the temple" suggests the reminders of God's promises and providential protection. It is in that setting that the devil pressures Jesus for a public display of power that is about trust: leaping from the highest turret into thin air. Again Jesus quotes Scripture with trust in its efficacy, countering the devil's readiness to misuse the Word (Ps. 91, offered as a formula for spectacle) with the Word faithfully used to establish that real trust needs no spurious proofs of God's care: "You shall not tempt the LORD your God" (Deut. 6:16).

Once more the scene shifts in the third temptation, now to a very high mountain affording a view of the kingdoms of the world and their glory. All this is promised — without suffering. In the background of this temptation is the view of Psalm 2 whereby the anointed ruler would have universal dominion, with the nations of the earth as his inheritance and the ends of the earth as his realm. Buttressing this boast is the claim that all these are the possessions of the devil to give away.

The deception of the proposal is again pierced by the Word on Jesus' lips, the great call to fear the Lord your God and serve him alone (Deut. 6:13). As Jesus will soon teach his disciples and others, no one can serve two masters (Matt. 6:24), so the lethal temptation to split the soul into divergent loyalties before God is exposed. Wholeness of response is the basis of integrity. Jesus shall walk the way of suffering and death in order to claim his crown of universal rule. His is the kingdom of grace, which is not won by bribery or manipulation, but by way of unswerving love and undiluted obedience to the Father.

Here again is teaching regarding sin. Whatever sways the people of God from the path of trust, obedience, and the service of God is satanic and idolatrous. Jesus says to the tempter what he will say to Peter, who also had visions of sovereignty without suffering and kingship without a cross: "Begone, Satan!" (cf. 16:23; 25:41).

Jesus is the only human being in this narrative. The wilderness has only earth and sky to offer, and the sinister enemy who invades the scene. The devil fails to gain the foothold and is forced to leave the field. Surrounding Jesus and every struggling child of God (6:13) are the everlasting arms of the heavenly Father. In the beginning the Spirit led Jesus out to the battleground. In the end angels come and minister to him, as they will do again for him — and for us (18:10; 26:53).

F. Dean Leuking

Third Sunday after the Epiphany, Year A

First Lesson: Isaiah 9:1-4
(Psalm 27:1, 4-9)
Second Lesson: 1 Corinthians 1:10-18
Gospel Lesson: Matthew 4:12-23

In this Gospel, events unfold in a rapid sequence of prediction and fulfillment. John was arrested. Jesus withdrew from the Jordan plain for Galilee, but not to the security of home (cf. 10:37; 19:29). Of the Evangelists, Matthew alone tells how Jesus almost immediately set aside Nazareth with its close associations with family and old occupations (cf. 12:26-40; 13:55-56) and established his base at Capernaum (8:5; 9:1; 17:24). Matthew stresses the geography of this move to the town "by the sea, in the territory of Zebulun and Naphtali."

The old tribal lands of Zebulun and Naphtali were the first portions of Israelite territory to be swallowed up by Tiglath-pileser III and reorganized as Assyrian provinces in 732 B.C., ten years before the rest of Israel was subjugated. Isaiah had proclaimed that the first territories to feel God's wrath would also be the first to receive the news of the coming of salvation at the birth of the messianic king (Isa. 9:1-7).

Throughout the opening four chapters of his Gospel, Matthew has traced the fulfillment of old hopes by attending carefully to the geography Jesus covered. Here once again prophecy appears to provide a blueprint of Jesus' well-known movements away from the river, "across the Jordan," settling "by the sea" at the city of Capernaum. None of this is accidental. Nor would it be true to Matthew's purpose to ascribe these movements to fear (4:12) or calculation on Jesus' part. All of these movements lie deep in the mind of God, leading Jesus on his appointed path. Every step of the way has to do with the fulfillment of God's saving purpose.

Furthermore, Galilee was no isolated pocket of purely Jewish settlements. It lay astride the international trade routes as well as traditional paths of invaders, and had always been open to Damascus and Syria to the north, Egypt to the south, Phoenicia and the Mediterranean to the northwest and west. Jewish and Gentile communities occupied this region, living side by side, and precisely in Galilee, not in Jerusalem, Jesus begins his ministry, silently prefiguring the universal mission to the world he would proclaim (28:19).

This Gospel narrative makes it clear that Jesus is no forerunner like John, as much as their ministries are linked. Nor does he come bearing the judgment John so eagerly sought. Matthew applies to Jesus stunning words from Isaiah 9:1-2. *He* is the great light rising and shining (2:2, 9) upon people whose whole existence is described as "sitting in darkness and in the region and shadow of death" (cf. Ps. 23:4). He is light and will give light, by his teaching and healing, by his suffering and his rising, and through the community of his disciples (Matt. 5:14-16). It is a magnificent Epiphany message!

The phrase "from that time Jesus began" (v. 17) is followed by the infinitive "to preach." The identical phrase appears again in 16:21, this time with the infinitive "to show" following. Now comes the content of the preaching or showing. Even though the phrase appears but twice in Matthew, it has the look of a formula introducing something of major importance. Some students of Matthew's Gospel see it as an important indicator of Matthew's view of the unfolding of Jesus' ministry.

In any case, "Jesus began to preach," and the public work of Jesus is defined as preaching the nearness of the kingdom of God. In all too many cases today, the term "preaching" has associations with scolding, harping on moral platitudes, or dwelling on the obvious or the irrelevant. In the Scriptures, however, "to preach" *(kēryssō)* is not to deal in shopworn or secondhand goods, but to announce as a herald *(kēryx)* the news that is both gut-wrenching and glad beyond all expectation.

Like John, Jesus also heralds: "Repent, for the kingdom of heaven is at hand." It is surprising that Jesus does not choose here a brand-new word, different from the word of John (3:2). But John and Jesus belong together in this truth (11:11-19; 17:9-13), and the call to repent is the beginning of the good news of the kingdom (13:14-15). The kingdom of heaven is present even in the Christian community as a countercultural force, untamed and raw, summoning us away from all easy ruts to the new life of righteousness. From time immemorial God's people had prayed that his rule might come on earth as in heaven (6:10), that the enemies of God and the haters of God's people might be cast down once and for all, that the new age might dawn speedily and soon, in our time and in our days. Jesus announces that the time is at hand! But how near is it? And when does near become actually here? At his birth? His baptism? His arrival onto the scene in Galilee? When tempted? When crucified? When raised from the grave? Nothing is gained by isolating one of these and declaring it alone as the moment of the dawning of the kingdom. The kingdom comes in and through Jesus, in and through his birth and ministry, his death and resurrection. It comes in the undivided wholeness of his life. It comes in the power of God which is always accompanied by the mystery of God's timing and the sure intention of his grace.

It is Matthew's theology, if we can so term it, to assert that Jesus in the splendid entirety of his being is the epiphany of God, the gracious coming forth of the reign of God. This is the central affirmation running throughout the Gospel of Matthew (1:23; 18:20; 28:20). In Jesus the new is here; yet the kingdom is also yet to come in power at the eschatological end (10:23; 16:28; 26:24) when all the nations will be gathered before the throne of God for judgment (25:31-46). It is also then that the brilliant light will shine gloriously beyond all ambiguity and opportunity (13:43). That time is known only to God, let all future visionaries note, and the community is simply summoned to turn from calculation to vigilance of another sort altogether.

This theological note in Matthew speaks to Christians today who do not agree with one another about the time or the nature of the kingdom. As lines were drawn sharply in first-century Judaism over these matters, so Christians today differ and argue. Will the kingdom be an earthly or heavenly rule? Will it be the reformation of this world and glorification of the present Jerusalem, or the fresh creation of a new-world land and the divine gift of a new Jerusalem? Will it involve the slaughter of unrighteous and insolent nations, or their conversion? Is the coming kingdom an inner, spiritual reality, triumphant wherever individual hearts are renewed? Or does it promise the rebirth of the entire universe (19:28), a new heaven and a new earth in which righteousness dwells?

Jesus' announcement of the coming sovereign sway of God prepares readers for the rest of the Gospel all the way through to the declaration of the Great Commission issued by the risen Lord (28:18ff.). Between this initial announcement and that climax, Jesus will everywhere steadily provoke audiences not only by proclaiming the nearness of the kingdom, but especially by challenging dearly held definitions of the kingdom, by implying that the powers of the kingdom are at work in him, and by stubborn insistence that righteousness is the one indispensable and infallible sign of the presence of the kingdom. Ancient Jews and Christians alike envisioned the coming of the kingdom in terms of prodigious crops and astonishing fruitfulness of the earth. Matthew's Jesus steadfastly fixes his gaze on the fruit of obedience and love as the signs of the presence of the kingdom.

With the call to repentance and the announcement of the kingdom at hand, we expect something spectacular to happen. Yet in Matthew's next scene Jesus is shown talking to some common laborers! Matthew's strategy is to use anticlimax to subvert sour expectations, in order to open up new possibilities. In the call of the fishermen Simon and Andrew, the subtle nature of the kingdom of heaven is coming, because Matthew identifies it with discipleship. Here we see Jesus choosing his disciples, the reversal of the normal practice of rabbinic recruitment at the time. He meets these men at their workplace, a family fishing business, yet calls them to abandon their trade for a new vocation. The call to discipleship demands more than an assent of the heart; it invites an uncompromising break with business as usual, which is a truth of high importance for the church in this and any day.

F. Dean Leuking

Fourth Sunday after the Epiphany, Year A

First Lesson: Micah 6:1-8
(Psalm 15)
Second Lesson: 1 Corinthians 1:18-31
Gospel Lesson: Matthew 5:1-12

I begin with a brief orientation to the Sermon on the Mount as background for the discussion of the texts for the Fourth, Fifth, Sixth, Seventh, and Eighth Sundays after the Epiphany. Three main streams of thought from the world of first-century Judaism intertwine in the Gospel of Matthew: apocalypticism, Pharisaism, and wisdom. Of these, apocalyptic thought is the most pervasive in the First Gospel.

Apocalyptic theologians believed that when God created the world, all entities were fully what God intended them to be, and they lived together in community in mutually supportive relationships (Gen. 1-2). However, after the fall, the world is no longer fully the place God wanted it to be. Satan and the demons seek to wrest the world away from God. This old world contains sin, idolatry, poverty, social oppression, sickness, violence, and death. To demonstrate God's righteousness, God will initiate a cosmic cataclysm in which God and the heavenly hosts destroy the power of Satan and create abundance, freedom, health, and eternal life. All things can again relate to one another as God intends. This new world is known as the realm (reign, dominion, rule) of God. Immediately prior to this cosmic transformation, the world will undergo a tribulation, a time of suffering, as Satan and the demons resist the divine invasion.

Matthew 4:17 states the central theme of the First Gospel: the realm of heaven (NRSV: "kingdom of heaven") is becoming fully manifest through the ministry of Jesus Christ. The phrase "realm of heaven" is Matthew's equivalent to "realm of God."

These motifs underlie much of the Sermon on the Mount. This sermon articulates a core of Jesus' teaching to help the church interpret its situation and to show how the church can live as a community of the new world in the midst of the old.

Matthew follows Jewish tradition in regarding mountains as places of revelation or instruction (4:8; 8:1; 15:29; 17:1, 9; 24:3; esp. 28:16). As the sermon unfolds, the Matthean Jesus, much like a rabbi with an apocalyptic worldview, interprets it in continuity with Jewish tradition.

Jesus speaks especially to the disciples. Most scholars agree that Matthew uses the figures of the disciples as a way of speaking to the church. While this instruction primarily has the disciples in view, the wider crowds also hear it and respond positively (7:28). Jesus follows ancient rabbinic custom by sitting to teach.

Nine beatitudes begin the Sermon on the Mount. The term "blessed" echoes the Jewish understanding of blessedness as God's provision for fullness of life, including knowledge of God, rightness of relationships, and material security (e.g., Pss. 1; 128; 144:12-15). However, when conventional security fails, blessedness still comes from recognizing God's presence and purposes. Israel, waiting for divine mercy, is blessed even as it waits (Isa. 30:19). Martyrs can be blessed because they die faithfully witnessing to the divine sovereignty (e.g., 4 Macc. 10:15; 12:1). Matthew's beatitudes are eschatological, as Matthew joins other writers in widening "blessing" to include participation in the divine rule in the new world (e.g., Dan. 12:12; 4 Macc. 17:18; 18:19; Rev. 1:3; 14:13; 16:15; 19:9; 22:7, 14). People in those circumstances are blessed because they recognize the realm of God working through their circumstances or promising to transform their situations.

These beatitudes are statements of fact. They are not imperatives. They prompt listeners to recognize the presence and blessing of the reign of God.

My colleague, Holly Hearon, points out that the only equivalent expression to "poor in spirit" in ancient literature occurs in the Dead Sea Scrolls where it speaks of God giving courage to those who have been beaten down by people and situations that are oppressive and unfaithful (1QM 14.7). The crushed are blessed not because they are presently happy but because the reign of God will restore their worlds.

While mourning in Israel could refer to a broad spectrum of sadnesses (e.g., at the death of a spouse), it came to have a specialized meaning of

mourning the brokenness of the community caused by sin or repressive outside forces (e.g., Isa. 60:2-3; 1 Esdr. 8:66-77; 9:1; 9:45-50; 2 Esdr. 9:38–10:15).
Like individuals who go through a period of mourning after the death of a
loved one as preparation for future living, the community mourns as preparation for the rule of God. Repentance is sometimes a part of mourning.
Their comfort is the reign of God.

Psalm 37:8-11 is the background of the beatitude in behalf of the meek.
In the psalm the faithful lose their land to wealthy wicked. The psalm is an
assurance that the wicked will lose their power and the land will be returned. In Matthew's day idolatrous Rome controls the land. Matthew
hears the notion of inheriting the land apocalyptically: the meek will be
blessed as the entire world is regenerated in the reign of God (e.g., Isa. 65:17-
25; 2 Bar. 29:3-8; Matt. 19:29). Later, Matthew uses the same term for meek
to refer to Jesus (11:29; 21:5) and to disciples (18:4); the death of Jesus and
the suffering of the church are signs of meekness that will be reversed in the
reign of God.

In Jewish literature in antiquity, the visceral images of hungering and
thirsting are sometimes used of the faithful who have been marginalized,
impoverished, or dispossessed and who seek for God to reconstitute their
lives (e.g., Pss. 42:1-3; 107:4-9, where much of the same language occurs as in
Matt. 5:6; Isa. 55:1-2; 65:13; Sir. 24:21; 51:24). God's righteousness is preeminently God's activity of setting things right in the world now (e.g., Isa. 51:1-
6) and in the world to come (e.g., 2 Esdr. 8:36; 16:52). Righteous persons are
rightly aligned with God's intent to restore. The affirmation "they will be
filled" calls to mind the eschatological banquet (e.g., 1QSa; 1 Enoch 62:14;
Matt. 8:11-12; 21:1-10; 26:29). Those who hunger and thirst for the cosmic
transformation of the realm of God will share in the eschatological banquet.

In the Septuagint (the translation of the First Testament from Hebrew
into Greek) the Greek terms *eleos* and *eleoō* (rendered in Matt. 5:7 as "mercy"
and "receive mercy") translate the Hebrew ḥesed. The latter is a relational
term invoking God's covenantal loyalty, steadfast love, compassion, (e.g.,
Exod. 34:6; Num. 14:18; Neh. 9:17; Pss. 86:15; 103:8; 145:8; Jer. 32:18; Joel
2:13; Jon. 4:2; Nah. 1:3). Divine ḥesed is the paradigm relationship in
covenantal community (e.g., Hos. 6:6; T. Zeb. 5:1; 8:1). The life of the community is to mediate ḥesed. Not surprisingly, such mercy is characteristic of
the eschatological age (e.g., Wis. 3:9; 2 Macc. 2:7; 7:29; Pss. Sol. 14:6). When
the disciples exhibit such covenantal loyalty, they enact the community of
the new age. Matthew illustrates such ḥesed in action through providing for
the poor (Matt. 6:2-4), in mutual relationships (9:13; 12:7), and in extending
forgiveness for restoration of relationship to one another (18:23-35).

In Jewish thought the heart is a central locus of thought, will, and emotion. Behind the expression "pure in heart" is the notion of a "divided (or evil) heart" *(yeṣer haraʿ)*. The pure heart thinks and wills one thing: faithfulness to God and the divine purposes for community (e.g., Deut. 6:4; Pss. 21:3-4; 119:2, 10). The divided heart is not singular in its faithfulness but also serves evil (2 Esdr. 3:20-36; 4:30; James 4:8). The divided heart leads to the collapse of self and community (e.g., Matt. 7:21-27). The pure in heart are blessed because they seek to be singularly faithful to God's regenerating purposes, and "shall see God" when the divine rule is fully manifest.

In a peaceful community, relationships are as God intends, including material provision for all. Such peace, of course, characterizes the eschatological world (e.g., *1 Enoch* 11:2; 71:15-17). Inhabitants of that world are sometimes called children of God (e.g., *1 Enoch* 62:11; *T. Jud.* 24:3; cf. *Jub.* 1:23-24). In this beatitude, which resonates with Psalm 34:15, making peace is characteristic of persons who respond favorably to the realm of God. Matthew calls attention to attitudes and behaviors that help bring about peace in community (e.g., 5:21-26, 38-47; 18:21-35).

The final two beatitudes work in tandem. 5:10 recalls a general principle while 5:11-12 applies that principle to the situation of Matthew's church. Jewish literature recalls the recurrent rejection of the prophets (Matt. 23:29-32; cf. 2 Chron. 36:15-16; Neh. 9:26; Acts 7:51-52). Many apocalyptic writers believe that their communities are persecuted. Powerful forces resist the message and messengers of God. In the beatitude, "those who are persecuted for righteousness' sake" are those who are persecuted because they witness to the dominion of God. This beatitude functions as pastoral counsel: people joining the community witnessing to the apocalyptic transformation of the world should expect conflict.

The final beatitude shifts from third person to second person, thus suggesting that Matthew is speaking directly to a congregation that is persecuted (cf. Matt. 20:19; 21:35-36; 22:6; 24:9-14). Matthew 10:16-23 depicts the persecution as taking place at the hands of synagogue leaders who subsequently delivered the witnesses to the Gentile government. The synagogue had the authority to discipline its members by means of the lash, but could not put anyone to death. The beatitude intimates that the synagogue authorities spoke falsely about the disciples. The final line encourages community members to "rejoice and be glad," not because they are persecuted but because they keep alive the tradition of the prophets and will be included in the heavenly world, that is, in the realm of God.

Ronald J. Allen

Fifth Sunday after the Epiphany, Year A

First Lesson: Isaiah 58:1-9a, (9b-12)
(Psalm 112:1-9, [10])
Second Lesson: 1 Corinthians 2:1-12, (13-16)
Gospel Lesson: Matthew 5:13-20

The church is the "salt of the earth." Salt has multiple associations in Judaism in antiquity. Salt brings out the flavor in food (Job 6:6) and acts as a preservative (e.g., salted fish). It is a basic necessity for life (Sir. 39:26). It averts destruction (1 Esdr. 8:20). Covenants were sealed by heavily salted meals (Num. 18:19). 2 Chronicles 13:5 speaks of a "covenant of salt." Newborn children were rubbed with it (Ezek. 16:4). Salt was sprinkled on sacrifices, thus becoming associated with God's gracious activity (Exod. 30:35; Lev. 2:13; Ezek. 43:24). Some of the rabbis use salt as a metaphor for wisdom. Some early Christians spoke metaphorically of salting as a part of the coming of the new world (Mark 9:49-50).

The salt is not the thing itself (e.g., meal, sacrificial victim, covenant). The church is not the reign of God. But like salt pointing to larger dimensions of actions (e.g., eating, offering sacrifice, making covenant), it points to that reign.

Much salt used in Palestine was taken from salt deposits on the edge of the Dead Sea. These deposits also included gypsum, which looks much like salt. Gypsum, when mistakenly used as salt, would give the impression of "salt that has lost its flavor" and is good only to be cast into the street.

However, the verb "has lost its flavor" is a double entendre. For the verb (*morainō*) can also be rendered "has become foolish." The fool does not know (or follow) God (e.g., Pss. 14:1; 53:1), and that can result in condemnation (e.g., 2 Esdr. 4:19). Foolishness is an important Matthean theme (cf. 5:22; 7:26; 25:1-13). The fool does not recognize the dominion of God, and is condemned. This insight is reinforced by the fact that Judaism uses the expression "being trampled under foot" to speak of judgment (e.g., Isa. 14:19, 25). If the church loses its saltiness, that is, fails to witness to the divine realm, it faces condemnation at the final judgment (e.g., Matt. 7:21-29; 24:45–25:46).

We can understand 5:14-16 similarly, though we must handle the symbolism of light carefully. Racism is reinforced by the recurrent use of the language of light, day, and whiteness in association with God, Jesus, the church (and other positive values), as well as the use of black, darkness, and night for sin, evil, and the devil.

Genesis 1:3-4 is a primary clue to the function of light in Matthew 5:14. Prior to the first day of creation, the chaos was dark. Light allows us to see the world as it really is. This perspective is behind Isaiah 42:6, in which the vocation of Israel is also described as being "a light to the nations." The nations are Gentiles — people who do not fully know or serve the God of Israel. Israel is to be a demonstration plot of the way that God wants all peoples to live.

The reference to the city set on a hill may simply make use of geographical fact. However, more likely the reference evokes associations with Jerusalem. Isaiah 2:2-4 describes Jerusalem as a city in which God's purposes of righteousness are enacted in all relationships. Of note, Gentiles will come to Jerusalem in order to learn the ways of God (cf. Isa. 18:7; 25:6-8; 45:14; Mic. 4:1-3). For some Jewish people Jerusalem is a symbol of eschatological activity and revelation (e.g., 2 Esdr. 9:26–10:49; 13:35-36; *2 Bar.* 81:1-82; cf. Rev. 2:1–22:6). These resonances suggest that the church is a community through whom Gentiles come to the knowledge of God as a part of the manifestation of the divine reign (e.g., Matt. 2:1-12; 4:15-16; 28:16-20).

Verse 15 assumes a typical Palestinian house that has only a window or two, or perhaps none. A lamp is needed. In order to provide maximum light, it would be put on a shelf fairly high on the wall or on some other kind of stand. The basket is probably a small one used for measuring grain. A lamp left under a basket uses up the oxygen and goes out.

The church is to be that kind of light in the world. Otherwise the community may lose its opportunity to shine. For, as noted, the church will be judged at the final tribunal (e.g., Matt. 7:21-29; 24:45–25:46).

The church lets its light shine through good works (5:16). The church does not engage in works to earn a place in the divine realm (works righteousness). Rather, the works are a response to the gracious presence of the realm. Works express the church's identity as community of the new aeon. This theme is drawn from Judaism, in which works of love and mercy are marks of identity (e.g., Sir. 32:16; for examples, see Isa. 58:6-7; Tob. 1:17; 4:16). Good works in the First Gospel are signs of the reign of God. A list of such works is offered in the commentary for the Ninth Sunday after the Epiphany.

In verse 17 Jesus affirms the continuing validity of the law and the prophets for the community of the new age. In the first century the terms "law" (Torah) and "prophets," at minimum, included the books attributed to Moses and the major writings of the prophets. From the first-century apocalyptic perspective, the purpose of the Torah is to guide the community in a life that optimizes the capacity for blessing in the old age. Enacting Torah marks Jewish identity. A faithful community eschews idolatry and conducts its relationships according to Torah, for example, loving God singularly, caring for the poor, maintaining justice in the community. The prophets compare and contrast the vision of common life articulated in Torah with the actual behavior of the community. The prophets call the people to conform their life to Torah so that all in the community can be blessed.

The Matthean Jesus says he has come not to abolish the law and the prophets but to "fulfill" *(plēroō)* them. While this notion is greatly debated in the commentaries, its point seems to me self-evident. The law and the prophets were God's temporary provision for people in the old age. Now the life of community that they foreshadow will become fully manifest in the reign of God, particularly after the return of Jesus.

This interpretation is reinforced by 5:18. The mentions of heaven and earth passing away and all things being accomplished refer to the apocalyptic cataclysm (e.g., cf. Matt. 24:29-34). Until the apocalyptic transformation, not one letter of the Torah will pass away, not even one stroke of a letter. These expressions may refer to the smallest letter of the alphabet (one letter = *iota*) and decorative strokes of ancient scripts. Torah and its way of life are normative for the community (as in 2 Esdr. 9:37; *2 Bar.* 4:1).

These ideas lead a conclusion that startles many Christians. Matthew calls persons who come into Jesus' community to live in the way of Torah. Matthew assumes that Christian Jews will be Torah observant. Some interpreters think Matthew expects Gentiles who come into Jesus' community of the new age to convert fully to Judaism. Other interpreters believe that Matthew sees Gentiles becoming similar to the God-fearers — Gentiles who worship the God of Israel and observe many precepts of Torah but are never completely initiated into Judaism (e.g., God-fearing men are never circumcised). Even if Matthew does not presume full conversion, Matthew calls all in the community, including Gentiles, to honor Torah and to live in ways that embody "the weightier matters of the law: justice and mercy and faith" (23:23).

This theme continues in verse 19. Some communities in antiquity believed that the reign of God would have its own social structures (e.g., Mark 10:37, 40; Matt. 20:21, 23; Luke 22:30; note the motif of multiple heavens in *1 Enoch* 39:3ff.; 2 Cor. 12:2). However, these social structures would not be amenable to the abuses of power that characterize the social pyramid of the old world. According to verse 19, those who break even the least commandment and teach others to do the same will be least in the reign of God. Such teachers are included within the dominion of God but are accorded a low social stratum (cf. Matt. 11:11; 18:4; cf. 20:20-28).

Verse 20 presumes the Jewish notion (cf. our remarks on Matt. 5:6, 10 above) that God expects the faithful to live in righteousness, that is, witnessing to the righteousness of God in community. Torah guides the community in this way. Matthew urges Christian Jews to a righteousness that is higher than that of conventional Pharisees. Their problem? They do not live out the best of their own tradition. They are hypocrites who espouse Torah and the prophets but do not live accordingly (e.g., Matt. 23:1-36). Indeed, they manifest unrighteousness.

Matthew does not call Christians to a righteousness that is higher than that of Torah. Quite the opposite: Jesus calls Christians to the righteousness of the Torah. If the Christian community does not act out such righteousness, they will not enter the reign of God (e.g., Matt. 7:21-29; 24:45–25:46).

Matthew calls Christians to a righteousness that is higher than that of conventional Pharisees. Matthew himself was likely a Christian Pharisee. In the first century, Matthew speaking as Pharisee to Pharisee may have been understood as a self-criticism within the community that had been typical of the classical prophets and that became a hallmark of Pharisaism. However, subsequent generations of Christians have used such remarks to degrade and even dismiss Judaism, and hence to contribute directly to anti-Semitism. The preacher needs to help the congregation name and reject these phenomena. They are inappropriate to a community witnessing to the realm of God.

Ronald J. Allen

Sixth Sunday after the Epiphany, Year A

First Lesson: Deuteronomy 30:15-20
(Psalm 119:1-8)
Second Lesson: 1 Corinthians 3:1-9
Gospel Lesson: Matthew 5:21-37

Christians sometimes refer to Matthew 5:21-37 as "antitheses," that is, statements in which the teachings of the Matthean Jesus are antithetical to those of the First Testament. This way of speaking and thinking is misleading. For the Matthean Jesus does not declare the tradition dead. Instead, Jesus interprets Torah much like a rabbi with an apocalyptic world-view. First-century Judaism was not a monolith but was pluralistic. Different schools of Judaism interpreted Jewish tradition in different ways. Jesus is the primary expositor of Torah for the school of Christian Judaism.

From the period of the First Testament into the first century (and through today), Judaism reinterpreted its tradition in new situations. In Matthew 5:21-48 the Matthean Jesus does not alter Torah, but interprets several passages in light of the apocalyptic transformation now under way.

The prohibition against murder in Matthew 5:21 is found in Exodus 20:13 and Deuteronomy 5:17. The claim that the murderer is liable to judgment echoes Exodus 12:12; Leviticus 24:17; Numbers 35:16. Murder is wrong because it ends relationship, eliminates the possibility that the deceased can be blessed, and destroys community. The perpetrator presumes the prerogative of God to end life.

According to verse 22, the same effects occur in community because of anger and its expressions in insulting a person or declaring a person to be a fool. At the last judgment people in angry relationships are consigned to eternal hell (cf. 2 Esdr. 7:36-44). Helping people resolve anger was a concern shared by other Jewish communities of the time (e.g., 4 Macc. 3:3; T. Dan 3:1-4:7).

The text does not prohibit anger as such. Anger is a feeling that simply comes upon a person. The text details the consequences of anger (hell) and, in verses 23-24, provides pastoral guidance for resolving anger.

If people are leaving gifts (i.e., materials for sacrifice) at the altar and remember brothers or sisters who have something against them, worshipers are to leave their gifts and seek reconciliation. The person who is aware of the broken relationship (regardless of who caused the rupture) is responsible for initiating restoration.

Verses 25-26 are an analogy of these principles in action. A debtor is about to be taken to court by a creditor. The debtor will be thrown into prison. However, the debtor can avoid imprisonment by making friends with the accuser. Likewise, persons in situations of anger can avoid the destructive results of anger only by restoring broken relationships. For a parable that makes a similar point, cf. Matthew 18:23-35.

Matthew, however, is caught in a contradiction between the teaching of this passage and other dynamics within the congregation. Matthew appears to be hostile toward many conventional Pharisees. Even if passages such as 23:1-36 are understood as prophetic self-criticism, underlying anger seems quite apparent. According to the logic of this text, Matthew's community needs to restore their relationship with traditional Pharisaism. This situation reminds today's preacher of the importance of relentless self-criticism, lest the church miss the opportunity to actualize the new age, and condemn itself.

In 5:27-30 the focus shifts to adultery, which is prohibited in Exodus 20:14 and Deuteronomy 5:18. In Judaism adultery referred to sexual relationships between a woman who was married (or engaged) and a male other than her spouse. The sexual relationship is intended to express and create a covenantal bond between the two people. As the partners come together in intimacy, they become "one flesh" (Gen. 2:24), that is, as fully responsive to (and responsible for) one another as two people can be in the old world. The sexual relationship in a covenantal relationship between a woman and a man is an especially expressive form of covenantal community. Such sexuality represents the bondedness that God wills for all. The two covenanted human beings becoming one flesh bespeak the intimacy of the divine covenant with humankind. Becoming one flesh is designed to encourage sexual partners and their relationship so that their own experience of covenantal solidarity is deepened and their contribution to the other communities of the world is magnified.

Adultery is a lie that destroys community. Indeed, it is an act of coveting (Exod. 20:17). Adulterers enjoy the pleasure of sex, but they neither express nor create a covenantal bond. Instead of deepening covenantal commitment, adultery creates guilt and suspicion. Others in the community do not know whether adulterers can be trusted to live in covenantal relationship in broader arenas of life. On the effects of adultery, especially in a context of idolatry, see Wisdom 14:22-26.

According to verse 28, lust in the heart destroys community as surely as physical acts of adultery. Lust is sexual desire for another person without regard for covenantal commitment that causes relationships and community to collapse (e.g., Sus. 1:8, 11, 14, 56).

Verses 29-30 prescribe radical treatment for urges toward lust: tearing out the eye and cutting off one's hand. The eye and the hand are the two body parts that are central to the act of adultery. Otherwise one's whole body will be thrown into eternal hell.

We must understand these prescriptions figuratively. Some other religions in antiquity practiced self-mutilation, but Judaism did not. The Jewish people steadfastly maintained that God wanted people to serve God in their wholeness. A story in 4 Maccabees illuminates how this language was understood in Judaism in the first century (4 Macc. 8:1–12:19; cf. 2 Macc. 7:1-2; 8:5–9:9). The tyrant Antiochus commanded seven brothers to eat defiling foods. They refused. The tyrant dismembered them. Although they did not cut off their own body parts, the story uses dismemberment to emphasize the importance of faithfulness. The alternative, eternal residence in the fires of hell, is much worse.

Verses 31-32 reframe the community's understanding of divorce. The Matthean Jesus refers to Deuteronomy 24:1. The husband had exclusive right to divorce. In case of divorce the husband was to write the former wife a certificate so that members of the community would know that she was no longer married and could enter a new sexual relationship without committing adultery.

In the first century Jewish interpreters debated the application of this commandment. The school of Hillel said divorce could take place for multiple reasons. The stricter school of Shammai maintained that sexual defilement alone could allow divorce.

Jesus says flatly that, with one exception, divorce is no longer to be practiced in the community of the new age. Jesus does not institute a new legalism. In 19:4-8 he indicates the reason for this principle. Moses created the certificate of divorce to accommodate hardness of heart: some men and women cannot learn to live together. However, that perspective was a concession to the old age. The manifestation of the realm of heaven sufficiently alters the conditions for relationships that divorce is no longer necessary. Indeed, so changed are the dynamics of the new world that, according to verse 32, a husband who divorces his spouse causes both his former spouse and her new husband to commit adultery, thus invoking the destructiveness resulting from adultery (cf. 5:27-30).

The exception is "unchastity." This much-debated phrase probably refers to adultery or fornication (a broad term including most forms of sexual expression outside a covenant between a man and a woman, e.g., rape, sodomy, illicit sexual relationships among family members, prostitution, adultery). The Matthean church evidently found the presence of the new age insufficiently realized to bring the full range of sexuality into conformity with refraining from divorce altogether (cf. Mark 9:50). A concession to brokenness is still needed even among the disciples.

In 5:33-37 Jesus paraphrases Exodus 20:7; Leviticus 19:12; Numbers 30:2; Deuteronomy 23:21; and Psalm 50:14. In antiquity people often swore by God when they needed to guarantee the truth of what they said about serious matters. For instance, Ruth not only swears by God to stay with Naomi but invokes God to inflict on her a curse if she violates her pledge to her mother-in-law (Ruth 1:17). People who swore falsely or did not carry out their oaths were punished. Judaism repeatedly stressed the importance of speaking and swearing truthfully (e.g., Sir. 23:7-11).

People sometimes swore by God's name directly. However, verse 35 intimates that people in Matthew's day swore by other things that served as stand-ins for God, for example, by heaven, which is the throne of God; by earth, which is the divine footstool (Isa. 66:1; cf. Philo, *Special Laws* 2.1.5); by Jerusalem, known as the city of the great sovereign (Ps. 48:2); or by the head. Matthew later charges that swearing, and multiple abuses, are characteristic of the Pharisees (23:16-22).

However, the Matthean Jesus instructs the disciples not to swear at all. Like divorce, taking an oath was practiced because of the brokenness of the old age. In the realm of God human hearts and relationships are transformed so that oaths are no longer necessary.

By using the double affirmative ("Yes, Yes") and the double negative ("No, No"), Matthew underscores the point that a disciple's word is trustworthy. By adding "anything more than this comes from the evil one," Matthew implies that the practice of the conventional Pharisees (23:16-22) is in league with the devil. This unfortunate motif is a part of Matthew's polemic against the Pharisees.

The contemporary church can certainly be expected to witness to the realm of God by enacting these new world qualities within its own common life. The preacher needs to help the community wrestle with the possibilities and difficulties posed by enacting these attitudes and behaviors in the larger world with its old age characteristics.

Ronald J. Allen

Seventh Sunday after the Epiphany, Year A

First Lesson: Leviticus 19:1-2, 9-18
(Psalm 119:33-40)
Second Lesson: 1 Corinthians 3:10-11, 16-23
Gospel Lesson: Matthew 5:38-48

The beginning of the commentary on the lection for the Sixth Sunday after the Epiphany indicates that Jesus' teaching in Matthew 5:21-48 is not antithetical to the First Testament and to Judaism, but seeks to interpret Jewish themes for the situation of the Matthean church from the perspective of the manifestation of the reign of God. The passage for today fits into this pattern.

Matthew 5:38 articulates a principle that is stated several times in the First Testament (e.g., Exod. 21:14; Lev. 24:20; Deut. 19:21). At one time unlimited retaliation was a part of life in the ancient Near East. If someone gouged out my eye, I could retaliate by removing both of the offender's eyes and the eyes of everyone in the offender's household (if I could find a situation in which to do such things). The idea of "an eye for an eye" is an attempt to limit retaliation. The offended party may inflict the offending party in proportion to the offense. By the first century c.e., the Jewish people had refined this principle even further. People could make restitution with money or goods rather than by extracting retribution in kind.

These efforts attempt to maintain the community as community. Unlimited retaliation could destroy the very resources (human and otherwise) that are needed for common life to continue.

Jesus reinterprets this principle for the community of the new world (v. 39a) and offers five examples of how it can come to life in the Matthean community (vv. 39b-42). The examples demonstrate perspective and behavior in particular instances that listeners can apply in other situations. This passage presumes the Roman occupation of Palestine as background.

The principle is, "Do not resist an evildoer" (v. 39a). Behind this counsel is the confidence that *God* will soon initiate the invasion of the cosmos to complete the full manifestation of the dominion of God that will end the dominion of Caesar. From the apocalyptic point of view, the vocation of the church is not to dethrone evil powers. God will do that through the apocalypse. Active resistance is in league with the old age by making use of human use of force (whether physically or in a legal setting) that often ends in brutality (see on Matt. 5:9 above). By contrast, God exercises power in the new world. However, the community *is* called to witness to the presence and character of the divine realm to Caesar and the Roman minions. The apocalyptic theologians hoped that demonstrations of faithfulness would bring about the repentance of the unfaithful (e.g., Rev. 9:20-21; 16:9, 11).

A slap in the face was an acid insult (e.g., Isa. 50:6; Lam. 3:30), and on the right side of the face especially so because it required either the back of the right hand (a particularly degrading action; 1 Esdr. 4:30) or the left hand. (The latter was perhaps denigrating because the left hand often functioned as toilet paper.) The disciple is to turn the other cheek. Behind this action is the apocalyptic belief that divine power is often demonstrated by actions that appear to be weak (e.g., the crucifixion of Jesus). Turning the other cheek is possible because the reign of God will provide security for all.

Verse 40 calls to mind a legal setting. People in the ancient world typically wore an inner garment (a shirt or coat) and an outer garment (a cloak). Because the outer garment served as a cover for sleeping and protection, Jewish policy mandated that it be returned each evening (Exod. 22:26-27; Deut. 24:12-13). Person A (a creditor?) sues person B for the inner garment. Perhaps person B has used the inner garment as pledge for a debt. Person B is voluntarily to turn over both garments. The behavior of person B witnesses to the dominion of God in which God clothes all. In the meantime, person B trusts God in the manner of Matthew 6:25-33.

Verse 41 recalls the Roman custom of impressing Jewish residents of Palestine to carry Roman loads for a mile. Disciples are to carry such loads a second mile. In the reign of God, such forced labor is replaced by rest (cf. 11:28-30).

Verse 42a invokes one of the most important practices of Judaism for providing for the poor in the old age: opening one's resources to the poor and giving alms (e.g., Exod. 23:10-11; Deut. 15:4-11; Prov. 14:21, 31; Isa. 58:6-8; Tob. 4:7, 16; 12:8-9; Sir. 7:10; 29:3). The dominion of God will replace poverty with abundance, but until it does the church is to demonstrate God's will to bless all in the community by providing for the poor (cf. Matt. 6:2-3, 19-21; 26:11 in conjunction with Deut. 15:7-11).

Verse 42b continues the same theme. Judaism provided for Jewish people to borrow without interest (Exod. 22:25; Lev. 25:36; 4 Macc. 2:8-9). Borrowing was an old-aeon mechanism to help distribute material resources so that the level of blessing in the community could rise (Sir. 29:1-13). In the first century, however, moneylenders often charged exorbitant interest in order to fatten their profits. They would refuse to loan to borrowers who looked risky. In the dominion of God, borrowing will not be necessary. In the meantime, the community of the new age is to act as a faithful Jewish community by making loans without usury.

The final segment of this part of the Sermon on the Mount claims that Jewish tradition directs love of neighbor and hatred of enemies (5:43). While the former is well attested (e.g., Lev. 19:18), Judaism nowhere prescribes hatred of enemies, though some strands of Judaism describe hatred toward enemies in response to their heinous deeds (e.g., Pss. 119:113-15; 139:19-22). The Jewish community debated whether neighbors should be understood only as comrade Israelites or as all persons. Matthew speaks as if the listeners take neighbors to be persons with whom they are in positive relationship.

The reign of God, however, restores all relationships to the mutual encouragement and support of the world in Genesis 1–2. Consequently, the disciples are to witness to the divine rule by loving their enemies and praying for those who persecute them (v. 44). In this way they both anticipate the completion of the divine realm and identify themselves as children of God, that is, the community that recognizes that the transforming of the cosmos is under way (v. 45a). On persecutors in the Matthean context, see the comments on 5:10-12.

Loving the enemy and praying for the persecutor are grounded in God's own pattern of relating with the world (v. 45). As God promised Noah, God provides sun and rain for the whole human family (Gen. 8:22). Indeed, an important strand in Judaism repeatedly asserts the divine sovereignty and impartiality (e.g., Deut. 10:17-18; 1 Kings 8:41-43; 2 Kings 5:1-19; Wisd. of Sol. 5:18; Sir. 35:15-16). It is inherent in God's nature to provide for both evil people and good, righteous and unrighteous. This aspect of God's character will be most fully expressed when the divine reign is fully operative.

According to verse 46, when people love persons with whom they are already in positive relationship, they are simply reproducing behaviors that are typical of the old age. Even tax collectors, the epitome of the old world, do as much. Tax collectors were Jewish people who conspired with Rome to extort heavy taxes from the Jewish people and were despised by many of their Jewish compatriots.

In the ancient world a greeting on the street acknowledged the personhood of the one greeted, and it implied a covenantal bond between the two parties. According to verse 47, when people only greet persons with whom they are already in relationship, they are again only replicating old age attitudes.

The realm of God creates a community of peoples who have been separated and alienated. Love for the enemy prefigures this restored community in the midst of the fractious communities of the old order.

The root meaning of the term "perfect" is undivided, whole, complete (e.g., 2 Macc. 12:42; T. Jud. 23:5). When verse 48 admonishes the community to be perfect, it means perfection in the sense of treating other people in the same way God treats people in the divine realm, that is, in a way that is undivided or whole. A parallel from the First Testament is the holiness of God that begets holy living in the community (Lev. 19:2; 20:26; 21:8). In the new world God will regenerate all relationships. The Matthean Jesus instructs the disciples to live in the present on the basis of the power of the new world that is already operative.

This teaching draws on the popular Hellenistic concept that human persons and communities achieve identity, in part, by imitating exemplars. Imitation not only produces behavior but forms character. People become faithful by imitating faithful people (e.g., 4 Macc. 9:23; 13:9; *T. Ben.* 3:1; 4:1) and even by imitating God (e.g., *T. Ash.* 4:3; *Ep. Arist.* 210, 280-81).

The theological core of verses 43-48 is in some tension with the theme of eternal condemnation found in the First Gospel. If God is truly gracious and provident toward all, and if God is consistent, then I believe God's providence and grace should extend for all into the complete manifestation of the realm of God.

Ronald J. Allen

Eighth Sunday after the Epiphany, Year A

First Lesson: Isaiah 49:8-16a
(Psalm 131)
Second Lesson: 1 Corinthians 4:1-5
Gospel Lesson: Matthew 6:24-34

Today's lesson should begin at Matthew 6:19 because 6:24 assumes 6:19-23. According to 6:19a, many people try to make themselves secure by storing up treasures (money and other material goods). However, such treasures belong to the old age moth, and rust destroys materials in the old aeon (e.g., Job 13:28; Isa. 51:8; Mal. 3:11; Hos. 5:12). Thieves steal, especially in an economically insecure world like that of Matthew, in which many people are impoverished.

Instead Jesus admonishes the disciples to store up "treasures in heaven" (Matt. 6:20). What are these treasures? Christians are often surprised to discover that in Matthew's world "treasures in heaven" refers to almsgiving (Sir. 29:8-12; more broadly of "good works," see Tob. 4:9; 2 Esdr. 6:5; 7:77; 8:33; *2 Bar.* 14:12; *Pss. Sol.* 9:5; *1 Enoch* 38:12). People store up treasure in heaven, that is, participate in the realm of God, by sharing material resources with those in need. Almsgiving provides material help to the poor,

41

serves as a sign of God's will to bless all with abundant resources for life in the new world, and loosens the grip of the wealthy on their wealth.

Matthew 5:22-23 is an illustration. A healthy eye passes light into the whole body. In Judaism the eye is a symbol of the capacity to perceive (e.g., Prov. 23:6 [KJV]; 28:22 [KJV]; Sir. 14:10; *T. Iss.* 3:4; 4:6). Indeed, in Proverbs 22:9 [KJV] a good eye leads one to share bread with the poor (cf. Deut. 15:9; 28:54-56; *T. Ben.* 4:2-4). We paused earlier over the symbolism of light (on Matt. 5:14-16, see the Fifth Sunday after the Epiphany). In the same way, almsgiving allows the heart (the center of the self) to be healthy so that the whole self can function as a faithful member of the covenantal community. But when the eye is unhealthy, the body is full of darkness (cf. Tob. 4:7; Sir. 14:8; Matt. 20:15). People who do not perceive the importance of almsgiving and other practices of covenantal community live in darkness. When Matthew says, "How great is the darkness!" the reference is to everlasting condemnation (e.g., 8:12; 22:13; 25:30).

The Greek of Matthew 6:24 contains the Aramaic *mammon* (wealth, mammon), which personifies wealth. Wealth is not simply a possession but can function as a deity that people serve. 6:24 resonates with 5:9 (the statement that those who have an undivided heart are blessed). The heart cannot be divided between God and wealth.

This verse sets before the listener the choice of either serving God (epitomized by the practice of almsgiving) or serving wealth. The story of the rich young person illustrates the tragedy of the latter (19:16-30). Matthew frequently uses the figure of a servant serving a master to speak of the last judgment (e.g., 18:23-35; 21:33-44; 24:45-52; 24:14-31). These associations inform 6:19-24. People who serve wealth invite eternal condemnation.

6:25-34 assures listeners that they do not need to amass mammon in order to be secure. The circumstances of the Matthean community might prompt some in the community to question whether God is still provident for them. As noted in connection with 5:10-12, the community believes that it is persecuted by the traditional synagogue. Families are breaking apart, thus creating economic uncertainty (e.g., 10:21-22, 34-39). Social conditions are deteriorating as a result of the tribulation (24:3-28).

6:25-34 intends to encourage the community's confidence in God's providence. Even in an economically and socially precarious time, the congregation is not to store up treasures on earth and serve mammon, but is to engage in a life of common provision for all through almsgiving and other practices represented by almsgiving.

While the term "worry" can refer to general anxiety, in the first century it was particularly characteristic of the tribulation (e.g., Mark 13:11; Matt.

10:19; 2 Esdr. 2:27; 3:3). People feared both the suffering of the last days and the possibility of losing faith before the apocalyptic cataclysm. They naturally struggled to maintain life as they knew it. This struggle is represented in verse 25 by anxiety about food, drink, and clothing.

In verses 25b-34 the Matthean Jesus assures the congregation that they need not suffer eschatological anxiety. The passage does not downplay the importance of material resources (e.g., food, drink, clothing); God "knows that you need all these things" (5:32b). The new world will be a material realm, albeit a world of abundance in which things do not decay. The passage reminds the community that they need not suffer eschatological anxiety now or in the future because God provides.

Rather than simply assert such confidence, Jesus asks the disciples a question (v. 25b) and offers three examples (vv. 26, 27, 28-30). The question invites listeners to reflect for themselves on these matters. By participating in the three analogies, listeners imaginatively experience divine provision.

In Palestine birds had a precarious existence. They did not engage in structured activities to stave off anxiety (sowing, reaping, gathering), yet God fed them (v. 26; cf. Pss. 104:12; 147:9; Pss. Sol. 5:9-10). When we hear this brief statement, we feel fed.

The precise meaning of verse 27 is debated. The central expression could mean "add a single hour to your life span" or "add one cubit to your height." Either way the essential point is the same: given the limitations of this broken age, human beings cannot increase their ability to provide for themselves (either through increased life span or increased size and strength).

The lilies (flowers) likewise do not engage in old-age behaviors (toiling and spinning) to secure themselves. Spinning is associated with women. Many Jewish people remembered the reign of Solomon as the high point of opulence in Israel (e.g., 1 Kings 3:13; 10:14-26; 2 Chron. 9:13-18). However, even Solomon's most elaborate garments pale in comparison with the splendor of flowers.

The "grass" of verse 30 is no longer the splendid flower, but is ordinary grass. In parts of Palestine that are semiarid, grass grows only during the few months of rain. When that season ends, the grass becomes brown and brittle and is good only to be burned. During its green season, however, grass has its own beauty. While the passage is not an allegory, the listener cannot miss the association of "grass" with the fragility of humankind (e.g., Isa. 40:6-7; cf. Ps. 103:15). If God so clothes the grass, with its short life, how much more God clothes the faithful.

To be anxious is to manifest Gentile uncertainty (v. 32). Indeed, people are idolatrous when they think they can provide for themselves. God has created the world so that it can provide.

Verse 33 directs listeners to "strive first" for the reign of God and the divine righteousness. (These ideas are discussed in connection with the Fourth Sunday after the Epiphany). Matthew does not imply that by "striving" or "seeking" people can work their way into the realm of God. Nor does the author imply a business deal: if people strive, God will give. To the contrary, the realm comes as a gift. In some Jewish circles striving was equivalent with study, that is, becoming cognizant of the presence of the reign of God and responding appropriately (e.g., Ps. 37:3-4; Wis. 7:11).

The community is to witness to the reign of God today, without being anxious about difficulties (e.g., persecution, economic and social uncertainty) that may come tomorrow (v. 34). Indeed, Jesus may return from glory tomorrow and end present anxiety by completing the establishment of the reign of God.

A very practical question arises. How does God provide? The creation imagery of verses 26-30 (e.g., birds, sowing, reaping, lilies, growing, grass) evokes Genesis 1 and 8:22. At creation God endowed the world with structures of providence. After the fall and flood God reaffirmed these phenomena. Furthermore, for Matthew God meets the material needs of the faithful through their own common life as well as through the support of others. In the Jewish world almsgiving is a means that God instituted in order to provide for those in need. When the church witnesses to the realm of God to persons outside the ecclesial circle, these persons become agents of providence through the ancient custom of hospitality (e.g., 10:9-10, 40-41; 25:31-46). The Matthean community can trust God to provide through these means, even in the midst of persecution and economic and social collapse.

Ronald J. Allen

Second Sunday after Pentecost, Year A

First Lesson: Genesis 6:9-22; 7:24; 8:14-19
(Psalm 46)
Second Lesson: Romans 1:16-17; 3:22b-28, (29-31)
Gospel Lesson: Matthew 7:21-29

Ninth Sunday after the Epiphany, Year A

First Lesson: Deuteronomy 11:18-21, 26-28
(Psalm 31:1-5, 19-24)
Second Lesson: Romans 1:16-17; 3:22b-28, (29-31)
Gospel Lesson: Matthew 7:21-29

According to verse 21, this climactic passage in the Sermon on the Mount is addressed to the Matthean congregation. Disciples address Jesus as "Lord, Lord." This text epitomizes a dramatic theme in the First Gospel: Christians must exhibit integrity between their words and deeds or face condemnation. Matthew is prophetically consistent on this point. Matthew accuses non-Christian Pharisees of inconsistency between the tradition they espouse (words) and their behavior (deeds) for which they will be judged and condemned (e.g., 12:1-8, 9-14, 22-32, 33-37, 43-45; 15:1-20; 16:5-12; 21:33-45; esp. 23:1-36). However, in 7:21-29 the Gospel writer levels the same gavel on the church, with the same consequences. Membership in the church does not spare people from the great judgment at the end of history. This theme runs throughout the Gospel and reaches its most intense expression in 24:45–25:46.

Those who will enter into the realm of God are those who do the will of God (5:20b). What is this will? For Matthew it is revealed through Torah as interpreted by Jesus. Here is a representative, nonexhaustive list of elements of the divine will: repentance as a first act of response to the recognition that the divine realm is becoming manifest (4:17); honoring Torah (5:17-20); resolving anger (5:21-26); maintaining marital relationships (5:27-33); speaking so that one's word can be trustworthy without swearing (5:33-37); refraining from resisting evil (5:38-42); loving the enemy and practicing the impartial generosity of God (5:43-48); almsgiving (6:2); praying for the divine reign (6:6-13); practicing forgiveness (6:14-15; 18:21-35); judging cautiously (7:1-5); acting mercifully (9:10-13); performing miracles (e.g., 10:7-

45

8); announcing the coming of the rule of God while testifying before authorities (10:16-20); seeking the lost (18:10-20); keeping the weightier matters of the law — justice, mercy, and faith (23:23); multiplying the community's witness to the realm of God (24:14-30); feeding the hungry, giving drink to the thirsty, welcoming the stranger, clothing the naked, visiting the prisoner (25:31-46); taking the gospel to Gentiles (28:16-20). These qualities may be summarized by the notion of witnessing to and embodying the restoration of all relationships in the realm of God.

In calling for consistency between words and deeds, the First Gospel does not downplay the importance of language. According to 12:36-37, on the judgment day people will have "to give an account for every careless word you utter; for by your words you will be justified, and by your words you will be condemned." The immediate literary context is Jesus' warning against blasphemy against the Holy Spirit (12:22-32). Such blasphemy invites condemnation. In addition, a larger reciprocal understanding of the relationship between words and deeds is implied. Just as a good tree brings forth good fruit (and a bad tree bad fruit), so our words (and thoughts) from the heart shape our character and behavior (12:33-34). The language of "fruit" is a traditional Jewish expression for behavior. The key to whether a tree (a human being) yields good fruit or bad is the content of the heart. Our behavior indicates whether we have a good heart or bad, that is, whether our language is sincere.

On the judgment day some people will say they prophesied in Jesus' name, or cast out demons, or did many deeds of power, and therefore should be part of the eternal and complete realm of God (7:22). The office of prophet emerged early on in the church's life. A prophet received messages from the risen Jesus and spoke them in the assembly. In this way the risen Jesus could continue to instruct the church, especially in regard to its problems. (Indeed, some scholars think parts of the Sermon on the Mount came from such prophets.) However, 7:15-19 and 24:11, 24 indicate the presence of prophets who prophesied falsely in the community, probably by advocating lawlessness (24:12; cf. on 7:23 below), or foolishly limiting the scope of the apocalyptic cataclysm (24:23-28), or foolishly trying to predict its date (24:36). The reference to bearing bad fruit in 7:16-20 indicates that they did not manifest behaviors characteristic of the full range of the will of God.

The early church also contained exorcists and persons who performed deeds of power (miracle workers). 24:24 suggests that they worked great signs, but that their signs led the church astray (cf. 12:38-42; 16:1-4). Like the false prophets, these persons probably also failed to live the full range of behaviors that manifest the will of God.

46

According to 7:23, Jesus acting as cosmic judge will deny relationship with these persons (see similarly 25:11-12). The NRSV calls them "evildoers," but a better translation is "lawless ones." In the First Gospel, to be lawless is to overlook parts of the Matthean interpretation of Torah. As a part of the ongoing polemic against the Pharisees in the First Gospel, Matthew accuses them of lawlessness (23:28). To the casual observer, according to Matthew, they appear to be obedient. But they do not attend to the "weightier matters of the law: justice and mercy and faith" (23:23). On the command "Go away from me, you evildoers [lawless ones]," see Psalm 6:8 (Septuagint).

Matthew 7:24-27 is a comparison that underscores the importance of recognizing the manifestation of the reign of God and responding by enacting the Torah of the new age. The conjunction of hearing and doing is fundamental to Jewish identity (e.g., Deut. 31:12).

Those who hear and do the words of Jesus are like the wise persons who build their houses on rocks. The storm cannot destroy them. In the broader wisdom tradition, the term "wise persons" refers to people who can discern the ways of God in the world and align themselves with those ways (e.g., Prov. 2:6). In the Gospel of Matthew, to be wise has the further particularity of recognizing the present and coming manifestation of the divine rule and responding appropriately with the lifestyle of the divine realm (e.g., 10:16; 24:45-52; 25:1-13).

The wise person chooses a site to build a home that provides a rock foundation. The mention of "rock" is a triple entendre. Of course, it refers to the stone that provides a solid foundation. Judaism also frequently uses the term to describe God (e.g., Pss. 18:2; 62:2). This occurrence of the term in the First Gospel points forward to 16:18, in which the confession of Peter that Jesus is the Christ, that is, the apocalyptic redeemer, is the rock on which the church is founded. 16:18 also recalls 7:24-27. The solid rock that is the confession that Jesus is the Christ includes living the covenantal life of Torah.

The description of the storm is typical of Palestine. When a storm comes up suddenly, the soil cannot always absorb the mass of water. The usual paths for runoff are overwhelmed. The area is flooded. The water rushes like a torrent down the wadis, pushing things before it. Furthermore, the storm of 7:25 includes fierce wind.

Jewish people sometimes associate the imagery of rain, flood, and wind with the power of chaos, and even of judgment (Isa. 28:17; Ezek. 13:11-14; Hos. 8:7). Some of this language recurs in the Gospel of Matthew to bespeak the situation of the Matthean congregation (8:23-27; 14:22-33).

Those who hear the words of Jesus but do not act on them are like those who build their houses on the sand. Sand is unstable. The house may even be in the middle of a wadi. A wadi is essentially a very large ditch through which excess water rampages. However, during the dry season a wadi can look harmless.

The storm destroys the house. As noted earlier, in the broader wisdom tradition the fool does not know (or follow) God, which can result in condemnation. In the Gospel of Matthew, to be foolish has the particularity of failing to recognize the present and coming manifestation of the divine rule through Jesus Christ (cf. 5:13; 25:1-13). The foolish are blind to the ways of God (23:17).

The fall is the condemnation that follows the great judgment after the apocalyptic cataclysm.

Matthew does not advocate works righteousness in these regards. People are received into the realm of God by grace. Entrance into the realm of God creates a realm identity that must be expressed in all aspects of life — heart, mind, body, and actions. When people act in ways that are contradictory to their identity, they must either repent (and reform) or lose a place in the common life.

Ronald J. Allen

Third Sunday after Pentecost, Year A

First Lesson: Genesis 12:1-9
(Psalm 33:1-12)
Second Lesson: Romans 4:13-25
Gospel Lesson: Matthew 9:9-13, 18-26

Chapters 8 and 9 of Matthew, which provide the context for today's Gospel, present Jesus in a kaleidoscopic series of images: healer, exorcist, teacher, physician, bridegroom, lord, servant, Son of David, Son of Man, and Son of God. But there is an ominous note in the progression. What begins (8:1-4) with Jesus' ministry of transforming power and promise comes to a close with Jesus denied as a blasphemer, in league with the prince of demons (9:34). Nine miracle stories are packed into these two chapters — ten, in fact, with the addition of the somewhat complex verses of today's Gospel (18-26), which report two interwoven miracle stories. They are arranged in three clusters of three miracle stories each, linked by reports dealing with discipleship matters, including today's Gospel account of the calling of Matthew, which evokes instant hostility from the Pharisees (9:9-13).

The Gospel reading today begins with the call of Matthew. It follows immediately upon the healing of the paralytic and Jesus' declaration of the priority on sin forgiven as the essence of being whole (9:1-8). "As Jesus was walking along" — from Capernaum — suggests that the location was not far from the border between the territories of Philip and Herod Antipas. There was a road there which crossed the border near Capernaum. It was customary for customs officials to set up their booth and collect duty on goods in transit. Matthew was collecting import and export duties for Herod in all likelihood, a practitioner in a despised profession (v. 11).

It has been thought by some that the Matthew referred to here (the name Levi is found in Mark 2:14 and Luke 5:27) is a subtle device for Matthew to introduce himself. That is possible. It may also be that the author of this Gospel is here honoring the memory of one of the great past founders of his community. In any case, the author is presenting a powerful event that depicts the nature of discipleship in the new age. Jesus calls to himself people totally lacking in all ordinary qualifications of piety, rectitude, or deservedness. This is an important preaching point for amplification; everything about discipleship is based on the radical grace of Jesus' call: "Follow me." The response is immediate. Matthew "rose and followed him." The account resembles the earlier calling of Peter and Andrew (4:18-22). The commanding authority of Jesus brings a compelling response. Nothing is said about the interim arrangements that would need attention after leaving all and following Jesus. The focus is on Jesus. This is a picture of what happens when the kingdom of heaven is drawing near.

Jesus' messianic authority, revealed in the calling of Matthew as well as the miracles reported in this text, opens up the twofold issue in which his ministry is already engaged. First, Jesus does not employ his authority for judgment, but rather for compassion and mission. Second, his compassionate use of his own authority issues in judgment nevertheless, for his mighty works demand response and therefore evoke a decision and produce a division. This twofold issue has been building throughout the narrative. The crowds who witnessed the healing of the paralytic "were filled with awe and glorified God, who had given such authority to human beings" (9:8). This is paired with the Pharisees, who take offense at him, challenging his authority to eat with tax collectors and sinners (v. 11).

Jesus' response to the Pharisees acknowledges the inevitable division his ministry brings. His words reflect his awareness that he brings into the world a distinction as sharp and radical as that between life and death (8:22). Who he is and what he brings differ from human views of piety as sharply as feasting differs from fasting (9:14). All that he is and brings is new and wonderful. The good news he brings will not be trimmed to fit into existing frames. He is not a patch to be sewn on the current religious piety, not a tame and mellowed wine that can be poured into the old and fragile wineskins (9:16-17). He comes as the fulfillment of God's promise, not as an accretion to the accumulated piety of human origin. And so his coming signifies cleavage. He seeks the sinner and forgives him. He separates himself from the righteous, not because they are righteous but because they would use their righteousness to assert themselves and oppose the higher righteousness of love, the divine compassion that flows through Jesus' words and works.

To this compassion of Jesus the church is summoned, and by his authority the church is equipped. Today's Gospel presents both. To be with Jesus as those called by him and healed by him is to behold his glory, the awesome glory of his authority and the winsome glory of his compassion. And, we must add, his terrifying glory before which people divide, to the right and to the left, for weal or woe, and forever.

Another insight into the calling of Matthew is how Jesus relates "follower" to "apostle" (10:2). The concept of being a disciple of a rabbi was not new, of course. Jesus drew on the familiar Jewish legal institution of the authorized follower or messenger, *shaliaḥ* in Hebrew. The main idea was that of a conferred authority, or power of proxy, which made one's *shaliaḥ* as that man himself, thus completely capable of representing the sender and wholly subordinated to the sender's will. The word therefore came to Jesus and to Matthew already fraught with the idea of a decisive authorization by a higher authority and a resolute belonging under that authority on the part of the one sent, so that the will of the sender counted supremely.

This insight offers needed truth for today's church, which can be either too torn by loveless authority or too hapless through no sense of authority at all. The former makes the human churchly institution so central as to obscure the Lord. The latter veers off into subjective isolation, as if Jesus' Lordship conferred nothing decisive upon the church. The former threatens the congregation with dead formalism. The latter makes the church vulnerable to the lure of whatever sells in the surrounding culture. The remedy for both lies in the compassion and the authority of Jesus Christ, as today's Gospel declares.

Now the scene shifts to a leader of the synagogue who bursts on the scene in a state of numbness: "My daughter has just died, but come and lay your hand on her and she will live" (v. 18). Mark and Luke tell his name, Jairus. He kneels before Jesus with an anguished cry that only a bereaved parent can know. And now, it is not Matthew who immediately gets up and follows, but Jesus who immediately "rose and followed him with his disciples" (v. 19).

Yet another cry for help intervenes as Jesus joins the distraught father. "A woman who had suffered a hemorrhage for twelve years came up behind him" and, reaching out in faith, touched the fringe of his garment (cf. a similar appeal in 14:36). Instantly, as Jesus speaks the word (8:8), she was made well. Matthew uses the term *sōzō*, "save." It occurs three times in two verses. The woman trusted Jesus and was made well, whole, saved, by his word (1:21).

He continues to the ruler's house, where the professional mourners and flute players have already assembled in the ritual of lamentation. The custom endures to this day in many cultures. I have witnessed this scene in Kenya: relatives and hired mourners arrive to circle the hut of the deceased person with crying that can be heard at some distance. Upon completing the third time around, the lamentation stops abruptly. All sit down for tea and the latest news from the neighborhood. Somehow formulaic tears always have a crocodile character.

Jesus' authority emerges as he clears the scene of mourners and mockers, who "laughed at him" (v. 24). Both groups signify unbelief, just as the healed woman models faith. She believed and was made whole; others laughed and were cast out. Matthew's account lacks the *"talitha cum"* which Mark includes. It may be that Matthew's community is more Greek and further from the Aramaic language than Mark's.

The two miracles are neatly interwoven. The healing of the woman serves to give a sense of time passing and also of spatial movement from the banquet hall to the ruler's house. But the two miracles are linked in other ways. Mark says the woman had been ill for a dozen years and that the girl was twelve years old. The ruler calls his child "daughter," and Jesus uses the same word when he addresses the sick woman. The ruler wants Jesus to touch his daughter, and the woman believes that her touching Jesus will be her salvation.

Thus the two stories complement each other. The woman exemplifies deep but simple faith. The dead girl cannot serve as a model of faith, but her story shows that the authority of Jesus extends beyond illness, even an illness of twelve-year duration, into the realm of death itself (16:18). He has all authority. Throughout chapters 8 and 9, Matthew has emphasized the limitless authority and compassion of Jesus and the absolute necessity of faith. Here they are brought together in a seamless narrative that develops both themes.

F. Dean Leuking

Fourth Sunday after Pentecost, Year A

First Lesson: Genesis 18:1-15; (21:1-7)
(Psalm 116:1-2, 12-19)
Second Lesson: Romans 5:1-8
Gospel Lesson: Matthew 9:35–10:8, (9-23)

The lection includes the opening portion of Jesus' second long address in Matthew, and begins with words almost identical to 4:23, the verse that inaugurated the first such address, the Sermon on the Mount. The preceding section, from 4:23 through 9:34, has portrayed Jesus in ministry. 9:35 both summarizes the work Jesus has done and serves as the transition to his disciples joining in that work. This is a turning point in the narrative, and in Jesus' work as it is broadened to include those he has called into ministry with him. Jesus' extended comments on ministry include all of chapter 10, but the lection is shorter and may end at either verse 8 or 23.

Jesus views the crowds drawn to him by his work with compassion rather than pity or condescension or revulsion or despair. Echoing several similar Old Testament situations, he sees them as oppressed, wandering, and leaderless, as "sheep without a shepherd" (cf. Num. 27:17; 1 Kings 22:17; 2 Chron. 18:16; Jer. 23:1-6; Ezek. 34:1-10; Mic. 5:2-4). Where others might gaze on such a group and see only desperate, even overwhelming, neediness, Jesus sees in them great potential. "Jesus, the embodiment of God's will, is the compassionate shepherd . . . [who] sees [the crowds] as a bumper crop ready for harvesting" (Thomas G. Long, *Matthew* [Louisville: Westminster John Knox, 1997], p. 113). What is needed are laborers to help him gather this harvest into renewed and renewing life with God. And so Je-

52

sus instructs his disciples to pray for "the Lord of the harvest" (cf. Ps. 24:1ff.: "The earth is the Lord's and the fullness thereof").

Presumably the disciples do so pray, only to find that they are to be the laborers. They realize "somebody should do something," and find they are the "somebodies" in the eyes and wisdom of God. Jesus calls them to himself and shares his authority with them that they might be empowered to do precisely the work he has been about. Heretofore only five of the twelve have been identified in their calling, but now the entire list is given, the names presented two by two as if to suggest that they will go forth in that manner to their work (cf. Mark 6:7). While the familial relations of some of the Twelve are mentioned, Peter the first, Matthew the tax collector, Simon the Cananaean, and Judas the betrayer are identified more specifically. Peter's role is gently affirmed as a first among equals. The telling contrast of having Matthew, the despised Roman collaborator, and Simon, a zealot committed to the violent overthrow of Rome, as well as one who will fall away to the point of betrayal makes clear the inclusive nature intended for the Christian community. By "uniting them to himself, [he can] unite them to each other" (Frederick Dale Bruner, *The Christbook: A Historical/Theological Commentary* [Waco, Tex.: Word, 1987], p. 370). Since the Twelve are in the process of being transformed from those who follow into those who are "sent out" in ministry on their own, Matthew understandably and rightfully calls them "apostles" in 10:2 (his only use of the word in his account).

Jesus' instructional speech to the Twelve begins at 10:5b, and may be broken down into three sections: 5b-8a, describing the apostles' work; 8b-15, addressing economic and hospitality matters; and 16-23, speaking of how to handle the opposition they will encounter. In accord with other New Testament passages (cf. Matt. 15:24; Rom. 1:16) and with Jesus' previous analysis of the crowds' condition, the primacy of going to "the lost sheep of Israel" first is affirmed. Jesus' intention is that the apostles stay close to the needs of "the least of these" (see Matt. 18:10; 25:40). The apostles are to speak ("proclaim the good news") and do ("cure the sick, raise the dead, cleanse the lepers, cast out demons"), as the latter bears witness to the truth of the former. Again, the wording repeats Jesus' own activities and draws the church into them.

Verses 8b-10 speak of economic issues. By grace the Twelve have been called into their work and equipped for it. They are not to profit from what has been freely given them. The people to whom they are sent already live under crushing financial burdens. The good news is not to burden them further. It is a gift in a world obsessed with financial security. In a time dominated by getting, taking, acquiring, and taxing, the church is to speak of and live by "another way" lest the gospel be subordinate to a god named mammon (see 6:24). The disciples are to travel extremely lightly, without any hint of ostentation. The instructed lack even of sandals and staff in that terrain is most likely hyperbole intended to underscore Jesus' seriousness about simplicity (Long, p. 117).

Verses 11-15 seem almost an answer to the apostles' unrecorded question of how they are then to provide for their most basic needs in light of Jesus' admonishment of simplicity. The answer has to do with accepting hospitality. When the disciples enter a new community and find someone who is worthy, by which Jesus means one who is receptive to their word and work and who welcomes them into his or her home, there they are to remain. They bless the house with peace and remain there, refusing any better offers that may come along during their stay. If hospitality is not extended to them, they are not to fight for acceptance but to move on, shaking the dust from their feet as they leave. This latter refers to the Jewish custom of shaking off the dust acquired on clothing and shoes while in non-Jewish areas as one reentered Jewish lands, lest anything unclean be brought in (Bruner, p. 378). The quintessential biblical examples of the lack of hospitality to God's messengers, Sodom and Gomorrah, are named as the example of how those not "worthy" shall be judged. The disciples are thus freed from concern and for their work elsewhere.

Empowered with such gifts for ministry, the apostles may be overconfident in the anticipated success of their work. So, Jesus cautions them in verses 16-23 that they will meet significant opposition. Yes, they have been made able to do the Shepherd's work, but they do so as sheep among wolves. When one chooses to work among the lost, one can expect to be treated like them by worldly powers. In an astonishingly mixed metaphor, they are to be "wise as serpents and innocent as doves." Snakes and birds could hardly be more dissimilar, but the implication is that those in ministry need not be naive but also not cynical; both thin-skinned enough to be empathetic and thick-skinned enough to withstand criticism; both angry at injustice and gentle in the overcoming of it, just as the Shepherd is both fully human and fully divine (cf. Paul's words in 2 Cor. 4:7-12).

Jesus' words of warning in the remainder of the lection make clear that his message will elicit hostile reactions in many, as has been true even from his birth (see 2:16ff., Herod's slaughter of the innocents). Those in ministry are to trust God to give them the needed words for their defense before Gentile authorities (to whom Jesus also will be handed over) and are to flee to new towns to continue their work if possible. The message and power with which the apostles, and by extension the church, have been entrusted will "comfort the afflicted and afflict the comfortable," and the latter will not take their affliction without the harsh response their considerable resources make possible.

The disciples are here transformed from recipients to givers, and clearly instructed as to the nature of their work. They are to "go and do likewise" (Luke 10:37) according to what they have heard and seen Jesus do. The blessed become the bestowers of blessing, and thereby come into greater fullness of discipleship. Many come to church seeking the gifts Christ brings, but there comes a time in the discipleship journey when such gifts must not only be received but passed on.

The work of the church is clearly delineated here: proclamation and all manner of healing. If the church is to be faithful, it must cure the sick, raise the dead, cleanse lepers, cast out demons. These tasks are not to be taken literally, but as the criteria for determining the focus and shape of the church's work in its particular setting. The church is called to continue and expand its ministries of healing for the many urban, rural, and Third World poor who have cripplingly limited access to health care. While Jesus indeed raised the physically dead and we may not, his word through the church can bring new life to those dead in despair, apathy, grief, workaholism, hedonism, substance abuse, and the absence of meaning. While leprosy, thanks almost exclusively to the work of Christ's church, is on the wane in much the world, surely AIDS patients continue to be treated as lepers by many, as do those suffering mental illness. And the demons of violence, materialism, hatred, and division possess many in the world. The church cannot be the church and ignore these calls to service any more than the disciples could have done so and been deemed faithful. The call to ministry is old and ever the same; the forms it takes are ever new.

Lawrence W. Farris

Fifth Sunday after Pentecost, Year A

First Lesson: Genesis 21:8-21
(Psalm 86:1-10, 16-17)
Second Lesson: Romans 6:1b-11
Gospel Lesson: Matthew 10:24-39

The Sundays following Pentecost recall the power of the Spirit which is essential for the successful mission of the church. Yet that essential power and promised success do not preclude being betrayed, persecuted, and even forced to flee from one place to another (Matt. 10:21-23). Like their Master, Jesus' disciples may have no place to lay their head (8:20).

This lection forms the last part of Matthew's Missionary Discourse (10:5-42). In its narrative introduction Jesus' mission is summarized in terms of his compassion for the crowds, who were like sheep without a shepherd (9:35-36). Out of such compassion Jesus incorporates his disciples into his mission because "the harvest is plentiful, but the workers are few" (9:37). Jesus also shares his authority with his disciples so that they can do precisely what he was doing: proclaiming the good news of the kingdom, healing every disease, and casting out demons (9:35; 10:7).

Like their Master's mission, the disciples' initial mission is directed exclusively to "the lost sheep of the house of Israel" (10:6; 15:24). Nevertheless, it is clearly Matthew's intention that the words of this discourse be understood as applying equally to the later commission to make disciples of all nations (28:19). For embedded in this discourse are words borrowed from or parallel to Jesus' Olivet Discourse, which speaks of their witness to all nations (10:17-22; Mark 13:9-13). Thus, whether they go to Israel or to the nations, the expectation of opposition and the need for courage and hope remain the same. In the immediate context, whether the promise that the disciples "will not finish going through the cities of Israel before the Son of Man comes" (Matt. 10:23) refers to an ongoing Jewish mission until the parousia, or whether it was fulfilled in the resurrection and appearances of the Son of Man, in Pentecost, or even in the judgment on Jerusalem, Matthew clearly teaches a mission to the nations that includes Jewish Israel. Wherever they go in their mission to the nations, wherever they manifest compassion for the crowds by giving witness to Jesus and the kingdom, Jesus warns that, like him, they will face opposition, betrayal, and death (10:16-21). Above all else, they must never be afraid (10:26). In this discourse Jesus gives reasons for such courage, hope, and lack of fear.

First, Jesus makes use of a proverb to illumine his disciples' situation. Students or servants occupy a position lower than that of their teacher/ master. Although they must aspire to be like him, they can never achieve a status equal to their master's (23:8, 10). Jesus' disciples are called to imitate their Master. Thus they must expect not only to be engaged in Jesus' mission, but also to suffer as Jesus suffered. If Jesus as master and head of the house is called Beelzebub/Beelzebul, so will his disciples. Although the derivation of this term is uncertain, whether Lord of the flies or Lord of the dwelling, in Matthew it is clearly a satanic epithet referring to the prince of the demons (12:24, 26). Like Jesus, his disciples will be considered not agents of God's compassion, salvation, and liberation, but rather agents of demonic oppression and enslavement. Yet whenever the disciples hear that epithet (or others like it) hurled at them, they will know that their troubles are like their Master's. And simply knowing that is to receive courage to endure troubles as Jesus did (1 Pet. 2:20-21). Even in suffering, identity with Jesus banishes fear and produces hope.

The second section in this lection (Matt. 10:26-31) provides three additional reasons for courage and hope. Since fear in the face of persecution is natural, Jesus issues three commands which provide reasons not to be afraid. While the first is in the aorist tense (a categorical imperative) and the other two are in the present tense (which could be translated "stop being afraid"), most interpreters believe this nuance should not be stressed. Instead, the focus falls simply on not being afraid. They should not be afraid, first, because God will see to it that what is presently concealed will be disclosed. In the final judgment the truth will be seen to be victorious over all who opposed it and tried to suppress it. Holding to this eschatological perspective and out of compassion for the crowds who need direction, the disciples must proclaim the truth openly and courageously. They must not give in to such fear of human opponents as to silence their proclamation or lead them to compromise the truth. The mystery of God hidden since the creation (13:35) must be publicly broadcast because the final judgment will fully unveil that mystery and reveal who belong to God's kingdom of truth.

The most that any opponent can do to silence the truth is to kill the witness. Yet, contrary to appearance, physical death does not destroy one's existence nor snatch one out of the Father's hand (John 10:29). Because Jesus died and rose again, disciples must not fear death. Instead, God is the only one to be feared, that is, to be held in awe and reverence because he alone is the judge "who is able to save and destroy" (James 4:12). While a few interpreters suggest that it is Satan who destroys soul and body in hell, the New Testament never counsels Christians to fear Satan because Jesus has already gained the victory over him. The New Testament does teach that while God is the God who saves, he is also the final judge who can consume his enemies (Heb. 12:29). Thus, even while facing persecution and death, the disciples should derive courage and hope from the awareness that God will judge in favor of those who confess Jesus and lose their lives for his sake (Matt. 10:32, 39).

Disciples must live by faith, not by sight; with hope, not with fear. They do not have all the answers to questions of evil and suffering, nor to the apparent victories of evil and the lie over truth and justice. Still they live with the assurance that God is in control and that his providence governs not only the life of the sparrow but also, and especially, the lives of his servants. God knows them intimately in ways their fellow human beings do not, for he has even numbered the hairs of their head (10:30). Hence even their troubles fall under God's providence. Consequently, they can face their troubles with hope and without fear. God is in control.

The most basic reason for courage and lack of fear is the absolute centrality of Jesus in the present and the future. Because Jesus reveals the present redemptive rule of God and is therefore the criterion for future judgment, no other person or relationship can be as significant as the relationship to Jesus. Allegiance to Jesus must manifest itself in public confession, in the refusal to be cowed or silenced by fear. Such allegiance is honored by Jesus before the Father (10:32-33). On the other hand, public denial of Jesus in the face of trial or bodily harm is evidence of lack of allegiance. Such lack also has consequences for one's standing before the Father. One's standing in the judgment depends on whether one stands up for Jesus in the present.

In this missionary discourse, standing up for Jesus means facing great difficulties. The era of universal peace still lies in the future; for now, in the present, Jesus has brought a sword which causes the divisions and oppositions characteristic of the period of the eschatological woes. While divisions may be of various kinds, the text stresses divisions in the family. This emphasis echoes Micah 7:6, where those who wait for the Lord discover that their enemies are members of their own household. In cultures where the family is elevated to an absolute status, allegiance to Jesus on the part of some can become a shattering intrusion. Where allegiance to Jesus precludes participation in the ceremonies and cultic rites on which familial and/or societal unity is based, his disciples will experience ostracism or something worse. Such was the experience of both Jewish and Gentile converts already in the first century. Human families are important as part of God's created order, but the family of God transcends the biological family because it is the family that does the will of God (Matt. 12:46-50). Of course, the ideal would be where there is no opposition because one's entire family joins the family of God. Thus Jesus demands that following him requires taking up one's cross, whether that be experiencing familial hostility, public trial, or martyrdom. A disciple is not above his Master; instead the disciple's life is shaped by the contours of the life of the Master.

In the twentieth century many Christians have experienced the troubles that Jesus describes. The rise of anti-God and anti-Christ totalitarian regimes produced more martyrs to the faith than in any previous century. Jesus' disciples have had to decide whether their ultimate allegiance was to their families, to the state, or to Jesus. Because of their identity with Jesus, many chose to bear a cross as real as his.

Many parts of the church have not had to face such opposition. For them the threats and fears are more subtle. The common cultural belief that faith is not to be voiced in public, that faith is merely subjective opinion holding no claims to public truth, silences many. Where public opinion prefers silence to engagement in religious matters, where many believe that the public voicing of religious beliefs promotes division rather than the social good, many Christians find it easier to opt for silence over shouting from the rooftops. Yet being silent lacks compassion for the crowds and constitutes a denial of Jesus. Since God's redemptive rule in the present and the future has been revealed in Jesus, that good news must be made known by those who follow Jesus. No present threat constitutes an adequate justification for silence.

David E. Holwerda

Sixth Sunday after Pentecost, Year A

First Lesson: Genesis 22:1-14
(Psalm 13)
Second Lesson: Romans 6:12-23
Gospel Lesson: Matthew 10:40-42

The possibility of persecution looms large in Matthew's Missionary Discourse. Jesus warns those he sends that they will not find the way easy. At almost every turn of the way there will be opposition, betrayal, and even death. Yet at the conclusion of the discourse there is a hint that all will not be bleak. Some will receive Jesus' representatives, and for such persons the reward will be great.

The basic promise underlying this passage is contained in God's covenant with Abraham:

> I will bless those who bless you,
>   and whoever curses you I will curse;
> and all peoples on earth
>   will be blessed through you.   (Gen. 12:3)

According to Matthew, Jesus is the one through whom this covenant is fulfilled, for he is the son of Abraham (Matt. 1:1), the promised shepherd who restores Israel (2:6) so that his disciples can carry out Israel's task of being the light of the world (5:14). Consequently, God's blessing once promised to Abraham and his descendants continues to fall upon Jesus' disciples and those who receive them. In fact, the act of receiving a disciple is simultaneously an act of receiving Jesus and the Father as well (10:40).

How should we understand this? Why should an individual's or a nation's response to a human follower of Jesus be considered a response to Jesus and God himself? There are two possibilities: a disciple is either Jesus' legal representative or agent, or an incarnational presence of Jesus and the Father — or both. Judaism was acquainted with the concept of legal representation based on delegated authority by which the person's agent (*shaliaḥ*) was equal to the person himself. The agent had the authority to act on behalf of the person who commissioned him. Jesus certainly delegated authority to his disciples and commissioned them to speak and act on his behalf (10:1, 7-8; 28:18-20). Yet this commission included not only the authority but also the power to speak and act as Jesus did (10:7-8). Such speaking and acting owes its power to the presence of the Spirit within them (10:20). The Gospel of John also assumes the concept of legal agency in presenting both Jesus and his disciples, yet it clearly moves beyond mere legal agency to an incarnational presence. The Father is so actually present in Jesus that seeing Jesus is seeing the Father (John 14:7-11). Similarly Jesus and the Father are present in the disciples (John 14:23; 17:21-23). Although Matthew's emphases are not the same as John's, it is intriguing that specifically in connection with the Great Commission Jesus promises, "Surely I am with you always, to the very end of the age" (Matt. 28:20). In the light of this promise, receiving a disciple of Jesus would entail also receiving Jesus because he is actually present in or with his disciples. Jesus is Immanuel, "God with us" (1:23).

What does it mean to receive a disciple? Initially Jesus' blessing applied to those who in a literal fashion hospitably welcomed the apostles and accepted their message. Such persons received the blessing of peace (shalom), the blessings of the kingdom of God (10:11-14). But this act of receiving Jesus' disciples and Jesus himself did not end with the death of the apostles. According to Jesus' seed parables, the power of the kingdom of God resides in the Word of God, in the proclaimed message (Matt. 13). This power was experienced first in Jesus' own proclamation of the kingdom and then in the proclamation of apostles commissioned to speak on his behalf. Because the one sent is as the one who sent him, the word of the apostles is for the church the word of Jesus, the apostolic word now contained in the New Testament. Therefore, receiving the apostles means accepting the truth and experiencing the power of their word contained in the New Testament. By so doing persons receive Jesus himself and, in receiving Jesus, receive the Father also. In this way Jesus continues to make disciples equipped to speak on his behalf and endowed with his continuing presence. How the world treats Jesus' disciples, how it responds to Jesus' message and presence in the message and presence of his church (16:18-19), becomes the criterion for blessing and peace. In this way the promised blessing of the nations through God's covenant with Abraham and his descendants continues to find fulfillment.

The blessing contained in receiving Jesus' disciples is explained further in three parallel sentences about receiving a prophet, a righteous person, and a little one. While some interpreters discover a hierarchy of offices in these verses (apostles in v. 40, prophets as itinerant preachers, righteous as local leaders, and little ones as laity), and others find three distinct groups (teachers, those who in obedience to the teaching live righteously, and children or others with little standing in the community), most treat these

61

three as an instance of synonymous parallelism which views the disciples from three different perspectives. Each perspective applies to the same group, to all disciples who represent Jesus.

The pairing of "prophet" and "righteous" occurs also in 13:17. There Jesus pronounced his disciples blessed because they saw and heard what "many prophets and righteous men" had desired to see but did not. Thus Jesus identifies his disciples, in distinction from those who heard but did not understand, with the privileged line of the Old Testament covenant people who were waiting for the fulfillment of God's promises.

The prophets had been sent to recall Israel to the demands of righteousness stipulated in the covenant. The righteous in Israel were those who listened to Moses and the prophets and faithfully kept the covenant and its righteousness. In this light it would be possible to distinguish prophets as teachers from the righteous who live in accordance with the prophetic teaching. However, it is questionable whether in Matthew such a distinction should be made. Because Jesus aligns his disciples with both the prophets and the righteous and assigns them the task of teaching all that he commanded, it is possible to conclude that for Matthew the righteous are also teachers of righteousness (28:20). An additional consideration is found in Jesus' warning not to listen to prophets who only prophesy but do not do "the will of my Father who is in heaven" (7:15-23). Every disciple must do good deeds (5:16) and possess the greater righteousness which includes fulfilling the true intention of God's commandments (5:17-20). In the final judgment the righteous are characterized as those who performed acts of hospitality and mercy for Jesus' needy brothers and sisters (25:34-40). Thus in Matthew prophets must not only teach but also walk in the ways of righteousness, and the righteous must not only do good deeds but also teach the ways of righteousness.

Two Old Testament stories from the lives of Elijah and Elisha illumine the meaning of receiving a prophet/righteous man because he is a prophet/righteous man. Both the widow in Zarephath and the Shunammite woman extend acts of hospitality to Elijah and Elisha because they acknowledge them as prophets/men of God, and both women receive a gift of life from God when the prophets bring their sons back to life (1 Kings 17:7-24; 2 Kings 4:8-37). Thus the act of receiving is basically an act of hospitality or kindness motivated either by the acceptance of the message or the attractiveness of the lifestyle of the witness, or both (Matt. 10:11-14). The one receiving is responding to the power of the Word of God spoken or to its visible, life-changing results in the one speaking. The reward is essentially the life-giving presence of Jesus and the Father. One can speak of the reward also as peace (10:13), or eschatologically as the inheritance promised to all God's people. This inheritance is as broad as the kingdom of God, which ultimately embraces the new heavens and earth in which God is fully present and righteousness dwells. This promise of the kingdom is at the same time the promise of eternal life (25:34, 46).

While the categories of prophet and righteous could be categories of honor or respect (although in Matthew the emphasis falls on the tasks implied), the last description of a disciple as "one of these little ones" moves in a different direction. This category is synonymous with Jesus' use of "little children," for in 18:5 Jesus makes the same promise that "whoever welcomes a little child in my name welcomes me." Little children and those who are like them are the greatest in the kingdom (18:1-10). Thus the little ones are those who are childlike, self-effacing, and humble as Jesus is humble in heart (11:29). They do not quarrel about matters of precedence or who is the greatest in the kingdom, but rather, like Jesus, live as servants (20:25-28). As little children who have been privileged to receive the revelation in Jesus, they stand in contrast to the wise and the learned (11:25). Such emphases are similar to Paul's theme that God chose the foolish and not the wise, those of lowly rather than noble birth, the weak rather than the strong (1 Cor. 1:26-29). In the parable of the sheep and the goats, the little ones are those who are hungry and thirsty, strangers, naked and in need of clothing, sick and in prison (25:35-40; cf. Isa. 58:7; Ezek. 18:14-16). Whoever responds to the needs of these little ones because they are Jesus' disciples is responding to the presence of Jesus and will receive the reward of the presence of Jesus.

The disciples of Jesus have the wonderful privilege of being not only the legally designated representatives of Jesus who as his agents speak on his behalf, but also of actually re-presenting the presence of Jesus in word and deed. This privilege carries with it no worldly prestige. Instead, it is the high privilege of being fools for Christ's sake, of living as servants for the sake of extending God's presence and blessing to a needy world. As the apostle Paul writes, "We have this treasure in jars of clay to show that this all-surpassing power is from God and not from us" (2 Cor. 4:7). How individuals and nations respond to this presence of God in the witness and life of Jesus' disciples determines whether they receive God's blessing or not (Gen. 12:3; Matt. 10:40-42). Their welcoming or hostile response to Jesus' disciples is their welcoming or hostile response to the Father and to the one he has sent.

David E. Holwerda

Third Sunday of Advent, Year A

First Lesson: Isaiah 35:1-10
(Psalm 146:5-10)
Second Lesson: James 5:7-10
Gospel Lesson: Matthew 11:2-11

This Advent lesson is occasioned by doubt and disappointed hope. For this reason it may be an unusually relevant Advent lesson. After two thousand years of celebrating what happened in the birth and ministry of Christ while waiting for his return, the church also knows something about doubt and unfulfilled expectations.

This particular occasion of doubt is especially surprising because it is voiced by the one who heralded Jesus' coming. This event so shocked earlier interpreters that some discounted John's own doubt and suggested that he sent his disciples to Jesus only to have their faith strengthened. But such an interpretation fails to understand John's own expectations.

The doubt of John the Baptist was real. Although he was the prophet sent by God to announce the arrival of the messianic Deliverer, he was now sitting in Herod's fortress-prison at Machaerus on the eastern side of the Dead Sea (Josephus). John's own announcement of the imminent arrival of the kingdom of God had been filled with themes of approaching wrath and judgment on the evildoers. The fire had been kindled, and they would be thrown into it (Matt. 3:10). Neither Judaism as a whole nor John the Baptist anticipated the arrival of the messianic kingdom without such judgment. Even the Old Testament itself seemed to blend together salvation and judgment as simultaneous events. Isaiah 61 had prophesied in a single sentence both the acceptable year of the Lord's favor and the day of judgment of our God. Yet when Jesus read that passage in the synagogue, he stopped in midsentence and omitted the announcement of judgment (Luke 4:19). This delay of the final judgment, found also in the parables of Jesus (e.g., parable of the tares), is teaching which clearly originated with Jesus. Today is the day of grace, and God's judgment is being delayed. This delay or this present failure to eliminate evil and to openly judge the oppressors of God's people lies at the heart of Judaism's rejection of Jesus' claim to be the Messiah. To-day also, now in the light of Jewish suffering throughout the Christian era and especially in the Nazi Holocaust, Jewish rabbis ask, how can Christians claim that Jesus is the Messiah who has already inaugurated the kingdom of God?

Thus, even though John was a prophet, he expected both blessing and judgment as simultaneous happenings, as the Old Testament had announced. The Malachi prophecy describing the messenger who prepares the way spoke also of the refiner's fire (3:2) and of the day of the Lord which burns like a furnace (4:1), called a "great and dreadful day" (4:5). Perhaps it was precisely because he was a prophet of the Lord that John could not understand why he should be sitting in prison while the one who sets the prisoners free, the messianic Lion of the tribe of Judah, was walking on the streets nearby. When would judgment fall on the oppressors of Israel as God had promised?

John had described Jesus as the "coming one who is stronger than I" (Matt. 3:11). Where, asks John, is the evidence? So he sent disciples to ask Jesus, "Are you the one who was to come, or should we expect someone else?" A shocking question from the one who filled Elijah's shoes, yet understandable. Even a prophet like Elijah was not free from doubt.

John had heard of the deeds of Christ but doubted because of what the Messiah had not done. Jesus replied only in terms of what he had done, his teaching and his miracles ("what you hear and see"). Two perspectives inform the significance of Jesus' answer. First, Jesus' description of his deeds echoes especially Isaiah 35:4-6 and 61:1 (as well as Isa. 26:19; 24:18). Thus Jesus' miracles are signs which signal the preparation of God's people for walking on the highway, called the Way of Holiness, back to Zion, the city of God (Isa. 35). His preaching of good news to the poor is evidence that God is fulfilling his promise to sow righteousness in the earth so that his praise will spring up before all the nations (Isa. 61:1, 11). Hence the deeds of Christ are the fulfillment of prophecy. Secondly, as placed in Matthew's Gospel, Jesus' answer summarizes and interprets all that is recorded from Matthew 4:17 to 11:1. Each of the miracles prophesied had actually occurred in Jesus' ministry, especially among the ten miracles recorded in chapters 8-9. Only the healing of lepers had not been prophesied, but this miracle could be either part of an Elisha typology (2 Kings 5) or simply subsumed in the spirit of Jesus "healing every disease and sickness" (Matt. 9:35). Preaching good news to the poor was also central to Jesus' ministry (4:17, 23; 5:3; 9:35). In Scripture "the poor" often designates the people of God who are oppressed. On the one hand, this term has economic connotations designating people who are materially poor. On the other hand, it is not exclusively an economic category, for it also designates God's people who, as poor and needy, look to God to deliver them out of all their troubles, whether material, political, or spiritual.

By stressing the positive qualities of his deeds, Jesus declares that he is the one who fulfills the Old Testament prophecies even though the final judgment of evil has not yet occurred. In this way he invites John to overcome his doubts and continue to believe: "Blessed is the one who does not fall away because of me." This verb can be translated "to take offense at," and hence to surrender faith and fall away. The deeds Jesus performed should be an adequate basis for faith even though faith has not yet seen all that it expects of the promised Messiah. Even if the Messiah lifts no hand to rescue John from prison and allows him to be beheaded, John should not take offense at him. Neither should we. It is always the miracles that Jesus does not perform for us that easily form a stumbling block for faith. However, since Jesus' manner of establishing the kingdom of God is shaped also by Isaiah's prophecies of the suffering servant (Isa. 53), we are encouraged not to take offense at a Messiah and kingdom that gains its victory over the nations through suffering and even martyrdom. The evidence for the arrival of the kingdom in Jesus is convincing, sealed by his own resurrection and ascension. He is already placing his people on the highway that leads into the city of God, for his miracles announce that that event is already under way.

After interpreting his own ministry for John, Jesus also interprets the ministry of John for the crowds. Yet in speaking about John, Jesus continues to speak about himself. He asks the crowd what they expected to see in the desert where John had appeared. While the desert or wilderness had associations with sin and the demonic, it also evoked thoughts of God's protection and preparation of his people for entrance into the Promised Land. On the basis of Isaiah 40:3, the Qumran community hoped by their life of repentance and obedience in the wilderness to prepare the way for God's promised redemption. Thus the crowd had gone out to John in the wilderness looking for prophetic signs of redemption and not merely for a reed swayed by the wind (a metaphor for weakness, indecisiveness) nor for the accoutrements of royalty. But the prophet they found, says Jesus, was more than a prophet. For John the Baptist not only prophesied but was prophesied about. As the object of prophecy, he was the promised eschatological prophet who would prepare the way for the revelation of God's glory. Since John is that prophesied prophet, Jesus is that promised presence (glory) of God.

The prophecy referred to is essentially Malachi 3:1 with overtones of Exodus 23:20 (a combination found in Mark 1:2 and also in Judaism). The Exodus component suggests an analogy between entrance into the Promised Land and entrance into God's coming presence and kingdom. In these prophecies God is the speaker, and the Malachi prophecy states explicitly that the messenger will prepare the way before *me* (God). In Matthew 11:10

there is a change from "me" to "you": ahead of *you, your* way, before *you.* Who is this "you"? In the context of Matthew's Gospel, it is obvious that Jesus stands in God's place and that in him the promised glory of God had been revealed. This switch from "me" to "you" is not to be explained as an arbitrary use of an Old Testament text, but rather as an interpretation of the text in the light of its fulfillment. From a Christian perspective Jesus is in fact the promised presence of God (1:23). Thus God himself exegetes his promises by what he does in sending his own Son. Hence all language about John the Baptist as messenger is inextricably related to the significance of Jesus Christ.

In the light of Malachi 3:1, Jesus interprets the relationship of John the Baptist to the kingdom of heaven in two sayings. While this lectionary reading concludes with the first saying and omits the second, more difficult saying, in both sayings John represents the end of the Old Testament era by announcing the imminent arrival of the promised new era of salvation. Wearing the mantle of Elijah, John represented the law and the prophets. As such there had not been anyone greater than John, for he alone had the privilege of announcing the arrival of God's promised kingdom, whereas all the other Old Testament prophets could only inquire as to when and how it would appear (1 Pet. 1:10-11). In this history-of-redemption perspective John was greater than the rest, yet even the person who is least in the kingdom is greater than John. For after announcing the kingdom's imminent arrival and pointing to Jesus as the one greater than he, John was removed from the scene. Like Moses, who saw the Promised Land from afar but did not enter, John saw the historical arrival of the kingdom but did not enter (i.e., he never became one of Jesus' disciples). This does not mean that John does not share in God's salvation, for he shares just as Old Testament people do (Matt. 8:11). From a history-of-redemption perspective John is a bridge figure connecting old to new, an Old Testament figure standing on the threshold of the new era who does not receive the baptism of the Spirit, which only Jesus could provide. Thus even those who are least in the kingdom enjoy greater blessings and privileges than John.

In this Advent lesson two objects of prophecy are encountered: the one who prepares the way for the arrival of God's kingdom and the other who ushers it in. Both announce the arrival of God's promised presence, and Jesus demonstrates its arrival in word and deed. The kingdom of God is already forcefully making its way (11:12). "He who has ears to ear, let him hear" (11:15). Let no doubt stand in the way.

David E. Holwerda

67

Seventh Sunday after Pentecost, Year A

First Lesson: Genesis 24:34-38, 42-49, 58-67
(Psalm 45:10-17)
Second Lesson: Romans 7:15-25a
Gospel Lesson: Matthew 11:16-19, 25-30

Jesus' self-revelation often shines most brightly in contexts of misunderstanding and unbelief. In such moments Jesus reveals the mystery of his identity and the blessings given to those who perceive it, but also the judgment that falls on those who see but do not perceive. Jesus' claim in this passage to be the exclusive revealer of the Father has been likened to a thunderbolt from the Johannine sky because the high christological claims are identical.

The presence of such a Revealer and his predecessor, John the Baptist, created a critical moment for the people of that generation. Its failure to recognize the urgency of that revelatory moment led Jesus to announce judgment on those who refused to repent and believe. Because of their unique privilege, their accountability in the coming judgment would be greater than that of the pagan cities Tyre and Sidon (Matt. 11:20-24).

That generation was privileged because John the Baptist was the greatest of the prophets, for he had been chosen to be the messenger who, as the promised Elijah, prepared the way of the Lord. If John was so great, then Jesus was even greater as the inaugurator of the promised time of salvation who by miracle and message proclaimed that the kingdom was now forcefully making its way. Jesus was already leading God's people on the highway, called the Way of Holiness, that leads to the city of God (11:4-5; cf. Isa. 35). In the face of such greatness, why did that generation in its entirety not respond? Jesus answers with the parable of children playing in the marketplace.

This parable has received two interpretations based on whether the voice of the children represents "this generation" or Jesus and John the Baptist. The currently popular interpretation favors the latter. It hears the voice of the children as the voice of Jesus and John. Like a flute player piping a wedding dance, Jesus voiced a message filled with notes of grace and joy inviting that generation to dance with joy at his wedding feast (Matt. 9:15). But John voiced a gloomier message, like a dirge inviting people to lament and beat their breasts in the face of the coming fiery judgment. This interpretation assumes that the comparison is not between "this generation" and "the children," but rather between "this generation" and the theme of the entire parable. "This generation" is then not like the children who invite but like the others who refuse to play the game. The major objection to this interpretation is that then Jesus speaks before John, inverting not only the historical order but the order found in verses 18-19.

In the second interpretation the words spoken by the children become "this generation's" own reasons for rejecting John and Jesus, reasons which correlate with their negative assessments in verses 18-19. John had appeared robed as a prophet, living an ascetic life in the wilderness, teaching fasting and repentance, and announcing judgment and doom, for "the ax is already at the root of the trees" (3:10). "This generation" found that message too harsh to accept and would have preferred a less severe prophet, one that responded to their invitation to dance with joy before the Lord. They believed they were entitled to such festivities without radical repentance. Yet when Jesus came announcing the wedding feast with no need to fast, his own personal fellowship with tax collectors and sinners was such a radical reversal of the conduct approved by the righteous that they accused him of being a sinful libertine. Apparently "this generation" preferred to have Jesus participate in a more solemn game because they believed the time of salvation had not yet come and the time of mourning was not yet over.

In either interpretation the outcome is basically the same. This unbelieving and unrepentant generation could accept neither the stern message of John nor the joyful message of Jesus. Neither message seemed to them to strike the right balance between their understanding of their own righteousness and the presence of sin/sinners in the world. John was too harsh on them, and Jesus was too soft on sinners.

Jesus' response to this rejection is intriguing: "Wisdom is justified by her works." "Wisdom" embraces all of God's revelation, whether special revelation through the prophets and apostles (Luke 11:49) or general revelation through the creation order (Prov. 8). Consequently, Wisdom reveals righteousness and justice and brings peace and life. Whereas in Luke, John and Jesus are the children of Wisdom as bringers of revelation, in Matthew Jesus is identified as the actual embodiment of Wisdom (11:19, 25-30; 23:34). As the fullness of Wisdom, Jesus is greater than the wisdom of Solomon (12:42). How can this claim be justified, or how can one know it to be true? Only by heeding Wisdom's call, by accepting Jesus' testimony and deeds. "Taste and see that the LORD is good" (Ps. 34:8). The proof is in the "eating." While the ultimate justification of Wisdom's claim will be found in the eschatological arrival of God's city, the truth of these claims can be known in the present by those who believe. For the blessings of Wisdom can be experienced only by those who do what Wisdom says. On the other hand, those who do not heed Wisdom's call will experience neither God's gift of life or peace either in the present or in the future (Prov. 1:22-33; Matt. 11:22).

The revelation of Wisdom is always a sovereign activity of God. Consequently, even in "that time" of rejection (11:25), Jesus praises his Father as the sovereign Lord of heaven and earth who both hides revelation and gives it, hiding it from the wise and learned and giving it to little children. "Wise and learned" is a pejorative category referring to a worldly wisdom divorced from knowledge of the Lord, a wisdom which God says he will destroy (Isa. 29:14; 1 Cor. 1:9-10). Humility is essential to perceiving the revelation God gives, a willingness to be taught as a child. It requires an acknowledgment of the fact that true wisdom cannot be discovered by human effort alone but must be revealed by God (Job 28:12-28). Hence both in the hiding and in the giving of revelation God's sovereign good pleasure is revealed. In this process human pride has no place, for God esteems only those who are humble and contrite in spirit and tremble at his word (Isa. 66:2).

As Wisdom had been entrusted with the mysteries of God and with the task of revealing them to humanity (Prov. 8:14ff.), so now Jesus has become the full embodiment of God's revelation and, therefore, the exclusive mediator of true knowledge of God. Jesus' knowledge of God is superior to all human traditions, for Jesus receives his knowledge of God's promised salvation and kingdom directly from his Father. His knowledge is in fact the knowledge the Father himself possesses. Consequently, even Judaism's understanding of the Wisdom and Law of God (Torah) must be amplified, corrected, and enriched by this one who is himself Wisdom and Torah. Only Wisdom as God's Son knows the Father, and only the Father truly knows the Son. Revelation flows from this mutual knowledge of Father and Son. Yet even Jesus' revelation of the Father remains a sovereign act, for the Son chooses those to whom he reveals the Father.

As the Revealer of the Father, Jesus invites all who are wearied and burdened to come to him for rest. Who are they? In the original setting they would include those wearied by the burdens placed on them by religious leaders who "tie up heavy loads and put them on men's shoulders, but they themselves are not willing to lift a finger to move them" (Matt. 23:4). But the invitation must not be restricted to a single circumstance. It includes all who live under the burden of sin and under the ignorance of God's ways, and who suffer from the frustrations and burdens of living in an imperfect world. For all such Jesus is the source of rest because he is the bearer of perfect knowledge of God and the inaugurator of his kingdom and its salvation. In the Old Testament promised rest is associated with God's presence (Exod. 33:14) and with following the ancient paths established by God (Jer. 6:16). Jesus is both the presence of God (Matt. 1:23; 28:20) and the interpreter and fulfiller of God's commandments (Matt. 5-7). Hence those who come to Jesus experience the rest promised to those who live in God's presence and walk in his ways. This rest in Christ is the beginning of the promised eternal Sabbath rest for the people of God (Heb. 4:3-11).

Paradoxically rest cannot be found apart from taking on a yoke. A yoke symbolizes work, for it enables an animal or a human being to perform a task (pull a plow, carry water). A yoke both restrains and enables. It is simultaneously a burden and a possibility. The question confronting humanity is, whose yoke or what yoke does one put on? No one lives without a yoke. God freed Israel from slavery in Egypt by breaking "the bars of your yoke and [enabling] you to walk with your heads held high" (Lev. 26:13). But when Israel failed to assume the Lord's yoke by serving him, God placed an unbreakable iron yoke on her neck, a harsh and uncomfortable burden under which Israel would have an anxious mind, eyes weary with longing, and a despairing heart (Deut. 28:47-65).

Humanity has but two choices: either take on Jesus' easy yoke that gives freedom, peace, and rest or take on some other yoke that destroys freedom, peace, and rest. In Jesus' day Judaism spoke of taking on the yoke of the Torah and the yoke of the kingdom of God. Although Jesus did not consider the law of God itself to be burdensome (Ps. 119, "a delight"), he does criticize the ongoing developments of the oral Torah as a heavy burden (Matt. 23:4). Later the apostle Paul characterizes that understanding of God's law as a source of spiritual slavery (Gal. 4:24-25). By way of contrast, Jesus describes his yoke as fitting, easy to wear, and kind, and Paul describes it as the way of freedom (Gal. 4:26, 31). The burden Jesus places on those who come to him is light both because he enables them to meet its demands and because those demands perfectly fit human beings created for fellowship with God and with one another. For the demands of this yoke are to love God above all and one's neighbor as oneself. Love is a gentle yoke, not burdensome or wearying, but light, easy, pleasant.

If the yoke is to be easy and the burden light, one thing more is necessary: to learn from Jesus himself how to walk the ancient paths that lead to the peace and rest of the kingdom of God and to inheriting the earth. Jesus was gentle, loving, forgiving, humble, and meek. He assumed the yoke of loving God above all and his neighbor as himself, and he inherited or gained title to the earth (Matt. 28:18; 1 Cor. 3:21-23). It is the meek who will inherit the earth, not the violent ones (Matt. 5:5; Ps. 37:7-11). It is inherited by

71

faith, not by force. Jesus assumed the yoke of the kingdom of God and gained the world. Those who humbly come to him, who live by faith, take on his yoke, and walk the ancient paths he walked, will receive the same inheritance both now and in the future: righteousness, rest, and peace.

David E. Holwerda

Eighth Sunday after Pentecost, Year A

First Lesson: Genesis 25:19-34
(Psalm 119:105-12)
Second Lesson: Romans 8:1-11
Gospel Lesson: Matthew 13:1-9, 18-23

C hapter 13 of Matthew's Gospel opens the third of Jesus' five discourses which form the organizing pattern for most of (but not all) Jesus' sayings. Briefly noted they are: chapters 5-7, the new community is called to practice the higher righteousness; chapter 10, the new community in its mission encounters hostility; chapter 13, the new community brings forth things new and old in its teaching and parables; chapter 18, the new community practices forgiveness and reconciliation; and chapters 24-25, the new community readies itself for the coming of the Son of man.

In the chapters just preceding this third discourse, two themes have been emphasized, along with the conflict they bring. First, Jesus is the unique Son of God (11:25-27) and the one in whom God chooses to establish his reign (12:28). Second, powerful enemies, however, will oppose him and will not rest with anything less than his death (9:34; 11:12; 12:24). Jesus and his fledgling disciples stand on one side of this conflict, and on the other side are the religious leaders. The crowds are caught in the middle and are faced with the question of what they are to do. They must struggle with their dilemma of wondering how it can happen that Jesus as the Son of God is not everywhere and always persuasive.

Chapter 13 picks up on this dilemma of the people, which has been growing, as the preceding chapters tell. Jesus truly is the one in whom the ancient promises and prophecies are fulfilled, and his appearing renders his disciples more blessed than all the righteous ones who came before (13:16-17), even though his identity is hidden and his authority may fail to impress. His followers must not despair that God's plan is deficient, even when present circumstances veil its power. Jesus summons hearers to seize the kingdom, despising tribulation or persecution, ignoring ridicule or anything else that makes discipleship costly, for the kingdom is supremely worth possessing.

One reason the disciples, and the crowds with them, are puzzled by the course of history is their failure to understand that the field on which life is lived is not neutral. Satan also sows bad seeds in the world. All who receive the good seed of the word of the kingdom proclaimed by Jesus and understand it are described as citizens of the kingdom (v. 38) and righteous (vv. 43, 49). On the other hand, weeds also spring up and flourish alongside the wheat in the kingdom. They closely resemble the righteous and live in the community with them but are in reality citizens of an evil empire (v. 38), and they are described as causing others to stumble (11:6) and as doing deeds of lawlessness (13:41). At the close of the age the righteous will shine like the sun in the kingdom of their Father (13:43), while the evil will weep and gnash their teeth (13:42, 50). So the parables focus relentlessly on what God is doing in the world through the ministry of Jesus and on the choices set before the people right now.

The parable of the sower and the seed makes the theological point that when God became human in Christ Jesus, all the usual defenses and self-preserving safeguards were set aside. The messianic king comes in defenselessness. The planting of God is exposed and vulnerable. Birds can devour it, the sun can wither it, and the thorns can choke it (13:1-9). Later in the chapter, in the verses following the Gospel for today, the teaching continues that the householder cannot — does not — prevent the enemy from sowing seeds where he has sown wheat (13:24-30). God, it would seem, has no nets that can selectively catch only good fish; his fishermen haul in good and bad alike (13:47-50).

And yet — the failure of the seed indicts the soil and the sower, and not the seed; the good seed on good soil bursts forth in bounty. If the devil sows weeds among the wheat, that is a sure sign that the wheat is God's planting, for that proud spirit attacks only works of God. And the event proves it so; though humans have no authority to execute judgment and uproot the devil's weeds, yet at the close of the age the Son of Man will execute judgment, burn the weeds, and bring home his wheat. The nets of God that gather good and bad alike sweep toward shore, and the eternal sorting comes.

73

The Christology of the parables, especially this one, is high indeed. The Messiah is a servant (12:17-21) and the kingdom is a "secret" (13:11). The splendor of the messianic fulfillment begins with the very opposite of splendor, with a Servant-Messiah whose only weapon is the word. He shall *proclaim* justice to the Gentiles (12:18). He goes the insignificant way of ministry to those whose ruined and desperate lives make them like the bruised reed and the smoldering wick (12:20). He is the Messiah who will not assert and defend himself but ministers in defenselessness. He will not wrangle or cry aloud (12:19). And yet it is just this Servant who shall triumph and bring God's cause to a triumphant issue, for he is the Lord's own chosen servant in whom God is well pleased, with God's Spirit on him to give his word victorious power (12:18). He shall bring justice to victory; he shall make the right and good and holy will of God everywhere prevail, so that all nations find their sure ground of confidence in him.

The kingdom is a mystery, a "secret." The words Jesus uses to explain the purpose of his teaching in parables — "To you it has been given to know the secrets of the kingdom of heaven" — recall the second chapter of Daniel. There the word "mystery" (translated "secrets" in Matt. 13:11) refers to the vision of King Nebuchadnezzar and its interpretation. It signifies the counsel of God which only God can reveal and will reveal, by his action "in the latter days" (Dan. 2:28). The "mystery" embraces God's whole governance and guidance of history to its ultimate goal — the goal, namely, that God shall reign supreme and reign alone. That guidance and governance takes surprising ways, in the face of massive and impressive forces marching through this world (Dan. 2:31 — the past century has seen enough of them). But at the end God shall intervene, and the rival forces will be ground to dust while God's kingdom will be like a great stone which fills the earth (Dan. 2:31-35).

Against this background of prophetic imagery, and with the metaphor changed to seed which brings forth productively in good soil, the mystery of the kingdom unfolds itself. Mystery, in the New Testament, is never total, enduring obscurity, but the grace of God made manifest in God's way and time. Good soil means lives of faith, for the seed of the word of the kingdom is accessible only by faith. The "mystery" is given to those who mark Jesus as the kingdom of God in person. For the others there is the fate of seed rejected by hardened soil, rocky and thorny soil — that is, lives where no receptivity is made for faith to take hold.

And so the revelation which enriches the believing disciples becomes an instrument of judgment on those who disbelieve and contradict. That which clears the soil of rock and thorn becomes an instrument of judgment on all that clutters and opposes the penetration of the good seed of the gospel.

Jesus himself is the good soil as well as the seed. He is called and chosen by the word from heaven. He holds fast that word, living with simple trust and joy under pressure of rejection, obeying God all the way to the cross, caring nothing for his own security, thus bearing much fruit (John 12:24).

Is there anything truly hard or obscure about this parable? Is not every word and image clear and plain? Is not the call a clarion summons for people to hear in Jesus' words the voice of God and see in Jesus' deeds the dawning of the reign of God (11:2-6)? If that is missing, then his Sabbath breaking is irresponsible, his claim of Sonship blasphemy, his death deserved, his resurrection a hoax, and the call to discipleship a fraud.

These are strong words for the church. Despite the familiarity of the parable, its somber note of judgment sounds three times over in the application (hardened soil, thin soil, thorny ground), while the good soil has its singular reference. Blessed are those who preach with courage and, with unsentimental directness, lay out the realities of a hardened heart, a shallow response, a cluttered soul that rejects and chokes off the word of the kingdom. And blessed are those who hear the word gladly, planting it deep in the good soil of trust, obedience, and adoration. How the world needs such soil and its fruits!

F. Dean Leuking

Ninth Sunday after Pentecost, Year A

First Lesson: Genesis 28:10-19a
(Psalm 139:1-12, 23-24)
Second Lesson: Romans 8:12-25
Gospel Lesson: Matthew 13:24-30, 36-43

This parable — the parable of the weeds among the wheat (13:24-30) — and its interpretation (13:36-43) appear only in the Gospel of Matthew within the New Testament. It appears as the second in a collection of seven parables in Matthew 13. The others are the parable of the sower (13:3-9), which precedes it, and five others that come after: the parables of the mustard seed (13:31-32), the leaven (13:33), the treasure in the field (13:44), the pearl of great price (13:45-46), and the dragnet (13:47-50).

One of the more interesting features within the reading is that the parable is even given a name. At 13:36 it is called "the parable of the weeds of the field." That indicates that the naming of parables goes back to the earliest times. The name given has been used consistently.

Although the parable does not appear elsewhere in the canonical Gospels, it does appear in the apocryphal *Gospel of Thomas* (logion 57) and runs as follows:

> Jesus said, "The kingdom of the father is like a man who had [good] seed. His enemy came by night and sowed weeds among the good seed. The man did not allow them to pull up the weeds; he said to them, 'I am afraid that you will go intending to pull up the weeds and pull up the wheat along with them.' For on the day of the harvest the weeds will be plainly visible, and they will be pulled up and burned." (Quoted from *The Nag Hammadi Library in English*, 3rd ed., ed. James M. Robinson [San Francisco: Harper Collins, 1988], p. 132)

It is debated whether this unit is dependent on Matthew's Gospel or represents an independent tradition known to the author of the apocryphal gospel. That issue need not be resolved here. What is of more interest is that the *Gospel of Thomas* (whose composition can probably be set somewhere in the era A.D. 150-200) reflects a form of gnostic theology and spirituality. The implications of that will be noted below.

As with many other "parables of the kingdom," this one begins with a comparison between the kingdom and what follows (13:24). The "kingdom of heaven" is Matthew's characteristic term, used by him (and only by him in the New Testament) thirty-two times instead of "kingdom of God" (used by him only four times). The kingdom is not compared to a man sowing, but to that which follows in the parable as a whole: as in the case of this picture, this story, so it is in the case of the kingdom of heaven. The introductory formula used here is found frequently in Matthew (cf. 18:23; 22:2; 25:1).

The man sows "good seed." Later we learn that the good seed is wheat (13:25, 29, 30).

An enemy comes into the field and plants weeds (13:25), which are mentioned subsequently also, using the same term (13:26, 27, 29, 30). The Greek word translated here (and in RSV, NIV, and NRSV) as "weeds" is highly significant. It is *zizania,* which is sometimes translated "tares" (KJV) or "darnel" (NEB). Its botanical name is *Lolium temulentum,* a troublesome plant for the farmer. It is similar in appearance to wheat and can be identified easily only when ripe. It is urgent that it is removed prior to milling, for if the two are milled together the flour will be spoiled.

Between the sowing and the harvesting, however, the good and bad plants grow up together and side by side. Dialogue between the slaves and the landowner establishes that no one knows for certain who planted the weeds, except that it was an enemy (13:26-28a).

Although the slaves suggest that they could pull up and gather the weeds, the master forbids it. The problem is that the roots of the weeds are intertwined with those of the wheat. Also, since the plants all look very much alike, one cannot always tell which is which. And there is an important detail not to be missed in 13:30. The master speaks of "reapers" for the first time — and they are persons other than the slaves — who will be in charge of the harvesting to come.

The parables of the mustard seed and the leaven (13:31-33) and a saying about the purpose of parables (13:34-35) follow our parable but are not a part of the assigned reading. The two parables will be a portion of the Gospel reading for the following Sunday. The purpose of parables does not appear in the lectionary.

The reading resumes at 13:36-43, the interpretation of the parable of the weeds among the wheat. Like the parable itself, this unit appears only in the Gospel of Matthew. It consists of an allegorical interpretation. The term "allegory," a loanword from Greek (itself a compound, combining words for "other" and "speaking"), means literally "speaking otherwise than one seems to speak," but in common English usage it means "an extended metaphor" in which meanings are assigned to virtually every detail narrated in a story or, in our case, a parable.

Since the end of the nineteenth century, particularly due to the influence of the massive work on the parables by the German scholar Adolf Jülicher, parable interpretation has moved away from the use of the so-called allegorical method, in which there was typically an item-by-item interpretation of a parable with reference to doctrines of the Christian church.

Nevertheless, even if the modern interpreter does not make use of the allegorical method, it is necessary for the interpreter to recognize allegory whenever it is embedded within the text itself, and it is surely necessary to recognize an allegorical interpretation when it is present. The interpretation contained within 13:36-43 is clearly an allegorical interpretation. Various equivalencies are set up: the one who sows the good seed = the Son of Man (Jesus); the field = the world; the good seed = the children of the kingdom; the weeds = the children of the evil one; the enemy = the devil; the harvest = the end of the age; and the reapers = the angels. No fewer than seven equivalencies are thus made.

The interpretation ends with a portrayal of the final judgment, in which there will be a separation of the good from the bad (13:40-43).

The interpreter must make a decision, and that is whether to focus on the parable alone or the parable and its interpretation. The parable alone (without the interpretation) emphasizes patience. Jesus had fellowship with persons both good and bad (tax collectors, sinners, etc.). That kind of ministry can raise questions: Should not the community of Jesus be pure, or be purified? Other groups, such as the Pharisees, the Qumran community, and various gnostic groups, were committed to purity (however defined). The parable counsels against such an idea. The followers of Jesus are and will continue to be a mixed group *(corpus mixtum)*. Whoever thinks he or she can discern the good and the bad can be deluded; they "look" so much alike, and their "roots" are intertwined. The judgment of God will take place at the end, and that will be done not by the slaves (the disciples of Jesus) but by the "reapers" (metaphorically, angels sent by God).

The meaning of the parable in Matthew's Gospel stands out with clarity especially when compared to the version in the *Gospel of Thomas*. The latter version lacks the explicit command to allow both the weeds and the wheat to grow together until the harvest, the most likely reason being that such a command would imply a call for the coexistence of gnostics with persons of the material world (or even ordinary Christians!), and for the gnostics that would be intolerable.

The church is made up of all kinds of people; it always has been. Certain voices may call for it to be a community made up purely of those judged to be righteous. But the parable teaches the need for patience. Even the most well meaning and discerning of persons is not always good at making judgments; no one can know the heart. The weeds and the wheat look very much alike! And sometimes an attempt to discern which is which can be disastrous to the body as a whole. There is comfort in the thought that the judgment will take place at the end, supervised by Christ.

If the interpretation is included, a shift is made. None of what has gone before is canceled, but the theme of warning comes to the fore. The righteous will be in the kingdom of the Father, and evildoers will go into the furnace of fire. So Christians are to take heart (13:43b) and not be false. Whoever claims to be among the righteous ones must live up to what he or she professes, and not be false.

Arland J. Hultgren

Tenth Sunday after Pentecost, Year A

First Lesson: Genesis 29:15-28
(Psalm 128)
Second Lesson: Romans 8:26-39
Gospel Lesson: Matthew 13:31-33, 44-52

The reading consists of five parables. Any one of them could be the basis for a complete sermon: the mustard seed (13:31-32), the leaven (13:33), the treasure in the field (13:44), the pearl of great price (13:45-46), and the dragnet (13:47-50). And then there are some closing verses (13:51-52) about the disciples' ability to understand, plus the saying about the scribe trained for the kingdom. To deal with the entire reading as a unit demands a lot of imagination — and restraint.

Each of the five parables is a "parable of the kingdom." Each one begins with the phrase "the kingdom of heaven is like. . . ." That does not mean that the kingdom is like a mustard seed, leaven, and so on, pure and simple, but that the kingdom is like what transpires in these stories.

The last of the five parables (the dragnet, 13:47-50) is very much like the parable of the weeds in the field (13:24-30, 36-43), the Gospel for the previous week. It portrays the gathering of good and bad alike, followed by a sorting out at the end. It refers to the final judgment, as its interpretation (13:49-50) makes clear. The preacher might not want to duplicate the theme of the previous Sunday. If there is a desire to use the parable, a nuance that appears in this parable and not the other should be noticed. As fish are gathered in the sea by nets indiscriminately, so the church in its mission makes no discriminations in its evangelization of the world. Judgment is left to the end, when God and his angels will carry it out.

But the theme of final judgment reminds all who hear and read the par-

79

able that they are accountable before God. While both "good" and "bad" are gathered into the kingdom (cf. 22:10) and, by implication, into the church, a transformation of the "bad" is expected by means of instruction and assimilation into the community. Those who are not transformed will be cast out at the end (cf. 22:11-14). The purpose of such an affirmation is not simply to describe the end, of course, but to exhort people to press on to observe those things that Jesus has taught (28:20) as they live out their lives in the world.

The other four parables can be treated as two sets of twin parables. The first two (the mustard seed and the leaven) are sometimes, and properly, classified as "parables of growth" (as well as "parables of the kingdom"). Other parables of growth include the sower and the seed growing secretly. The other two parables in our assigned reading (the treasure and the pearl) are about discovery and consequent joy.

Versions of the four parables treated hereafter are found also in the *Gospel of Thomas* (logia 20, 96, 109, and 76, respectively). Although their differences from the Matthean parables are interesting, discussion of them would probably serve more to complicate our work here than to enhance it. Knowledge of the differences is not likely to help the preacher in this case.

The parable of the mustard seed (13:31-32) appears to be based on versions of it in both Mark (4:30-32) and Q (cf. Luke 13:18-19). It shares much in common with Mark's version, but it differs in three respects, and in each case these items are found in Luke's parallel (indicating probably use of Q): (1) the clause "which a man took," (2) reference to a "tree," and (3) the ending words "the birds of the air made nests in its branches."

The mustard seed was proverbially the smallest of all seeds in antiquity, as attested in both Hellenistic and rabbinic sources (see also Matt. 17:20). The mustard plant known in the Near East can grow to six, twelve, or even fifteen feet in height. The distinction between the seed and the plant is thus not simply a difference along a continuum; there is a tremendous contrast in size. The imagery of birds making nests in the branches of the treelike plant is eschatological symbolism from the Old Testament, in which all the nations come to rest in the branches of a tree, the kingdom of God (Dan. 4:12; Ezek. 17:23).

What is the meaning of the contrast between the seed and the huge plant? The contrast is striking, to say the least: so much comes from so little. So it is with the kingdom. Even though Jesus and his followers were such a tiny group, and even though the kingdom seems at times virtually invisible, one can have faith in its final coming in fullness. It will be glorious and include an ingathering of the nations.

In the parable of the leaven (13:33) a major contrast is made as well. It doesn't take much leaven (a small unit of fermented dough in biblical times) to leaven three measures (*sata tria* in Greek) of flour. (The three measures in question here would amount to roughly one and one-eighth bushels total.) A small amount of yeast placed within such a huge amount of flour produces an enormous amount of bread. So it is with the kingdom.

The next two parables of the kingdom use imagery of discovery, joy, and their consequences. In the first of these (the treasure in the field, 13:44), one need not get into questions of legality and morality ("Shouldn't the man tell the owner about the treasure?"). It is better simply to stay with the story. The man stumbles on the treasure, rejoices greatly, sells all, and obtains the field. In the second (the pearl of great price, 13:45) the one who discovers the pearl is a wholesale dealer who travels about searching for pearls to sell. Although the word "joy" does not appear in the text, it spills over from the previous little parable, and it is evident that in liquidating all his assets he is overjoyed, and he obtains the pearl.

Is there a theme common to the two parables? In each case there is a discovery, followed by joy (explicit or implicit) and then a consequent action. The comparison would mean that, for the disciple, realizing the reality of the kingdom comes as a surprise, like a discovery, and that the only possible response to it is a commitment that risks all without reserve. God's presence and reign are often hidden below the surface of life, but we experience little epiphanies of it at surprising, unplanned moments. The twin parables differ, however, in some details. Those differences shed light on differences in human experience. Sometimes epiphanies of the kingdom are surprising, and they are left as surprises. In other cases people are involved in a search for the meaning of life to begin with, as in the second of the parables. If they happen upon the kingdom, it is still a surprise, for it is more than what was sought after. The quest is more than justified. And all one can do is relegate everything else to second place and commit oneself to the kingdom, God's gracious rule in our own lives, as well as in nature and history.

The reading for the day closes with a question from Jesus to his disciples about understanding the parables of the kingdom, and the disciples' reply that they do understand. Understanding is an important theme in Matthew's Gospel. Whatever else it is, according to this Gospel, it is a prerequisite for discipleship. The enigmatic saying about the scribe trained for the kingdom (13:52) is, in many ways, a prescription for the teacher in the church. According to Jewish tradition, the scribe is one who derives teachings from what is old (the Scriptures and oral traditions) and from what is new, which can include the interpretation of texts in light of one another and insight generally. So the teacher in the church draws teachings out of the Scriptures and the words of Jesus, thereby gaining new insights to transmit to others.

The preacher may want to concentrate on the four little parables, leaving the dragnet aside (since its meaning is so similar to that of the reading for the previous Sunday). If so, the two sets of twin parables can be dealt with to illumine two major aspects of the kingdom of God (or heaven). The one is the certainty of its coming and effects, regardless of any and all appearances to the contrary, even if it does not seem to be making its way into our lives. One can trust in God's will to bring about God's own rule. The other aspect to highlight is that, indeed, the kingdom does make itself known in surprising times, places, and persons. And those epiphanies stir us, as they stirred others in centuries gone by, to place things into perspective so that the kingdom is our joy and task.

Arland J. Hultgren

Eleventh Sunday after Pentecost, Year A

First Lesson: Genesis 32:22-31
(Psalm 17:1-7, 15)
Second Lesson: Romans 9:1-5
Gospel Lesson: Matthew 14:13-21

"**N**ow when Jesus heard this, he withdrew. . . ."

The Greek verb translated "he withdrew" is *anechōrēsen*. The same verb occurs three times in eleven verses in chapter 2. Each time the "withdrawal" was a response to a dangerous situation.

In 2:12 the Magi were warned not to return to Herod, and they "withdrew" to their country by another road. Similarly, Joseph was warned about Herod's intentions, and he "withdrew" to Egypt (2:14). Again, when Joseph was in Egypt preparing to return to Israel, he was warned that Archelaus, Herod's son, was in power. Because of the danger, Joseph "withdrew" to Galilee (2:22). The pattern continues in 4:12. Jesus heard that John the Baptist had been arrested, and he "withdrew" again to Galilee. In 12:14 a Sabbath controversy moved the Pharisees to conspire against Jesus "to destroy him." When Jesus heard it, he "withdrew."

Here in 14:13 it occurs again. Following John the Baptist's grisly execution by Herod, "[John's] disciples came and took the body and buried it; then they went and told Jesus" (14:12). Upon hearing the report, Jesus withdrew. The report, however, also included 14:1-2: "At that time Herod the ruler heard reports about Jesus; and he said to his servants, 'This is John the Baptist; he has been raised from the dead, and for this reason *these powers are at work in him.*'" Thereupon follows the report of the birthday party and the resulting execution of John in response to the request of Herodias. Reporting the execution of John did not in itself pose a threat to Jesus. Rather, it was Herod's fear that the powers at work in Jesus were the powers of the resurrected John. If the "powers at work" in Jesus were those of Herod's executed prisoner, the resurrected prisoner would be the greater danger. The first execution would require another. Jesus was in danger because Herod feared the powers he saw at work in him. Therefore, "when Jesus heard this, he withdrew from there in a boat to a deserted place by himself" (v. 13).

It was the withdrawal to a deserted place that set the stage for a new display of "these powers at work in [Jesus]." The contrast between the powers at work in Herod that brought death to John the Baptist at a birthday party and the powers at work in Jesus that fed five thousand hungry people in a deserted place could hardly be more sharply drawn.

The powers at work in Jesus can be best known and appreciated if we watch the unfolding of four tensions and trace their resolutions in the story.

The first tension arises between Jesus and the crowd. "Now when Jesus heard this, he withdrew from there in a boat to a deserted place by himself. But when the crowds heard it, they followed him on foot from the towns. When he went ashore, he saw a great crowd" (vv. 13-14a). That is the first tension in the story. It is the tension between Jesus wanting privacy and the press of the crowd. It is a tension that we can understand even today, removed by generations and cultures from the Galilee beach.

Jesus sought privacy in order to pray. As the story reveals, Jesus did not get the opportunity he sought until later that evening (v. 23). In the face of the threats, Jesus was sustained by his relationship to God in prayer. His primary identity according to Matthew was "the Son of God" (v. 33). He sought privacy to pray, but the gathering crowds would not let him go. They anticipated his destination, walked the distance, and awaited his arrival.

How is this tension between Jesus' desire to pray privately and the press

83

of the crowd resolved? "When he went ashore, he saw a great crowd; and he had compassion for them and cured their sick" (v. 14). One need look no further than this story to understand the meaning of *esplangchnisthē* (he had compassion). It is the ability to be moved *by* the needs of others and then to move *toward* them in mercy. Jesus resolved the tension with compassion, and he healed their sick.

The second tension in the story followed immediately. "When it was evening, the disciples came to him and said, 'This is a deserted place, and the hour is now late; send the crowds away so that they may go into the villages and buy food for themselves.' Jesus said to them, 'They need not go away; you give them something to eat'" (vv. 15-16).

What is the tension here? It is between the disciples and Jesus over who is responsible for supper. The disciples give the primary responsibility to Jesus, instructing him to send them away. The secondary responsibility is given to the people to buy food for themselves. The disciples see their situation in the deserted place at the late hour and conclude that Jesus and the crowd have responsibility for supper.

Jesus turns the table on them: "They need not go away; you give them something to eat" (v. 16). The tension mounts. Neither side gives in.

How is the tension resolved? The disciples took inventory of their resources. "We have nothing here but five loaves and two fish" (v. 17). Jesus responded by issuing a call to discipleship: "Bring them here to me" (v. 18). The long-standing and recurring debates in the church regarding God's responsibility and ours for the needs of the world are addressed here by Jesus. It is not a matter of who is responsible; it is a matter of bringing what we have to him as his disciples. Discipleship is not merely a matter of managing limited resources; it is a matter of giving what we have in faith, hope, and love in acts of worship. If compassion resolves the first tension in the story, discipleship resolves the second.

The third tension is one that will be immediately recognized by North Americans. It is the tension between supply and demand. It is the law of the marketplace in a free economy. The five loaves and two fish were a meager supply for the yet unnumbered crowds Jesus commanded to sit on the grass. The story is crafted to create suspense after suspense as we listen for the tensions to be resolved.

How is this third tension resolved? In spite of the variations among the six miraculous feeding stories in the Gospels, all converge here: Jesus made it enough. The meager supply, cradled in the hands of Jesus, became enough to feed the multitude.

Matthew's church would not have missed the eucharistic overtones in the story. No one there was likely to ask our twenty-first-century question: Is this story about the Eucharist or about feeding the hungry multitudes? For the earliest Christians, this is a story that gives meaning to the Eucharist in a world where the compassionate Christ cares about healing the sick and feeding the hungry.

The eucharistic gestures and words of Jesus were familiar and therefore unmistakable. The liturgy of the upper room is clearly anticipated here on the shore. "Jesus took a loaf of bread, and after blessing it he broke it, gave it to the disciples, and said, 'Take, eat; this is my body'" (Matt. 26:26). He *took* the five loaves and two fish. He *looked up* to heaven in a gesture of invocation. He *blessed, broke,* and *gave* the loaves to the disciples. While four of the six reports of miraculous feedings include the distribution of the loaves *and* the fish (Matt. 15:32-39; Mark 8:1-10; Luke 9:10-17; John 6:1-15), this feeding of the five thousand here and in Mark 6:30-44 entails only the blessing, breaking, and giving of the *loaves* to the disciples. The eucharistic meaning of the event is thereby heightened.

The tension between the small supply and the great demand is resolved in the hands of Jesus, who made the loaves enough. But the disciples were not merely spectators of Jesus' act of compassion; they were participants. This is a discipleship story. From the diagnosis of the situation to the distribution of the bread, Jesus involved his disciples. Jesus "gave [the loaves] to the disciples, and the disciples gave them to the crowds" (14:19). Thus the manner in which Jesus made the small supply enough provides an enduring message for the church. The church knows now that disciples of Jesus cannot feed the hungry without sharing in the Eucharist, nor can they share in the Eucharist without feeding the hungry. Separating our relationship to Christ in the Eucharist from feeding the hungry would lead to frustrating fanaticism or demoralizing despair.

The first three tensions in the story have been resolved. The fourth tension does not get resolved. It has to do with the abundance. The story begins with scarcity and ends with abundance. It portrays an eschatological vision of the reign of God that is calculated to astonish us. The listener is left amazed at the abundance and cannot help wondering what happened to the twelve baskets of leftovers.

For all practical purposes the story could end with the words "And all ate" (v. 20). What else is needed? The compassionate Jesus, through the ministry of his disciples, made a meager supply of bread enough for the multitude. Is that not astonishing enough?

But the punch line of the story doesn't stop. "And all ate *and were filled.*" This was more than a snack to carry them over until they could buy food in the villages as the disciples had originally urged. This is an abundance which occasions in us the dominant question in the Gospels: "Who is this Jesus?"

There is more: "And all ate and were filled; *and they took up what was left over of the broken pieces, twelve baskets full.*" There was more bread in the end than there was in the beginning. But the end is not yet. *"And those who ate were about five thousand men"* (v. 21). What could astonish us more? Just this: *besides women and children* (v. 21).

The final tension is not resolved. We will need to live with it: What happened to the leftovers? The story lifts us from our economy of scarcity in which accumulating, hoarding, and protecting material goods are marks of our culture and opens our eyes to see an economy of shared abundance for all.

The powers at work in Jesus were a threat to Herod. But the powers at work in Jesus are for the salvation of the world. Jesus is not a resurrected John, but the incarnate Son of God, the Messiah of Israel, and the Savior of the nations. Bring what we have to him and watch for the abundance.

Roger E. Van Harn

Twelfth Sunday after Pentecost, Year A

First Lesson: Genesis 37:1-4, 12-28
(Psalm 105:1-6, 16-22, 45b)
Second Lesson: Romans 10:5-10
Gospel Lesson: Matthew 14:22-33

"Now when Jesus heard this [the report of the beheading of John the Baptist], he withdrew from there in a boat to a deserted place by himself" (*kat' idian*, 14:13). But the crowd intercepted Jesus, and his retreat was suspended until verse 23: "And after he had dismissed the crowds, he went up the mountain by himself (*kat' idian*) to pray." The purpose of Jesus wanting to be "by himself" is finally disclosed and fulfilled.

Jesus' sending the disciples "on ahead" to the other side of the sea (v. 22) implies that he intended to join up with them again. More importantly,

Matthew reports the dismissal of the disciples and the crowds in a manner calculated to emphasize that Jesus was "by himself": "When evening came, he was there alone" (v. 23). Jesus at prayer, alone on the mountain, is the setting for the story of the storm that follows. The content of Jesus' prayer is not disclosed and therefore does not contribute to the story. But Jesus' prayer retreat is essential to the events that follow in that it sets the stage for the disciples to experience the absence of Jesus when the storm hits.

The story of what happened on the lake is actually the convergence of three stories that are concentrically arranged around the person of Jesus. The largest story is the Gospel according to Matthew, which portrays Jesus as the Son of God, the Messiah of Israel, and the Savior of the nations. The middle-sized story is that of the disciples braving the storm alone on the lake until Jesus comes — a story that appears also in Mark (6:45-52) and John (6:16-21). The third and smallest story about Peter and Jesus is wrapped in the other two and is reported only by Matthew. Seeing the relationship of the three stories concentrically is helpful for understanding the text and suggests homiletic possibilities.

The dominant issue in the Gospels concerns the identity of Jesus of Nazareth. Who is this Jesus? That issue surfaces in the three stories in this lection: "Take heart, it is I; do not be afraid" (the medium-sized story, v. 27); "Lord, if it is you, command me to come to you on the water" (the small story, v. 28); and "Truly you are the Son of God" (the large story, v. 33). While Jesus' mission is intimately related to his identity and is sometimes explicitly expressed (Matt. 16:16 and 21), here Jesus' identity becomes explicit but his mission remains implicit in the drama. He appears in the story as the one whose presence created and then calmed the fears of his followers, who called, saved, and judged Peter, and whose presence overcame the power of the storm. Whether explicit or implied, Jesus' identity and mission cannot be separated in the Gospel reports or in the faith of the church.

The middle-sized story begins with Jesus being alone in prayer on the mountain and the disciples being alone in the boat on the lake. The absence of Jesus is important to furnish the stage on which the action took place. In the time of Jesus' absence, the wind arose against them and the waves battered the boat. If the disciples were afraid of the storm, as we may well speculate, Matthew does not report it and preachers do well not to embellish it. Fear does not come into play until "early in the morning" when Jesus "came walking toward them on the sea" (v. 25). Like Matthew's beleaguered church, the disciples were about to be tested not by the storm itself, but by the presence and word of Jesus.

87

Not recognizing Jesus, the disciples feared that something unnatural (or supernatural) was against them in the presence of this mysterious figure. The verb translated "terrified" *(terassō)* often describes the fear that arises from a combination of natural and unnatural phenomena. It describes the fear of Herod upon hearing the Magi ask concerning the birth of the king of the Jews that was heralded by seeing "his star" (2:3). It describes Zechariah's fear when an angel of the Lord appeared beside the altar of incense while he was on duty in the temple (Luke 1:12), and the fear of the disciples who mistook the risen Jesus for a ghost when he appeared to them in the room (Luke 24:38). These terrors bordered on dread because of the presence of powers from beyond nature.

The real test for the disciples, however, came not from what they saw, but from what they heard. The voice came: "Take heart [courage], it is I; do not be afraid" (v. 27). All three expressions have deep and extensive roots in the Scriptures. "Take heart" recalls Moses' word to Israel on the edge of the Re(e)d Sea, pursued by the Egyptians and doomed to destruction: "Do not be afraid, stand firm, and see the deliverance that the LORD will accomplish for you today" (Exod. 14:13). "It is I" *(egō eimi)* echoes the word of the Lord to Moses at the burning bush: "I am who I am" (Exod. 3:14), and reverberates in all of the "I am" sayings of Jesus in John's Gospel. "Be not afraid" was spoken by the angel to Joseph in Matthew 1:20; by Jesus when he sent the Twelve on their mission in 10:26, 28, 31; by Jesus to Peter, James, and John on the Mount of Transfiguration in 17:7; and by the angel and the risen Christ to the women in 28:5, 10. Taking hold of the threefold word of Jesus can enable the church to hear God's word to his people in times of crisis.

Jesus' unrecognized presence was a threat to the disciples in the storm on the lake, but it was his word that tested them. Would they trust his threefold word to them? It is no wonder that one of the earliest and most common art images in the early church was a boat on the water. Would the church trust the word of Jesus whose unrecognized presence was with them when the winds of persecution were against them?

The story of the disciples in the storm is interrupted by Matthew to include the small story of Peter and Jesus. The small story within the story begins with Peter responding to the word of Jesus: "Take heart, it is I; do not be afraid." If Jesus' words were a test of their trust, Peter passed the test — almost. He hurled his own test to Jesus across the water: "Lord, if it is you, command me to come to you on the water" (v. 28). In characteristic fashion, Peter prefers the role of the tester to the role of the tested. His words resemble the words of Satan in tempting Jesus in the wilderness: "If you are the Son of God . . ." (4:3, 6). Peter's testing of Jesus was ill conceived, and he would soon learn that the disciple is not greater than his master; he would be the tested one. Given time, Peter's testing of Jesus on the water would ripen into telling Jesus how to go about being the Christ (16:22), thus bringing upon himself the rebuke of Jesus, "Get behind me, Satan!" (16:23).

Jesus responded to Peter's test with a single word of command: "Come" (v. 29). The whole drama turns on that bit of conversation between Peter and Jesus. Peter had heard Jesus' command to come and follow him earlier (4:19), and now the call to come to him on the water was a fresh test of Peter's discipleship.

The story unfolds quickly. Peter stepped out of the boat and began to walk toward Jesus on the water. All the images of the sea as the picture of primordial chaos came to life before Peter's eyes and beneath his feet. The words of Psalm 107:25-30 provide the script for the drama:

> For he commanded and raised the stormy wind,
>   which lifted up the waves of the sea.
> They mounted up to heaven, they went down to the depths;
>   their courage melted away in their calamity;
> they reeled and staggered like drunkards,
>   and were at their wits' end.
> Then they cried to the LORD in their trouble,
>   and he brought them out from their distress;
> he made the storm be still,
>   and the waves of the sea were hushed.
> Then they were glad because they had quiet,
>   and he brought them to their desired haven.

Distracted by the storm, Peter was afraid, he began to sink, and he cried out, "Lord, save me!" (v. 30). And Jesus reached out and took hold of him.

Interpreters are quick to point out that Peter's life and character are summarized in this story. Nearly everything we know about his discipleship in the Gospels can be related to the movements of this drama. Even the rebuke, "You of little faith, why did you doubt?" (v. 31), has both milder and more severe counterparts in his life. Those of us who live in more polite societies and therefore neither give nor receive rebukes easily may be inclined to wonder why Jesus could not have found something to praise in Peter for his noble effort. But this story is not about cultivating self-esteem; it is about the grace of the Son of God who saved a disciple from death before his faith could qualify him for anything. Jesus' rebuke told the truth in love and gave Peter yet another lesson in discipleship.

The two stories that I have called the middle and small stories merge into the large story which is the Gospel according to Matthew. When Jesus and Peter got into the boat, the wind ceased from weariness. The language personifies the wind as though it had engaged in a fierce struggle with the Son of God and then gave up. The identity of Jesus in the first two stories ("it is I" and "if it is you") is confessed by the disciples in the boat in an act of worship: "Truly you are the Son of God."

The identity of Jesus as the Son of God runs through Matthew's Gospel. The voice from heaven at the baptism of Jesus testified that "This is my Son" (3:17). In the earlier story of Jesus in the storm on the lake with his disciples (8:23-27), the disciples woke the sleeping Jesus with a call to save them from perishing. Jesus rebuked the disciples for their little faith and then rebuked the wind and sea. The storm ceased and the disciples were amazed and wondered aloud: "What sort of man is this, that even the winds and the sea obey him?" The stilling of the storm in chapter 8 results in the question that is answered by the confession of the disciples in chapter 14: "Truly you are the Son of God." Two chapters later the confession of Peter in 16:16 stands as a milestone in Matthew's portrayal of Jesus' identity: "You are the Messiah, the Son of the living God." That confession was uttered again by unlikely persons at an unlikely time and place; the Roman centurion and his comrades at the cross of Jesus uttered in fear: "Truly this man was God's Son!" (27:54).

Midway though the Pentecost season, this is a good time to refresh the faith of the church with the confession of Jesus' identity which has been sealed for all time in the baptismal formula of the church: "Go therefore and make disciples of all nations, baptizing them in the name of the Father and of the Son and of the Holy Spirit" (28:19).

Roger E. Van Harn

Thirteenth Sunday after Pentecost, Year A

First Lesson: Genesis 45:1-15
(Psalm 133)
Second Lesson: Romans 11:1-2a, 29-32
Gospel Lesson: Matthew 15:(10-20), 21-28

In the section that precedes the story of the Canaanite woman, Matthew (15:1-20) reshapes the Marcan tradition (Mark 7:1-23) of Jesus' conflicts with the Pharisees over the traditions of the elders. In Mark the emphasis is on debates over purity laws; in Matthew the focus is on the traditions of the elders, that is, those matters not spelled out explicitly in the Torah. In the context of Matthew's predominantly Jewish Christian community, who were struggling to define themselves in relation to Jews who did not follow Jesus, the questions of which traditions to keep and which to let go were pressing ones.

The conflicts in the Gospel between Jesus and the scribes and Pharisees were undoubtedly mirrored by the debates within Matthew's own community. These were made even more difficult with the increasing numbers of Gentiles seeking admission. Matthew gives us a glimpse of this family quarrel, which is resolved by a pronouncement by Jesus that it is not external observance alone that reflects right relation with God; it is what proceeds from the heart (15:18-20).

With that the scene shifts and questions about boundaries between old and new, Jew and Gentile, male and female, sick and well, holy and demonic press anew as a Canaanite woman and the plight of her possessed daughter confront Jesus (15:21-28).

Matthew leaves the geographical locale unclear. He does not indicate that Jesus actually entered the region of Tyre and Sidon as does Mark. He leaves the impression that Jesus only goes in that direction, perhaps in keeping with his own command to his disciples not to go into pagan territory (10:5). The woman comes forth from those regions and meets him en route. Whereas Mark (7:26) had labeled her a Syrophoenician, Matthew designates her as Canaanite (v. 22), evoking the name of the ancient inhabitants of the land, Israel's foes of old.

The woman's cry, "Have pity on me, Lord, Son of David" (v. 22), is reminiscent of other cries heard in the Gospel. When the disciples were tossed about in a storm on the Sea of Galilee, they pleaded, "Lord, save us! We are perishing!" (8:25). In that instance Jesus got up and rebuked the winds and sea and chided them for their fear and their little faith (8:26). In another episode Jesus tells Peter to come to him across the water, but seeing the wind, he begins to be afraid and to sink, and he cries out, "Lord, save me!" (14:30). Again Jesus reaches out his hand and catches him and says, "You of little faith, why did you doubt?" (14:31). And again, a father of a boy who suffered from epilepsy calls out to Jesus, "Lord, have mercy on my son" (17:15). The disciples had been unable to heal him. Jesus tells them it was because of their little faith (17:20).

Throughout the Gospel, Jesus immediately responds to anyone who cries out to him for mercy or salvation or healing. His initial silence toward the Canaanite woman is stunning. The foreign woman even uses the Jewish title "Son of David" (1:1; 9:27; 20:30; 21:9, 15) and calls Jesus "Lord." Still, Jesus does not respond — the only instance in the Gospels where he ignores a person who approaches him in need.

The disciples' response is no better. They want Jesus to get rid of this bothersome woman, but it is not clear whether they want him to just send her away or to give her what she wants so as to be left in peace. Jesus' reply is that she is not part of Israel to whom he is sent (see also 9:36; 10:6; 18:12). The woman's situation seems impossible, as she bears the weight of her daughter's illness, in addition to Jesus' refusal and the disciples' annoyance. Despite Jesus' rebukes, she does him homage and pleads once again for help. Like the Magi (2:11), the man with leprosy whom Jesus makes clean (8:2), the ruler whose daughter Jesus raises back to life (9:18), and the disciples who witness Jesus' rescue from the water of the sinking Peter (14:33), so this mother bows down in worship before Jesus. She renews her plea once again: "Lord, help me."

Jesus' second reply is more shocking still, as he declares that it is not right to take the food of the children and throw it to the dogs. There is no softening this ugly insult. In addition to its obvious connotations, an allusion to Isaiah 56:10 may be heard, where those who are blind and without knowledge are like "dumb dogs." The Mishnah likewise dubs as "dogs" those not versed in Torah. The "children" are the people of Israel, while those outside, the Gentiles, are "dogs."

Undaunted, the woman retorts that even dogs get the scraps that fall from the masters' table. She does not deny Jesus' self-identification as the Messiah of Israel, but challenges him to extend the horizons of his mission: Is there no mercy for the outsider in his expansive love? In her persistence she echoes Jesus' own words to his disciples. He had been teaching his followers to persist in the face of rejection (Matt. 5:10-12; 10:16-25), to absorb the pain of insult rather than return insult for injury (5:38-48), to pour out their lives in service to even the lowliest child (10:42). While his own disciples seemed slow to understand, always having only "little faith," this woman, this foreigner, absorbs the silent slap and responds to the racist slur not with hostility but with unflagging faith.

The episode is cast as a turning point in Jesus' own understanding of his identity and his mission. The healing of the Canaanite woman's daughter is instantaneous and portends the healing effects of Jesus' mission that will extend beyond the boundaries of Israel. The story mirrors the very struggles of Matthew's community as they wrestle with their own understanding of the limits of their mission. Like Jesus, who in the encounter with this insistent woman of faith changes from icy silence to annoyance and hurling of insults, to finally being moved to recognize her great faith and her need for healing, so Matthew's community journeys from silent separation from the Gentiles to conflictual encounters, to embracing an active mission to include them, as reflected in the Great Commission at the end of the Gospel: "Go therefore and make disciples of all nations" (28:19).

A number of threads from the Gospel intersect with contemporary situations. In communities that struggle with exclusivity of any sort, the episode with the Canaanite woman presents a powerful story of Jesus' own transformation in his ability to perceive this woman as one of his own, not as ancient enemy, but as one to whom the bounds of his love could extend. If Jesus was like us in all things but sin, he would have shared his own people's sense of boundaries, marking them as God's own chosen ones. And he understood his mission to be only to his own people. While the prophets spoke of the ingathering of all nations in the eschatological age (as the image of the birds of every kind dwelling beneath the sheltering boughs of Israel in Ezek. 17:23), it took time before Jesus and his followers understood the full implications of a mission to include Gentiles. It was a long and arduous process before followers of Jesus reinterpreted the "traditions of the elders" and the law and the prophets in such a way as to actively seek out Gentiles as full participants in the renewed Israel. The conflicts behind both the episodes in Matthew 15, over the traditions of the elders and the healing of a Canaanite, were not struggles between Christianity and Judaism, but were family conflicts as two siblings of the same mother eventually defined themselves differently and went their separate ways. Preachers will want to be wary of reading this chapter of Matthew in ways that foment anti-Semitism.

The story of the Canaanite woman and Jesus can help believers today grapple with questions of inclusion and embracing of diversity. This Gospel invites believers today to embrace a Jesus who had the ability to change his perception of the outsider, one he considered a "dog," to see her as a child of the promise to whom his salvation fully extended. It is this Jesus who can help Christians today be converted from racism, sexism, nationalism, ethnocentrism, homophobia, and myriad other obstacles to perceiving the "other" as sister or brother.

The figure of the Canaanite woman is also one that can help steel a believer to speak out strongly and persistently on behalf of the world's needy children. Despite being ignored, insulted, and disregarded, the Canaanite woman does not desist until she has secured healing for her daughter. She is an icon of God's persistent care for the most needy, as she gives voice to the needs of one who is helplessly caught in demonic power. She impels believers to commit themselves to action on behalf of the most vulnerable of our world.

Barbara E. Reid

Fourteenth Sunday after Pentecost, Year A

First Lesson: Exodus 1:8–2:10
(Psalm 124)
Second Lesson: Romans 12:1-8
Gospel Lesson: Matthew 16:13-20

Today's Gospel takes us to a crucial turning point in Jesus' ministry, when he sets before the disciples who he is, what he will do, and what both mean for the disciples and their role. For that purpose he takes them northward from Capernaum toward the headwaters of the Jordan River into the district of Caesarea Philippi. To this day it is a refreshing, appealing place, well suited for the truth Jesus will reveal to his disciples.

Jesus asks the key question: "Who do people say that the Son of Man is?" And Peter speaks for the Twelve in giving the celebrated answer: "You are the Christ, the Son of the living God." It is not as though the disciples only then recognized him as the Messiah. All along his relationship to them had been messianic: they had heard the imperious grace in his call to follow him, they had seen the authority of his word worked out in the mighty deeds of healing he performed, they had learned the terms on which he commissioned them and sent them out into Israel, they had sensed the fearful judgment implicit in his parables. In all this they were given signs of the Messiah who called them to follow.

Now at Caesarea Philippi Jesus' question signifies the intensifying of the commitment he seeks from them, a commitment made in view of the coming cross. Jesus bound them now to the Christ who was to die. He bound them so firmly as to make them definitively separated now, not only from Jesus' enemies, but also from his admirers who saw in him a John the Baptist returned from the dead or an Elijah come back to life. They were separated from all who said what humans could say about Jesus, who gave him a place and a function in preparation for the kingdom but did not see in him the presence of the reign of God. Therefore the confession was now explicitly to the Christ, the anointed Son of the living God. No other title could so commit a man or woman. Once one had said "Christ," one bound oneself to follow the Christ, no matter where that following might lead.

The term "Son of Man" frames all that is revealed between verses 13 and 28. Matthew had constructed the narrative in such a way as to interpret this puzzling title by means of the confession of Jesus as the Christ of God. Will the disciples be able to understand the necessity of the cross both for the Christ and for their own mission? That is the issue.

Jesus' response to Peter's confession comprises three short verses, each of which has three parts: a thematic statement and a pair of parallel clauses expanding and expounding the theme. Jesus' first word to Peter contains a beatitude (cf. 5:3; 11:6; 13:16), with the added clauses spelling out the grounds of the blessing: "Blessed are you, Simon Bar-Jonah! / for flesh and blood has not revealed this to you / but my Father who is in heaven." In John 1:42 Peter is called "son of John," and this may be a variant on that naming. But it may also be that Matthew's intention is to associate Peter and all the disciples with the prophet Jonah both in confessing and in experiencing death and resurrection (cf. Matt. 12:39-40; 16:4).

The second triad of blessing/conditions follows in v. 18: "And I tell you, you are Peter, / and on this rock I will build my church, / and the powers of death shall not prevail against it." For centuries Christians have struggled with the meaning of Peter as the rock. Among the several traditions to which interpreters have appealed are these: (1) a reference to Isaiah, who summoned Israel to "look to the rock from which you were hewn, / and to the quarry from which you were dug" (51:1-2); (2) a reference to rabbinic sources which viewed Abraham not only as the rock from which Israel was hewn but the rock on which God founded the entire world; (3) a reference to the great cosmic rock sealing the entrance to heaven and hell upon which the temple of Jerusalem was thought to rest; (4) a reference to the Qumran community, which was governed by a council of twelve laymen and three priests, a community described as established on an unshakable foundation and precious cornerstone; (5) other New Testament references in which Jesus (Matt. 21:42; 1 Cor. 3:11) and the apostles (Gal. 2:9; Eph. 2:20; Rev. 21:14) are described as the foundation of the new community.

However one chooses to interpret the reference to Peter as the rock, it is certain that the new name has nothing to do with any solid, rocklike, or unflinching features in Peter himself. In fact, Peter is fully capable of base misunderstanding as well as astonishing confession, so he is addressed in rapid succession both as foundation rock (16:18) and as stone causing others to stumble. The new name is his, not because he is a miracle worker, not because he is a visionary or prophet, not because he is the head or ruler of the new community, nor even because he is doer of charity or of deeds of righteousness. He is called the rock because he has faith and confesses that faith in Jesus as the Christ of the living God. For no other reason does he receive the new name and its attendant promise.

Peter is the symbol of all who follow Jesus. In Peter, whether boldly treading the waters or sometimes sinking like a rock, whether full of understanding or often of little faith, whether confessing him or denying him, Jesus sees what building material he has for his church. It is material that must be shaped altogether by grace. That is why Jesus sees in him the whole future community of disciples and confessors. Jesus looks away from Pharisees and Sadducees and scribes (15:1-20) and, gazing upon Peter and the Twelve, sees the church (the term occurs only here and in 18:17), the new community which bears the gospel into the world until the end of time.

Jesus is "the Son of the living God" (16:16), and therefore not even the powers of death can conquer his community. What is meant by "powers"? Literally the phrase means "the gates of Hades," which could refer to Satan's evil power in general, or to the apparently invincible power of the grave over all living things, or to the deadly power of persecution (cf. 12:25-29).

Confessing Jesus means saying no to other powers and other leaders, thereby opening the disciples to their wrath and persecution. But Jesus, "Son of the living God," shares his own indestructible life with members of his community. Beyond all loss he promises a mighty harvest (13:3-8), beyond persecution and martyrdom, resurrection and shining like the very sun (13:43). The seeming invincibility of Hades will never consume and destroy the people of God. On the contrary, Hades will not be able to resist the power of heaven, liberating and resurrecting, at work in Jesus and the community. What immensely empowering promise here for the church of this and every age!

The third and final unit of Jesus' word to Peter, like the first two, again consists of three parts: "I will give you the keys of the kingdom of heaven, / and whatever you bind on earth shall be bound in heaven, / and whatever you loose on earth shall be loosed in heaven." To Peter and the Twelve Jesus gives keys (Rev. 1:18; 3:7; Isa. 22:22), here interpreted as authority to bind and loose. In ancient rabbinic literature the terms "bind" and "loose" refer to forbidding and permitting actions, to the formulation of authoritative legal decisions, declaring that certain ordinances of the Law are or are not binding upon particular people in particular situations. So binding and loosing refer to the regulations of the ethical life of a religious community by means of authoritative teaching, such as Jesus offered in the Sermon on the Mount (esp. Matt. 5:21-48). Binding and loosing therefore inevitably involve admitting people to or excluding people from the community. Thus, in response to Peter's confession, Jesus declares his intention to build a new community whose teachers will not be Pharisees and Sadducees and scribes (15:1-20) and whose teachings will not be the traditions of the elders (15:2-3).

To whom is leadership ascribed for this new community? Everything in the Gospel points to Jesus Christ alone as the head. How shall he lead? Through his word. Who is Peter's successor? Matthew's Gospel itself. On that foundation the church shall stand, and hell's worst will not be able to hold it back.

F. Dean Lueking

Fifteenth Sunday after Pentecost, Year A

First Lesson: Exodus 3:1-15
(Psalm 105:1-6, 23-26, 45c)
Second Lesson: Romans 12:9-21
Gospel Lesson: Matthew 16:21-28

The Gospel lesson is Jesus' announcement of what lies ahead for him in Jerusalem: great suffering, death, and the resurrection on the third day. His disclosure brings to fulfillment the ancient prophecy of a Messiah who would come as the servant who would suffer (Isa. 53), the prophecy of Simeon that the Christ child he held in his arms would be destined for the fall and rising of many in Israel and a sign that would be spoken against (Luke 2:34-35). The ominous charges against Jesus (blasphemy, Matt. 9:3; collusion with Satan, 10:25; 12:24), the plots to destroy him (12:14), and the growing resistance of the Pharisees and scribes against him (15:1-20; 16:1-4) combine to make his announcement of the cross anything but a surprise.

And yet Peter reacted to the announcement with vehement rejection of any such end for Jesus. His reaction is the enduring sign of how thoroughly he, and the church with him, missed Jesus' crucial word "must" which prefaced the announcement (16:21). Behind that little word (*dei* in the Greek text) lay not only the murderous plotting of those determined to destroy Jesus, but the mystery of God's own plan to give his Son into suffering and death for the salvation of the world. The cross was not a tragic intrusion, but is of the very essence of Jesus' mission and ministry. Jesus declared with regal authority his acceptance of what was coming. By no means was he simply a victim of evil, a helpless straw swept along on the stream of events, manipulated and taken by surprise at any turn. He set his face steadfastly toward Jerusalem and went the way of the cross, willingly, knowingly. He repeated the announcement of his coming suffering and death to the shocked, disoriented disciples (17:12, 22-23; 20:17-19; 26:2), naming Jerusalem and the events there as the goal of his journey.

Peter's vehemence in rebuking Jesus' announcement is answered by Jesus' greater vehemence in words that contrast so vividly with the commendation of Peter following his confession of Jesus as the Son of the living God (16:16). Peter the Rock is now rebuked as the spokesman for Satan, the stumbling block, whose mind is not on the side of God but on human things (v. 23). The sharp term "stumbling block" (*skandalon*) recalled the Isaiah 8:14-15 warning of God's truth, meant as a rock of sanctuary but turned into a stone over which one stumbles as sinful human presumption crashes against the granite of the divine holiness. Jesus gave a twofold command in this sharp retort to Peter. He is to "get away," since such a misunderstanding of the cross blocks the way of obedience to it. Jesus wants Peter, and the church with him, to follow "behind me!" for that is where followers belong who will take up their cross as his disciples.

In Dietrich Bonhoeffer's well-known phrase, it is to costly discipleship that Jesus calls the church in this great passage. Discipleship is inseparable from the cross which Jesus first carried; being a disciple means bearing the cross of servanthood in his name. Think of how this word of Jesus sounds in today's climate of popularized religion, calculated to conform to the cultural expectations that bigger is better and comfortable affluence the unquestioned sign of divine favor. Can the hard word of the cross of Christ and the reasons he had to endure it even get a hearing in an atmosphere so unwilling to allow the truth that purposeful living comes by dying to the well-stroked ego and that fulfillment is the secret learned through servanthood? Jesus' announcement of his cross is as offensive now as it was to Peter. How might such a hard word be faithfully spoken in our time? Such boldness in proclamation proceeds from a sober awareness of how pervasive is the perceived wisdom that bearing a cross is revolting and disgusting. But the text itself, in its brevity and directness, is witness to Jesus' own boldness in contradicting deeply held convictions about life. He does not offer arguments or reasons for taking up the cross in following him. He calls people to himself. In belonging to him in trust and devotion, it will become clear that discipleship is not losing life but finding it in a depth and richness never known before. Jesus makes the most sweeping claim, "Whoever would save his life will lose it, and whoever loses his life for my sake will find it." The task is not to blunt the claim or to offer it as an option to those already inclined. The task is to hand on this abundant text with obedience and commitment, without apology or compromise.

In his call to any who would become his followers to deny themselves and take up their cross (Matt. 16:24), Jesus asks the question about what truly profits life. Does profit, then, really lie in gaining the whole world but at the cost of forfeiting life (v. 26)? That question is anything but rhetorical when asked in the face of the riveting appeal of wealth gained by acquisitive means undisturbed by ethical norms, or instant affluence gained by megadollars won through lottery luck, or millionaire status conferred by answering game-show questions. The problem Jesus raises by his probing question is not only for the few who become the rich and famous. Jesus' question reaches all who are caught up in obsessive fascination with what it would be like to live in that stratospheric realm, but without counting the cost of being sucked into its fatal grip. In this question of Jesus there is an echo of his parable of the rich fool (Luke 12:16-21). What is the profit, finally? Or, to rephrase it, is there any thing, any object, which one would not gladly give in return for his life, that is, pay over in order to ransom or prolong life? Fear of loss prevents people from taking up the cross. But Jesus makes the strange promise that taking up the cross in his name, which is another way of describing discipleship, is gain. Counter to the wisdom of the world, taking up the cross leads to saving, finding, gaining one's life!

Blessed is the preaching that speaks this hard truth with a Christ-given love that leaves no illusions about gaining and losing life. The church lives by the Word of the cross of Christ, the Christ who judges any will that opposes him on his divinely marked course as a satanic will, a stumbling block. In the light of this text, faith is not simply the acknowledgment that God exists. It is commitment to Jesus the crucified and risen Lord, and the abandonment of any attempt to set aside the central place of the cross. It means, positively, thinking the thoughts and willing the will of God, being "on the side of God," being God's partisan in every decision and in every act. Living under the Word of the cross means growing in the stature of Christ's whole Yes to God and his whole No to all that is of sin. It means going Christ's way into the daily rounds of life, finding one's life by losing it.

Nothing, not even the happy prospect of winning the world for God, is to make Christ's followers break the wholeness of this commitment to God in and through the cross. Thus people become pure, fit for worship and ministry in the world. Shouldering the cross is a consciously personal and responsible act, made possible by daily repentance and renewal of baptismal grace. The result is active discipleship, lived out under the tension of responsibility to a Lord who will come again in glory to repay everyone for what has been done (Matt. 16:27). Only in the power of the cross and resurrection of the Savior is it possible to anticipate that final judgment with hope, trusting that the one who shall come to judge the world is the one who has already come as Savior.

The closing verses of the Gospel lesson present Jesus as the eschatological judge. In another place Matthew pictures Jesus as advocate (25:31-46). Whether judge or advocate, Matthew's Jesus comes with no millennial speculation about which to argue. What counts are the practiced deeds of mercy and love. His summary declaration that some of those present will not taste death before he comes (v. 28) is a difficult saying. Take it as his word to every generation to remember who they are and what time it is. When he comes as judge and advocate, what will count is not titles or possessions but faithful, unselfish, cross-formed living. Here, as throughout Matthew's Gospel, the praise is for that integrity whereby right confession is joined with right deeds.

F. Dean Lueking

Last Sunday after the Epiphany (Transfiguration), Year A

First Lesson: Exodus 24:12-18
(Psalm 2)
Second Lesson: 2 Peter 1:16-21
Gospel Lesson: Matthew 17:1-9

Readers of this text regularly recall Exodus 24 and 34. After "six days" Jesus' face shines like the sun, a circumstance that reminds one of what happens to Moses' face in Exodus 34:29-35 (cf. Exod. 24:16, where God calls to Moses out of the cloud on the seventh day). Further, as in Exodus 24:15-18 and 34:5, a bright cloud appears, and a voice speaks from it. And the onlookers — a special group of three (cf. Exod. 24:1) — are afraid (cf. Exod. 34:29-30). All this, moreover, takes place on a mountain (cf. Exod. 24:12, 15-18; 34:3); and Moses and Elijah, who converse with the transfigured Jesus, are the only figures in the Old Testament who speak with God on Mount Sinai (called Horeb in Kings), so their presence together makes us think of that mountain and the epiphanies that took place there. As so often in Matthew, then, Jesus is like Moses, and his history is something like a new exodus. In the early part of the fourth century, Eusebius wrote: "When Moses descended from the Mount, his face was seen full of glory, for it is written . . . [Eusebius quotes Exod. 24:19]. In the same way only more grandly our savior led his disciples 'to a very high mountain, and he was transfigured before them, and his face did shine as the sun, and his garments were white like the light.'"

The heavenly voice, which seems to mix Psalm 2:7 ("I will tell of the decree of the LORD: / He said to me, 'You are my son; / today I have begotten you'") and Isaiah 42:1 ("Here is my servant, whom I uphold, / my chosen, in whom my soul is well pleased"), is probably designed to reinforce this idea that Jesus is here like Moses. For Deuteronomy 18:15 and 18, which Acts 3:22-23 sees as fulfilled in Jesus, foretell the coming of one like Moses, to whom the people should "listen."

If Matthew 17:1-9 sends thoughts back to several Old Testament texts, it also recalls texts within Matthew itself. There is, for example, an obvious connection with the baptismal narrative. "This is my Son, the Beloved; with him I am well pleased" (17:5) is a verbatim repetition of the voice of the baptism (3:17). So the transfiguration, in the middle of the story, confirms a declaration made at the beginning of Jesus' public ministry.

But the most interesting links for theological and homiletical explication are with the passion narrative. For the transfiguration has a twin of sorts in 27:32-54. After the centurion and those with him see the miraculous signs attendant upon the crucifixion, they too fear exceedingly (27:54), just as the disciples do in 17:6. Only in these two places does Matthew say that people were "exceedingly afraid" *(ephobēthēsan sphodra)*. The link is small, but it prods one to observe that also common to the transfiguration and the crucifixion are the confession of Jesus as God's "Son" (17:5; 27:54), the presence of three named onlookers (17:1, three male disciples: Peter, James, and John; 27:55-56, three female disciples: Mary Magdalene, Mary of James and Joseph, the mother of the sons of Zebedee), and the number six ("after six days," 17:1; "from the sixth hour," 27:45). Moreover, these shared features exist in the midst of dramatic contrasts:

The transfiguration	The crucifixion
Jesus takes others (17:1)	(27:31) Jesus is taken by others
elevation on mountain (17:1)	(27:35) elevation on cross
private epiphany (17:1)	(27:39) public spectacle
light (17:2)	(27:45) darkness
garments illumined (17:2)	(27:28, 35) garments stripped off
Jesus is glorified (17:2ff.)	(27:27ff.) Jesus is shamed
Elijah appears (17:3)	(27:45-50) Elijah does not appear
two saints beside Jesus (17:3)	(27:38) two criminals beside Jesus
God confesses Jesus (17:5)	(27:46) God abandons Jesus
reverent prostration (17:6)	(27:29) mocking prostration

Between Matthew 17:1-8 and 27:27-56 there is a curious confluence of similar motifs and contrasting images. We have here pictorial antithetical parallelism, something like a diptych in which the two plates have similar outlines but different colors. If one scene were sketched on a transparency and placed over the other, many of its lines would disappear.

What is the significance of this? The two scenes represent the extremities of human experience. One tells of spit and mockery, nails and nakedness, blood and loneliness, torture and death. The other makes visible the presence of God and depicts the divinization of human nature. So Jesus embodies the gamut of human possibilities; he is the coincidence of opposites in one person. Perhaps this is one of the reasons he has always been so attractive and inspiring: he shows forth in his own person both the depths of pain and anguish which human beings have known and what we all long for — transfiguration into some state beyond such pain and anguish. Jesus is the great illustration of both pain and hope; he is humanity exalted and humanity glorified.

How does Matthew 17:1-9 fit into its immediate context? Jesus' appearance in glory anticipates or foreshadows both his resurrection and his Second Advent — maybe one could liken the transfiguration to a movie preview — and so helps to confirm the prophecy of his resurrection in 16:21 and his prophecy of the second coming in 16:28. There is also a close connection with the confession at Caesarea Philippi (16:13-20), for both there and on the Mount of Transfiguration Jesus is proclaimed to be the Son of God. There is, to be sure, a major difference in that in the earlier story the confession of Jesus as Son of God comes from Peter, whereas in the latter God speaks. But this only makes 17:1-9 set the divine seal of approval upon Peter's pronouncement. Further, the two passages are related insofar as both qualify Sonship with suffering service. Just as 16:13-20 is followed by 16:21-23, which holds forth the necessity for suffering, so 17:1-8 interprets Jesus' Sonship in terms of Isaiah's servant ("in whom I am well pleased"; cf. Isa. 42:12).

The history of the interpretation of the transfiguration leads to fruitful reflections. In 2 Peter 1:16-21 the story functions as an apologetic, for it vindicates belief in Jesus as God's beloved Son and as the recipient of divine honor and glory. It also serves to uphold what 2 Peter 1:19 calls "the prophetic word," which probably refers to the promises of the Second Advent or, more precisely, to the transfiguration as an anticipation of and so prophecy of that advent. Christ's glory at his first coming assures believers that his promise of a second advent is sure.

In the second-century *Apocalypse of Peter* 17, the transfiguration is recounted in response to the disciples' request that they behold the fate of the righteous after death. Furthermore, when Peter asks where the righteous ones dwell and inquires about their world, the scene expands to include the paradise of God, with its lights and flowers and trees and fragrances and fruits. So here the transfiguration is a preview of what heaven will be like and an illustration of what awaits Christians.

Perhaps the most common interpretation in Christian history is that found in the apocryphal *Acts of Peter* 20 and *Acts of Thomas* 143: the transfiguration is a revelation of Christ's heavenly or divine nature, a revelation of Jesus as he always was and is. On this view, Jesus was not really changed; rather, the disciples were enabled to perceive what was always the case. On this reading Matthew 17:1-8 reminds one of the story in 2 Kings 6:15-17, where the eyes of Elisha's servant are opened so he can see the invisible horses and chariots of fire around Elijah.

One part of the story of the transfiguration remains intractable. What is the significance of the three booths that Peter wants to build (17:4)? Some think there might be a connection with the Feast of Booths, which Jewish tradition sometimes associated with eschatological expectation. Is Peter then expressing his conviction that the transfiguration is a harbinger of the end of the world? Cyril of Jerusalem wrote: "Peter, thinking perchance that the time of the kingdom of God was even now come, proposes dwellings on the mountain, and says that it is fitting there should be three tabernacles. . . . But he knew not, it says, what he was saying, for it was not the time of the consummation of the world, nor for the saints to take possession of the hope promised to them." Others have simply surmised that Peter wishes to prolong the blessed moment, or that his request comes from a desire to observe the feast that is at hand, or that he assumes that the saints in heaven have dwellings and so will need them when on earth. Whatever Peter has in mind, and whatever his mistake might be — Is it that he wants to linger when he cannot? Is it that he wants to build the booths instead of letting God take things in hand? Is it that "one for you and one for Moses and one for Elijah" implies the parity of the three named? — the cloud and its voice interrupt him. His job is not at this point to do or to teach but to listen.

The final verse of today's reading has Jesus enjoining secrecy: the disciples are not supposed to tell what they have seen until the Son of Man is resurrected (v. 9). The command presupposes that some things should be proclaimed only in the light of Easter because some things can only be rightly understood in the light of Easter.

Dale C. Allison

Sixteenth Sunday after Pentecost, Year A

First Lesson: Exodus 12:1-14
(Psalm 149)
Second Lesson: Romans 13:8-14
Gospel Lesson: Matthew 18:15-20

The whole of Matthew 18 has to do with maintaining the integrity of the Christian community, both in terms of making sure that the least (vv. 1-6) and the lost (vv. 10-14) are protected and retrieved should they stray, and in terms of addressing the power of sin to destroy the community. That Christians should exist in isolation from one another is not entertained even as a possibility. But it follows, then, that sin cannot be construed as a matter simply between the individual and God, as if it had no impact on others. Whether one has by an act of omission or commission harmed or neglected another or has led him or her astray, or whether one has wandered or been injured oneself, the matter is serious — so serious that Jesus does not hesitate to speak in such hyperbole as to say that it is better that one maim oneself than that one sin (vv. 7-9). Yet Jesus is also thoroughly realistic about the possibility of repeated sin (vv. 21-35). It is in this context that Matthew deals with church discipline, in what has been called the most distinctly ecclesiastical passage in his Gospel (McNeile); the intention is clearly the protection of all, not harshness.

We may note that this is the second of only two explicit references to the church in all the Gospels (the first is Matt. 16:18), and the usage here is rightly seen as at least slightly anachronistic: it clearly refers to the local church and assumes that the local church exists in a distinct, organized form (as it did not at the time of Jesus' earthly ministry). We may also note that the passage is a unity, with the result that verses 19 and 20 ought not be cut out of the context and used as a global, independent teaching on prayer, as we might be tempted to do: a striking structural parallelism consisting of "if" *(ean)* clauses at the beginning of verses 15, 15b, 16, 17, 17b, and 19 may be observed. Furthermore, verse 19 starts with "again": the same issues are at stake that have been under discussion. Even the term used for "any*thing*" *(pantos pragmatos, any matter)* clearly has a legal sense in 1 Corinthians 6:1. Thus we have here a specific promise of guidance for the church in matters of discipline — a more restricted affirmation than those of Matthew 7:7 or 21:22. The nature of this guidance, though, accentuates the importance of what is at stake. The promise is of the very presence of the resurrected

105

Christ, put in a way that echoes the rabbinic affirmation that the Shekinah glory — the presence of God — is present where two gather to study Torah (Hagner).

Whether we should understand the passage as referring to action that a member of the community should initiate only if the sin at issue is against himself or herself is not certain: it is not clear whether or not the phrase "against you" *(eis se)* is original. That is, the text may have a more general meaning, referring to action that is appropriate whenever a sin (presumably one that is more than trivial) comes to one's attention. If we assume an intended resonance between the brother or sister who is "gained" in verse 15 and the one who is at risk of being "lost" in verse 14, we may conclude that more than just personal reconciliation is in any case at stake in verses 15-20. The consequences are large: the sin that alienates one from one's brothers and sisters and hence from the church puts the sinner at risk of perishing. Pursuing the offender, then, is not properly seen as a matter of meddling intrusively in business that is not one's own, but rather as both a responsibility and an act of care. (Granting, of course, that we who are also sinners are always at risk of putting a pious mask over anything-but-caring vendettas.)

The progressive nature of the procedure to be used in confronting an offender takes into account the commonsense notion that one does not want to spread anything disruptive or damaging to anyone's reputation any more widely than strictly necessary to produce repentance (cf. Prov. 25:9; "repentance" is not mentioned explicitly but is surely intended in the question of whether the offender "listens"). The series of steps envisions one making every possible effort to regain or retain every member of the community; but the final step of insisting on the excommunication or ostracism of the obdurate from the community also takes seriously the impossibility of preserving the integrity and identity of the church itself if, say, not offending or not hurting someone's feelings should become an ultimate value. (The requirement of two or three witnesses has obvious resonances with Old Testament law, though there the witnesses required are to the deed itself [e.g., Deut. 19:15]; and it carries over into other New Testament legal proceedings [2 Cor. 13:1; 1 Tim. 5:19].)

One of the most difficult questions facing the interpreter of this passage is how to understand the promised result of following the recommended procedure: that somehow the earthly judgment reached by leaders of the church corresponds to heaven's (God's) own judgment (almost identical language is used in Matt. 16:19, though there, where Peter alone is being addressed, the verbs are singular; and a parallel idea is found in John 20:23). In rabbinic thought the primary sense of "binding" and "loosing" had to do with what particular conduct was to be disallowed or allowed according to Torah, the Law of God: the rabbi, on the basis of his expert knowledge, would determine whether one was or was not, in a particular case, acting in accord with God's will. A secondary usage so applied the terms as to condemn or acquit those who did not or did obey these interpretations of the Law, and thus the tie to church discipline is a natural one. But should we read these verses as meaning that God promises to ratify our decisions? The Roman Catholic Church, with its high view of church tradition as authoritative because guided unfailingly by the Holy Spirit, has been more ready to reach this conclusion than have many Protestant interpreters. The latter note that the grammar of the passage is difficult: to be precise, in each clause a second-person aorist subjunctive (*ean dēsēte,* or *lysēte,* whatsoever you have bound, or loosed) is followed by verbs in the future plus the perfect participle (*estai dedemena,* will have been bound; *estai lelymena,* will have been loosed). Many Protestant interpreters have taken this construction to imply not that God *ratifies* human decisions in these circumstances, but rather that prayerful human decisions will, by the Spirit's guidance, faithfully *reflect* the decision already made by God; that is, the judgment of the church will correspond to God's already fully determined will. It is still, of course, a very strong assertion — so strong that many will blanch and be willing to say no more than that, by God's grace, the church's decisions *may* have this character, but not that any superficially "correct" procedure will assure that they *do* (any more than agreement among participants and gathering in Jesus' name will, in what could seem like a magical way, force God's hand; the prayer that is answered is the prayer that, by grace, is in accord with God's will [vv. 19-20]).

Even if we take it at its mildest, though, a passage like this one confronts us sharply with how different the church is today from the one Matthew envisioned. It is not just that excommunication or ostracism do not "work" as they did in Matthew's day, since a person disciplined in one church community can simply walk down the street and join another if he or she chooses. Multiple options and the anonymity of modern societies make meaningful church discipline peculiarly difficult. But apart from the pragmatic questions, and apart from the swing of the pendulum toward too little discipline as a reaction to the horrific too-muchness of, say, the Inquisition or even the abuses of seemingly arbitrarily confining fellowships alive in our own memory, there are fundamental substantive problems. For one, we seem to be suffering from a pervasive confusion about what community requires. We in our society seem to be lonely and isolated and speak a great deal of the *need* for community, yet there is real question of whether we are willing to face the constraints on our own behavior, or to engage in the persistent care for others, that the whole of Matthew 18 would suggest that community requires. Do we have such trouble both with discipline and with forgiveness in part because we have such trouble taking sin, in its effects on us and on others, seriously? Are we too afraid of having someone meddle with our own choices to dare to question the actions of others? Most importantly of all, could it be that we have become jaded enough, or hopeless enough, that we no longer believe the Lord himself takes these matters so seriously that he promises personally to be involved with our efforts specifically with regard to them?

Marguerite Shuster

Seventeenth Sunday after Pentecost, Year A

First Lesson: Exodus 14:19-31
(Psalm 114)
Second Lesson: Romans 14:1-12
Gospel Lesson: Matthew 18:21-35

If the whole of Matthew 18 is concerned with maintaining the integrity and character of the Christian community, including the firm discipline of the *unrepentant* offender (vv. 15-20), then the question of forgiveness of the *repentant* offender comes quickly to the fore. (While the term "repentant" is not used in this passage, the idea is implicit throughout.) Only full and free forgiveness makes genuine restoration of offenders to the community possible and keeps the community from becoming harsh, rigid, and punitive in its ethos. But might not promiscuous forgiveness undercut moral seriousness and make the church's standards meaningless after all?

Peter's question assumes that one does, after all, have to draw the line somewhere, as anyone concerned with discipline surely knows. Something about Jesus' teaching and style has led him to conclude that the rabbis' tradition of drawing that line at forgiving a person three times (for the same sin) is insufficiently generous, so he offers seven times, a number symbolizing fullness. Jesus' well-known response, "Not seven times, but, I tell you, seventy-seven times" (or "seventy times seven" — the phrase can be read either way), points away from all lines and limits, all remembering and scorekeeping, all establishing of museums and conducting of museum tours, with respect to the faults of others. It harks back to the unlimited revenge of which Lamech boasted ("If Cain is avenged sevenfold, / truly Lamech seventy-sevenfold," Gen. 4:24) in the spiral of destruction after the fall, countering it with the unlimited forgiveness that must mark the new order inaugurated by the coming of Jesus.

Jesus' larger answer to Peter's question, though, is not a number — not even a number pointing beyond itself — but a story. And if Peter listens closely, he will find that the story shifts the terms of his question altogether and places him not in a safe and comfortable position on the outside, as a well-qualified judge seeking information, but in a very awkward and vulnerable position on the inside, as a sinner who has already received mercy beyond all possible deserving.

There was a king who wished to settle accounts with his slaves, we read. The "king" language connects to the reference to God in verse 35, and the "lord" *(kyrios)* language throughout fits both God and king, so the allegorical quality of the story is hardly in doubt. And there was a particular slave who was a debtor; in Matthew, sin is more than once seen as debt, as when we pray in the Lord's Prayer that our debts *(opheilēmata,* 6:12) might be forgiven, with that dangerous concluding clause, "as we forgive our debtors." The slave in question owed, we might say, a zillion dollars, more than we can even conceive: that may be the sense of a "myriad" or ten thousand talents. According to Josephus, in 4 B.C. only six hundred talents were collected in taxes from the whole of Judea, Idumea, and Samaria. It would take an ordinary worker more than 150,000 years to earn such a sum, were we to understand the number literally. That the man and his family should be sold into slavery and the proceeds put against the debt was simply the customary punishment for debtors; the return on their sale would scarcely touch the actual sum owed. Under such circumstances, the slave's protestation that if the king would only be patient he would pay all, exemplifies the absurdly unrealistic boldness that comes of desperation. In response to this desperate plea, the king forgave the debt, fully and freely. He didn't extend the time limit; he didn't make a fine display of indulgence; he didn't add a list of conditions and qualifications. He simply forgave (the same verb, *aphienai,* is used regularly for the forgiveness of sins).

Then comes the depiction of the astonishing obduracy of the human heart, the incomprehensible and uncomprehending blindness by which hu-

109

mans fail to see the needs, motives, and circumstances of other human beings as fundamentally like their own. The one who, but moments ago, had
not a shred of a right to which he could cling to save himself, hastens to assert his rights over against another, another whose debt in fact could easily
have been paid. It was, after all, only one six-hundred-thousandth of the
debt the first slave owed, a debt comprising maybe a scant third of a year's
wages, a debt maybe a tenth the size, proportionately, of the home mortgage
an ordinary American with ordinary credit could qualify for. To a plea put
in almost exactly the same language as he himself had used so recently (vv.
26, 29), the slave turned a deaf ear and threw his fellow slave in jail.

Retribution was swift and sure. The king withdrew his leniency and delivered the wicked servant to the torturers (most translations soften this
term) until his impossible debt should be paid in its entirety. And the parable closes, "So my heavenly Father will also do to every one of you, if you do
not forgive your brother or sister from your heart." The conclusion leaves
one gasping, for it is framed in such a way as to point to everlasting torment
for those who fail to forgive.

We dare not ignore the fact that Scripture repeatedly makes clear that
there are consequences for our behavior. God is hardly depicted as a benevolent grandfather who overlooks his little darlings' foibles and misadven-
tures as things they will outgrow as they get older. Hardly. But the mysterious sternness of God is not something at which we can safely stare for too
long, and it is not the essential point of the parable. The essential point is
that of verse 33, that we are to act toward others as God has acted toward us.
And indeed, if we judge with just judgment, the sins of others toward us can
only be construed as petty compared to the forgiveness we ourselves require
from God. Yes, even repeated sins, or especially repeated sins: Dare those of
us who struggle, say, even with a diet or an addiction or a hurtful personal
style, and find our best efforts defeated again and again, suppose that we do
not require forgiveness beyond all reasonable limits if we are to keep going
at all? Do not *especially* these sins that we repeat again and again — not so
much the grand sins that would require heroic moral effort but the petty
ones that we surely *should* be able to conquer — show us our helplessness in
the face of sin and our utter lostness apart from God's mercy? In this sense,
the "little" sin we cannot defeat is altogether like the "big" debt we cannot
pay.

Reasoning alone doesn't quite do it, though: The requirement is that
the forgiveness must be from the heart (v. 35), and how can heart attitudes
be coerced by reason? It may be more that being offered forgiveness is like
being given as a gift a can whose contents are under pressure; as soon as you

open the can, the contents will spill out. If they have *not* spilled out, you may be sure that you have not actually opened the can. That is to say, truly receiving forgiveness leads so intrinsically to the overflowing of forgiveness to others that the two simply cannot be separated. (It may be, in fact, that the identification of the first slave as "wicked," verse 32, is a way of making clear that he never was a true disciple; had he been, he would have forgiven [Gundry].)

Consider: Can we even believe in the possibility of God's forgiveness for us, much less receive it, if we are utterly unable to forgive? How could it be that we should truly receive God's forgiveness without its altering our attitude to others? The thing is impossible. Everywhere in the Gospels, knowing the love of God is linked indissolubly with the love of neighbor. Forgiving and being forgiven cannot in their very nature be torn apart.

Note, too, that the more our willingness to forgive others flows from the deep humility of knowing how much we have been forgiven, the less our efforts to forgive others will take on that aura of an act of superior merit that can do more to destroy a relationship than did the original fault. Many people have commented that as hard as forgiveness may be, it is easier than being forgiven. When done from a position of supposed moral virtue, forgiveness can be the ultimate power play; and instead of restoring normalcy to a relationship, it creates the sort of inequality that leaves the recipient feeling one-down and resentful — not a position from which an individual is likely to do better in the future, and not the best way to reestablish mutual freedom and harmony in the Christian community.

It turns out, then, that Peter's question was not so innocent as it sounded. It really could not be answered at all except by showing Peter, and us, to be in a quite different position than we tend to suppose ourselves to be when we put such questions.

Marguerite Shuster

111

Eighteenth Sunday after Pentecost, Year A

First Lesson: Exodus 16:2-15
(Psalm 105:1-6, 37-45)
Second Lesson: Philippians 1:21-30
Gospel Lesson: Matthew 20:1-16

In a world in which a keen conviction of what we rightly have coming to us is so endemic that the smallest children are more than ready to protest, "It's not *fair*," at the smallest perceived slight, it is hard to avoid the impression that the story of the laborers sent to the vineyard at different hours, but all paid the same amount, is calculated to offend. Or if not precisely to offend, at least to shock hearers into considering the possibility that the kingdom of grace is so utterly unlike the kingdoms of this world that all bets, and especially all tidy calculations of merit and means, are off. It comes in a setting just prior to Jesus' fateful entrance into Jerusalem (chap. 21), where he will triumph by the most upside-down means imaginable, dying in a manner itself certain to offend all pious sensibilities. It is preceded by teaching on money and rewards in chapter 19, where Jesus makes clear that this world's goods are a positive barrier to the reception of God's greatest good. It is followed by the incident later in chapter 20 where the mother of James and John lobbies Jesus for positions of honor for her sons, and Jesus teaches all the disciples that the one who would be first must be the slave of all, even as Jesus himself was. In this setting of reversals, the story of the laborers in the vineyard illustrates the saying of 19:30, that many that are first will be last, and the last first (as the "for," *gar*, with which 20:1 begins shows); and lest anyone miss the point, it closes with a somewhat stronger version of the same saying.

The story may also be directed at Peter's question of 19:27, where he asks what the disciples, who have left everything to follow Jesus, may expect to receive, and Jesus promises them rewards in heaven. The tale serves as a warning as the Lord reaches out to many others: the disciples must not fall prey to the spirit of grumbling characterizing those hired first in the parable — by analogy to the disciples' having been called first. In no case is receiving the kingdom and its gifts predicated on any form of worthiness, including length of service. In no case must a miracle of grace be confused with something that could be deserved or earned. If we can find no "motive" for God's love for the unrighteous, we are equally to seek none for his love for the righteous.

In the parable itself, the analogy of the master of the household to Jesus and of the workers to the disciples is plain, and the vineyard was, of course, a common Old Testament symbol for Israel. Perhaps, that the master went out again and again to hire laborers implies a particular urgency about the work, with the harvest being analogous to the last judgment (Hagner). It is also possible, though not certain, that the workers hired last should be understood to have been overlooked by other employers because of some presumed unworthiness, like the "sinners" Jesus invited to follow him, or perhaps believing Gentiles. In any case, the marketplace was where day laborers would normally gather to look for work. The denarius promised to the first laborers hired was a standard day's wage, enough to live on, but not much more — hence the practice of paying laborers daily (Lev. 19:13; Deut. 24:4-15). To be hired late could mean belt-tightening for one's entire family. Thus the generosity of the master in the parable simply provided what was necessary for life to each of the workers. Yes, it was more than they had any reason to expect: the master has promised them only "whatever is right," leading to the logical assumption that it would be a due proportion of the daily wage. But it was still only what was genuinely needed.

Why couldn't Jesus have just left it there? Many of us could find it in our hearts to be grateful for the generosity of the God who gives the least and the last barely enough. Why, instead of making that perfectly pleasing point, did he have to go on not only to show everyone getting the same amount, but also to depict the master handing out the day's wages in reverse order, positively setting up those hired early to presume that, since the last hired got a full denarius, the first would surely get proportionately more? Yes, the master addressed one of the grumblers kindly, as "Friend," before asserting his freedom to do as he wished with his own goods. And he reminded the man that he had not received any less than he had agreed to: grace is more, not less, than justice. But had Jesus not wanted to show something about sin — envy, presumption, resentment — as well as about grace, all he would have had to do was have the master pay the early workers their denarius first and send them away.

"Is your eye evil because I am good?" the master said. That is, are you envious? Envy presupposes the thought that one has somehow been badly or unfairly treated. Someone else has gotten away with something, or someone has somehow received a better deal than one got oneself. The idea further presumes that one has grounds on which one can stand to make a claim — an idea inimical to the fundamental character of grace. Grace is not grace if it is qualified by superior virtue in the recipient. Sinners are not sinners if some of them are less completely dependent on grace than others. Besides, if one has enough oneself, why would one even *want* more than someone else, unless out of some sort of pride and self-righteousness? That it seems so odd to put the question that way — so normal, so natural, is our desire to want more — shows the depth of our sin. The more we insist on our tit-for-tat way of thinking, the more baffled and angry we will be at God's whole way of dealing with us.

Note that it is not, of course, those who received the unexpected bonus who grumbled, or who engaged in a season of soul-searching to see if someone might have deserved this good fortune more than they did. Most of us do not have sensitive consciences about undeserved blessings, especially if we do not construe them as being at anyone else's direct expense. We do not get an "evil eye" by looking at ourselves, but by looking at others. But "What do [we] have that [we] did not receive? And if [we] received it, why do [we] boast as if it were not a gift?" (1 Cor. 4:7). Even to be hired to work in the vineyard, to labor in and for God's kingdom, is already to be caught up by God's power and to work out of that power. It raises no claim on God.

Look at it from another angle. Is it really such a great coup to be hired late rather than early — to spend the greatest part of a day, or a life, waiting fruitlessly? Is even laboring during the heat of the day, or bearing a scorching wind (a sense the word *kausōna*, v. 12, may have), really worse than having one's hopes of a meal fade with every degree the sun descends in the sky? Even apart from the need for sustenance, work is a creation ordinance, and those who for reason of age or disability or any other cause are deprived of the opportunity for work often feel the lack keenly simply at the level of purpose and meaning in life. Yes, work is often stressful, difficult, monotonous in this fallen world, but not to have work at all is worse. Surely the analogies in the spiritual realm are clear. Difficulties and strain beset many aspects of the Christian life; the heat of the day may indeed be hard to bear. But once we have been called by Christ to work as his disciples in the vineyard, would we really prefer to go back to the uncertainty of waiting in the marketplace? Really?

Yes, there is a sharp challenge here to our sinful tendency to bring God to the bar of our self-serving "justice." But the tremendously good news of this parable is that God's grace is so great, so surprising, that it can provide *enough* no matter how late in the day it has become. It is not *too late* even on the deathbed, even in the jail cell, even after the repeated failures at whatever one has repeatedly failed at, because the recipient need not add anything to that grace but simply receive it in order for it to do its life-giving work. Oh yes, one must still behave as a disciple while there is light: even the last worker hired went to the vineyard; but should the sun threaten to set on one's life in mere minutes, it is still not too late. And we may trust that in heaven those who labored all their lives long will discover that heaven's "enough" makes all earthly comparisons petty and meaningless.

Marguerite Shuster

Palm/Passion Sunday, Year A

First Lesson: Isaiah 50:4-9a
(Psalm 31:9-16)
Second Lesson: Philippians 2:5-11
Gospel Lesson: Matthew 21:1-11

Paradoxes, seeming contradictions, dual meanings abound in this text for the day the church calls Palm or Passion Sunday. It is in the exploration of these that Matthew's telling of Jesus' entry in the holy city of Jerusalem offers rich insight into the nature of the Messiah. Geography often matters symbolically to Matthew, and Jesus' journey to the city of his death begins tellingly on the Mount of Olives, which was associated with Jewish messianic expectations (cf. Zech. 14:4) (Frederick Dale Bruner, *Matthew: A Commentary*, vol. 2 [Dallas: Word, 1990], p. 748).

Jesus sends not one but two disciples to secure two animals for his journey into the city. Clearly Jesus can ride only one animal, and it may be simply that the unridden colt is companioned by its mother in order to keep it calm. (It would seem unlikely that Matthew has mistaken the parallelism of the Zechariah quotation to mean two animals.) A wag familiar with farm animals once suggested that this is Jesus' greatest miracle: successfully riding a donkey that had never before been ridden! The disciples go and find all just as Jesus had told them it would be, either because he had prearranged matters or had divine foreknowledge of unfolding events, or both (see below). Somewhat curiously, the phrase "the Lord needs them" appears in Jesus' instructions to the two disciples, raising the issue of what indeed the Lord needs in the way of help in accomplishing the divine purpose. It should be noted that what the Lord needs here is borrowed rather than purchased, suggesting an interdependence which stands in some contrast to contemporary notions of the need for ownership and independence. Very characteristically, Matthew marks this event as a fulfillment of what was spoken by the prophet. However, here he in fact conflates the words of two prophets in his citation, Isaiah 62:11 and Zechariah 9:9, and curiously omits the phrase "triumphant and victorious is he!" from the middle of the latter.

Notice the many double-sided issues in these few verses. Jerusalem is at once the holy city and "the city that kills the prophets" (Matt. 23:37). Jesus sends two disciples to get two animals when he can clearly ride only one. Do events happen by previous planning or divine knowledge? In all of these, Matthew is seeking to convey the two natures of Christ — fully human and fully divine (Thomas G. Long, *Matthew* [Louisville: Westminster John Knox, 1997], p. 233). Both aspects must be held in mind together if Jesus is to be comprehended in full. Jesus is "the *Crucified* Messiah, the *Modest* King, the *Lowly* Lord, the *Human* God" (Bruner, p. 748). The omitted phrase from Zechariah makes clearer the fact that this king is humble, unlike the kings of the earth so familiar to Herod, Pilate, and Caesar. Jesus in his humanity may have arranged the loan of the animals, but in his divinity he would not have needed to. Thus again is his dual nature affirmed by the very ambiguity of the text in regards to that matter. Following this Matthean emphasis, Dietrich Bonhoeffer said, "If Christ is not fully human, how can he save us? If Christ is not fully divine, how can he save us?" This is the central point of Matthew's recounting of the first Palm Sunday.

Once the animals are secured, the two disciples put their cloaks on both donkey and colt and Jesus sits on the garments. Some of those coming to Jerusalem for the Passover celebration join the procession as Jesus descends from the Mount of Olives. Though he rides on a donkey rather than a warhorse (thereby symbolizing peace rather than militarism), the crowd seems to catch the royal symbolism of the act and carpets his path with their cloaks and branches cut from trees (compare royal triumphal entry stories in 1 Kings 1:32-40 and 2 Kings 9:13). The donkey Jesus rides is a beast of the people, a working beast that identifies Jesus as being in solidarity with those familiar with the animal. It is humble and stubborn in the burden it is bearing, even as the one who rides it this day is humble and determined to fulfill his calling.

The crowd starts chanting phrases taken from Psalm 118:25 and following. The words "Son of David" do not appear there, but again underscore Jesus' identity as being in accord with the great king whose city he is entering. The "Hosanna" can be understood as both a prayer ("save us," as in the psalm) and as an acclamation of praise in keeping with the double entendre character of the passage pointing to Christ's dual nature. And again, it can be argued that God both did not (the crucifixion) and did (the resurrection) save the Son of David (Bruner, pp. 750-51).

Matthew says, "The whole city was in turmoil, asking, 'Who is this?'" when Jesus entered. The "whole city" in its ignorance stands in contrast to "the crowds" who knew Jesus to be at least a prophet "from Nazareth in Galilee." Both groups will be presented with the opportunity to learn that Jesus is more than a human prophet or human king in days to come. "Turmoil" as a translation for *eseisthē* (from the verb *seiō*, "to shake") is too mild. Matthew's readers would recognize the cosmic, earthshaking significance of what is happening in this story, even if the inhabitants of Jerusalem do not. The Messiah has come. This is the first of several seismic shocks in the coming days (see 24:7; 27:51; 27:54; and 28:2), a "shaking of the foundations," to use Paul Tillich's term. There is an apocalyptic character to what is coming to pass in this event that may be sensed, if not understood, by those present. Apocalyptic times set house against house and sibling against sibling. Seeing the text through apocalyptic lenses opens the door for understanding how people could (in the popular misconception of Palm Sunday) go from allegedly loving Jesus to killing him in just five days. As Jesus' birth troubled Herod and "all Jerusalem," so his death and new birth will trouble and shake Jerusalem and far beyond.

Rome held the Jews in captivity as surely as had the Egyptians. And the people looked for a deliverer based on their trust in God's promises borne to them by their prophetic sacred writings. But the given Messiah does not, as is often noted, fulfill popular expectations. Not only was that true then, it is true now. "Who is the Christ?" is the question behind this text, and the answer is of the both/and variety: both human and divine, both militant and nonviolent, both crucified and resurrected, both obedient and triumphant, both royal and humble, both empowering and not overpowering. The text calls its hearers to the hard but utterly essential struggle with Christ's dual nature. Grasping either aspect of Christ without its counterpoint distorts the gospel. The modern church in its quest for an understandable, easily communicable gospel is tempted to oversimplification. We may marvel, even shake our heads, at the long and bitter struggles waged in the early church to articulate in creedal form the answer to this essential question. Such debates can indeed delay or substitute for the work of compassion and justice to which our Lord calls us. But this Palm Sunday lection affords the opportunity to wrestle with the mystery of Christ's nature, or at the very least to remind God's people that it matters immensely even if it cannot be articulated simply nor grasped totally.

There is a loneliness and quietude about Jesus as the procession unfolds, the piercing loneliness of being misunderstood. He speaks not a word. It is as if he knows all too well that the affirming crowds and the curious city will not be able to grasp the mystery of God's work through him. And what they do not understand, what contradicts their present belief, they will seek to destroy. The church affirms something of this loneliness in its affirmation of Christ's unique and dual nature. Christ seeks those who will endeavor to explore the mystery of his uniqueness in their quest for God that thereby he may find himself in the community of disciples he ever sought to form in his life, death, and resurrection.

Lawrence W. Farris

Nineteenth Sunday after Pentecost, Year A

First Lesson: Exodus 17:1-7
(Psalm 78:1-4, 12-16)
Second Lesson: Philippians 2:1-13
Gospel Lesson: Matthew 21:23-32

The first half of today's lesson, Matthew 21:23-27, is a dialogue in which the chief priests and elders ask Jesus why he does what he does and who has given him the authority so to act. We should probably imagine that their words are occasioned especially by Jesus' protest in the temple (vv. 12-17). But the query presumably covers also Jesus' provocative deeds in general (including the entry to Jerusalem, where he does not discourage the crowds who hail him as the Son of David) as well as his teaching, which has astounded people (7:28). If so, the question is about Jesus' presumption both to act as messianic king and to teach as he does. The question betrays a deliberate blindness, of course, for Matthew has established Jesus' authority for those with eyes to see (cf. esp. 7:29: "he taught as one having authority"; 9:6: "so that you may know that the Son of man has authority on earth to forgive sins"; and 9:8: "When the crowds saw it, they were filled with awe, and they glorified God, who had given such authority to human beings"). The question of the high priests and elders is in fact ludicrous if read in the light of Matthew's conclusion: the authorities are asking for the credentials of the one who can say, "All authority in heaven and on earth has been given to me" (28:18).

If Jesus were to answer the question with "I do these things by human authority," he would of course contradict his own bold behavior and annul his ministry. But were he to answer, "I do these things by divine authority," he would be laying explicit public claim to messianic status and risk Roman investigation of sedition. Obviously a clever trap has been laid. Readers infer that the members of the Sanhedrin are crafty individuals.

But Jesus is equally shrewd. In response to his opponents' challenge, he poses a counterquestion. Was "the baptism of John" — the phrase stands for all of John's ministry — "from heaven," that is, from God, or was it of purely human device? In this way Jesus cleverly circumvents the ambush that has been laid for him. He avoids making a public statement about himself — something he elsewhere refrains from doing (cf. 16:20; 17:9) — and moves attention from himself to his opponents. Suddenly the question is no longer what Jesus thinks but what his opponents think. Moreover, just as the opening question seemingly left Jesus with only two unsatisfactory responses, so too are the Jewish leaders now left with two unpalatable possibilities. Dilemma matches dilemma. Unlike Jesus, however, the authorities will be unable to match his clever comeback.

What would happen if the leaders were to endorse John's baptism as being from heaven? The problem for them is that, earlier in the story, John has publicly testified to Jesus (3:11-13). So acceptance of John would require acceptance of Jesus. That is, the leaders cannot endorse John without endorsing Jesus. But if the chief priests and elders declare John's ministry to have a human origin, they would alienate the populace, who honors John as a prophet (21:26). So to avoid losing an argument (v. 25) or raising the ire of the crowd (v. 26), the chief priests and elders feign ignorance and run from the truth, as all of us so often do. But in this there is no victory. To confess no estimate of John only reveals blindness to the obvious. The leaders accordingly indict themselves, and their own lack of authority is made plain. Instead of saving face, they look cowardly.

When the authorities consider answering "From heaven," perhaps we are to think that they suspect the truth but cannot honestly face the implications. Their motivation for keeping silent in any event is fear of entrapment. As Calvin remarked, "They do not inquire what is true, nor do they put the question to their own conscience." Bengel said something similar: "That is an evil mind which, in a holy subject, does not look at the truth but assumes what serves its purpose."

Jesus terminates the discussion by matching refusal with refusal. His closing words ("by what authority I do these things") reproduce his opponents' opening words (v. 23: "By what authority do you do these things?") and create an inclusion. Thus the discussion comes to a close with all the questions going unanswered. But Jesus' authority is not placed in doubt by his refusal to answer. Rather is it indirectly confirmed: he need not submit to questioning at the hands of the chief priests and elders. His refusal is in fact veiled affirmation of his own stupendous authority.

Matthew 21:23-27 is not so much about John the Baptist or even about Jesus — the main point is certainly not that he is a skilled debater or clever philosopher — but about the chief priests and elders. Its first purpose is to characterize certain principals in the subsequent drama. Here we learn that the leaders, upset by the Messiah's deeds, inquired of him "without reason or respect, a thing that was plain to all" (Calvin), and further, that out of cowardly expediency they responded to his questions by lying against the truth, thereby demonstrating that their own authority was not from God. As if that were not enough, they showed themselves to be spiritually less perceptive than those over whom they presumed to preside as privileged members of the Sanhedrin; the multitudes — here sharply distinguished from their leaders — at least recognized John's prophetic status. The effect of all this is to set the passion of Jesus within a moral context. Jesus' death is not the upshot of an unfortunate misunderstanding on the part of uninformed authorities; instead was it brought about by the plotting of self-serving men of ill will. The passion narrative, in other words, depicts not an innocent blunder or a genuine misunderstanding but a dramatic struggle between good and evil.

21:28-32 functions as a sort of addendum to verses 23-27. Jesus first utters a brief parable (vv. 28-30), and then we get the application and commentary on it (vv. 31-32). The parable relates two encounters and their issues. The differences and similarities between the two encounters and their issues are formally reflected by the dissimilarities within the parallelism:

The first episode	The second episode
The father goes to one son	The father goes to another son
The father asks him to work in the vineyard	The father asks him to work in the vineyard
Curt refusal: "I will not"	Respectful affirmation: "I (will), Lord"
Later he changes his mind and goes	He never goes

The second half of 21:28-32 opens with Jesus asking a nonrhetorical question, "Which of the two did the will of the father?" to which his opponents give the only reasonable answer: "The first." This answer calls forth an accusation that, unlike verses 28-30, is undisguised polemic: the chief priests and the elders approve of behavior which is unlike their own. So they are hypocrites.

Verses 31-32 allegorically interpret verses 28-30. The father represents God. The first son represents toll collectors and prostitutes, those lax in the law who come to obey God through John's ministry. The second son represents the chief priests and the elders, those who, despite their religious profession, disobeyed God by not believing in John. The main function in the broader context is to characterize the Jewish leaders who oppose Jesus.

The use of "Lord" (*kyrios;* the NRSV has "sir") in verses 30 adds pathos, for it makes the contradiction between word and deed more acute. One is reminded of 7:21: "Not every one who says to me, 'Lord, Lord,' will enter the kingdom of heaven; but the one that does the will of my Father who is in heaven." Three items are shared: "Lord," entrance into the kingdom, and doing the will of the Father. 21:28-32 is thus an illustration of 7:21. Speech without deeds is dead.

"Toll collectors and prostitutes" occurs in the New Testament only here and in verse 32. It is likely that Jesus himself was accused of being in the company of harlots. In the Greco-Roman world the slur (often baseless) was commonly made against men who banqueted with women. In any case their mention is effective: the chief priests and the elders — like Matthew's readers — would have had nothing but utter disdain for prostitutes. These last were, like toll collectors, outside the law and, additionally, associated with the Roman soldier camps. To put them ahead of the Jewish leaders dramatically proves that those leaders "could not be further from the position they boasted of" (Calvin): they were beneath both the unjust and the unchaste.

Chrysostom urged that the two children of our parable "declare what came to pass with respect to both the Gentiles and the Jews. For the former, not having become hearers of the law, showed forth their obedience in their works; and the latter having said, 'All that the Lord shall speak, we will do, and will hearken' (Exodus 19:8), in their works were disobedient." This interpretation of our parable in terms of salvation history has dominated Christian exegetical history. The list of its proponents is long. And it is not implausible. Matthew 21:43 can be taken as confirmation, and both toll collectors and prostitutes were generally reckoned as being beyond the bounds of Torah and were therefore appropriate symbols for Gentiles.

Some recent exegetes, however, have rightly begun to question the consensus of the past. Nothing since Jesus' arrival in Jerusalem has directly addressed Jewish/Gentile relations. Indeed, the section has encouraged the reader rather to think in terms of believing and unbelieving Israel. More-over, our parable is explicitly about different responses to John the Baptist, not Jesus or the Christian kerygma. The most natural interpretation, then, is that which finds in our pericope three items — (1) depiction of a divided Israel, (2) illustration of the first (the chief priests and elders) becoming last and the last (toll collectors and prostitutes) becoming first, and (3) charac-terization of Jesus' opponents as hypocrites. The advent of the Messiah's forerunner, like the advent of the Messiah himself, compels Israel to make a decision that splits her asunder: there are believers and unbelievers. The for-mer tend to come from disenfranchised groups, whereas the latter include individuals of power and prestige who sin knowingly.

Dale C. Allison

Twentieth Sunday after Pentecost, Year A

First Lesson: Exodus 20:1-4, 7-9, 12-20
(Psalm 19)
Second Lesson: Philippians 3:4b-14
Gospel Lesson: Matthew 21:33-46

Of all the parables of Jesus, this one surely ranks near the top of the ten-sion and drama scale. A clash arises between some thoughtless tenant farmers and some innocent servants of a property owner. Before we know it, the conflict has ended with the wicked death of the owner's son. The whole scene is quite vivid. Matthew lays out the landscape details of the farmstead with a precise picturelike quality. He lets us in on the arbitrary cruelty of the beating, killing, and stoning. We even get to listen in on the inner workings of the landowner's mind ("They will respect my son," v. 37) and the internal scheming of the tenants ("This is the heir, let us kill him and get his inheri-tance," v. 38).

Yet perhaps what holds our attention more than anything else through-out this parable is the exaggeration of the story pieces themselves. Every-thing gets stretched. Every action pushes the envelope of probability. What farm owner would operate with this absurd level of patience? Who would put up with such abuse if he or she automatically had the power to attack it? And since when would a harvest moment elicit such homicidal behavior on the part of tenant farmers, farmers who stand to gain nothing through their cruelty? All of this exaggeration and improbability adds to the drama of the story. It pulls us into a theological quest for what Matthew is trying to accomplish.

Many interpreters suggest that this must be a parable of judgment, scissored as it is between two other accounts of judgment — the parable of the two sons and the parable of the king's wedding feast. But that's a simplistic rendering. For not only may the story of the two sons be about much more than judgment. This scenario of some tenants rebelling against innocent emissaries of their boss has layers of theological depth that rest well below the surface appearance of judgment. The one layer to which I'll give focus for preaching purposes is that one marked by the subject of *ownership*. Simply put, the human tendency to behave less like guests in God's creation and more like management comes alive in this parable. From start to finish, we see confusion and conflict resulting from human beings who mistake what belongs to someone else for their own possession. This confusion over ownership constitutes the theological heartbeat of the parable.

Notice how the story opens. Verse 33 has six verbs in it alone, all attributed to activities of the owner. In those verbs — "planted," "put," "dug," "built," "leased," "went" — we learn of the owner's absolute love for and absolute ownership of the property. His proprietary rights are total. What happens on that land happens entirely according to his dominion. But he exercises those rights and that dominion with utmost care and respect. He not only goes to great lengths to care for his vineyard. He also trusts the tenants to be responsible in his absence. When Matthew informs us that the owner "went away," these tenants attempt to steal or divert what has only been entrusted to them, not given to them. They rewrite the lease contract in their head to read with the kind of autonomy we're prone to read into our modern circumstance: "It's my life to live. I make my own decisions. I'll choose the obligations I wish."

The fact that the land is "leased" to the tenants gives a clue to the source of the conflict that emerges. It's a conflict of ownership. These tenant farmers are employees, not independent contractors. They are part of a lease agreement. They may behave as if they own the farm and work for themselves. But the truth of the matter is that they're accountable to the owner.

Certain privileges and responsibilities go with being related to God and God's sovereignty. Trying to rewrite the terms of those privileges, or escape the responsibilities that accompany them, may engender a momentary feeling of freedom. But God remains the sovereign owner of everything we are and have, regardless of how we act. And not even coercion and cruelty can wrest from God what belongs to God and somehow make it our own.

So when the tenant farmers contemplate obtaining the inheritance of the owner, they're playing with the idea of owning what is not theirs to own. Since an inheritance is not something one gets for oneself or coerces for oneself, the very notion of inheriting the vineyard is a futile exercise. By its very nature, an inheritance is a gift that one cannot earn or arrange. The vinedressers in our story stand out for their confusion over ownership and loan.

A preacher might explore the many ways in which we claim for ourselves what has only been entrusted to us. While it may feel good to seize the life we think we deserve, God has other plans in mind for such selfishness. "He will lease the vineyard to other tenants who will deliver him the produce at harvest time" (v. 41). This apparent favor of God toward those who understand the ownership issue properly can be construed in very anti-Jewish ways. The preacher should treat the parable with extra care on this front. To suggest that the people of Israel were the wicked vinedressers from whom God took the land, only to give it to responsible Gentile or Christian types, would be an unfortunate interpretation. We're all capable of rejecting the word and authority of God. We all deserve to be thrown out of the vineyard.

The christological glow of the parable is obvious. It would have been natural in the faith life of early Christians to identify the murdered son in the story as the Christ figure himself. The association is natural for us as well. If the servants who undergo the brutal treatment from these employees represent the prophets of Israel being persecuted (as seems to be the author's intent — see also 23:29-39), then the introduction of *the* son, as representative of Jesus the Messiah, seems logical. The son arrives as the ultimate gift of the owner's confidence, full of his Father's authority. He is the most unique emissary; no one else is related to the owner of the vineyard quite like he is. He is also the final emissary; no one will come after him. Surely "they will honor my Son," the landowner reasons.

When the peasant farmers kill this son in the weird belief that they would come into possession of the soil pushing up at their toes, they haul him out of the vineyard before they kill him. Jesus suffered a similar fate, dying outside the city limits of Jerusalem (cf. Heb. 13:12; John 19:17). And Jesus met his death, mocked about his rule and challenged about his ownership of life. "If you are the King of the Jews, then come down and save yourself."

Jesus obviously draws on the vineyard imagery from Isaiah 5:1-7, translating that prophet's word quite freely. In Isaiah the vineyard also is planted and tended with great care, only to end in tragedy when the vines yield bad grapes instead of good ones. But the biggest difference is in the owner of each vineyard. Isaiah's "beloved" planter destroys the vineyard out of anger for its production of wild grapes. The owner in Jesus' parable displays absurd patience! What owner of a cherry-tree farm in Wisconsin, or a blueberry grove in Maine, or a hillside of grapes in Napa Valley would behave with such patience, sending agent after agent to collect the produce, only to have their lives destroyed? The answer of course is none. No one we're familiar with in our circles of life would ever display this kind of persistent attention. Why not attack the tenants, for goodness' sake!

When talking about the astonishing mercy of God, however, it all begins to make sense. The great lengths to which God goes for us should elicit loyalty, not disgust. God's incomprehensibly steadfast character and undying love ought to provoke gratitude, not sinful behavior. But when we confuse the ownership and loan issue, mistaking what has been entrusted to us as in fact our own, there's no telling what we'll do to have our way. Even violence may enter the picture.

It is the season for collecting fruit, we are told. And Jesus is interested in whether we are ready and willing to produce "the fruits of the kingdom" through our lives. His demand for fruitful living is a demand for changed lives. And if we're willing to get the ownership matter straight, and comprehend how much of us God properly owns, we have a good chance of loving God and our neighbor as we ought.

One final note: the sudden switch in this parable from agricultural to architectural imagery may confuse. Some view the excerpt from Psalm 118 as out of place and "a later addition to the text." A preacher, however, gets to make use of this shift in creative ways. Here is the promise of new life in the midst of brutal death, erupting in the middle of the parable. It's the exceeding greatness of God overcoming all rejection. It's the redemptive chance for wicked tenants to become faithful builders.

Peter W. Marty

Twenty-first Sunday after Pentecost, Year A

First Lesson: Exodus 32:1-14
(Psalm 106:1-6, 19-23)
Second Lesson: Philippians 4:1-9
Gospel Lesson: Matthew 22:1-14

Matthew alone reports this paired set of fierce parables. Luke 14:16-24 is parallel in some details. There are a great banquet and the weak excuses made by those who choose not to go. It ends with the inclusion of the odd and uninvited and thus makes the same final point about the Gentile mission, but although it sheds some light on Matthew 22:1-10, it is a different story and a gentler one. We must stay within Matthew's context to understand the full power of this pericope.

This double parable comes as one of Matthew's additions to Mark's collection of controversies that take place after Jesus' entry in Jerusalem. The whole section might easily be subtitled "How to get yourself killed." The length of this section in Matthew and the additional material lend impact to the unfolding drama. Matthew's account of Jesus in Jerusalem matches Greek drama in its sense of inevitability and impending catharsis. At every turn Jesus' words and behavior intensify the conflict that will lead to the cross.

There two parables, here so deftly combined into one, seem at first to make the preacher's job more difficult. I will deal with them separately at first because I think that when one has done so it becomes possible to recombine them in the end and to see the genius of the evangelist's editing.

Another reason to separate them is that the first part needs to be treated from two angles — first as a controversy account that speeds the way to crucifixion and second as an allegory addressed more directly to the church. The account plainly has a double function in the evangelist's telling of it.

First, then, the preacher needs to see it in its context as one of the encounters that hastens the way to the cross. Jesus is identifying his own mission with that of the prophets who were rejected before him. This kind of parable directly accuses those who obstruct the Kingdom of God. Chapter 21 ends, "the chief priests and the Pharisees . . . realized that he was speaking about them."

There is little mystery, then, about the meaning of the parable in the situation where Jesus told it. It summarizes a frequent theme. God calls, but his people reject his call and the prophets who issue it. Like the prophets before him Jesus turns the sharpest critique on the leaders, shepherds, and upper classes. Note that in this parable there are still plenty of riffraff left to invite to the king's wedding banquet. Those who accompanied Jesus into Jerusalem earlier are not the target of this critique. He is speaking about the chief priests and the Pharisees, and for his pains he will suffer like the prophets before him.

The historical meaning of the parable presents a problem in our era. It is vulnerable to a rough supersessionist interpretation, as if it argued for God's rejection of the Jews. As Romans 9-11 makes clear, God has done no such thing. Surely Matthew cannot mean to imply such a thing, since he is writing for a heavily Jewish community of believers in Jesus. What we need to see here is a typical prophetic critique of Israel, which in the New Testament becomes a warning to the Church and not a condemnation of Israel. Anti-Semitic distortion of this kind of New Testament literature should not frighten us off from the parable, although the preacher may find occasion to point out that the parable is not anti-Semitic in intent not least because it is absurd and anachronistic to imagine that either Jesus or Matthew could be anti-Semitic.

One of the reasons that the parable cannot rightly be read as anti-Semitic or anti-Judaic is that in its allegorical sense (which is literally apparent without stretching) it is a word to the Church. Following in the prophetic tradition of the fiery, angry love of God for his faithful people, the risen Christ speaks this parable to the Church just as the "historical Jesus" proclaimed it to warn against the disastrous leadership of the chief priests and Pharisees. In each case it is uttered in love.

God sends various waves of prophets to invite his people to the wedding banquet of his Son. They reject them with increasing harshness, first rejecting then killing them. Finally, God punishes them severely, but he is not done. He shows greater grace and love by extending his reach and invitation, bringing in the overlooked, the unworthy, and ultimately the gentiles. Apart from the identification of a Son, the parable announces in a different key what we find in Jeremiah and Isaiah.

As the meaning was clear to the chief priest and Pharisees, it is also clear to the Church. The Gentile mission resulting from Jesus' rejection by the leaders of his own people is to continue, and we are warned not to take the king's invitation lightly. This is a command performance, not a matter of preference. It would not be a bad occasion for the preacher to take on the voluntarism of the American church. God expects his people to show up for the wedding banquet of his Son.

And if God has called you off the streets (or from Luke's highways and hedgerows) — and if you are Gentile he *has* called you off the streets — then you had better appreciate the invitation and show it respect. You too can be punished if you respond with disdain. You don't need to kill any prophets to rouse the king's wrath. Taking the invitation lightly and showing up in your cut-offs may get the same reaction.

Once we see the historical and allegorical significance of the first parable, the second becomes as easy as I indicate in the above paragraph. Matthew is speaking to Jewish and Gentile Christians. Both depend on God's patience, and the Gentiles cannot just come barging in without respecting the truth and Torah that God has revealed to Israel. Swinish Gentile behavior must be left behind.

Note how much this is like the concerns that Paul tackles. Gentiles do not have to become Jews, but they do have to be clothed in the righteousness of Christ and leave immorality and idolatry behind. Jews are not rejected, but they are accountable for their history and their misplaced zeal and presumption in the past. Paul himself would of course be the chief example.

This fierce double parable is thus deeply *ecclesial.* It is concerned for the mission of the church, for the faithfulness of the church, and for the inclusiveness of the church. As in the Old Testament the people of God are the bride. The pericope is deeply *christological.* It identifies Jesus as the Son for whom the king throws the wedding banquet, and response to him is the measure of faithfulness. The pericope is also *sacramental.* The marriage banquet is transparent to the eucharist, and the wedding garment is powerfully suggestive of baptism.

Finally, the pericope is profoundly *moral.* God's people are expected to be obedient to God and his prophets. Jesus and the Pharisees do not disagree at this point — only about the nature of such obedience. The inclusiveness of the Kingdom of God is not an easy tolerance. It is not antinomian, as it is so often misinterpreted among more liberal Christians these days. Nor does the invitation of God leave the status quo untouched, as more conservative American Christians might be tempted to think.

The invitation is generous and it is broad, but it is not an invitation to a come as you are party, and it does not make the colossal error of the contemporary self-esteem movement. It does not pretend that "you are just fine the way you are." You are not — you are troubled, confused, sinful, mortal, perhaps sick or in deep distress. The Gospel is not the announcement that any of us is just fine the way we are. Rather, God loves so much that he will not leave us unchanged.

It is not our banquet, as so many bad contemporary communion hymns seem to imagine. It is the marriage supper of the Lamb. God wants us there as what God has made us to be, not as the mess we have made of ourselves.

The Gospel is an open invitation to the marriage supper of the Lamb, but it knows that the way in goes through the waters of baptism. Those who accept the invitation will not reject the new and holy identity that God offers them. They will accept and wear the wedding garment. (Note how the logion at the end — "For many are called, but few are chosen" — fits well and reinforces the parables on virtually all of these points.)

You don't get an invitation like this every day. Come, you are wanted, but the only way to accept an invitation as good as this one is to clean up, dress up, and rejoice in the new identity you receive by coming to this banquet.

Leonard R. Klein

Twenty-second Sunday after Pentecost, Year A

First Lesson: Exodus 33:12-23
(Psalm 99)
Second Lesson: 1 Thessalonians 1:1-10
Gospel Lesson: Matthew 22:15-22

This passage commences a series of discussions that runs through the remainder of chapter 22. Jesus first engages the Pharisees and Herodians (vv. 15-22). Then he opposes the Sadducees (vv. 23-33). Then he has a discussion with a Pharisaic lawyer (vv. 34-40). Finally he again disputes a group of Pharisees (vv. 41-46). Taken together, the four passages continue the negative characterization of the authorities in Jerusalem and show all reason and argument to be on Jesus' side. He is the master of the debate from beginning to end. One feels in the exchanges the powerful difference between Jesus' incisive and memorable declarations and the forgettable words of his opponents, who are reduced to uttering the obvious (vv. 21, 42). There is here no real debate but a majestic authority whose utterances leave opponents with nothing much to say. Believers are of course in the very same boat as those opponents: Jesus is the last word; there is no arguing with him.

The Pharisees and Herodians open by flattering Jesus: "We know that you are sincere, and teach the way of God in accordance with truth, and show deference to no one; for you do not regard people with partiality" (v. 16). This comment and those that follow are of course ironic: Jesus' opponents speak the truth unwittingly. Moreover, the words serve to distinguish Jesus from his adversaries, for unlike him, they are not sincere but "hypocrites" (v. 18). They additionally flaunt their leaders' irrationality. It should be as obvious to them as to the reader that Jesus cannot be moved by adulation. In their own eyes, however, their flattery may be, as Chrysostom urged, designed to encourage Jesus to speak his mind without regard to the Roman authorities.

The identity of the "Herodians" is, despite their being conveniently described in most of the commentaries, unknown. It is possible they were Essenes, for Josephus tells us that the Essenes won the favor of Herod the Great. Most, however, speculate that they were in any case supporters of Herod and his policies. They are mentioned only here in Matthew and nowhere outside of the Gospels.

The question to Jesus is, Does the divine will permit paying taxes to Caesar? The word here translated "taxes" refers to the Roman *census,* a tax upon agricultural yield and personal property. The latter was collected through census, or registration (Luke 2:1-5; Acts 5:37), and probably amounted to one denarius a year. Although Jewish authorities (including the Sanhedrin) helped collect the tax, many Jews resented it and objected on religious grounds. Indeed, although Roman taxation had been a reality since 63 B.C., the census of A.D. 6 or 7, when Judea came under direct Roman control, encouraged a revolt; and resentment of Roman taxation contributed to the unrest that culminated in the later revolt against Rome in A.D. 70. Thus the question of our verse, a question that in one form or another always arises outside a theocracy, was a real one for first-century Jews. It was hardly formulated for this occasion.

Jesus, reading the hearts and minds of his opponents, asks for a coin (v. 19). He could make his point without the coin. But the use of a visual aid, of nonverbal communication, adds drama, while the coin being in the possession of the questioners highlights the insincerity of their query: at least they have no qualms about using pagan money. They have brought a coin with the emperor's image and blasphemous inscription into the holy precincts of the temple. (Evidently Jesus and his followers have no money on them, or at least not the right type of coin.)

The "denarius" was the coin in which taxation was calculated and paid. Many Jews would have used the coin without much thought, despite its bearing a "graven image." Certainly that is the presupposition of our verse: some of Jesus' hearers will have a silver coin to hand. The denarius of our story is almost certainly one minted in Lugdunum in Gaul. It had on the obverse a head of Tiberius along with his name, and on the reverse the image of a seated lady (peace personified, perhaps as the emperor's wife, Livia). Copper coins without Caesar's image were, however, produced for daily use, and according to one source, the Essenes refused to either carry or even look at the denarius.

Jesus clearly speaks while holding up the coin, showing no hesitation in handling or looking at Caesar's coin. The answer to his question — "Whose head is this, and whose title?" — is a foregone banality — "The emperor's" — which contrasts with the memorable words that follow. The opponents, although they speak, have nothing to say.

Jesus' words — the verb "give" literally means "give back," so the thought may well be that in giving the coin to Caesar one is simply returning to him what is his — distance him from those who opposed supporting Rome. At the same time, the inclusion of giving to God what is God's relativizes the political obligation. There is here no firm principle of loyal submission to the state. Implied rather is a reservation regarding the state, a lack of reservation regarding God. While obedience to God can, as in the current instance, coexist with doing what the state requires, obligation to the former obviously overshadows obligation to the latter. So there is no simple yes or no, no straightforward rule, but the imperative to weigh the demands of two (very unequal) authorities, one of which endures, one of which passes away. When those demands are not at odds (as here), obligations to both can be met (cf. Rom. 13:1-7; 1 Pet. 2:17). In cases of conflict, however, it is manifest which authority requires allegiance. Our text has thus rightly been cited to curb the powers of the state. God, who after all determines what is Caesar's and what is not, is sovereign over the state. In the end, no one can serve two masters (Matt. 6:24), and all that truly matters is obedience to God.

Beginning with Tertullian, many have identified "the things that are God's" with human beings. If coins with Caesar's image and inscription belong to Caesar, then human beings created in God's image (Gen. 1:26) belong to God. Perhaps our verse does indeed allude to Genesis 1:26.

Some have found our passage in harmony with the Lutheran doctrine of the two kingdoms: life has two spheres, the sacred and the secular, each with its own demands. It should be kept in mind, however, that the two spheres can hardly be kept apart, and that although Jewish tradition tended to view governments as divinely placed, and while Christian tradition followed, it is not clear that this thought belongs to our pericope. Indeed, some commentators have argued that "render to God" so outweighs "render to Caesar" as to make the latter ironic or unimportant, a matter (as Kierkegaard had it) of indifference. While they go too far, our passage remains relatively cryptic, and theological assertions about God's relationship to the state will wisely ground themselves in other Scriptures (e.g., Rom. 13). There is here no precise theory of governmental authority.

Whether one considers Jesus' answer to his opponents clever or profound or both, the performance is impressive and unforgettable. Jesus not only avoids a well-conceived trap but additionally communicates his own teaching. Moreover, that teaching is expressed in the briefest compass, preserved in just a few words. Here again is the speaker of the Sermon on the Mount, the man able to put worlds into aphorisms. The reader of Matthew 22:15-22 not only feels admiration but also knows that here is a teacher without peer; and that feeling and knowledge in turn reinforce our Gospel's portrait of Jesus as the great teacher whose words are to be observed until the end of the age.

22:15-22, continuing upon 21:23–22:14, is more polemic against the Jewish leaders. Here they take counsel against Jesus, seek to manipulate him through flattery, behave as "hypocrites," and fail to confess their defeat when outdone — they simply move on. The negative characterization could hardly be bleaker. In this way the pericope anticipates chapter 23, or more precisely, offers partial justification for the attack there unleashed.

Dale C. Allison

Twenty-third Sunday after Pentecost, Year A

First Lesson: Deuteronomy 34:1-12
(Psalm 90:1-6, 13-17)
Second Lesson: 1 Thessalonians 2:1-8
Gospel Lesson: Matthew 22:34-46

A representative of the Pharisees, one of their learned experts in the law, continues the series of hostile challenges begun in 21:23. That the Pharisees are said to be "gathered together" has reminded some of Psalm 2:2: "the rulers gather together / against the LORD and against his anointed." Whether or not that verse is alluded to, the Pharisees are said to tempt Jesus. It is not precisely clear wherein the temptation lies. Are we to suppose that the lawyer expects Jesus to answer by annulling part of the law (cf. Matt. 5:17-20) or to denigrate certain statutes? Perhaps the verb simply indicates bad faith.

Again the issue regards the Torah, and again Jesus speaks the truth without becoming ensnared. His summary of the law and the prophets, which recapitulates the unifying theme of his own words and deeds, simply combines, against all possible complaint, two traditional Jewish summaries, the commandment to love God found in Deuteronomy 6:5 (part of the Shema, Judaism's closest thing to a creed) and the commandment to love neighbor from Leviticus 19:18 (which Rabbi Akiba reportedly called "the greatest principle in the law"). Indeed, when Jesus quotes Deuteronomy 6:5, in which "heart," "soul," and "mind" represent the entire person, he is quoting from a text pious Jews recited every morning and evening.

Leviticus 19:18 is quoted three times in our Gospel, more than any other Old Testament text: 5:43; 19:19; 22:39. The first citation expands the meaning of neighbor to make it universal: even the enemy is to be loved. The second citation reveals Leviticus 19:18's status as a fundamental summary of the moral demands of the Decalogue (cf. Rom. 13:8-10; Gal. 5:14). The third brings the love of neighbor into innermost connection with the commandment to love God and thus, in typical Matthean fashion, fuses religion and ethics.

Sometimes exegetes have claimed that Jesus' nonpolemical response is somehow novel. But, as already observed, he simply puts together two famous Old Testament verses. Moreover, the *Testament of Issachar*, a Jewish document from perhaps the first century, commands one to "love the Lord and your neighbor" (5:2). One should also remember that the Decalogue, in which the first table concerns piety toward God, the second table right be-havior toward others, was sometimes thought of as a summary of Torah, and that the two verses Jesus quotes have so often been, from Tertullian to the Book of Common Prayer, viewed as summarizing the two tables. Indeed, Philo the Jewish philosopher referred to those who obey the commands of the second table as "lovers of persons" and those who obey the commands of the first table as "lovers of God."

That Jesus' answer is not startlingly original is confirmed by Luke 10:27, where it is not Jesus but a lawyer who says the chief commandment is to love God and one's neighbor. So we have here an example of something important and characteristic but not unique. This should not trouble us. As Samuel Johnson put it, we are more often required to be reminded than in-formed. And the reason was given by Pascal: "All the good maxims are al-ready current; what we need is to apply them." This was already mostly true in Jesus' day.

Love of God, like love of neighbor, is not firstly an attitude or affection but — as the example of Jesus shows — a way of life, the sweat of labor for an-other, "the free service of our wills" (Calvin). This is why, unlike an emotion, it can be commanded, and why, as Tertullian wrote, it is "visible."

Matthew does not clarify "as yourself." Augustine found here approval of self-love and even put love of self alongside love of God and neighbor. But there is no support for such a reading elsewhere in Matthew, which has so much to say about denying and losing and crucifying the self (10:38-39; 16:24-26). Probably the point is instead that, as in 7:12, it is presumed that we look after our own interests, and that just as we are real and sincere in our sinful self-love, so we must be real and sincere in our love of others.

Jesus, although asked for the greatest commandment, answers with two which are inextricable. One is reminded of 1 John 4:20-21, where the com-mand to love God cannot be separated from the commandment to love brothers and sisters. But Matthew does not indicate exactly how the two commandments to love relate to one another. Theologians through the cen-turies have made up the lack. In the fourth century Evagrius Ponticus ar-gued that love of neighbor is love of God because it is love of the image of God. Theodoret of Cyrrhus, a fifth-century Syrian bishop, urged that as contemplation is to action, so love of God is to love of neighbor: the one is the foundation of and inspiration for the other. We imitate what we love; so to love God is to imitate the one whose love is catholic (5:43-48). The twelfth-century abbot Ailred of Rievaux contended, on the contrary, that "love of neighbour precedes love of God": the latter grows out of the former. Martin Luther argued that while our neighbor is needy, God needs nothing, so true service to God must always be for the sake of the neighbor: "Even the preaching of His glory and our praising and thanking Him take place on earth in order that our neighbours may be converted and brought to God thereby." Adolf Harnack thought the Gospel places love of neighbor beside love of God because "the love of one's neighbour is the only practical proof on earth of that love of God which is strong in humanity."

Although all these proposals are worth pondering, Evagrius's claim may be especially congruent with the rest of Matthew. For there is some sense in which, according to Matthew, God is in others. Especially striking is 25:31-46. In this Jesus, the functional presence of God (cf. 18:20; 28:20), is the direct recipient of acts of love done to others: "as you did it unto the least of these. . . ." Service to neighbor is service to Christ, which means service to God. Chrysostom was right: "to love God is to love one's neighbour." One recalls the old saying, found already in Clement of Alexandria: "You have seen your brother; you have seen God."

In 22:41-46 Jesus abandons his defensive posture for the offensive. His questions, unlike those of his opponents, go to the heart of things, for they concern Christology: "What do you think of the Messiah? Whose son is he?" The foregone answer of the Pharisees, "David's," is only half the truth. The other half, unpronounced by Jesus but clear from the rest of the narrative, is: God's.

Jesus' first question, "What do you think regarding the Messiah?" is completed by the second, so that the meaning is: "Whose son is the Messiah?" Although the question is designed to draw forth a conventional answer, "Son of David," it simultaneously hints at another title, "Son of God."

The argument makes two assumptions. First, in accordance with Jewish tradition David composed Psalm 110 (cf. the superscription), and second, Psalm 110 is prophetic and, more specifically, messianic. It follows that David wrote about "[the] LORD" (= God) speaking to "my Lord," and that this last must be the messianic Son of David (cf. Matt. 22:42). We have here an apparent contradiction. For how can one standing at the right hand of God and addressed as "Lord" be David's "son"? A son may address his father as "Lord" (cf. 21:30), but a father does not so speak to his son. The silence of the Pharisees shows that they have no solution to the hermeneutical riddle, even though it is superficial for the Christian reader, who knows that all is resolved in Jesus, to wit: although the Messiah is of the lineage of David, he will also be exalted to God's right hand and there reign as "Lord." The "Son of David" — neither the title nor its content is rejected or denigrated — is therefore not an earthly king or David's simple successor but a descendant of the former king whose destiny surpasses his forebear. Beyond this, Jesus is already, before Easter, God's Son, in which capacity he is even now greater than David or any son of David (cf. 12:42: "greater than Solomon").

Our pericope is a concatenation of christological themes. The subject is "the Son of David." But the question, "Whose son is he?" reminds the reader that Jesus is also the Son of God. Moreover, both "Christ" and "Lord" appear here; and it may further be worth remarking that in 26:64, Psalm 110:1 is cited to depict Jesus' vindication as the Son of Man of Daniel 7. All this is most appropriate. For the fundamental theme of 20:29–22:46 is response to Jesus, that is, evaluation of who he is; so what ending to the entire sequence could be more fitting than one that sets forth Jesus' manifold identity?

Dale C. Allison

Twenty-fourth Sunday after Pentecost, Year A

First Lesson: Joshua 3:7-17
(Psalm 107:1-7, 33-37)
Second Lesson: 1 Thessalonians 2:9-13
Gospel Lesson: Matthew 23:1-12

Matthew 23:1-12 falls into two parts. After the brief introduction (v. 1), verses 2-7 polemicize against the scribes and Pharisees, who desire public acclaim. The five verses after that, which are introduced by "But you," contain prohibitions and generalizations that demand humility. So verses 8-12 are the antithesis of 2-7.

As in the Sermon on the Mount, Jesus here addresses the crowds and the disciples. The objects of Jesus' polemic, the scribes and Pharisees, are addressed only indirectly: he speaks against the leaders, not to them. Is it assumed that they are so hardened that imperatives would be wasted on them, because the incorrigible do not repent?

Those Jesus addresses directly ("you") are told that they have one teacher, one father, and one master. Hence Christology and theology shape their behavior. It is otherwise with those whose conduct is condemned. Those who sit on Moses' seat and lengthen their fringes and love to be called "Rabbi, rabbi" are not, in our passage, related either to God or Christ. Rather, they are related to other people, and their behavior is dictated not by authentic religious considerations but by perceived public opinion. Our passage thus depicts the same antithesis as Ephesians 6:6 — there are, on the one hand, those who live for the eyes of others and, on the other hand, "the servants of Christ who do the will of God from the heart."

What is meant by "Moses' seat" in verse 2 is unknown. It may either refer to a literal chair for synagogue authorities or be a metaphor for teaching authority, something like the "professor's chair." In any case, only here are the Jewish leaders presented in a positive light: their words should be heeded. The command is remarkable and seemingly out of accord with the rest of Matthew. How can Jesus enjoin obedience to his opponents? Some have suggested we have here a pre-Matthean tradition out of harmony with the rest of the Gospel. But probably the best solution is that Matthew 23:2-3 acknowledges the social fact that the scribes and the Pharisees control access to Torah. That is, in a world in which most people did not have any books at all, knowledge of the Bible had to come from those who read it in the synagogues. So Jesus may well be saying that one should obey what the leaders teach when they sit in Moses' chair, that is, observe the Scriptures they recite. But since their interpretations and actions are problematic, as is so clear from the rest of this chapter and the rest of Matthew, one cannot emulate their behavior, which reflects their mistaken understanding and application of Moses and the prophets. Implicit is the lesson that we can have access to the truth and even proclaim it and yet not live it.

To castigate one's opponents as hypocrites (vv. 3-4) interested in pleasing others (vv. 5-7) was standard fare for ancient polemics, Jewish and Greco-Roman. It goes without saying that the charge was always credible, for even if the best of scribes and Pharisees were admirable people who faithfully practiced their religion, hypocrisy belongs to the human condition and so can always be found in the enemy camp. This is ironically demonstrated by the fact that the rabbis themselves, the descendants of the Pharisees, earnestly stressed the need for consonance between word and deed.

If Jesus' commandments are "light" (11:30; cf. 1 John 5:3), those of his opponents are, by implication, "heavy," as verse 4 teaches. The reader inevitably thinks of the Halakic rules Jesus counters in chapters 12 and 15. Even so, it is not, as Calvin realized, a question of hard rules versus easy rules or even more versus less. The Sermon on the Mount blasts that notion. The opponents' yoke is so heavy probably because its proponents, as verse 4 states, lift no finger to help — just as Jesus' commandments are "light" because he is a gracious, helping presence (28:20). Obviously few things are easier than moving a finger; so not to do even that is to do nothing.

The "phylacteries" of verse 5 are *tepillin*, the two black leather boxes containing parchment Scriptures that, since at least the second century B.C., were commonly worn on the upper left arm and forehead following the literal understanding of Exodus 13:9, 16; Deuteronomy 6:8; 11:18. Rabbinic sources know that they could be used in an ostentatious or hypocritical manner, and the *tepillin* found at Qumran with the Dead Sea Scrolls vary considerably in size, which recalls Jesus' charge about "making broad." One recalls the superstitious uses Christians have made of crosses.

"Fringes" (v. 5) were made of blue and/or white threads and were worn on the four corners of the rectangular outer garment, in accord with Numbers 15:38-39 and Deuteronomy 22:12. The text presumes that the scribes and Pharisees who make their tassels long — the Torah prescribes no length or number, and the rabbis debated the issue — do so to draw attention to their piety. Jesus' attack clearly is not against a scriptural ordinance but against its observance for self-glorification. Indeed, Matthew 9:20 and 14:36 tells us that Jesus himself wore tassels on his garment. In accord with 5:17-20, he lived according to the law and so wore fringes.

In Numbers 15:38-39 the fringes are sewn into garments so that they may be looked upon, thus reminding one of the commandments of the Lord, that one should "do" them. Verse 40 continues: "So you shall remember and do all my commandments." But the scribes and Pharisees, according to Matthew 23:2-3, do not do the commandments. So on them the fringes do not serve their lawful purpose.

The desire condemned in verses 6-7 for the "place of honor" at dinners (cf. John 13:23-25; James 2:2-3), that is, the place nearest the host, and for the "best seats" in synagogues is self-explanatory, as is the wish to be greeted with a title of respect, that is, hailed as important, by those of lower rank in the marketplace. But Jesus teaches that the first will be last (19:30; 20:16), so he must condemn the impulse.

Unlike the scribes and Pharisees, authorities in the church are to shun titles (vv. 8-10). Such titles are inconsistent with the demand for humility and mutuality and the need to restrict certain appellations to God and Christ. Brothers and sisters are equals, and none should be exalted by unnecessary adulation. Authority is grounded in the risen Christ; therefore, all earthly authority is derivative, rooted outside itself, which fact should impart humility to the bearers of such derivative authority.

The most natural interpretation of 23:8-10 is that the injunctions against "rabbi," "father," and "instructor" constitute a general prohibition against all ecclesiastical titles. Thus there is no more room for "bishop" or "the most reverend" than "rabbi." If so, one could scarcely find a biblical text so little heeded. Indeed, the practical difficulty of getting along without titles is such that one wonders whether our verse was ever more than an unrealized hope — although occasionally some individuals, such as Francis of Assisi, have eschewed honorifics.

Verses 11 and 12 issue a general call for humility, the paradigm example of which is Jesus (20:26-28). Chrysostom nicely expressed the point: "Not only does he forbid setting heart upon the first place but he requires following after the last." The section ends on an eschatological note — "will be humbled" and "will be exalted" refer to the final judgment — which reminds us of the sad maxim that "many people want to be pious but few are prepared to be humble" (La Rochefoucauld).

One final note. Christian history instructs us that all the vices that Matthew 23 attributes to the scribes and Pharisees have attached themselves to Christians, and in abundance. While Eastern Orthodox bishops have, despite 23:6, enthroned themselves at the fronts of churches, Pentecostal leaders have sat on raised stages during revival meetings; and in the Old American South the pews were often ranked according to social status. Christian leaders of all stripes have, against the spirit of 23:7-12, bestowed on themselves honorifics, including "father" and "teacher" and "bishop"; and of course, many post-Constantine churches have gloried in pomp and circumstance. In view of all this, common sense and sound theology require that Matthew 23 should not encourage us to imagine that we are unlike others or better than they. The chapter should provoke not self-congratulations because Christians are better than those Jesus condemns, but self-examination because we are just like those Jesus condemns. It is fitting that the polemic of Matthew 23 has, throughout sermonic history, been turned against the church itself. And how much more is this true in our time, when the church is more aware than ever of its historical misunderstanding and mistreatment of the Jewish people.

Dale C. Allison

First Sunday of Advent, Year A

First Lesson: Isaiah 2:1-5
(Psalm 122)
Second Lesson: Romans 13:11-14
Gospel Lesson: Matthew 24:36-44

The preceding portions of Matthew's great eschatological discourse are partly designed to quell uninformed eschatological enthusiasm: the end is not yet (see esp. vv. 6, 8, 14, 23-26). This is a lesson that seemingly needs to be relearned by many within each Christian generation, including our own. But the intended effect of countering uninformed enthusiasm is not apathy. This is why our section seeks to instill an appropriate eschatological vigilance. Ignorance concerning the date of the end (v. 36), although necessary, is dangerous, for it may lead to spiritual lethargy. But Matthew wants it instead to lead to moral preparation. For the end may come at any time. One must accordingly be ever prepared to give an account of oneself to the divine justice, from which there is no escape (25:31-46).

Verse 36 marks a transition in the discourse: it brings to a close the previous section and introduces verses that unfold the practical implications of Jesus' eschatological utterances. Its declaration of eschatological ignorance grounds the entire section: one must be ever prepared for what may come at any time.

The verse, which is perhaps the first verse in Matthew to suggest a real limitation to Jesus' knowledge, states something also found in rabbinic sources. For instance, the *Mekilta* on Exodus says, "No one knows when the kingdom of David will be restored to its former position." Some in the ancient world, as in ours, attempted to calculate the date of the end. But Jesus, like the later rabbis, negates all such endeavors, which have always proved wrong. If the angels and the Son, leading characters in the eschatological scenario, do not know something, it must lie beyond all others.

Although Irenaeus, in the second century, could take our saying at face value, older Christian theologians often struggled with Jesus' declaration of ignorance. Certain copyists omitted the saying from Matthew. Origen wondered whether Jesus might not be referring to the church, of which he is the head. Ambrose attributed "nor the Son" to an Arian interpolation. Athanasius suggested that Jesus only feigned ignorance. The Cappadocians thought that the Son did not know the date on his own but only through the Father; or, as Gregory of Nazianzus put it: "He knows as God and knows not as man." Chrysostom, in a prize example of bad exegesis, simply denied that Jesus was ignorant of anything: "neither is the Son ignorant of the day, but is even in full certainty thereof." Here is one point at which the early orthodox tradition failed us. Modern theologians have been more willing to emphasize, in harmony with the creeds, that Jesus' humanity was real and so have often come to terms with our saying as an expression of the radical self-emptying of God in the incarnation.

Verses 37-39 take up the old idea that it will be at the end as it was in the beginning, and make the flood a prototype of the last judgment or end of the world (cf. 2 Pet. 3:6-7). But our saying goes its own way in focusing neither on the sins of Noah's generation — the rabbis excluded that generation from the world to come — nor on Noah's righteousness, but on the unexpected nature of the cataclysm that overtook the world while people went about their daily business unawares. Following as it does the dramatic narration in 24:3-28, our line implies that, even in the midst of the eschatological tribulation, life will for many continue as ever.

Verses 40-41 supply two additional illustrations of judgment unexpectedly falling on people while they go about their daily chores. The first concerns two men doing the same thing, the second two women doing the same thing (grinding at a mill was considered women's or slaves' work). The divergent fates show that God's sudden judgment annuls external similarities (cf. 13:30).

In verses 40-41 one is taken and one is left. But are the righteous taken to meet the Lord in the air? Or are the wicked removed by angels and cast into fire? The text is not clear about this. But the verb used here ("taken") means "taken [to safety]" in 2:13, 14, 20, and 21, and the picture of angels taking the saints to meet the Son of Man was probably common in early Christianity (cf. 1 Thess. 4:17), so it may be best to think that the intended image is akin to the story of Enoch's rapture (Gen. 5:24) or Elijah's ascension (2 Kings 2:11).

Verse 42 draws the obvious lesson from the preceding illustrations. Given our ignorance of the end's date, leisurely repentance is foolish. Fear of being caught off guard should motivate one to watch. The simple parable in verses 43-44 (cf. 1 Thess. 5:2; 2 Pet. 3:10; Rev. 3:3; 16:15) continues the point. The image is of a thief breaking through the mud wall of a house.

Looking back over the whole, Matthew 24:36-44 offers us a collection of scenes from everyday life — people eating and drinking, people marrying and being given in marriage, two men in a field, two women at a mill, a man asleep in his house, a thief going about his business. These images of day-to-day existence stand in stark contrast to the unusual and even surrealistic

141

events depicted in the first part of Matthew 24 — wars, famines, earthquakes, flight from the abomination of desolation, darkened luminaries, a sign in the firmament, the Son of Man on the clouds of heaven. The transition from the extraordinary to the ordinary well serves Matthew's purpose. Those whose imaginations hold the terrors and hope of things to come still live in the often mundane present, and their eschatological expectation does not undo the fact that they must still work in the field and grind at the mill.

Many Christian interpreters have applied 24:36-44 to death rather than to the second coming (so already Chrysostom in the fourth century). This is understandable. For while death comes to us all, only one generation will see the end. So Christian interpreters have often used our text to teach what the rabbis taught — that one should repent a day before one's death — which of course means that one must repent daily, because one never knows when death will come. The unpredictable date demands constant preparation.

Whether one transfers the exhortations of Matthew 24 to the death of the individual or prefers to maintain Matthew's focus on universal history, it remains true that our behavior is inevitably altered if we keep before ourselves the end of things. The point is effectively made in a story told by the ancient Greek historian Herodotus. Solon, a wandering philosopher from Athens, once came to Sardis, where he met the great king of Lydia, Croesus, who had vast wealth and much power. The king, after showing his honored guest the royal palace and treasuries, vainly asked, "Who is the happiest person you have seen?" Croesus wished to hear of his own blessedness. Solon, however, surprised him, declaring that Tellus, a man Croesus had never heard of, was the most blessed. Tellus had dwelt in a prosperous city, fathered five sons, lived to see his grandchildren, died a glorious death in battle, and received the honor of a public funeral on the spot where he fell. The king could not understand why Tellus was more blessed than he, so he asked Solon for an explanation. In response, the wise man observed that he could call no one blessed before death. Why? Because a life still lived is a life not yet complete, and who knows what the future will bring? The rich may become poor, the conqueror may become vanquished, the powerful may become powerless. Good things do not make for happiness unless they endure. It is wisdom to "Look to the end, no matter what it is you are considering. Often enough the divinity gives a person a glimpse of happiness, then utterly ruins that one."

It takes little to put a Christian spin on this story. All we have to do is think of the divine judgment that, in the end, awaits all of us. Happiness cannot be declared true happiness unless it is destined to endure. For it is the final outcome that determines the meaning of all that goes before. It is the issue of things which puts them in perspective. It is the end of the story that interprets the preceding narrative. And as it is with the individual, so is it with all of history, which is why Christianity speaks of the second coming of Christ. The victory of the cross and resurrection in the middle of history would hardly remain unaffected if it were not somehow confirmed by history's outcome.

While all this makes excellent sense, and while there are modern theologians such as Wolfhart Pannenberg who have accordingly made the future central to their theologies, it is hard, when we are eating and drinking and at work, to keep things in perspective and conduct our affairs in the light of the consummation of things. This is due in part, no doubt, to the fickleness of human nature. Constancy of purpose derived from a fixed gaze on the future is rarely achieved, for our minds resist being harnessed toward one end. They are too restless and too readily distracted and too afraid of death. So thought of our individual end or of the end of all does not, as a matter of record, much inform our lives.

Beyond the handicap created by our fickle natures, perhaps modern technology fights against us. For, through its magical gifts, desires and whims of the moment can now be instantly gratified. Lights come on with a switch, water flows with the turn of a faucet, food is only a swing of a door away. These and so many other newfangled things tend, through habit, to make us impatient, and are not impatient people less likely to spend much time reflecting on the future?

In a world geared toward the immediate fulfillment of everyday desires, it is not easy to look to the end. But this is what Matthew 24 requires. For it knows that only the end will tell us the meaning of the present, that only the outcome can give us true perspective. Perhaps, then, it would be profitable, from time to time, to imagine ourselves on our deathbeds, or to put ourselves within Matthew's eschatological scenario. Maybe such exercises might help refine our sensitivity to what really matters. In any event, Jesus requires us to see through the present to what is to come, to yank our minds away from the present to dwell imaginatively on the future, in which we will all, sooner or later, have to face God without excuse.

Dale C. Allison

143

Twenty-fifth Sunday after Pentecost, Year A

First Lesson: Joshua 24:1-3a, 14-25
(Psalm 78:1-7)
Second Lesson: 1 Thessalonians 4:13-18
Gospel Lesson: Matthew 25:1-13

The parable of the wise and foolish maidens is found only in the Gospel of Matthew. It is located in a section devoted to events at the end of the world, the so-called Eschatological Discourse (Matt. 24:1–25:46). It is framed by two other parables that, like it, anticipate the final judgment: the parable of the faithful and wise servant (24:45-51) and the parable of the talents (25:14-30).

A puzzle for the modern reader or hearer is to figure out what the purpose of the maidens in this scene could possibly be. The NRSV helps in this regard by translating the term *parthenoi* (lit. "virgins") as "bridesmaids."

To describe marriage customs in any era is tricky, since there are so many variations, but some things are known about ancient Jewish marriage customs that occur typically, and these appear in the parable as well.

Marriage was, in a sense, a process that consisted of two main steps. The first step involved an agreement, the marriage contract (*kiddushin* or *'erusin*, the "betrothal"), that was arranged by the parents (or with their consent). From that point on the couple was legally married. The betrothal could be dissolved only by divorce.

The second step was the celebration of the marriage itself (the *nissuin*), which typically took place up to a year later, and which was followed by a marriage feast. Then the couple began to live together. The couple was usually quite young (the bride about twelve to thirteen years old, the groom about eighteen). Details typical of ancient weddings and important for interpreting the parable include (1) festival processions of both the bride and groom (individually) to the house where the wedding would take place (see Ps. 45:13b-15 regarding a bride's procession; 1 Macc. 9:39 for a groom's procession); (2) the conducting of the marriage ceremony (including prayers and blessings) at the home of the groom's parents; and (3) a marriage feast afterward, which could last for several days.

The picture provided at the outset of the parable is that the groom is on his way to his parents' home, where he will meet the bride and join the festivities — both the ceremony and the feast. The ten bridesmaids "went to meet the bridegroom" as he approached the house, expecting to escort him and to go into the house with him.

The difference between the wise and the foolish maidens is that, from the beginning, the wise have extra oil with them while the foolish do not. The wise are therefore prepared for a possible delay in the coming of the groom.

As it turns out, the groom is delayed until midnight. Why that is so is not important. There is no need to know. But it is obviously not usual, nor expected. All ten maidens fall asleep while waiting.

When the groom does come, all awake and begin to trim their lamps, an expression meaning to put them in order, getting the wicks positioned rightly and adding oil, which is precisely what the foolish lack. The result is that the wise are able to go out to meet the groom, escort him into the house, and enter into the festivities. The foolish, on the other hand, must go to purchase oil for themselves. And since they are not present, they are left out. There is no point in raising the question of where the foolish can buy oil in the middle of the night. While the question is legitimate, any answer to it simply ruins a good story!

When the foolish bridesmaids return, they ask to be admitted to the marriage festivities, using language that recalls that of Matthew 7:21-23. The maidens are refused entry. There is a finality to what is spoken by the bridegroom in 25:12, as also with the shutting of the door in 25:10.

The command to keep awake (25:13) is not part of the parable itself but an interpretive comment, and it refers to the day of Christ's second coming. Similar sayings appear at 24:36 and 24:42. In those places it is declared that the day of Christ's (second) coming may be very soon. Here, however, it means that his coming might be later than expected.

Several allegorical elements can be discerned in the parable, at least at the Matthean level. That fact can make a modern interpreter uneasy. After all, as is well known, major works on the parables of Jesus — at least since the pathbreaking work of Adolf Jülicher — have insisted that the allegorical method of interpretation is to be avoided.

But of course, while that is true, the presence of allegorical elements within a parable itself should be recognized and dealt with by the modern interpreter. And in this parable there are several, five of which are reviewed here. (1) A marriage feast can represent the gathering of the Messiah and his people (cf. Matt. 22:1-14; Rev. 19:9), and it has those overtones here. (2) The bridegroom most likely represents Christ (cf. Mark 2:19-20; 2 Cor. 11:2; Eph. 5:25-27; Rev. 19:7, 9). (3) His delay and subsequent coming represent the delay and yet the inevitability of his parousia (cf. 2 Cor. 11:2; Rev. 19:7-

145

9). (4) The closing of the door and the refusal to allow the foolish maidens in represent the final judgment. (5) And the wise and foolish maidens represent those who are prepared for the final judgment and those who are not, respectively.

The question must now be raised about what kind of preparation is being prescribed. And here there is no end of possibilities. Interpreters, for example, have speculated about the symbolism of the oil that the wise have with them, suggesting that it represents faith, good works, or both. But there is a different way to look at the situation. What distinguishes the wise maidens from the foolish ones is that the wise are ready for an extended wait. That means, then, that the key to the parable is to be found in the distinction. And the symbolism, within the arena of Matthew's Gospel and community, would be important for Christians. That is that no one knows when Christ will come. It may be later than expected. Be ready for the long haul.

Within early Christianity, as attested often in the New Testament, the accent was on the nearness of the parousia. That is implied even in the similar sayings of 24:36, 42 and is a common theme elsewhere (Mark 13:32-37; 1 Thess. 4:15-17; Rev. 22:12-21). But in this parable the other side of the matter is exposed. True, one knows neither the day nor hour of his coming (25:13) — and, in fact, it may be later than expected. So whether it is soon or far away, one must be prepared.

No one can know the timing of the end, the coming of the Lord. For most people the end may well be their own death. But there is also the end of all things, the beginning of the new, with the coming of Christ. The New Testament pictures the coming of Christ the bridegroom and the final judgment as both soon and, in this case, distant. No one can know the day or the hour. Since Christ's coming might be soon, one must take care and get ready. But since it might be far, one ought not to grow weary in doing good. Every person must come to terms with living in the world, the place given by God for his children, over time. For modern Christians, that includes care of the earth and making peace for the sake of future generations. It is necessary to plan for the long haul, remain faithful, be wise, and stay strong.

Like virtually every other passage in Scripture, this one can be interpreted as both threat and promise, law and gospel. Often the theme of Christ's coming is taken to be a threat. The end is near! But it should be realized that in biblical thought "the end" is never really the end. The end of this world is the doorway to the new — the new age, the new creation. The coming of Christ and the end of all things is finally good news. The Bridegroom is coming, and he will admit all those to his kingdom who await his coming with perseverance. The present is a time of waiting, but joyful waiting, like awaiting a festival of marriage.

Arland J. Hultgren

Twenty-sixth Sunday after Pentecost, Year A

First Lesson: Judges 4:1-7
(Psalm 123)
Second Lesson: 1 Thessalonians 5:1-11
Gospel Lesson: Matthew 25:14-30

Luke has a parable which is similar to but also different from this Matthean parable (Luke 19:11-27). Whatever the explanation for this (Jesus told one parable which has acquired two rather different versions in the course of transmission, or Jesus himself told two variations on the same plot), each parable as it stands in each Gospel has its own integrity, which is only spoiled by cross-reference. The preacher does well to ignore the parallel.

As with many of Jesus' parables, it is important not to rush into interpreting the story (often with too allegorical results) before understanding it in terms of its own verisimilitude and logic. The man going on a journey is a very rich aristocrat with vast property, and his slaves or servants are his staff who run his estates and affairs. It was normal in the Greco-Roman world for slaves to occupy very responsible positions. The sums with which they are entrusted are very considerable (a poor man could live at subsistence level for fifteen years on just one talent). (It is interesting to note that with the word "talent" this parable has actually contributed to the vocabulary of the English language. The use of "talent" to mean a natural ability derives from interpretation of the talents in this parable as signifying gifts of that kind. But the preacher needs to beware of the prejudice in favor of a particular interpretation of the parable that this word usage creates in many readers.) The three slaves are of differing status, according to their already proven competence in business dealings, and so the sums entrusted to them vary.

147

The arrangement is a kind of investment on the master's part. Of course, he expects a return for his money. For the servants, it is an important chance to prove themselves and so perhaps attain further advancement in the master's household. This is a situation in which they can succeed or fail, and have much to win or to lose.

The master's confidence in the first two servants proves justified. They are rewarded with further responsibilities. The invitation to each to "enter into the joy of your master" could be an instance of the eschatological significance of the parable breaking through the realism of the story, as it certainly does in verse 30. In that case, the reference would be to the joy of the messianic banquet, just as verse 30 certainly refers to hell. But the invitation could be realistic: the servants are to share in their master's celebration of his homecoming, all the merrier for the appreciable profits the two servants have made for him since he went away. The storytelling device of the three servants might lead us to expect the pattern repeated in the case of the first two servants to recur again in the third case. But in fact, we already know what the third servant has done with his one talent (v. 18). We expect different treatment from the master, but we cannot yet tell what that will be.

In entrusting the third servant with only one talent, the master had judged this servant's business acumen less reliable than that of the others. However, the servant's failure lies not in being no good at business, but in not even trying. He did what was generally regarded as the *safest* thing to do with money: he buried it. His explanation is that he knew his master to be rapaciously and ruthlessly interested in profit. This is the implication of verse 24, on which one exegete comments that the man is "an absentee landlord who bleeds the land dry." So the servant was terrified of what might happen if he traded with the money and lost most of it. Or was it really, as the master accuses him, that he is just lazy (v. 26)? Knowing that his master would be pleased with nothing but profit, why did he not at least put the money in the bank, where it would have accrued some interest, paltry though that would be? The bank would have posed a very slight risk (it might be robbed), and so presumably the servant was such a coward he feared even that risk. But his action — whether due to fear or laziness — was plainly stupid. Had he tried to make profit, he would have risked his master's displeasure if he failed. But not even trying to make profit was certain to provoke the master's anger. He knew this because he knew his master to be interested only in profit. By not taking a risk he took the one sure way to lose.

The saying in verse 29 also occurs elsewhere in the Gospel traditions in a different context (Matt. 13:12; Mark 4:25; Luke 8:18). As an isolated saying, it might seem to be a cynical comment on the unfairness of life: the rich get richer and the poor get poorer. But its context in this parable (whether or not it originally belonged there) reveals its logic as that of financial investment. To the one who has made a profit, more will be entrusted, but from the one who has not made a profit, even his initial loan will be taken back.

The parable could well have ended there. The punishment of the slave in verse 30 steps outside the story's own world into the traditional imagery of final damnation. Other Matthean parables also do this (22:13; 24:51). It is not an indication that the whole story is an artificial allegory. Rather, it is an indication, to readers who reach it at the end of the story, of the way they should now reflect on the meaning of the parable: it concerns nothing less than people's eternal destiny.

The parable compares the business of life in the service of God to the business of commerce. It compares the use of all God has given one — not just specific "talents," but all that one has and is — in God's service, with the use of a financial loan in order to make a profit for the investor. The reason the master is furious with the third slave is that, for a businessman, the whole point of money is to be used and spent and circulated in order to make more money. Money merely hoarded might just as well be thrown away. In the same way, what God has given us — our selves, our lives, our faith, our abilities, our gifts, our possessions — is given in order to be spent and put into circulation. Our lives are to be expended in God's service, becoming thereby the source of further blessings for others and for ourselves. Only in that sense is God like the rapacious investor interested only in profit. He expects returns from the loans he makes us. To try merely to preserve them is to lose them. This applies even to the gift of eternal life. For in the parable's final transition from story to eschatological imagery, the servant who has lost his talent in the story loses his eternal self in final reality.

In order even to keep his talent the servant had to risk it. If he did not risk it, he was bound to lose it. This has a certain truth with reference simply to life as such. We all know that no one can really live by playing safe all the time. But it is even more true of life lived for God. All that God gives us is given to be risked in new ventures in God's service. Every new step in living for God is a risk. But if we stand still — paralyzed like the third servant by the fear of failure, clinging for safety to what we already are and have — we in fact lose what we have. We can keep it only by risking it in going further. And every successful risk leads to being entrusted with more, again to be expended and risked. Jesus elsewhere summed it up: "Those who want to save their life will lose it, and those who lose their life for my sake will find it" (Matt. 16:25 and several parallels).

Jesus could have told a parable with the message: "Life is a risk. In the business of living we can win, but we risk losing." The parable he actually told has a much more interesting and profound message: "You can take the risk or not, but if you do not you are bound to lose."

Oliver Quick's comment is worth pondering: this parable "so far from teaching any prudential or utilitarian morality, sounds the call to a more heroic adventure than any which the Christian Church on earth has ever led the main body of its members to attempt. It is the very condemnation of a merely cautious defensive policy which finds its chief aim in survival and security."

Richard Bauckham

Christter the King, Year A

First Lesson: Ezekiel 34:11-16, 20-24
(Psalm 100)
Second Lesson: Ephesians 1:15-23
Gospel Lesson: Matthew 25:31-46

The passage appears within the Eschatological Discourse of Matthew's Gospel (24:1–25:46), and only there among the Gospels, bringing the section to a close. Although often called the parable of the final judgment or the parable of the sheep and the goats, it is not truly a parable. It is an apocalyptic discourse with a parabolic element — the simile of a shepherd separating the sheep and the goats — which occurs at the very beginning (25:32-33). That imagery is dropped and never returned to again. All else portrays a judgment scene.

The coming of the Son of Man, seated upon his throne, is declared. Angels are present, even "all the angels," as though heaven has been emptied of its angels. "All the nations" are present too (so the balance of terms — all angels, all nations). The nations are present for judgment to be pronounced upon them. As the Greek shows, however, the judgment is not upon the nations themselves (requiring the neuter plural *auta*). The people of the nations are the ones being judged (so the masculine plural, *autous,* is used). The NRSV does well in saying "he will separate people one from one another" (25:32) to highlight the point.

The imagery of sheep and goats being herded together but then separated by the shepherd is a familiar one. One can still see the practice of herding sheep and goats together among the Bedouins. But the sheep and the goats need to be separated on certain occasions, as when the goats are milked and the sheep are sheared.

The term "shepherd" gives way to "king" at 25:34, and the latter is used for the main figure again at 25:40. The people, however, address him as "lord" (25:37, 44).

The words of the king to those on the right (25:34-36) commend them for the service they have rendered him. The things they have done are actions performed to alleviate typical problems of the unfortunate — hunger, thirst, being an alien, lacking clothes, illness, and imprisonment. These good deeds are called "deeds of lovingkindness" *(gemilut hasadim)* in rabbinic literature. The problems listed, which the righteous alleviate, are typical of those found in Old Testament lists (Deut. 15:7-11; Isa. 58:7-10; Pss. 37:21; 41:1; cf. also Tob. 4:16; Sir. 7:32, 35; and 2 Esdr. 2:20 in the apocryphal/deuterocanonical writings) and other ancient Jewish sources.

A dialogue ensues (25:37-40). The people addressed by the king know nothing at all about this. The king has to explain everything to them. By doing good for others, they were doing good to him.

The words of the king to those on the left (25:41-43) rehearse wording similar to that expressed to those on the right, except that those on the left have not done what they ought to have done. What they have not done is to care for typical problems of the unfortunate. They are condemned to eternal fire.

The final judgment will take place (25:46), and the separation will be final.

The passage has been interpreted in three primary ways among modern interpreters. Probably the most familiar runs this way. The passage portrays the last judgment, when all (Christians and non-Christians alike) will be judged. The judgment will be based on how people deal with the unfortunates of the world. There is hope even for non-Christians, persons who do not know the gospel or Christ, for the good that they do is service to Christ. Christians will be saved too, of course, because they confess Christ, but the attention is on all the peoples of the world. Whoever serves the unfortunates serves Christ, even if they do not know him by name.

A second interpretation of the passage is that all the peoples of the

151

world will be judged on how they have treated Jesus' disciples, that is, Christians. When Jesus speaks of "one of the least of these, my brothers and sisters" (25:40, 45), he is referring to his disciples, since he uses similar terminology in speaking of them in 10:42; 18:6, 10, 14 ("one of these little ones"), and 11:11 ("the least in the kingdom of heaven").

A third interpretation is a variant of the second. That is that the judgment will be based specifically on how the peoples of the world have treated Jesus' missionaries. All six of the troubles listed can happen to them (for examples, cf. Acts 16:23; 1 Cor. 4:10-11; 2 Cor. 6:5; 11:27). Within the Gospel of Matthew itself there are sayings that give some support to this view. The disciples are to travel without provisions (10:9-10, 42), and so they depend on others for food and drink. Some will experience persecution (10:17; 23:34), which can lead to imprisonment. But whoever receives a missionary receives Jesus (10:40), and whoever rejects such a one will be accountable at the final judgment (10:14-15). So, the point is made, Jesus says in this discourse that all will be judged on how they treat his disciples as they travel about as missionaries in the world.

The distinction between the second and third interpretations is a fine one. To make a distinction between disciples and missionaries is itself one that the Gospel of Matthew does not seem to make. In any case, the choice for the interpreter seems to be between the first interpretation above, which for convenience we can call the "universalist" one (since it has to do with the treatment of all people, whether Christians or not), and the second and third, which for convenience we can call the "particularist" one (since it has to do with the treatment of a particular group of people, i.e., Jesus' disciples, Christians).

Although the particularist interpretation has good arguments in its favor, there are even better arguments in favor of the "universalist" one. The following reasons are offered:

1. The sufferings of those ministered to include problems typical of human suffering in general in the Old Testament (see above), rabbinic works, and Greco-Roman literature. The misfortunes listed are not specific to missionaries, but are common to the lot of humanity.

2. The sayings about the disciples as "little" (Gk. *mikros*) in 10:42; 18:6, 10, 14 or as "least (Gk. *mikroteros*) in the kingdom" contain words in Greek that differ from the word "least" (*elachistos*) used in 25:40, 45. In fact, the Greek terminology may point to a deliberate distinction between the disciples and those who are the "least of these."

3. The persons on the right and left are astonished to hear that they have or have not served the king. If those on the right had served the repre-

sentatives of Jesus, and had done so knowingly, why would they be surprised? If those on the left had turned away Jesus' missionaries, why would they need an explanation for their condemnation by Jesus?

4. The passage is located within a lengthy eschatological discourse (24:1–25:46) and actually concludes it. Throughout the discourse the theme of final judgment is strong. Jesus tells his disciples that they must be faithful (24:45-51), wise (25:1-13), resourceful (25:14-30), and now — in our passage — merciful to the needy whom they encounter (25:31-46). The disciples, the Matthean community, and all of humanity are ultimately to be judged on whether they do works of mercy or not. It would be strange to conclude this long discourse with a passage that turns at the end to the welfare of the disciples in the world.

5. Rhetorically, the passage affects its audience, ancient or modern, in such a way as to move persons to care for those who have suffered or are currently suffering. As it is read, the hearer inevitably examines his or her conscience and memory. It is not likely that such a response by the hearer is mistaken.

What is obvious for the interpreter is that, according to this text, God's judgment on the world will be carried out by Christ. He is the one who lived among us as hungry, thirsty, and without a home. He knows about these problems of human suffering. He identifies with the poor and the homeless, the suffering. The proper response of God's people is to work for the betterment of the poor, the sick, the homeless, the suffering. Doing good for them is one form of service to Christ.

Lest it seems that the passage teaches "works righteousness," the interpreter should recall that any passage of Scripture addresses, at best, an aspect of the Christian life. None provides a complete, well-rounded dogmatics!

There is also a message here for Christians about working with others who are not Christians. Christians can join up with other religious groups and organizations in doing good for the poor, the sick, and the homeless. They too are doing service unto Christ, whether they know it or not. In the end Christ will acknowledge their service as well as that of Christians. It just so happens that Christians are aware of such service in ways the others are not.

Arland J. Hultgren

153

Resurrection of the Lord, Year A

First Lesson: Acts 10:34-43
(Psalm 118:1-2, 14-24)
Second Lesson: Colossians 3:1-4
Gospel Lesson: Matthew 28:1-10

Chapter 28 is the necessary ending to Matthew's story. Without the resurrection, Jesus' words would be vacant and his opponents exonerated. With it, Jesus is vindicated, his cause and authority confirmed, and his opponents disgraced. "The empty tomb is . . . a kind of trophy of God's, symbolizing his victory over the foes of Jesus, who up to his death effectively exerted their power against him, but who with his death have now come to the limit of their power" (Ulrich Wilckens).

The story of Jesus' resurrection, which has been foretold by Jesus again and again (16:21; 17:9, 23; 20:19; 26:32), has also been foreshadowed, for the story of the resurrection of the saints in 27:51-53 resembles 28:1-10 in several striking respects:

The death of Jesus, 27:51-53	The resurrection of Jesus, 28:1-10
"and behold"	"and behold"
earthquake opening of tombs	earthquake opening of tomb
guards are afraid	guards are afraid
witnesses (the resurrected)	witnesses (the guards)
go to the city	go to the city
women witnesses (including Mary Magdalene and another Mary)	women witnesses (including Mary Magdalene and another Mary)

Clearly what is both prophesied and foreshadowed is of supreme importance.

The women at the tomb are the antithetical correlation of the guards, who are introduced in the previous paragraph, 27:62-66. Both groups gather at Jesus' tomb (vv. 1, 4). Both see an angel (vv. 2-5). Both feel fear (vv. 4, 8). Both leave the tomb in order to tell others what has happened (vv. 8, 11). And both are told by others what they should say (vv. 7, 10, 13-14). The difference lies in this, that while (we assume) the women tell the truth to the disciples, the guards tell a lie about the disciples. So by putting the two groups side by side, we see two representative responses to Jesus and the gospel.

As just noted, the response of the women is the same as that of the guards — they all fear. But whereas the women's fear dwells within faith, the fear of the guards — the last nameless walk-ons — dwells within unbelief (v. 11). This makes for a contrast with 27:54, where the guards who experience an earthquake and other wonders fear and come to faith. Here the ineffectual guards, who illustrate that God brings human might to naught, experience an earthquake and other wonders but do not come to faith. Ironically they, not Jesus, are the dead ones (v. 4: they "became like dead men").

The women go to the tomb having observed the Sabbath and waiting until the following dawn. The literal dawning of a new day has often been understood to symbolize the advent of a new period in history, and Christian tradition has seen Easter Sunday as the day of a new creation, the so-called eighth day. Maybe Matthew's first readers already thought in these terms, because Judaism was certainly familiar with the notion that a new (eschatological) era would commence after a period of seven world days or weeks of years (cf. Dan. 9:24-27).

Why do the women come to the tomb? "To see the tomb" (28:1) is unexplained. Mark's explanation — to anoint Jesus (Mark 16:1) — is, for whatever reason, missing. It is possible that visitation of the newly entombed was common practice among Jews. There is a rabbinic text that speaks of visiting graves until the third day in order to prevent premature burial — something sadly not all that uncommon until very recent times (as readers of Edgar Allan Poe's "Premature Burial" will remember). In any case, the women who come to the tomb, whatever their motive, arrive in sadness and leave with joy. Their expectation of finding only the mundane has been shattered by the absolutely unexpected.

The women's expectations are undone in three specific ways. First, the tomb is not closed by a stone (intended to keep out animals) but open. Second, the women discover not Jesus but an angel (vv. 2-3; is this the same angel that appeared in the very first chapter of Matthew?). Third, when they do find Jesus, he is not dead but alive (vv. 8-9). So Jesus enters their lives again as he did before, by undoing expectations.

Chapter 28 records an earthquake (v. 2) and a resurrection. Beyond that, the angelic appearance in verse 3 recalls both the eschatological vision of Daniel 7:9 (see also 10:6) and Matthew 17:2, where the transfigured Jesus anticipates the glory of resurrected existence. So Jesus' resurrection is a sort of end of the world in miniature. This carries over a theme from the previous chapters. If the great eschatological discourse prophesies the end of the temple (24:2), earthquakes (24:7), handing over to death (24:9, 10), "falling away" (24:10), and heavenly darkness (24:29), all these things reappear in the passion narrative, where Jesus is handed over (26:47-50), the disciples fall away (27:56, 69-75), there is darkness (27:45), the earth quakes (27:51), and the temple is symbolically destroyed (27:51). Jesus' end correlates with the end of the world. The pattern implies that, when the Messiah enters into suffering and death and then is raised to new life amidst signs and wonders, he foreshadows and anticipates or perhaps even begins the eschatological scenario. So if it is the end of a story that determines the meaning of what goes before — this is certainly true of Matthew's story of Jesus — then the Gospel may allow us to see the meaning of history by giving us a sort of preview of its end.

Although we have heard only of the guards' fear, the angel, who proclaims the Christian message in terms that recall the primitive confession in 1 Corinthians 15:3-5, apparently addresses the women with "Do not be afraid." Calvin commented: "Soldiers, accustomed to tumult, were terrified and so struck with panic that they fell down half-dead: no power raised them from the ground; but in the like alarm of the women, a comfort soon came to restore their spirits."

The angel interprets the empty tomb ("he has been raised") and then offers supporting evidence ("see the place where he lay"). Jesus has, in the language of 22:30 (and in refutation of Sadducean belief), entered into "the resurrection" and become "like the angels." He has, to repeat, experienced the end of history.

The promise through the women to the disciples that Jesus will go before them into Galilee is an amazing demonstration of forgiveness. In Matthew 10:32-33 Jesus says plainly that everyone who acknowledges him before others will be acknowledged before his Father in heaven, and that those who deny him before others he will deny before his Father in heaven. All the disciples have in effect denied Jesus by forsaking him at his arrest. And Peter has publicly denied Jesus. So here forgiveness qualifies or, perhaps it is not too much to say, overturns Jesus' solemn pronouncement. Despite the fact that they have not confessed him before others but rather denied him, Jesus offers them a second chance and will meet them in Galilee.

Verses 9-10, which are very close to John 20:11-18, recount a very brief appearance of Jesus, who becomes, in addition to the empty tomb and the angel, the third witness to the reality of the resurrection. The verses depict the proper response to the risen Lord — worship; and because Jesus' words about Galilee repeat those of the angel ("Do not fear," "go," "tell his disciples/my brothers, "go to Galilee," and "there you/they will see him/me" are common to vv. 7 and 9), they throw additional emphasis upon the climax to come — the great commission with which Matthew ends.

The women, upon seeing Jesus and hearing him speak, immediately recognize him (contrast Luke 24:16; John 20:14) and bow before him. No mention is made of doubt (contrast Matt. 28:17). The taking hold of Jesus' feet (cf. John 20:17) is unexplained. It may be an act of supplication. But throughout worldwide folklore, ghosts often have no feet; if the text presupposes this idea, then the grasping of feet indicates that Jesus is not a spirit — precisely the same thought found in Luke 24:37-43.

Two final comments. First, the resurrection — the full meaning of which only becomes apparent in Matthew 28:16-20 — makes Jesus himself an illustration of his own teaching. He is, like the prophets before him, wrongly persecuted because of his loyalty to God, and he gains great reward in heaven (cf. 5:10-12). He finds his life after losing it. He is the servant who becomes great, the last who becomes first.

Second, there is, whether intended by the author or not, a very happy contrast between chapters 2 and 28, the only two places where angels are active participants in the story. In the former, the Gentile Magi inform Herod and the Jewish leaders in Jerusalem, including the chief priests, of events surrounding the advent of the Messiah. In the latter, Gentile soldiers announce to the chief priests of Jerusalem the events surrounding the resurrection of Jesus. In the former, the king opposes the infant Messiah and tries to kill him. In the latter, the leaders counter the resurrection by setting a guard at the tomb and, when that fails, by promulgating a false rumor. In the former, the faithful Magi worship Jesus and rejoice with great joy. In the latter, the faithful women worship Jesus and go on their way with great joy. Thus the story comes full circle.

Dale C. Allison

Trinity Sunday, Year A

First Lesson: Genesis 1:1–2:4a
(Psalm 8)
Second Lesson: 2 Corinthians 13:11-13
Gospel Lesson: Matthew 28:16-20

This passage constitutes the climax of Matthew's Gospel and ties together his most central themes, especially about Jesus' identity and his commission for his followers.

The passage instructs us, first of all, about Jesus' identity, climaxing the revelation of his character offered through the rest of the Gospel. It portrays Jesus as the one with supreme authority in all creation (28:18), climaxing the recognition of Jesus' authority on earth (7:29; 8:9; 9:6, 8; 21:24). Moreover, John the Baptist, Jesus himself, and his disciples had already preached God's coming kingdom (3:2; 4:17; 10:7); this claim that God invested Jesus with all authority makes clear that Jesus is the king in God's coming kingdom (25:31, 34). The passage also presents him alongside the Father and the Spirit (28:19), which must have startled the first Jewish disciples to hear it: the Father was God, and Judaism also recognized the Holy Spirit as God's divine Spirit. To link Jesus with the Father and the Spirit this way was tantamount to calling him divine! The passage further presents Jesus as "with" his people (28:20); this image also portrays Jesus as divine. The Gospel earlier introduced Jesus as "God with us" (1:23) and claimed that where even two of his disciples gathered, he was among them (18:20) — a claim Jesus' contemporaries had traditionally reserved for God's own presence.

But the passage also climaxes Jesus' commissions to his followers, and as such teaches us about the church's responsibility. We might understand the church's responsibility as presented in this passage under three headings: cross-cultural missions, evangelism, and Christian education. This is because the crux of Jesus' commission, based on his universal sovereignty (28:18), is to disciple the nations (28:19), a commission that we are to carry out in three ways. The Greek contains one imperative ("make disciples") surrounded by three subordinate participles: going, teaching, and baptizing.

Jewish teachers customarily made disciples by training those who volunteered to follow them; these disciples would in turn pass on this teacher's views when they became teachers themselves. But unlike most other Jewish teachers, Jesus recruited many of his own disciples directly (4:19, 21; 9:9), and taught that we make disciples only for him, not for ourselves (23:8).

158

The nature of the discipleship he required was radical: disciples must suffer for him (8:21-22; 10:25), even sharing the death of the cross (16:24). Even if the disciples initially failed to take up the cross to follow Jesus — the Romans had to draft a bystander to do what they failed to do (27:32) — the Gospel announces that in time many disciples would persevere through suffering (24:9).

Yet Jesus also expanded the pool for discipleship: not only among Israel, but among all the other nations as well (28:19). Given the commission to disciple "the nations," "going" probably implies that our ministry must often cross cultural boundaries. Jesus earlier told his disciples to "go" only to Israel, not to the Gentiles, in their preaching of the kingdom (10:5-7); here he revokes the earlier limitation. This climaxes an emphasis on reaching and embracing Gentiles, probably directed toward Matthew's Jewish Christian audience. As such it might have implications today for racial reconciliation, cultural sensitivity, and cross-cultural ministry.

This theme runs from start to finish throughout the Gospel. Matthew's genealogy, unlike most genealogies, includes some women; all or nearly all are Gentiles (1:3, 5-6). Gentile astrologers come from the east to worship Jesus (2:1), in contrast to a king of Israel who acts like the pharaoh of Moses' day (2:16). Such models come not only from the east but also from the west (8:11) and elsewhere: Roman centurions, among the most hated of Gentiles, become models of faith (8:9-11; 27:54), as does a Canaanite, symbol of Israel's despised ancient enemies (15:22, 28). God can turn even stones into spiritual descendants of Abraham (3:9); Jesus ministers in Galilee "of the Gentiles" (4:15); Jesus delivers some demoniacs in Gentile territory (8:28); and Peter first confesses Jesus' messiahship in Gentile territory (16:13). Gentile Nineveh and Sheba compare favorably with Jesus' contemporaries (12:41-42), and Sodom turns out to be no worse than his contemporaries (10:15; 11:23-24). The nations are judged, according to the interpretation of many scholars, according to how they have responded to the gospel's messengers (25:32, 40; cf. 10:11, 40-42). Most significantly, the good news of the kingdom must be preached among all peoples before the end will come (24:14) — the sort of preaching our passage envisions.

Second, Matthew speaks of "baptizing," which might translate roughly into our idea of evangelism today. In Matthew's day Jewish people baptized Gentiles who converted to Judaism; John probably offended his culture by baptizing Jewish people for repentance as if they were Gentiles (3:6, 9). Because baptism could function as an "act" of conversion, this part of discipling the nations involves calling people to respond to the good news of the kingdom. John proclaimed repentance in light of God's coming reign

159

(3:2); Jesus proclaimed the same message (4:17), and instructed his disciples to do the same (10:7). Repenting in light of the coming kingdom means preaching that it is God to whom we must give account; if we wish to be ready for the day of his unchallenged rule, we must submit to his rule in the present time. Although we continue to announce God's reign, since Jesus' resurrection we announce more specifically the reign of Jesus and the need to submit to him (28:18). Some people today, even in some churches, regard evangelism, especially cross-cultural evangelism, negatively, often in response to the wrong ways it has sometimes been done in the past. But those in the churches who hold this view should consider carefully the implications of their position: without cross-cultural evangelism, the church would have mostly ceased to exist by the end of the first century, and would never have expanded beyond the Jewish people. We share with others what excites us most; an expositor of this passage might help our audience to understand the critical importance of sharing our faith and suggest practical ways we can most effectively carry out this mandate in our cultural settings today.

The idea of witness in this passage is one for which its context prepares us. After the male disciples abandoned Jesus in fear (26:31-35, 56), only the women followed to the cross and the tomb (27:55-56, 61). Consequently, these courageous women become the first witnesses of the resurrection, providing a true report of what happened (28:1-10); Jesus commissions them to "go" (28:10) as he later commissions all his disciples (28:19). By contrast, the guards act in fear and greed, giving a false report (28:11-15). Their example is a negative one in Matthew's passion narrative: fear is what caused Jesus' disciples to abandon him and Peter to deny him (26:56, 69-75). His passion narrative also warns against monetary incentives to bear false witness; Judas betrayed Jesus for the biblical price of a slave (26:15), in contrast with the woman who lavished expensive affection on Jesus (26:7-13). The church's witness must be modeled on that of the women, Jesus' first witnesses, not on that of the guards.

Third, followers of Jesus make disciples by Christian education — specifically, by instructing new believers in Jesus' teachings. Ancient writers could arrange their biographies in topical as well as chronological order, and Matthew arranges the largest bulk of Jesus' teachings in his Gospel into five main discourse sections: the ethics of the kingdom (chaps. 5–7: how a repentant person submits to kingdom values in advance); principles for evangelism (chap. 10); the presence of God's kingdom (chap. 13, the kingdom parables); relationships in the kingdom (chap. 18); and the future of the kingdom (chaps. 23–25, including judgment on the religious establishment both in A.D. 70 and for all generations until Jesus' return). Of course, Matthew collects especially those teachings most relevant for his audience, and Jesus first offered these teachings in a culture quite different from our own. But when we understand what these teachings meant in their first historical settings, we can think of many analogous situations that invite us to hear afresh Jesus' words for our generation.

Such a program of cross-cultural evangelism and training seems a daunting task, especially given the rapidly expanding populations in the least-evangelized regions of the world today. But Matthew's Gospel closes with a reminder that we are not alone in our task. Just as Jesus noted that the good news would be preached among all nations before the end, Jesus here promises that he will remain with us in our task of discipling the nations until the end. We may wish to remember that in Matthew's day, followers of Jesus remained an insignificantly small percentage of the Mediterranean world, and could embrace this command and promise only by great faith. Whatever our obstacles today — and they are many — the first generations of the church managed to believe and spread their message in the face of greater hostility. Miraculously, they multiplied into the numbers of Christians today that the first generations could hardly have imagined.

Yet even among the many who call themselves Christians, there is often inadequate grasp of the real demands of discipleship. This is why we must remember that true discipleship involves not only conversion but Christian education. For it is only true and faithful disciples who may disciple nations to the one for whom they speak.

Craig S. Keener

Second Sunday of Advent, Year B

First Lesson: Isaiah 40:1-11
(Psalm 85:1-2, 8-13)
Second Lesson: 2 Peter 3:8-15a
Gospel Lesson: Mark 1:1-8

Mark begins his gospel with a fanfare: the story about to be told is nothing less than the first installment of the good news of what God has done in his Son Jesus Christ. God's great act in Jesus is the beginning of a whole new era in human history, and is nothing less than the coming of his Son.

Clearly such a move on God's part cannot take place in a vacuum. Were the Son of God merely to appear without any preparation, there would be no way to identify him or make much sense of what he did. Crucial moral, spiritual, and conceptual preparation is essential. The whole history of Israel at this point is a pertinent backdrop. The revelation of God in Israel is the conceptual and spiritual cradle for the coming of Christ. God's dealings with Israel provide the swaddling clothes for the life of Jesus Christ. They tutor a people to receive God's decisive and final act of healing and redemption. Mark signals this by conflating material from Isaiah, Exodus, and Malachi. The coming of Jesus is no bolt from the blue; it happens in God's good time once the platform has been put in place through the centuries.

The final plank in the platform is the ministry of John the Baptist. In his own way he fits neatly the pattern of a prophet sent by God, hence it is not surprising that folk took him very seriously. His role is quite precise: he is to prepare the way. His job is to prepare the people for what is to come, to cut a straight path so that folk can get where God wants them to be. Everything he does works toward that purpose: the location of his work in the desert, the central act of baptism for which he is remembered, the content of his message, the lifestyle he embraces, and the description of the one to come.

John operates on the level of an extraordinary audiovisual aid. His location in the wilderness signals that what God is about to do can lead to either rebellion or deliverance. His baptizing the people indicates that the time has come for a new beginning that calls for personal response. His proclaiming of repentance calls for a readiness for a change of mind. His offer of forgiveness shows forth the readiness of God to release people from the guilt of

162

their sins. His strange attire recalls that of Elijah, and also signals that the one to come may not be the kind of grand military figure who will use violence to get his way. John does not show up with grandeur and force in a limousine or an army tank; he does not dine at the best restaurants; and his wardrobe is not that of the brightest and best. He represents a reversal of all earthly values; indeed, he stands out as a stark figure that strips the hearer to the essentials of human existence. Thus he clears the way for a clean and uncluttered look at the one who is to come.

John's designation of the coming one is terse and compelling. Like everything else about John, it cuts straight to the chase. The one to come is more powerful; he is of superior status; and he will baptize not with water but with the Holy Spirit. These descriptions are deliberately opaque and open-ended. They are more formal than material, leaving a lot to be filled in by the one who comes. They work precisely because they provide enough to kindle the imagination in anticipation but not enough to satisfy the intellect as they stand. They propel one to look and see for oneself, all the while indicating the general drift of what is to come.

Given what John has already signaled, we know that the power to be exhibited by the one to come is of an unusual kind. It is not the power of brute force and political violence. Yet his superior status is real, so real that John is not worthy to bend down and untie the thong of his sandals. The specific role of the one to come is to baptize in the Holy Spirit. The coming one is to immerse people in the Holy Spirit, to plunge them fully into the life of God intimately and personally.

This is an extraordinary description of the purpose of the coming of Jesus Christ. It should not, of course, be set against the general sense that Jesus has come to save or that he has come, say, to give his life as a ransom for many. Nor should this designation of the role of Jesus take away from the manifold role of Jesus as healer, prophet to Israel, exorcist, teacher, and the like. All this other work and all these other roles of the one to come are folded into a bigger purpose, namely, baptism in the Holy Spirit. This is so crucial that it is found as the single agreed purpose of the work of Jesus in all three synoptic Gospels. The final purpose of the coming of Jesus is to bring about the acquisition of the Holy Spirit. Forgiveness, spiritual healing, restoration of right relationship, deliverance from the demonic, incorporation into the people of God, and a host of other things matter. Yet they are all subordinate to one overarching goal: the baptism in the Holy Spirit secured by Jesus Christ.

We can trace the significance of this text in three ways.

First, in coming to see the grand thing that God has done in Jesus

Christ, we need tutoring before, during, and after our encounter with him. The church rightly insisted that the Old Testament is indispensable. If Jesus simply showed up and announced he was the Son of God, the word "God" would have little or no content and we would flounder in consternation and confusion. The history of Israel provides essential content to the name and character of God, so that in speaking of Jesus as the Son of God, those who first discerned this knew what they were asserting. To be sure, exposure to Jesus transforms and enriches what they knew of God, but there has to be some sort of idea of the divine to get the gospel off the ground in the first instance. John's role was to draw attention to this preparation in Israel and to bring it to a fitting climax.

Second, in coming to see who Jesus is, we all need time and space to ponder what is before us. The urge to move in for immediate decision must be tempered with adequate reflection, with pondering these things in our hearts, and with sitting down and counting the cost before we make fools of ourselves. God is both urgent and patient in his dealings with us. The good spiritual director provides both specific direction and room for rumination. Retrieving this is urgent in the renewal of evangelism in our day. Coming to know and follow Christ is a momentous undertaking. In meeting Jesus for the first time, most people scarce know what to make of him or what to do with him. We all need personal time and space to come to terms with him. On one side this stems from our confusion, our blindness, and our readiness to read our own aspirations and ideas into his life and work. We are deeply embedded in our natural ways of acting and thinking and resist moving beyond our comfortable categories. On the other side the coming of Jesus is a radically new event. It takes us by surprise; we naturally want to set it aside as impossible, as too good to be true, or as a piece of ancient mythology. We are at a loss to know what to say or do. We are shaken to the foundations of our being. Hence for both internal and external reasons, we need help in getting our bearings. This is precisely what John furnishes in his day. Even those who have long been privy to God's special revelation in Israel need renewed assistance in discerning the signs of the times. We need similar help from the church in our day.

Third, the final end of Christ's coming is to immerse and baptize us in the Holy Spirit. Debate about the meaning of this should not erode the crucial place it has in the purposes of God for his people. The recovery of this emphasis is one of the great treasures of the last century within Protestantism. It has long been buried in the church's practice and memory. It was central in the first public announcement concerning the ministry of Christ. Luke picked it up in his careful account of what happened on the Day of

Pentecost. This work of Jesus remains pivotal in the experience and work of the church in every age.

William J. Abraham

First Sunday after the Epiphany (Baptism of the Lord), Year B

First Lesson: Genesis 1:1-5
(Psalm 29)
Second Lesson: Acts 19:1-7
Gospel Lesson: Mark 1:4-11

John's fundamental role was to prepare the way for the coming of Christ. His appearance in the wilderness signals that something truly significant is afoot, for the wilderness was a prime location for a divine encounter that brought either blessing or judgment. Baptism signified a change of mind and the forgiveness of sins. Folk were to get ready by coming to terms with their past failure, by turning around, and by facing in a new direction in their thinking.

People gathered in large numbers from Judea and Jerusalem. John's popularity was not in doubt. Baptism was the common route from the pagan world into the Jewish community; here the Jews themselves are baptized. Baptism reinforces the call to be ready for something new. Insiders to the faith of Israel were summoned to confess their sins and be on the lookout for God's fresh intervention.

John's lifestyle matches his role as forerunner. His clothes and diet are sparse and minimalist. There is not a hint of anything grandiose, politically powerful, or militaristic. The contrast to the normal suggests that people should be ready for the unexpected and the surprising. They should be prepared for what breaks with conventional ways of thinking about God's coming in history.

John's message is directed away from himself to the one who is coming. The details are sparse, cut back to the bare essentials. He is more powerful than John is, and he is of greater status, for John is not worthy even to stoop and untie the thong of his sandals. The role of the coming one is to baptize in the Holy Spirit. This is a cryptic but extraordinary description of the work of Christ. The language of baptism speaks of immersion, of being saturated and snowed under in the life of God. It is a powerful vision of the coming of Christ. The location of this revelation at the very beginning of the narrative gives baptism in the Holy Spirit a theological primacy in accounts of Christ's role; the fact that it's underwritten by a prophet means that baptism in the Holy Spirit is not incidental to the coming of Christ but at the very core of his work; the contrast with water baptism drives home this message even further.

The identity of the coming one is unveiled immediately with the appearance of Jesus. By being baptized by John, Jesus endorses the ministry of John. There is no mention of confession of sin on the part of Jesus; his baptism with sinners shows his unrestrained identification with sinners. He joins them in their confession without himself confessing any sin.

This reaching down to sinners, in turn, receives divine approval with the opening of the heavens and the descent of the Spirit. The gentleness of the Spirit appearing as a dove on one who is to be more powerful than John shows that the power at work in Jesus and bestowed by him on others is no conventional power. It is a power made manifest in weakness and tenderness.

The voice from heaven drives home the divine approval, for the Father is well pleased with the Son. Moreover, the identification of Jesus as the Son, the Beloved, fills out John's vision of the greater status of the one to come. Jesus is not a mere prophet; he is not some adopted human agent who becomes through the Spirit the Son of God; he is the Son of God. We now know, albeit implicitly, why there was no confession of sin: we are dealing with the divine in our midst.

Pondering these texts brings home in a striking way the significance of the baptism of Jesus for the church today.

First, baptism is not an optional extra that we can take or leave at will. It is a pivotal event in the life of the believer. Jesus fully endorses the use of external symbolic rites; indeed, he goes out of his way to lead in subjecting himself to immersion in water. In subjecting ourselves to baptism, we resist the temptation to reduce the faith to mere inwardness, subjective piety, personal intellectual rumination, and the like. We acknowledge our dependence on others; we recognize the indispensability of the church in the work of God; we inject ourselves willingly into the practices of the Jewish tradition. We tell the world that we cannot make it on our own.

Moreover, we look to God to work through the practices of his people, through mundane material reality. Our faith is a materialistic faith; God works in, with, and through water. God meets us as an objective reality outside of ourselves and our inward doubts by fixing his action and his presence to something we can see and feel in our bodies. We are not left lingering in a spiritual world of feelings and thoughts; we are plunged in a real, tangible world of water that cleanses and refreshes us. In short, God meets us as embodied creatures of flesh and blood, and God floods us with his presence in the practices of the church.

Second, these practices clearly involve response on our part. Baptism requires repentance and confession of sin; it is a physical event intimately related to spiritual reorientation. And baptism is not merely an isolated physical occurrence; it is an integral component of a complex process of initiation. Since the Reformation, Christians have had questions about the correct ordering of the various components of initiation. Should repentance and confession, for example, precede baptism? Or can baptism, as happens in the case of infants, precede confession of sin and explicit turning to God? This is a futile discussion. What matters is fullness of initiation and a living faith in the action of God in the sacrament of baptism. In gratitude and wonder, all the baptized should look back on their baptism as an objective location of divine action. God has freely subjected himself in humility to work through the water of baptism. So the act and remembrance of baptism provide an invitation and spur to self-examination, to confession of sin, and to genuine, ongoing reorientation of our lives. The physical and the personal, the objective and the subjective, the inward and the outward — these are joined in an intimate union in the journey of faith.

Third, baptism is not just an objective physical reality joined to confession of sin and repentance; baptism mediates the presence of the Holy Spirit. It leads to immersion in the Holy Spirit, so that we are indwelled by God and participate in the very life of God. What Christians call salvation can aptly be described as the acquisition of the Holy Spirit. From the onset of the journey of faith the Holy Spirit is present in our lives. The Spirit comes to convict us of our need, to make us aware of our sin, to reveal to us the beauty of the Savior, to give us new birth, to bring forth the fruit of the Spirit, to empower us for service in the kingdom and in the church, and the like. The crowning climax of this process is to be totally immersed in God, to be baptized in the Holy Spirit. This is how John graphically summarizes the whole purpose of the coming of the Son.

Conventional theology has obscured this crucial point in three ways. In much academic theology the work of the Holy Spirit has been reduced to mere talk of divine grace, as if the unmerited favor of God, wonderful as it is, can stand as a substitute for the intimate immersion of the believer in

God that is at stake here. Alternatively, much theology has collapsed the work of the Holy Spirit into the activity of the church, thus confusing the bearer or agent of the Spirit with the reality of the Spirit. Much popular theology, especially in the Pentecostal tradition, has reduced the presence of the Spirit to the merely psychological, insisting on various feelings and experiences as constitutive of immersion in the Spirit. The relations between the Spirit and grace, between the Spirit and the church, and between the Spirit and human experiences of the Spirit are all worthy of the most sensitive reflection. However, the ultimate and primary goal of the Christian life must ever be kept in view; the final outcome is the full acquisition of the Holy Spirit, graphically captured here in the language of baptism and immersion.

Participation in the life of the Holy Spirit is the hidden secret of the church's life. Bestowed through the Son by the will of the Father, the Holy Spirit brings a gentle power into the world that redeems it from within, beginning with the creation of children of God. Through the Spirit we participate in the same Spirit which came upon Jesus in his baptism. Through the Holy Spirit we become subject to the rule of God that has come among us in the life of the Son.

William J. Abraham

First Sunday in Lent, Year B

First Lesson: Genesis 9:8-17
(Psalm 25:1-10)
Second Lesson: 1 Peter 3:18-22
Gospel Lesson: Mark 1:9-15

Lent is clearly designated in the church as a season of preparation. How better to begin the journey on which we now embark than by pondering the beginning of the ministry of our Lord on earth. The golden thread that runs through Mark's terse summary of three crucial episodes at the outset of his ministry is that of preparation. John has already prepared the people to hear and see Jesus; God now prepares Jesus for his ministry among the people, a ministry brought to a climax in his passion and crucifixion.

John's ministry aroused all sorts of queries. Clearly John had made a deep impact, for many had heeded his call to baptism, repentance, and forgiveness. Jesus leaves no doubts as to the status of John. His acceptance of baptism at the hands of John is a ringing endorsement of his integrity and message. Jesus is fully on board with God's new move in the history of Israel. His baptism is also a clear move to identify with people where they are. He does not stand aloof from our sin but reaches down into the water with us where we are. There is no hint that he needs to be baptized or to repent and be forgiven. The move Jesus makes in baptism is that of drawing alongside us in our need. He descends into our world as it is, ready to step into the effects of our sin and self-destruction.

There is also a clear indication in Jesus' baptism that baptism is associated with the coming of the Holy Spirit upon us and within us. This was commonplace in later Christian initiation. In baptism the catechumen turned toward God, was cleansed of sin, and was buried with Christ. Equally the new disciple received the gift of the Holy Spirit. This in no way suggested that the Holy Spirit was absent or inactive before this decisive moment in the journey. Yet the coming of the Spirit, hovering and descending like a dove, comes now in a new and full manner upon the Lord. Equipped with the Spirit, Jesus has at his disposal all the resources of heaven. The power of God is shed abroad to make possible the life and works of God in the world. Even the Son of God is dependent on the active presence and power of the Holy Spirit to do his work for the Father.

It is not enough, however, just to be the Son of God, it is also crucial to recognize and live out of that identity. Hence the word of revelation here is vital. "You are my Son, the beloved; with you I am well pleased." Our confidence and bearing are inextricably bound to our sense of identity. This is well recognized in the place we assign nowadays to our racial or national identity. Once our identities are interiorized, we live our lives in ways that are profoundly shaped by our sense of who we are and where we have come from. In Christ his identity as a Jew is now enfolded into his identity as the Son of God. It is only fitting that this should be highlighted in a decisive way at the moment he steps into the waters with us and receives the Holy Spirit for the work that lies ahead.

Yet we must be careful not to move too quickly. The Holy Spirit is not a holy laborsaving device who bypasses the hard grind of temptation and spiritual discernment. On the contrary, the Holy Spirit intensifies the need to work through the tough choices that confront those who would do

God's work in the world. Matthew and Luke spell out the details. Jesus has to resolve the choice between offering bread and circuses or the Word of God, between deploying dramatic miracles or resting in quiet trust in God, and between going after the glory the world offers and worshiping God alone. Mark is content to record the reality of demonic temptation, its persistent manner over forty days in the wilderness of testing, the peace Jesus has with wild beasts, and the ready provision of the angels through it all. The core issue is that the work of Christ requires deep moral and spiritual preparation that operates with the world as it is, shot through with the demonic at every major turn. The Holy Spirit does not spare us this leg of the journey; the Holy Spirit dumps us right in the middle of it and insists that we deal with it head-on. The world in which we operate is indeed saturated with evil; Jesus enters into and confronts its attractive options directly and persistently. The Holy Spirit propels him and us into periods of intense testing in order to equip us for ministry in the world as it is.

That world has already taken note of John; indeed, it has bundled him unceremoniously into prison. However, the preparation to which Jesus is subject really does work. Despite the fate of John, he launches his ministry in Galilee with the joyous proclamation of the good news. The heart of that good news is not some new idea, nor some grand philosophical scheme, nor some guilt-driven ideology, nor a new code of behavior. It is a terse announcement and a call to response. While it may take a library of books to fathom its content, it can be written on a postcard or form the headlines in the daily newspaper.

The announcement and the response each have two components. "The time is fulfilled, and the kingdom of God has come near." In other words, the great day has at last arrived, and the rule of God in human history is upon us. The days of waiting are at an end; God's moment to move has dawned. His active plan to rule is now at hand; the divine administration of the world is about to be inaugurated. So "repent and believe in the good news." In other words, be radically open and ready to turn to what God is about to do, and believe the good news you are about to witness in Israel's history. Be ready for an intellectual turnaround that takes you in a different direction, and look upon what is happening not as bad news but as good news.

What is the significance of these texts for this season of the year?

First, we can and should find time to turn aside and come to terms with our spiritual journeys. Lent was originally a period of intense scrutiny, self-examination, and spiritual stocktaking for new believers. It was the last step before baptism when believers faced up to the full demands of following

Christ. The church found it so effective that it instituted it as a refresher course year in and year out. Hence in Lent we are driven back to the elemental issues of the faith. We are confronted again with baptism, with our primary identity as children of God, with the coming of the Holy Spirit into our lives, with the ever enduring battle with the demonic, and with the ever available resources of God.

Second, we can and should find time to rejoice during this season in the arrival of God's kingdom among us. The bad news of the persistence of evil is ever before us; it screams at us daily across the world. We face it head-on without sentimentality or evasion in this season of the year. But the good news is equally persistent. God has not abandoned his creation; in his own time he has come among us; his kingdom has arrived in our midst; this remains now, as of old, the greatest news that has ever been told. In Lent we let that stand as a summons to renewal and hope while we grapple with the elemental forces of human existence that are ranged against us.

Third, both these exercises are a means to an end; the turning aside to face evil and the rejoicing at the coming of the kingdom prepare us for sharing the good news with the world. The world, of course, is driven hither and yon with slogans, mission statements, sound bites, and newspaper headlines. By nature we are like the two men in the Irish pub; they wanted to know two things: Who did it? And did he get caught? Mark's summary of the message of Jesus is at home in this world. He nails the issue concisely and precisely. We must do no less in our day and generation. It will not do to send a library of books or the most recent video. We must cast aside our intellectual inhibitions and our love of complexity and nuance. We must reach down to people where they are and deliver the good news in simple and accessible form. "The time is fulfilled, and the kingdom of God has come near; repent, and believe in the good news."

William J. Abraham

171

Third Sunday after the Epiphany, Year B

First Lesson: Jonah 3:1-5, 10
(Psalm 62:5-12)
Second Lesson: 1 Corinthians 7:29-31
Gospel Lesson: Mark 1:14-20

After a terse but rich account of the preparation of the people by John and the preparation of Jesus by the Father and the Holy Spirit, Jesus now begins his ministry. Two elements of his work are identified at the outset: the proclamation of the kingdom of God and the gathering together of a close band of disciples who will carry on his work after his death and resurrection.

The temporal and physical contexts of his initial proclamation are important. Jesus operates at a time after John has been arrested. Already we can see the potential conflict between Jesus and opponents, a conflict that erupts in a string of confrontational episodes in chapter 2. We can sense the suspense already, although we have no idea of the details to come. Just as John was "handed over," so Jesus will too be "handed over." Moreover, Jesus begins his ministry not in the great centers of power like Jerusalem, but in Galilee, signaling that the ground has to be further prepared before he can speak directly to the powers that be. Everything will have its time — God's time in fact.

Potential opposition does not deter Jesus in the least. His message is a message of good news, good news that can be seen both as about God and from God. The crucial content of the good news concerns the coming of the kingdom of God. The language is clearly political in content, for it concerns a kingdom. The kingdom is not about philosophy, ethics, or abstract spirituality; it is about God's rule in history here and now. There is a hard edge to kingdom discourse; it suggests that we cannot reduce what is at stake to interior piety or the world to come; current public and political issues are in view. To his hearers this would be obvious, for in Israel religion and politics, ethics and politics, were inextricably connected.

The core of the declaration is that God's rule, God's sovereign reign, has drawn near. The kingdom is no longer far away; it is upon us. The timing is in God's hands. This is not a timing determined by human authorities or by human ingenuity; the timetable is developed by God, and on God's timetable it is now time to move to inaugurate his kingdom.

The appropriate response to this is to repent and believe in the good news. Repentance means a change of mind that leads to a change of behavior. In repentance a person's intellectual and spiritual horizons are radically reshaped by the arrival of the kingdom, so much so that there is a change of heart and behavior. Emotions are entirely secondary; they may or may not be in place; what matters is a change of mind and direction. This is more likely if one really grasps that what one is encountering really is good news. We are not likely to change if we cannot see the new direction as contributing in a deep way to our future welfare. Hence the call to believe the good news. A real effort has to be made to set aside our fears and our skepticism and replace them with trust and hope.

No rationale or reasons beyond this promissory note of the kingdom being near are given. The call goes out, the invitation is made, and we are expected to respond. This is driven home in the call of the first disciples. Jesus, passing along the Sea of Galilee, simply calls Simon and Andrew while they're at work on the shore, and they respond immediately. They constitute the beginnings of Christ's community, the model for all to follow in their readiness to respond. They are to follow Jesus, not some party, or ideology, or philosophy. Their new vocation is to be fishers of people, suggesting that their work will be demanding for them and radically transforming for those they catch. The same readiness to follow is exemplified in the response of the sons of Zebedee. Simon and Andrew were fishing from the shore, suggesting that they were too poor to buy a boat. In contrast, James and John were more upscale, possessing both a boat and hired hands. Social and economic differences are entirely irrelevant to the call to follow. Given the time that has dawned, given the arrival of the kingdom, given the good news involved, given the authority and identity of the one who is calling, there is no time for delay or deliberation. All the called can do is leave their work on the spot and take off with Jesus.

Already, as the story unfolds, we can see that the preparation and timing brought about by God are working. These themes are amply developed in the whole of chapter 1, as Jesus sweeps through Galilee and takes it by storm. His preaching is forthright and to the point, and he has effectively called together a nucleus of disciples. He is about to take on the demonic and heal Simon's mother-in-law, and by the end of the day the whole city will be gathered about the door. To be sure, the human agents play their part, yet the underlying sense is that God is on the march in the ministry of Jesus. The time for God's rule has arrived, and we can see its initial impact in human history. John may languish in prison, but he had a real place in God's visitation of Israel, and the one he had pointed to and baptized has now taken center stage. God is no fool, and already there are those who are prepared to risk everything to get on board and follow the lead of his Son.

What is the significance of these developments for following Christ today?

First, there should be no doubt as to the center of Christ's message. It is constituted by the good news that the kingdom of God really has arrived in human history. This has been and remains the core of the gospel. God has shown up in Israel to rule; the opposition to this is real and even effective; but the eventual victory of God is secure. The gospel is precisely this. It is not the announcement of some generic theism, or a call to moral renovation, or an offer of celestial fire insurance for the life to come, or a network of pious platitudes about how to become more religious. The gospel is the arrival of God's new order in the world. Long prepared for and eagerly awaited in Israel, it is the good news that God's rule has arrived. To be sure, this will be bad news for those who want to be in charge of the universe, and they will not stand by and abandon their role of running the world. Yet the truth is simply this: God's sovereign reign has drawn near in human history, and in the end nothing will prevent its being established. This remains the heart of the gospel for all time.

Second, the first response to this is intellectual. It is not a matter of looking within ourselves and discovering what we need, what we have done wrong, or where we need comfort and consolation and then turning to God to take care of our list of particulars. The first order of business is to focus on what God has done in Jesus. We have to get outside our obsession with our problems and ourselves and look upward and backward to these pivotal events on God's calendar for the world. We have to catch sight of God's agenda, internalize its priorities, and let it become the cornerstone of our thinking. Thereby we can turn in a new direction and bring our lives into line with what God is doing. We can then resist the temptation to reconstruct God's agenda so that it fulfills our felt needs or our schemes for the world and ourselves. The great good news is that it is in this and only this that the world and we are set on our proper course.

Third, in responding in this manner we have very little to rest on beyond the word and call of Jesus. There are no external intellectual props, no extended seminars to weigh the matter carefully, and no prior testimony to trust. We are confronted with the naked word of Jesus, and we are given an ultimatum that we can accept or refuse. The starkness of the first response to Jesus is almost terrifying. These first disciples hear his call to follow him and drop everything to respond. Of course, this is a special calling, for to them will be entrusted the keys of the kingdom and the awesome responsi-

174

bility to hand on its treasures to the world and to future generations. Yet that same call and that same response echo down the ages to all who hear the good news of the arrival of God's kingdom in history.

William J. Abraham

Fourth Sunday after the Epiphany, Year B

First Lesson: Deuteronomy 18:15-20
(Psalm 111)
Second Lesson: 1 Corinthians 8:1-13
Gospel Lesson: Mark 1:21-28

Having announced in summary form his message and called the first batch of disciples, Jesus moved to Capernaum. On the Sabbath he entered the synagogue and taught there. In the course of his teaching he is confronted with a man with an unclean spirit. Both his teaching and his exorcism evoke wonder and joyful surprise.

Mark tells us nothing of the content of his teaching. His interest is entirely focused on the astonishment it evokes. It is the manner rather than the ideas that get attention. "He taught them as one having authority." The authority of Jesus at this point is direct. It is not derived from his status as, say, a prophet, or from his native ingenuity, or from his school pedigree. Indeed, it is set over and against the authority of scribes who derive their authority from their learning and skill as passed on through pertinent training. We are left to ponder what is behind such authority. No explanation is given, not even a hint. We have to come to terms with Jesus in himself; we cannot at this point find a foothold for an external warrant that would give him authority.

At least, this is how it is until the crying out of a man with an unclean spirit abruptly interrupts the story. The question aroused by the authority of Jesus is answered indirectly. Jesus is addressed as both "Jesus of Nazareth" and "the Holy One of God." The first is easily ascertained; indeed, we already know that Jesus came from Nazareth. The second designation is elu-

175

sive, yet it speaks plainly of an intimate relation between Jesus and God. Jesus is "the Holy One of God." We also know this about the teacher: there is immediate conflict between him and the demoniac. The demons inside this man rightly fear that he has come to destroy them.

Jesus wastes no time in confirming their worst fears. In keeping with standard practice he casts out the demons, but not before he has commanded them to be silent. Their departure is a dramatic event: they send the man into convulsions and cry with a loud voice as they leave.

By now everybody is paying attention. They are all amazed and look for an adequate explanation of what has transpired in their midst. There is a new teaching unaccompanied by conventional warrants, and there is immediate obedience to the command of Jesus. Not surprisingly his fame spread throughout the surrounding region of Galilee.

These events, the teaching with authority and the dramatic exorcism, cut right across modern ways of teaching and of conceiving reality. They conflict with two central dogmas of the last three centuries. First, the teaching of Jesus comes without the presentation of relevant evidence. There are no data, arguments, warrants, or any of the standard paraphernalia of modern common sense or of the modern academy. There is also not a whiff of relativism, nor a sniff of postmodern playfulness, nor a puff of personal opinion. There is the stark directness of the teaching of Jesus, akin to the stark command to follow without explanation. In modern categories this comes across as an arbitrary appeal to dogma or to accept the mere word of Jesus. Yet Mark does not see it this way. Jesus is clearly identified as the Holy One of God by the demoniac; we have a new and direct source of warrant that stands on its own feet. And where ordinary people are concerned, Jesus sets the mind on edge, evoking astonishment and further inquiry. As of old, Jesus breaks the mold and invites us today to reconstruct our conventional ways of thinking.

The encounter with the demoniac is even more disconcerting. Seen at its best, we are introduced to a world of the psychological; hence we look for pertinent remedies in the world of psychiatry and counseling. Seen at its worst, we are dragged into a prescientific world of demons and angels; in short, we are introduced to a religious underworld of irrelevant mythology. Yet neither of these options will suffice. On the one hand, exorcism works by means of direct command and involves the driving out of agents that mysteriously invade the human person. The parallels with modern mental illness are nonexistent. On the other hand, modern naturalistic and scientific accounts of the world do not in themselves secure their omnicompetence. Their universal application is a matter of faith, a plausible faith because of the success of science, no doubt, but a faith nonetheless. Challenging this reductionistic faith in the secular is a vast body of testimony to the reality of the demonic; anyone with personal pastoral experience in this arena will have little difficulty following and accepting what has happened here. Those with a rich and complex ontology can readily take on board the findings of modern science and keep intact belief in the demonic, even though this breaks in a radical manner the conventional options available in our contemporary intellectual culture.

Where does this leave us in pondering the significance of this short episode for today? The waters run deep, but we do well to enter them boldly.

First, the gospel confronts us with another world, a world that was once alive for most people but is now lost to the cultural elite of our times. The temptation to tame and domesticate this world so that we can fit it neatly into our inherited categories and explanations is intense. Yet this temptation must be resolutely resisted without defensiveness or nostalgia. The ministry of exorcism brings us face-to-face with a form of evil that we would prefer to forget. We are aware, of course, of evil in our hearts, and we are acutely aware in the contemporary world of evil at work in social structures. Jesus confronts here yet another level of evil, that of the demonic. Hollywood loves to present this world from time to time, rolling out its version of the demonic every decade or so. Unfortunately the Hollywood version does not help us in this arena. There is a dramatic and noisy dimension to the demonic, but, as we can see from Mark, this is muted in Scripture. Moreover, the demonic can recognize immediately the presence of the divine. It is as if radical evil has a way of immediately discerning the presence of good; it takes a spiritual agent to recognize another spiritual agent. The episode here in Mark calls for a radical reorientation in our conception of reality.

Second, we can make this drastic intellectual transition because in Jesus we see immediate victory over the powers of evil. Evil naturally evokes fear. We rightly take seriously the destructive powers that confront us in cases that require exorcism. Hence we should turn in such instances to specialized help. It is a sign of the renewal of the church in our day that many churches, including the mainline churches, have resources available in this arena that would have been ignored or scorned a generation ago. The Orthodox and Roman Catholic churches have never abandoned this ministry. What makes exorcism possible is the healing power of Jesus available now through the ministry of his church. As Christ's body, we are equipped with the power of the Holy Spirit to confront the powers of evil and deliver the captives from bondage. This work should be done without fuss; it should be kept out of the limelight; and it should follow the fundamental pattern set here by Christ himself.

Third, we should be well aware how strange all this will appear to many in our day. Hence we should practice a principle of reserve. That principle states very simply that some things can only be said after other things have been said. Christ's admonition to be silent is eminently prudent. In Christ's day the problem was less with the demonic than with the nature of the divine. It took time for folk to unpack what was involved in the presence of the Holy One of God. All sorts of misconceptions had to be weeded out; the truth had to be planted so that it could grow over time. In our day, after centuries of demythologizing and secularization, we often have to build the whole fabric of faith from the bottom up. We need to be acutely aware of the deep assumptions that underlie the rejection of both the divine and the demonic. Happily we have extraordinary resources available in the renewal of Christian philosophy in the last half-century to help us. Yet in the end we need to expose people to Jesus himself. He is at the heart and center of God's revelation to the world. Sooner or later we have to come to terms with his unique authority over us. This is not the authority of personal opinion or of arbitrary dogma. It is a form of divine authority that expands our current intellectual horizons in wonderment and joyful surprise.

William J. Abraham

Fifth Sunday after the Epiphany, Year B

First Lesson: Isaiah 40:21-31
(Psalm 147:1-11, 20c)
Second Lesson: 1 Corinthians 9:16-23
Gospel Lesson: Mark 1:29-39

Literary context. This narrative marks the end of the first phase of Jesus' public ministry in Capernaum. Following his baptism, temptation, and the call of Simon, Andrew, James, and John (1:16-20), they went to Capernaum (1:21). Jesus is surrounded by sickness, disease, distress. He is recognized by demons as the Holy One of God (1:24), but as a mere miracle worker by the people. He is hounded by people seeking healing and is hunted down by his own disciples while he prays. He cannot escape the clamoring crowds or the constant needs that surround him. Mark is signaling that Jesus' ministry was taking off like a rocket. It would have devoured a mere mortal.

Literary structure. This Sunday's pericope is part of a larger narrative that unfolds in six scenes.

1:21-28: On the Sabbath Jesus entered the synagogue, where he taught with authority and healed a man with an unclean spirit. He commanded the demon to be silent and cast him out of the man. His fame spread like wildfire. This was the Gospel lection for the Fourth Sunday after the Epiphany.

1:29-31: Leaving the synagogue, Jesus and the four disciples "immediately" enter Simon and Andrew's house. Douglas Hare says this is to be taken literally. Archaeological evidence suggests that this spacious house was contiguous to the synagogue (D. Hare, *Mark* [Westminster/John Knox, 1996], p. 29). Matthew says it was Peter's house (8:14). Inside this home there is sickness. Simon's mother-in-law lay sick *(katekeito)* with a fever. Taking her by the hand, Jesus raised her up *(ēgeire);* she was healed instantly and began to serve *(diēkonei)* them.

1:32-34: At sundown, that is, when the Sabbath was officially ended, townspeople brought "all" *(panta)* who were sick and all those possessed with demons (note: these are two different categories) to Simon's door. The whole city *(holē hē polis)* turned out to watch. Jesus cured many *(pollous)* who were sick with various diseases and cast out many demons, which he would not allow to speak.

1:35: Well before dawn, literally when it was very early at night *(prōï ennycha lian),* Jesus stole away to a deserted place *(erēmon topon)* to pray. A. T. Robertson, in volume 1 of his *Word Pictures in the New Testament,* says it was between 3 and 6 A.M. Mark uses a variation in chapter 16 when the women went to the tomb very early *(lian prōï)* on the first day of the week to anoint a dead body.

1:36-38: While Jesus was praying, Simon and his companions searched for him *(katadiōxen),* literally: pursued, searched eagerly, hunted for him. Why are they searching? Because everyone (in Capernaum) is looking *(zētousin)* for him (lit. looking for what one possessed and has lost). Jesus refuses to return, saying they must go to neighboring towns so he can preach *(kēryxō)* there also.

1:39: Jesus went throughout Galilee preaching in the synagogues and casting out demons.

Homiletical possibilities. This passage suggests many possibilities for preaching. Fruitful sermons might consider, among other topics, the centrality of healing in Jesus' ministry and its implications for us; the character of Jesus' leadership; the stewardship of time; and mission versus evangelism.

Preaching, teaching, and healing are always connected in Jesus' ministry. His healings were both public (the man in the synagogue, the multitude at Simon's door) and private (Simon's mother-in-law). He healed various diseases and cast out demons (exorcising the minions of Satan which attack the mental and spiritual dimension). No one was turned away. Many were healed. The commentators do not think that Mark is highlighting the fact that many, not all, were healed. (See the discussion of Robert Guelich, *Mark 1–8:26*, Word Biblical Commentary 34 [Word, 1989], p. 66.) Nevertheless, this passage affords an excellent opportunity to discuss the healings in the context of Jesus' public ministry. The healings here do not seem to depend on the faith of the beneficiaries, but on the purposes of the healer. One thing is clear: Jesus has the desire and the power to touch, to cure, and to heal people who come to him. The healings are more about the character of the healer than of the healed. They signal God's miraculous inbreaking power over infirmity and the powers of evil. That hasn't changed. Any church that follows Jesus Christ is ipso facto in the healing business. How are we manifesting the healing power of Christ?

The passage also indicates several dangers that Jesus recognized. People often seek Jesus for purely personal gain, not to repent and become disciples but to get their infirmities healed and their needs met. Jesus' explicit, later warning concerning Capernaum (Matt. 11:23 and Luke 10:15) indicates that the deeds of power performed there were sufficient to save Sodom but apparently did not produce repentance in Capernaum. We sometimes focus so much on the activity of ministry and "success" in strictly human terms that we mistake it for the kingdom of *God.* Jesus understood the limitations of healing as well as the grace it involved.

Jesus might have cut and run, like someone bailing out of a relationship because it is simply too demanding, too hectic, too all-consuming. Or Jesus could have exploited his easy success at Capernaum for fame and fortune. He does neither. For Jesus the healings point to something greater, which only the demons (spirits) can recognize. For him, and thus for us, the healings are always secondary, subordinate to and supportive of his dominant mission of preaching the inbreaking of the kingdom of God.

This passage tells us a great deal about Jesus' character and behavior as a leader. Secular literature offers many models. See, for example, Peter Drucker's classic, *The Effective Executive* (New York: Harper Business, 1967), or Stephen Covey's runaway best-seller *The Seven Habits of Highly Effective Peo-*

ple (New York: Simon & Schuster, 1989). Christian authors have also tried to catalogue the traits of effective leaders. See, for example, Calvin Miller, *The Empowered Leader: Ten Keys to Servant Leadership* (Nashville: Broadman, 1995); John Maxwell, *The Twenty-one Irrefutable Laws of Leadership* (Nashville: Nelson, 1998). You might contrast these to the leadership of Jesus described in this passage:

Authority: Jesus spoke and acted decisively, effectively, calmly, simply.

Compassion: He gave himself generously to all people from every station.

Humility: He spent time alone in prayer seeking God's will and strength.

Vision: He did not succumb to the blandishments of the crowd or the pressure of his disciples, but remained focused on and faithful to the mission.

A congregation, a person, could do worse.

This passage can also be explicated in terms of busyness or the stewardship of time. The passage is literally ordered by the sun: preaching in the synagogue on the Sabbath, healing in the afternoon (before the evening meal); healings after sundown, prayers before dawn, traveling to the next town to preach and cast out demons. The curse of postmodernity is "I just don't have enough time." A sermon might compare the way we misuse and fritter away our time. Some of us waste time, others fail to prioritize and spend our time unwisely. Compare this to Jesus' schedule and then explore what accounts for the difference. Jesus is extremely busy but never rushed, never too busy to deal with problems he encounters on the way, never too busy to heal, to pray, to go. Is it a matter of his priorities, his energy, his identity, or all three? What does this tell us about the futility of increasing human effort and the perfect freedom that comes when we are resting in God's creative, life-giving power and will?

Finally, this passage shows that the old debate between mission and evangelism is a false one. Was Jesus a healer or a preacher? Some Christians emphasize the caring ministries. Some emphasize spiritual formation/prayer. Some emphasize outreach. This story shows that Jesus held these in tension. Effective ministry doesn't choose one over the other. Jesus healed many. He prayed. But he also moved out to spread the word. In truth, his healings and exorcisms supported his preaching and teaching, and vice versa.

Stephen W. Ramp

Sixth Sunday after the Epiphany, Year B

First Lesson: 2 Kings 5:1-14
(Psalm 30)
Second Lesson: 1 Corinthians 9:24-27
Gospel Lesson: Mark 1:40-45

H e touched him. Jesus touched the man with leprosy. A leper is unclean and not to be touched. In fact, the leper was isolated from Jewish society: "The person who has the leprous disease shall wear torn clothes and let the hair of his head be disheveled; and he shall cover his upper lip and cry out, 'Unclean, unclean.' He shall remain unclean as long as he has the disease; he is unclean. He shall live alone; his dwelling shall be outside the camp" (Lev. 13:45-46).

We see in the New Testament several health problems that might cause social ostracism. The woman with the flow of blood was unclean (Mark 5:24b-34), though she dared to touch Jesus rather than vice versa.

> If a woman has a discharge of blood for many days, not at the time of her impurity, or if she has a discharge beyond the time of her impurity, all the days of the discharge she shall continue in uncleanness; as in the days of her impurity, she shall be unclean. Every bed on which she lies during all the days of her discharge shall be treated as the bed of her impurity; and everything on which she sits shall be unclean, as in the uncleanness of her impurity. Whoever touches these things shall be unclean, and shall wash his clothes, and bathe in water, and be unclean until the evening. (Lev. 15:25-27)

Having a disease or health problem surely was terror in the ancient world. Little was known about illnesses and even less about cures. Even so, for people like the leper or the woman with the flow of blood, being unclean must have been more painful than the disease itself. Being unclean, they were isolated from their family and their community.

For the most part, in the Jesus tradition faith creates the possibility for healing. This story does not change the Marcan pattern. The leper comes to Jesus with the faith that he can be healed. The response of Jesus bears some reflection, even though it is not the primary point of the narrative. Jesus had compassion on the leper. That isn't always the case. No compassion is mentioned in the healing of Peter's mother-in-law, or the paralytic, or Jairus's daughter. It is difficult for us not to assume that Jesus had compassion on anyone who was ill. But the Jesus tradition would have us believe that there was more than compassion involved. The real issue was separation from family and community. The pain was not so much the chronic disease as the isolation of quarantine.

Jesus was really sorry for the situation in which the leper found himself. The Greek word for compassion could be correctly translated as it was in the King James: "His bowels were moved with compassion." In contrast with the Jewish world, the Western world has different locations for emotional and cognitive functions. For us decisions are made by the mind, while in the biblical world decisions are made by the heart (Mark 2:8; Luke 3:15). For us compassion comes from the heart, but in Hebrew thought compassion comes from the guts. One might argue that a quarantine is more gut-wrenching for a family than the disease itself. It is worth considering. Despite the above observation, this passage does present a unique situation. The leper does not ask for mercy like the blind Bartimaeus (Mark 10:48), but asks Jesus to choose whether he will heal him or not — a cognitive request (also in the parallel in Luke 5:12-16)! Following his compassionate reaction Jesus does make an affirmative cognitive response!

We are not certain about the type of leprosy described in these stories. Scholars generally agree that the word "leprosy" in the Bible does not refer to the disease we call leprosy. The extensive discussion in Leviticus 13–14 gives us the impression of a fungus or inflammation that discolors the skin, causes it to flake off, and yet can invade also fabrics and house walls. In contrast to the leprosy we know, the biblical leprosy could be cured rather quickly. Regardless of skin color, the person was declared healed when the mottled effect disappeared: "But if the disease breaks out in the skin, so that it covers all the skin of the diseased person from head to foot, so far as the priest can see, then the priest shall make an examination, and if the disease has covered all his body, he shall pronounce him clean of the disease; since it has all turned white, he is clean" (Lev. 13:12-13).

Naaman the Syrian was cured (his flesh was like a young boy's) of this disease simply by obeying the prophet of God (2 Kings 5:1-14). Jesus also effects an immediate cure here and in the story of the ten lepers in Luke 17:11-19. We cannot tell whether the skin was returned to its original color or was the same color as the mottle. In any case, the leper was asked to show himself to a priest, just as Leviticus had order. By showing himself to the priest, the leper was then able to return to his family and community. As we have seen, the issue was not simply that he had a disease, but that he had been excommunicated. Only the priest could assure the Jewish community that the man no longer was unclean.

We are not certain why the leper was unclean. Was excommunication some form of a wellness program? It doesn't seem likely. The Bible doesn't speak about wellness programs for unclean people. Was this form of leprosy a communicable disease? Did isolation of the unclean person save the community from a serious health hazard? One would like to believe that, but it doesn't seem likely. We don't know why this fungus called leprosy was unclean, nor do we know why men with sexual emissions or women with a flow of blood were also unclean. From our knowledge of unclean foods we would suspect that irregularity is the problem. God made the world in a certain ordered fashion. When animals developed that altered that pattern, they were called unclean. People were also created in a clearly defined manner. If they were born with a defect, became visibly diseased, or their body didn't function correctly, then they were unclean.

Jesus touched the unclean leper. His touch made him acceptable. Once the priest pronounced him well, he could return to his family. Or better yet, once the church touched a person who was unclean or ill, that person became a part of the faith community. Was the person cured? We don't know. We do know that he or she once again had a family, and furthermore, became a functioning part of early Christian ministry. It is nearly invariable that healing by Jesus also involves ministry. For example, Peter's mother-in-law became a deacon (*diakonia*, 1:29-31). The leper became a preacher (from the noun *kērygma*) and spread the word around the countryside so that Jesus could hardly move. The community role of the leper was in direct contradiction to the so-called messianic secret. In verse 44 Jesus had told the leper not to tell anyone what happened and who did it. Many of the healing narratives in Mark include the warning not to tell anyone (1:34; 5:43; 7:36). The *locus classicus* for the messianic secret occurs in Mark 8:27-30, where Jesus actually asks the disciples what they think about him:

> Jesus went on with his disciples to the villages of Caesarea Philippi; and on the way he asked his disciples, "Who do people say that I am?" And they answered him, "John the Baptist; and others, Elijah; and still others, one of the prophets." He asked them, "But who do you say that I am?" Peter answered him, "You are the Messiah." And he sternly ordered them not to tell anyone about him.

When Peter gives the supposed correct answer, Jesus tells the disciples not to tell anyone. Readers at the turn of the century thought the messianic secret was created by Mark to explain why the historical Jesus was known as the Messiah only after his death and resurrection. According to Mark, then,

Jesus was the Messiah but would not allow it to be proclaimed. That reading of the secret no longer holds sway, but explanations are hard to come by. There was, of course, a strong Jewish messianic expectation. A son of David would always be on the throne of Israel (2 Sam. 7:12-14). Jesus the healer, the servant, the friend of the unclean did not fit the messianic expectation. So he asked people not to talk about it.

In any case, the leper found a community where he found caring and purpose. One wonders why we isolate those who are ill from family and friends. Why do we tend to take away their purpose for living? Is it to save their lives? For what purpose? Is it to protect family and friends? At what cost? Or, as in this story, is the touching itself the beginning of real healing?

Graydon F. Snyder

Seventh Sunday after the Epiphany, Year B

First Lesson: Isaiah 43:18-25
(Psalm 41)
Second Lesson: 2 Corinthians 1:18-22
Gospel Lesson: Mark 2:1-12

First of all, we must make a decision about the origin of this passage. Few readers would doubt that we have two stories here. The story of the paralytic, a healing story, stops with the phrase "when Jesus saw their faith" in verse 5 and begins again in verse 10 with "he said to the paralytic." The narrative would read like this:

> When he returned to Capernaum after some days, it was reported that he was at home. So many gathered around that there was no longer room for them, not even in front of the door; and he was speaking the word to them. Then some people came, bringing to him a paralyzed man, carried by four of them. And when they could not bring him to Jesus because of the crowd, they removed the roof above him; and after having dug through it, they let down the mat on which the paralytic lay. When Jesus

saw their faith, . . . he said to the paralytic, "I say to you, stand up, take your mat and go to your home." And he stood up, and immediately took the mat and went out before all of them; so that they were all amazed and glorified God, saying, "We have never seen anything like this!" (2:1-5a; 10b-12)

The remaining verses record a controversy story between Jesus and some Jewish leaders. It involves the power and right of Jesus to forgive sins and uses, as the subject, the same paralytic we see in the healing story. Mark likes insertions. For example, he inserted the healing of the woman with a hemorrhage into the story of Jairus's daughter (5:21-43), and the cleansing of the temple into the fig tree story (11:12-25). So we will deal with these as two separate narratives.

The healing of the paralytic follows the normal pattern of New Testament healing stories: a crowd gathers, a healing problem presents itself, Jesus heals, the result is described, and the crowd expresses amazement. In this narrative, as in most other synoptic healing stories, the context reflects the ministry of the early church. Jesus was in the (his!) house speaking the word. Four friends brought to the house a fifth friend who was paralyzed. Because of the crowd they could not come close to Jesus, so they made a hole in the roof and lowered the paralytic down by ropes. Jesus was astounded! He might have been distressed by the damage done to his house, but there is no further mention of the hole. It is the faith of the four friends that attracts attention. Nothing is said about the paralytic himself. We do not know if he asked the other four to take him to Jesus; we do not know if he believed Jesus could heal him. We do know the four friends believed Jesus could heal their paralytic friend and would stop at nothing to arrange an encounter.

For those who are more individualistically oriented, this has to be a puzzling story. Jesus healed the paralytic because of the faith of the four friends. That is, the community of faith (meeting in the house of Jesus!) could effect the healing of someone else whether he or she believes or not. Often personal faith, at least implicit faith, was the key factor in a healing event (5:34). But there are other occasions when the faith of one could heal another. The faith of a synagogue leader, Jairus, healed his daughter (5:36). The faith of the Syrophoenician woman healed her daughter (7:24-30). The faith of a father healed his epileptic son (9:24).

Turning now to the controversy story, we must note a surprise. In the Jesus tradition illness or disability is not connected with the sin of the individual. It comes as a surprise because in the Hebrew Scriptures illness invariably results from sin. God sends illness and heals:

> See now that I, even I, am he;
>> there is no god besides me.
> I kill and I make alive;
>> I wound and I heal;
>> and no one can deliver from my hand. (Deut. 32:39)

In Hebrew poetry healing and being saved (from sin) can be found in exact parallelism. That is, they are identical:

> Heal me, O Lord, and I shall be healed;
>> save me, and I shall be saved;
>> for you are my praise. (Jer. 17:14)

The pious Jew who is sick can pray:

> As for me, I said, "O Lord, be gracious to me;
>> heal me, for I have sinned against you." (Ps. 41:4)

The connection between sin and illness is so consistent that it is difficult to see what happened between the Hebrew Scriptures and the Jesus tradition. In the Jesus tradition illness and disability may simply have happened (leprosy, flow of blood, blindness, withered hand, epilepsy), or it may be due to the presence of an unclean or evil spirit (the Gerasene demoniac; see Mark 1:23; 1:34; 3:11). In the Mediterranean world illness could often be attributed to demonic forces. The early Christians were well aware of the pervasive nature of evil spirits in the Greco-Roman world. In 1 Corinthians 10 Paul argues that the problem of food does not involve idols, but demons (*daimones*) that were probably the spirits of the dead: "No, I imply that what pagans sacrifice, they sacrifice to demons and not to God. I do not want you to be partners with demons. You cannot drink the cup of the Lord and the cup of demons. You cannot partake of the table of the Lord and the table of demons" (1 Cor. 10:20-21). One does not find in the Hebrew Scriptures reference to this constant presence of evil spirits that could cause damage and illness. To be sure, some Second Temple materials attribute illness to evil spirits (4QPrNab), but they are few. So for most us it is not really clear why the Jesus tradition shifted from sin as the cause of illness to accidental causation or sometimes the presence of invasive unclean spirits. Nevertheless, Jesus demonstrated the power to heal and cast out demons.

This controversy story in which Jesus forgives sins almost stands alone in the Jesus tradition. It reads:

187

He said to the paralytic, "Son, your sins are forgiven." Now some of the scribes were sitting there, questioning in their hearts, "Why does this fellow speak in this way? It is blasphemy! Who can forgive sins but God alone?" At once Jesus perceived in his spirit that they were discussing these questions among themselves; and he said to them, "Why do you raise such questions in your hearts? Which is easier, to say to the paralytic, 'Your sins are forgiven,' or to say, 'Stand up and take your mat and walk'? But so that you may know that the Son of Man has authority on earth to forgive sins." (Mark 2:5b-10a)

We find the parallel stories in Matthew (9:2-8) and Luke (5:17-26), both adaptations of the Marcan story, of course. In addition, Luke has Jesus forgive the sins of the woman who washed his feet with her tears (7:47). Other than that, Jesus does not forgive sins. If we are correct about the insertion of the forgiveness story into the paralytic story, then actually there is no occasion in the Jesus tradition where forgiveness of sin connects with healing.

In a real sense the scribes or teachers were correct. How could Jesus forgive sins? Sin is alienation in the community: hate, anger, jealousy, theft, adultery. Forgiveness requires the reconciliation of such alienations. The Jesus tradition makes that clear: "If another member of the church sins against you, go and point out the fault when the two of you are alone. If the member listens to you, you have regained that one. But if you are not listened to, take one or two others along with you, so that every word may be confirmed by the evidence of two or three witnesses. If the member refuses to listen to them, tell it to the church; and if the offender refuses to listen even to the church, let such a one be to you as a Gentile and a tax collector" (Matt. 18:15-17).

Forgiveness occurs when members of the faith community are reconciled to each other. Now it all begins to fall in place. The forgiveness story occurred in the house of Jesus. Forgiveness (i.e., reconciliation) may/must occur there. They were all in the house of Jesus because that is where the new faith community brought their paralyzed friend. He was healed by the faith of his friends — a faith that could overcome alienation.

The issues here are monumental. Can there be forgiveness of sin without reconciliation? But there is even more. Does sin cause illness and disability? Or can they be "natural," or even simply accidental? Can health only come through faith and forgiveness, or can healing be achieved by medicine, drugs, and therapy? Despite the witness of the Jesus tradition, during the Middle Ages illness was considered a result of sin. It wasn't until the advent of the left wing of the Reformation that illness was disassociated from sin and medicines could be freely used.

Graydon F. Snyder

Eighth Sunday after the Epiphany, Year B

First Lesson: Hosea 2:14-20
(Psalm 103:1-13, 22)
Second Lesson: 2 Corinthians 3:1-6
Gospel Lesson: Mark 2:13-22

Literary context. No two commentators agree precisely on Mark's organizational schema. Nevertheless, it is helpful to place the pericope in its literary and theological context. Drawing on Patrick Flanagan's *Gospel of Mark Made Easy* and Douglas Hare's *Mark*, I offer this suggestion:

Jesus Stirs Notoriety and Controversy	1:40–3:12
Healing the leper	1:40-45
Five Conflict Stories	2:1–3:6
Paralytic/forgiveness of sins	2:1-12
Call of Levi/dinner with sinners	2:13-17
Questions about fasting/feasting	2:18-22
Picking grain on the Sabbath	2:23-28
Healing on the Sabbath	3:1-7
Great multitudes come to be healed	3:7-12

Our pericope, 2:13-22, contains two controversy stories and a theological rejoinder or explanation by Jesus. Situated in Capernaum, these events occur early in Jesus' public ministry.

Literary structure and exegesis. This is a complex passage that appears to be woven together by Mark from several traditional sources. This structure will easily support an expository sermon, treating each verse and then drawing out one or two overarching themes as you conclude. I will provide a wooden translation designed to highlight homiletical possibilities.

189

2:13: [Jesus] went out again (palin) by the sea; all the crowd (pas ho ochlos) was coming to him, and he was teaching them. The townspeople of Capernaum (2:1) flocked to hear Jesus by the sea and listened to him repeatedly. Contrast this with the hostile questions and attitudes of the religious authorities. Seminary students generally find it much harder to preach in a preaching class or in chapel than out in rural churches where "real people" are hungry to hear someone stand up and proclaim the gospel. Some congregations are like the crowds by the sea; others are extremely judgmental and critical.

2:14: And as he passed by, he saw Levi, the son of Alphaeus, sitting in the tax office [toll booth], and he said to him, "Follow me." And rising up, he followed him. This is the call of Levi. But who was Levi? Many commentators think Levi and Matthew (Matt. 9:9) are the same person. Walter Wessel, in *The Expositor's Bible Commentary*, suggests that Levi was his given name and Matthew his apostolic name. Others believe Levi was not one of the Twelve but was part of a wider circle of followers who remained in Galilee. This view is supported by the fact that Mark does not list Levi among the Twelve in 3:16-19. In any case, Levi was an unlikely disciple. A. T. Robertson's description is masterful: "An unlikely specimen was Levi (Matthew), son of Alpheus, sitting at the tollgate [telōnion] on the Great West Road from Damascus to the Mediterranean. He was a publican [telōnēs] who collected toll for Herod Antipas. The Jews hated or despised these publicans and classed them with sinners [harmartolōn]" (*Word Pictures in the New Testament* [Nashville: Broadman, 1930], 1:270). They were hated because they did business with Gentiles, were toadies for the government, and overcharged and skimmed money for themselves. "Sinners" is a generic term meaning the ritually impure who made no attempt to observe the law. "Toll collectors and sinners" is almost a formula for lowlifes, the ancient equivalent to "pimps and prostitutes" or "drug lords and pushers." In any case, Levi arose and followed him: *ēkolouthēsen* is the same verb used with the four fishermen in 1:16. When called, Levi dropped everything and followed — *went with* Jesus.

2:15: And it happened that he [Jesus] reclined/dined (katakeisthai) in the house of him [probably Levi], and many tax collectors and sinners were reclining/dining with Jesus and his disciples — for there were many, and they were following (ēkolouthoun) him. Many in this despised class were followers of Jesus. Perhaps churches in decline may not have enough sinners. Sinners have a way of attaching themselves closely to Jesus. To follow Jesus also means to recline and eat together. According to Jeremias, Jews sat for regular meals but reclined on pillows and rugs on festive occasions or to honor special guests. This suggests that Levi had thrown a banquet following his call (Robert Guelich, *Mark 1–8:26*, Word Biblical Commentary 34 [Word, 1989], p. 101).

Preachers might want to contrast this leisurely style of enjoying a meal with our contemporary habits of wolfing food on the run or while sitting glued to a video monitor.

2:16: *The scribes (grammateis) of the Pharisees (Pharisaiōn), seeing that he ate with sinners and tax collectors, began saying to his disciples, "Why does he eat with tax collectors and sinners?"* Mark thickens the plot with several vignettes. Jesus' laxity offends the establishment types. Every church, every denomination, has them: people who love to uphold the tradition and who raise their eyebrows and their voices when someone dares to break with it. They are custodians, keepers, of the tradition. And they are offended when Jesus is mingling with outcasts and reprobates. Jesus is not fasting with pietists, but feasting with the impure (which is good news!). The hawkeyed scribes (lawyers) of the Pharisees ask a barbed question: Why does *he* eat with these undesirables? Notice, they do not ask Jesus directly. Perhaps they are not so bold. They prefer to ask his followers, hoping to discredit Jesus or confound his followers.

2:17: *And having heard [this] Jesus said to them, "The strong ones (ischyontes) have no need of a physician, but rather the ones having illness. I did not come to call the righteous (dikaious) but sinners (hamartōlous).* What a refreshing approach. When accused, Jesus does not dissemble or cover up. He cheerfully admits the charge. You're absolutely right. My mission is to the weak, the sick, the infirm, not the healthy (mighty, powerful, well). Clearly, Jesus is employing a clever rhetorical strategy. They asked: Why does he eat with these people? He answered: I'm a doctor. Surely no one would deny that sick people need a physician. But when he adds the phrase about sinners and the righteous, he raises the ante. Now the questioners, and we, must ask: Which are we? Are we sinners, or are we righteous? Is his statement one of law (accusation) or gospel (comfort)?

In 2:18-22 we find a similar exchange. This time the issue is fasting, or rather the fact that John's disciples and the Pharisees fasted but Jesus' troops did not. People noticed this and asked Jesus about it. Note: in Matthew, it was John the Baptist's disciples who raised the question (Matt. 9:14). This means Jesus was catching it from the traditionalists and the pietists. Mark's version does not say who raised the question. Whoever it was, their question challenged the impiety and lack of moral seriousness of Jesus' followers. If they were serious (like us), they'd fast! Why don't they? Jesus replied simply, They can't! What do you mean, they can't fast? Jesus asked, Would it be right for the wedding guests to fast in the presence of the bridegroom? The answer is obvious. The whole point of a Jewish wedding was to celebrate the groom's great joy. The feast could go on for days. The guests' obligation was to enjoy themselves and share the groom's happiness. It wouldn't be right for them to fast, would it? asked Jesus. He'd outmaneuvered them again.

Jesus offers two more illustrations. You can't patch an old garment with a new piece of cloth. Why not? They're incompatible. You can't put new wine in old wineskins because they're incompatible. New wine requires new wineskins. Who could argue with that?

Once again, Jesus has bested his questioners rhetorically. They were criticizing the fact that Jesus was not doing the old thing properly, and Jesus says, in effect, "You're absolutely right. The new thing and the old thing are not compatible. I'm doing a new thing. It calls for a feast, not a fast, for new wineskins capable of holding new wine." Mark is a shrewd theologian. Jesus' answers also question us: Are we prepared to join Jesus' celebration of grace, forgiveness, justice, and love? Or are we trying to patch old garments with a little religion on the side? Do we truly see that the old wineskins will not do, or do we stand with the critics who find fault with this eschatological extravagance and the sheer joy of sharing Christ's joy? Those who fast instead of feast miss the point perfectly. The *Westminster Catechism* puts it succinctly: "Q. What is the chief aim of [humanity]? A. To praise God and enjoy Him forever."

Conclusion. This is not your father's Oldsmobile. Nor is this the messiah we expected. Jesus confounds the religious experts, the pietists, and those who walk by common sense and sight. Those who have right thinking (*ortho dokein*) often find that they are blind to the new thing that Jesus is doing in their midst.

Mark tells us in these short stories that Jesus calls not the righteous, but sinners. He communes with the least, the lost, with those who are weak, weary, and sick, with those who know they need a physician. Oh, taste and see that the Lord is good.

Stephen W. Ramp

Ninth Sunday after the Epiphany, Year B

First Lesson: Deuteronomy 5:12-15
(Psalm 81:1-10)
Second Lesson: 2 Corinthians 4:5-12
Gospel Lesson: Mark 2:23–3:6

Second Sunday after Pentecost, Year B

First Lesson: 1 Samuel 3:1-10, (11-20)
(Psalm 139:1-6, 13-18)
Second Lesson: 2 Corinthians 4:5-12
Gospel Lesson: Mark 2:23–3:6

The opening words of this two-pericope lection, "One sabbath," and the closing words, "destroy him," provide a disturbing *inclusio*. Though still in the early stages of Mark's narrative, we are becoming sensitized to the signal that is sent by the seemingly innocuous time-phrase "One sabbath." More than a mere literary device marking temporality, it is a conflict hot button. As was the case in 1:21, and will be the case in 6:2, Jesus' activity on the Sabbath provided a magnet of attention for the disciples, the crowds, the demons, and the religious leaders. What follows will be conflict in both the natural and supernatural realms, creating the reading experience of being jostled by tension, agitation, anger, questioning, power plays, awe, amazement, and unbelief. One thing is for sure: Jesus + Sabbath = Conflict.

Sabbath day observance and synagogue service are far from business as usual when Jesus comes to town, a fact which challenges contemporary services of worship which are stale, boring, and perfunctory despite the church's dual confession that (1) this is the Lord's day and (2) Christ is truly present wherever two or three gather in his name (most assuredly, we say, in the preaching and sacraments). Could the Jesus Mark insists creates Sabbath disturbances (an oxymoron?) wherever he is present be the same Jesus who is present with us? Who is threatened by his presence today? Who is awed? Who is prompted to unholy alliances for destruction? Whose authority is pushed to the breaking point? Whose imagination is stretched and strained beyond the old and safe categories in ways that demand a rethinking of Scripture, tradition, God, everything we thought we were doing for God, and everything we thought God was doing for us?

On the one hand, though, the case the Pharisees — who are first mentioned here in Mark's Gospel; prior to this, only "the scribes" (2:6) and "the scribes of the Pharisees" (2:15) are present when Jesus acts — have against Jesus is a strong one. As God's quality-control experts, they were only doing their job when they observed Jesus' disciples "harvesting" on the Sabbath. But their case was not airtight. Rather, it provided the occasion for debate, a customary and sometimes contact sport for rabbis. Deuteronomy 23:25 seems to side with Jesus' disciples: "If you go into your neighbor's standing grain, you may pluck the ears with your hand, but you shall not put a sickle to your neighbor's standing grain." Either the disciples' plucked quantity raised the Pharisees' eyebrows or they were operating from a stricter perspective than the Deuteronomy text (a "hedge around the Law"). Their assumption is clear: the Sabbath law has been broken, a serious infraction which carries the death penalty (Exod. 31:12-17). What is Jesus' excuse as their leader?

Rather than state case law, Jesus leapfrogs to a Davidic reference, something he will do later in Jerusalem to please the crowd and taunt the religious leaders (cf. 12:35-37). All other references to David in Mark are shouted to Jesus by fringe characters in the short span of sixteen verses: blind Bartimaeus shouts, "Jesus, son of David, have mercy on me!" and the crowds at the triumphal entry shout, "Blessed is the one who comes in the name of the Lord! Blessed is the coming kingdom of our ancestor David!" Such shouting of messianic assertions for Jesus emphasizes the prevalent hearing impairment to Jesus' identity.

But interestingly, Jesus' reference is technically incorrect. 1 Samuel 21:1-6 tells us that Ahimelech was actually the high priest during the episode to which Jesus refers. In the parallel texts, neither Matthew (12:1-14) nor Luke (6:1-11) names the high priest, which could be their way of correcting Mark by silence. If, historically speaking, Mark quotes Jesus correctly, then Jesus was either wrong in his citation or intentionally "gets it wrong" to tweak them in defiance of their authority standards for precision. Indeed, Jesus was not above deconstructing a text (Mark 12:35-37) in order to get a rise out of his opponents, which puts a different spin on our common perceptions of "What Would Jesus Do?"

The thrust of Jesus' response is contained in the two pronouncements which bring to a close the first of our conjoined pericopes: "The sabbath was made for humankind, and not humankind for the sabbath; so the Son of Man is lord even of the sabbath." The first pronouncement attempts to unhinge Sabbath day observance from the penally oppressive practice of Sabbath that had developed by the first century. Because of the accrued regulations for Sabbath keeping, the day arguably had evolved into an event which was more work to keep than if they had no day of "rest" at all. Moreover, Jesus' declaration of the Sabbath as a gift from God to humankind for humankind's benefit not only restores early biblical conceptions of the Sabbath, but also anticipates (even overlaps?) rabbinic teaching concerning the sanctity and meaning of the day. In his classic work *The Sabbath*, Abraham Heschel draws from both Scripture and the rabbinic commentary: "The art of keeping the seventh day is the art of painting on the canvas of time the mysterious grandeur of the climax of creation. . . . Our keeping the Sabbath day is a paraphrase of [God's] sanctification of the seventh day" (*The Sabbath* [New York: Harper Collins, 1951, 1999], p. 16). Law and discipline frequently threaten to eclipse love and delight, however, and this is what often happened in the near "deification" of the Sabbath law. Sabbath frequently turned from gift into curse. It is, however, the spirit of the law which must be retained, even in the strictest observance of law. The rabbis were often as passionate about understanding the Sabbath as gift as Jesus was. The ancient rabbinic text *Mekilta* 31:13 reads: "The Sabbath is given unto you, not you unto the Sabbath." Heschel comments: "The ancient rabbis know that excessive piety may endanger the fulfilment of the essence of the law." *Genesis Rabbah* 19:3 reads: "There is nothing more important, according to the Torah, than to preserve human life. . . . Even when there is the slightest possibility that a life may be at stake one may disregard every prohibition of the law." Heschel sharpens the point: "One must sacrifice mitzvot (commandment) *for the sake of [human beings] rather than sacrifice [human beings] 'for the sake of the mitzvot'*" (Heschel, p. 17, emphasis Heschel's).

Jesus not only calls the Pharisees to the best within their tradition for understanding the Sabbath, but he trumps the tradition by the second pronouncement: "so the Son of Man is lord even of the sabbath." Perhaps they accepted his argument from Scripture and tradition; they may have even agreed to disagree. This second assertion, however, would require their ire if they realized that "Son of Man" was a self-reference. It is only the second time Jesus has used the phrase in Mark, but it will be Jesus' favorite term of self-designation in the Gospel. Widely debated, its meaning must be tallied by the total disclosure of Jesus' character throughout the Gospel, especially over against the identity tags that others thrust upon him. At this point in the Gospel, the term has been used to designate authority in two powerful and threatening (to the religious leaders and their conception of God) ways: (1) the Son of Man has authority on earth to forgive sins (2:10), and (2) the Son of Man is lord of the Sabbath. The first claim sets Jesus up as God, "who alone can forgive sins." The second sets him up as at least the new David (if not God here, too) who, if necessary, can perform Sabbath bending since he, not the Sabbath, is the greater. Indeed, if the Sabbath is a divine gift, then the giver has the right to alter the gift as he deems fit.

Apparently, that same day Jesus went into the synagogue. The reader has become attuned (as in 1:21) to the equation Jesus + Synagogue + Sabbath = Conflict. The situation was tense: a man was in need of healing; Jesus the healer is there; and "they" (read: Pharisees) are there, waiting to pounce at the slightest infraction of the law. Jesus calls the man forward and puts forth the question of the day: "Is it lawful to do good or to do harm on the sabbath, to save life or to kill?" It was, of course, a debated point, and could have been construed as an invitation to argue the issue. Tradition did allow for the superseding of strict Sabbath observance in order to save a life, as we noted above from *Genesis Rabbah* and Heschel's commentary. The Mishnah, too, notes: "If a man has a pain in his throat they may drop medicine into his mouth on the Sabbath, since there is doubt whether life is in danger, and whenever there is doubt whether life is in danger this overrides the Sabbath" (*m. Yoma* 8:6). The prevalent prescription of the day appears to be expressed well by the synagogue leader in Luke 13:14, who was angry with Jesus for healing *unnecessarily* on the Sabbath: "There are six days on which work ought to be done; come on those days and be cured, and not on the sabbath day." The sense is that Jesus was flaunting his healing on the Sabbath, thus diverting people's attention to him and his work rather than to God and the sanctification of the day to God. This sense of "necessity" is key. It is what turned the Pharisees against Jesus. For Jesus it was necessary that the fractured be made whole, regardless of the day, perhaps even because of the day. For the Pharisees, what was one more day with a withered hand or demon possession? Better sanctified than sorry. For Jesus, what better way to sanctify the day than to overcome brokenness?

"But they were silent." The debaters held their tongues. For whatever reason, they did not dignify his question with a response, hoping instead that he would further defy them. And he did, in *anger*. The human Jesus is the Jesus that Mark portrays, and that humanness comes through most clearly in his times of anger and exasperation with people — Pharisees, disciples, and even those who come to him in need (cf. esp. 1:40, where the textual variant "anger" instead of "pity" is to be preferred as clearly the more difficult reading, but also in view of the context, wherein Jesus had just refocused from his runaway healing ministry and back to his "coming out," namely, "to proclaim the message," and is immediately confronted again by human need for healing; see also 7:1-23, 24-30; 8:11-13, 14-21, 33-34; 9:19-29; 11:12-14). "He looked around at them with anger; he was grieved at their hardness of heart. . . ." The Pharisees' view of "necessity," which kept people in their condition of brokenness for the sake of legal observance, Jesus interprets as the condition of "hard hearts." They were neither open nor expectant that God might do a new thing, a restorative thing on the day of sanctification. No longer stewards of the day for God, they were self-appointed owners of the Lord's day, the gatekeepers for what was right and what was wrong, what could and should be done and what was unnecessary to do.

Jesus' anger is frequently overlooked by Christians for whom such emotion is threatening to their preconception of Jesus as meek and mild, the always-kind and accommodating Jesus. But the rabbis would notice not only the incongruity of Jesus' unnecessary works of healing on the Sabbath, but also the problem of his anger on the Sabbath. Heschel taps into tradition again: "The Sabbath must all be spent 'in charm, grace, peace, and great love . . . for on it even the wicked in hell find peace.' It is, therefore, a double sin to show anger on the Sabbath. 'Ye shall kindle no fire throughout your habitations on the Sabbath day' (Exodus 35:3), is intended to mean: 'Ye shall kindle no fire of controversy nor the heat of anger.' Ye shall kindle no fire — not even the fire of righteous indignation" (Heschel, p. 29). When the day is deified, then defacing it by heretical activity and attitude is blasphemy.

"'Stretch out your hand.' He stretched it out, and his hand was restored. The Pharisees went out and immediately conspired with the Herodians against him, how to destroy him." Little is known of the Herodians, yet this comment by Mark foreshadows Jesus' warning about "the yeast of the Pharisees and the yeast of Herod" (8:15) and the linking of the two parties in attempts to trap Jesus (12:13). One way of construing this unholy alliance is to see that all powers, both religious and political, are already in alignment against Jesus, even powers that do not themselves ordinarily get along. Yet alliances between enemies often form when a greater threat to both presents itself. The enemy of my enemy is my friend, at least until the greater enemy is destroyed. The cumulative effect of Jesus' actions and attitude adds up to a need for all threatened leaders to figure out a way to eliminate him. Already by 3:6 in Mark's story, the seeds for Jesus' end are planted and the plot is under way "to destroy him."

Jesus reframes Sabbath as a gift from God. Nowhere in Jesus' ministry does he proscribe the Sabbath day or its observance for his followers. In fact, the implication in his words and actions is that Sabbath as gift will continue in perpetuity for Jesus' followers. There is an ongoing need for Christians to reclaim this gift and open it anew for their own benefit. Our freedom *from the law* as those "in Christ" has not resulted as of late in a freedom *to the law* and all its God-intended benefits for our spiritual shaping and maturation. Some Christian communities, in fact, practice a kind of new

197

and ironic legalism which functionally forbids Sabbath observance. Since we don't *have* to keep the Sabbath in the legalistic ways "they" did, and since there is danger of deifying it as they did, we don't keep it at all, and we persecute those who do as "legalists" or "fundamentalists." A new kind of antinomianism asserts itself, which flaunts our enlightened freedom *not to have to obey* the command. Rather than having a day every week separated from the others for the purpose of freedom — "a day of detachment from the vulgar, of independence of external obligations, a day on which we stop worshipping the idols of technical civilization, a day on which we use no money, a day of armistice in the economic struggle with our fellow [humans] and the forces of nature" — instead we often vulgarize the day and call that Sabbath observance. The Sabbath is not a day "to shoot fireworks or to turn somersaults, but an opportunity to mend our tattered lives; to collect rather than to dissipate time." Indeed, it was the Romans who anxiously sought after "bread and circus games" to fill their recreational free time, the ancient equivalent of our pizza and football. "But man does not live by bread and circus games alone. . . . The Sabbath is the most precious present mankind has received from the treasure house of God" (Heschel, p. 19). What would it look like to receive the Sabbath anew as a gift of God? The sermon on this text could explore creative ways that the Sabbath could be reinitiated into the church's life for its own rest and good, for the social good, for personal transformation, and for witness to the world as to who our God is and who we are as this God's covenant community. In other words, the sermon would explore the reasons for the Sabbath in the first place, as well as those aspects of the Sabbath which Jesus readjusted, with a view to renewed reverence, obedience, and expectancy. The broader issue in this text is the nature of gift receiving and law keeping. How do we receive what God gives, keeping the commands as gifts of God's grace and covenant, while refraining from legalism and power games. Deification of a law changes the law into something else, as does the antinomian reaction to strict law observance. The middle way of faithfulness to what God has given and to what God calls us to in obedience is reception without destruction, observance without manipulation. This is the live, tensive stance of faith, which recognizes the nature of Christian reception of God's gifts and observance of God's laws to be acts of stewardship. We are stewards of what God gives, especially those gifts which disclose God's and our identity and purpose in the world. The Sabbath gift cuts to the heart of identity disclosure on both the divine and human levels and thus became then and becomes now a flash point for theology, worship, and discipleship.

André Resner, Jr.

Third Sunday after Pentecost, Year B

First Lesson: 1 Samuel 8:4-11, (12-15), 16-20; (11:14-15)
(Psalm 138)
Second Lesson: 2 Corinthians 4:13–5:1
Gospel Lesson: Mark 3:20-35

This section opens with Jesus entering a house, possibly the house of Simon Peter in Capernaum. As Jesus enters, a crowd presses around and seeps inside. Mark leaves us to guess exactly what Jesus might be doing and how it involves the crowd. Whatever it is leaves Jesus and the disciples so indisposed as to be unable to grab a bite to eat and prompts Jesus' family to attempt an intervention. Perhaps Jesus is embarrassing them. They set out to rein him in, concluding from his behavior that he is clearly out of his mind. So what is Jesus doing in the house?

Thoughtful speculation about Jesus' activity might lead in any number of directions, but strong clues point in the direction of exorcism. Mark clearly presents Jesus as an exorcist, and his first detailed description of Jesus' public ministry involves an exorcism in the synagogue in Capernaum. Later that same evening Jesus drives out many demons. And just prior to the section under discussion, Jesus chooses the Twelve and begins equipping them not only to preach but also to cast out demons. And who could doubt that Jesus playing the exorcist before the crowd might qualify as the sort of activity that would prompt his family to question his sanity and give occasion for the teachers of the law to speculate negatively about the source of his power.

Calling Jesus' sanity into question was a serious enough charge, but the teachers of the law go a step further. While his family concludes that Jesus is quite literally "beside himself," the teachers of the law suggest that not only has he stepped outside himself, but something else has stepped in. Jesus, they say, uses the demonic to cast out the demonic. While his family may slander Jesus by questioning his sanity, the teachers of the law blaspheme the Spirit, the source of Jesus' power.

Jesus puts family concerns on hold as he responds to the suggestion of the teachers of the law. He points out what little sense it makes to suppose that Satan would cast out his own demons. And then Jesus further observes that even if what the teachers of the law suggest about him is true and Satan is so confused as to be pitted against himself, this nevertheless would be an indication that Satan's end is surely in sight, since "a house divided against itself cannot stand."

Jesus then moves to identify the source of this massive disruption of Satan's kingdom by telling a parable. Suppose you wanted to rob the house of some great big bruiser of a guy, a man with bulging biceps and rippling muscles. Only a fool would try to rob a guy like that without somehow taking him out of the picture, perhaps by tying him up. Only then could you go into his house and carry off his prize possessions. Through his story Jesus both acknowledges the strength of Satan and points to himself as the stronger one who has come to bind and despoil the strong one. The house Jesus enters is this world, and the valuables with which Jesus makes off are the ransomed lives of those he releases from demonic bondage.

After Jesus addresses the teachers of the law, Mark then places a saying on his lips which offers both forgiveness for the misdirected efforts of his family and stern warning to the teachers of the law. Human sin and blasphemy is all forgivable, but those who blaspheme against the Holy Spirit can never be forgiven. By coming to the settled opinion that Jesus' work was animated and empowered by the demonic, the teachers of the law placed themselves outside of the realm where forgiveness is possible.

Having addressed the accusations of the teachers of the law, Jesus now turns more directly to the misdirected efforts of his family. Jesus' mother and brothers arrive, and word of their arrival passes up through the crowd: "Your mother and brothers are here." Jesus gently rebuffs the intrusion of his family; looking around at the gathered crowd, he says, "These are my mother and brothers." In so doing, he acknowledges that the power of the Holy Spirit working through him not only works to despoil Satan, but creates a new family-like community. After his resurrection, the Holy Spirit would also guide Jesus' mother and brothers into this new family.

But Jesus' family and the teachers of the law are not the only ones who are less than excited about Jesus the exorcist. Many Christians today aren't all that excited either. Jesus the exorcist embarrasses modern Christians too. We have gotten comfy with the idea of Jesus and religion going together, but we wish he would stop with the exorcisms. "If you have to dabble in the supernatural, Jesus, why not do a few faith healings. Better yet, though, concentrate on preaching and teaching." We modern people know how to handle a teaching and preaching Jesus, but exorcism embarrasses us. Demons went out with the Middle Ages. We're inclined to agree with Jesus' family. People who begin to act like the world is overrun with evil supernatural beings belong in institutions.

And so we conspire with his family to have Jesus the exorcist put away. We move to leave that Jesus locked up between the covers of the New Testament. But getting rid of Jesus the exorcist doesn't make evil go away. Our world is full of examples that show that evil or something like it is alive and well. Some instances of it have led thoughtful Christians to once again speak of possession or demonization. And people who find themselves living and raising children in a world shot through with evil wonder to whom they might turn. Getting rid of Jesus the exorcist still leaves us with a world full of evil.

Maybe we have acted prematurely. Maybe we do need Jesus the exorcist as much as we need Jesus the teacher and preacher. Maybe it's time to swallow our embarrassment with him and take a second look at Jesus the exorcist. What can he tell us about our world? Can he help us begin to face the evil around us?

As lovely as the world may look on the surface, Jesus' activity as an exorcist points to hidden spiritual dangers, a world of principalities and powers that are forever busy, as the old hymn puts it, "striving, tempting, luring, goading into sin." Jesus the exorcist alerts Christians to the reality of a world of spiritual dangers. "Go out there with your eyes open," we hear him say. "Expect to be tempted. Realize that when bad things happen, evil powers may well have a hand in them. Don't naively suppose that life ought to be like a leisurely afternoon at the beach and then blink in surprise when some sort of evil explodes into the middle of your existence." Jesus announces that we live in a world held hostage by formidable evil powers, powers always on the prowl.

Maybe Jesus should not have told us. Ignorance is bliss. If it's true — all that talk about demons and demonic powers — our world is a less comfortable place than we often like to think. Talk of the demonic can be scary. "Don't be afraid," says Jesus the exorcist as he casts himself as the robber in his little story about binding the strong man. We don't expect to see Jesus cast in the role of a robber, but according to his little story, Jesus is the one who has come into the world to steal the devil's stuff. And if you look at what's happened throughout the world and down through the ages, you can see that Jesus has had quite a successful career in larceny. He has strategically begun to ransack the devil's house. Just look at all the millions of people Jesus has taken from the household of the devil and brought safely into his Father's house. He never could have done that if he had not first tied the powers of evil in knots.

True, demonic powers still haunt our world like hidden land mines on a tranquil beach. And yes, they still do a great deal of damage. But the parable of Jesus the exorcist in Mark 3 teaches us that our Lord has exerted his power over the powers of evil in our world. Jesus has tied up the devil and is busy robbing him of his hostages. And as evil forces seem to make their presence more obvious at certain times and in certain places, perhaps it is time for the church to reappropriate the old rite of exorcism in Jesus' name and to be sure that it includes renunciation of evil in its baptismal vows.

As those baptized into his name gather for worship, Jesus surveys the crowd. See, he says, these people are my brothers and sisters, these people free from the grip of the devil, these people who walk through this evil world doing the will of my Father. These people are my family. You belong to me now; don't let the evil powers frighten you. You're mine.

John M. Rottman

Fourth Sunday after Pentecost, Year B

First Lesson: 1 Samuel 15:34–16:13
(Psalm 20)
Second Lesson: 2 Corinthians 5:6-10, (11-13), 14-17
Gospel Lesson: Mark 4:26-34

Mark 4:26-34 consists of two separate parables (vv. 26-29 and vv. 30-32) and concluding sayings (vv. 33-34) that are part of the larger parables discourse in Mark 4. The first parable (vv. 26-29) is found only in Mark and is the first Marcan parable that is explicitly about the reign of God. But its point is elusive. Is the focus on the sower, the process of growth of the seed, or the harvest?

If the focus is the sower, it is not clear who he represents. One possibility is that the farmer stands for God, who is active in bringing the divine realm to fruition even if this remains imperceptible to humans. This interpretation is supported by the allusion in verse 29 to Joel 3:13, where the harvesting metaphor connotes God's visitation of punishment upon the nations. God's "sleeping" (v. 27) can be understood as human perception that God seems removed from human concerns, when God seems silent (Pss. 22:2; 35:22) or hidden (Ps. 13:1) or apparently needs to be awakened (Pss. 35:23; 44:23). But a further difficulty remains unresolved. How can it be that God does not know how the seed sprouts and grows (v. 27)?

Another possibility is that the sower represents a Christian disciple who goes about the work of evangelization, not always comprehending but allowing God's action to bring it to fullness. From this angle the "not knowing" is quite coherent with Mark's depiction of the disciples. There is also a connection between 4:26-29 and the Gethsemane scene (14:32-42), where sleeping and rising and incomprehension of the disciples converge. A difficulty with this interpretation, however, is that elsewhere in Mark the disciples' incomprehension is cause for rebuke from Jesus. Moreover, the part of harvester usually belongs to God or Christ.

A third possibility is that the sower represents Jesus. The seed that he scatters (as in 4:14) is the word. In its original setting this could be a parable of reassurance that despite present appearances, his preaching will bear a good harvest. His sleeping and rising has echoes in the subsequent episode (4:35-41), where Jesus' disciples rouse him during a frightful storm. This may also be an allusion to Jesus' death and resurrection.

In the setting of Mark's community, the parable may reflect their experience that Jesus seems absent to them during their time of present suffering while they await the parousia. The parable offers assurance that the process of growth toward the end time is proceeding according to God's plan. That Jesus does not know the timing of the end is not problematic in light of 13:32.

Other interpretations focus not on the identity of the sower but on the manner of growth of the seed. In its original context it may have been directed toward those who thought that greater human observance of the Law could hasten the coming of the messianic kingdom. The parable, then, advocates patience and asserts that the reign of God is God's doing according to God's timing, and is not dependent on human action.

One other possibility is that the emphasis of the parable is neither on the seed nor the sower, but on readiness for the harvest. The farmer may not know how the seed sprouts and grows (v. 27), but he certainly is not idle. He goes about his normal routines: scattering seed, sleeping, and rising. The sower monitors production first of the blade, then the ear, then the full grain in the ear. The emphasis falls on the farmer's ability to recognize the critical moment when the grain is ripe and at once the harvest must be reaped. This is the moment when God's time and human time intersect, when tranquil human rhythms are disrupted by the full manifestation of God's power and call for immediate response.

The parable of the mustard seed (vv. 30-32) at first blush appears to be one of contrast: a tiny mustard seed grows into the greatest of all shrubs. Botanically speaking, mustard does not grow to be the greatest of all shrubs, nor is it the smallest of all seeds; hyperbole is used to drive home the contrast. However, mustard seed was proverbial for its tiny size (Matt. 17:20). For some scholars Jesus spoke this parable to his discouraged disciples to reassure them that although his ministry did not seem to amount to much at the outset, there would come a time when he would have a huge, universal following. This interpretation of the slow but inevitable growth of the church as the locus of the reign of God was most popular in the nineteenth century with the rise of evolutionary science.

The detail of the sheltering tree has been interpreted in light of passages such as Daniel 4:10-12, where a tree with nesting birds symbolizes a powerful nation gathering other peoples under its sway. Similarly, in Ezekiel 17:22-24 Yahweh plants a cedar shoot atop the mountain heights of Israel, which becomes a majestic tree beneath which birds of every kind shall dwell. Just as Ezekiel envisions the end-time gathering in of all the Gentile nations, like nesting birds, under the sheltering embrace of Israel, so Jesus points toward the end time when all will be drawn into the bosom of the renewed Israel.

Alternatively, the parable may be a parody of Ezekiel's cedar with a comic twist. The key is in the contrast between mustard, a common garden weed, and cedar, the most majestic tree, as an image of God's reign. The reign of God does not have to be imported from faraway Lebanon, nor does it come with an impressive power. Rather, it is found in every backyard, erupting out of unpretentious ventures of faith by unimportant people — but which have potentially world-transforming power.

Furthermore, wild mustard, often regarded as a pesky weed, is impossible to eradicate once it has infested a field. So too is the tenacious faith of those who seem to be of no account. From this perspective another point emerges: the reign of God, like wild mustard that menaces the cultivated field, is a threat to the upper classes who live off the toil of the poor cultivator. Not only is the mustard dangerous, but also the needy birds it attracts can be destructive to the crop. The weedlike reign of God poses a challenge to the arrangements of civilization and those who benefit from them. This interpretation poses a disturbing challenge to the hearer: Where is God's reign to be found? With what kind of power is it established? Who brings it? Who stands to gain from its coming? Whose power is threatened by it?

The final two verses (vv. 33-34) are the conclusion of the whole complex of parables in Mark 4 and complete the framework opened with verses 1-2. Mark 4:33-34 reiterates what is asserted in 4:11-12: parables are enigmatic speech that cannot be understood by those who have chosen to remain on the outside. But to those who choose to follow Jesus, the mystery is gradually unfolded. One must decide whether to place oneself inside the circle "around Jesus" (4:1, 10) or to stand with the unperceiving outsiders.

Both parables in this Gospel present a number of preaching possibilities. The preacher would do well to focus on only one main point. One aspect of the first parable worth consideration is that God is the source of all productivity. In a culture where people find themselves caught in the webs of overwork, where increased productivity and increased profit are the supreme goals, the parable of the growing seed could offer an invitation to recognize God's grace that does not depend on human efforts. This parable could point toward a renewal of Sabbath observance, by which a disciple's life can be lived by a more balanced rhythm of sleeping and rising, working and resting. In this way believers glorify God by performing the productive work of the sower but recognize that the growth of the seed ultimately depends on God.

Another variation of this theme is that the parable of the growing seed, when addressed to poor people who labor mightily in the employ of others for bare subsistence, may offer a vision of eschatological rest. As in the case of the sower who does nothing to bring about the harvest, there will be no more backbreaking toil for poor laborers in the fullness of God's realm.

Another direction the preacher can take from the first parable is to emphasize the necessity of living the rhythms of Christian life so as to be ready for the decisive end-time moment, whether that be the end of one's own life or the parousia. A farmer cannot reap a good harvest if there has never been any seed sown or tended.

The preacher might also focus on assurance that God is at work even when the divine action seems imperceptible or unintelligible. In its original setting the parable of the growing seed may have assured followers of Jesus that the word he preached would eventually bear a good harvest, even if the beginnings seemed very modest.

From the mustard parable the preacher could also choose to focus on the locale of the reign of God and its manner of coming. It is not imported from far off, but comes with every small venture of faith by ordinary believers who act in the power of the crucified and risen Christ. Such ventures pose a challenge to oppressive systems of power just as mustard run wild can overtake cultivated fields. These kinds of efforts also shelter the little ones who, like the birds of the air, depend on God's benefaction for existence (Luke 12:24). This subversive power of radical faith, like mustard gone to seed, is impossible to root out once it has taken hold.

The final verses of the Gospel urge the preacher to make clear how important is the challenge that faces the hearer of these parables. They are not peaceful stories about birds and plants and rhythms of nature. Rather, they pose difficult challenges to conversion. The choice must be made whether to be included with the "insiders" who struggle to understand and follow Jesus or to stand outside looking but not seeing, hearing but not listening (4:12).

Barbara E. Reid

Fifth Sunday after Pentecost, Year B

First Lesson: 1 Samuel 17:(1a, 4-11, 19-23), 32-49
(Psalm 9:9-20)
Second Lesson: 2 Corinthians 6:1-13
Gospel Lesson: Mark 4:35-41

S ebastian Junger's book *The Perfect Storm* relates the fates of a number of ships during the 1991 "storm of the century." One ship in particular, the fishing vessel *Andrea Gail,* illustrates the peril of the seas. The crew of the *Andrea Gail* entered the storm of the century the way you walk into a room: one minute all was calm with light and variable winds, the next minute the sea began to boil, churned up by winds of forty knots, gusting to ninety knots. In just one hour the barometric pressure dropped 996 millibars and the waves had kicked up to seventy feet!

There comes a point when physics takes over. If a boat heads into a wave that is higher than the boat is long, it will get pitchpoled end to end to its doom. Or if a wave that is higher than the boat is wide hits from the side, it will capsize. The *Andrea Gail,* though a large ship of seventy-two feet, eventually met waves even higher, and so pitchpoled to the bottom of the North Atlantic.

Jesus' disciples were not ocean-faring sailors, but they knew enough to sense these same dynamics. So when one night a gale blew up from out of nowhere, it did not take long before they knew the end was near. Exhausted from a day of teaching, Jesus was fast asleep in the stern. So they awaken him and rebuke him for his lack of concern for their welfare. But then, with great wonder, they witness Jesus still the storm with no more than his voice. In the calm after the storm the disciples hear the unsettling question, "Do you *still* have no faith?"

In addition to being a memorable Sunday school tale, this lection is clearly a central story in the larger Gospel witness to Jesus. All four Gospels include some version of this incident. There's something so vital in this story that no Gospel could be complete without it. But it is not simply the eye-popping nature of the miracle that prompted Matthew, Mark, Luke, and John to insert this story into their Gospels. After all, there are any number of miracles that can be found in only one or two of the Gospels but not all four.

The Evangelists were not averse to leaving out miracle stories. But this miracle had to be included. Why? Many commentators say the reason is that this story is a vital vignette that teaches much about the life of the church and the role faith is supposed to play as we navigate the often rough seas of our life together in this world.

The wider context helps to make this clear. Mark 4:35-41 comes at the end of a string of parables (the sower, the growing seed, the mustard seed) and at the beginning of a series of miracles. The parables testify to the reality of God's kingdom in this world while also making clear that for now it is no more outwardly impressive than a seed — indeed, in the parable immediately prior to this passage, the kingdom is compared to the tiny mustard seed.

In these parables Jesus conveys that although it is the most awesome reality in the universe, for now the kingdom of God comes in whispers. The power of salvation is there, but outward razzle-dazzle may well be lacking. Indeed, in the parable of the sower the message of the gospel is so vulnerable that it can be snatched away by birds, choked out by weeds, or withered by noonday sun.

Following Mark 4 Jesus quickly performs several miracles: he exorcises demons, raises a little girl from the dead, and heals a woman who had an unceasing menstrual flow. Then in chapter 6 Jesus feeds five thousand people from a single loaf of bread, following which he walks on water and calms yet another storm. (This second calming may form the immediate literary frame for this section of Mark.)

Thus Mark 4 is surrounded by a remarkable set of contrasts. On the one hand, the kingdom of God, though powerful, looks weak to those who can only look at it with secular vision. On the other hand, Jesus no sooner says this than he performs miracles which reveal his cosmic Lordship. This simple carpenter's son somehow is able to tame creation, root out the demonic, conquer death, rout disease, feed the hungry.

But nestled right into the middle of all that is this little story. Once the storm had subsided, the disciples get chided for their lack of faith. What did Jesus mean by that rebuke? Perhaps he meant that by this time the disciples should have known that God was within Jesus. It wasn't simply that the disciples should have known that *of course* Jesus could have calmed the storm. True, following all the miracles they had seen up to this point the disciples could have known that with a mere snap of his fingers Jesus could end even the fiercest of storms.

But in Mark's Gospel the miracles of Jesus are never the key. Hence the Marcan "messianic secret" by which Jesus again and again insists that no one talk about his miracles. Jesus is the Messiah, the Christ of God, and his miracles highlight and underscore that fact. Yet Jesus does not want to reveal himself as the Messiah — at least not through his miracles. Again and again Jesus makes clear in Mark that he wants his identity to be revealed through his *teachings*. Because if you look at only the miracles without understanding the greater depths of Jesus' parables, you will misunderstand the Gospel and Jesus himself. What Jesus is all about is humility, self-sacrifice, a life of quiet service to the glory of God. Jesus has come to die, and all his teachings point forward to the cross. But if you remove the cross from your line of vision, then Jesus becomes only a cosmic Mr. Fixit, a Wizard of Oz kind of figure whose only purpose is to help you realize your heart's desires.

So when at the end of Mark 4 Jesus rebukes the disciples for their lack of faith, it is not their lack of faith in his ability to perform miracles that he is rebuking, but their lack of faith in being able to see that within this man from Nazareth the kingdom of God was hidden the same way a mustard seed is hidden in the soil. *God* was in Jesus such that the disciples could have known that storm or no storm, the boat was not going to sink! But just to show that even after Jesus' rebuke the disciples *still* did not get it, the last word in Mark 4 has the disciples exclaiming over *the miracle*.

For centuries commentators and preachers have seen in this story the lesson that life will have its share of storms. Believers are not promised exemption. In all the miracles that Jesus performed, he never claimed that just this kind of healing, just this kind of reviving of a child's dead body, would happen to *all* who believe. Quite the opposite, Jesus often predicted that disciples could expect trouble, persecution, hardship.

But in and through it all we are to remember that the one thing the world cannot change is the fact hammered home in Jesus' parables: the kingdom of God is *within* us. There is a curious line in 4:36 which says that the disciples took Jesus out in the boat that night "just as he was." What does that mean? In all likelihood it means that Jesus just stayed where he had been sitting in the boat most of the day. At the beginning of Mark 4 Jesus pushes just offshore in a boat and teaches the crowds from there. So when Jesus suggests they cross over to the other side of the lake, Jesus didn't have to move.

But there's something about that line "just as he was" that intrigues. Accepting Jesus "just as he was" presented the disciples with their greatest challenge — maybe it remains a challenge today. After all, the picture of Mark 4 is so humbly simple: there's Jesus, bobbing around in a boat, teaching parables that almost no one understood. Jesus never taught crowds from a fancy rostrum behind a bunting-draped lectern. No, his venues were vastly more modest — just an old wooden fishing boat with peeling paint, rusty oar holders, and ratty sails. From this little boat in the middle of a modest lake in a quiet corner of Palestine, Jesus talked about seeds and birds and trees, and most people went away scratching their heads and wondering when in the world they'd get to see one of those spine-tingling miracles they heard tell of.

The disciples took Jesus out "just as he was." The challenge was to look at this man and nevertheless see God. The challenge was and is to believe in God's kingdom despite a world so filled with storms. That's not easy. Yet faith believes that so long as Jesus is in the boat, then whether or not any given storm is quelled, the church will not be finally or eternally swamped.

Scott Hoezee

Sixth Sunday after Pentecost, Year B

First Lesson: 2 Samuel 1:1, 17-27
(Psalm 130)
Second Lesson: 2 Corinthians 8:7-15
Gospel Lesson: Mark 5:21-43

Mark combines two miracle stories — that of Jairus's daughter and that of the bleeding woman — into an intense, suspenseful drama with three scenes. As a unified narrative, the text becomes more than simply an account of two unrelated miracles; it becomes an announcement of Jesus' interruption of the social order and his creation of a new community. In his encounters with Jairus and the woman, Jesus shatters conventional social expectations and breaks down the barriers between insider and outsider, clean and unclean.

The first scene of this very Jewish drama opens with the note that Jesus has "crossed again" to the other side of the sea, having just performed an exorcism in Gentile territory (5:1-20). At the very beginning there is a hint that Jesus is crossing boundaries and creating new possibilities for community. Immediately upon his arrival, several key characters and a central conflict of the drama are introduced. A great crowd, which will play an important role later in the story, surrounds Jesus. Into their midst a prominent man of the community — Jairus, a leader of the synagogue — comes and throws himself at Jesus' feet, begging Jesus repeatedly: "My little daughter is at the point of death. Come and lay your hands on her, so that she may be made well and live."

Already, strange things are transpiring. In front of a large crowd, a leader of the synagogue risks humiliation by throwing himself at the feet of an itinerant teacher and healer. He places his reputation and status on the line for the sake of his daughter, who will die at any minute if someone doesn't heal her. This opening scene depicts the love of a father for his daughter (at a time when daughters were not valued as much as sons) and creates a sense of urgency (cf. Matt. 9:18-26, in which the girl is already dead). The scene ends with Jesus — and the crowd — going with Jairus, who is surely trying to hurry everyone along so they might arrive before his daughter dies.

The second scene presents an extraordinary interruption into this story, particularly if one keeps in mind the urgency of Jairus's situation. In this scene the action slows down, and Mark provides many details and much conversation (compare Mark's account to Matthew's and Luke's). First, a new character appears in the crowd. She has no name, but is described only by her condition: "Now there was a woman who had been suffering from hemorrhages for twelve years. She had endured much under many physicians, and had spent all that she had; and she was no better, but rather grew worse." The description is a kind of downward spiral which places the woman at the bottom of the social and religious ladder. She is not only suffering from a devastating illness, but she is unclean. In fact, she has no business being in the crowd; she quite literally risks her life by entering the crowd and coming into contact with others. She has been betrayed by the medical system, has lost all her money, and has only gotten worse. She literally has nothing left to lose.

Having heard about Jesus, the woman comes up behind him and touches him. Immediately she is healed by power that comes forth from Jesus. This unusual healing, in which Jesus appears to be a powerful, magic object, sets up the conversation that follows. The point is that the woman is *already* healed. Jesus could easily continue on his urgent mission to Jairus's daughter. There is no need to stop. Jesus' work is done — if physical healing is all that matters.

Jesus, however, stops and asks who touched him. The disciples, understandably skeptical, note that many people are bumping up against him in the crowd. How can he ask, "Who touched me?" But Jesus persists, knowing something extraordinary has happened. And the woman, possibly knowing she has been "caught," possibly fearing she will be punished for touching him and others in the crowd while unclean, comes before him in fear and trembling. The conversation that follows (as Jairus stands anxiously beside the road watching the whole thing!) marks the extraordinary interruption Jesus enacts in the social order.

The woman, first of all, tells Jesus the whole truth. Jesus listens to her story: "Once my life was different . . . ; began to bleed . . . twelve years . . . weaker and weaker; the physicians, oh, the physicians . . . ; no more money . . . ; worse . . . ; I knew if I could just touch you, you could heal me. . . ." There is great power in being able to tell our own story, and Jesus hears the woman into speech. (Jairus must be in an absolute panic by now, shocked that Jesus would spend time with such a woman while his daughter is on the verge of death.)

Then Jesus speaks to the woman and changes the world. "Daughter," he calls her. He restores her to the family of Israel, makes her once again a part of the community in which she had been an outcast. Echoing the love of Jairus for his daughter, Jesus suggests that God has the same love for this woman. In the presence and power of Jesus, the old barriers between insider and outsider, clean and unclean are broken down, and a new community is created.

Then he continues: "Your faith has made you well." The Greek word for "made well" is *sōzō*, which can also mean "saved" (*sōzō* actually weaves throughout the text in an intriguing way — see vv. 23, 28, 34). Something much larger than a physical healing is at stake; salvation is happening. And Jesus affirms the woman as an active agent in this process: your faith has saved you. No longer is she just a passive victim of the "system"; she has become an agent in her own salvation.

Finally Jesus concludes, "Go in peace, and be healed of your disease." Go in the wholeness of shalom, and be healed of your disease (the Greek word here is a narrower word for healing). Jesus sends the woman forth with a blessing. In the course of the conversation, she has gone from being a cursed outsider to a blessed insider. Jesus' words to the woman literally raise her from the dead socially.

During Jesus' conversation with the woman, people come from Jairus's house with the news that his daughter is dead. There is no need to bother "the teacher" anymore. Jesus, however, simply tells Jairus, "Do not fear, only believe." And having seen the faith of the woman and Jesus' interaction with her, Jairus has some reason to trust Jesus' words. The second scene ends with the stakes raised considerably. The challenge before Jesus now is that of raising the dead, not healing the sick. But we also have been given a glimpse of the power of Jesus and the possibilities of faith.

The final scene takes place at Jairus's home. The interpretive challenge revolves around Jesus' words to the mourning crowd (probably professional mourners): "The child is not dead but sleeping" (v. 39). Perhaps Jesus is making a theological statement. In the presence of Jesus, death has no more power than sleep. Or perhaps Jesus is telling the truth, and he really doesn't raise the girl from the dead (though the Greek verbs in vv. 41 [*egeirō*] and 42 [*anistēmi*], which are used elsewhere of Jesus' resurrection, at least suggest the possibility that Jesus does raise her). Or perhaps Jesus is misleading the crowd on purpose. Perhaps he does not want to be known at this point as someone who has the power to raise the dead. Such an interpretation would be consistent not only with Mark's emphasis on the cross, but also with Jesus' actions in the story. He only allows a few people to view his actions and "strictly orders them" to tell no one of what he has done. At the very least, Jesus' power to raise the dead remains ambiguous and hidden here. While Jesus' power over death and his own resurrection may be foreshadowed in this story, Mark leaves enough ambiguity to keep the attention focused primarily on the path to the cross.

By the end of the drama Jesus has raised/healed the daughter of Jairus, a man at the top of the social and religious ladder, and Jesus has raised (socially) and healed (physically) the bleeding woman, a social and religious outcast. The two are forever held together in one story and community (as the number twelve, symbolic of the Jewish community, suggests; vv. 25 and 42). As the drama began with Jesus having crossed the barrier between Gentile and Jew, the drama concludes with Jesus having crossed the social and religious barriers within the Jewish community. This social miracle deserves our attention as much as the personal ones.

Charles L. Campbell

Seventh Sunday after Pentecost, Year B

First Lesson: 2 Samuel 5:1-5, 9-10
(Psalm 48)
Second Lesson: 2 Corinthians 12:2-10
Gospel Lesson: Mark 6:1-13

Earlier lectionaries parceled up this lesson into two Sundays' worth of readings, much like Bibles with subtitles suggest it could be divided. The first six verses focus on the rejection of Jesus by his relatives and peers. The last seven verses address the sending of the twelve disciples out into the great big world. These two chunks of Scripture might be treated as separate entities, completely independent of one another. After all, they do have a very different look and sound about them. But just as Mark places them side by side, so modern lectionary planners sat down one day and determined that — Yes! — these two segments of Scripture should not be separated casually. The content of their message is connected. Let's have a look.

If Jesus can seem amorphous at times, or at least hard for the believer to imagine in concrete terms, Mark 6 offers a marvelous glimpse of his down-home humanity. We find that he is close to other people, engaging the passions of those who know him well. He has a hometown, a place of roots, a location where the neighbors are known by name. In this chapter we learn some of the most detailed information that the Bible offers about the identity of Jesus' family.

The tone of Jesus' reception by his family and "friends" is hardly warm. Their language is shaded with negativity. They seem to appreciate the results of what they see Jesus doing, even if it puzzles them in large measure. But they do not appreciate *him*. They do not accept *him* for who he is. In their negative assessment we get a taste of the challenging task Jesus will face in his ministry, all the way to the cross. We see some demanding features of what the full mission entails for those who choose to follow him.

The Nazareth townspeople are astonished by what they see and hear. "Where did this man get all this? What is this wisdom that has been given to him? What deeds of power are being done by his hands!" This astonishment does not carry an admiring tone. It possesses a sharp and skeptical edge. The pivotal verse in the text is verse 3: "And they took offense at him." They find it impossible to appreciate his merits. They reject him. The NRSV translation of "taking offense" may be too mild of a take on the word *skandalos*. The NAB has it: "They found him too much for them." The NEB puts it: "They fell foul of him." In our day we might exclaim, "Who is this wise guy? His roots are no different than our own!"

So from where does this lack of sympathy originate? Why the pointed language from a crowd that is said to include even his own sisters? Several possibilities come to mind. First, the reluctance of his own kin to hold him in honor may be either an inability or an unwillingness to recognize Jesus as the bearer of salvation. To believe that this particular one is God-appointed may just be too hard for the Jewish community in Nazareth to accept. How could one of their own, whom they knew from his youngest years, be divinely sent? If *he* is divinely sent, then so must be Bobby and Samantha and Zachary who live next door!

Second, the neighbors and relatives of Jesus may have been struck by some chord of irritability, knowing as they did from close observation many of the personal behaviors of Jesus. In our own day celebrities are best loved at a distance. In fact, their distance from admirers often contributes to their status. Would our public be as enamored with its most cherished celebrities if we had to share the same household chores and personal routines with them day after day and year after year? It's worth pondering if we're interested in contemplating the cool reception Jesus received from those closest to his upbringing. One can deduce from this text that a confident faith in Jesus Christ is certainly not based on any physical proximity to him. As we find out, it's based on a willingness to commit to his way.

The comment about Jesus' lineage — "Is not this the carpenter, the son of Mary?" — deserves special notice. Such a remark, which excludes any reference to a father, would have been very unusual in ancient times. Indeed, it would have served as an insult in Jewish society. It may be an indirect reference to Joseph having already died. More likely though, it's a slur upon the legitimacy of Jesus' birth. It has the smell of the kind of rumor that can float around irritated or jealous people.

Third, the rejection of Jesus by his fellow villagers may be a result of their overfamiliarity with his ways. If you know someone very well, it becomes easy to lose a sense of wonder for what he brings or who she is. You take such a one for granted. You assume the person to be capable only of what you're capable of. You expect ordinariness. How could Jesus possibly be as amazing as he seems to be when his own neighbors know exactly who he is and where he has come from. If an exotic wonder-worker is what the people want, Nazareth seemed to them like the last place in the world to grow one.

The lack of sympathy among Jesus' closest neighbors and family contributes a certain pathos to the story. His "own people" reject him. It isn't Jewish society in general. His own people fail to believe in him. Twice previously in Mark the family of Jesus demonstrates a lack of faith in him (3:21, 31-35). Now derision is added to that absence of faith. It's one thing to be rejected by people who don't know you very well. It's quite another to be rebuffed by your "own." Mark indicates that Jesus didn't fare well in their estimation. And though "he was amazed at their unbelief," he did not stop his work or stick around to argue. He moved on from there.

A preacher might want to explore what is meant in verse 5: "And he could do no deed of power there, except that he laid his hands on a few sick people and cured them." It's one of the most candid statements in the Gospels that seems to point to the limitations in Jesus. It's reminiscent of that confusing healing incident when Jesus touches a blind man's eyes, only to have the man see fuzzy-looking trees instead of people (8:22-26)! Is Mark connecting the power of Jesus here with the faith of the people? If so, their shortage of faith may explain the shortage of power-filled deeds.

Whatever is crippling his power in the Nazareth community, Jesus delivers a clear signal to anyone willing to listen — the work of the Lord is not easy. If he can be rejected so summarily in what should have been a favorable hometown environment, others can certainly expect more of the same in less hospitable regions. Jesus' personal experience is instructive. The gospel is often not a welcome word. Anyone bearing its message had better be ready to encounter a fair share of unbelief. Shaking off sandal dust on front porches and moving along from ungracious territory will prove to be very prudent advice.

To prepare his disciples for the toughness of the mission ahead, Jesus spends a great deal of energy outlining what can and can't be taken along. In fact, he has more to say about their luggage than about the mission message itself. One gets the impression that he is more interested in stripping them of basic necessities than outfitting them for an adventure of unknown proportions. Why the emphasis on such spartan provisions? Why all the prohibitions of standard suitcase items? The answer rests in Jesus' profound concern for the shape of his messengers' lives. If the messengers should get in the way of the message they bring, all of their goodwill in bearing the message in the first place will be for naught. In Eugene Peterson's contemporary language translation of this verse, Jesus says, "Don't think you need a lot of extra equipment for this. *You* are the equipment." Jesus' disciples are not taking a vacation. They are being sent. And there is a huge difference between the two.

Jesus seems well aware of the human proclivity to turn to possessions for security in uncertain times. When we do not know the precise twists and turns of every road in front of us, we have been known to use possessions to assure ourselves that we have a life. This is a particularly acute problem in our North American affluence of today. Provisions for the journey can substitute for faith if we're not careful. Jesus makes no peculiar call for asceticism here, as if provisions have no place in life. He just doesn't want people disappearing beneath the weight of their treasures when they have something as important as the good news to live and share.

The one thing that Jesus authorizes his disciples to bring along for the journey is a stick. Whether that stick's chief purpose is to propel their walking forward in the face of adversity, or whether its best use arises as a friendly reminder — to poke each other with every time one might begin trusting in his or her own self-sufficiency! — doesn't matter. The suggestion from Jesus remains the same: do not let rejection or yourself get in the way of the good news.

Peter W. Marty

Eighth Sunday after Pentecost, Year B

First Lesson: 2 Samuel 6:1-5, 12b-19
(Psalm 24)
Second Lesson: Ephesians 1:3-14
Gospel Lesson: Mark 6:14-29

The story of John the Baptist's confrontation with Herod Antipas is a grim reminder of the perils that injustice backed by power breeds. Yet this account is also full of lessons that God's people need to hear today, lessons about faithfulness and the cost of faithfulness; about the dangers of lust, self-deception, injustice in marital relationships, a leader's failure to acknowledge responsibility and the corporate consequences of his behavior; and about the cost of failing in these areas.

Most of us today prefer stories with happy endings, and in a sense the gospel promises us a happy ending for the faithful. Good Friday culminates in Easter Sunday, and we know that in the final judgment God will vindicate those who suffer for his will in the present. But Mark records the story of John not simply to direct us to our future hope, but to remind us that faithfulness to God often costs us something in the present.

Some of our hearers may be tempted to confuse the Herod of this account, Herod Antipas, with his relatives Herod the Great (the tyrant who killed the children of Bethlehem) and Herod Agrippa I (who executed John's brother James in Acts 12). It is important to distinguish these figures, though all three provide examples of exploiting power in unjust ways. Josephus provides us many details about Herod Antipas, including his notorious affair with his brother's wife.

When people involve themselves in extramarital affairs or other sins, they often rationalize away the consequences of their actions, and Antipas seems to have been no exception. The affair was unpopular, but most of Antipas's lackeys would have been wiser than to have reminded him of this. A prophet like John did not have the option of politically correct silence, however: under Israelite law, Herod was guilty of both adultery and incest. This was a breach of God's law as well as an injustice against Antipas's first wife, against Herodias's husband, and against everyone else involved.

Antipas was glad to listen to John (6:20), but he did not change his behavior; like many wealthy Greek patrons who paid philosophers to lecture at their banquets, he seems to have preferred being entertained by hearing a renowned figure to heeding that figure's message. That human flaw preceded Antipas's time (Ezek. 33:32), and we may suspect that it also outlived him.

What complicated the situation and probably forced Antipas to keep John in prison was politics: Antipas's first wife was a Nabataean princess, and when she learned that Antipas planned to divorce her for Herodias, she fled to her father, Aretas IV, king of the Nabataeans. Aretas took Antipas's unjust behavior as an insult, creating tension not only between himself and Herod Antipas but within the latter's realm: many Nabataeans lived in Antipas's territory of Perea and, in the event of a conflict, would have sided with the Nabataean king against Herod Antipas. But rather than dealing with his own behavior as the source of the problem, Antipas wished to prevent the prophet John from stirring further dissatisfaction in his realm. Prophets were welcome so long as they stayed out of politics — or at least what Antipas regarded as politics! Thus the tension between the two rulers grew, eventually (after John's death) leading to a war in which Aretas soundly defeated and embarrassed Herod Antipas. Only by Rome's intervention did Herod keep his kingdom, and Josephus declares that his subjects thought this situation was God's punishment for killing John the Baptist.

But even if Antipas could tolerate John personally while ignoring his message, some other hearers had more tender consciences. Josephus portrays Herodias as a manipulative schemer like Mark does, but Mark focuses on how Antipas set the stage for John's execution with his drunkenness, lust, and pride in front of others. Following what was then a non-Jewish custom of throwing a birthday party for himself, Herod got himself very drunk and had Salome, Herodias's daughter, dance suggestively before his male guests. Though Salome's exact age is debated, she was probably in her early teens. Whatever her age, she would have known that it was disgraceful for a female member of the royal household to have to appear in the male section of the banquet; in fact, the book of Esther told of a drunken Persian king who divorced his wife Vashti precisely for refusing to disgrace herself in such a manner. Though she was a princess, Salome was being subjected to degradation and sexual harassment!

But in Mark, the story of Salome represents a reversal of the story of Esther, with an opposite and terrible outcome. In his drunkenness, Antipas promised Salome the same thing the Persian king eventually promised Esther: half his kingdom, if she wanted it. Because Herod was only a tetrarch under Rome, he had no authority to give away his kingdom, so Salome went out to ask her mother for a more practical benefit. She had to go out because women banqueted in a separate section of this Perean fortress named Machaerus, as in many wealthy banquet halls of the day. (Herodias had not been able to watch the dance, but it was widely known in the ancient world that parties sponsored by the Herod family often included lewd elements.)

When Herodias demanded John's head, Salome added a detail that fit the banquet setting: she wanted it served on a platter. Herod reluctantly kept his word; his sins of lust, unfaithfulness, and swearing had trapped him. Antipas suffered for his sin, but John suffered more immediately for it. The present world is not always just, and it includes many innocent victims; but John was more than an innocent victim in this case — he was a martyr. By compromising his message John could have escaped death; by refusing to deny truth regardless of the cost, he became a forerunner of Jesus in death as well as in ministry.

Here is where the biblical story of John closes, but history offers a few more details that Mark's audience may have known. Mark focuses on John's faithfulness and Herod's depravity. But by calling Antipas a "king" (6:14), he may also provide a hint that he knows that Herod's lifestyle eventually caught up with him. Unlike Herod the Great and Herod Agrippa I, Herod Antipas was never officially a "king"; he was merely a tetrarch (Matt. 14:1; Luke 3:1). But when Herodias's brother Herod Agrippa I became king of Judea, she insisted that her husband Herod Antipas should also be a king. The title "king" was one the emperor granted only rarely to rulers under him, but Herodias kept insisting that her husband should petition the emperor for the title "king" of Galilee.

The emperor Gaius Caligula had made Agrippa king because they had been party buddies in Rome before Gaius became emperor. When Antipas requested the title, however, the emperor regarded the request as treason, hence promptly banishing him to Gaul, where he and his wife Herodias spent their last days. One can only wonder whether in the end they remembered the challenge of the prophet they had silenced.

Often doing God's will demands suffering. When we challenge popular forms of injustice or immorality, we often invite disdain and sometimes even persecution from those who prefer unjust or immoral lifestyles. John's courage provides us both a warning of the cost of faithfulness and an example of such faithfulness. His example is relevant for both the Christian witness of our hearers and our own task as stewards of God's message. Not all ministries require the same model of confronting culture John provides (Matt. 11:18-19), but all do require the same fidelity to God's message, even when it is unpopular.

But while later history sheds some light on Mark's story, the context of the rest of it teaches us even more fully the lessons Mark wished to emphasize. The verses that immediately surround our story tell us about discipleship. In this context Mark devotes only three verses to the victorious public ministry of Jesus' followers (6:12-13, 30), while discussing in much greater detail the suffering of Jesus' forerunner. This is because the disciples do not yet realize the cost of their ministry: the prophet John's suffering foreshadows the suffering of Jesus (6:14; 8:28; 9:12-13), which in turn foreshadows that of his disciples (8:31-35; 10:38-45; 13:13).

Yet this context not only announces that doing God's work involves suffering along with victories. It also reveals the frailty of the people that Jesus often chooses to follow him. Our story of John closes with his disciples performing the final act that would be expected of John's sons had he had any: they bury him in a tomb (6:29). This act took courage; in that culture, asking for the body of one publicly executed could at times invite the wrath of officials who had instigated the execution. The behavior of John's disciples makes all the more startling the later failure of Jesus' male disciples, who fearfully left that work for a courageous Sanhedrist (15:43-45). The example of John and his followers shames us when our own claims of Christian discipleship fall short of their standard. Their example summons us to a deeper level of Christian discipleship, and to consider which things matter most in light of eternity.

Craig S. Keener

Ninth Sunday after Pentecost, Year B

First Lesson: 2 Samuel 7:1-14a
(Psalm 89:20-37)
Second Lesson: Ephesians 2:11-22
Gospel Lesson: Mark 6:30-34, 53-56

These verses focus first on Jesus' relationship with his disciples, but this theme is quickly overtaken by that of Jesus' relationship with the crowds — the two foci of Jesus' Galilean ministry as Mark narrates it. Verse 30 is the only point at which Mark calls the disciples "the apostles" (meaning "those sent out"), appropriately since they are returning from the mission on which Jesus had sent them (6:7). Just as Jesus himself had sought "a deserted space" for his own spiritual refreshment (1:35; cf. 1:45), so he now invites those who have begun to share in his ministry as his delegates to do the same (v. 31). But just as Jesus himself had failed to escape the crowds (1:36-38), so in this case the extraordinary eagerness of the crowds to be with Jesus literally crowds out the spiritual needs of the disciples (v. 33). As participants in his ministry, they are subject to the same missionary imperative as he. The dire need of the people takes precedence.

These verses (vv. 30-34) climax in a potent evocation of Jesus' feeling for the people's need. He sees them as "sheep without a shepherd" (v. 34), an Old Testament phrase which pictures the nation of Israel left without leaders (Num. 27:17; 1 Kings 22:17; Jdt. 11:19). It relates, of course, to the common image of a king or national leader as shepherd. Some commentators think Mark alludes especially to Numbers 27:17, where Moses asks that God appoint a successor for him so that Israel may not be left leaderless, and God answers the prayer by appointing Joshua. In that case the phrase might evoke the idea of Jesus as a new Moses, the expected prophet like Moses, which coheres with the location in the wilderness (v. 31) and the feeding miracle which follows (vv. 35-44). But in the messianic context which Mark's narrative has created, it is perhaps more likely that the image of the shepherdless flock recalls Ezekiel 34, where God denounces the shepherds (rulers) of Israel for exploiting instead of caring for the flock, in effect leaving the flock scattered with no shepherd to search for them (vv. 5-6). Implicit in Mark's phrase would be a critique of Herod Antipas (prominent earlier in this chapter of Mark) and other Jewish rulers as shepherds who grow fat at the sheep's expense (cf. Mark 11:17). Also implied would be the restoration of the scattered flock, when God himself will shepherd his

220

sheep, searching, gathering, pasturing, and healing them (Ezek. 34:11-16). In Ezekiel 34 this is God's own activity (vv. 11-22), but God's appointment of the Davidic Messiah as shepherd of his people is also mentioned (vv. 23-24). This fits well with Mark's gradually emerging depiction of Jesus as not only the human Davidic Messiah but also divine (2:7; 4:41; cf. 6:48-50).

What identifies Jesus here as the true shepherd, the one who has come to restore Israel, is his compassion (v. 34). This is the good shepherd's attitude toward his flock (cf. Zech. 11:5: the shepherds of the flock doomed to slaughter "have no pity on them"). It is God's compassion for his people, enacted by Jesus. We might well expect Jesus' compassion to lead to a miracle, as it does in Mark 1:41; 8:2; 9:22; and in verses omitted by the lectionary (6:35-44), it does inspire the miracle of the feeding of the multitude (as also in 8:2). But its immediate effect is that Jesus teaches the crowds. It is spiritual leadership they lack and their spiritual hunger that Jesus initially feeds with his teaching. Though Mark records relatively little of Jesus' teaching compared with Matthew and Luke, he constantly refers to it and clearly depicts it as central to Jesus' mission. The teaching and the miracles belong together, in that in his teaching Jesus instructs the people about the kingdom of God while in his miracles he provides illustrative instances of its coming.

The theme of the divine shepherd of Israel showing compassion for his flock can also link verses 53-56 to verse 34. In Ezekiel 34 a key role of the shepherd which the rulers of Israel have neglected and which God promises to provide for his people is that of healing the sick, binding up the injured, and strengthening the weak (Ezek. 34:4, 16).

The enormous popularity of Jesus with the crowds, already apparent in verses 31, 33, is even more evident in verses 54-56, where Mark's narrative style effectively conveys the excitement and the magnetic attraction of Jesus wherever he goes. It is primarily as a healer that Jesus is popular. The desperate enthusiasm of the people to bring their sick to him for healing is, as far as it goes, a form of faith. That they begged to touch even the fringe of his cloak (v. 56) might suggest a magical notion of his supernatural power, but the story of the woman with a hemorrhage, which Mark has already told (5:25-34), illuminates this. Her touching of Jesus' cloak (5:27-28) Jesus understands as an expression of faith (5:34). So, if anything, the willingness of the people in 6:56 to be content with touching even the fringe of his cloak, confident that that will be sufficient, suggests even greater faith. (The "fringe" here may refer to the tassels [ṣiṣit] which Jesus, as an observant Jew, wore at the four corners of his cloak, in accordance with Num. 15:38-39; Deut. 22:12; cf. Matt. 23:5.) The faith manifested by the recipients of miracles in Mark is a very down-to-earth desire for healing and confidence that

Jesus can heal them. It is much the same with the faith Jesus expects his disciples to express in prayer (Mark 11:22-24). Whatever we say about the problem of unanswered prayers for healing and the dangers of raising false expectations and inducing guilt, we should also beware of pouring cold water on the simple, eager trust which Mark portrays in so many of those representative people who come to Jesus for help and healing in the Gospel. Readers of Mark should be able to put themselves among the crowds thronging to Jesus in the marketplaces (v. 56), carrying their sick friends, relatives, and neighbors to him with their prayers, begging his healing compassion for them.

Though some modern interpreters could wish that he did, Mark by no means plays down Jesus' miracles. They occur mostly in the first half of the Gospel (up to 8:30), which climaxes in Peter's confession that Jesus is the Messiah (8:29). In the second half of the Gospel the theme that Jesus as the Messiah must suffer becomes dominant, climaxing in the centurion's confession that the crucified Jesus is the Son of God (15:39). But this does not mean, as some have suggested, that Mark sets a theology of the cross in the second half of the Gospel *against* a theology of glory in the first half. Rather, he lays out Jesus' identity as the Messiah in two complementary phases. In the first half of the Gospel Jesus is rightly recognized, on the basis of his miracles, as the Messiah who acts with divine authority and power to implement God's rule in the world in the form of victory over evil, sin, suffering, sickness, death, and material need. The miracles demonstrate this in concrete instances of God's compassion for those who are subject to evil, sickness, and deprivation, taking effect in their liberation. It is important that this purpose of God in the messianic redemption Jesus is accomplishing be established in the first half of the Gospel, before the second half can show that the way to the kingdom cannot be solely through works of power but must also be through the suffering and death of the Messiah and his followers. Putting the healing miracles of our passage in this overall Marcan context can enable the preacher to indicate that God's ultimate purpose is redemption from all that oppresses and diminishes human life, that this purpose can take effect in miracles of healing today, anticipating the final coming of the kingdom of God in power, but that also, in Christian disciples' following of the crucified Jesus, God gives paradoxical meaning and purpose to some suffering. Jesus is present with us both as the powerful healer to whom we may bring the sick and also as the man of sorrows who comes alongside us in our suffering and helps us to bear its burden for the sake of the kingdom of God.

Richard Bauckham

Fifteenth Sunday after Pentecost, Year B

First Lesson: Song of Solomon 2:8-13
(Psalm 45:1-2, 6-9)
Second Lesson: James 1:17-27
Gospel Lesson: Mark 7:1-8, 14-15, 21-23

*L*iterary context. This unit appears to interrupt a series of miracles performed by Jesus:

Acts of Power:		
Feeding the five thousand	6:33-44	
Jesus walks on water	6:45-52	
Healing at Gennesaret	6:53-56	(frantic crowds pursue Jesus)
Controversy over Jewish tradition	7:1-23	
Acts of Power:		
Syrophoenician woman	7:24-30	(a Gentile)
Healing the deaf-mute	7:31-37	(a Gentile)
Feeding the four thousand	8:1-10	(set in Gentile territory?)

Mark's placement of the controversy highlights the disingenuousness of the legalists' critique. Jesus was wildly popular in the rural areas among the common people. No sooner did he get out of a boat than people recognized him and started running about, gathering the sick on mats and bringing them to him and begging him for permission to touch the fringe of his garment. These people were desperately seeking Jesus. And Jesus was well received by Gentiles.

In marked contrast, the Pharisees and some of the scribes from Jerusalem came as critics. These members of the establishment traveled out from the city to observe and investigate, perhaps in order to make a report on all the commotion. When they spied some of Jesus' disciples eating bread without washing their hands, they pounced on this technical infraction of tradition. This calls forth a powerful response from Jesus.

Literary structure. In its present form this is a controversy narrative between legalists, representing the tradition of the elders, and Jesus, representing the new order. On closer examination the passage consists of several units that are skillfully woven together:

7:1-8	Controversy with legalists over hand washing before eating
7:9-13	Tradition of the elders versus the commandments of God

7:14-16 Jesus calls the multitude and delivers an apothegm on
defilement

7:17-23 Jesus enters the house and explains the apothegm to the
disciples

Seen in this light, Mark was working with units dealing with ritual purity and tradition (7:1-13) and Jesus' teachings on defilement (7:14-23). These topics are related but not identical (see Robert Guelich's helpful discussion in *Mark 1–8:26*, Word Biblical Commentary 34A [Waco, Tex., 1989], pp. 360-61). Preaching on the tradition of the elders versus radical obedience to God's new order, for example, would not necessarily deal with what really defiles a person.

Unfortunately, the preacher's task is further complicated by the Revised Common Lectionary's treatment of the text. The ecumenical task force appointed by the Consultation on Common Texts chose to create a third option — a truncated unified narrative — deleting verses 9-13 (Jesus' example of how the Corban doctrine nullifies the fifth commandment to honor father and mother) and verses 17-19 (the first part of Jesus' explanation of the "parable" to the disciples). While not absolutely necessary, the omitted material gives a clearer sense of what is at stake in these controversies. The preacher should decide in advance whether it is preferable to read and preach on 7:1-13 or 7:14-23, or to include the omitted verses and treat 7:1-23 as a single unit.

Other exegetical issues. Verses 2-5. Some of the disciples were eating the loaves with defiled hands (*koinais chersin*), that is, unwashed (*aniptois*). The syntax suggests that Mark's intended audience does not know about the Jewish rites and defiled hands. The narrator explains that defiled meant "unwashed" and then gives a more detailed explanation of Jewish customs. The parenthetical explanation of the infraction suggests that his intended audience was not Jewish. In accordance with the tradition of the elders (i.e., oral tradition, not Scripture), the Pharisees and all the Jews never eat without washing their hands, always wash things from the market before eating, and hold to many other customs such as the washing of cups, pots, and kettles. A. T. Robertson, in his discussion of Matthew 15:2 in his *Word Pictures in the New Testament*, points out that hand washing before meals was not a requirement of the Old Testament. Rather, it was prescribed in great detail by the oral tradition of the rabbis, later codified in the Mishnah around 200 C.E. One washed one's hands before and after the meal, using clean water that was contained in cups and pots that were also ceremonially "clean." The statement that this was done by "all the Jews" appears hyperbolic. It was the Pharisees who strove to integrate temple rules into everyday living.

The NRSV says they "do not eat unless they *thoroughly (pygmēi)* wash their hands." Bruce Metzger notes that the word literally means "with a fist," but some copyists omitted it and others changed it to read *pykna*, "often" or "thoroughly." Others think it refers to the practice of using a cupped hand (Guelich). Years ago Wellhausen claimed, "No one knows what *pygmēi* means!" (Guelich, p. 364).

Verses 5-8. The religious authorities asked Jesus, "Why do your disciples not walk *(peripatousin)* according to the tradition of the elders *(paradosin tōn presbyterōn),* but eat with impure hands?" Here the tradition of the elders refers to specific and very detailed regulations handed down *(paradidomai)* by rabbis in the oral tradition, which was considered binding on observant Jews.

Jesus' response is both strange and noteworthy. He responds with a vigorous ad hominem on the questioners, calling them hypocrites and accusing them of subverting the commandments of God with their niggling legalisms. Was he employing the old adage, "The best defense is a good offense?" Or was he refusing to take the question seriously? It has the appearance of a genuine question, but Jesus peers behind the form of the question to the heart of his questioners. They are not sincerely seeking information. They are using a question to launch an attack.

Jesus cites from memory a verse from Isaiah. Scholars note that Mark has reworked this material to make the point that the legalists mistake lip service for heart service and human conventions for God's commandments. Jesus doesn't directly answer the question of hand washing. Instead, he attacks the premise of the hand-washing ritual, claiming that the questioners are holding to human tradition and abandoning the commandments of God. He answers their attack with an attack of his own: human tradition abandons and perverts the very commandments of God. This is a very serious charge — one that will preach.

Verses 9-13. The fifth commandment requires one to honor parents (Exod. 20:12; Deut. 5:16). The Holiness Code prescribes the death penalty for cursing father or mother (Lev. 20:9). Thanks to the casuistry and sharp practices of the legalists, a son was permitted to avoid the requirements of the commandment to honor one's parents by swearing an oath *(korban)* of "Corban," or gift. This oath was deemed to designate the property for a worthy cause, often the temple, thereby exempting it from the commandment to support a parent. Technically it was a case of giving priority to the specific oath over the general commandment. Jesus saw that this effectively nullified *(akyrountes)* the word of God. This comes from *akyroō*, to make void, as in canceling a will. A. T. Robertson, in volume 1 of *Word Pictures in the New Testament*, concludes, "The moral force of God's law is annulled by their hairsplitting technicalities and immoral conduct."

You do many things like this, said Jesus. In other words, this is a pattern to evade, pervert, nullify the commandments of God.

Verses 14-16. Jesus calls the crowd and delivers an apothegm: It's not what goes in but what comes out of a person that defiles. This appears to be the answer to the original question about not washing. We are not told whether the crowd understood. The disciples did not.

Verses 17-23. Jesus left the crowd outside and entered the house. Here he explains the defilement apothegm. The reason food does not defile is anatomical. It goes in and passes out without affecting the heart. Defilement is not caused by external forces. Behaviors defile, but the source of evil behaviors is one's heart. Jesus is probing the causes of evil behavior. Once again he pushes the disciples past the form to the substance, past the symptoms to the causes. If this be true, the parenthetical in verse 19 ("Thus he declared all foods clean") misses the point perfectly. Jesus wasn't talking about food. He was talking about hearts.

Homiletical possibilities. In addition to those topics already mentioned, sermons on this pericope might treat justice verses equity. Equity was developed in England as a way to do justice when the law provided no remedy. The Chancellor of the Exchequer, an ecclesial officer, could hear a matter and decide on the basis of equity or fairness when the law was silent. This eventually produced courts of common law and courts of equity presided over by chancellors. Jesus clearly has this distinction in mind when he notes how the law can pervert justice. The movie about the liberation of Ruben "Hurricane" Carter demonstrates the distinction between law and equity exquisitely.

Other homiletical possibilities might include: how God regards tradition, or the two sides of tradition, good and dark; lip service versus heart service; what really defiles a person?

Stephen W. Ramp

Sixteenth Sunday after Pentecost, Year B

First Lesson: Proverbs 22:1-2, 8-9, 22-23
(Psalm 125)
Second Lesson: James 2:1-10, (11-13), 14-17
Gospel Lesson: Mark 7:24-37

The Gospel reading for this Sunday is a pair of healing stories, each with an odd or troubling feature. In the first story Jesus seems to treat a woman seeking his help with uncharacteristic rudeness, and in the second he employs what might appear to us as strange or even offensive technique in healing a deaf man.

In the first story a mother comes to Jesus on behalf of her troubled but cherished child. She comes because her daughter's agony has become her agony. But she arrives at anything but the ideal moment. Jesus is completely tuckered out. He's preached out, prayed out, and peopled out. He's headed north and holed up in a safe house. Across the border he attempts to conceal himself from the intrusive crowd while on retreat with his disciples.

But someone or something has blown his cover. Careful as the disciples have been, someone has discovered the secret hideaway. There's a knock at the door. Outside stands a woman from the area, a mother, a Syrophoenician. She has come to see if Jesus will do something for her demon-possessed daughter. She comes to Jesus hoping that he might do something to heal her deepest sorrow.

Perhaps she knows it is a long shot. He's a Jew and she's Syrophoenician, and between the two stand centuries of bad blood. He is a man, she is a woman. She is intruding and he is tired. But for her daughter she must try, and so she knocks at the door and then falls at Jesus' feet. "Please, gracious teacher, please, please heal my precious little girl. Cast out the demon. It's turned our lives into a living hell." And she waits for him to answer. Her biggest fear is that he will tell her to go away or will be unable or unwilling to do anything.

She makes her request, and then Jesus delivers his troubling response: "It is not right to take the children's bread and throw it to the dogs." Now Jesus' words to this mother might lead us to suppose that he means to turn her away. Let the children eat first, Jesus says. It is not right to take the children's bread and throw it to the puppies. The word Jesus chose, a diminutive, is less harsh than it might initially sound. But placing the needs of children before the puppies establishes a pecking order, if not of persons, at least of tasks. Jesus' intention to instruct his disciples is a higher priority than healing the masses.

The woman must wonder for a moment precisely what Jesus' response could mean. Does he mean that for now he can only help his own, the Jews? Or does he mean that his time with his disciples is too precious to be distracted by problems like hers and her daughter's. He seems to be testing her with his words.

She acknowledges his right to set priorities even as she voices her confidence in him. "What you say is right," she concedes, "but even the puppies under the table receive some of the crumbs. Even a crumb of your power would be sufficient to do what you are able to do for me and my daughter."

Jesus expresses his appreciation of her answer. And though her answer is clever, he is not so much impressed by its cleverness as by the faith bound up in this woman's response. Her answer says I need you. I know you can do what I ask. Please help.

And Jesus responds to her faith by violating the normal order of things and casting the evil spirit out of her daughter. There's not even much fanfare in her case: he heals her without so much as lifting a finger. "Because you answered with faith," he says, "I have healed your daughter." He casts out the demon without razzle-dazzle, using a word extending over a distance. And the text informs us that when the woman arrives home, she finds her daughter resting comfortably on cool sheets. The evil spirit is gone. She had asked in faith, and Jesus had healed her deepest sadness.

People today still entertain fears of being turned away when bringing their deepest sorrows and agonies to Jesus. God might be available to prominent religious leaders, but when it comes to attending the prayers of religious nobodies, people are tempted to fear that God may turn them away, not do anything, consider them unworthy. And so, unlike the Syrophoenician woman, people may be inclined to not even take their problems and troubles to Jesus.

But should people today expect a miracle or be open to that possibility? God does sometimes respond to prayers for healing by working a miracle. God sometimes seems to violate the expected order of things in response to particular requests.

And yet there always have been those with strong faith and besetting diseases who were not healed. They asked for healing, but their disease progressed unabated. And in those instances we might be inclined to suppose that Jesus did nothing, turned them away at the door.

Yet even when God does not work a miracle of physical healing, Jesus always heals his children when they come to him. Sometimes he steadily brings them into closer and deeper relationship with him, giving contentment and peace even in the face of death. Sometimes he breaks the power of addiction and evil in their lives. Sometimes he heals emotional wounds. Even when he allows them to die, they are not beyond his healing power. Death ushers them into the great and final healing of those who go to be with Christ. When his children ask, he never turns them away at the door. Jesus never fails to give his children the bread of his healing power.

In the second story Jesus employs a healing strategy that could only be called unorthodox. Jesus has left Tyre via a circuitous route leading north to Sidon and then down to the Sea of Galilee in the Decapolis region. There some people bring an inarticulate deaf man to Jesus and challenge him to lay his hands on him and heal him. Is the crowd looking for a show at the expense of this deaf one? Jesus takes him aside, away from the crowd.

Jesus commences healing the man with techniques that stand in sharp contrast to the "word at a distance" approach in the previous story. He begins by putting his fingers into the man's ears. He then spits and touches the man's tongue. Presumably he spits on his finger and then touches the man's tongue. The precise nature of these actions remains a matter of speculation. Jesus seems to be making contact symbolically or ritually with the defective parts of the deaf man. Spit seems to have been regarded as having healing properties and may have been a familiar feature of certain healing rituals. But why in this instance Jesus touches and spits when at other times he simply speaks a healing word is unclear.

If touching and use of spittle were familiar features, the source and character of Jesus' healing ministry was anything but magical manipulation. He acknowledges the source of his healing power by looking up toward heaven, symbolically the location of God, and groaning or sighing. The nature of Jesus' sighing or groaning is also unclear. While Mark may not have had the Spirit in mind in recording this feature, it suggests the groaning of the Spirit interceding for those who belong to Jesus (Rom. 8:26). Jesus then speaks in Aramaic, *"Ephphatha"* (Be opened). Why Mark preserves the Aramaic in this instance also pushes the reader in the direction of speculation. Was the strange word meant to heighten the drama for his Greek readers? Perhaps the detail telling of this incident points to its unusual and memorable character or its degree of difficulty among the healings that Jesus did.

However one understands it, Jesus' efforts result in the man's immediate healing. He hears perfectly and now speaks clearly. And Jesus responds by urging "them" to silence: "Don't tell." But it is not clear who the third-person plural has in view. Clearly it is more than the man, but a smaller group than the crowd. Perhaps the man and Jesus' disciples or a group of his friends are intended. Jesus may very well enjoin silence to discourage the crowd from pushing his ministry in the direction of a full-scale healing ministry. But the amazement of those who witness the healing spills out, overwhelming people. Here is a healing sign pointing to Jesus: "He does all things well." The deaf hear and the mute speak.

This story may urge a certain amount of restraint in critique of those engaged in healing ministry. Strange healing approaches should not be reason in and of themselves for rejecting a particular healing ministry. And perhaps even today there are instances in which God makes use of certain ritual features that go beyond a simple prayerful word. Sometimes God seems to use a mix of conventional and unconventional approaches. There is often much mystery surrounding why and how God heals even today. While people may be inclined to value miracle healings in their own right, God wants people to see in them signs that point to the greatness of Jesus and the presence of the kingdom of God.

John M. Rottman

Seventeenth Sunday after Pentecost, Year B

First Lesson: Proverbs 1:20-33
(Psalm 19)
Second Lesson: James 3:1-12
Gospel Lesson: Mark 8:27-38

This is the hinge text in Mark's Gospel. With the fifteen-mile journey "out of the loop" to Caesarea Philippi, Jesus shifts his focus from the crowds to the disciples. Though they will return to Galilee, and to interaction with the crowds, this text begins a block of intensive discipleship training that leads to Jerusalem's threshold. Specifically, Mark tightens the lens to issues pertaining to Jesus' identity and mission and the implications for the disciples' identity and mission.

Structurally the section is the first within the blind-man healing frame,

8:22-26 and 10:46-52. This frame to "The Intensive Discipleship Training Section" functions, as one could argue all the miracles function in Mark's Gospel, on both the literal and figurative levels. On the literal level, those who could not physically see receive their sight from Jesus, a fact which suggests that the long-anticipated messianic age is at hand (cf. Isa. 29:18; 35:5; 42:7, 16; Ps. 146:8; Matt. 11:5; Luke 4:18; 7:21-22; John 9:25-30). On this level Mark's emphasis is that when the King is present, all subjects should be able to set their eyes on him and see him truly. The King's presence and the onlookers' future demand such sight. And indeed, miraculously they do see.

On the figurative level, Mark deploys the blind-to-sight stories as commentary on the nature of discipleship: it is a process of coming to see, to perceive, and to understand who God is, who Jesus is as the anointed one, and who we are in the light of his self-disclosure. The process is dependent, too, on Jesus' leading and Jesus' words and touches. Though Bartimaeus has faith, the first blind man is healed with no mention of his faith. For Mark healing is a divine activity. Mark ties healing to faith inconsistently. Our faith may attend it, but Mark hinges wholeness on God's work, not humanity's right response. (This point is made with subtlety in Mark 9:28-29 when the disciples wonder why they could not perform what was probably a routine exorcism compared to others "they" had performed [cf. 6:7-13, 30]. Jesus' rebuke, "This kind can come out only by prayer and fasting," reminds them, just as prayer and fasting remind one who submits to these disciplines, that it is God alone who is in control.)

Like the blind man (8:22-26) in the pericope immediately preceding the Caesarea Philippi jaunt, the disciples are starting to see, though not clearly as of yet. The blind-yet-coming-to-sight man can tell after Jesus' first touch that what he sees are indeed people, yet they are still as fuzzy as trees. So Peter will tell all that he perceives Jesus to be the Messiah, yet on closer examination his conception of Jesus as Messiah is blurred. Jesus' leading of the disciples is Mark's way of displaying the subsequent "touches" Jesus gives his blind disciples. Such "touches" come in the form of their being with him, seeing his work, listening to his words, and joining in *his* work. All these will bring greater clarity as to his identity and mission. Indeed, Mark sets up blind Bartimaeus (10:46-52) at the back frame of this "Intensive Discipleship Training Section" (8:22–10:52) as the ideal disciple. Bartimaeus sits for all to see at the city gate of Jerusalem. Though the world scorns him, in the gospel world Bartimaeus is the paradigm. For Mark it is the blind who lead the blind.

In 8:27-38, however, the disciples' vision correction is still in process. At this stage Jesus examines them to see what they now see after almost eight chapters of following and observing him. This "midterm" exam consists of two questions. The first is, "Who do people say that I am?" It seems an innocent enough inquiry, and as posed in the form that Jesus does here, namely, as third-person speculation, it is a safe, generic, abstract probe. "And they answered him, 'John the Baptist; and others, Elijah; and still others, one of the prophets.'" Every identity claim for Jesus says something about the one who makes it, that is, what that person "sees." Like Herod, those who believe Jesus is John evidence a strong belief in the resurrection (cf. 6:14, 16). If they are referring to Herod himself, they may also be alluding to Herod's paranoia about resurrection: he just can't shake this prophet who calls him to moral account! Those who believe Jesus to be Elijah show a good understanding of the tradition. They know that for the Messiah to come, "Elijah must come first." Jesus as Elijah is an exciting possibility for these, for, if Jesus were Elijah, then the Messiah would be just around the corner (cf. 9:11-13). (This is why each Gospel begins with John the Baptist furtively depicted as Elijah, for those who have eyes to see and ears to hear. Mark's reference to John's clothing is intended to signal the alert reader to Elijah's wardrobe in the same way that it did for King Ahaziah in 2 Kings 1:1-8.) "One of the prophets" is an enigmatic assertion that reveals the conviction that someone extraordinary was among them.

So far, so good for the disciples. In fact, the query to this point looks like a typical Christology class in seminary. Even though it takes some research, it is nevertheless a safe and sometimes even interesting exercise to rehearse, discuss, and debate what "others" think *about* Jesus. Sticking to what Schleiermacher, Barth, Bultmann, Schillebeeckx, and Soelle say about Jesus' identity and mission can keep the whole matter in the realm of theological gossip, safely distanced from the claim that Jesus himself makes on each person's life, heart, and ultimate allegiance. It can even become a new exercise in prideful, one-upmanship behavior, since GPA will determine the valedictorian of this Christology class.

Jesus, however, warned against such grubby ways of differentiating one another in his kingdom work (9:33-37; 10:35-45). Caesarea Philippi was not meant to be a continuing-education weekend in speculative theology or competition as to who the best student was, so Jesus turns to question number two, which moves the exam from the safe and abstract to the existentially demanding: "But who do *you* say that I am?"

What could have been a question for long contemplation, even hesitant and halting confession, Peter seemingly answers without so much as a hairbreadth of a pause: "You are the Messiah." Peter's completed exam hits the professor's desk first. But is he correct? Or did he bomb?

The reader of Mark knows that Peter is right, in a sense. We were given the punch line in the first line of the Gospel. But Jesus frustrates his students. He doesn't grade the tests, nor does he return them. Rather, "he sternly ordered them not to tell anyone about him." This command to messianic secrecy is, of course, a well-known feature of Mark's narrative and is in fact a strategy of Jesus' own self-disclosure, a revealing which must not be prematurely co-opted. His nondenial of Peter's assertion, however, appears to have been taken by Peter as an affirmation. In spite of the "stern warning," Peter apparently runs ahead in his own mind to the implications of Jesus being the Messiah. Simultaneously Jesus begins to explain to them his own spin on his identity. He couches his description, however — the first passion prediction — in terms of the "Son of Man" again. Narratively, this strategy functions in Mark as a way for Jesus to reveal his identity and mission free of the ideological baggage that the term "Messiah" brought with it. It is this ideological baggage and its imposition on his own person that Jesus tried to avoid by means of the "messianic secret" and the use of "Son of Man" as self-designation. For although the disciples seemingly had left everything behind to follow Jesus, at different points on the journey it became clear that they had brought with them certain "internalized nets," like a latent ideology of messiahship that conflicted with Jesus' vision.

Peter shows that he missed the subtle shift to "Son of Man" terminology. As Jesus begins to teach them plainly for the first time exactly what his mission entails, namely, that "the Son of Man must undergo great suffering, and be rejected by the elders, the chief priests, and the scribes, and be killed, and after three days rise again," Peter is appalled. It appears that from the moment Peter had identified Jesus as the Messiah and received his silent confirmation, he had also begun imposing upon Jesus everything he thought the Messiah ought to be and do. In all likelihood, Peter's conception of Messiah was grand and Solomonic in proportions — a kingdom of worldly might and power. (One cannot know, of course, from an historical perspective what Peter's conception of the Messiah was. As Jacob Neusner has asserted in *Messiah in Context*, at the time of Jesus the concept of Messiah was a "blank screen" upon which anyone could project his or her own fantasies or wishes. The backdrop that the Gospels portray, however, is the militaristic one which was at odds with Jesus' own portrayal of himself as the suffering servant Messiah.) So, when Jesus began his description of the suffering Son of Man, Peter saw it as an affront, and frankly, as a misguided and misinformed picture of Jesus' true identity. It is striking that even though Jesus was speaking in the third person and describing someone he calls "the Son of Man," Peter rightly takes the description to be about Jesus, the one Peter now "sees" as a mentally muddled Messiah.

But isn't Peter correct? Isn't Jesus the Messiah? The conflict that exists between Peter's assertion and Jesus' own self-description highlights the difficulty of confessional statements. Though seemingly correct, Peter's confession is actually dead wrong. One could say that Peter's mistake was in not reading the instructions before writing his exam. Though Jesus' question, "Who do you say that I am?" seems to lend itself to a simple declarative answer, even a fill-in-the-blank response, it is in fact an essay question. Simply to say "Jesus is the Messiah" isn't necessarily to say anything meaningful unless we know more fully what is meant by "Jesus" and "Messiah." This is why the ultimate answer to the question "Who is Jesus?" and "What is the nature of *his* messiahship?" can only be answered by the narratives we call Matthew, Mark, Luke, and John, narratives which concretely display for us Jesus' own life, words, and actions. The only way the disciples could have rightly answered the question was not by a pithy saying, creedal proposition, bumper sticker, or silk-screened T-shirt, but by continuing to leave their nets behind, including all the new ones they discovered they were still smuggling onto the discipleship journey, and follow Jesus all the way to his Jerusalem.

Because the identity question is so crucial and can only be answered narratively and over time, the church, the continuing community of Jesus' disciples, must return perpetually to these paradigmatic narratives of Jesus' self-disclosure. The Gospels have an ongoing iconoclastic function in the church's theological and ecclesial imagination, challenging the static formulations and abstractions of his identity and personhood which are devoid of narrative envelope. The creed needs the story to understand what it says it believes. Kierkegaard said it long ago: you can tell the Christians by their lives — concretely manifested human experience — more than by their words. Christian confession that follows Jesus' lead is incarnational — enfleshed witness. Words that tell the truth come out of lives that live that truth, that follow that Truth, first.

Peter's own actions subsequent to his confession explain what he really means, what he really sees and doesn't see. He appears almost to interrupt Jesus' first passion prediction by an action that could be construed as sensitive pastoral care. Having heard Jesus' self-description, Peter pulls Jesus aside to correct him — actually, more strongly, "to rebuke him." The star pupil senses his duty to correct the well-meaning but misinformed professor. But note that Peter refrains from embarrassing Jesus in front of the others. Jesus' conception of the Messiah and thus of Jesus' identity and mission could not be more at odds with Peter's own. Peter owes it to Jesus, to God, and to the future kingdom to help Jesus get it right. Peter here is the ambitious know-it-all character played by Holly Hunter in *Broadcast News,* who is told what was intended to be an ironic and corrective statement by her producer: "It must be terribly burdensome to always be the only person in the room who knows all the right answers," to which she responds as if understood by someone for the first time, "Yes, it is."

Jesus does not prove to be as pastorally sensitive as Peter. Interrupting Peter's rebuke, Jesus turns his back to Peter, faces the others, and rebukes Peter: "*Get behind me, Satan!* For you are setting your mind not on divine things but on human things."

To this point in Mark's Gospel the only characters to correctly identify Jesus have been demons. And now the first human being in Mark's narrative to get Jesus' identity "correct" is named "Satan." Peter's exam finally has been returned to him with the comment, "Though this exam appears to merit an A, I must nevertheless fail you because YOU ARE SATAN!" Why the accusation and why with such force? Because Peter is attempting to impose on Jesus who he ought to be rather than taking the posture of learner and listener that Jesus could disclose his identity for himself. Peter's narrative envelope for "Messiah" is the wrong story. Jesus names this posture boldly: "For you are setting your mind not on divine things but on human things." Peter's concealed nets, his latent messianic ideology which he never relinquished, reveal themselves.

Everything hinges on this. Everything is at stake here — everything that these people are, everything that Jesus is. If their internal landscape is not shaped and reshaped by God, and most specifically by Jesus' own disclosure before them in word and deed, then the kind of disciples they are becoming and the kind of kingdom they will lead will be merely human. This is why Jesus' demand and claim on them here, at the beginning of their intensive discipleship training, is for the cruciform mind-set. And it is a mind-set that is available to all who follow, not just those who appear to be closest to him. True apostolic succession consists of those in every age who continue the journey of the cross that Jesus first walked: "If any want to become my followers, let them deny themselves and take up their cross and follow me. For those who want to save their life will lose it, and those who lose their life for my sake, and for the sake of the gospel, will save it. For what will it profit them to gain the whole world and forfeit their life? Indeed, what can they give in return for their life? Those who are ashamed of me and of my words in this adulterous and sinful generation, of them the Son of Man will also be ashamed when he comes in the glory of his Father with the holy angels."

This text continues to make demands on hearers and readers. The Jesus of Mark asks each Christian and each community of believers, "Who do you say that I am?" The retreat to the safe, abstract forms of discussion *about* God, *about* Jesus, and *about* the role of the church in the world is little more than a contemporary avoidance strategy from the more crucial issues. Faith communities which carry it further and differentiate disciples by the greatest to the least on matters pertaining to "gossip theology" (i.e., "Who do *people* say that I am") perpetuate a different vision than Jesus'. The more crucial issues, the ones on which our very lives hang in the balance, have to do with the piercing and existentially challenging question that Jesus continues to foist on us: "Who do *you* say that I am?" An answer is required, and the answer will be judged with a broader criterion than mere doctrinal and creedal correctness. Remember: those most creedally correct in Mark's Gospel are mostly demons. The true disciples in Mark's Gospel aren't necessarily those who "speak" most clearly. Discipleship in Mark is first of all a matter of "seeing" Jesus and following him wherever he leads regardless of what you understand or do not understand. Part of the good news of this text is that Jesus *does* call Peter "Satan" but *does not* kick him out of the group of disciples. Six days later, Mark tells us, Jesus takes Peter, James, and John up to the Mount of Transfiguration. You could choose a safe route of discipleship where your goal is to never give Jesus occasion to have to call you "Satan." Another, more risky, form of discipleship might be to take the journey so seriously that you risk at every turn being called "Satan."

Tradition says the Gospel according to Mark is actually Peter's story related to Mark in Rome. If so, one of Peter's last acts of leadership, as arguably the lead apostle of Jesus' group, was to be radically confessional about his own failures as a disciple. Mark's story is the most explicitly revealing of the disciples' thickheadedness, and Peter leads the way. This kind of confession puts a different spin on the nature of kingdom leadership and apostolic succession. The claim this text makes is for the church and for theological education for future church leaders to do more than abstract "God-talk," but to extend the actual, existentially challenging demands of the gospel of Jesus Christ to would-be followers. Every theological assertion has a concomitant relationship to one's life. In addition, this text reminds the church, its leaders, and its teachers that Jesus ultimately is the teacher and the leader. The church's task, and every leader's and teacher's task, is the humble expectation and anticipation of Jesus' continuing lead and continuing self-disclosure. Kingdom leaders are characterized most clearly by the fact that they are, first and last, Jesus followers.

André Resner, Jr.

Second Sunday in Lent, Year B

First Lesson: Genesis 17:1-7, 15-16
(Psalm 22:23-31)
Second Lesson: Romans 4:13-25
Gospel Lesson: Mark 8:31-38

Lent is the season when the Christian faith dispels all illusions of a Disney World paradigm for life. Only a few weeks ago the church celebrated Advent and Christmas with songs and stories. We have been able to gloss over the slaying of the infants and romanticize the birth narratives. No such possibilities emerge from the somber final weeks of the pilgrimage to Jerusalem. Beginning in chapter 8, Mark is a Lenten book, recording the growing restlessness of Jesus and the increasing confusion of the disciples as they struggle to understand dark prophecies of suffering and death.

Following the gift of sight to a blind man at Bethsaida, Jesus begins to work on the spiritual blindness of the disciples. He asked them about the speculation as to his identity and role by those outside their land (8:27), and then about their own understanding of his person and mission. Peter declared that Jesus was the Christ, but what did that mean to Peter? The identity of Jesus has remained a subject of debate through the centuries. Not all Christians agree as to his nature or mission.

What might have been an exhilarating moment of discovery and anticipation was turned to foreboding by Jesus' declaration of impending suffering by "the Son of Man." The tendency of modern Christians to be critical of Peter's confusion and outright resistance to the thought of suffering and rejection for the Messiah is unfair. Jesus self-identification as "Son of Man" would seem to confirm Peter's declaration. The popular messianic thought of that period based on Daniel 7 and the apocryphal book of Enoch anticipated a figure who could bring judgment and punishment on the unrighteous and vindication of the righteous: "There came one like a son of man . . . and to him was given dominion and glory and kingdom, that all peoples, nations, and languages should serve him." The kind of Messiah that Jesus described was different from Peter's concept.

Jesus "began to teach them." Here marks a critical turning point in Jesus' training of the disciples. Mark used "began" frequently, but here we have the sense of an intensification of the instruction of the disciples and Jesus' increased anxiety of what now appeared to him to be inevitable. The time was short, and the disciples were unprepared for what lay ahead.

Mark writes that Jesus' prediction of his rejection, death, and resurrection was spoken "plainly." Mark wrote after the resurrection and wanted to emphasize that that event was a part of a divine plan that had been revealed to the disciples but not comprehended by them. Mark is not kind to the disciples, especially to Peter. Here Mark portrays an arrogant disciple who takes Jesus aside to correct his theology. Peter wanted to protect Jesus from himself. He might have been afraid that Jesus' public image as a Messiah would be tarnished by such statements. Christians today are still uncomfortable with the notion of a suffering servant Messiah or one that reveals a possible weakness. Rather than taking Jesus aside to rebuke him, many other Christians choose to just ignore the painful parts of the passion. Churches tend to leap over Good Friday, going from the grand parade into Jerusalem of Palm Sunday to the triumphant shout of Easter Sunday.

Peter the proclaimer of good news quickly transforms himself into a "Satan," adversary of God. Docetic theology is popular in an indulgent society where pain and discomfort are to be avoided at all costs. Just as there are those who want to deny the Holocaust, there are those who want to minimize the suffering of Jesus. It is easier to deny than to deal with the horror of evil. The Greek is forceful in verse 31; Jesus said he "must" suffer. Mark made emphatic that suffering and rejection were a part of God's plan for the Christ. The humanity of Jesus required the experience of unjust suffering. Of the four writers of the Gospels, Mark placed the greatest stress on the humanity of Jesus.

After his private conversation with Peter, Jesus called together all the disciples and "the crowd" that was always nearby. It was clear to Jesus what obedience to God would mean for him and for those who followed him. Jesus from that point forward made clear the cost of sharing his mission. Contemporary preaching seems determined to proclaim cheap grace that promises secular success and a life of ease to those who follow Christ. Jesus' words of warning are addressed not only to the disciples and the crowd present that day, but to "anyone" through the centuries who would follow him.

What did Jesus want them to do? In what way are followers of Christ to deny self? The great spiritual writers suggest that the path to oneness with Christ begins with the purgation of self. If we are to take seriously the idea that the "self" was breathed into humankind by God (Gen. 2:7) and was a part of the creation which God said was good, then we should tread carefully around this issue. The false self (or fallen self) is the self that comes between a human and God. A person must be willing to give up selfishness and preoccupation with self in order to discover the true self in Christ.

The "cross" was not mentioned in verses 31-33, and the connection of the two sayings may well be the editorial work of Mark. Certainly the connotation attached to the use of "cross" would be quite different to hearers or readers before and after the crucifixion. The cross could be considered in terms of criminal conduct, as convicted felons were counseled to carry their cross to the place of execution. One's cross might be one's sinful self, which could be linked to the renunciation of selfishness. As the cross applied to Jesus, it was a necessary part of his mission. Jesus bore his cross not because of his offenses but as a result of the offenses of others. It was a part of the cost of his discipleship. The history of the early church is replete with stories of martyrs who lost their lives (bore their crosses) in the service of Christ. Later, when James and John ask for special places in the kingdom, Jesus asked them, "Are you able to drink the cup that I drink, or to be baptized with the baptism with which I am baptized?" (10:38). In both instances Jesus invited those who follow him to a commitment that may entail suffering and death.

The generations of humankind continue to be "adulterous and sinful." The Jewish nation was one established on the scriptural codes handed down through the centuries. Evasion of the law was more common than obedience to the law. W. C. Fields, an early comedic movie star, was purported to have said that he studied the Bible looking for loopholes. That is a popular pursuit of those who read the Bible at all today, if public morality is any indication. It will not be difficult to make a case for this generation being "adulterous and sinful." Lent is an appropriate season to look honestly at the American culture that pays lip service to Christianity. Many professing Christians pick very carefully the arenas in which they are willing to admit their faith or talk about Jesus. The percentage of people who take Jesus and his teachings seriously is much smaller than that which seems to be embarrassed by him. This passage clearly states that there will be rewards for those who persevere in their identification with Jesus and punishment for those who are "ashamed" of him. The first Sundays of Lent sound notes of judgment, a subject most Christians would just as soon ignore.

The Gospel lection for this Sunday begins with suffering and sorrow but ends in hope. The "Son of Man" will ultimately have dominion and establish the kingdom in glory. The titles "Son of Man" and "Son of God" are somewhat synthesized in verse 38. Jesus, "Son of Man," will come "in the glory of his Father with the holy angels" to reign. The rejected suffering Jesus will return as the triumphant Christ.

This lesson is a troubling one for those who want religion to be the source of comfort and success. We, like Peter, want to take Jesus aside and tell him just to skip the ugly part. If, however, there must be pain, we want to leave all that to Jesus long ago and far away. We certainly do not want to entertain the thought that we might be any part of the problem, as was Peter. This is one of those passages that require reality therapy.

What is the life that most of us seek? Fame and riches, here and now, are the primary values of American culture. Pleasure seeking is the order of the day, and many establishment Christians are not ready to renounce the life they enjoy. How can you lead people to examine life and contemporary materialism and to consider the Christian alternative?

Raymond Bailey

Last Sunday after the Epiphany (Transfiguration), Year B

First Lesson: 2 Kings 2:1-12
(Psalm 50:1-6)
Second Lesson: 2 Corinthians 4:3-6
Gospel Lesson: Mark 9:2-9

The transfiguration story is strategically positioned in Mark's Gospel. The first phase of Jesus' ministry commenced with the heavenly acclamation, "You are my Son, the beloved one. I am very pleased with you" (1:11). At every point of his subsequent ministry this Sonship is affirmed, implicitly ("Who indeed is this that even the wind and the sea obey him?") or explicitly ("I know who you are, the Holy One of God!"). But with the announcement of the passion, a new phase in Jesus' ministry is introduced. The Marcan Evangelist must assure his readers that Jesus still enjoys heaven's favor and that his mission still has validity. The Evangelist achieves this by a heavenly endorsement where not only do we hear God again claiming Jesus as his Son, but we witness Jesus in the company of two of ancient Israel's greatest figures: Moses and Elijah.

Several scholars have argued that Mark's account of the transfiguration was originally a resurrection appearance story. In some second-century Gnostic traditions the resurrection of Jesus is described in language that clearly parallels the transfiguration account, for example: "Then a great

240

light appeared so that the mountain shone from the sight of him who had appeared. And a voice called out to them, saying, 'Listen to my words that I may speak to you'" (*Letter of Peter to Philip* [Nag Hammadi Codices VIII] 134.9-16). Another significant example is seen here: "What then is the resurrection? It is always the disclosure of those who have risen. For if you remember reading in the Gospel that Elijah appeared and Moses was with him, do not think the resurrection is an illusion" (*Treatise on the Resurrection* [Nag Hammadi Codices I] 48.3-11). The phrase "Elijah appeared and Moses was with him" comes right out of Mark 9:4. Yet this Gnostic text speaks of the post-Easter resurrection, not the pre-Easter transfiguration. There are other problems with the theory that the transfiguration story originated as an Easter story. Among other things, it has been observed that at many points the transfiguration account differs from the resurrection accounts found in the New Testament Gospels. It is not at all clear that the earliest accounts of Jesus' resurrection involved the kind of luminosity depicted in the transfiguration.

There are many features about the transfiguration that have led commentators to conclude that this episode is intended to have some sort of typological connection to Exodus 24 and 33–34, passages which describe Moses' ascent up Mount Sinai where he meets God and then descends with the tablets of the Law and with a shining face. The following specific parallels between Mark's account (9:2-8) and Exodus are evident: (1) the reference to "six days" (Mark 9:2; Exod. 24:16), (2) the cloud that covers the mountain (Mark 9:7; Exod. 24:16), (3) God's voice from the cloud (Mark 9:7; Exod. 24:16), (4) three companions (Mark 9:2; Exod. 24:1, 9), (5) a transformed appearance (Mark 9:3; Exod. 34:30), and (6) the reaction of fear (Mark 9:6; Exod. 34:30). Another suggestive item that should be mentioned is that in Exodus 24:13 Joshua is singled out and taken up the mountain with Moses. Since "Joshua" in the Greek Old Testament is frequently rendered "Jesus," the early church may have seen in Exodus 24:13 a veiled prophecy, or typology, that came to fulfillment in the transfiguration, where once again Moses and Jesus are together.

According to Mark, Jesus "was transfigured" *(metemorphōthē)* and his "clothing glistened and became exceedingly white" (vv. 2-3). The closest parallel is probably to the shining face of Moses (Exod. 34:30), but the faces of other saints are described as shining (see 2 Esdr. 7:97, 125; *1 Enoch* 37:7; 51:5; compare Luke 9:29, which specifically mentions Jesus' face). The clothing of the saints also will shine (see Dan. 12:3; Rev. 4:4; 7:9; *1 Enoch* 62:15; *Eccles. Rab.* 1:7, 9: "he will renew their faces and will renew their garments"). In one tradition it is said that when Elijah was born, "men of shining white appear-

241

ance greeted him and wrapped him in fire" (*Lives of the Prophets* 21.2). There are stories of transfigurations of the Greco-Roman gods. One thinks of Demeter, whose transfigured person filled a house with light (*Homeric Hymns* 2.275-80).

Mark's depiction of Jesus is also reminiscent of Daniel's vision of the "Ancient of Days," whose "clothing was white as snow, / and the hair of his head like pure wool" (Dan. 7:9). The "one like a son of man" approaches the Ancient of Days (i.e., God) and receives authority and kingdom (Dan. 7:13-14). Perhaps in his transformation we should understand that Jesus, as the Son of Man, has taken on some of the characteristics of the Ancient of Days when in his presence (much as Moses' face begins to shine with God's glory). If this is correct, then the transfiguration should be understood as a visual verification of Jesus' claim to be the Son of Man who will come in the glory of his Father with the holy angels (see Mark 8:38; Dan. 7:10).

Moses and Elijah are said to have appeared and to have spoken to Jesus (v. 4). These two are often paired up. The two witnesses of Revelation 11:3-12 could very well be Moses and Elijah (on Moses compare v. 6 with Exod. 7:17, 19; on Elijah compare vv. 5-6 with 2 Kings 1:10). (However, Elijah is sometimes paired up with Enoch; see 2 Esdr. 6:26; *Apoc. of Elijah* 4:7-19, which appears to be dependent on Rev. 11.) According to one rabbinic midrash, God promises in the future to bring Moses with Elijah (*Deut. Rab.* 3:17 [on Deut. 10:1]). The rabbis compared Moses and Elijah at many points: "You find that two prophets rose up for Israel out of the tribe of Levi; one the first of all the prophets, and the other the last of all the prophets: Moses first and Elijah last, and both with a commission to redeem Israel. . . . You find that Moses and Elijah were alike in every respect. . . . Moses went up to heaven [cf. Exod. 19:3]; and Elijah went up to heaven [cf. 2 Kings 2:1]. . . . Moses: 'And the cloud covered him six days' [Exod. 24:16]; and Elijah went up in a whirlwind [cf. 2 Kings 2:1]" (*Pesiq. R.* 4.2). This rabbinic comparison is probably an elaboration of older traditions in which Moses and Elijah were believed to be involved in some way with the last days.

It is likely that Peter had concluded that the last day had arrived when some of the great events of the first exodus would be repeated (such as manna in the wilderness and God's presence among the people). To commemorate the exodus Jews celebrated the Feast of Booths by living in small booths or huts for seven days (Lev. 23:42-44; Neh. 8:14-17). But the feast was also understood by many as looking ahead to the glorious day of Israel's deliverance.

The heavenly voice interrupts Peter (Mark 9:7) and may be partially intended as a rebuke (i.e., "listen to Jesus, not to Moses or Elijah"). The time of

Moses and Elijah is over. It is time to heed the words of Jesus. The heavenly voice recalls the words uttered at the time of Jesus' baptism (1:10-11) and serves as a second divine endorsement: Jesus' talk of rejection and death has not disqualified him from his messianic task. He is still God's Son, and his message, now placed in a new light, must still be heeded.

Craig A. Evans

Eighteenth Sunday after Pentecost, Year B

First Lesson: Proverbs 31:10-31
(Psalm 1)
Second Lesson: James 3:13–4:3, 7-8a
Gospel Lesson: Mark 9:30-37

Preachers get attracted to this text because of the close attention Jesus gives children. Let's face it: when life does not run smoothly, or evil rears its ugly head, or prideful behavior gets the best of us adult types, there are always children to turn to for rejuvenating the human spirit and restoring confidence in the human race. Or so we figure. To hear the Lord focusing special attention on little children catches our fancy. A certain contentment settles over us as we contemplate the beauty of God creating children. It's an attractive thought to our ears.

But any interpretation of this passage should avoid all quick contentment, just as it ought to skip right past any thoughts that border on sentimentality for children. When Jesus embraces a child and plops the little one in the midst of his disciples, he is not glorifying childhood. There is no mention of anything resembling sweetness, tender eyes, or childlike innocence. Not in this passage anyway. At issue for Jesus here is the reversal of values that constitute the kingdom of God. Whereas adults possess all sorts of abilities to give, to rank, and to control, children have none of these. They are first and foremost *receivers* in life, and powerless ones at that. To welcome such helpless ones, whose very life depends on the gift of being able to receive life from others, is to welcome Jesus. While the disciples are busy strategizing over the topic of personal greatness, Jesus presents them with a new flowchart for organizing the kingdom of God. And children are at the top of the chart!

It is well known that children in the ancient world did not fare well when it came to respect. They did not count for much. It wasn't because parents forgot to love them, but because children had no legal status. They also had no productive capabilities, at least as the world tended to measure productivity. In the Greco-Roman world, children were the least-valued members of society. A father had the right to punish, sell, pawn off, or even kill his own child. Treatment of children in the Jewish community was more positive. But even there, Jewish children could be diminished socially and religiously. In Mark 10:13-16 we find the disciples shooing children away from Jesus and Jesus getting irate over their action. In the Judaism of our own day, children are not required to adhere to the commandments before the bar mitzvah (twelve years), since they are not considered mature.

Attitudes toward children have improved markedly over the centuries. But one thing has remained very much the same. We still view children as apprentices "on the way to" full humanity. We're always training them to be something for the future rather than appreciating them for the blessing they already are. One cannot be a full human being, a complete citizen, a respectable contributor to society — our adult reasoning assumes — until adulthood. Even the apostle Paul noted the devalued nature of childhood. "When I was a child, I thought and acted like a child . . . but when I became a man [a full human being], I put away childish ways."

In a house in Capernaum Jesus engages the hearts and minds of the disciples on this subject of receiving children (v. 33). Whenever he ends up in a house alone with the disciples, we can be pretty sure that a moment of personal instruction is at hand. Evidently, togetherness inside a house provided both the ideal time and place to gain their undivided attention, free from the distracting pressures on the outside. The disciples were silent on this particular day, having just argued over who among them was the greatest.

In preparing to preach on this text, time would be well spent contemplating this silence among the disciples. It's a strange thought to consider a group of adults who are busy one minute playing a talkative game of "who's more significant?" yet completely silent the next minute. What's behind their silence? Is it shame for being caught in the act of bantering about greatness? Is it embarrassment over the silliness of never having outgrown their childhood bragging instincts? Is it disgust for their willingness to argue in self-aggrandizing ways instead of pondering why God would allow the Messiah to suffer and die (v. 31)? Whatever it is, we get the impression that they were talking along the road in the language of "asides," complete with private remarks about being in the limelight, when Jesus calls their bluff, catching them in the midst of this ruthless ambition.

The conversation the disciples had regarding greatness is familiar human behavior. Who hasn't dreamed about praise or fame, if even for a fleeting moment? It's part of the human condition. We are all shareholders in the global business of an inferiority complex. Besides, we get little tastes of glory every now and then when life runs our way. And we easily misconstrue that glory for honor. James and John, to note two immediate examples, were convinced that their special audience with Jesus on the Mount of Transfiguration constituted unusual status. Fresh from that oxygen-thin experience, they were certain of their seat locations to the right and the left of the throne. And Peter, who had boasted of sufficient faith for walking across water, was not to be outdone on the pride front. These disciples and others, complete with all their desire for greatness, were the ones Jesus addressed in the strangeness of that silent circle.

"Whoever wants to be first must be last of all and servant of all." When Jesus breaks the silence and initiates instruction on this truth, he repackages the language of desire into the vocabulary of requirement. It all points to the creation of a new community with altered priorities. This new community would be one where the least of humankind would count. And the least would not only count, they would be embraced. Jesus hooks his disciples' interest in desiring greater things by using the verb "want" — "Whoever *wants* to be first. . . ." But in so highlighting the desire for greatness, Jesus specifies a requirement for smallness — "[that one] *must* be last of all." And lest the disciples interpret being "last" as some easy maneuver, some self-deprecating behavior, Jesus attaches an "and": "*and* [that one] must be servant of all." Jesus tacks on this expression of outward service as a *must*, to ensure that his people will not distort the truth and blessing of new community, twisting it to their own ambitious ends.

Note that Jesus does not shy away from the concept of rank. As far as God is concerned, there is a rightful place for rank. It's just that the ordering of such things as rank and status has been flipped upside down with the servant Jesus now scheduled for death, and the child now labeled as central. The Greek origins for the words "child" and "servant" share a common root. They can mean the same thing. And what do they have in common? Both a child and a servant live life on the receiving end of things. Neither one possesses, to any notable degree at least, the power of being able to give — a power that most of us take for granted. When we possess the power to give, we also hold the power to control. Whether we give someone a compliment

245

or a raise, whether we give that person medicine or advice, we are fundamentally in a position of control as we deliver these goods.

Children catch the eye of Jesus because they lack this capacity to control situations. It's not part of their daily experience. Like servants, children do not get to dictate the terms for living. They are (and in the first century they most certainly were) dependent, helpless, and nonproductive beings. Little children cannot employ you, they cannot drive you to soccer games, they cannot lend you money. Quite explicitly, children live in a receiving mode of existence.

No wonder the disciples were unable to understand what Jesus was saying when he told them of his impending suffering and death (v. 32). Jesus was speaking of his role as a servant, one who lives on the receiving end of life. He was not in a position of control such that he could dictate the terms for living or dying. Quite the contrary, he was at the mercy of others. In fact, Jesus refers to his vocation in third-person language (v. 31). He uses the passive voice to articulate his own helplessness in the face of others who possess control. "The Son of Man is being handed over," Jesus says. At issue in this text is the disparity between a grasping behavior that seeks worldly greatness and a receiving behavior that relies on grace.

Jesus not only embraces a child in the midst of these now silent disciples. He also identifies himself with the little child embraced. "Whoever welcomes one such child in my name welcomes me." However the disciples would choose to treat that child would be some indication or measure of their own faith in Jesus. For a child is like a servant. And a servant is like a child.

Peter W. Marty

Nineteenth Sunday after Pentecost, Year B

First Lesson: Esther 7:1-6, 9-10; 9:20-22
(Psalm 124)
Second Lesson: James 5:13-20
Gospel Lesson: Mark 9:38-50

L iterary context. In Mark's narrative this pericope is in the catechetical materials that follow Peter's confession of Jesus as the Messiah (8:29) and precede the disciples' arrival in Jerusalem (11:1). The whole section might be titled "Preparing the Disciples on the Way to Jerusalem" (8:31–10:52).

First Passion Announcement	8:31–9:1
Second Passion Announcement	9:30-32
Catechetical Vignettes	
Who is the Greatest?	9:33-37
Stopping False Exorcists	9:38-40
Warnings about Hellfire	9:41-50
Divorce Controversy	10:1-12
The Place of Children	10:13-16
A Rich Man Refuses	10:17-22
Midrash on Wealth	10:23-31
Third Passion Announcement	10:32-34

Literary structure of the pericope. The pericope consists of five discrete literary units connected by certain key words, phrases, and images.

9:38-40: John presents a problem: We (i.e., the disciples) tried to stop someone who was casting out demons (apparently successfully) in your name *(en tōi onomati sou)* because he was not following us. Jesus disagreed: anyone who performs a deed of power *in my name* is not our enemy. Whoever is not against us is for us.

9:41: Anyone who provides a cup of water to someone *en onomati hoti Christou este* — literally, while naming or calling on the name, because you are Christ's — will be rewarded. This looks back at the exorcist who cast out demons in the name of Jesus, and also looks forward. Whoever helps you because of my name, even something as trivial (little) as giving a cup of water, will be rewarded.

9:42: Conversely, whoever causes a little one *(mikron)* to stumble *(skandalisēi)* will receive a different kind of reward; death by drowning would be preferable. This verse sets the theme, tone, and rhetorical form for what follows: better to embrace a horrible temporal consequence now and avoid stumbling (skandalon) than to embrace stumbling and face the inevitable and unthinkable eternal punishment.

9:43-48: These verses build on the argument from the lesser to the greater: better to amputate your hand, your foot, and gouge out an eye to avoid sin and to enter life (tēn zōēn) than to keep your appendages and be thrown into Gehenna, the place of the dead, where the worms never die and the fire is never extinguished (pyr asbeston). This reference is to the ominous last verses in Isaiah 66: Israel will be restored; then the whole world will come and bow before the Lord. "And they shall go out and look at the dead bodies of the people who have rebelled against me; for their worm shall not die, their fire shall not be quenched, and they shall be an abhorrence to all flesh." The message is clear: stumbling, if not arrested in this life, will produce a horrible, eternal result.

9:49-50: The "fire" in Gehenna leads into a discussion of salt. Everyone will be salted with fire. Salty salt is good; unsalty salt is not. Jesus concludes with another apothegm: Have salt in yourselves and be at peace with one another. It is not clear whether the association is purely linguistic and poetic or fire and salt are theological opposites: both burn, but fire destroys, salt preserves. Therefore, be salt: be preserved from sin and live in peace.

Homiletical approaches. Here I will propose several ways of appropriating the text.

Context matters. It helps enormously to read these verses in their literary context. Jesus announced that he must go to Jerusalem and die, but the disciples are in denial. They cannot fathom this ending. With time growing short, Jesus bears down. He makes short dogmatic pronouncements without much explanation: "Whoever is not against us is for us"; "If your hand causes you to stumble, cut it off"; etc. On a literally reading, one would reasonably expect to encounter many self-mutilated Christians in the world. We do not, because the context tells us that Jesus was stretching language to the breaking point to make an emphatic point: the kingdom of God is bizarre, paradoxical, weird. Jesus alone understands the deepest paradox of all: by losing your life for Christ's sake, you receive it. They cannot grasp this yet, so he offers them glimpses, images, shot through with mystery and awe. This new kingdom offers compassion for little ones and the downfall of their oppressors; eternal life, not death; peace, not unquenchable fire. The language is symbolic, hyperbolic, and deliberately scandalous to our sensibilities.

In the name of Jesus. When Jesus sent out the Twelve in pairs to preach, he also gave them authority to cast out demons, and they did (6:7). The disciples had achieved some success at this, but they were not able to heal the boy whose father sought their intervention. Only Jesus could do it (9:14-29). John's concern about the man who was casting out demons *(daimonia) in your name* relates to the exorcism Jesus performed, but it follows immediately on the heels of Jesus' first prediction of his passion. Jesus announces his death, and the disciples are talking about some fellow engaged in the unauthorized practice of exorcism. His transgression was not that he cast out demons, but that he did it "in your name." This was objectionable because this illicit exorcist was not following them *(ēkolouthei hēmin)*.

The disciples had a point. Jesus had given *them* authority over unclean spirits (6:8). No doubt they felt some proprietary rights in this privilege. Perhaps they understood at a deeper level that using the name of Jesus without following him is not right. It's cheating. The disciples were focused on a temporal problem: What should we do about the unauthorized use of our trademark, our logo, our franchise? From a temporal perspective this is a legitimate question. Microsoft, Coke, IBM, Amazon spend millions of dollars in legal fees preventing the unauthorized use of their name. People have made fortunes reserving names on the Internet and then selling them to businesses that need the name. The law recognizes the value of a name.

Jesus isn't concerned about the trademark issue. In fact, he says it's positive whenever someone does a mighty deed of power *(dynamin)* in his name. Microsoft calls it stealing. Jesus calls it good because by using the name you become part of his ministry and success. It's a ministry of multiplication, not subtraction. Such is the kingdom of God. We do things in the name of our employer, in the name of our alma mater, in the name of our civic club and even our church. Query: What are we doing in the name of him who is above all names?

Hellfire and damnation. I have heard many sermons, but none on the warnings in this text. Mainline preachers are much more squeamish when it comes to such texts than the people who warm the pews. Christians deserve to know what Jesus was talking about.

The first point is that Jesus is dead serious about sin. The problem is stumbling, *skandalon.* Commenting on the parallel text in Matthew (5:29) in his *Word Pictures in the New Testament,* A. T. Robertson rejects the Authorized Version's translation as misleading: "If thy hand offend thee, cut it off." Robertson prefers "causes thee to stumble" or "ensnares ye." "It is not the notion of giving offence or provoking, but of setting a trap or snare for one. The substantive *(skandalon)* means the stick in the trap that springs and closes the trap when the animal touches it." Whatever is diseased should be removed so the body can be healthy. What Jesus is after is not self-mutilation, but self-mastery. In any case, he was dead serious about sin.

If we persist in sin, the result is a foregone conclusion: Gehenna. Quebec's archbishop Phillip Carrington provides this detailed description of Gehenna: "Gehenna was the valley of Hinnom on the east side of Jerusalem, which had once been the site of the worship of the horrible heathen deity, Moloch; now, apparently, offal and rubbish was thrown there, and we may picture it with fires perpetually smouldering and rotten carcases committed to the fires; perhaps even the bodies of criminals and outcasts. Here the bodies of the heathen would be cast in the days when they would be defeated in the wars of the Lord; there they burn and stink" (*According to Mark* [Cambridge: Cambridge University Press, 1960], p. 207).

A. T. Robertson adds that Gehenna should be distinguished from Hades, a neutral place where dead spirits depart. Gehenna is the place of unquenchable fire. "Our word asbestos is this very word." Because of the earlier sacrifice of children to Molech, Gehenna was an "accursed place . . . used for the city garbage where worms gnawed and fires burned. It is thus a vivid picture of eternal punishment."

The point is not to scare the hell out of people. Nor is it to convince people that they can avoid the torments of hell by their own efforts. Rather, the text paints a vivid picture of the exact dilemma we would face — a remedy we lack the ability to apply — without the amazing grace of Jesus.

Stephen W. Ramp

Twentieth Sunday after Pentecost, Year B

First Lesson: Job 1:1; 2:1-10
(Psalm 26)
Second Lesson: Hebrews 1:1-4; 2:5-12
Gospel Lesson: Mark 10:2-16

Readers need first to be assured that the question asked Jesus is not frivolous. It was — and is — a question debated within the religious community. By the time the oral law was written down in the Mishnah around

200, the topic had been debated sufficiently among teachers to have resulted in definable positions. As in many rabbinic debates, the issue revolves around the close reading of biblical instructions. The debate came to focus on Deuteronomy 24:1: "Suppose a man enters into marriage with a woman, but she does not please him because he finds something objectionable about her, and so he writes her a certificate of divorce." The legal debate centered on the phrase "something objectionable." According to one opinion (the students of Shammai), the phrase is to be taken narrowly to refer only to infidelity. According to another opinion (the students of Hillel), the phrase is to be taken broadly to refer to anything objectionable — even what we would regard as the most trivial of reasons. While modern readers may find the grounds for holding a position weak and the viewpoints exaggerated, the debates reflect important discussions of actual practice within the community. Those unfamiliar with legal debates have the same reaction to contemporary case law. Law is effective, however, only as it is applied, and it is not a trivial matter on what grounds divorce is permitted. In fact, the very survival of society depends on such matters. And in the discussion between Jesus and his interrogators, both parties assume that God is involved in both the giving and the interpretation of the law.

Many people in our culture have a far lower estimate of law and its importance. Lawyers are viewed with suspicion. Involving lawyers in matters of divorce, according to popular wisdom, insures that the dissolution of a marriage will be unpleasant. The assumption seems to be that such family issues are better left as private matters. Easily forgotten is that marriage and divorce are public legal matters involving laws and legal rituals and courts. While marriage may be a sacrament in some Christian traditions, from the perspective of the state, marriage is a legal contract which can be formalized by pastors acting as agents of the state — as well as by other legally recognized authorities. Couples and the children for whom they are responsible are afforded the protection of law because society recognizes the vulnerability of such basic social units and their importance to the larger community.

In ancient societies, primarily agricultural, where women rarely owned property, marriage laws determined the circumstances under which women and children would be guaranteed support. The elaborate and intricate discussions of the grounds for and the precise procedures governing the dissolution of marriages indicate what was at stake. Without the protection of the law, women — especially mothers with young children — were at the mercy of their fathers and husbands. Seen positively, the law provided the structure within which families could live justly together and thrive; seen negatively, the law protected the most vulnerable members of society against the powerful.

The situation has not changed. Even in this country, which allows women to own property and to earn wages as well as men, women and young children remain the most vulnerable members of the society. Liberal divorce laws and the failure to enforce child support have resulted in a dramatic rise in the poverty rolls, which are made up principally of young women with children.

Jesus' response to the question is to interpret the laws regarding divorce by appeal to the intention of the Creator in Genesis: God intends that marriage (leaving mother and father and clinging to one another) be permanent. His response is even more extreme than in Matthew, where he echoes the position of the school of Shammai ("except for unchastity"). His interpretation for the disciples is even more pointed: anyone — man or woman — who marries after divorce commits adultery.

The passage is remarkable for its placement in Mark's Gospel, where much of what Jesus says and does could be — and is — construed as antisocial. When Jesus' family makes its first appearance in the story, they come to take Jesus away, believing he has lost his mind (Mark 3:20-21). His response to his mother and brothers is to speak of family in almost cultic terms: "Those who do the will of God, these are my brothers and sisters and mothers" (3:31-35). Later, in speaking to his followers about what is to come, Jesus again speaks of family in negative terms: families will be turned against one another because of Jesus (13:12). They obviously cannot be counted on for social stability any more than can the synagogue or the state who will persecute Jesus' followers. Jesus' contemporaries — at least the pious and the responsible members of society — had good reason to view him as potentially antisocial and as politically destabilizing.

His comments in this portion of the narrative indicate that Jesus is not an enemy of law. God intends that life be lived in ordered, structured environments that provide support and nurture for those who are most vulnerable. For those whose allegiance to Jesus has meant the complete disintegration of their economic and social and political life, Jesus promises a new family and a new order: "Truly I tell you, there is no one who has left house or brothers or sisters or mother or father or children or fields, for my sake and for the sake of the good news, who will not receive a hundredfold now in this age — houses, brothers and sisters, mothers and children, and fields with persecutions — and in the age to come eternal life" (10:29-30).

It is significant that the lectionary reading includes Jesus' comments about children as well as divorce. The two topics are related. The issue has to do with the obligations of society to its most vulnerable members. That may not be the way Christians generally read such passages. Some respond by defending the injunction against divorce as reflecting an absolute order God has given — including, in many cases, specific ordering of households in which the superiority of fathers and husbands is the primary agenda. Others, presumably including many who have been divorced, are offended by Jesus' alleged attack on individual rights. What both groups may fail to understand is the point of law. It is the structuring of human society necessary to life together. If our corporate actions are unregulated, the strong will thrive and the powerless suffer. Divorce has to do primarily with providing a safe environment for women who, like young children, may need defenders in the world of the wealthy and strong.

Reading Jesus' comments in the context of the larger Gospel makes it clear that his instructions are by no means an unambiguous guide to church policy. It is clear that believers will suffer the loss of family. Parents will turn against children and spouses against one another "for my sake and the gospel's sake." Paul's first letter to the Corinthians indicates one aspect of the problem. Paul can tell the Corinthians that "the Lord" has spoken against divorce while recognizing that believers may have no choice in the matter (1 Cor. 7:12-16). His firm statement forbidding divorce is immediately qualified ("but if she does . . ." [7:11]). Christian life is lived in the midst of a broken world, and believers are by no means exempted from the forces that tear at basic relationships.

That some will experience the words as hurtful is not surprising. The law works by punishing disobedience and transgression. A proper response is not to define the problem away by trying to explain Jesus' words as somehow appropriate to an ancient culture or as a patriarchal bias. It is to ask how God deals with brokenness, which is of course the main theme of the Gospel story. "Those who are well have no need of a physician," Jesus told his pious critics, "but those who are sick. I came not to call the righteous but sinners." Jesus gives his life as a ransom.

Crucial here is that God, who created and sustains the world, is committed to the well-being of the human family — which means particular attention to those who are most vulnerable. Laws regarding divorce, like laws regarding children's rights, remain necessary for the protection and well-being of families. The Jesus who makes such statements warns elsewhere that even these most basic social units may fail and that there is mercy for sinners and a place for the broken. But that mercy should not obscure God's intention that the world should be a place where trustworthy relationships are cultivated and encouraged.

Donald Juel

Twenty-first Sunday after Pentecost, Year B

First Lesson: Job 23:1-9, 16-17
(Psalm 22:1-15)
Second Lesson: Hebrews 4:12-16
Gospel Lesson: Mark 10:17-31

This text on discipleship uses Mark's strategy of contrasting between "insider" characters (the disciples) and "outsider" characters. Here, however, the contrast is carried out differently. Mark's normal contrast confounds expectations in the sense that the "outsiders" are usually more insightful than the "insiders." This is part of Mark's message: those who seem to be in power are actually weakest (cf. Herod and the Pharisees); those who are seemingly most perceptive are actually blind (religious leaders and disciples); those who seem to have left all to follow on the journey have actually smuggled items on board which threaten to capsize the ship (the closest disciples); those who are furthest from the kingdom know Jesus' identity best (demons, blind beggars, the Roman centurion). And vice versa, those who are blind are in the position to see best; those who come with nothing in their hands will be filled; those who come with no prerequisites for leadership are qualified for the advanced class in discipleship.

Here, however, the tables are turned. Just when we, the reader, are becoming accustomed to Mark's topsy-turvy world of the gospel, we are confounded again. The outsider who appears at the start of the story to have the ideal posture and question is shown by the end to be tragically outside. Clearly, this was a key story for the early church. Each synoptic witness tells it.

Several elements in the text highlight the scene before us. "As he was setting out on a *journey*." The word for "journey" here is the Greek *hodos* ("journey," "road," "way," or "path"), which in Mark is a technical term for *the* journey that Jesus is on to Jerusalem as the suffering servant Messiah (cf. 10:32, 52). No mere temporal phrase, the reference to Jesus' journey coupled with the man running up to Jesus indicates a sincere attempt by the man to get on the road too, or it represents an interruption and distraction to Jesus' intended path. In Mark's Gospel disciples are characterized as being *on* the way with Jesus or *in* the way of his intended purposes.

The man's posture and question indicate the kind of humility and seeking that would seem to characterize Jesus' ideal disciple: "[He] knelt before him, and asked him, 'Good Teacher, what must I do to inherit eternal life?'"

On closer inspection, though, these pious gestures could be a smoke screen for a more selfish concern. The man's posture, reverent address to Jesus, and question belie his desire to possess the one thing he had not figured out how to acquire on his own. Being rich and fastidious in his keeping of the commandments (and a "ruler," according to Luke), the man had everything he wanted here and now, but what about later, after life? How could he secure his eternal destiny, be sure that it was as secure as his 401 (k)? Jesus was this man's opportunity to take care of his eternal securities, and it appeared to be going well when Jesus couched the capacity to "inherit eternal life" in terms of keeping the commandments. For if that were the dance, then this man had been practicing the right steps since he was a child. He had earned eternal life by his lifelong ability to pull up his Torah bootstraps. "Teacher, I have kept all these since my youth."

It is not clear what prompted Jesus' next response, whether it was the man's tone of voice, his facial expression, his sincerity, or his genuine joy in discovery that he had already turned the key on eternal life. But Mark tells us something about Jesus' response to this man that we do not hear regarding any other character in the synoptic tradition: "Jesus, looking at him, loved him." Everything has changed now. Jesus goes beneath the surface of every layer that separates this man from true discipleship — beneath the layer of his politeness, his public piety, his political correctness, the signs of his being blessed by God with wealth, and his obvious and well-known religious and moral accomplishments — everything is peeled back as Jesus lays bare the true Achilles' heel that threatens this man's embarkation on *the* journey to eternal life which, for Jesus and everyone who would follow him, travels through Jerusalem and entails a cross. "You lack one thing: go, sell what you own, and give the money to the poor, and you will have treasure in heaven; then come, follow me."

This man's fatal flaw was what he "owned" — actually, what he thought he owned, but even more, how it actually owned him. His desire to "inherit eternal life" is revealed here as a desire to possess eternal life, as long as it doesn't cost him any current assets. It is often pointed out that Jesus is not against possessions, wealth, or money per se but the power they assert when one is owned by them. It isn't money but the love of money that is the root of all evil. True. But such elaboration and knowledge is often used as a clever excuse to own and pile up assets in the name of both Jesus and an enlightened understanding of what Jesus really meant. No one knows but God, of course, what actually goes on in each human heart — which hearts are controlled and threatened by the material goods they possess. But Jesus doesn't negotiate with the man in this text. He draws a line in the sand. The issue for this man's soul, as it probably is for most privileged people in this world, is not *eternal* life but *temporal* life. Take care of where your heart, where your life, is *now*. Do that well, do that with purity of conscience before God, and eternal life will take care of itself. Take care of your earthly assets in a stewardship that is defined by the cruciform journey to Jerusalem that you're on when you truly follow Jesus, and your treasure will be exactly where it needs to be for eternal life, in heaven. *"So, sell it all, give it to the poor, and come, follow me."* Ask yourself, what's the worst thing that could happen if you took Jesus' radical words radically seriously?

The man saw this as no metaphor. "When he heard this, he was shocked and went away grieving, for he had many possessions." He wasn't the only one who was shocked. I imagine everyone within earshot stood slack-jawed at Jesus' words. Jesus only makes the moment more incredulous when he says, "How hard it will be for those who have wealth to enter the kingdom of God!" Though we agree with Jesus in a kind of ho-hum manner because we're so used to hearing Jesus say such things about the rich, the disciples are perplexed. They operated out of that ancient conviction that if one had wealth, that was a sign of God's blessings, and conversely, if one was poor, sick, or troubled, that was a sign that God, or many gods, was against that person, probably because of some sin or sins in his or her life. It's good that we have outgrown such naive notions.

To drive the point home by means of absurdity, Jesus paints a picture for them: "Children, how hard it is to enter the kingdom of God! It is easier for a camel to go through the eye of a needle than for someone who is rich to enter the kingdom of God." Some commentators through the years have tried to soften the radicality of Jesus' words here by saying that there was a gate of passage called "The Eye of the Needle" through which camels could pass, but only with difficulty, by bending low. That's to miss Jesus' point entirely. The disciples show they get it: "Then who can be saved?" They are absolutely exasperated by the proposition since it leaves them powerless, helpless, bordering on despair, which is exactly where faith has the possibility to begin. "Jesus looked at them and said, 'For mortals it is impossible, but not for God; for God all things are possible.'" So even God can get a camel through the eye of a needle? That is good, and humbling, news for all camels everywhere.

Peter has been doing some thinking while Jesus has been speaking. I know, uh-oh. But he has put the rich man incident together with Jesus' words and linked those to the disciples' own leaving of nets, family, homes, businesses — seemingly everything — and asks, with a hint of excited anticipation, "Look, we have left everything and followed you." In other words,

"We did what he couldn't do! What do we get?!" Now I, as astute observer of Jesus' actions with the disciples for ten chapters, expect Jesus to bring the hammer down on Peter in some reorienting, humiliating way. But Jesus doesn't. He instead blesses Peter by illustrating, in many ways, what the rich young man missed out on in his inability to give up what he thought were riches: "Truly I tell you, there is no one who has left house or brothers or sisters or mother or father or children or fields, for my sake and for the sake of the good news, who will not receive a hundredfold now in this age — houses, brothers and sisters, mothers and children, and fields with persecutions — and in the age to come eternal life. But many who are first will be last, and the last will be first."

This is one of the most remarkable statements by Jesus in the entire Gospel tradition. As a completion to the entire section, he further emphasizes that the rich man's question about how to inherit eternal life was misguided. For discipleship is about temporal life that spills out onto eternal life, and both are due to the impetus and sustenance and needle-threading genius of God. The journey to which Jesus calls us in this world leads to the one we hope for in the world to come. Moreover, our fear of leaving behind our securities in this world by embarking on the journey to "God knows where" is assuaged by Jesus' promise here of the hundredfold blessing which awaits all who take the risk of the discipleship path. This promise begs to manifest itself concretely in the persons who follow. Moreover, preaching can helpfully reflect on the stories where this promise has come true in the lives of believers who have acted on it and received it. Preaching the promise of this text means recounting the stories of the mothers, fathers, children in Christ, even the "fields with persecution" that we have shared with fellow pilgrims on the journey. Each story concretizes the ways that the promise has come true in the lives of those we have been blessed to know and love and to be loved by along the journey.

André Resner, Jr.

Twenty-second Sunday after Pentecost, Year B

First Lesson: Job 38:1-7, (34-41)
(Psalm 104:1-9, 24, 35c)
Second Lesson: Hebrews 5:1-10
Gospel Lesson: Mark 10:35-45

This text follows immediately on the heels of Jesus' final passion prediction in Mark's Gospel. Even though the disciples clamored early on in the journey for Jesus to teach them directly rather than using the sideways language of parables (4:10-34), his direct method of communication employed since 8:27 is not any more effective.

After the first passion prediction, Peter rebuked Jesus and quickly was renamed, not "Rock," but "Satan" (8:27-33). After the second, Mark tells us that the disciples "did not understand what he was saying and were afraid to ask" (9:30-32). The third is preceded by the disciples' amazement and fear at Jesus' resolute walk on the road toward Jerusalem. The current story is Mark's commentary on their reaction to and misappropriation of the third and final passion prediction in Mark's story.

This text is the final story before the ending blind-man frame to the intensive discipleship training section (10:46-52). This episode brings us virtually to Jerusalem's threshold, and shows how far the disciples have come in their understanding of Jesus, themselves, and the kingdom. Jesus' intent throughout this segment of the journey was to focus on their development: "They went on from there and passed through Galilee. He did not want anyone to know it; for he was teaching his disciples" (9:30-31). The focal point of his teaching has been his own identity as the soon to be betrayed, rejected, killed, and rising "Son of Man." Such identity disclosure was crucial for their own development as leaders who would follow, hopefully, in Jesus' footsteps.

If they had been taking good notes through their final course, they would now conceive of themselves as disciples/leaders who:

- deny self for Jesus' sake and the sake of the gospel, risking and accepting worldly shame (8:34-38);
- are focused on Jesus and his words above all others (9:7);
- remain humbly dependent on God's power to do God's work (9:14-29);
- do not play the game of competitiveness, one-upmanship, glory grasping, but choose the role of least of all and slave to all (9:33-37);

- relinquish control for who does what and how they do it in the kingdom; in other words, giving up the need to be God's quality-control experts (read: control freaks) for anything that's done for God (10:38-41);
- keep children at the center of their work, even when it appears distracting (9:36-37, 42-48; 10:13-16); and
- do not become overburdened by possessions, but receive the gift of the hundredfold promise (10:17-31).

Essentially, Jesus was deconstructing the forms of leadership — both religious and political — that his disciples would have been most accustomed to seeing. As they grew in their ability to "see" that Jesus was indeed the Messiah, they would naturally make the connection that they would be his cabinet. This meant they would be in power, they would be the religious leaders. The only categories for leadership they had were what they had seen and experienced through the Pharisees, the Sadducees, the scribes, and Herod. Jesus recognized, however, that the form of leadership these groups now carried out was lethal, and would be toxic in the kingdom for which he was giving his life and for which he was preparing his disciples to lead. This explains the warning that prefaced Jesus' focused teaching of the disciples: "Watch out — beware of the yeast of the Pharisees and the yeast of Herod" (8:15). Just a pinch of their style of leadership — power-hungry grasping, hierarchical and paranoid control — would destroy the church of Jesus Christ.

So, how are the disciples coming along? "James and John, the sons of Zebedee, came forward to him and said to him, 'Teacher, we want you to do for us whatever we ask of you.' And he said to them, 'What is it you want me to do for you?'" What follows had to be one of the most disappointing moments in Jesus' time with the disciples. James and John, the sons of Zebedee, the sons of thunder, those called at the very beginning of Mark's story, those in the most inner circle of Jesus' followers, have the opportunity to reveal how close they are to Jesus' vision of kingdom, of discipleship, and of leadership. "And they said to him, 'Grant us to sit, one at your right hand and one at your left, in your glory.'" Again, they prove that they had not left all when they followed him. Some nets are harder to let go of than others. The nets of their messianic ideology, those surreptitious nets of desire for personal power and glory, of use and manipulation of those we know to get what we want — these are the nets the disciples had failed to let go. Jesus, incredulous at their request, responds with thick understatement, "You do not know what you are asking. Are you able to drink the cup that I drink, or be baptized with the baptism that I am baptized with?" Jesus' response had in mind his upcoming rejection and crucifixion, everything that he had

259

been telling them about for three chapters now. But they show how drastically they had missed even his most recent teaching. "They replied, 'We are able.' Then Jesus said to them, 'The cup that I drink you will drink; and with the baptism with which I am baptized, you will be baptized; but to sit at my right hand or at my left is not mine to grant, but it is for those for whom it has been prepared.'" Jesus' own "cup" and "baptism" he promises them. They are eager; he is reluctant — all because of a different conception of what has to be drunk, a different understanding of just what sort of reality they are about to be immersed in.

"When the ten heard this, they began to be angry with James and John." Probably because the ten had not thought to angle Jesus for these positions of honor first. Jesus attempts one last word of orientation to his vision: "So Jesus called them and said to them, 'You know that among the Gentiles those whom they recognize as their rulers lord it over them, and their great ones are tyrants over them. But it is not so among you; but whoever wishes to become great among you must be your servant, and whoever wishes to be first among you must be slave of all. For the Son of Man came not to be served but to serve, and to give his life a ransom for many.'"

It would have been quite untasteful for a Jewish person to have someone compare the way he acted to the way "Gentiles" typically act. Jesus aims this racially charged criticism at the disciples in yet one more attempt to help them "see" that Jesus' messiahship, their discipleship, and their subsequent leadership are to be characterized by completely different kinds of actions and attitudes. Jesus highlights the hierarchical way that most leadership structures function, where those in power exert force over those beneath them. So one pictures an angry CEO calling in his VP and chewing him out over some matter. The VP takes it on the chin like a good employee and backs out of the CEO's office apologetically. But the minute he's in his office he calls in the next in the chain of command, continuing the pattern of abuse and intimidation all the way to the last on the totem pole. The last then slithers out to his car, drives home, and inflicts his chain-reaction "lording it over" power game on whoever is there to receive it. This domino effect of verbal and sometimes physical abuse often affects the weakest at the end of the line, namely, children, whom Jesus lifted up again and again throughout this intensive discipleship training section as those:

- whom the disciples ought to welcome, for in welcoming children we welcome Jesus and God too (9:35-37);
- whom the disciples ought to not scandalize, or they will suffer severe punishment (9:42-48);

- whom the disciples ought not to prevent coming to Jesus, "for it is to such as these that the kingdom of God belongs" (10:13-15);
- whom the disciples ought to learn from how to receive the kingdom of God (10:15-16);
- whom the disciples ought to bless, as Jesus did (10:16); and
- whom the disciples ought to receive, as part of God's hundredfold blessing to disciples (10:30).

Again, to reorient them to the kind of leadership appropriate to Jesus' vision of the kingdom, Jesus points them to his own way of being as the paradigm. "But it is not so among you; but whoever wishes to become great among you must be your servant, and whoever wishes to be first among you must be slave of all. For the Son of Man came not to be served but to serve, and to give his life a ransom for many."

Part of the demand of preaching the gospel is that one reads Scripture with a view to the claim that God makes, that the gospel makes, on people in the text. That claim exerts itself in the ways the text, and the immediate text's context, portray God's activity to judge and bring salvation into a situation, to create a new and redemptive situation that goes beyond human capacities, but also the way that God's new and redemptive situation invites humans to participate in redemption with all their heart, soul, mind, and strength. The faithful preacher must also ask questions beyond the text's display of this gospel gift and claim, notably, what does this gospel and claim look like in my own life and in the world here and now? As the preacher rummages around in his or her own experience, in the experience of the community of faith, and in the experience of those who in their lives have displayed the same gospel gifts and claims that the text has exerted, the preacher focuses as a witness on those illuminating narratives which give our preaching life, flesh-and-blood concreteness. Often these narratives will by necessity require confessions of failure, and corrections given, that ultimately functioned as part of the gospel of the event. The story of James and John coming to Jesus and asking this question is a confession of ignorance and blindness, and an embarrassing correction by Jesus. How often is our preaching as confessional and revealing as the apostles'? Of course, one key is that the apostolic stories that continued were self-effacing stories which pointed to Jesus, and to the disciples' own failure. The disciples in Mark rarely if ever do or say the right thing. Preaching the gospel is witness to Jesus, to his ministry, to God's work of judging and redeeming love that creates a community which perpetuates that memory and instantiates that same redeeming activity.

André Resner, Jr.

Twenty-third Sunday after Pentecost, Year B

First Lesson: Job 42:1-6, 10-17
(Psalm 34:1-8, [19-22])
Second Lesson: Hebrews 7:23-28
Gospel Lesson: Mark 10:46-52

This is the second blind-man healing story in Mark. It functions as the climax of the intensive discipleship training section, providing the concluding frame to the block of material that began with the first blind-man healing story in 8:22-26. At the site which was famous for the walls coming down as a result of Israel's faith and God's miraculous activity, Jesus encounters a blind beggar named Bartimaeus sitting at the roadside. Faith and the miraculous commingle again outside Jericho's city gate.

Being blind, a beggar, and by the roadside are all key narrative markers in Mark's Gospel, and each functions on both the literal and figurative levels. In Mark's story Jesus is indeed walking on the road leading out of Jericho, but "road" (*hodos*) is a technical term in Mark's narrative for Jesus' path of faithfulness — that of the suffering servant Messiah who goes to Jerusalem to give his life as a ransom for many. The disciples are following Jesus on the road, but they do not comprehend *his* "road," *his* version of messiahship, kingdom, or Jerusalem. *They* are the blind, those who ought to be begging to "see" what only Jesus can reveal to them, but their own visions of power and glory (9:34; 10:37, 41-42) obscure what he has to show them, keeping their sight fuzzy at best (8:24 + 8:32) and totally dark at worst (9:32; 10:32). Blind Bartimaeus functions for Mark to show what a true disciple looks like. If the disciples have "eyes to see," they will perceive that, in this story, it is the blind who lead the blind. It is the physically, literally blind who lead the figuratively and spiritually blind.

As Jesus leaves the town, word gets to Bartimaeus that it is "Jesus of Nazareth" who is the cause of the large and raucous crowd. Bartimaeus overhears Jesus' human identity marker, namely, the *man* Jesus from the *no-account town* of Nazareth. With only this information, Bartimaeus begins to shout out a different identity claim: "Jesus, *Son of David*, have mercy on me!" The townspeople "sternly ordered him to be quiet," which sounds a lot like what Jesus always did to the demons who identified him in messianic terms. But the townsfolk's motive in silencing Bartimaeus is different. In all likelihood they are embarrassed by him. He's not the one they want at the front of the welcome wagon committee for the celebrity, miracle-working prophet Jesus. But Bart is undeterred. In fact, one senses his desperation: this is his chance. Who knows if he will ever have another opportunity to be in Jesus' presence? And what if Jesus really can do what Bart has heard that he has done — heal his own blindness? So Timaeus's son cries out all the more, even as he was censured by his neighbors: *"Jesus, Son of David, have mercy on me!"*

Once again this is an interruption to Jesus' journey, a hindering of his progress toward Jerusalem (cf. 10:17). But as before, Jesus stopped and called the man. In what appears to be a mocking tone, the townspeople say to Bartimaeus, "Take heart; get up, he is calling you." And he does just that. "So throwing off his cloak, he sprang up and came to Jesus. Then Jesus said to him, 'What do you want me to do for you?'" Do you recognize the question? It is exactly the same question that Jesus had put to James and John when they came to him wanting Jesus to do for them whatever they asked (10:35-36). I picture James and John standing there beside Jesus when he asks Bartimaeus their question, and Jesus shooting a quick glance in their direction. John looks down and scuffs the ground with his toe. James looks away and whistles. Jesus looks back at Bartimaeus as he begins to speak: "My teacher, let me see again."

As Mark's portrait of the ideal disciple, Bartimaeus the outsider, the blind beggar, shows James and John what they should have asked and how they should act. Note Bartimaeus's actions:

- Hearing that Jesus is at hand, he shouts his confession at the risk of public shame and scorn. Those things matter less than his confession and the possibility to be with Jesus.
- When called by Jesus, he responds immediately and at the cost of his "cloak." His reaction reminds us of the disciples back in chapter 1, hearing Jesus' call, responding without hesitation and leaving behind their possessions. Throwing off his cloak was a risky and costly move for Bartimaeus, in that it was probably his only outer garment, and being blind and the seeming scorn of his town, there was no guarantee that he would find it again. It is symbolic of his willingness to leave all to be with Jesus. (This move by Bartimaeus also stands in stark contrast to the later incident in Gethsemane when Jesus was arrested. Whereas the disciples at first gave up everything to follow Jesus (including their clothing), when faced with the reality of his arrest, they give up everything to flee [including their clothing, 14:51-52].)
- Faced with Jesus' question, "What do you want me to do for you?" Bartimaeus answers correctly, in contrast to James and John. His simple

request is that he might just "see." It is, perhaps, the one thing that Jesus wishes his disciples would want most: just to see, just to "get it," to understand who Jesus really was, what the nature of his messiahship is, and who they are as his disciples in light of that. Jesus hopes his disciples, in their ignorance and failure, will give up grubbing for position and power and trying to make the kingdom happen in worldly and short-term ways.

- When Jesus tells Bartimaeus to "go," literally, to "go away," or to "go his way," Bartimaeus shows that he really has understood, that he really does see and wants what Jesus wants, by following Jesus on *"the way,"* which in the next verse leads to Jerusalem, which for Mark's Jesus is a code word for "the cross."

For Mark discipleship doesn't get any better than what we see in Bartimaeus. He displays the kind of humility, dependence, riskiness, and courage that characterize those in any era who seek to be Jesus' true disciples. In humility he comes as an ignorant beggar with the simplest but most important request a disciple can have: "Just let me see." Such a request requires the necessary insight that sight is dependent on Jesus' ability to render it. We cannot self-correct our nearsightedness, farsightedness, or presbyopia (old-sightedness). Humility is a continuing characteristic of the disciple who truly sees. And such humility asserts itself in a keen sense of one's dependence on Jesus and on Jesus' community of faith. When one is truly blind, one must learn to receive dependence as a gift rather than a threat to our American right and responsibility to independence. Moreover, disciples are required to have a certain perspective on possessions which allows them to give whatever holds them back from God's call. Faith sits, leaning forward, ready to leap at the opportunity to answer God's call whenever it might come, and it shows itself willing to shed whatever holds it back from the journey. Bartimaeus shows us what having "ears to hear" and "eyes to see" really looks like. And courageously, Jesus' disciples know when to stand up for what they believe, even when it may cost them public shame. There are times when our confession puts us in a situation of shame, but faith sees that it's worth the risk.

The kind of humility, dependence, riskiness, and courage that Bartimaeus exhibits is expressed well in the familiar Clara Scott hymn, "Open My Eyes That I May See."

Open my eyes, that I may see
Glimpses of truth Thou hast for me;

Place in my hands the wonderful key
That shall unclasp and set me free.

Open my ears, that I may hear
Voices of truth Thou sendest clear;
And while the wave notes fall on my ear,
Everything false will disappear.

Open my mouth, and let me bear
Gladly the warm truth everywhere;
Open my heart and let me prepare
Love with Thy children thus to share.

Refrain:
Silently now I wait for Thee,
Ready, my God, Thy will to see;
Open my ears, illumine me,
Spirit divine!

André Resner, Jr.

Palm/Passion Sunday, Year B

First Lesson: Isaiah 50:4-9a
(Psalm 118:1-2, 19-29)
Second Lesson: Philippians 2:5-11
Gospel Lesson: Mark 11:1-11

In preparation for his entry into Jerusalem, Jesus sends ahead two disciples. The instructions he gives them and the events that follow show that arrangements had been made. The Marcan Evangelist is not privy to these arrangements (nor is he privy to those that were made to secure the upper room; see 14:12-16). We should not assume that Jesus has demonstrated supernatural knowledge (i.e., he knew a colt would be tethered in the street and that onlookers would surrender it if the right words were spoken). What is demonstrated is Jesus' mastery of the situation. It may also hint at his assumption of political authority, at least on par with Roman authority.

Jesus' celebrated entry is similar to as many as twelve other entries, as recorded in 1 and 2 Maccabees and in Josephus. These entries follow a more or less fixed pattern. Major figures involved in entries include Alexander, who enters Jerusalem, is greeted with ceremony, and is escorted into the city where he participates in cultic activity (*Antiquities* 11.8.4B5 §§325-39); Apollonius, who enters Jerusalem accompanied by torches and shouts (2 Macc. 4:21-22); Judas Maccabeus, who returns home from a military victory and is greeted with hymns and "praising God" (1 Macc. 4:19-25; *Antiquities* 12.7.4 §312); Judas Maccabeus again, who returns from battle and enters Jerusalem amidst singing and merrymaking, followed by sacrifice (1 Macc. 5:45-54; *Antiquities* 12.8.5 §§348-49); Jonathan brother of Judas, who is greeted by the men of Askalon "with great pomp" (1 Macc. 10:86); Simon brother of Judas, who enters Gaza, expels idolatrous inhabitants, cleanses idolatrous houses, and enters the city "with hymns and praise" (1 Macc. 13:43-48); Simon brother of Judas again, who enters Jerusalem and is met by crowds "with praise and palm branches, and with harps and cymbals and stringed instruments and with hymns and songs" (1 Macc. 13:49-51); Antigonus, who with pomp enters Jerusalem, then the temple precincts, but with so much pomp and self-importance that he is criticized by some for imagining that he himself was "king" (*Jewish War* 1.3.2 §§73-74; *Antiquities* 13.11.1 §§304-6); Marcus Agrippa, who enters Jerusalem, is met by Herod, and is welcomed by the people with acclamations (*Antiquities* 16.2.1 §§12-15); and Archelaus, who, hoping to confirm his kingship, journeys to and enters Jerusalem amidst acclamation of his procession (*Antiquities* 17.8.2 §§194-239).

The "Mount of Olives" is selected as the official starting point for entry into the city. This makes sense, for it overlooks the city and the eastern side of the Temple Mount itself. But it also makes sense in view of Jesus' interest in acting out an agenda informed by themes and images in the prophecy of Zechariah: "On that day his feet shall stand on the Mount of Olives, which lies before Jerusalem on the east" (Zech. 14:4). The departure from the Mount of Olives, in order to enter Jerusalem, mounted on a colt, is the beginning of a series of elements drawn from Zechariah. With the exception of Mark 14:27, where a quotation is found on the lips of Jesus, the allusions to Zechariah are implicit and there is no reason to think that they represent the theology of either the Evangelist or his tradition. What we have here are significant fragments of Jesus' theology, especially as it relates to his relationship to Jerusalem.

The Marcan entrance narrative, in which Jesus mounts a colt, appears to be deliberately modeled after Zechariah 9:9: "Tell the daughter of Zion, Behold, your king is coming to you, humble, and mounted on an ass, and on a colt, the foal of an ass." Other scriptural influences have been suggested, such as 1 Samuel 10:2-10. But this act is to be traced to Jesus, not to a community imagination inspired by the prophetic Scriptures. Mark's account (11:1-11) does not quote the passage from Zechariah, but the Matthean and Johannine accounts do (Matt. 21:4-5; John 12:14-15). Mark's failure to exploit an important proof text argues both for his Gospel's priority and for the essential historicity of the account. The explicit and formal quotation of Zechariah 9:9 in Matthew and John is consistent with their scriptural apologetic, an apologetic that seems to be primarily fashioned with the synagogue in mind. Commentators are divided over the question of the original significance of the entrance, with many seeing it as messianic and many suggesting that the messianic significance is later interpretation. In all probability the act was indeed originally messianic, which in later tradition was exaggerated.

According to Mark, Jesus enters Jerusalem mounted on a "colt" (pōlos), which may mean a young horse, not necessarily a young donkey. Mark's Roman readers would have had no reason to imagine anything other than a horse (it is Matthew who cites Zech. 9:9 and speaks of a donkey; see Matt. 21:1-7). The actions of Jesus' followers (v. 8) are reminiscent of honors accorded Israel's past rulers. Throwing garments on the colt and on the road in front of the colt reminds us of the royal anointing of Jehu and how Israelites placed their garments on the steps before him (2 Kings 9:12-13). The branches placed before Jesus recall the reception that Judas Maccabeus, Israel's great intertestamental leader, received after purifying the temple (2 Macc. 10:7). Riding the colt, which may or may not have called to mind Zechariah 9:9, would also have been reminiscent of Solomon, David's son, who rode his father's mule and was proclaimed king (1 Kings 1:32-48).

Mark also says no one had ever sat on the colt (v. 2). This does not mean it was unbroken and therefore potentially difficult to ride; it could have been used to carry baggage. Mark's point in mentioning this detail probably has to do with Jesus' honor; that is, the animal on which Jesus rode was not a common one; it was special. It had not been used before (for animals or things reserved for special use, see Num. 19:2; Deut. 21:3; 1 Sam. 6:7; and in nonbiblical literature, see Homer, *Iliad* 6.94; Horace, *Epodes* 9.22). According to Mishnah *Sanhedrin* 2:5, no one may use an animal on which a king rides.

Thus the "newness" of the animal, in that no one else has used it, seems to be the point.

The shouts that meet Jesus, "Hosanna! Blessed is he who comes in the name of the Lord! Blessed is the kingdom of our father David that is coming!" (vv. 9-10), allude to Psalm 118:26 and are consistent with the imagery of Jesus mounted on the royal mule, much as Solomon did shortly before the death of his father David (1 Kings 1:32-40). The crowd interpretively adds to Psalm 118 the words: "Blessed is the kingdom of our father David that is coming!" (Mark 11:10). The coherence with the interpretive tendencies preserved in the Psalms Targum is especially suggestive. In verse 22 it speaks of the rejected boy (instead of stone, as it is in the Hebrew) who was a son of Jesse and is worthy to be appointed king and ruler. Although initially rejected by the builders (i.e., the religious authorities; see CD 4.19; 8.12; Acts 4:11), David will be later blessed by the builders from the temple precincts: "Blessed is the one who comes in the name of the word of the LORD" (v. 26). The ruling priests then celebrate David's kingship by sacrificing a lamb (v. 27). How ancient this Aramaic tradition is cannot be determined with certainty, but the association of Psalm 118:26 with the kingdom of David suggests that elements of this interpretive tradition lie behind the words of the enthusiastic crowd. (For more on Psalm 118 in Jesus' thinking, see commentary on Mark 12:1-12 below.) There can be no doubt that the people that make up Jesus' following anticipate the speedy appearance of a Davidic kingdom. That Jesus would only one week later be crucified as "King of the Jews" (Mark 15:2, 26) is compelling evidence that this was indeed what the crowd hoped would come about under Jesus' leadership.

The awkward conclusion (v. 11: "and when he had looked round at everything, as it was already late, he went out to Bethany with the twelve") is evidence that the triumphal entry did not conclude the way its planners, including Jesus, had hoped. It does not imply that Jesus was a gawking first-time visitor of Jerusalem. The city of Jerusalem did not welcome the prophet — perhaps Messiah — from Galilee, as had those among his following. When Jesus finally entered the temple precincts, there was no priestly greeting. Jesus was ignored. All that he could do was look over the precincts and then retire to Bethany with his disciples. This quiet, anticlimactic conclusion foreshadows the storm of controversy that will break out the following day when Jesus returns to the temple precincts.

Craig S. Evans

Twenty-fourth Sunday after Pentecost, Year B

First Lesson: Ruth 1:1-18
(Psalm 146)
Second Lesson Hebrews 9:11-14
Gospel Lesson: Mark 12:28-34

The opening verse (v. 28: "And one of the scribes came up and heard them disputing with one another") makes clear that the question of the Great Commandment was asked shortly after the question of levirate marriage and the resurrection (12:18-27). A scribe is impressed with Jesus' ability and so asks him, "Which commandment is the first of all?" The pericope consists of the question (v. 28), Jesus' reply (vv. 29-31), the scribe's approving response (vv. 32-33), and Jesus' commendation (v. 34). The Marcan Evangelist has added the opening "And one of the scribes, approaching and hearing them disputing, and seeing that he had answered them well," as well as the concluding "And no one any longer dared to question him." The Evangelist may also have added most of verse 33, where the scribe repeats the two commandments.

If the exchange is thoroughly Jewish in perspective and advanced nothing of the early church's distinctive claims, why was the tradition preserved? Pre-Marcan tradents no doubt found the material useful because of the scribe's enthusiastic agreement with Jesus, which included the assertion that the double commandment "is much more than all whole burnt offerings and sacrifices" (v. 33). The Marcan Evangelist found the material useful because it supplemented well his depiction of Jesus besting temple authorities within the temple precincts themselves. Why, even one of their own had to admit that there were principles that took precedence over the temple cultus. For a community rejected by the cultus, and therefore rejected by the synagogue of the Diaspora, the scribe's assertion would be reassuring and of some apologetic value.

Interrogation comes from a scribe who has seen how well Jesus has answered the questions put to him. The question put forth in this instance is not a trick question, nor is it designed to entrap Jesus. Unlike his response to the previous questions (12:14-15, 19-23), which Jesus countered with questions of his own, this time Jesus answers in a straightforward manner. The scribe asks which commandment is first (or most important) of all (v. 28). Jesus replies by quoting Deuteronomy 6:4-5, the famous Shema, as the "first" commandment (vv. 29-30). The Shema denotes three passages (Deut. 6:4-9;

11:13-21; Num. 15:37-41) and was to be recited every morning and evening. Although the opening words, strictly speaking, are not a commandment, affirmation that "the LORD our God is one LORD" is implicitly an injunction to recognize and obey the only God. The only God is identified as Yahweh. The commandment proper that follows presupposes this identity. A comment in Josephus (*Apion* 2.22 §190) reflects similar thinking: "What, then, are the precepts and prohibitions of our Law? They are simple and familiar. The first that leads (all of the commandments) concerns God." Jesus then quotes part of Leviticus 19:18 as the "second" (v. 31). The quotation matches the LXX exactly, which in turn is an exact translation of the Hebrew. Appeal to Leviticus 19:18 to sum up one's duty to humanity finds an important parallel in the tradition ascribed to Rabbi Aqiba: "'. . . but you shall love your neighbor as yourself.' Rabbi Aqiba says, 'This is the encompassing principle of the Law'" (*Sipra Lev.* §200 [on Lev. 19:15-20]). Hillel's negative form of the Golden Rule is also relevant, in that it finds the whole of the Law summarized in a single principle: "What is hateful to you, do not do to your neighbor; that is the whole Law" (*b. Shab.* 31a). Of course, Jesus provides not one (i.e., the "first") commandment, but two (i.e., a "second" as well). However, in this also he is not unique, for the idea of love for humans as a complement to love for God is found elsewhere in Jewish thinkers and writers of late antiquity. According to Philo (*De decalogo* 109-10), "lovers of men" and "lovers of God" only attain virtue by half if they are not both lovers of men and of God. The idea of love of God and love of humanity is expressed in many texts (e.g., *T. Iss.* 5:2: "love the Lord and your neighbor"; 7:6: "I loved the Lord and man with the whole heart"; *T. Dan* 5:3: "Love the Lord with all your life and one another with a true heart"; Philo, *De specialibus legibus* 2.63: "But among the vast number of particular truths and principles [are] two main heads: one of duty to God . . . one of duty to humans").

The scribe finds Jesus' reply succinct and compelling, commenting that to love God with all that one is and has and to love one's neighbor as oneself "is much more than all whole burnt offerings and sacrifices" (vv. 32-33). His comment is a remarkable admission, suggesting that Jesus' teaching potentially renders the temple activities of the priests redundant. As such, in the Marcan context it represents one more criticism of the temple establishment.

The combination of "whole burnt offerings and sacrifices" occurs more than one hundred times in the LXX, so it may be regarded as a set phrase. The scribe's confession that love of God and love of one's neighbor are "much more than all whole burnt offerings and sacrifices" reflects various great statements in the prophetic tradition. The prophet/priest Samuel tells the disobedient King Saul:

Has the LORD as great delight in burnt offerings and sacrifices,
    as in obeying the voice of the LORD?
Behold, to obey is better than sacrifice,
    and to hearken than the fat of rams.   (1 Sam. 15:22)

Hosea, the prophet to the northern tribes, declares the word of the Lord:

  For I desire steadfast love and not sacrifice,
    the knowledge of God, rather than burnt offerings.   (Hos. 6:6)

See also Isaiah 1:11; Jeremiah 6:20; Amos 5:22; Micah 6:6-8; Psalms 40:6 (LXX 39:7); 51:16 (LXX 50:18). The scribe's enthusiastic endorsement of Jesus' theology is in keeping with the prophetic tradition and with Jesus' own general principles (cf. the appeals to Isa. 56:7 and Jer. 7:11 in Mark 11:17). This endorsement thus highlights again Jesus' competent knowledge of Scripture and his impressive ability to engage the scribes in debate.

The scribe's assertion that "to love one's neighbor as oneself, is much more than all whole burnt offerings and sacrifices" finds potentially two interesting parallels from the Dead Sea Scrolls. The first comes from 1QS 9.4, which anticipates the time when the Qumran community will "atone for iniquitous guilt and for sinful unfaithfulness and as good will for the earth better than the flesh of burnt offerings and the fat of sacrifices." The second comes from 4Q266 10 i 13, a fragment of the Damascus Document, which looks to the time when "he [the Messiah] will atone for their sin better than meal and sin offerings." These two texts may envision a time when ritual sacrifice may no longer be necessary, perhaps suggesting that in the coming of the Messiah atonement would be effected apart from animal sacrifice. This perspective is consistent with Jesus' eschatology and may shed light on his criticism of the temple establishment in 11:15-18.

Jesus commends the scribe for his answer: "You are not far from the kingdom of God" (v. 34a). The accuracy of the scribe's answer indicates that he is "not far from the kingdom of God," that is, he is close to entering the ranks of those who have responded to the message of the kingdom. The "kingdom of God," of course, has been the essence of Jesus' proclamation from the very beginning (cf. 1:14-15; 4:11, 26, 30; 9:1, 47; 10:14, 15, 23-25; 14:25). To be "far" from God or from the kingdom of God is language that recalls exile and diaspora (e.g., Isa. 57:19: "Peace, peace, to the far and to the near, says the LORD; / and I will heal him"; Ezek. 11:15; Zech. 6:15; 10:9), which, according to New Testament theology, has been rectified by Christ's mission (cf. Eph. 2:13: "But now in Christ Jesus you who once were far off have been brought near in the blood of Christ"). Why does Jesus regard the scribe as "not far from" the kingdom, rather than as having "entered" the kingdom? Perhaps the Evangelist expects his readers to assume that all that remains for the scribe is repentance, as both John the Baptist and Jesus called for (cf. 1:14-15; 6:12). In an earlier exchange (10:17-31), wealth had prevented another man from entering life (i.e., the kingdom). What prevents the scribe on this occasion we are not told (or did he later repent?). As the heavenly "Son of Man" (2:10, 28; 3:28; 10:45; 13:26; 14:62), Jesus has the authority to make pronouncements regarding one's nearness or remoteness to the kingdom.

Jesus' critics are beaten; they have been bested in argument at every point. Indeed, even one of his antagonists has been nearly converted, so powerful is Jesus' teaching and debating skills. Not until he is later arrested and brought before the high priest "did anyone dare to ask him a question" (v. 34b).

Craig S. Evans

Twenty-fifth Sunday after Pentecost, Year B

First Lesson: Ruth 3:1-5; 4:13-17
(Psalm 127)
Second Lesson: Hebrews 9:24-28
Gospel Lesson: Mark 12:38-44

"As he taught, he said, 'Beware of the scribes. . . .'" We are accustomed to seeing the scribes as the "bad guys who wear the black hats," the ones of whom we are to be most suspicious. We, as privileged readers, know about the "scribes," that "scribes" is a shorthand way for Mark to name the most violent and manipulative of opposition and conflict to all that Jesus is and that God wills.

It would have been a shocking assertion to the people of the day, however. The scribes in the first-century mind were those who had an integral role in each of Judaism's denominations, namely, the Pharisees and Sadducees. The scribes would have been considered the most religious and the most pious, those men (literally) who had given up everything to serve and worship God and to study and teach the sacred Scriptures. They were the gatekeepers for the kingdom, the go-betweens for the people to God. Jesus' condemnation of them would have been shocking to most, and perhaps delightful for the few who suspected they were hypocritical powermongers but would not necessarily have had the courage to say so out loud.

But Jesus names their sins: pride, focusing on their public persona and privilege, but even worse, extortion. "Beware of the scribes, who like to walk around in long robes, and to be greeted with respect in the marketplaces, and to have the best seats in the synagogues and places of honor at banquets! They devour widows' houses and for the sake of appearance say long prayers. They will receive the greater condemnation." All these pious acts of self-promotion are familiar to frequent readers of the Gospels: Jesus is the greatest critic of the misuse of prayer and position in religious leadership for personal gain. But the accusation "They devour widows' houses" stands out. The widow and the orphan had a special place in God's compassion and sense of justice. The law and the prophets both thundered God's heart and will for these powerless ones in society (cf. Exod. 22:22; Deut. 10:18; 24:17-21; 26:12-13; 27:19; Isa. 1:17; 9:17; Jer. 7:6; 22:3; 49:11; Zech. 7:10; James 1:27; 1 Tim. 5:3). To think that the very ones who were to most defend and uphold widows would be those who manipulated them was reprehensible. But what evidence did Jesus have that such was the case? It is easy to take potshots at certain people, especially those who do not like us, but how is what Jesus saying not mere gossip or slander?

> He sat down opposite the treasury, and watched the crowd putting money into the treasury. Many rich people put in large sums. A poor widow came and put in two small copper coins, which are worth a penny. Then he called his disciples and said to them, "Truly I tell you, this poor widow has put in more than all those who are contributing to the treasury. For all of them have contributed out of their abundance; but she out of her poverty has put in everything she had, all she had to live on."

Many a stewardship campaign has kicked off using this text and this widow's example as exemplar extraordinaire. The preacher bellows the conclusion: "So this widow, with the little she had, gave it all to God's work. *What about us?* Are we as willing to show the kind of faith that hurts? Can we give until it hurts, until it really costs us?"

But is Jesus raising this widow up as an example of the way people ought to give? Does Mark intend this story to function as a stewardship text for "giving until it hurts"? It is not likely, especially in this context. After just naming the chief reason to "beware of the scribes" as "they devour widows' houses," we see a scene where one widow's house does indeed get swallowed whole.

Jesus and his disciples sit watching people put money into the thirteen donation chests that sat in the temple court. That they were out in the open invited a kind of competition and show of charity. But even in the most corrupt of situations there are still some who operate from pure hearts and motives. Jesus, seeing what others could not, names what he sees. He sketches another picture of the topsy-turvy world of the gospel: here is what "the greatest is the least" looks like. And what appears to be the least is the greatest (cf. 10:31).

Jesus is not concerned with money or the show of it. In fact, he has already charged the Jerusalem temple as being spiritually bankrupt in its material wealth (11:17). Does he here, then, commend a kind of giving which would render an already impoverished widow completely devoid of anything to live on? And would he commend such a "selfless" act of giving knowing that she gives to a corrupt system run by prideful, power-hungry, widow-devouring, God-despising priests who have poisoned the well of God's kingdom and even now are plotting to kill God's anointed (3:6; 13:13)? Moreover, the scribes' perspective on her giving would be quite different from Jesus'. For them, tallying up the two small copper coins was probably more bother than it was worth, just like those who despise pennies, nickels, and dimes in the collection plates on Sunday mornings. It's much easier and quicker to add check totals to the deposit slip (and we can also see who gave the largest sums by noticing the names of the checks) than to laboriously count and add the change. Yet the change usually comes from the poorest, the least able to give, and those whose hearts are purest.

But doesn't Mark narrate this story for a purpose, and isn't that purpose most obviously the generosity of the widow? Just because something is narrated in Scripture does not mean that Scripture is calling its readers to emulate that activity. Scripture's narration is not necessarily a condoning or authorizing of the narrated activity as blessed. Moreover, just because Jesus is reported to have said something about someone's behavior does not mean he is endorsing it or encouraging its emulation, even if his words could be used for our ends on stewardship Sunday.

I believe that Jesus' words here are to be taken as lament. Having just warned his followers about the widow's-house-devouring-scribes, he says, in essence, "There goes another one, just like I told you." It is a lament that is continued in chapter 13, where the disciples are awed by the temple's appearance because the stones of which it is made are so impressively large. Like the impressive amounts of money given by the rich, size can be deceiving. Jesus deconstructs their picture just as he is in Jerusalem to deconstruct their entire religious system. Jesus' words concerning the widow are a lament and a deconstruction of what they thought they saw.

However, his lament of the widow's plight contains a message of good news, of gospel. For the good news of this text is that in spite of this woman's plight at the hands of the corrupt religious leadership, in spite of her well-intentioned but ignorant giving to a sick system which was preying on people just like her, God sees what's going on. God sees her plight; God knows her situation, her heart; and God is doing something about it. Jesus embodies in this story the one who knows better than even we do who the bad guys are and who the good guys are. Jesus is the one who can lament the corruption and then go about giving his life to bring down every stone of it so that not one remains upon another. I have known many who, because of "what they know" about organized religion and the hypocrites they have known in religious leadership, refuse to go to worship, refuse to be involved in church activities, refuse to give any financial support to the system.

Moreover, they take potshots at the poor, ignorant folks who continue to be duped by the charlatans and money-grubbing sophists who pass themselves off as God's prophets, God's ministers, God's priests today. Jesus here shows us a situation where an innocent is caught within a corrupt system. She is doing all she knows how to do, all she has been led to do by the only authorized leadership she has ever known, and it takes the form of her giving her last bit of solvency to them. But God sees her, too. God knows what is going on in her heart, what motivates her giving. And the same God who is in the process of taking down the religious corruption that has sucked her dry, honors her for what she has done.

This text functions then as a divine lament about corrupt religious leaders who prey on the goodwill and good intentions of especially the poor. It functions as a warning to such people that God sees, God knows, and God is working to dismantle such corruption. It serves too as an encouragement to the faithful not to give up. Continue to serve God, know that even when you do something to support what you thought was a worthy person or cause, God knew what your motives were. God is bigger than our ignorance, bigger even than those who use God and manipulate God's innocents to their own ends and profit. God is even bigger than all the institutions that wear God's name and do what they do ostensibly as God's servants, yet actually function as self-serving instruments for self-promotion and self-gain. God is on the side of the "little person," the powerless, the one who cannot stand up against the slings and arrows of the world's Goliaths. And God sees, and knows, and is working toward a just end.

André Resner, Jr.

Twenty-sixth Sunday after Pentecost, Year B

First Lesson: 1 Samuel 1:4-20
(1 Samuel 2:1-10)
Second Lesson: Hebrews 10:11-14, (15-18), 19-25
Gospel Lesson: Mark 13:1-8

These verses open the chapter known as the "little apocalypse" or the "Marcan apocalypse." The characterizations are not terribly helpful. The term "apocalypse" has been chosen in view of visionary material, drawn largely from Daniel, that has a place in other "apocalyptic" literature. References to "tribulations," "desolating sacrilege," and the coming Son of Man all derive from biblical imagery. The chapter's function within the Gospel, however, has little to do with the genre of apocalyptic literature even if it shares aspects of such a worldview. The extended forecast is part of the passion story. Jesus' inexorable march to his confrontation with the religious and political authorities that will mean his death pauses for an extended prediction, given by Jesus to his intimate circle of disciples, that offers a glimpse of what disciples — and readers, who are addressed directly at the end of the chapter — can expect of the time beyond the end of the Gospel.

The setting deserves some comment. The occasion for Jesus' discourse is the disciples' admiring comments about the temple (13:1). These comments follow the story of a widow who places her last coins in the temple treasury (12:41-44) — which in turn follows Jesus' castigation of the religious authorities who "devour widows' houses" (vv. 38-40). While the story of the poor widow has been generally viewed as an example of faithful stewardship, it actually serves as justification for Jesus' prediction that not one stone will be left on another, that they will all be thrown down, in Jerusalem.

Jesus' characterization of the temple as a "bandits' lair" (11:17, quoting Jer. 7:11) is now given some specificity. The leadership is corrupt, concerned with appearance while drawing sustenance from the poor and powerless whom they ought to protect. The temple and its leadership will no longer live off such people. There will not be left one stone on another. Though perhaps not obvious in the pericope itself, the ability of religious institutions to draw life from people by absorbing time and energy and money rather than freeing them for a life of service in the world leads to the prediction of the temple's demise and is surely a topic on which a preacher might focus.

The chapter raises an interesting set of historical questions. Does Jesus' forecast of Jerusalem's destruction reflect knowledge of what actually occurred in 70 C.E. — when Roman legions and their prisoners literally dismantled the entire city, breaking down every building and wall? While this is not a necessary conclusion, many find it convincing that Mark was written shortly after the temple's destruction. Certainly all readers subsequent to 70 have read the story in light of the history that followed. Jesus' forecast proved to be true.

Since the prediction of the temple's fate is tied to events leading to "the end," we may wonder if the author believed the end of the world was at hand and that the war with Rome was part of the events that would bring history to a close. While there is evidence for such notions within other Jewish groups and in early Christianity, Jesus points out in Mark that the dramatic signs mark only the "beginning of the end." "The end is not yet" (13:7). Toward the conclusion of his forecast, Jesus suggests that the end is not far off. "Truly, I say to you, this generation will not pass away before all these things take place" (13:30). Yet, two verses later the statement is qualified: no one knows the precise time of the end except the Father. What is clear is that the author believed the events surrounding the destruction of Jerusalem and the persecution suffered by Jesus' followers were part of a larger conflict between the forces of good and evil that would end only with Jesus' return.

One of the striking things about the chapter is its somber tone. The future the disciples could anticipate would include natural disasters (famines and earthquakes), wars, and — as later verses spell out — social dislocation, including the breakup of families and community strife. It is a strange counterpoint to Jesus' announcement that "the kingdom of God is at hand" and his healings and exorcisms with which the story begins. It also sounds strangely like a summary of the "news" on the front page of local newspapers. Jesus' words are unnervingly realistic. Following Jesus will not provide an escape from difficulties and suffering; in fact, it may make life more difficult. The chapter does not offer any explanation. It presumes that the world is in the grip of evil from which Jesus is liberating people. And it speaks of a day when that liberation will be complete, when the Son of Man sends his angels to gather the elect from the corners of the earth.

For all its somberness, however, the chapter is hopeful. That hope is sounded even in these opening verses. The terrible sufferings ahead are only the prelude to a new day. The point can be missed in the old King James translation: "This is the beginning of the sorrows." More helpful is the NRSV: "This is but the beginning of the birth pangs." Like the natural imagery on which Jesus draws in the parables about the kingdom earlier in the Gospel, in which humble beginnings may conceal the bounty of the harvest that is sure to come, the unfolding of the world's future is compared to the experience of childbirth. The immediate future promises suffering and agony, but these are signs that God's promised reign is near. A new age is about to be born.

In living in such a world, everything depends on knowing what sufferings mean — or better, where life is headed. Jesus offers no interpretation of suffering that suggests some positive function. Much of the difficulty in life is rather due to the bondage of a world that has no room for such a one as Jesus. The story of his own fate at the hands of the Jewish and Roman authorities only confirms the sketch of a world whose most noble and respected authorities will regard Jesus' disciples as enemies. For those with eyes to see, however, signs of the demise of these institutions are already visible. The temple curtain tears at the moment of Jesus' death. Those whose adherence to the temple requires that Jesus be rejected will themselves be rejected. Not one stone will be left on another. The history of promise, though hidden deep within a future that looks dark and foreboding, will finally deliver. The sun will rise on a new world when the Son returns on the clouds of heaven to gather the elect. All will see.

Is there reason to believe such promises? The truthfulness of the good news is invested precisely in that question. On the one hand, there is no way to answer before history comes to its conclusion. Everything depends on what God is yet to do. On the other hand, what God has yet to do is bound up with what God does in Jesus' ministry. If the world has no place for the one whom God calls "my Son," who comes to give his life as a ransom, what will God do in response? Trusting God with the future depends completely on what God will do when Jesus has been tried, mocked, and executed. Jesus' forecast points ahead to the climax of the story.

Donald Juel

First Sunday of Advent, Year B

First Lesson: Isaiah 64:1-9
(Psalm 80:1-7, 17-19)
Second Lesson: 1 Corinthians 1:3-9
Gospel Lesson: Mark 13:24-37

It has been widely agreed since the early twentieth century that Jesus was (among other things) an apocalyptic prophet. He looked for the imminent and dramatic action of God. His was the praxis of a prophet (N. T. Wright). He speaks words of judgment and speaks confidently of his relationship to the Father and to the Father's coming kingdom.

Yet academic readings of the New Testament, even as they grant the apocalyptic aspects of Jesus' proclamation, have often taken a skeptical view of prophecies like those in this Gospel reading. The view became standard that such pericopes were prophecies after the fact, that "the little apocalypse" of Mark, retained by the other synoptics, was a post–A.D. 70 commentary of the church on the fall of Jerusalem.

Those whose traditions have been molded by such New Testament scholarship need in this case to take that scholarship with a large grain of salt. Even if the interpretation and redaction of Mark's Gospel are colored by a final date after A.D. 70, such a collection of warnings by Jesus surely fits his preaching and practice as seen in the rest of the Gospel accounts. N. T. Wright's invitation to picture Jesus sitting on the Mount of Olives overlooking Jerusalem and instructing his disciples about the impending doom is a far more credible scenario than the idea that the church invented the little apocalypse from whole cloth. It is also fully consistent with the witness of the prophets before Jesus.

If we thus dispel a skeptical view of the little apocalypse and in so doing honor the better angels of modern scholarship, the true canonical power of the text lies open. Jesus throughout his ministry, and surely near the end as the powers of darkness gathered forces against him, shared with his disciples both warnings and promises. Like Jeremiah, he grieved prophetically over the judgment that God's people were yet again inviting. He predicted the fall of Jerusalem and apocalyptic chaos in the generation of his own disciples. He was not the first to do so or the first to be right about it. It is as simple as that.

For the church today the season of Advent makes room for such a note of judgment, as it prepares us to celebrate the gracious end of God's judgment in the incarnation of his Son. Just as the prophets ever looked hopefully to the new and restored Jerusalem, the church hears Jesus' warnings in the context of her messianic hope. There are both prophetic judgment and prophetic comfort here.

There are three segments in this selection, and they follow coherently on each other.

Verses 24 to 27 set the apocalyptic scenario. These are the days "when the stars begin to fall." Though that may sound traumatic, the days are not merely dismal. They will lead to the coming of the Son of Man and his gathering of the elect.

Verses 28 to 31 call on the disciples to be watchful. Jesus alerts them that these things will transpire in their own generation. Jesus' prophetic words are sure; they would see disaster. The Father's action would be accompanied by distress. The final segment, verses 32-37, warns against trying to prepare for the time of trial by chronological speculation, that foolish but perennial temptation. Since only the Father knows the chronology, the best the disciples, then or now, can do is to stay alert and be faithful.

Still, we should not be too harsh in our view of those who have tried their hand at chronological speculation. Even after skeptical views of the text are brushed aside, the issue of chronology remains. If this prophecy was about the Son of Man's return, it did not happen in that generation. (It's also as simple as that!) The church needs to deal with the "delay of the parousia." But we are not without tools. Mark was dealing with it already in writing his Gospel, and note well: he is not at all dismayed by it.

There is good reason for that. The Gospel story ends with the resurrection of Jesus. The end has broken in, and the prophetic promise has already begun to become true. The delay of Jesus' return is in that sense no problem at all — all the worry about it is just another case of modern scholarship scratching where it does not itch. There is no such itch in the New Testament, and Mark's account is untroubled. After the "little apocalypse" comes the passion . . . and the resurrection.

This is not to deny the existence of a serious hermeneutical challenge. If we are not going to abuse the text in a lame effort to predict the Lord's return, how shall we preach over nineteen hundred years later as we await his return? How shall we do so without falling into an excessively realized eschatology which would collapse apocalyptic into the life of the church, the personal life of faith, or one of the various lame new age appropriations of Jesus?

The work of Wolfhart Pannenberg and others over the last century is helpful. Only in understanding the centrality and importance of Jesus' apocalyptic preaching can we understand what the resurrection means, as Paul already makes clear in 1 Corinthians. When we understand that the resurrection of Jesus is the beginning of the end time, then we can live quite comfortably with the delay of Christ's return. For what it accomplishes is to open space for the proclamation and life of the gospel. The delay of the last judgment is a good thing — not least because it is God's decision to do so.

The last time I preached on this text, I dealt with it in the following manner.

Our experience is still the same as that of the Evangelists, even if they did not imagine the year 2000 jubilee. We know that there will be a lot of history after Jesus, and for all the evils that history has brought, it has also brought a magnificent array of witnesses, of worship, of wonders of God's mercy.

If it had stopped then, there would have been no Saint Augustine, no Saint Francis, no Martin Luther, no Mother Teresa, no Gregorian chant, no Gothic cathedrals, no Bach. And come to think of it, there would have been no you and I, no Christ Church, York.

We should just grant that God knows what he is up to in giving all this time and space, in giving his church a long history. The same question, then, is there for us as it was for the writers of the Gospels — what do you do if you believe that Jesus will come back but probably not so soon as had once been thought?

And to that question, I think there is for the preacher a fairly straight-forward answer that comes right from the text. We are: (1) to live as if his return were just around the corner and (2) to recognize the signs of his rule and presence now.

Here local situations will dictate the content. The first point can be developed around Jesus' warning to keep alert. Christians are not always very alert. They are far too rarely on tiptoe to see where God is calling them, challenging them, or inviting them. The church can be awfully somnolent. It is beset by every manner of temptation, as is the individual. Where, the preacher can ask, have you been sleepy? Where has our congregation been sleepy? What would it look like to wake up?

The second point is of course closely related, but it is not the same. Christians need to be reminded that Jesus is present through the work of the Spirit in the life of the church, in Word and sacrament. They need to be reminded of the way the kingdom is manifested in meeting the needs of others. They need to have it reaffirmed that God is acting in those personal and social apocalypses that expose our idolatry and false hopes.

In reflecting on this essential piece of New Testament apocalyptic and in keeping in mind the truly eschatological nature of the Gospel, it is also important not to repudiate utterly realized eschatology. The kingdom really has broken in (or in good Advent language, *dawned*) in the coming of Jesus. While it must not be equated with the life of the church or the faith of the individual Christian, it does manifest itself there. While it is not yet, it is in some very important ways present already. That is another reason why the New Testament is not much troubled by the delay.

The eucharistic hymn widely used in Advent, "Let All Mortal Flesh Keep Silence," celebrates the presence of the kingdom in the Eucharist. It is present likewise in the faith, the faithfulness, and the good works of God's people. God has decided that there will be a lot of history after the resurrection. In that space and time God's people continue to hope and watch and stay alert, even as they remain confident that the Son of Man's coming is not confined to the distant future or to another reality. The sermon can and should explain and encourage one of the church's most basic prayers: "Come, Lord Jesus."

Leonard R. Klein

Resurrection of the Lord, Year B

First Lesson: Acts 10:34-43
(Psalm 118:1-2, 14-24)
Second Lesson: 1 Corinthians 15:1-11
Gospel Lesson: Mark 16:1-8

Mark 16:1-8 is challenging text for Easter Sunday. The text does not meet the liturgical and emotional expectations that most worshipers bring to this climactic Sunday of the Christian year. Although the messenger in the tomb does proclaim that Jesus has been raised, there is no triumphant, joyful celebration of Jesus' resurrection in the story. Rather, the text ends with frightened silence and disobedience. And contemporary worshipers are not the first ones to be troubled by this ending. Most scholars today agree that verse 8 is the original conclusion of Mark's Gospel. Verses 9-20 were apparently added at a later date, probably to give the Gospel a more satisfying ending. The preacher and congregation who struggle with this text on Easter Sunday stand in good and faithful company!

Despite the text's difficulties, preachers should linger with Mark 16:1-8 and let its witness be heard, even if it cuts against the grain of traditional expectations. Mark's reminder that the resurrection can be disturbing and frightening provides an important complement — even a corrective — to our rush toward triumphant joy. Easter Sunday of Year B is a good time to remember that Easter is a *season* lasting fifty days. There will be plenty of time for further reflection upon and celebration of the resurrection. Everything does not have to be said on the first day. On this Sunday, let Mark have his say.

When one does linger with this text, one confronts the unexpected and shocking character of Jesus' resurrection, as well as its direct relationship to the way of the cross. The three women, the only ones who remain faithful to Jesus after the desertion and betrayal of his disciples, rise early on the first day of the week, having rested on the Sabbath, and go to anoint Jesus' body. Although they are doing what they can to be faithful to Jesus, the women continue to function in the old world, a world governed by the power of death. They go to anoint Jesus' body; they go to deal with Jesus as a corpse, as one who himself has succumbed to the power of death. Along the way they ask themselves, "Who will roll away the stone for us from the entrance to the tomb?" (v. 3). The women, Mark emphasizes, expect the old world to be in place, a world of predictable cause and effect in which stones placed over tombs on Friday will inevitably be there on Sunday. While the women do demonstrate faith and courage in going to the tomb, they carry a world with them, the old world in which death has the final word.

Then, bit by bit, this old world is dismantled and everything is thrown off balance. The women "look up" and discover that the large stone has already been rolled away. While numerous human explanations are possible for this development, it is clear that something is out of kilter. Then the women enter the tomb and, instead of Jesus' corpse, encounter "a young man, dressed in a white robe, sitting on the right side." The figure is depicted as an angel — a messenger — possibly one of the white-robed martyrs from the apocalyptic tradition (Ched Myers, *Binding the Strong Man: A Political Reading of Mark's Story of Jesus* [Maryknoll, N.Y.: Orbis, 1988], pp. 397-98). The women are "alarmed," as their discoveries begin to turn their world upside down.

The presence of a messenger is appropriate for what follows. The young man does indeed have a message for the women. And this message marks a momentous turning point in Mark's Gospel. In place of Jesus' physical presence, we now find the proclamation of the gospel, the core of which is announced by the messenger: "Do not be alarmed; you are looking for Jesus of Nazareth, who was crucified. He has been raised; he is not here." The kerygma has replaced the corpse: Jesus of Nazareth, who was crucified, has been raised from the dead. That is the news that challenges the power of death and turns the predictable cause-effect world on its head.

No wonder the women are frightened. If something as certain and inevitable as death is no longer predictable, the world has changed dramatically. As the Misfit, a character in Flannery O'Connor's short story "A Good Man Is Hard to Find," put it: "Jesus was the only One that ever raised the dead, and He shouldn't have done it. He has thrown everything off balance" (in *Three by Flannery O'Connor* [New York: New American Library, 1955], p. 142). If stones are rolled away without human effort, if Jesus really is raised from the dead, what other human assumptions about wisdom and folly, power and weakness, will likewise be proved false? If the very power of death has been overcome, what other kinds of power and domination will likewise be overthrown? What other kinds of disturbances will God work in the world and in our lives? The women may be frightened precisely because they grasp the implications of Jesus' resurrection.

But there is another reason the women may be frightened. The messenger continues: "But go, tell his disciples and Peter he is going ahead of you to Galilee; there you will see him, just as he told you." Jesus is going ahead of them to meet them and the disciples back in Galilee, the context of their everyday lives and the place where their discipleship began. What a daunting prospect. Having betrayed and deserted Jesus, the disciples must encounter him again in Galilee. And at this point no one knows what shape that encounter will take.

Jesus is loose in the world. He is not in our present as a lifeless corpse or in our past as a distant memory. Rather, he goes ahead of us into the future to meet us there and claim us, not on our own terms, but on his. We can no longer deal with Jesus as a dead body, safely buried in a tomb, but now we encounter him as a living reality. There is no escaping him, no containing him, no forgetting him. Business as usual is no longer safe because Jesus goes ahead of us to call us to discipleship again and again. The resurrection is not a onetime event in the past, but the promise of more surprising, disturbing encounters to come. Mark thus proclaims that the resurrection is not primarily about empty tombs, but about the living Christ who continues to encounter us in the world and call us to discipleship.

This discipleship involves the way of the cross. Jesus promises to meet the disciples back in Galilee, where the story began. The disciples — and the readers — are directed back to the beginning of Mark's Gospel in order to take up once again the way that leads to the cross. Resurrection here is not primarily a word about life after death, but rather a confirmation of Jesus' way in the world and a call to discipleship along the path of the cross. While such discipleship can now be taken up in a world in which the power of death has been defeated — good news, indeed! — the path nevertheless remains the costly path of the cross. The women are probably right to be afraid upon hearing that Jesus goes before them to meet them and the disciples back in Galilee. Not only has the world been thrown off balance, but the way of the cross, at which the disciples failed so miserably, remains the path they must walk once again.

The response of the women takes us into the struggle of discipleship in Mark's Gospel. The women, who have up until this point been Jesus' most faithful followers, now become disobedient. They have heard the gospel proclaimed, and they have been given a mission to the disciples. In response, however, "they said nothing to anyone, for they were afraid" (and in the Greek there is a double negative, which makes this statement extremely forceful). Just as the disciples had been disobedient as Jesus moved toward the cross, so now the women are disobedient to the calling they have been given by the messenger. Jesus' resurrection is no guarantee of faithfulness. The Word proclaimed can lead to disobedience. The struggle of discipleship continues even after the resurrection.

"They said nothing to anyone, for they were afraid." The Gospel seems to come to a "dead end," despite the resurrection. Literally no one in the story remains faithful. And there appears to be no way that the news will be spread and people will be called to the risky journey of faith and discipleship. Here, however, we can discern the brilliance of Mark's Gospel. There is one group remaining who can carry the Word into the world, meet Jesus in the context of everyday life, and take up the path of discipleship. And that group is the readers (Mary Ann Tolbert, "Mark," in *The Women's Bible Commentary*, ed. Carol A. Newsome and Sharon H. Ringe [London: SPCK; Louisville: Westminster/John Knox, 1992], p. 274)! To borrow an old cliché, Mark throws the ball into our court. The disciples have failed, the women have failed. But we have heard the proclamation: "Jesus of Nazareth, who was crucified, has been raised. He is going ahead of you into Galilee; there you will see him," and begin the journey of discipleship anew. That is the calling of Easter, which Mark sets before the church.

Charles L. Campbell

Fourth Sunday of Advent, Year B

First Lesson: 2 Samuel 7:1-11, 16
(Psalm 89:1-4, 19-26)
Second Lesson: Romans 16:25-27
Gospel Lesson: Luke 1:26-38

The importance of this text to the Advent season can hardly be over-stated. This liturgical context has, quite appropriately, focused readerly attention on *the child* to be born, especially as that child's birth is both predicted (1:31) and explained (1:35), and as that child is called by name (Jesus) and numerous titles (1:31-33, 35). A focus on the baby to be born is in line with the observation that this account — like many in Luke 1–2 — has much in common with Old Testament annunciation stories. These stories usually include an announcement of imminent birth, the name of the child to be born, and insights into the child's future (see, e.g., Gen. 16:7-13 [Ishmael]; 17:1-21 [Isaac]; 18:1-15 [Isaac]; Judg. 13:2-25 [Samson]). The connections between these stories and the annunciation highlight that the God at work in the opening chapters of Luke is the same God that was at work in the saints of old, and that what God was up to back then is the same thing God is up to now. The connections also invariably invite comparison (and contrast) between Jesus and these figures.

Another close parallel that invites comparison is the birth of John the Baptist (1:5-25, 57-80). Luke has structured the births of John and Jesus in parallel — as a diptych. The many similarities and connections serve to unite these two boys in the plan of God as well as to highlight Jesus, who is clearly depicted as the superior (see 3:16-17; 7:18-30).

These three factors — the Advent context, the Old Testament parallels, and the parallel structure of the Lukan birth narrative — tend to highlight the child in the account, and particularly the child to be born to Mary. How-ever, there are other parallels between 1:26-38 and the Old Testament be-yond the annunciation-of-birth type. To be more specific, the annunciation to Mary in 1:26-38, as well as to Zechariah in 1:8-20, closely follows the pat-tern of prophetic call narratives first established in the calling of Moses (Exod. 3:1-12; see the Old Testament lesson [Exod. 3:1-15] for the Fifteenth Sunday after Pentecost, Year A, for further details) but is also found else-where, for example, in the calling of Isaiah (Isa. 6:1-13; cf. the Old Testa-ment lesson [Isa. 6:1-8, (9-13)] for the Fifth Sunday after the Epiphany, Year C). This text can be easily outlined according to this pattern. This pattern, while not neglecting the importance of the birth of the Christ child, nevertheless also highlights the importance of Mary herself, especially concerning the *nature* of her duty and her radical *obedience* to God's call.

1. *The divine confrontation (1:26-27)*. The "sixth month" is the sixth month of Elizabeth's pregnancy (1:24); the notation serves to connect the previous scene with the present one, not to mention the two mothers and their two children. The angel Gabriel also connects the two: he is the same angel that appeared to Zechariah in the temple (1:19). But despite the close connections and parallel structures, there are marked differences between these two accounts. Prior to this point Luke has centered on Judea and its religious center: the temple in Jerusalem. Now the scene shifts to the north — to Galilee and its ill-reputed town of Nazareth (cf. John 1:46). Earlier Luke focused on a priest, Zechariah, of the priestly order of Abijah, and his wife Elizabeth, also of priestly descent (via Aaron; 1:5). But now he turns to a young girl (perhaps twelve to thirteen years of age, the typical age of betrothal) named Mary. We known nothing of her lineage whatsoever — at least not until 1:36, when Elizabeth is described as her "relative" (*syngenis;* the term is nonspecific), perhaps indicating that they share the same lineage, though this is not certain. Apart from her name, we are also told that Mary is a virgin. The Jewish concept that lies behind this term includes any young, unmarried woman of marriageable age, but in Mary's case "virgin" is a technical term, for she "has not known a man" (1:34). Luke also tells us that Mary was engaged to one Joseph, from the house of David. The differences between engagement then and now should be noted. Joseph and Mary were, by our accounts, "married" (the bride-price had been paid, etc.), but Mary would have continued to live with her family for a year, at which point the wedding became "official" via consummation (for further details regarding marriage customs, age, and so forth, consult Joel B. Green, *The Gospel of Luke,* New International Commentary on the New Testament [Grand Rapids: Eerdmans, 1997], pp. 85-86 and 86 n. 17). In Mary, then, we find an extremely young girl (who may have not — or only barely — reached puberty), sexually chaste, with no elaborate pedigree, living in a despicable town in something of a liminal state between her husband-to-be and her father.

2. *The introductory word (1:28)*. It is to this unlikely girl in this unlikely situation that God sends Gabriel, who greets her and names her: "Favored One." No wonder Mary wondered what sort of greeting this might be (1:29)! Given the great attention to Mary throughout the Christian tradition, one might be inclined to view her favored status as *the reason why* God chose her. But Luke is not interested in such behind-the-scenes reasoning. Mary is favored *because* she has been chosen. There is not — to our eye at least — any in-

herent or explicit reason given for her selection. Instead, there is much to the contrary (see above). Indeed, Mary is but a lowly servant (1:48), but this is exactly the kind of person that Luke (and God!) loves to exalt in his pattern of *status reversal* where the poor and humble are lifted up and the rich and proud are brought down (cf. 1:52-53). Of course, as the narrative will make clear, God has — as usual — made an excellent choice in selecting Mary.

The angel also tells Mary that "the Lord is with you." Such words are said to mighty warriors like Gideon (see Judg. 6:12, 16) and to godly prophets like Moses (Exod. 3:12) and Jeremiah (Jer. 1:8) in their calls. Could Mary be called to a similar, divinely ordained — perhaps even *prophetic* — task? As Gabriel pauses we are left to wonder, with Mary, about the meaning of this greeting.

3. *The commission (1:30-33).* The pause is short-lived, however. Gabriel goes on to instruct her to have no fear (this is frequently said to the saints and warriors of the Old Testament — e.g., Gen. 15:1; 26:24; 46:3; Num. 21:34; Deut. 1:21; 3:2; Josh. 8:1) and reiterates that she has found favor with God. At this point in the call narrative structure comes the commissioning proper. For Mary the mission is to conceive a child. When she gives birth to this child — a boy — she is to name him Jesus. Motherhood is Mary's prophetic vocation. This will be a glorious vocation — her child is destined for greatness (1:32-33; 2:29-32) — Mary's soul can only magnify the Lord (1:46-55). She will treasure this mission (2:19, 51). But this vocation will also be painful — a sword will pierce her own soul too (2:35). She will hear her son say that his mother and brothers are those who hear the word of God and do it (8:21). Mary and Jesus' brothers do just that in Acts 1:14. But Mary does it here as well — before the child who will utter these words is even born (see below).

If Mary is called like the great prophets of old, then Jesus is her oracle. If she is called like the great warrior-deliverers of old, then Jesus is her weapon (cf. 2:34-35). In either case, her vocation pales in the face of the vocation of this child. He will be "great" like John (1:15), but is destined to be much, much more. He will be called the Son of the Most High (1:32), and the Lord God will give him the throne of David. Lest this throne be allegorized, Gabriel promises Mary that Jesus will *reign* over the house of Jacob forever and that his *kingdom* will never end (1:33).

These terms are loaded — especially in the politically charged context of the first century and in the eschatologically charged opening chapters of Luke. It will take a whole Gospel (and perhaps a sequel as well!; cf. 2:31-32; Acts 1:6-8) for this child to fulfill these terms, to fill them out, not to mention to redefine many — if not all — of them.

Be that as it may, it is worth noting that many of the prophets are called to failure. Their prophetic preaching will bring termination (Isa. 6:9-13), destruction (Jer. 1:10a), rebellion (Ezek. 2:1-7; 3:7-11). Mary's calling will involve no such failure. She *will* have this child, *will* name him Jesus; he *will* be great, *will* be called Son of the Most High, *will* receive the throne, *will* reign forever, and there *will not* be an end to his kingdom. Success, not failure! Of course, the great irony of the Gospel is that this boy's success will come through what appears — to most at the time (cf. 24:21) — to be a fantastic failure (23:26-56).

4. *The objection (1:34).* If before Mary was perplexed, she is now downright confounded. "How can this be?" she asks, and proceeds to explain the situation to Gabriel, who is apparently ignorant of the details regarding human procreation (!). The question could be an honest one, simply asking for more information, but the form of the call narrative typically includes an objection following the commission (see Exod. 3:11, 13; 4:1, 10, 13; Judg. 6:15; Isa. 6:11; Jer. 1:6). The objections in these cases serve as a means by which the called tries to get out of the calling. It is quite possible that Mary's question functions similarly — this is an unnatural task, after all, and will no doubt complicate matters, especially with Joseph (cf. Matt 1:18-25).

5. *The reassurance (1:35).* The objection element of the call form is followed by the reassurance, wherein God's activity is often highlighted and magnified. Such is certainly the case with the annunciation, as Gabriel assures Mary that this birth will be *God's* doing: the *Holy Spirit* will come upon her, the *power of the Most High* will overshadow her. The child will be *holy,* the *Son of God.* The task may be confusing and complicated, maybe even objectionable, but God will see to it.

6. *The sign (1:36-37).* Calls in the Old Testament also sometimes involve the giving of signs, whether these are asked for or not. Gabriel seems to give Mary a sign by directing her attention to Elizabeth and revealing that she is pregnant (1:36). If old, barren Elizabeth is already in her second trimester, then certainly God can work with the opposite problem: a young girl who happens to be a virgin. "For nothing will be impossible with God" (1:37).

The giving of a sign signals the end of the call form, but Luke is not yet done, and neither is Mary. Amazingly, she has the last word; this is unparalleled in any of the examples of calling in the Old Testament. And what a last word it is! "Here am I, the servant of the Lord; let it be with me according to your word" (1:38). Mary uses language rich in biblical allusion: "Here am I" *(idou)* is what Abraham, Samuel, and Isaiah — among others — say when they hear God call their names in the Greek Old Testament. But Mary says it even better than they did: she says it *after* she learns the details of God's plan. She also calls herself the Lord's servant or *slave* (cf. also 1:48). By both means, Mary depicts herself as one who is ready and willing to — indeed, who *must* — do God's bidding. As if this weren't enough, Mary wishes that this transpire exactly as Gabriel has stated. This last sentence may contain a wordplay. 1:37 said that no thing — literally "word" *(rhēma)* — was impossible for God. Now Mary says, "May it be according to your word" *(rhēma)*. This seemingly-impossible but not-really-impossible word/thing will now be the word/thing that comes to pass with Mary.

Mary's response is, in sum, one of the best statements of human response in the Bible. Isaiah responded eagerly, but was rash: as soon as he discovered the details of his mission, he objected. But Mary, *after* learning the details of her calling, *despite* an objection (?), *nevertheless* responds with radical obedience. She hears the word of God, believes it, and does it — and is blessed for it (see 1:45; cf. 8:15, 21). "For Luke she is the first Christian disciple" (Raymond E. Brown, Karl P. Donfried, Joseph A. Fitzmyer, and John Reumann, eds., *Mary in the New Testament: A Collaborative Assessment by Protestant and Roman Catholic Scholars* [New York: Paulist, 1978], p. 126). She is also the first female prophet in Luke (note also Anna in 2:36). She will go on to prophesy in the Magnificat (1:46-55), where many prophetic themes are present (in the diptych structure of the birth narrative, 1:46 is parallel to 1:67, where Zechariah "prophesies" the Benedictus [1:68-79]). Her main prophetic calling, however, is delivering Jesus, the Oracle of God.

Brent A. Strawn

Fourth Sunday of Advent, Year C

First Lesson: 2 Samuel 7:1-11, 16
(Psalm 89:1-4, 19-26)
Second Lesson: Romans 16:25-27
Gospel Lesson: Luke 1:39-45, (46-55)

The scene portrayed in Luke 1:39-55, commonly called the visitation, cannot be rightly understood without consideration of its pivotal role within Luke's infancy narrative as a whole. Luke 1 and 2 is constructed as a "diptych," a painting drawn on two panels. One panel tells of the birth of John the Baptist; the other recounts the coming of Jesus Christ. There is usually a structural relationship between the two panels of a diptych, and so it is with the infancy narrative. The two representations are remarkably parallel. The John panel begins in 1:13 with an angelic promise to the aged Zechariah that his equally aged wife, Elizabeth, will bear a son. That son, John, will have a remarkable ministry before the Lord. The angel then appears to the young Mary in 1:26-38, and in a similar manner promises Mary, a virgin, that she too will bear a son. The parallelism is not confined to content, however. In both panels the angel declares, "Do not be afraid." In both there is a reasonable objection to the promise: "We're too old!"; "I am a virgin!" Finally, in both panels there is an angelic response to the objection.

The scenes are not completely parallel, however. In various ways Luke demonstrates the superiority of Jesus over John. The most obvious of these is that a birth to aged parents is unusual; a birth to a virgin is impossible. For our purposes the most important distinction is that Mary, despite her questioning of the angel, is granted a sign while Zechariah, whose objection is very similar, is punished for his incredulity. The sign for Mary is the fulfillment of the promise to Zechariah; his wife, Mary's relative Elizabeth, has conceived in her old age. Note the manner in which Luke carefully prepares the way for the visitation. On the John side of the diptych, the final word is a note that Elizabeth hid herself away (1:24-25). The final word of the angel to Mary is a reference to this very secret. Because the pregnancy is a secret, it can function as a sign. Mary then sets out to visit her kinswoman, the scene that is the subject of today's text. The parallelism also continues after the visitation. On both sides of the diptych, the child is born; an aged and pious Israelite, Zechariah for John and Simeon for Jesus, sings a hymn of praise to God; and the child's growth is described. Much of this common pattern is modeled after the Old Testament descriptions of the births of various heroes of the faith.

The place of the visitation within the infancy narrative is now clear; it is the link between the two parallel stories. In this scene alone the characters of the two panels come together. We will also expect, however, that the scene, in accord with Luke's theological intent and the flow of the narrative itself, will portray the superiority of Jesus. It will make clear which story really matters. This pericope is the narrative equivalent of the poetic statement concerning the Baptist in the prologue to the Fourth Gospel: "He was not the light" (John 1:8).

So it is that "upon hearing Mary's greeting, the child leaped in [Elizabeth's] womb" (Luke 1:41). This prenatal greeting hearkens back to the angel's promise that John will be the forerunner of the Lord (1:16-17) and draws the mind forward to his role in the body of the Gospel (3:1-20). It has already been noted that both sides of the diptych are influenced by Old Testament accounts of the births of heroes of the faith. Elizabeth's greeting and blessing are also shaped by the Scriptures of Israel. Her words to Mary echo the greetings both to Jael (Judg. 5:24) and to Judith of an apocryphal book (Jdt. 13:18). The faithfulness of both women is instrumental in the saving of Israel, though the analogy ought not be pressed too far. The means of salvation in both cases is assassination! Perhaps it would be fair to say, however, that these echoes do remind the observant reader that the salvation to be wrought through these present events is more than personal; it is for the people as a whole. This corporate understanding is reinforced when another allusion is identified. Elizabeth's words echo the farewell of the aged Moses to Israel in Deuteronomy 28:4: "Blessed shall be the fruit of your womb." That blessing is to be accorded Israel if it is obedient. This understanding also leads us forward to the body of Luke's Gospel. Elizabeth's words are not only an echo of what has been; they are an anticipation of what is to come. In 11:27 there is another blessing on Jesus' mother. A woman shouts out, "Blessed is the womb that bore you and the breasts that nursed you!" But Jesus replied, "Blessed rather are those who hear the word of God and obey it!" A right hearing of God's word always issues in obedience. In precisely this way Mary is worthy of blessing, for she has heard the angel's word and has obeyed by coming to her kinswoman. Elizabeth's blessing rightly culminates therefore with a final word: "And blessed is she who believed that there would be a fulfillment of what was spoken to her by the Lord." Hearing, believing, obedience, and blessing — these are the keys to the story.

The visitation culminates in Mary's magnificent hymn of praise. This hymn, like the other hymns of Luke's infancy narrative, the Benedictus and the Nunc Dimittis, culminates in a promise/fulfillment/praise progression. We have already noted the promise, that Mary will bear a special son. The sign promised by the angel, the pregnancy of Elizabeth together with the greeting by Elizabeth and her unborn child, shows that the promise has been fulfilled. Note the previous words: Mary believed that there would "be a *fulfillment* of what was spoken to her by the Lord." Now comes the praise, Mary's Magnificat. The progression promise/fulfillment/praise is homiletically helpful. It suggests a possible structure for the sermon.

As is the case with Elizabeth's greeting, the Magnificat is shot through with Old Testament allusions. Almost every phrase finds a parallel in the Scriptures of Israel. Nor is the kinship a matter of words only. The synonymous and antithetical parallelism that fills the hymn is the distinguishing mark of Hebrew poetry. Likewise, its overall structure — word of praise, reason for praise, extended in this and many cases — is common in Israelite poetry. The beautiful hymn was probably used in the worship of the early Jewish Christian church. Some have even argued that it comes from the church of Jerusalem itself. If even the more general supposition is true, it is more testimony to the Jewishness of the early Christian church. The magnificence of the poetry, which has inspired many truly magnificent musical compositions, is not diminished by this dependence on the Old Testament. Rather, we see in this hymn the way those who live within a tradition can use the language of the tradition to weave a rich new tapestry. That the threads of the tapestry have been used before but adds to their luster.

Another progression in the hymn is from the personal to the corporate. The hymn begins with personal references, *"My* soul magnifies. . . . The Mighty One has done great things for *me."* From verse 50 on, however, all references are corporate: God has lifted up the "lowly," filled the "hungry," helped "his servant Israel." The Hebrew word behind the New Testament Greek rendered "lowly" is particularly interesting. Not only does it refer to those who are objectively "poor," but in the Psalms it also serves as a common designation of Israel. Finally, it represents those who, having nothing else to depend on, cast their trust completely upon the Lord. It is these folk whom the Lord, then and now, has reached out to save.

The tense of the verbs is worthy of note. The aorist (past) tense normally represents something completed at a point in the past. But how can it be said that the wonderful things spoken of in this hymn have already happened? Sometimes they are treated as if the verbs were really present tenses describing what God habitually does (cf. the well-known hymn based on this text, "Tell Out My Soul"). Others argue that they refer to future events, but the speaker is so confident of them that she can speak as if these things had already happened. A more nuanced version of this is that the singers of the hymn do in fact look back on something that has already happened, something that makes them so sure that God has triumphed that they can speak of all the rest of God's victory as sure and certain. For Mary that something is the fulfillment of the Lord's promise through the angel. For the early Christians the events that gave them such certainty were the life, death, and resurrection of Jesus Christ.

Stephen Farris

Nativity of the Lord (Christmas Day), Years A, B, C

First Lesson: Isaiah 9:2-7
(Psalm 96)
Second Lesson: Titus 2:11-14
Gospel Lesson: Luke 2:1-14, (15-20)

The Christmas story as recounted by Luke is a marvel of the storyteller's art. Simple as it appears, the narrative connects the birth of Jesus both to the history of salvation and to the history of the wider, public world. Within this lovely story are references back to the Old Testament and forward to Luke's two-volume account of Jesus and the birth of Christianity.

The first section of our text tells of the birth of Jesus itself. A historical difficulty arises at the outset. Luke dates the birth of Jesus by reference to a census ordered by Emperor Augustus when a certain Quirinius was governor of Syria. It is known that there was a census when the Romans took over direct rule of Palestine in A.D. 6. At that time Quirinius was indeed stationed in Syria and in charge of affairs in the region. Luke thus seems to stand in direct contradiction to Matthew, who places the birth in Herod's reign, for it is certain that Herod died in 4 B.C. More conservative scholars note the reference to "first" in verse 2, however, and assert that Luke may be referring to a census earlier than the one described above. What can be stated with more certainty is that it appears to be Luke's desire to set his narrative of Jesus Christ in a world context. "A decree went out from Emperor Augustus that all the world should be registered." Similarly, when Jesus' ministry begins there is another reference to the public affairs of the Roman Empire (3:1). Luke wishes to say of Jesus what Paul will tell the Roman governor Festus, "This was not done in a corner" (Acts 26:26). In the first century Jesus might appear insignificant to the world, and it was important to tie his story to the great world in which Augustus and Quirinius figured so prominently. Now, of course, Augustus is chiefly remembered, and Quirinius only remembered, because in their time Jesus was born in Bethlehem.

The journey to Bethlehem once again links Jesus to David (cf. 1:32, 69). That Jesus was a descendant of David is an important theme in early Christianity. See, for example, the early Christian confession in Romans 1:3-5. Once in Bethlehem, Jesus is born, wrapped in cloth bands, and laid in a manger. This should not be interpreted, as in so many sermons, as a consequence of sheer indifference on the part of the innkeeper. A clean, quiet stable might well have been preferable to a crowded inn. Rather, it carries the mind forward to the ministry of Jesus. "Foxes have holes, and birds of the air have nests; but the Son of Man has nowhere to lay his head" (Luke 9:58). In the immediate context, there must be something surprising for the shepherds to recognize as a sign; the unusual replacement cradle and perhaps also the cloth bands function in this way. Scholars have seen allusions to various Old Testament and intertestamental texts in this description. Perhaps only a link to Isaiah 1:3 is convincing. There the donkey knows its manger but Israel does not know its Lord. If Israel now wants to know its Lord, it may see him in a manger.

The story then proceeds to the third angelic visitation of Luke's Gospel, in this case to the shepherds. The figure of the shepherd is a particularly rich biblical image. Perhaps the reader of this story will remember that David, who likewise had been born in Bethlehem, had been a shepherd. Perhaps the hearer, if well versed in Scripture, will remember the promise that God himself will act as shepherd to Israel. Some have suggested that behind this part of the infancy narrative is a reflection on the promises of coming salvation in Micah 4 and 5. In those chapters there is specific mention of Bethlehem, of God's savior as shepherd, and of a "tower of the flock" as a place of honor. A consideration of that part of Micah that contains so much of the key vocabulary of the infancy narrative may assist the preacher in preparing the Christmas sermon. It is not the case, however, that shepherds were held in honor in the first century. They were poor, and the demands of their trade made it difficult, even impossible, for them to fulfill the demands of the law. Perhaps with the reference to the shepherds there is an anticipation of the body of Luke's Gospel. There the one who tells the parable of a shepherd who seeks and saves the lost will associate chiefly with the poor and the outcast. As the story begins, so it will continue.

It is, then, to "certain poor shepherds" that the angel comes. As with Zechariah and Mary, the angel will say, "Do not be afraid," words that were already a beloved old Bible phrase in the first century. (Because these words were ancient and traditional in the first century, the equally ancient and traditional "Fear not!" is actually a superior translation for our time.) The message of the angel is crammed with theologically loaded vocabulary. The thing which God has done is "good news." It is a "great joy." It is public, that is, it can be witnessed by all the people (here certainly Israel). It is not a matter of the future only; it is visible "today," a key word for Luke (cf. 4:16). The one who has come is characterized as Christ or Messiah. He is also "the Lord," a title reserved elsewhere in Luke 1–2 and in the Hebrew tradition as a whole for God, but elsewhere in Luke-Acts as a characteristic title for Jesus himself. The unusual circumstances of the birth, known already by the reader, are then communicated as yet another sign.

After a sign one might expect praise, and so it is: the birth of Jesus is hailed by an angelic chorus. It is interesting to note that when Jesus enters Jerusalem, the disciples shout out a very similar word of praise (19:38b). The angelic chorus is difficult to translate. The translation problem comes from a textual difficulty that is reviewed in any thorough commentary but cannot be discussed here. The lovely and moving rendition of the King James Version divides the song into three parts. The third part of the hymn then becomes "Good will towards men." Another option is to attach the goodwill to the people, "to those of goodwill." In this reading the song falls into two parts, a word about God and word about humanity. That is to say, peace comes to those who exhibit goodwill. This division into two parts is correct, but another understanding of "goodwill" is preferable. Parallels in the Dead Sea Scrolls now make it almost certain that the "goodwill" is an attribute of God, not of people. It is that divine favor by which God reaches out to humanity to rescue and save. Glory belongs to God in heaven. Peace belongs on earth to those whom God favors. The coming of Jesus and the peace that he gives is a direct consequence of that divine favor.

The word "glory" is a key one in this passage. Because of verse 9, many churchgoers imagine the word refers to a bright light. This is too concrete a reading. The "glory" language is reminiscent of Old Testament theophanies, manifestations of God's presence. God's presence, even through an angel, overwhelms the senses as brightness can overwhelm the eyes. "Glory" also appears in verse 14. Clearly, "Bright light to God in the highest" would make no sense whatever. It may help to remember that the root of the word "glory" in Hebrew comes from the verb "to weigh or to be heavy." We still use the word "weight" as a way of giving respect. "Her word carries weight." "He's a heavyweight." Or a leftover hippie might simply say, "Heavy!" To give God glory is to recognize that power and honor and might belong not to Augustus or Quirinius or their contemporary equivalents, but to God and to God alone. "Glory to God in the highest!"

In the story the shepherds demonstrate an obedience (cf. Mary in 1:39-55) simply by going. Feet, it seems, can be indicators of faithfulness. There then occurs a note which is often overlooked in the Christmas story. The shepherds tell what they have seen and heard and what Mary hears and treasures in her heart. Faithfulness is not a matter of the feet only, but of the mouth, the ear, and the heart also.

The response, as is often the case in the body of the Gospel after one of Jesus' wonders, is praise. The shepherds glorify God. Once again the progression is promise, fulfillment, praise. Unlike the other such progressions in these narratives, no words are supplied for the shepherds' praise. In the interest of the wider parallelism with the John the Baptist narrative, the hymn of praise for the birth of Jesus is saved for the next section of the chapter.

Stephen Farris

Nativity of the Lord (Christmas Day), Years A, B, C

First Lesson: Isaiah 62:6-12
(Psalm 97)
Second Lesson: Titus 3:4-7
Gospel Lesson: Luke 2:(1-7), 8-20

L uke introduces for us the true king, a ruler greater yet humbler than the most powerful ruler that seemed to set the agenda for the world known to Luke's first audience. An expositor of this passage today might recall the powerful and glamorous figures of this world that capture people's attention, then point back to how the greatest king of all came to us in a humble way.

The passage opens with a decree from Caesar Augustus concerning a universal tax census, calling attention to Caesar's power over Luke's world (2:1). This power covered all geographical regions in the empire and had economic implications for every individual; Caesar's decree also sets the stage for the events occurring in this passage, including the journey to Bethlehem. The informed reader, however, knows that God had decreed the Messiah's birth in David's Bethlehem long before Caesar decreed his tax census (cf. 2:5; Mic. 5:2). The narrative proceeds to develop the contrast between those who are powerful by the world's definition and the greatest of kings.

Because we lack complete knowledge of the ancient census system, some historical details surrounding the census remain obscure to us. In a later period, officials seem to have provided regular censuses every fourteen years; the practice seems less regular in this period, and the census may not have been implemented at the same time in all locations. People would return to where they held property, and it is possible that Joseph and Mary were originally from Bethlehem; pottery samples suggest that many settlers in Nazareth immigrated there from Judea. In Syria women were also taxed, which might explain why Mary would have to travel this late in her pregnancy — though given the circumstances of the pregnancy, Joseph may simply have had no one else with whom to leave her.

At the present time, although we know that Quirinius was governor during the later census in A.D. 6, and there is reason to believe that he held earlier offices, possibly in the same region, we do not possess exrabiblical evidence for who the governor was during the time of Jesus' birth. Luke could well mean that this was Quirinius's first governorship over Syria, using this statement simply to date the event. In any case, because it was more widely remembered that Quirinius was governor during the revolt of A.D. 6, Luke might also be raising the connection to help his readers sense the oppressiveness involved in a tax census, an oppressiveness that later provoked a serious Jewish revolt against Roman authority. In response to that revolt, Rome crushed Sepphoris, the epicenter of the revolt, some four miles from Nazareth. If any such associations are in view here — the matter is unclear — Joseph and Mary's meek compliance with the empire's demands is noteworthy. Yet from the standpoint of subsequent history, faith in the one true God posed a greater threat to the cult of Rome's emperor through this humble family than through violent revolutions in God's name.

Clearer in the situation is what the text explicitly tells us: Joseph and Mary were betrothed (2:5), and she was pregnant — possibly showing. Betrothal was much more serious than engagement today, having included an economic exchange between the families, and could be broken only by the death of one partner or by divorce. Nevertheless, the more conservative Galilean custom discouraged couples being alone together before the wedding; and even in Judean Bethlehem, which would have discouraged this less, pregnancy before the wedding testified to the commission of a terrible sin that tore at the social fabric. Although the reader knows that Mary is a virgin (1:34-35), the reader would also know that this would not be common knowledge in Bethlehem. If Caesar was the standard for nobility and respectability in the Roman Empire, this couple by contrast would be the object of gossip, and the circumstances of Jesus' birth viewed as questionable.

Not only the circumstances of Jesus' birth — Rome's oppression and negative attitudes toward Joseph and Mary — but also its location is noteworthy. The Christmas stories as retold today usually involve no room in the "inn," but Luke's account is actually more dramatic than this. Luke's particular term in Greek probably means not an inn but a "room" or "home" (2:7). It was not lack of hospitality in a local inn, but probably overcrowdedness of some relative's home, that forced the couple to seek refuge in a manger outside. Very early and probably reliable tradition — acknowledged even by non-Christian Bethlehemites in the early second century — identifies the spot as a cave behind the family home. Caesar had his impressive palaces in Rome; the greater king apparently arrived in a trough for feeding animals.

It is here, however, that the most striking contrasts with Caesar appear. God reveals his Son's birth to shepherds, members of a despised and lowly profession (2:8), people who might never be admitted directly to Caesar's court. Choirs in temples throughout the eastern Mediterranean celebrated Caesar's birthday, for he was counted the "son" of a god (the previous Caesar). Roman propaganda hailed Caesar as a "savior" and "lord" and announced "good news" of the Roman "peace" he had established. By contrast, heavenly choirs praise Jesus as the true Savior and bringer of peace (2:11, 14). The true God and his true Son did not rely on earthly power structures; they came among the broken. We might think today of examples of the broken and needy that would especially communicate the same images to our audiences.

It may surprise us that these shepherds would be looked down on by Luke's contemporaries. Certainly the Bible had painted favorably portraits of shepherds like Moses, David, and Amos; some Romans also looked with nostalgia on an older era of rural simplicity. But for the most part urban people in the empire viewed shepherds as low class; they appear in lists of professions apt to be uneducated and crude. Educated Jewish urban dwellers seem to have felt the same way, if later rabbinic lists provide an indication. (As shepherds first witnessed Jesus' birth, women first witnessed his resurrection; in both cases God chose those marginalized from the centers of power.) To some degree, fault lines between white-collar and blue-collar workers in our culture may convey the sense; images of uneducated field workers or herders in other parts of the world might drive home even better the sense of innate superiority some groups of people feel when they compare themselves with others. After hearers have an unguarded moment to identify with one side of that fault line or another, calling them back to the message of the text will confront them with either judgment or comfort: Jesus came to the lowly.

We recognize God's grace in the people he chose; but we also recognize it in the setting in which he revealed his plan to them. Although he had revealed himself to Zechariah during his prayer in the temple (1:8-11), the aged priest had responded with less faith than the young virgin, probably a teenager, from obscure Nazareth (1:26-28). Luke repeatedly emphasizes prayer positively in Luke-Acts, but while God often reveals himself to the prayerful (e.g., Acts 10:2-4, 9-10), he is not limited to this means (e.g., Acts 9:1-4; for a similar point, cf. Luke 18:11-14). The shepherds were watching over their flocks by night (2:8), which suggests that the season was warm; in colder seasons the sheep were normally penned in at night. (The date was not December 25, an otherwise arbitrary date later chosen to counter the Roman festival of Saturnalia; Jewish people normally did not celebrate birthdays as Gentiles did, hence earliest Christian tradition probably had no reason to preserve the exact date.) It also suggests that they were engaging in their occupations, which required watching the sheep, and perhaps entertaining themselves with conversation or playing their pipes.

Nor is the revelation in this passage one of minor significance. God's "glory" shone around them (2:9), as at Paul's conversion (Acts 9:3; 22:6) and Peter's escape from execution (Acts 12:7). In the Gospel of Luke itself, Jesus reveals his glory in a way that compares him favorably with Moses (9:31-32); Luke's audience would probably recall God revealing his glory to Moses at Mount Sinai. In other words, a momentous event in history is now taking place — and these shepherds alone are privy to it. They respond with fear (2:9), a not unusual response to a divine encounter (e.g., 1:12; Mark 9:6); the revealer's encouragement to the shepherds not to fear (Luke 2:10) is also characteristic of divine revelations (e.g., 1:13, 30; Matt. 17:7; Rev. 1:17). God and his agents may be awesome, but often they come to us to reveal God's love and mercy toward his people.

The angel promises a "sign" for them (Luke 2:12), as prophets sometimes had given kings and their people in the Bible (1 Kings 13:3; 2 Kings 19:29; 20:8-10; Ezek. 4:3), even a sign about a significant birth (Isa. 7:11, 14). They would recognize the baby somewhat by its swaddling clothes — a not unusual way to insure that a newborn child's limbs would grow straight — and especially by its lying in a feeding trough — which was unusual. Bethlehem was not large, so presumably they could run among the caves where they would find most of the feeding troughs till they found a child. But the angel's message reinforces the location of the Savior's birth, identifying him more naturally with shepherds than with nobles like Caesar.

Then the angelic choir, more majestic than any earthly temple choir that worshiped Caesar, announces that praises belong to Christ both in heaven ("in the highest") and on earth. It is the Lord Christ, not the lord Caesar (with his Pax Romana, a fiction of peace and Rome's nearly universal rule), who will establish true peace. Unlike some religious leaders in a different Gospel's story about a later period in Jesus' infancy (Matt. 2:6, 9, 16), these shepherds go to see Jesus for themselves (Luke 2:15-16). One might hope that their message to the community offered some vindication for Mary and Joseph, who had risked great shame in her virgin birth (2:17-18). That the shepherds glorify God for the revelation (2:20) rather than ignore it (cf. 17:18) fits another Lukan theme and invites us to follow their example.

This story fits the ethos of Luke's entire Gospel: Jesus is king of the marginalized. As the prophets had pointed out, the exalted God chose to dwell among the lowly (Isa. 57:15; 66:2). That is in a sense what the incarnation is all about, but Luke forces us to think of Jesus' coming in all the more concrete terms. Do we like to rub shoulders with the powerful in this world? Or do we sense God's presence and compassion among the broken, and identify ourselves with them in their brokenness? In the incarnation Jesus appeared among the broken, and the broken received him. Two millennia later, he still draws near to the lowly, and invites us to be the humble among whom he finds welcome.

Craig S. Keener

First Sunday after Christmas, Year B

First Lesson: Isaiah 61:10–62:3
(Psalm 148)
Second Lesson: Galatians 4:4-7
Gospel Lesson: Luke 2:22-40

The structure of Luke 1 and 2 falls into two roughly parallel parts, the story of John the Baptist and the story of Jesus. While the two stories are parallel, Luke also makes it entirely clear which of the two really matters. For that reason an extra scene, the presentation in the temple, to which there is no parallel in the John story, appears here. In many ways it functions as the climax of the infancy narrative as a whole.

The story begins with Mary and Joseph bringing the infant Jesus to the temple in Jerusalem for "their purification." It appears that Luke has combined for the purposes of his narrative two rituals prescribed in the Old Testament, the redemption of the firstborn and the purification of the mother. The firstborn, as Luke states, was particularly "holy to the Lord" and must be bought back for five shekels. There was apparently no requirement that this be done at the temple, though there is likewise no evidence that it could not be performed there. The purification of the mother is an entirely different ceremony. For forty days after giving birth to a male child a woman was ritually unclean. At the conclusion of that period, a sacrifice for purification of the mother was offered. For the poor the sacrifice was, as Luke correctly informs us, two young pigeons. Many commentaries tend to focus on what Luke may have known or not known about Jewish customs, but this issue, while doubtless interesting, is peripheral. The interpreter ought rather to consider first the symbolism involved in what Luke actually recounts in connection with these ceremonies. Firstly, Luke wishes to emphasize that Jesus is genuinely and rightly "holy to the Lord." But note that in the text the ceremony of redemption itself is not described. This is not historical incompetence on Luke's part, but deliberate symbolism. Jesus is never "bought back," but belongs wholly to the Lord. Luke will reinforce just this point in the following pericope, the episode of the boy Jesus in the temple at the age of twelve. Then and throughout his ministry he is about his Father's business. Secondly, the mention of the purification allows Luke to remind us that Jesus is from birth one of the "poor." We have seen this identification with the poor already in Mary's song; we will see it again throughout the Gospel. Finally, it is significant that the action takes place in the temple, the very center of Israel's spiritual life. The location may not have been legally necessary for the redemption of the child, but it is theologically and literarily necessary for the child's story. A scene in the temple, 1:5-25, has begun the infancy narrative. Another temple scene — in fact, two such scenes — now closes it.

In the physical center of the worship of Israel, the holy family meets a personification of the piety of Israel, one Simeon. Simeon, within the story of Jesus, is parallel to Zechariah in the John story. Like Zechariah, he is aged, pious, and just and represents all that is best in Israel. Simeon has been waiting for the consolation of Israel. The word "consolation" may contain a veiled reference to the Messiah. Like all the main characters of the infancy narratives, and like Zechariah in particular, Simeon has received a promise from the Lord. In this case it is that he will not die until he sees the Lord's Messiah. It is no surprise therefore that, like Zechariah, he will sing a particularly lovely hymn.

The beautiful hymn is widely known as the Nunc Dimittis, after the first two words of the Latin translation, the Vulgate. The meaning of the first line is quite simple, "Now I can die in peace." (The canticle is sometimes used as a closing hymn, especially in evening services. One wonders if the singers are aware of what they are really saying to God.) Here Simeon echoes the words of the aged Jacob, or more correctly, Israel, upon seeing his much-loved son Joseph (Gen. 46:30). The words may be even more reminiscent of the same point in the extracanonical retelling of the Genesis story, the book of *Jubilees*. There Jacob not only states his readiness to die but also blesses God. In this lovely hymn Simeon, like Jacob, blesses God. The juxtaposition of the words "master" and "servant" or, more rightly, "slave" suggests another image, the manumission of a slave. This is but a secondary meaning, however. The imagery of death as peaceful departure is paramount.

The reason why Simeon may depart in peace is that he has witnessed the Lord's "salvation." This is doubtless a wordplay on the Hebrew root of the name "Jesus," "the Lord is my salvation." Simeon is holding "salvation" in his arms. The gift of salvation is "according to your word." This is a reference to the specific promise to Simeon, but it is also broadly true of all humanity. The present salvation is a fulfillment of God's ancient promises, a theme already explicitly laid out in Luke's other infancy hymns. As a result, he may die in peace, that is, wholeness or "shalom." It is noteworthy that this key word appears also in Zechariah's song, to which this hymn is parallel. It is the task of the Messiah to "guide our feet in the way of peace." Similarly, according to the angels' song, peace will come to those on whom the good favor of God rests. That peace envelops Simeon even now.

The wording of the remainder of the hymn is drawn largely from the second part of Isaiah. Most interesting is the mention of the Gentiles. In some of the texts from Isaiah that form the background to the hymn, it is possible that the Gentiles merely witness the glory of Israel and do not share in it. The salvation would indeed be "in their face," in the contemporary slang phrase. That is also a possible reading here, but one that is terribly unlikely in the introduction to a two-volume work that will culminate in a mission to those very Gentiles. The salvation is also a glory for God's people Israel. Luke does not present Israel as completely rejecting Jesus. Israel at its best, as in Simeon, pious and faithful, frequenting the temple, understands and accepts God's purposes. Likewise, many follow Jesus in the Gospel, and in the first half of the book of Acts many thousands accept the gospel. But the gospel Jesus will bring is not an easy one. Luke knows very well that many in Israel will not imitate Simeon. Many will hate Jesus, and in the end they will crucify him. Later, especially in the second half of Acts, the good news is rejected by representatives of Israel. Israel will be divided by Jesus himself and then by the preaching of the gospel. So Simeon, once again like Zechariah, prophesies, "This child is destined for the falling and the rising of many in Israel, and to be sign that will be opposed." Too many sermons make the story of Jesus' birth little more than a charming tale of Christmas card prettiness. Even in the temple there is the shadow of the hatred that will lead to a cross. In both Matthew and Luke there is a dark side to Christmas. In Matthew it is the wailing of the mothers who will not be comforted, for their children have been slaughtered. In Luke it is a hard word to this one mother: "A sword will pierce your own soul too." It may be that no truth is ever received without opposition. But most certainly the truth of Jesus will not always be welcomed. The pain of rejection is there from the beginning.

But Simeon is not the only pious Israelite in the temple. An aged prophetess, Anna, also hails Jesus. Perhaps the welcome to the Savior is made more complete by the greeting of a woman to match the aged man. It may also be that just as Simeon parallels Zechariah, so Anna parallels Elizabeth. Certainly Anna, like Elizabeth, has a prophetic word to say concerning the child, though in this case the words are not given. It is specified, however, that she spoke to all those "who were looking for the redemption of Jerusalem." It is never just the famed preachers, the Peters and Pauls and their successors, who bear witness to God's purposes. Far more often it is through the quiet women like Anna or the faithful men like Simeon that the hope of redemption comes to God's people. Here we may also catch a foreshadowing of the climax of the Gospel in Luke 24. A certain Cleopas and an unnamed companion are walking toward Emmaus. When the risen Christ walks unrecognized with them, they say of him, "We had hoped that he was the one to redeem Israel." They do not yet know how justified was that hope. In the end the hope and peace of Simeon and Anna are only made complete when the risen Christ is recognized at last.

Stephen Farris

First Sunday after Christmas, Year C

First Lesson: 1 Samuel 2:18-20, 26
(Psalm 148)
Second Lesson: Colossians 3:12-17
Gospel Lesson: Luke 2:41-52

In an age when growing numbers of people express personal interest in "spiritual things" while shrinking numbers demonstrate familiarity with the basics of Scripture, the Bible has become something of an answer book for many people. To them it is an encyclopedic compilation of quick solutions for modern problems. It's the source for unambiguous answers to testy questions.

Parents who are hungry to fix their latest problem with a teenage son or daughter might get excited to learn of a biblical report on Jesus' adolescence. Surely, hopeful thinking would have them believe there is at least some practical wisdom in Luke 2:41-52, a passage where an exceptional twelve-year-old enters the public eye. Unfortunately, this brief story is the only biblical record containing any mention of Jesus' youthful years. Disappointingly perhaps, it offers nothing in the way of direct help for everyday adolescent crises. Jesus may be on the threshold of adulthood. But there is not a hint of insight about puberty issues for those who seek straightforward biblical answers to modern teenage problems.

What Luke does offer is a glimpse of Jesus beginning to make the break from some familial claims in order to commit himself more closely to God. It's a tension between earthly parents and one's heavenly Father that is apparent here, a collision between two competing loyalties. We can see this collision surface throughout the New Testament witness on discipleship. But here it is Jesus bringing to light his divine vocation. This is Jesus moving his life and purpose away from a private world into the realm of public significance.

Biblical scholars speak of the detached and separate feel of this text. To some it appears "tacked on" to the infancy narratives. It dangles loosely, reading almost better alone than connected. But what Luke accomplishes by inserting it here is the successful movement of Jesus out of the crib and into the world. He leaves the circle of his parents and the protection of his mother's arms and enters a great big world of need. It might have been easier to stay sheltered in the warmth of parental attachment than to enter the world of sin and death. But Jesus has come of age. He has found his voice

305

and taken his place. And that voice and place, we learn, are "in my Father's house."

The setup for Jesus' coming out and entrance into the religious community is a family trip. Jewish law prescribed that all males — and later women and children — would make three visits annually to Jerusalem for the three major festivals of Passover, Weeks, and Booths (Exod. 34:23). Whether or not every male or family managed this extensive travel probably had as much to do with their distance from the city as anything else. On this particular voyage the twelve-year-old Jesus and his parents became separated. Since children in ancient times transitioned into adulthood around the age of thirteen — there was no age cycle comparable to the modern teen experience — the "disappearance" of Jesus may not have been all that traumatic, young as he was. Even though he stayed behind in the temple and "his parents did not know it," it would have been natural for them to believe that he was with relatives or friends elsewhere in the caravan returning home. Entire villages were known to make the pilgrimage together.

If parental neglect is not the issue — and claims of thoughtlessness on the part of Mary and Joseph are equally ridiculous — a search for the missing Jesus nevertheless took place. When the parents finally find Jesus in the midst of the temple rabbis, there is distress in his mother's voice: "Son, why have you treated us so? Behold, your father and I have been looking for you *anxiously*." The sense here is more than uneasiness. It's anxiousness with pain. Luke uses *odynaomai* once elsewhere in referencing the torment or agony of the rich man (16:25). Is this the first indication that Simeon's prophecy of suffering will be fulfilled?

Who knows what transpired between the eyes of Jesus, squatting there in the temple, and the eyes of his parents, tired from the search and rescue operation. Stained glass windows in American sanctuaries don't give us this detail. Was it anger? Or puzzlement? Or the first recognition of true maturity in bloom? All that Luke lets us in on is that here was a pupil demonstrating unusual understanding, enough at least to evoke astonishment in his parents — and amazement from the gallery. Something in the way of Jesus, if not his eyes, communicated the sense that this child had indeed become "strong" and "filled with wisdom" (2:40).

Luke is very much at home with the word "amazement," *existēmi* (see, e.g., 8:56; 24:22; Acts 2:7, 12). He uses it in many different settings to refer to Jesus and the events surrounding him. In this instance Jesus is listening to the teachers, asking them questions, and evidently arriving at some brilliant answers himself. Who is this Jew of exceptional merit? Is he every parent's dream achiever or merely that precocious child displaying some scriptural acumen? More than likely Luke records this instructional moment to prepare the reader for later times when Jesus' questioning and teaching will get him into trouble with the religious authorities. For the moment, however, Jesus appears to these bright minds around him as one who possesses exceptional qualities. No one would guess that later on one of his first acts in the city would be to cleanse the temple (Luke 19:45-46).

Jesus said to his parents standing before him, "Why have you been searching for me? Did you not know that I must be in my Father's house?" Here lies the heart of the passage. In these short utterances of Jesus we see the beginning of his break away from familial attachments in order to identify more intimately with God the Father. He is doing so in the immediate presence of his parents, presumably for the first time. His commitment to the Father now transcends his love for the family.

If any one word indicates this emerging shift in allegiance, it is the word "must" *(dei)*. "I *must* be in my Father's house." Some translations have it, "I must be with my Father." Either way, the necessity of Jesus' special call and the requirements of his divine love — seen in that tiny word *dei* — end up characterizing his entire life. Luke repeats the must-ness of his vocation over and over again. "I must preach the good news" (4:43). "The Son of Man must suffer many things" (9:22). "I must go on my way today and tomorrow" (13:33). "The passover lamb must be sacrificed" (22:7). If all these signs of loyalty to the Father were in some way penultimate, the day of total commitment would arrive eventually. On that day Jesus would commit the entirety of his spirit into the Father's hands (23:46).

We have known of the name Jesus prior to this text. And Luke and Simeon and Anna have made us aware of his holiness. But in these early words recorded from his own mouth, we get our first indication that Jesus is God's Son. He has not abandoned his role in the family or his obedience to his parents. In fact, Luke takes pain to note the obedience of his return to Nazareth with his parents. But clearly he is conscious of the necessity — the must-ness! — of a closer relationship with his heavenly Father.

"Why have you been searching for me?" This mysterious line of Jesus prefigures a word that is strikingly similar to one we will get familiar with at the tomb. There two men will speak to some frightened women who are looking for Jesus' corpse: "Why do you search for the living among the dead?" In both cases we have the sense that Jesus constitutes a deeper reality than anyone around him can comprehend. Throughout the Gospel of Luke, the hidden statements of Jesus consistently confound his disciples (18:34). Mary herself struggles to make sense of her young son's sayings here in the temple. And just as she pondered in her heart the inspired events of Bethlehem (2:19), Mary chooses to keep these temple developments "in her heart" as well. What else do you do when faced with an adolescent who is said to be blessed with "divine and human favor" (2:52)!

Mary disappears from Luke's reporting after this, mentioned only once more, and then not even by name (8:19-21). But this shift away from Mary (and Joseph) to Jesus as the focus of Luke's message underscores the movement of Jesus away from strict familial attachments to a closeness with the Father. The temple scene opens with Mary and Joseph as the subjects of the action, traveling and searching. It closes with Jesus as the subject of the verbs: *"He* went to Nazareth, *accompanied by them. . . ."* In this subtle shift rests the challenge of every believer who loves both family and God — a loosening of the grip of the family embrace and a tightening of one's grasp of the Father's love.

Peter W. Marty

Second Sunday of Advent, Year C

First Lesson: Malachi 3:1-4
(Luke 1:68-79)
Second Lesson: Philippians 1:3-11
Gospel Lesson: Luke 3:1-6

A friend of mine once began a sermon on this text by saying that if you daydreamed during the first verse, you missed the whole point. Not only does Luke list the *dramatis personae* of some of the villains in the story that is about to unfold, but in so doing he does something even more important: he sets the ministry of Jesus in its wider historical context. In classical tones he pays respectful homage to the principalities and powers of the Roman imperium, just as he had done in the infancy narrative. Here also he adds the names of two key Jewish leaders. But there is a critical edge of irony in Luke's citation. Just as it was Jesus in the little town of Bethlehem — and not great Caesar Augustus — who is acclaimed by angels and shepherds as the real Lord and King, so the really important news thirty years later is about John the Baptist, not the notables Luke lists. They in fact play negative roles in the story, although through their abuse of power God will work out his purposes and bring salvation to the world.

But if you daydream through verse 1, you do indeed miss the point of Luke the historian. Everything that is about to transpire will occur in history, and the reader shares the same reality as the writer and the people who play roles in the story. We know the world in which all this takes place; we are part of it; we can see, understand, and believe.

The infancy narratives were introductory. They are past. The narrative of Jesus' ministry begins here in Luke 3, and it begins with the ministry of John the Baptist. Many faithful scholars have reached the conclusion that Jesus for some period of time lived as a disciple of the Baptist. Surely his gospel was preached in continuity with John the Baptist, even as it is contrasted with it on occasion. They share the faith of pious Israel and her hope for deliverance, although it is worth noting a key difference: Jesus enacts the kingdom in his fellowship with sinners and outcasts while John merely prepares for it with his severe message and call to repentance. In any case, to set the stage for Jesus, each of the canonical Gospels starts with the role and ministry of John the Baptist. Thus the preacher can set the stage for the rule of Christ among us here and now by paying attention to the words and ministry of John the Baptist.

He is, like Jesus, a prophet. His continuity with the Old Testament traditions is revealed in his message and behavior. It is also revealed in his persecution and execution. The excitement and fervor that he generated were, as the Gospels testify, a necessary setting of the stage for the Christ. John is preparing Israel for God's intervention — yet another typically prophetic act.

Of course, he is for the Gospels and for Jesus not just a prophet; he is also the fulfillment of prophecy. This all the synoptics establish with the citation from Isaiah 40. The Word of God is coming to fruition in John the Baptist. Jesus' "kinder and gentler" announcement of the kingdom is possible precisely because John is the prophet who prepares the way for the fulfillment of Second Isaiah's messianic hope. Note, for instance, how beautifully the last clause of the quote from Isaiah coincides with the message of the Christmas angel. "Glad tidings of great joy that shall be to all people" is the virtual equivalent of "all flesh shall see the salvation of God."

John the Baptist, like Mary, straddles the two Testaments and, like her, embodies both promise and fulfillment. The reflection of the church that finally issued in the "deisis," the image of the crucified Jesus flanked by his mother and the forerunner, was deeply biblical. They point to him for whom they each made room and prepared the way and who fulfilled the hope of Israel in which they were nurtured and in which their unique and unrepeatable roles were formed.

Advent is uniquely the time when the church focuses on prophecy and fulfillment, and the figure of John the Baptist presents a unique opportunity for the preacher to talk about both. It is a time for reflection on God's judgment against sin and his response to the crisis sin has created. John the Baptist's role and his call to repentance open possibilities for being specific about sin and repentance.

He proclaimed, says Luke, "a baptism of repentance for the forgiveness of sins." There is considerable risk that in our era of tolerance and cheap grace, part of the message of Advent, the part about repentance, will be missed. It is so tempting instead to preach about hope in the abstract or to rush Christmas and talk about glad tidings of great joy. The glad tidings are, however, in large part the announcement of forgiveness. The Advent preparation for Christmas involves repentance.

In truth, preaching about the gravity of sin and the need for repentance is enlightening and life-giving. Our era's desire to forget the reality and even the possibility of sin has not liberated or enhanced human life. It has diminished it. Denial of the gravity of sin leaves people witless and disabled in the face of the world's evils and their own shortcomings. Denial of sin has left Christians and non-Christians alike unable to understand their predicament, save in terms of the misdoings of others or the randomness of existence. The denial of sin has unleashed despair, confusion, and anger.

In a way, learning that you are a sinner can be part of the good news. It means knowing what the problem is, knowing that there is a God whom you have offended and to whom you can be reconciled. To name sin properly is already to name God and to open the possibility of forgiveness. John the Baptist is a great ally in the preacher's effort to proclaim this truth just before the easy and false peace and goodwill of the secular Yuletide.

While this is all to the good, in a merely chronological sense the liturgical placement of the ministry of John the Baptist is odd. After all, it took place thirty years after the nativity. But, as I said, the figure of John the Baptist straddles the Testaments. The reason for Christ's coming remains as true in his adulthood as in his infancy, and so Luke wisely places John's birth before Jesus'. He will similarly precede Jesus' ministry, and his proclamation rightly, then, precedes the Christmas celebration.

Among other things, John helps make it clear that it is the adult Christ, crucified and risen, whom we celebrate at Christmas. We would never approach this crib among the animals if he were not also the paschal Lamb and the Good Shepherd. Some years ago, to drive this point home, a Lutheran exegete wrote an article entitled "Christmas Never Saved Anyone." The article, like the title, was something of an overstatement. To be sure, we are not saved by the birth of Jesus apart from his death and resurrection, but his birth does not take place apart from his death and resurrection. Insofar as the Word's becoming flesh is already the beginning of the passion, the birth is already glad tidings of great joy and Christmas, because it is paschal, does save us. It is about the birth of a very necessary Savior. It is, as the Orthodox sometimes call it, "the winter Pascha," and the apocalyptic readings of Advent, especially those that feature John the Baptist, help us remember that all this is about sin, forgiveness, salvation, and the death and resurrection of Jesus.

And Christmas very much saves us — "a Savior which is Christ the Lord."

In addition to these rich themes of baptism, hope, repentance, sin, and history, the reading offers at least two specific and straightforward jumping-off points for the preacher.

One of these is to do the same kind of thing as Luke in the first two verses of chapter 3. Name the times, the when and where of our life. Then move forward from that to a description of their conditions, their sins, and their challenges. Remember in so doing that the big shots Luke lists are not the real power. God is, and they are only bit players in his work. Those who control power and wealth in this world seem to be the real players, but in the end they are not.

The second possibility is closely related to the first. It is to ask in what wilderness the voice cries out now. Where are the valleys that need to be filled and the mountains that need to be leveled? Don't restrict the question to asking who the big shots are, because there are rough ways aplenty among your hearers as well. It is too easy to address John's call to repentance to somebody who won't be there. Identify the "players," but be sure to address the call to repentance to those who are actually there.

Leonard R. Klein

311

Third Sunday of Advent, Year C

First Lesson: Zephaniah 3:14-20
(Isaiah 12:2-6)
Second Lesson: Philippians 4:4-7
Gospel Lesson: Luke 3:7-18

Each of the Gospels gives a different take on John the Baptist. In Matthew 3:1 his first word is "Repent," and he addresses his words of condemnation ("you brood of vipers") to the Pharisees and Sadducees; in Mark 1:7 he simply proclaims the worthiness of the one who is coming after him and is promptly arrested; and here in Luke his words condemn the entire multitude. The word for crowd here is not *laos* (Luke 1:18), which Luke tends to use to designate those who have a positive relationship to Jesus, but *ochlos*, used repeatedly later to refer to the multitudes Jesus faces (e.g., 11:14, 27, 29; most notably 22:47, accompanying Judas). The crowd approaches him because they have heard he is preaching "a baptism of repentance for the forgiveness of sins" (3:3). The passage is so much focused on John the Baptist that God's action in the text is easily ignored. The previous passage from Isaiah establishes that John is continuing God's work of salvation. John is proclaiming under compulsion of the Holy Spirit. When he calls the multitudes a "brood of vipers," he is not just being cranky or rude, he is being prophetic of the outcome of Jesus' life: they are like snakes who come out from under rocks when it is safe to do their poisonous deeds and later slither back under their rocks again. In asking them, "Who warned you to flee from the wrath to come?" (v. 7), he is prophesying the disastrous consequences of their current ways as well as affirming that in coming to him they still have a chance. His question is rhetorical — he knows the Spirit has warned them. His attitude seems almost to regret their coming and may echo something of Jonah's lament that Nineveh will repent if he preaches.

The baptism he will give is not to be received passively; it demands actions, specifically "fruits that befit repentance." The crowd must not presume that as children of Abraham they have a privileged standing before God; the rocks have a better future than they do if they do not repent, for God "is able from these stones to raise up children to Abraham" (v. 8). John switches metaphors: the trees of which the crowd are a part already have an ax laid to their roots. The matter is urgent, the time is now, the blow that will finish them is about to be struck. Either they produce, or they will be "cut down and thrown into the fire" (v. 9).

John's words strike the crowd with evident power, for they seek instruction: "What then should we do?" The same question is asked by the first converts of Peter in Acts 2:37. For all that John seems to have no love for this crowd, his responses to individual groups in the crowd demonstrate (a) true concern for the least fortunate in society, (b) recognition of various ways that the crowd has failed to live out God's justice and righteousness, and (c) John's care for those to whom he speaks, for he tailors his commands to the specific needs of each group he addresses. Those who have two coats should give one to someone in need; those who have food must share with those who have not. (These commands are similar to what the church lives out in Acts 2:43-47 and 4:32-35.) Tax collectors are to collect only what is owed, and the soldiers must not rob or lie and must be content with their wages. Repentance, in other words, is setting right what is wrong and is the appropriate preparation for Christ's coming. Of course, setting things right is God's concern, and the word John is speaking is in fact God's word to those people.

The two groups John specifically addresses would be expected to be in need of repentance. The tax collectors are a separate group that "also came to be baptized" (v. 12), or they are just part of the one crowd. In any case, they stick together, perhaps because they are despised for cheating and betraying their own people in working for Rome. The soldiers are members of an occupying army, yet as "children of Abraham," they are probably mercenary members of Herod's own troops who are of Jewish background and are assigned to take care of local policing matters under the authority of the high priest as magistrate (22:4); as members of the temple police, they are the same force that will come to arrest Jesus on the Mount of Olives (22:52). In spite of the established laws of Rome, they have considerable latitude to be a law to themselves. They too are hated and stick together, yet even with all of their power they are led collectively by the Spirit to ask John, "What should we do?" (3:14). Their presence here, at the beginning of Jesus' ministry, makes their later presence at his arrest a sign of their failure to repent and a decision against Jesus. While the tax collectors are said to have come "to be baptized," the soldiers are depicted as only asking a question — their interest may be more remote.

So compelling is John in his words and actions that an expectation moves through "all" the people (laos) as to whether he is the Messiah. The question is not voiced — they "were questioning in their hearts" (v. 15) — thus their awakened hope is to be interpreted as a work of the Spirit that John recognizes and answers without waiting to hear what is on their minds. No, he is not the Christ. So mighty and worthy is the Christ that John by comparison has no right even to do the lowliest of servant tasks for him, tending his sandals. While John baptizes only with water, the Christ will baptize with "the Holy Spirit and fire" (v. 16), a reference that anticipates Pentecost (Acts 2:3-4). The fire here is a fire of righteousness, purification, and judgment, presumably the same fire that will consume what God cannot tolerate, the unproductive trees (Luke 3:9) and the chaff that is left on the threshing floor after the Messiah takes the wheat into the granary (v. 17). John does not identify his own ministry of baptism with Jesus' ministry in the Holy Spirit except as preparation for the one who is coming and has the power to save.

John's preaching message is nowhere as detailed as it is here. There can be no question in Luke's community about the status of Christians baptized only with the baptism of John. John is preaching ethical reform and repentance, actions people must perform by their own will. He does not call people specifically to belief or to trust but to action, although he impresses upon them the immediacy of the Messiah's appearance. Christ later will call them to belief in the power of his death for their salvation. John thus stands as the last of the prophets and at the beginning of the time of salvation. To emphasize Christ as the beginning of a new age, Luke awkwardly moves John to prison (v. 20) before Jesus comes on the stage (v. 21); that will leave John's presence to be inferred at Jesus' baptism (v. 22).

John's ministry contributes to a larger picture of God at work in fulfilling God's promises. The people here are of a mixed sort: they are excited by the prospect that the Messiah might be among them even if they think John is he. John does not say, "You are wrong to think the Messiah is at hand"; he simply says, "You are wrong to think that I am the Messiah." Several signs indicate that the crowd is participating in something larger than themselves and beyond their control: (a) all of the multitude is drawn out to the desert to hear John, (b) upon hearing his words they are filled with a desire to repent, and (c) they all experience a profound sense of expectation. God is working to accomplish what God alone can accomplish.

God is still working to accomplish our salvation in Jesus Christ through the power of the Holy Spirit. That can be a very comforting message for today's church. There are things that we can do to get ready, and things that we need to do by way of repentance. Our actions have consequences. Ultimately, however, salvation is what God accomplishes for us. Just as preachers can read this text and focus on John's actions and effectively sideline God, so too we can miss out on what God is doing in events around us. Even today God may be awakening the multitudes to their need of God and to a hope growing within them of which God alone can be the author.

Paul Scott Wilson

First Sunday after the Epiphany (Baptism of the Lord), Year C

First Lesson: Isaiah 43:1-7
(Psalm 29)
Second Lesson: Acts 8:14-17
Gospel Lesson: Luke 3:15-17, 21-22

As Luke retold the story of Jesus for Theophilus and his like, somewhere in the Roman Empire after 70 C.E., two concerns were prominent for him. On the one hand he wanted to demonstrate the continuity of Jesus with the traditions and piety of Israel. This Jesus was no rebellious upstart intent on destroying the Roman "peace" by undermining the ancestral customs of the Jewish race, who were allowed to practice those customs as part of a Roman strategy to preserve that "peace." On the other hand, Luke wanted to show that Jesus was the culmination of those traditions and that piety, their logical conclusion and fulfillment. After the shattering of Jewish aspirations in the disastrous war with Rome, Luke presented to interested, informed, and God-fearing Gentiles the story of a transformed Israel, defined now not by race but by allegiance to the Messiah who had come among them: an Israel to which they might belong, beneficiaries together with Jewish people of the salvation of God.

Jesus emerges on the scene of history, then, not in isolation from its contingencies and his people's urgent longings, but in their midst. When Luke recounts Jesus' first appearance on the public stage, he recalls that the surrounding atmosphere was one of expectant fervor (3:15). Luke is especially fond of the word for "people" *(laos)* which he uses in this verse: it suggests the faithful people of God. For such pious folk the activity of John, preaching like one of the old prophets, raised the serious question whether he were the Messiah (the "anointed one") whom many anticipated as their God-sent liberator from foreign subjugation. This questioning about John draws us into the atmosphere surrounding the arrival of Jesus, who is to be the hero of Luke's story.

However, it is necessary for Luke also to stake out carefully the distinction of Jesus from all his predecessors in the charismatic-prophetic tradition in Israel. There is indeed one coming to fulfill Israel's dreams, but coming to do so in ways that are disruptive, uncomfortable, unexpected, and, above all, new. So Luke (unlike Matthew and Mark) emphasizes that it was in response to people's speculation about John's identity that John himself draws a stark contrast between himself and the one who is "coming" (vv. 15-

17). John's answer is to "them all," a typically Lukan note of universality. Much later, apparently, there were still those who had been caught up in the movement surrounding John who needed to be shown that Jesus now, not John, was the one to whom they must give allegiance (see Acts 18:24–19:7).

What, then, was the difference between John and Jesus? In John's words, the coming one was "mightier" than he (Luke 3:16). This is not a matter of mere degrees of dynamism; the distinction is qualitative. In a crucial sense Jesus *has* power; John has not. John regards Jesus as the master, for whom he is not even worthy to perform the duties of a slave. The distinction is dramatized in the contrast between the two "baptisms" they carry out. John baptizes with water — an outward symbol; the Messiah's Spirit baptism is the reality to which the symbol points (v. 16). John had warned of impending judgment (vv. 7-9), but the Messiah will be the very agent of judgment (v. 17). Winnowing, the separation of wheat from chaff by tossing grain into the air, was familiar from the Old Testament as a metaphor for judgment (e.g., Jer. 15:7; Isa. 41:15-16, where Israel as God's servant is the agent of judgment). John implies that the winnowing is already taking place, and the coming one's task will be to gather the wheat and burn the chaff.

We should note the significance of the two mentions of "fire": in Luke 3:16 the promise is that the coming one would baptize "you" with fire, indicating a process of purifying; in verse 17, burning the "chaff" with "unquenchable fire" is clearly a reference to the destruction of everything evil. But the process is essentially one. The people of God are to be caught up in a process of universal refinement in which all evil will be consumed to ashes. Jesus' own consciousness of being the agent of this process is revealed in 12:49. When the Holy Spirit fell at Pentecost, the visible flames were a sign that the days of the great sifting, in which God's people themselves would be purged, had indeed arrived (Acts 2:1-4, 15-21).

These words about the coming one not only contrast him with John; they continue John's ministry of warning. The hope of the people would have been for Messiah to deliver them from their enemies. But the focus of John's prophecy is on a fiery purification which would reach to the heart of their own community.

After these fiery words of John about the coming one, it is a surprise for Luke's reader, who knows the coming one's identity (as, according to Matt. 3:14, it was a surprise for John himself), when in the quiet scene of Luke 3:21, Jesus also is baptized after "all the people." The strange ordinariness of it is highlighted by Luke's mention of it almost in passing, in the middle of a sentence. Here is Jesus, undergoing the ritual along with the expectant ones, by no means announcing himself as the expected one. His submission to this baptism would have been a luminous sign for his followers in later years, and for Luke's audience or readers, that he identified with Israel's hopes, with the desire of many to make a new beginning with their God. It was the first signal of Jesus' sharing in the stigma of human sinfulness which Luke is to emphasize (see 15:1-2; 23:39-43). The characteristically Lukan glimpse into Jesus' intimacy with God (his praying, v. 21) underlines this picture of a simple, humble piety which filled the outward baptism with meaning.

Then, however, continuity cracks apart once again, and from heaven is revealed the other side of the picture, the unique status of this Jesus. Matthew and Mark record that Jesus saw the heavens opened, John that John the Baptist saw it; Luke simply records that it happened. Of supreme importance for him was not the question of who witnessed the event, but that it took place, a powerful though fleeting sign of a unique bestowal. In the form of a dove — the symbolic significance of which is uncertain — the Holy Spirit came down to anoint the one who was to baptize Israel with the Holy Spirit; in words resounding with echoes of God's ancient words to his appointed King (Ps. 2:7) and his faithful servant (Isa. 42:1), a voice speaks to assure him of his calling.

As we, like Luke but two millennia later, look back on this vignette of Jesus in and by the Jordan at the beginning of his career, and the testimony to him from John and from heaven, what light does it cast for us on the one we know as the Christ? Here, first, is an unmistakably human being, one who, moreover, fully shares the aspirations of many of his contemporaries in Judaism. He is one who prays — and there is no surer sign of a sense of being a dependent human. He is not, here, one who asserts himself or his calling as distinct from others (cf. Isa. 42:2), but one who identifies totally with his compatriots' sense of shame and yearning for a new start in the humiliating ritual of baptism. It is an extraordinary contrast to the picture of the one who gathers the wheat and burns the chaff.

And it is precisely at this moment of humiliation that the witnesses to his Christhood appear. These are as far from "proof texts" as can be imagined. Luke recalls the words of a prophetic witness (John), and the memory of a mysterious manifestation of God (the dove and the voice), not to win over the hostile to faith, but as part of the integrity of a picture drawn by faith in order to bring greater depth and clarity of understanding to a sympathetic enquirer (Luke 1:1-4). In fragile, fleeting ways, ways that most would in the immediate aftermath forget, the identity of *this* man as God's Judge, God's Son, God's King, God's Servant was marked out. Today's reader or hearer finds herself part of the story, for the Spirit baptism given by Jesus is still taking place in these final days which he ushered in. And it may well be the silent picture of the anonymous man praying by the water, not the fiery imagery of the threshing floor, which compels a contemporary person to take note of this Messiah and draws her into the fire.

Stephen I. Wright

First Sunday in Lent, Year C

First Lesson: Deuteronomy 26:1-11
(Psalm 91:1-2, 9-16)
Second Lesson: Romans 10:8b-13
Gospel Lesson: Luke 4:1-13

The final verse of this text, which is unique to Luke's account of the temptation, is a good place to begin on the first Sunday of Lent: "When the devil had finished every test, he departed from him until an opportune time." This rather foreboding conclusion to the story provides a critical link between the beginning and end of Lent — between the temptation and the cross. The "opportune time" when the devil will return is the time of Jesus' passion and crucifixion, when the devil will not simply test Jesus with words but attack him with actions.

The final verse in Luke's temptation story thus stands as a warning: don't try to understand the cross apart from the particular story of Jesus that runs from temptation to crucifixion. There is an essential narrative connection between Jesus' life and his death. The cross cannot be plopped down out of the blue as a magical transaction between God and individual sinners. Rather, the story of Jesus, and particularly his engagement with the powers of the world, gives the cross its distinctive meaning. While there are many other well-known connections between the temptation story and Lent (e.g., the wilderness, forty days, fasting), this relationship between the temptation and the crucifixion is one that is often overlooked but needs to be proclaimed. The temptation story, right at the beginning of the season, provides the context within which we approach the crucifixion during Lent.

This context is Jesus' engagement with and resistance to the powers of the world, here embodied in the figure of the devil. These powers are the great forces in the world that hold people captive; they are the institutions and systems, along with the driving spirit within them, that promise people life but in fact lead people along the way of death. These forces make people feel powerless before the immensity of the world's problems. They generate comments like the following: "No one really wants war, but the bodies and weapons keep piling up" or "No one really wants homelessness, but we can't seem to do anything about it."

Or "I'm not really *living*, but simply being driven along by forces beyond my control." These powers are characterized by domination and violence, and they seek to have their way at all costs — even the cost of crucifixion. The whole system of these powers, which Walter Wink has called the "Domination System," is embodied in the figure of the devil. Indeed, one might even, along with Wink, refer to the devil as the spirit of the Domination System. (See Walter Wink, *Engaging the Powers: Discernment and Resistance in a World of Domination* [Minneapolis: Fortress, 1992], esp. pp. 13-104. Although there is not space here for a detailed discussion of the "principalities and powers," one should not preach from this text without some reflection on these powers and Jesus' resistance to them. Wink's book is a helpful place to start.)

These are the powers that Jesus encounters in the wilderness, and they are the powers he resists throughout his ministry. They are the powers that ultimately will crucify him (as Paul asserts in 1 Cor. 2:8). In this initial struggle with these powers in the wilderness, Jesus begins to shape his identity and mission in absolute obedience to God. What is significant, however, is that by the end of the story we don't yet know the positive direction Jesus' mission will take. We learn that obedience to God lies at the heart of Jesus' identity, but we do not know where his journey of faithfulness will lead. In the temptation story, rather, Jesus' obedience and faithfulness take the form of *resistance*. Here at the beginning we simply learn what Jesus will *not* do. We discover the kind of Messiah he will *not* be, the means he will *not* take, the ends he will *not* pursue. The mission of Jesus, into which he has just been baptized, begins with resistance to the powers; it begins with a *no* to the powers and priorities that drive the world and lead to death.

In his obedience to God, Jesus says no to three particular temptations of the devil (the spirit of the Domination System). First, he refuses to use his power to secure his own survival. Jesus is famished, and the devil invites him to turn "this stone" (singular in Luke) into bread. The devil invites Jesus to use his power to meet his own needs, to insure his own survival. Responding, as he will each time, with a text from Deuteronomy, which was addressed to Israel in the wilderness, Jesus replies, "One does not live by bread alone." Like the people in the wilderness who lived on manna, Jesus affirms that dependence on God and obedience to God are more important than securing one's own survival. People can in fact suffer "death by bread alone," as is clearly evident in our consumer society. Jesus says no to making his own survival the top priority and to using his power to meet his own needs. And if he had not said no, if he had pursued his own survival, there would have been no cross.

Second, the devil invites Jesus to use his power to establish a political empire grounded in the ways of the world. Jesus can have all worldly power, which, disturbingly, has been given over to the devil, if he will simply worship the devil and follow the way of the Domination System. "All of the kingdoms can be yours, Jesus, if you will just lord your power over others and take up the sword of the nations. Take charge of the biological weapons, deploy some troops, command the implementation of a 'Star Wars' missile defense system. All the kingdoms can be yours — if you will just use the world's means of power: domination and violence."

But again, Jesus says no. To serve the devil in this way would be idolatry (something the powers, particularly the nation, always seek from people). To take this path would set Jesus on the way of the world rather than of God. So Jesus says no to this path of domination and violence. In fact, his no to this path runs throughout the temptation story. The only "weapon" Jesus uses (and will ever use) against the Domination System is the Word. The only sword Jesus will take up is the "sword of the Spirit, which is the word of God" (Eph. 6:17). Jesus doesn't use his power to destroy even the devil by means of violence or domination. Rather, he lives with the confidence expressed in Luther's great hymn, "A Mighty Fortress Is Our God":

> The prince of darkness grim,
> We tremble not for him;
> His rage we can endure,
> For lo! His doom is sure,
> One little word shall fell him.

Jesus says no to the path of violence and domination. And if he had not said no, if he had assumed the power of the world, Jesus would not have died on the cross.

The devil himself turns to Scripture for the final temptation, reminding us that even the Bible can be used in opposition to the will of God. Quoting

Psalm 91:11-12, the devil tempts Jesus to use God for his own ends, to make God an instrument for his own success and popularity. (For Luke, unlike Matthew, this temptation is the climactic one.) By jumping off the temple and having God's angels protect him before the eyes of all the people, Jesus could give the people dramatic proof of who he is; he could give them the kind of Messiah they want and avoid misunderstanding and rejection. "Come on, Jesus, God will protect you; the Scriptures say so. Use God just this once as a means to your own personal goals." This avenue, of course, is one the powers take all the time. How often, for example, do nations call on God in the midst of war and seek to make God a servant of their own goals in order to insure popular support. But again, Jesus says no. He will not test God in this way; he will not try to use God for his own ends. Faithfulness and obedience to God are more important than effectiveness. And again, if Jesus had not said no, if he had used God for his own popularity and success, he would not have been crucified.

So we return to the conclusion: "When the devil had finished every test, he departed from him until an opportune time." Jesus' resistance to the powers of the world, which begins immediately following his baptism, will lead to his crucifixion. The powers, in fact, must crucify Jesus because of the no he speaks to their way. Intent on their own survival at all costs, the powers must crucify the one who threatens their authority. Committed to domination by the sword, the powers must put to death the one who challenges their most basic values. Placing themselves above God and using God for their own ends, the powers must crucify one who names their pretensions and serves God alone. Here in the temptation story is the fundamental conflict — the conflict between the way of God and the way of the powers, between the way of life and the way of death — which eventually, at an "opportune time," will end on the cross. The crucifixion is no accident and no magical transaction isolated from the life and ministry of Jesus. The cross is a direct consequence of Jesus' resistance to the powers of death in the world. And between temptation and crucifixion, the church examines its own life of resistance during the season of Lent.

Charles L. Campbell

321

Third Sunday after the Epiphany, Year C

First Lesson: Nehemiah 8:1-3, 5-6, 8-10
(Psalm 19)
Second Lesson: 1 Corinthians 12:12-31a
Gospel Lesson: Luke 4:14-21

The Lukan Evangelist reports that Jesus returned from his wilderness temptations "in the power of the Spirit" (4:14). Luke's assertion is fully justified by his narrative. In 1:35 the angel Gabriel announces to Mary that the "Holy Spirit will come upon" her and that her child "will be called holy, the Son of God." By virtue of his generation by the Spirit of God, Jesus is holy and is God's very Son. Indeed, this logic appears to lie behind the interesting conclusion of the genealogy presented in Luke 3:23-38. In contrast to the Matthean genealogy, which begins with Abraham and moves to the present, the Lukan form begins with Jesus and works its way back in time, beyond the great Jewish patriarch Abraham, all the way back to "Adam, the son of God" (3:38). Adam may be called "son of God" by virtue of his creation by the Spirit of God (cf. Gen. 2:7). But unlike Adam, Jesus the Son of God does not yield to the devil's temptation (Luke 4:1-13). This is because the Holy Spirit had come upon Jesus at his baptism "in bodily form" (3:22), that is, in great power. Therefore Jesus is able to withstand Satan's every temptation and so is able to begin his ministry in Galilee "in the power of the Spirit."

In verses 16-21 the Evangelist Luke narrates Jesus' sermon in the synagogue at Nazareth. One must note that Jesus' center of operations was not his hometown Nazareth but rather Capernaum, situated on the northwest shore of the Sea of Galilee. The lack of support, even outright opposition, that Jesus experienced at the hands of his family and neighbors (see Mark 3:20-22, 31-35; 6:1-6) may very well account for this location.

Luke's account of this synagogue service is our oldest and most detailed description of what took place in the early synagogue. Since the return from the Babylonian exile (ca. 586-516 B.C.), the Jewish people spoke Aramaic. (See the account in Nehemiah 8:1-8 in which Ezra and his scribes read the Law of Moses and explain it to the people.) In the synagogue service a portion of the Hebrew Bible was read and then an "explanation" (or Targum) was given in Aramaic. This need is likely what gave rise to the custom of preaching a sermon after a brief reading of Scripture (see Acts 2:16-36; 13:16-41). By the end of the first century A.D. synagogue services consisted of the recitation of the Shema (Deut. 6:4-9; 11:13-21; Num. 15:37-41), the Eighteen Benedictions, the daily psalm, the priestly blessing (Num. 6:24-26), prayers, readings from Torah and the Prophets, and a homily.

We are told that it was Jesus' custom to attend the synagogue. He is handed the scroll of Isaiah, implying that Jesus was a recognized teacher and that Isaiah may have been one of his favorite books. Jesus' frequent allusions to this book bears this out. Jesus turns to Isaiah 61 and reads:

> The Spirit of the Lord is upon me,
> because he has anointed me to preach good news to the poor.
> He has sent me to proclaim release to the captives
> and recovering of sight to the blind,
> to set at liberty those who are oppressed,
> to proclaim the acceptable year of the Lord.   (Luke 4:18-19)

Jesus has quoted most of Isaiah 61:1-2, notably omitting the final clause, "and the day of vengeance of our God."

Luke's quotation is from the Greek translation (LXX) of the Hebrew Old Testament and is actually a combination of various parts of Isaiah 61:1-2 and 58:6 (61:1a, b, d; 58:6d; 61:2a; with 61:1c and 61:2b, c omitted). Isaiah 61 and 58 are linked by common words and ideas (*dektos* [acceptable] in Isa. 61:2 and 58:5, *aphesis* [release/forgiveness] in 61:1 and 58:6). Luke may understand *aphesis* in both senses. Another noteworthy detail is the replacement of the verb meaning "to call for" in Isaiah 61:2a with a verb meaning "to proclaim," thus suggesting that the anointed one does more than merely "call for" the acceptable day of the Lord — he actually "proclaims" its arrival. Of course, such a modification lends itself very well to the idea of Jesus preaching. The reference in Acts 10:35 to the person (in this case a Gentile) who is "acceptable" to God may allude to Luke 4:19.

The reading of this prophetic text has captured the interest of the congregation, for "the eyes of all in the synagogue were fixed on him" (4:20). Their interest is only heightened when Jesus declares, "Today this scripture has been fulfilled in your hearing" (4:21). Jesus' assertion that this Scripture has been fulfilled is very significant. It is to this passage that he appeals when a doubting, discouraged, and imprisoned John the Baptizer sends word, asking Jesus, "Are you he who is to come, or do we look for another?" (cf. Matt. 11:2-6; Luke 7:18-23). It is this passage that in all probability has shaped Jesus' understanding of mission more than any other. Jesus believes the Spirit of God is upon him. This claim is well supported by the healings and exorcisms he is able to perform "by the finger of God" (cf. Luke 11:20).

323

In the Lukan narrative, of course, the foundation for such a claim has been convincingly laid: Jesus was generated by the Spirit, was baptized by the Spirit in great power, was full of the Spirit when he entered the wilderness to be tested, and then emerged from the wilderness "in the power of the Spirit." The reader has been well prepared for the claim that the words of Isaiah 61:1-2 are fulfilled in Jesus.

According to Isaiah 61:1-2, Jesus is also "anointed." It is from this word that we have "Messiah" (Hebrew) or "Christ" (Greek). Jesus has been anointed (or christened) not by oil, as the kings of Israel in former times had been, but by God's Spirit. This makes him the anointed one, or Messiah, in a very special sense. This anointing qualifies him to "preach good news," which for Jesus means the proclamation of the kingdom of God, or the rule of God. The very essence of Jesus' proclamation, the "kingdom of God has come," probably is indebted to this passage and to other "good news" passages in Isaiah, such as 40:9 and 52:7, both of which in the Aramaic version of Isaiah read: "The kingdom of your God is revealed!"

The Lukan Evangelist situates this Nazareth sermon at the outset of Jesus' public ministry in order that its theme may serve a programmatic function. The question that this sermon raises concerns election: Who are the chosen people of God and on what basis? The Baptizer had raised this question one chapter earlier in Luke's Gospel when he warned the people of Israel not to think to themselves, "We have Abraham as our father" (3:8). Throughout Luke's Gospel, more than the other Gospels, the issue of election is addressed. One thinks of the parable of the prodigal son and the parable of the rich man and Lazarus. The Evangelist is keenly interested in who will enter the kingdom and sit at table with Abraham and the righteous.

The sermon also touches on the question of who will be blessed in the "acceptable year of the Lord." Jesus has quoted a popular passage of Scripture, and he has thrilled the congregation of his hometown with the solemn declaration, "Today this scripture is fulfilled in your hearing." The widespread assumption is that messianic blessings belong to Israel, while the judgments of the messianic era will fall heavily upon Israel's enemies. The residents of Nazareth thrill to Jesus' selection of Scripture, but will they find his interpretation of this Scripture acceptable?

Craig A. Evans

Fourth Sunday after the Epiphany, Year C

First Lesson: Jeremiah 1:4-10
(Psalm 71:1-6)
Second Lesson: 1 Corinthians 13:1-13
Gospel Lesson: Luke 4:21-30

After quoting parts of Isaiah 61:1-2, Jesus declares to the congregation in the synagogue of Nazareth: "Today this scripture has been fulfilled in your hearing" (Luke 4:21). The immediate reaction of the congregation is positive: "And all spoke well of him, and wondered at the gracious words which proceeded out of his mouth; and they said, 'Is not this Joseph's son?'" (4:22). This question should not be understood in a negative sense, as in the parallel in Mark 6:3: "'Is not this the carpenter, the son of Mary and brother of James . . . ?' And they took offense at him." No, in the Lukan context the reaction is positive, in the sense of being something too good to be true. If Jesus really is the herald of the good news, the anointed of the Lord, who proclaims the appearance of the kingdom of God, then surely wonderful benefits and blessings will be bestowed on the people of Nazareth, Jesus' longtime neighbors and family. Or so they assumed.

In Luke 4:23 Jesus makes it clear that he understands what the people expect of him. The proverb "Physician, heal yourself!" means that the healer or benefactor (in this case Jesus) should take care of his own and does not imply that Jesus himself has some deficiency or fault that needs correcting. The proverb is similar to proverbs found in both Greek ("A physician for others, but himself teeming with sores"; Euripides, *Fragments* 1086) and Jewish ("Physician, heal your own lameness"; *Gen. Rab.* 23:5) traditions. The saying in the *Gospel of Thomas* §31 probably represents a variant version of the synoptic saying: "A physician does not heal those who know him." The people of Nazareth expect Jesus to do the same things for them that he has done for the people of Capernaum. If Jesus pronounced that the Isaiah passage was truly fulfilled, then all could expect him to do wonderful things for them. In verse 24, however, Jesus disappoints this expectation by stating that no prophet is acceptable in his hometown. The irony is that the word "acceptable" *(dektos)* here is the same word found in verse 19, in which Isaiah 61:2 is quoted. The prophet who is to announce the "acceptable" year of the Lord is himself not "acceptable" to his own people (cf. John 1:10-11). Underlying this expression is the long tradition of the rejected, persecuted, and martyred prophets of Israel. Those prophets who spoke the word of

God often found themselves out of favor or "unacceptable" to the ruling political and religious establishments of their times. Instead of proclaiming what the authorities wanted to hear, the prophets of old spoke what God wanted said. Jesus' words here, and in Luke 13:34, reflect a Jewish tradition that Israel has routinely rejected and persecuted the prophets (2 Chron. 36:15-16; Pss. 78; 105; 106; Lam. 4:13; Acts 7:51-53). According to the pseudepigraphal work *The Lives of the Prophets* (cf. 1:1; 2:1; 3:1-2; 6:2; 7:2), Isaiah, Jeremiah, Ezekiel, Micah, and Amos suffered martyrdom. So it is in the case of Jesus in the Nazareth synagogue. The people hear that the messianic era is at hand, and in this they rejoice; but they hear that it will not entail what they expect, and in this they become angry.

In verses 25-27 Jesus explains and justifies his startling pronouncement by citing two Old Testament examples involving Elijah and his disciple and successor Elisha. That he singled out these two figures is particularly appropriate in light of the fact that Elijah was regarded as the prophet of the last days who would prepare the way for the Messiah (see Mal. 3:1; 4:5-6). If the last days are truly at hand, then the Elijah/Elisha tradition would surely bear some relevant significance. In verses 25-26 Jesus recounts the incident in which Elijah provides an unending supply of food for a Gentile widow and her son (1 Kings 17:8-16) and yet makes no such provision for any Israelite. In verse 27 Jesus tells of the incident in which Elisha healed Naaman, the Syrian army officer, of the dreaded disease leprosy (2 Kings 5:1-14; see Luke 5:12-14). In the minds of his Jewish listeners, it was offense enough to be reminded that Elijah ministered to a poor Gentile widow, but it was intolerable to be oppressed by Roman occupation and then be reminded that Elisha healed a soldier of Syria, a country which had oppressed Israel in an earlier time.

What makes all of this preaching so "unacceptable" is that the people of Jesus' time expected Messiah to come and destroy Israel's enemies, not to minister to them. With respect to messianic expectation the Jewish people of the first century held, by and large, to two basic beliefs: (1) every generation believed that the coming of Messiah was very near and that he would probably come in their own time; and (2) all believed that when Messiah would come, he would vanquish the Gentiles (and perhaps the corrupt of Israel) and restore and bless Israel. Isaiah 61:1-2 was felt to witness to this second belief. It was believed that the blessings described in this Old Testament passage were reserved for Israel alone, while the "day of vengeance" (that part of the quotation omitted by Jesus) was reserved for Israel's enemies. When Jesus announced that Isaiah 61:1-2 was fulfilled "today," he would have been understood as fulfilling the expectations of the first commonly held belief. However, when he announced that "no prophet is acceptable" and then cited the examples of Elijah and Elisha, he flatly contradicted the second belief. It was this contradiction that led to outrage and the attempt to kill Jesus by throwing him down the cliff. Nevertheless, Jesus passed "through the midst of them" and "went away." Whether or not Luke intends this escape to be miraculous is uncertain, for the passion of the crowd, once outside, may have abated somewhat. But what is certain is that Jesus' ministry was far from over.

In at least one of the writings of Qumran (11QMelch 2.9-16), Isaiah 61:1-2 is linked with Isaiah 52:7, which, judging from the paragraph indentations of the Great Isaiah Scroll of Qumran (= 1QIsaiah^a), was thought to be the opening verse of the Suffering Servant Song (52:7–53:12). In the Aramaic version of the Old Testament, known as the Targum, this servant song is clearly understood as messianic (see 52:13; 53:10). In 11QMelch 2.16 the reference to "peace" *(shalom)* in Isaiah 52:7 is revocalized to mean "retribution" *(shillum)*, thus underscoring the aspect of vengeance and retribution found in the Isaiah 61:1-2 passage. According to the people of Qumran, the appearance of the Messiah meant comfort for them and judgment for their enemies (see also 1QH 15.15; 18.14-15). This may very well have been a widely held view. Underlying these ideas of vengeance and retribution was the popular understanding of the militaristic Messiah. That Luke was familiar with such an understanding is seen in Acts 5:33-39, where Gamaliel reminds the Sanhedrin of the (apparently military) failure of two messianic claimants, Theudas (v. 36) and Judas the Galilean (v. 37). Josephus knows of this Theudas and two others. Theudas (ca. A.D. 45), he tells us, claimed that he was a prophet and could command the river to part *(Antiquities* 20.5.1). Here is likely an allusion either to Moses parting the Red Sea (Exod. 14:21-22) or to Joshua's crossing of the Jordan River (Josh. 3:14-17). Later we are told of a man from Egypt (ca. A.D. 54) who claimed to be a prophet at whose command the walls of Jerusalem would fall down *(Antiquities* 20.8.6). This sign was probably inspired by the story of Israel's conquest of Jericho (Josh. 6:20; cf. Acts 21:38). Finally, Josephus tells us of another "impostor" who promised salvation and rest if the people would follow him into the wilderness *(Antiquities* 20.8.10). Years later Israel would herself suffer terribly in following the popular messianic/military figures of Menachem (first war with Rome, A.D. 66-70) and Simon bar Kosiba (a.k.a. "bar-Kochba"; second war with Rome, A.D. 132-35).

It has been suggested by some commentators that Luke may have had in mind the year of the Jubilee (every fiftieth year), which is described in Leviticus 25:10-13 and was intended to be a year of "release" (or "forgiveness") for debtors. In the Qumran text mentioned above (11QMelch), Leviticus 25 is referred to in connection with Isaiah 61:1 and would seem to indicate that one of the tasks of the Messiah was to announce a year of Jubilee. Since the year A.D. 26/27 was a Jubilee year, it is possible that Luke understood this as the year that Jesus began his messianic ministry.

Craig A. Evans

Fifth Sunday after the Epiphany, Year C

First Lesson: Isaiah 6:1-8, (9-13)
(Psalm 138)
Second Lesson: 1 Corinthians 15:1-11
Gospel Lesson: Luke 5:1-11

Luke's story of the great catch of fish parallels Mark 1:16-20, which the Evangelist Luke has expanded, partly by utilizing other Marcan details (see Mark 4:1-2, where it is necessary for Jesus to preach to the crowds from a boat) and by drawing on his own special information. (Some scholars think Luke's information regarding the great catch of fish is somehow related to the similar episode in John 21:1-11.) Mark's account of the calling of Simon (Peter), James, and John takes place shortly after the baptism of Jesus (Mark 1:16-20). Although Jesus had begun to proclaim the kingdom of God (Mark 1:15), no reason is given for why these Galilean fishermen would be inclined to follow Jesus. But Luke's arrangement does provide a logical context. Jesus has been preaching all through Galilee (4:14-15, 31-32, 43-44), has performed numerous healings and exorcisms (4:33-37, 40-41), and has healed Peter's mother-in-law (4:38-39). The miraculous catch of fish provides a fitting climax, and it becomes easy for the reader to understand why Peter, James, and John would drop their nets and follow after Jesus.

Luke 5:1-11 also serves a function in Luke's narrative that is similar to the Nazareth sermon in Luke 4:16-30. The Nazareth sermon sets forth Jesus' program, asserting that messianic blessings will be extended to all people (cf. Luke 3:6: "all flesh shall see the salvation of God"), while the dramatic call of the disciples throws the program into motion by formally launching the Jesus movement.

In Luke 5:1 we encounter Luke's first usage of the expression, the "word of God," an expression that occurs frequently in both of his writings (see Luke 8:11, 21; 11:28; Acts 4:31; 6:2, 7; 8:14; 11:1; 13:5, 7, 44, 46, 48; 16:32; 17:13; 18:11). When the expression occurs in Acts, it refers to the gospel, the message of the church. In Luke, of course, Jesus uses it in reference to the kingdom of God. By using the same expression in both the Gospel and Acts, Luke provides a strong link between Jesus' preaching and the later apostolic preaching.

Luke's view of Peter calls for a brief discussion. In the Lukan Gospel Peter (who is called "Simon" consistently until Jesus changes his name to "Peter" in 6:14) enjoys a position of prominence among the disciples and a position of closeness, almost endearment, approximating the relationship between Jesus and the "beloved disciple" in John's Gospel. When one realizes to what extent the Evangelist Mark cast the disciples, particularly Peter, in a negative light and that Luke has utilized this Gospel as one of his major sources, one can appreciate the special effort this Evangelist has undertaken in rehabilitating Peter. Although probably not the only reason, it would seem likely that Luke desired to portray Peter as positively as possible in view of his future prominence in the early church, as can be seen in Acts 1–11.

Luke's special interest in Simon Peter is seen in the miraculous catch of fish. When Jesus desired to board one of the boats so that he could address the crowds, he chose the one that belonged to Simon (Luke 5:3). After the miraculous catch of fish it is Peter who cries out to Jesus (v. 8). Moreover, when Jesus speaks to the disciples (see Mark 1:17), Luke has him address Peter (v. 10). Elsewhere in Luke, Peter is portrayed as spokesman for the disciples (9:20, 33; 18:28, both of which come from Mark, but see 12:41) or is named as one of the two disciples sent to fetch the colt on which Jesus would ride into Jerusalem (22:8; see Mark 14:13, where Peter is not named). Although Peter's close association with Jesus (along with James and John) is not unique to Luke (see 8:51; 9:28), there are several noteworthy features involving Peter found in the Lukan passion and resurrection stories. Only in Luke are we told of Jesus' prayer in behalf of Peter, that his faith may not fail and that afterward, having recovered, he might strengthen his brothers (22:31-32). (In contrast, Mark's account leaves the reader very much in doubt with regard to Peter's condition.) This then leads into Peter's assertion, found only in Luke: "Lord, I am ready to go with you to prison and to death" (22:33). Later, when Jesus is arrested and Peter joins those standing by the fire (22:54-55), unlike Mark, who then takes the reader inside to Jesus and his accusers (Mark 14:55-65), Luke proceeds immediately with Peter's denials (22:56-60). Although there are several minor differences between the Marcan and Lukan accounts, the most noteworthy is where Luke alone tells us that after the cock crowed, "the Lord turned and looked straight at Peter" (22:61). Furthermore, whereas Mark tells us that after the cock crowed Peter went outside and "wept" (Mark 14:72), Luke says Peter "wept bitterly" (22:62). Luke's editorial activity has heightened the pathos of this scene, leaving the reader with a sense of empathy for the fallen Peter. Following Jesus' resurrection, Mark only mentions the angel (or "young man") at the tomb, who commands the frightened women to tell Peter and the disciples that Jesus will appear to them in Galilee (Mark 16:7), but no actual appearance is recorded (16:9-20 had not yet been attached to the ending of Mark's Gospel when Luke made use of this document). Luke, however, reports in 24:34 that the risen Christ did indeed appear to Peter. Luke also manages to cast Peter in a better light by omitting two of Peter's more embarrassing moments: his rebuke for disapproving Jesus' passion plans (see Mark 8:32-33) and his reproach by Jesus for sleeping instead of watching and praying (see Mark 14:37).

In Luke 5:5 Jesus is called "Master" for the first time in the Gospel of Luke. Whereas the other synoptic Gospels refer to Jesus as "Teacher" or "Rabbi," only in Luke is he called "Master," and only by his followers (see Luke 8:24, 45; 9:33, 49; 17:13). It is significant that the first to address Jesus in this manner is Simon Peter. It is an address of respect, but when the miracle of the catch takes place, Peter addresses Jesus with awe: "O Lord!" What makes the catch so extraordinary is that Jesus is by trade a carpenter and Peter and his friends are fishermen. They have toiled all night (when net fishing was optimal) and caught nothing. How does Jesus know that fish may be taken now? Somehow he does, for Peter makes such a great catch that assistance is required from another boat (5:6-7). Suddenly aware of his sinfulness, Peter cries out in verse 8: "Depart from me, for I am a sinful man." Peter is not asking Jesus to get out of the boat, but to "leave the vicinity," that is, wherever Peter is. In more fully coming to recognize who Jesus is, Peter is overwhelmed by his own sense of sinfulness and unworthiness and, in contrast, Jesus' purity and holiness. Jesus tells Peter, "Do not be afraid; henceforth you will be catching men" (v. 10). Literally, this statement may be translated: "You will be catching [or taking] human beings alive." Mark's version (1:17) reads: "I shall turn you into fishermen of men." It has been suggested that because catching fish brings harm to the fish (in that they die), Luke has rephrased the words of Jesus to avoid such an implication. The word that Luke uses (i.e., "catching [or taking] alive") is used in the

Greek Old Testament for saving the lives of persons from danger (for examples, see Num. 31:15, 18; Deut. 20:16).

Overwhelmed by Jesus' teaching and the presence of divine power as seen in the great catch of fish, the disciples "left everything and followed" Jesus (v. 11). This is the first time that the word "to follow" occurs in Luke's Gospel, where it often is used of Christian discipleship (see 5:27-28; 9:23, 49, 57, 59, 61; 18:22, 28). Josephus (*Antiquities* 8.13.8) states that Elisha "followed" Elijah (LXX 1 Kings 19:21). The expression "to follow after" means to be a disciple of a rabbi.

The main point of the episode of the great catch of fish is not the miracle itself, but Jesus' call to Peter to begin preparation for his ministry as an apostle. Jesus has been teaching throughout Galilee (4:44), has performed healings and exorcisms (4:33-35, 40-41), and now, through the catch of fish, has extended his first call of discipleship (5:11). The miracle itself provides an apt point of illustration for Jesus' words in verse 10: "Henceforth you will be catching men." Peter the fisherman, a man who had expended his energies trying to catch fish for a living, has now left his nets behind and has begun his life's training as one of Christ's apostles.

Craig A. Evans

Sixth Sunday after the Epiphany, Year C

First Lesson: Jeremiah 17:5-10
(Psalm 1)
Second Lesson: 1 Corinthians 15:12-20
Gospel Lesson: Luke 6:17-26

Luke's Sermon on the Plain has striking similarities to Matthew's Sermon on the Mount, yet there are significant differences. The detailed discussion of the relationship between these two sermons is best left to the commentaries. Our focus will center on Luke's distinctive shaping of Jesus' message.

Luke locates the sermon on a plain or a plateau within a range of hills, for he describes Jesus as coming down from a mountainside after a night of prayer. A crowd of disciples has gathered there together with people representing the whole of Israel who are waiting to be taught and healed. Some tried to touch Jesus because, as Luke characteristically describes, "power was coming from him" (cf. 4:14; 8:46). As in Matthew, the teaching is addressed particularly to the disciples, but of course Jesus' teaching must also be heard by those who are not yet disciples.

Luke's sermon, like Matthew's, begins with beatitudes and ends with the parable of the wise and foolish builders. But Luke's sermon is much shorter (30 verses to Matthew's 107), and it contains only four beatitudes compared to Matthew's eight. Yet Luke uniquely adds four woes that stand in antithetical parallelism to the beatitudes. These antithetical pronouncements must be understood in the context of what has been called Luke's theology of Jubilee or his theology of reversal. For Luke the arrival of God's salvation and kingdom is that time when God sets an upside-down world right side up. Salvation as reversal is deeply rooted in the prophets and in the Sabbath year and Jubilee legislation of the Old Testament (Deut. 15; Lev. 25).

Interestingly the Qumran community used the first verses of Isaiah 61 as a framework for relating a variety of texts, including Deuteronomy 15 and Leviticus 25 (11QMelch). In other words, they interpreted Isaiah's prophecy of God's restoration of Israel as an eschatology of Jubilee. Luke's interpretation of Jesus is similar. By placing Jesus' sermon in the synagogue at Nazareth at the beginning of his public ministry, Luke intends to announce that the jubilary themes of Isaiah 61 shape his entire Gospel. Isaiah 61 announces the year of the Lord's favor in which the poor hear good news and the oppressed are released. It is important to note that the Septuagint calls the year of Jubilee the year of Release, a release that includes release from both sin (Day of Atonement) and the social conditions of oppression.

This theology of Jubilee or reversal and release shapes Luke's presentation of Jesus' ministry. Already the Song of Mary is filled with themes of reversal and release, of God setting the present upside-down world right side up by knocking the rich and the proud off their seats of privilege and power and lifting up the humble and the poor by filling their needs (Luke 1:50-54). Then Zechariah sings of rescue and salvation from the enemy as well as salvation through the forgiveness of (release from) sins (1:74-77). In addition, many Lukan parables emphasize God's demands for the appropriate use of wealth, as in the parables of the rich fool (chap. 12), the shrewd manager (chap. 16), and the rich man and Lazarus (chap. 16). The story of Zacchaeus is presented as the paradigm of a disciple who carries out the jubilary themes governing the use of wealth (chap. 19). In the Sermon on the Plain, the antithetical relationship of the beatitudes to the woes emphasizes the same theme. Salvation entails being caught up into God's great work of eschatological reversal, of righting an upside-down world.

The Lukan beatitudes and woes contrast the conditions of the poor and the rich before God. Who are these poor and rich? Although there are four beatitudes and four woes, each set of four focuses on a single type, not four different types. The poor are those who also are hungry, who weep and are hated, insulted, and excluded. The rich are those who already are comforted and well fed, who laugh and are flattered. Thus both types reflect their economic conditions and social status. The poor are the powerless, the rich are the powerful. The poor find it difficult to fend for themselves, whereas the rich have no trouble making their way in the world. Consequently, in the Old Testament God established rights for the poor in Israel: the right to eat from a neighbor's field or vineyard to satisfy hunger (Deut. 23:24-25), the right to glean (Deut. 24:19), freedom from interest on a loan (Exod. 22:25), and if the poor sold themselves or their land for reasons of debt, they would regain their freedom in the Sabbath year of release (Deut. 15:12-18) and their land would be restored in the year of Jubilee (Lev. 25). In this way God sought to provide the poor with the economic base which is essential to guaranteeing both a livelihood and personal liberty (Jer. 34:13-17).

Such rights of the poor were an integral part of God's covenant with Israel as rooted in the exodus. The refrain "They are my servants whom I brought forth out of the land of Egypt" or "You shall remember that you were a slave in Egypt" grounds in God's redemptive act both the rights of the poor and Israel's obligations to maintain those rights (Lev. 25:38, 42, 55; Deut. 24:18, 22). These rights and obligations are also rooted in the goodness and justice of the created order. Hence, especially the Wisdom Literature declares that both the rich and the poor are equal before God because "the LORD is the maker of them all" (Prov. 22:2; cf. 17:5; Job 34:19). Both the righteous person and the righteous king are expected to know the rights of the poor and defend them (Prov. 29:7; 31:9).

Since this rich and extensive Old Testament background concerning the rights of the poor clearly informs the New Testament usage, the church may not overlook the social, economic, and political connotation of the term "the poor." It is obvious that Jesus in Luke does not. However, is this term restricted exclusively to the economic-social-political status of the poor?

The Old Testament also designates the people of God as "the poor" who look to God to deliver them out of all their troubles (Pss. 37:14; 40:17;

333

74:19, 21; Hab. 3:13-14). Similarly in Luke, Jesus addresses his disciples as the poor (6:20). Of course, this spiritual connotation in no way negates the social-economic-political connotations because both oppressed Israel and the oppressed disciples experience these aspects of oppression as well. That the poor in the beatitudes are the disciples is clearly indicated in the fourth beatitude, where hatred and rejection occur because of their relationship to the Son of Man. The rejection he experienced will fall on them as they proclaim "repentance and release from [forgiveness of] sins in his name to all the nations" (Luke 24:47). So in Luke's later account we read that "the apostles left the Sanhedrin, rejoicing because they had been counted worthy of suffering disgrace for the Name" (Acts 5:41; cf. Luke 6:22-23). Such "poor" disciples should take encouragement from the example of the Old Testament prophets and leap for joy, keeping their eyes fixed on the eschatological reward in heaven. Their present condition will be reversed.

The beatitudes are thus eschatological promises of blessing, blessings which, like the kingdom itself, are both present and future. The specific blessing of the kingdom is phrased in the present tense, a blessing experienced already now even though the kingdom has not yet fully appeared. The subsequent blessings are likewise kingdom blessings but promised in the future: the hungry will be satisfied, those who weep will laugh, the final reward for the rejected is received beyond this life. Complete satisfaction and joy will occur in the celebration at God's banquet table (Luke 14:15-24), where God will prepare a feast for all peoples (Isa. 25:6-9). On that day God will right the wrong.

Nevertheless, while there remains a future blessing still outstanding, God's future action must become the norm for his people's conduct already in the present. Because God's banquet for the poor and oppressed is promised for the future (Luke 14:21), God's people must already include the poor and oppressed in their present banquets (14:13-14). The shape of God's future must shape our present. In this way there is in the kingdom an anticipation of the future in the present. The spiritual significance of release must not be divorced from social-economic release from oppression. As the exodus obligated Israel to grant release to the poor and oppressed within their borders, so Jesus' gift of the forgiveness of sins and the year of God's favor must lead his disciples to actions which release others from all manner of injustice and oppression. The story of Zacchaeus demonstrates this jubilary meaning of salvation.

The woes pronounced upon the rich are also intended to impact present conduct, for woes are painful warnings of coming judgment if change does not occur. The rich are the powerful and well fed whose life is filled with laughter. They are envied and flattered by others because of their power and wealth. While this seems to be only a social-economic-political category, it too has a spiritual significance. The rich are aligned with the false prophets who spoke and acted according to their own inclinations and did not subject themselves to the revelation and will of God (6:26). Similarly, wealth and power not subjected to God's demands are life in a fool's paradise (12:13-21). God requires that wealth be used to care for the poor (Prov. 19:17) and to carry out God's kingdom work in this world (1 Sam. 25:23-31). If the rich do not acknowledge God's claim on their wealth, God's eschatological reversal will place them outside the eschatological blessing.

Thus both the beatitudes and the woes are intended to shape the lives of disciples who live in this world as citizens of God's kingdom. While the promise of a future in which there is no hunger, thirst, or weeping (Rev. 7:16-17) is a hope that is necessary to strengthen obedience and patient endurance in this life, the presence of the kingdom demands a manifestation of that future already in the present. That is why in Acts Luke records the community whose purpose was to see to it that "there were no needy persons among them" (Acts 4:34). Although the modern church is under no biblical injunction to follow the method of alleviating poverty adopted by the Jerusalem church, it must never forget that God's purpose in establishing the sabbatical year of release and the year of Jubilee was to see to it that there was no needy person among his people (Deut. 15:4). Such is God's will at all times. The method is up to us.

The social, economic, and political realms of life have a spiritual claim hovering over them. Money, wealth, and power have always been intended by God to be a means of grace (Calvin) by which all persons, including the needy, experience God's own care and favor. Hence the disciples of Jesus must hear in the woes Jesus' call to be a demonstration to the world of a community which knows the appropriate use of wealth. The time of Jubilee (the year of the Lord's favor) has been inaugurated by Jesus Christ. Woe to those disciples and that society which ignore the claim of the Creator and the Redeemer upon their wealth.

David E. Holwerda

Seventh Sunday after the Epiphany, Year C

First Lesson: Genesis 45:3-11, 15
(Psalm 37:1-11, 39-40)
Second Lesson: 1 Corinthians 15:35-38, 42-50
Gospel Lesson: Luke 6:27-38

The heart of Luke's Sermon on the Plain is focused on conduct. Since the beatitudes and woes announce God's action of righting an upside-down world, Jesus now commands conduct appropriate for living in the world which God is setting right side up. Such conduct is expected of disciples who hear and obey (6:27). Even though the disciples will continue to be subjected to the hostile actions of this world (6:22), their conduct must reflect God's new world whose standard and measure is God's mercy (6:36, 38).

In the light of the promised kingdom blessings (6:20-23), Jesus exhorts his disciples to conduct themselves in a manner appropriate to citizens of God's kingdom (6:27-38). Such appropriate conduct is expressed in four exhortations regarding the demand to love one's enemies. These enemies are clearly those who hate Jesus' disciples, exclude and insult them, and reject their name as evil because of the Son of Man (6:22). These enemies follow a standard of conduct which seems appropriate in a world turned upside down by human sin. In such a world love is considered appropriate only for those who are like oneself. For example, in the Qumran community it was the purity of a person's deeds and the degree of that person's intelligence that formed the standard by which a person was to be loved or hated. Those who did not meet that standard were to be hated and shunned. Many persons and societies have deemed it good advice to do harm to one's enemies and to do good only to one's friends.

In the Old Testament God commanded that one should love his neighbor as himself (Lev. 19:18). To the experts in the law in Jesus' day, this command seemed to create an opening for a debate about the definition of neighbor and to allow a distinction between the neighbor and the non-neighbor to whom the obligation of love did not apply. Jesus' parable of the Good Samaritan overthrew such casuistry. For the Good Samaritan conducted himself as neighbor toward one who under normal circumstances would not have considered him his neighbor (Luke 10:25ff.). Jesus' command to love one's enemies underscores his understanding of who the neighbor is, for by any "normal" definition the enemy is the nonneighbor.

Thus Jesus turns the ordinary categories and normal definitions upside down.

The love Jesus requires goes beyond mere emotion or attitude to action, for the love that can be commanded is an exercise of the will. Disciples must do good to those who hate them, bless those who curse them, and pray for those who mistreat them. Good deeds are the central expression of the command to love (Matt. 5:16). Besides doing good, the disciples must invoke God's favor on those cursing them and intercede with God for those mistreating them. In so doing they follow the example of Jesus (Luke 23:34), Stephen (Acts 7:60), and Paul (Acts 16:28-32). The motivation for such loving action is not a utilitarian scheme calculated to win over the enemy, although that could be the result. Instead, the basic motivation is found in the nature and action of God (Luke 6:36).

The meaning of loving the enemy and being merciful as God is merciful is illustrated by four examples. Undergirding each example is the willingness not to defend one's personal rights but rather to accept insult, abuse, and loss for Christ's sake and for the sake of showing love to one's enemy. Motivated by such love, Jesus' disciples may not retaliate or seek revenge. This need not exclude the possibility of using existing law to defend oneself, as Paul did in his appeal to Caesar. The ethic here is personal, governing relationships between the followers of Jesus and those who abuse them because they are. While such an ethic is often judged by an upside-down world to be an ethic of weakness, Jesus' disciples know that "the weakness of God is stronger than man's strength" (1 Cor. 1:25).

The illustration of turning the other cheek is a response to insult and rebuke. Matthew's reference to being struck on the right cheek refers to a rebuke with the back of the hand (Matt. 5:39). Although Luke's version is more generalized, it seems similarly to be an illustration of physical insult or rebuke (Luke 6:22). In such circumstances love must be patient and vulnerable, and when insulted it will not retaliate (1 Pet. 2:23). The second illustration is similarly altered by Luke to fit a more generalized situation. By reversing the order of outer garment (cloak) and inner garment (tunic), Luke removes the saying from Matthew's legal setting and applies it to a more general setting of theft of any kind. In Matthew someone sues for the tunic, which is not protected by the letter of the law, and the disciple is encouraged to respond by giving the cloak as well to expose the immorality of such legal casuistry. The moral reasoning in Matthew's illustration is this: if God saw fit to legally protect the cloak, which is necessary only for the night (Exod. 22:26-27), how much more would he protect the inner garment without which the person would be naked. For an audience not acquainted with such legal stratagems, Luke applies Jesus' saying to a situation of ordinary theft in which the outer garment is stolen and the inner garment becomes the gift.

The last two illustrations of loving one's enemies seem especially to be instances of overstatement for effect, because other passages in different circumstances require the opposite conduct (e.g., 2 Thess. 3:6-13). Even so, we must not lose the point of the sayings. Giving to everyone who asks may refer to requests made by beggars in need; as such, this command would fit with the parallel in Matthew 6 and the scriptural requirement of using one's wealth for the care of the needy. Others, however, have suggested that this command refers only to borrowing, and that then the command not to take back from one who has taken what belongs to you refers only to the loan that was made. This understanding would harmonize with the requirement to cancel debts in the sabbatical year (Deut. 15:2) and with Jesus' proclamation of the inauguration of the year of Jubilee (Luke 4). However, in its immediate context it seems this saying should not be so delimited. As unrestricted, the saying points clearly to the extravagance that love bestows, a loving action that imitates the extravagant generosity of God himself (Luke 6:38).

The immediate ground for such an extravagant expression of love is Jesus' statement of the Golden Rule: "Do to others as you would have them do to you." Although not unique, for similar "Golden Rules" are found in Jewish, classical, and Chinese traditions, Jesus' statement has a far more emphatic and positive tone. For example, Confucius said, "What you do not want done to yourself, do not do to others." But Jesus' formulation reflects the positive character of the Old Testament command to love one's neighbor as oneself, a love Jesus interprets as generous deeds even toward one's enemies.

To highlight further the radical nature of such love, Jesus contrasts it negatively with the love and good deeds found in the world of sinners (6:32-34). The world of sinners refers to those who act in ways not shaped by God's eschatological act of renewal in Christ which turns the upside-down world right side up. In this new world love and doing good is not a mutual exercise of reciprocal actions. This new world was a sharp contrast to the world of Jesus' day, which was governed by the relationship of patron and client in which all actions were controlled by a set of reciprocal obligations. The beneficence of the patron expected in return acts of loyalty and obedience on the part of the client. Virtually all human societies function under a similar code of ethics: if I do something good for you, you are expected to return the favor. Where acts of love and goodness are received but not returned in kind, such ingratitude brings a quick halt to any further acts of love and kindness. Jesus' disciples, however, must love, do good, and lend without self-interest, calculation, or any thought of any kind of reciprocating behavior.

The negative contrasts in these verses (6:32-34) are self-evident, except for the one about lending. Literally the command is to lend "despairing nothing," that is, having neither concern nor despair about repayment. Again the ground for such action is God's kindness even to the ungrateful and the wicked. In addition, God promises an eschatological reward far greater than any unrepaid loans (6:35). However, most interpreters believe that the literal meaning "despair" does not really fit and instead argue that the meaning must be shaped by the context. Then the focus falls on not getting "the same" (v. 34, lit. "sinners expect the same"). This means either not getting the loan back (either principal alone or with interest) or not expecting a person to whom you have given a loan to return the same favor to you when the need arises. In any case, under any of these interpretations Jesus requires that the loan be extended freely as an act of love and without considerations of self-interest, to meet the need of the other and not to satisfy one's own.

Even though there is a promised reward for such free demonstrations of love not contaminated by self-interest, the reward is given precisely to the person who acts without any thought of reward. Instead of future reward, the ground and motivation for such conduct is the fact that Jesus' disciples are sons and daughters of the Most High who reflect his loving nature and imitate his merciful deeds. As a result, such extravagant deeds of love extended even to the enemy become a boundary marker which sets Jesus' disciples apart from the "sinners," for such conduct reveals who God is, who the disciples are, and what the God-given nature of this world really is.

The final sayings in this lesson underscore the indiscriminate character of the love given and the love received (6:37-38). There are four sayings: two negative in form and two positive, with each of the two being parallel with the other. Not to judge another means not to condemn. Although disciples do discriminate between actions that are morally good or evil, they may not prejudge persons and so predetermine who will or will not be the objects of one's kindness. Forgiveness and gracious giving must replace condemning judgment because God gives lavishly even to the ungrateful and wicked. Like a grain merchant in the marketplace, God gives a full measure, pressed down, shaken together, and running over. His love is bestowed with a measure far greater than anyone deserves. That is why his sons and daughters must give indiscriminately the same overflowing measure of mercy to all without calculating the consequences. A warning is attached: "for with the measure you use, it will be measured to you." God's immeasurable love should beget in the recipient loving actions toward others. If instead condemnation replaces forgiveness and love toward others, condemnation will ensue. God rewards only those who act as he does.

The ethics of Jesus are not reserved for another world at some other time. God has already acted to restore his created world to its rightful character. Since righteousness and justice have always been the foundation of his throne and steadfast love and faithfulness continuously go before him, God's earth has always been full of his steadfast love (Ps. 89:14). Thus, when God in Christ turns the upside-down world right side up, he expects that in his children his own character will once more be manifested and his indiscriminate, noncalculating love will flourish. Jesus' disciples must remember that they are God's children and citizens of his new world.

David E. Holwerda

Eighth Sunday after the Epiphany, Year C

First Lesson: Isaiah 55:10-13
(Psalm 92:1-4, 12-15)
Second Lesson: 1 Corinthians 15:51-58
Gospel Lesson: Luke 6:39-49

The Old Testament announced that one day God's Word would create a new world of fruitfulness in which the righteous would flourish like a palm tree (Isa. 55; Ps. 92). That new world manifests itself throughout Jesus' sermon, and in the parables with which it concludes the focus falls on that expected obedient fruitfulness.

Obviously safety and security are not best guaranteed by having the blind leading the blind. In such cases disaster looms ahead. But who are the blind? In the Matthean parallel, the blind guides refer to the Pharisees who are offended by Jesus' teaching (Matt. 15:14). Here in Luke, however, the reference is to disciples who are blind to their own faults while judging others.

The disciples have heard Jesus' radical teaching of what love requires regarding the enemy, yet they will be tempted to fall back into a life lived under more ordinary standards of conduct. Like most of humanity, they will find it easy to see the sins of others while overlooking their own, even when the sins of others are but a tiny sliver compared to their own, which may be as large as a beam supporting a house. But such ordinary human conduct is a manifestation of self-righteous judgment, which Jesus calls hypocrisy.

Hypocrisy goes beyond the ordinary understanding of self-conscious pretense or two-faced conduct by which one consciously acts one way in public settings and another way in private. The Pharisees conducted themselves morally in both spheres but were called hypocrites by Jesus because they failed to see that they were sinners. They clearly saw the sins of their fathers, who had killed the prophets, but they believed they were not like their fathers because they honored the tombs of the prophets. They failed to understand that the sin of the fathers was also their own, a deeply rooted sin which became visible when they called for the death of Jesus the prophet (Matt. 23:27-32). Hypocrisy is blindness concerning the fact that one is a sinner, and its consequence is self-righteous judgment of others. Whenever a generation self-righteously condemns the sins of its forefathers, that generation stands in mortal danger because it is not aware of its own sins.

The disciples of Jesus who are called to live in God's new world must avoid hypocrisy. Instead they must honestly practice self-examination and self-judgment regarding their own sins. Only then will they not be blind leaders of the blind. Instead they will see clearly and so be able to help others to remove the specks from their eyes and overcome their blindness. The self-righteous person cannot help uttering severely harsh judgments of others. Only those who have themselves experienced forgiveness will be able to live a life of forgiveness. Only those who themselves have received mercy will be able to love the enemy.

Jesus' teaching must not only be heard but lived. His disciples are like students who, when fully trained, will be like their Teacher. Thus the disciples must arrive at the point where they are able to practice the radical love and merciful forgiveness that Jesus lived and taught. Jesus was not a hypocrite because his life, his words, and his deeds were always in complete harmony. What he taught, he practiced. Sin destroys the harmony between word and deed, belief and action. Hence to become fully trained so as to be like Jesus requires the acknowledgment of sin and its removal. Only then will Jesus' disciples not be blind leaders of the blind.

The second parable in the concluding section of the sermon shows why the removal of sin is the absolute prerequisite for carrying out Jesus' command of radically loving even the enemy (Luke 6:43-45). Nature teaches that good trees do not bear useless or inedible fruit, nor do bad or useless trees bear good fruit. Thornbushes or briers do not produce figs or grapes. The quality and nature of a tree are recognized by the fruit it produces. This natural truth is filled with spiritual implications. In the Song of the Vineyard, God lamented that although he had planted Israel as a vineyard on the earth, and even planted it with the choicest vines, when he looked for good fruit it yielded only bad. The reason for this strange produce was Israel's sin, for they called evil good and good evil. The consequence was not justice and righteousness in the land, but bloodshed and cries of distress (Isa. 5). The disposition of the heart determines what kind of fruit is produced. When the heart confuses darkness for light, darkness will rule the day and good fruit cannot flourish.

The condition of the heart is therefore the key to becoming like Jesus. Consequently, Jesus reacted against the idea that cleanness could be created by observing external laws governing clean and unclean. What comes out of a person makes the person unclean. Sin and evil come from the inside, which external washings cannot alter (Mark 7:1-20). This focus on the inside, the inner self or heart, is found throughout the Scriptures. Wisdom calls her children to guard their hearts because the heart is the source or wellspring of life (Prov. 4:23). Now in the new covenant God has written his law on his people's hearts, and it is with the heart that one loves and serves God (Jer. 31:33). The heart reflects the person (Prov. 27:19).

Jesus' application of this parable assumes this biblical focus on the condition of the heart. If a good person is recognized by good deeds, then goodness must be stored up in that person's heart. Similarly, if an evil person is recognized by evil actions, it is because evil resides in that person's heart. Consequently, if a disciple is to become fully trained so as to be like Jesus, that person's heart must be filled with goodness, for out of the overflow of the heart the mouth speaks (Luke 6:45). Such goodness comes only from the good seed which Jesus sows, the seed which is the Word of God, the source of all fruitfulness (8:5-15).

The third and final parable in the concluding section of this sermon is, as in Matthew's sermon, the parable of the wise and foolish builders. In both Gospels the theme of the parable has to do with obedience. However, the settings are different. In Matthew the opening appeal to the Lord occurs in an eschatological context in which the Lord rejects some who had considered themselves to be his disciples and had even performed miracles in his name. Yet on the day of judgment they were denied admission into the kingdom because they had not done the will of Jesus' Father in heaven (Matt.

7:21-23). The wise builder in Matthew is the one who performs the greater righteousness, the radically true intent of God's law as taught by Jesus in the Sermon on the Mount. The foolish builder is the one who fails to do God's will.

The context in Luke is not so directly eschatological. Instead the emphasis falls on Jesus' desire that his disciples in the present not be blind leaders of the blind, that they not only hear his teaching but enact it in deeds of love and mercy. The parable about the builders stresses the urgency of doing what Jesus says in the present. Luke's description of the man who "dug down deep and laid the foundation on rock" seems to reflect a Hellenistic house with a basement rather than a Palestinian house. Similarly, the flood seems to be the result of an overflowing river rather than a storm that brought rain gushing down from the mountains that filled the dry wadis, as in Matthew's account. However, the central teaching of both versions is the same: only the house built on a sturdy foundation can withstand the eroding force of floodwaters. Only a fool builds a house that cannot withstand the storms of wind and water.

Human life has a similar architecture. It requires a firm foundation. The rabbis taught that the rock which would give stability to human life was the law (Torah). Yet the Scriptures teach that while the law of God gives guidance in the ways of righteousness, the law cannot by itself produce the good heart that performs good deeds (Rom. 7–8). God condemned the false prophets for teaching that by merely whitewashing the wall of the building which was Israel they could cause it to stand in the storm of God's great day (Ezek. 13). Instead, God declared that only by giving his people a new heart and his Spirit would they be able to keep his commandments and manifest his holy Name to the nations (Ezek. 36:23-27). Jesus' word is not only teaching but also a life-giving power that enables his disciples to produce good fruit. Jesus' words are actually spirit and life (John 6:63). Hence disciples who wish to be fully trained so as to be like Jesus must build their lives on the foundation of Jesus' teaching and put his words into practice. Only then will they be those with "a noble and good heart, who hear the word, retain it, and by persevering produce a crop" (Luke 8:15).

Sometimes Jesus' teachings in the sermons both in Matthew and in Luke have been considered to be too idealistic for life in the real world. Even Christians sometimes think that while the teaching may sound good in church, it does not work in the marketplace. We all need to be reminded of the world in which we live, a world which God is setting right side up and in which Jesus calls his disciples to be leaven and light. We must also not forget that the world God created was also structured by God's justice and righteousness, by his faithfulness and steadfast love. Such is the real world, not the world turned upside down by human sin.

Living according to the structures of God's real world requires repentance and forgiveness of sins, a new and good heart, and the gift of God's Spirit. Those who come to Jesus and truly hear his words will receive, according to this Gospel, all those gifts and will be able to put Jesus' teaching into practice. Such a life is built on the only foundation that will provide stability and security amid the storms encountered in life as well as on God's great day of judgment. The attempt to make one's life secure on the basis of any other foundation is the foolish conduct that leads to disaster.

David E. Holwerda

Second Sunday after Pentecost, Year C

First Lesson: 1 Kings 18:20-21, (22-29), 30-39
(Psalm 96)
Second Lesson: Galatians 1:1-12
Gospel Lesson: Luke 7:1-10

Ninth Sunday after the Epiphany, Year C

First Lesson: 1 Kings 8:22-23, 41-43
(Psalm 96:1-9)
Second Lesson: Galatians 1:1-12
Gospel Lesson: Luke 7:1-10

The healing of the centurion's servant is a story of faith outside the circle where faith was expected. This centurion was a Gentile, not a Jew. Yet even so, this story is filled with echoes of biblical themes and anticipations. Echoes from the distant past are heard from Solomon's prayer of dedication asking God to hear the petition of the foreigner in the land and to do "whatever the foreigner asks of you, so that all the peoples of the earth may know your name and fear you" (1 Kings 8:43). Also the ancient psalmist invites the nations to "worship the LORD in the splendor of his holiness" (Ps. 96:9). Luke writes his Gospel in the awareness that the time for the Gentiles to worship the true God had come, and deliberately takes great pains to ensure that Gentile readers of his Gospel know from the beginning that the good news of Jesus is intended also for them (Luke 2:32; 3:6, 38; 4:25-27; 7:1-10). For Luke the faith of the centurion foreshadows the coming in of the Gentile world recorded in his book of Acts. This story of Gentile faith during Jesus' ministry is like Pentecost ahead of time.

However, it is at the same time an epiphany story, for it clearly reveals Jesus and the nature of his manifestation to Israel and to the world. This revelation echoes Jesus' proclamation in the synagogue at Nazareth (Luke 4). There the audience could not believe that this son of Joseph was capable of inaugurating the prophesied "year of the Lord's favor." In response to this unbelief Jesus warned that no prophet is acceptable in his hometown, and then he mentioned two Old Testament prophets who also in times of unbelief extended God's mercy to Gentiles. Elijah had been sent to the widow at Zarephath and brought her son back to life (1 Kings 17), and Elisha healed Naaman, the commander of the army of Aram (2 Kings 5), and also raised a widow's son (2 Kings 4). The echoes of these miracles performed by these two great Old Testament prophets are heard in Jesus' miracles of compassion in Luke 7, for following the healing of the centurion's servant Jesus also raises a widow's son. (In fact, the town of Nain lies just down the hill from Shunem, where Elisha raised the widow's son.) God's mercy had always been intended for more than just Israel. So Jesus acts in accordance with God's intentions. Yet his own generation did not believe him (Luke 7:33ff.).

Luke places this story after Jesus' Sermon on the Plain, just as Matthew locates it after the Sermon on the Mount. The traditional location of this sermon is on a hill or level place near Capernaum, and after Jesus had finished his teaching he walked down to Capernaum. Capernaum was an important village not only because of its many piers for fishing boats, but also because it was located near the important highway called the Via Maris, where tolls were collected as it crossed the nearby political boundary. That is why Herod Antipas stationed a centurion with his cohort of one hundred soldiers in Capernaum, to keep order and to oversee the collection of tolls and taxes. This centurion was not in charge of Roman soldiers, as is often assumed, because there were no Roman soldiers in Galilee before A.D. 44, but he was obviously a Gentile and not a Jew (7:9). Centurions were well paid, receiving fifty to one hundred times the pay of an ordinary soldier. Thus, even if this centurion had not increased his income by dishonest means, he would have sufficient wealth to make a significant contribution to the synagogue. Whether the statement that he built the synagogue means that he paid the entire cost or only made the largest contribution is impossible to know. In any case, the Jews credit him for having made possible their new synagogue in Capernaum. The remaining ruins of the synagogue at Capernaum are of a later synagogue in Hellenistic style built in the fourth to fifth centuries A.D.

Some have wondered whether this centurion was a proselyte. The story indicates only that he was friendly toward the Jews and that he loved the Jewish people. He is not described with the words applied to Cornelius the centurion, who was a "righteous and God-fearing man, who is respected by all the Jewish people" (Acts 10:22). Cornelius was not a proselyte but he was a God-fearer, one who had been attracted to the worship of Israel's God and who followed the moral demands of the commandments. The centurion in Capernaum loved the Jewish people and was generous toward them, and they had genuine respect for him. In fact, they respected him so much they told Jesus that he deserved to have Jesus heal his servant. Although the story says nothing about his religious affiliation with the Jews, perhaps it contains an echo of God's covenant promise that he would bless those who blessed Israel (Gen. 12:3).

The centurion valued his servant highly. This may mean simply that this servant had served his master well and was especially useful to him. But it may indicate also that the centurion esteemed him as a person and considered him his friend, for that was not unheard of in master-servant relationships in the ancient world. If so, the centurion desires to extend the life not only of a useful servant but also of one who is a friend. Jesus had healed in Capernaum before (Luke 4:31-41), so the centurion had heard about him. He asks some elders of the Jews to intercede with Jesus on his behalf. Here Luke differs from Matthew. The story in Matthew is abbreviated and describes the centurion himself as making the request directly of Jesus. But the conclusion of Matthew's account contains an additional saying found later in Luke about the subjects of the kingdom being cast out while others take their place at the eschatological feast with Abraham (Matt. 8:11-13; Luke 13:28-29). The omission of the Jewish emissaries from the story may be due to Matthew's emphatic theme concerning the rejection of unbelieving Israel which leads to replacement by Gentile believers.

Why the centurion felt it necessary to send Jewish emissaries to Jesus is not stated. His decision may have been governed simply by the patronal ethic of that era. Since he had acted as a patron to the Jews, he could expect that as clients they would willingly return the favor, and he may have assumed also that a mediated request by Jewish elders would be more readily received by Jesus. There may also have been a certain reserve in the face of a great teacher, just as when the Greeks wanted to see Jesus they made the request through Jesus' disciples (John 12:20-22). While all these reasons may have played a role, the most dominant factor was undoubtedly the centurion's expression of personal unworthiness (Luke 7:7).

Jesus honored the centurion's request through his Jewish emissaries and went with them toward the centurion's house. But before he arrived the centurion sent some friends to prevent Jesus from entering his house. While some suggest this was due to the centurion's sensitivity to the Jewish belief that they would become unclean upon entering a Gentile home, the centurion actually pleads his own unworthiness. In fact, not only does he feel he is not fit to have Jesus come under his roof, he also does not consider himself sufficiently worthy to come to Jesus. Thus the real issue is not the centurion's possibly courteous action to prevent Jesus as a Jew from becoming unclean, but rather his personal feeling of unworthiness when compared with Jesus.

In Luke's account no mention is made of any direct contact between the centurion and Jesus. Instead the centurion requests through his emissaries only that Jesus say the word and his servant would be healed. For he understood how words spoken with appropriate authority accomplished what was said. Since his own authority was derived from superiors and ultimately from King Herod, the soldiers and servants under his command had to do what he said. Similarly, he viewed Jesus as having the necessary authority to heal. All that was required was Jesus' willingness to speak the word. He may not have known that that was the purpose for which Jesus had come. (To derive from the centurion's statement of being under authority the implication that Jesus also is under authority and hence that Luke teaches a subordinationist Christology seems to move beyond the point of the story.)

The climax of the story underscores the centurion's humility and faith. To borrow a perspective from a similar story in John, faith that simply takes Jesus at his word and believes that it accomplishes what it says is true faith (John 4:46-53). Thus when Jesus heard his request, he was amazed by the centurion's faith and declared to the crowd, which included the Jewish elders, "I tell you, I have not found such great faith even in Israel." The man who stood outside the expected circle of faith believed, while those inside the circle often did not (Luke 7:29-35). The story ends simply with the notice that when the men who had been sent returned to the house, they found the servant well.

347

This story of the centurion's faith and the consequent healing of his servant clearly advances Luke's purpose in writing his Gospel. From Simeon's response to Jesus as a child to Paul's response in the face of Jewish unbelief, Luke celebrates Jesus as a light for the Gentiles who brings salvation to the ends of the earth (Luke 2:30-32; Acts 13:46-48; 28:28). In Luke there is a pre-Pentecost anticipation of what Pentecost inaugurates in its fullness. In addition, this story reveals who Jesus is and the nature of his mission. Jesus was anointed with power to bring in the year of the Lord's favor, the year of Jubilee or the year of Release. Jesus is God's Son who possesses the power and the authority to bestow God's promised blessings of release from all manner of oppression, including from sickness and, most basically, from sin (Luke 5:20; 24:47). Finally, the centurion's faith is that genuine faith which trusts Jesus' word to effect what it says even before the evidence is in. Not to believe before the evidence is in is to be characterized by Jesus as being of little faith (Matt. 8:26). Ultimately the faith of the centurion is the kind of faith Jesus requires of his disciples throughout the centuries. Jesus said to Thomas, "Blessed are those who have not seen and yet have believed" (John 20:29). Such faith is committed to the belief that the word of Jesus is the word of God which always accomplishes what it says.

David E. Holwerda

Third Sunday after Pentecost, Year C

First Lesson: 1 Kings 17:8-16, (17-24)
(Psalm 146)
Second Lesson: Galatians 1:11-24
Gospel Lesson: Luke 7:11-17

In the Lukan version of the Nazareth sermon (Luke 4:16-30), Jesus appealed to the examples of the great prophets Elijah and Elisha. The implication is that Jesus understood that messianic blessings would be extended to the marginalized, the apparent nonelect, and even to Gentiles. The episode of the raising of the son of the widow, which is found only in Luke's

Gospel, reveals several points of contact with the Elijah/Elisha stories, and once again appears to reflect Luke's special interest in the question of election, that is, who are the elect of God and on what basis.

The most noteworthy parallels between this story and the similar miracles in the ministries of Elijah and Elisha include the following: (1) the setting in Nain (Luke 7:11), which may be an allusion to the ancient city of Shunem (2 Kings 4:8); (2) arrival at the town gate (Luke 7:12; 1 Kings 17:10); (3) a grieving widow (Luke 7:12; 1 Kings 17:9, 17); (4) the death of the only son (Luke 7:12; 1 Kings 17:17; 2 Kings 4:32); (5) the speaking or crying out of the resuscitated son (Luke 7:15; 1 Kings 17:22); (6) the expression, borrowed verbatim from the Greek version of the Old Testament, "he gave him back to his mother" (Luke 7:15; 1 Kings 17:23); and (7) the recognition that "a great prophet has appeared among us" (Luke 7:16; 1 Kings 17:24). Although the widow in 1 Kings says, "Now I know that you are a man of God," the Aramaic version (i.e., the Targum) inserts the word "prophet," thus bringing the Lukan and Kings passages into closer agreement.

The city called Nain (from the Latin *Naim* and/or Hebrew *Na'im*, meaning "pleasant") may possibly be traced back to the preexilic city of Shunem, the original site of which is quite close to the newer city. Nain is perhaps derived from the second half of the name Shu*nem*. It has been suggested that the modern Arab village Nein may stand on the site. Even if such an identification cannot be made with certainty (some commentators think it cannot), it is quite possible that Luke saw a connection. The various other parallels between the raising of the widow's son and the similar episodes in 1 and 2 Kings would suggest that Luke did see a connection.

In all probability the widow's son died the very day of the funeral procession. It was customary among Jews of late antiquity to bury the dead on the very day of passing, unless death occurred in the evening. The corpse was washed, anointed with perfume, wrapped in linen, then carried amidst much weeping and wailing to the tomb. One year later family members would gather the bones of the departed and place them in an ossuary, or bone box.

The young man's body had been washed, anointed, and wrapped (not embalmed), and was being transported to the place of burial outside the city. Contrary to convention and expectations, Jesus says to the grieving mother: "Do not weep" (Luke 7:13). These words would have struck all as strange, for there was no more appropriate time for weeping than at the time of death. Jesus' words imply that there is no cause for grieving, for the young man will yet live. Jesus commands: "Young man, I say to you, arise" (v. 14). To the utter astonishment of all, the "young man sat up, and began

349

to speak" (v. 15). The young man's speaking signifies that he has awakened from death fully recovered. His sudden and unexpected movement was not some sort of convulsion, but an awakening and recovery from death. His speaking shows that he is conscious mentally; his sitting up shows that he is sufficiently strengthened physically. The funeral has indeed been canceled.

When the people see the miracle, they cry out, "God has visited his people!" This exclamation makes the reader recall the similar words of praise uttered by Zechariah after the naming of his son John (Luke 1:68). Although many of the people recognize in Jesus' ministry God's visitation, the religious establishment, particularly as represented by Jerusalem, does not recognize such a "visitation." For this reason, when Jesus reaches Jerusalem he weeps over the city, "because you did not know the time of your visitation" (19:44). This concept derives from the Old Testament. The idea is that God comes near to inspect the human condition (whether Israelite or Gentile) to determine what action ought to be taken. The visitation may involve judgment (Exod. 32:34; Pss. 59:5; 89:32; Isa. 23:17; Jer. 14:10) or deliverance (Gen. 50:24, 25; Exod. 13:19; Ruth 1:6; Ps. 80:14; Jer. 15:15).

Despite the many and significant parallels between Jesus' miracle and the miracles performed by Elijah and Elisha, there is a major difference, however, in that whereas Elijah must pray to God and three times stretch himself upon the dead lad before he revives, Jesus merely speaks the word of command and the dead one is raised up. Jesus' superior power is clearly illustrated and sets the stage for his response to the messengers of John: the hopeless now have hope, for Jesus, acting as the Lord's anointed, has begun to fulfill his messianic task, just as he had earlier announced (Luke 4:18-21). In this particular episode Jesus has remedied the worst possible tragedy, for in the death of her only son the widow has been left alone and the family line has come to an end. This is indeed an example of the good news of the Lord's "acceptable year." Such an episode contributes significantly to Luke's theology of messianic blessings being extended to the weak and the outcast or, in the words of Isaiah 61:1-2, which Jesus quotes in the Nazareth sermon, the "oppressed."

Luke concludes the episode by noting that "this report concerning him spread through the whole of Judea and all the surrounding country" (v. 17). By mentioning this the Evangelist prepares for the passage that follows, in which the imprisoned and discouraged John the Baptizer hears of Jesus' activities and sends messengers to him. John will be told all that Jesus has done, again in the words of Isaiah 61:1-2 (and Isa. 35:5-6 and 26:19), such as restoring sight to the blind, enabling the lame to walk, and raising the dead.

Craig A. Evans

Fourth Sunday after Pentecost, Year C

First Lesson: 1 Kings 21:1-10, (11-14), 15-21a
(Psalm 5:1-8)
Second Lesson: Galatians 2:15-21
Gospel Lesson: Luke 7:36–8:3

As preachers, this story is very familiar to us. It is such an important tradition that all four Gospels present an account of Jesus and an unnamed woman (Matt. 26:1-13; Mark 14:3-9; Luke 7:36-50; John 12:1-8). By comparing the stories we see that Luke has redacted the tradition substantially. Why? We may also wonder about the next pericope (8:1-3), which is attached to the lectionary selection. What can we discover about what the Spirit is saying to the church on the Fourth Sunday after Pentecost?

We know that Luke includes women as important characters in the Gospel narrative. He uses special and common traditions to emphasize the mutuality of women and men as witnesses to the healing, empowering, and preaching ministry of Jesus. A look at a broader context of the Year C readings from Advent to the Sundays after Pentecost confirms Luke's portrayal of Mary and Elizabeth, women of Jerusalem, women who witness Jesus' death and resurrection. Acts mentions women among multitudes of believers who listen to the apostles' preaching and believe in Jesus (Acts 5:12-16).

As the liturgical year moves to Pentecost and subsequent Sundays, we have the opportunity to reflect on Jesus' mission and ministry that begins in the synagogue in Capernaum (Luke 4:21-30). Then we hear how Jesus heals, preaches, and encounters the Baptist's envoys (5:1-7:35). Suddenly our pericope begins with no transition. In the story Jesus asks Simon a penetrating question: "Do you see this woman?" (7:44, NRSV). It is our question, too. What do we need to hear the familiar story with different possibilities? To feel its power? To identify with an unnamed woman? To proclaim a familiar story with renewed energy for our preaching?

Do we see this woman? Surely Jesus sees her. And he feels her tears, her hair, her kiss, and her anointing of his feet. The Pharisee Simon sees the woman who performs a servant's role on Jesus' behalf (7:36-39). He dismisses her, however, as a sinner, and Jesus too, because he does not recognize who the woman is (v. 39).

Do we see this woman? What we see, and especially how we see, often depends on which pair of interpretive lenses we put on. For most of us, historical lenses are familiar and easy. Nonetheless, reimagining with cultural

351

anthropology can help us to refocus. Social-scientific critics who are interested in the human dimensions of the text ask: What does the author communicate so that others would remember the story? What values are operative in the hearers' worldviews to affect the story? What behaviors are praised or condemned according to cultural codes? Two models illumine the Mediterranean world of Jesus' time.

The foundational model is honor/shame. An adult male has the responsibility of protecting the honor of the entire household in the public arena where he encounters other men in dialogue. Correspondingly, an adult woman, a responsible person in a household of other women, children, and slaves, has the responsibility of embodying "shame," that is, the values of the culture, by insuring that the household has integrity in the private, domestic sphere.

The second model is the importance of ritual meals. The purpose of a meal is to affirm statuses because of a shared, symbolic worldview. Etiquette includes behavior and attitudes toward bodily boundaries (skin, clothing) and structures (hands, feet, eyes). The honor of the household is the primary value. (For the importance of meals, see Jerry Neyrey, "Ceremonies in Luke-Acts: The Case of Meals and Table Fellowship," in *Social World of Luke-Acts* [Peabody, Mass.: Hendrickson, 1991], pp. 61-87.)

When we look at Luke's account of the story, we find a meal context (v. 36). The Pharisee is the presider. He affirms Jesus' status by asking him to dinner. They have equal status, or Jesus would not be at table. In verse 38, however, when Jesus allows the sinful woman to touch him, the Pharisee is worried that his table is dishonored and shamed. Why? The narrator offers us a distinctive clue: a woman of the city, a sinner, enters the room (v. 37). She is not an invited guest, yet she acts. Her multiple movements and gestures correspond to the first stage of a "traditional luxury meal" where servants wash the guests' hands and feet and anoint them with perfumed oils to eliminate body odors (v. 38). The woman, however, does not belong to the Pharisee's household.

The Pharisee knows that the woman polluted purity codes — boundaries (skin) and structures (hands, feet) — because of her activity on behalf of Jesus' person. Her presence in men's space is "a violation of where she should be." She intrudes upon the group and breaks acceptable boundaries of a ritual meal. Jesus, however, accepts the woman's activity. Like the woman, he breaks boundaries. He shames Simon the Pharisee when he introduces the parable about the debtors (vv. 41-42) as well as when he reminds Simon about his lack of hospitality (vv. 44-46).

For many preachers, literary lenses may be more comfortable or challenging. Comparing differences in narrative characteristics may deepen our awareness of the Lukan redaction on Mark. In the setting, Luke indicates a table of male guests whom Simon the Pharisee invites to dine with him (v. 36). Pharisees especially dine often as *Haburot*, friends, where no women are present because they lack equal status, whether in Jewish or Gentile society.

In characterization, Luke presents a Pharisee, and his status as host is repeated four times (vv. 36 [twice], 37, 39) while his personal name, "Simon," occurs only once (v. 40). The next character, "a woman in the city, who was a sinner," is a double generic name. Her sexual immorality includes religious and political impropriety. Anyone who could pay for her services is considered a potential traitor.

In developing the plot Jesus affirms the woman's servant status when he tells the debtors' story (vv. 41-42). When he recites Simon's omissions as host (vv. 44-47), he praises the woman as a responsible, grateful servant. Jesus addresses the woman directly (vv. 48, 50) instead of speaking about her to Simon (cf. vv. 44-46). Jesus confirms that her sins are forgiven, while others at the table question his authority to forgive sins (v. 49). Finally, Jesus gives her permission to leave in peace. This story is an open-ended narrative. We never hear about the woman again unless we can imagine her among the women in 8:1-3 who follow Jesus from Galilee.

When we exchange narrative lenses for our own contemporary lenses, we interpret the values and ideologies of the text from individual social locations. If female gender is considered an important analytic lens, several questions arise: Is the woman's social location changed? Is her "place" to continue as a mute servant? Will she be permitted to sit at table because her "sins, which were many, have been forgiven; hence she has shown great love" (v. 47)? The Lukan Jesus did not invite the woman to the table; he dismissed her in peace. Yet in dismissing her Jesus said, "Your faith has saved you" (v. 50). Like the woman with the hemorrhage (8:48), she becomes an exemplar of faith.

Ritual meals and table fellowship constitute major images for Jesus' community in Luke-Acts. Servants may gather at the table. In table scenes, however, Luke did not intend an inclusive table that is gender specific. Luke preferred a traditional Greco-Roman public/private sphere dichotomy that upholds an honor/shame model.

When women and men consider the implications of table fellowship today, they specify tables in homes, shelters, tents, and food pantries throughout the globe. They analyze economic, social, and political situations in each place by asking fundamental questions: Who is invited to the table?

Who provides the food? Who serves it? Who eats it? Who goes without food? Why?

When women and men read the story of Jesus and the woman with the ointment jar via contemporary lenses, they also see the dilemma of table fellowship in the church. While all may be welcome to the table of the Word, who speaks? Who is addressed? Who is left out? Why? While all may be welcome to the table of the Eucharist, who presides? Who serves? Who is nourished? Who is not fed? Why?

If table fellowship remains only a theme in the first-century gospel of Luke-Acts, the presence of the risen Jesus will not be evident in our world and in our church *now*. Jesus welcomed *everyone* at his table. As preachers, we believe in his invitation and respond by inviting inclusive table fellowship to our communities. It is in our proclamation of the gospel that we create and sustain new possibilities for the power of the Word in our midst. How willing are we to break boundaries? To speak about issues that hinder authentic table fellowship? To speak the truth in love so that everyone is included? Our commitment and convictions about the Word of God can be like the ointment that filled the house with unexpected fragrance, healing, and joy.

Mary Margaret Pazdan, O.P.

Fifth Sunday after Pentecost, Year C

First Lesson: 1 Kings 19:1-4, (5-7), 8-15a
(Psalms 42 and 43)
Second Lesson: Galatians 3:23-29
Gospel Lesson: Luke 8:26-39

The lectionary here introduces one of the longest and most difficult miracle stories in the Gospels, the healing of the Gerasene demoniac. In the synoptic Gospels it is one of a series of miracles in which Jesus shows his power over the winds and waves, evil spirits, persistent illness, and even death. Although Luke follows the order of stories he has taken over from Mark, the arrangement of materials still suits his own theological purposes. Scholars have noted, for example, that the arrangement of stories in this part of the Gospel parallels the arrangement of material in Luke 4:31-44. There also we find a series of four miracle stories, including an exorcism. As in Mark, the series of four miracles then leads to the call of the disciples. Our story is, of course, also an exorcism and is one of a series of four miracles. This second series of four miracles then leads, unlike Mark, to the commissioning of the disciples to heal and to proclaim. This ordering of the materials tells us to look for the effect of the event on the followers of Jesus. But it must also be remembered that the Gospel of Luke is but the first half of a two-volume whole. In the context of Luke-Acts as a whole, this story anticipates the Gentile mission and, in particular, is parallel to Paul's healing of a possessed slave girl in Acts 16.

Luke also tells the story in a way very similar to Mark, though a close reading of the text will show that he has cleaned up Mark's sometimes ragged narrative. But once again a narrative taken from Mark suits Luke's theological purposes.

The story begins with Jesus stepping ashore in the country of the Gerasenes on the far side of the Sea of Galilee. Older commentaries spend considerable time on the difficult textual problem here. Is it the country of the Gerasenes, Gadarenes, or Gergesenes? The problem is exacerbated by the fact that Gerasa, the best purely textual option, is a city more than thirty miles from the lakeshore. The pigs would have to have been Olympic-caliber running swine to reach the water from there, or even from the five-mile distant Gadara! For the preacher, however, the key point is that the country on the far side of the lake, whatever its name, is Gentile territory. This is shown by both archaeological investigation and the simple fact that in the country there are herds of swine. Already the gospel reaches beyond the boundaries of Israel.

In that country there lives a man possessed by an evil spirit. As a result, he is separated from normal human relations, surely one of the most dreadful consequences of the presence of evil. He is naked and does not live in a house but among the tombs, an appropriate symbolic dwelling place for one claimed by the powers of evil. Moreover, he has been in this state for a long time. When Jesus commands the unclean spirit, the man falls down before him and shouts out. A comparison to the parallel passages in Luke's structure is instructive. Demons do shout out when faced by Jesus' power (Luke 4:41), or even by the ambassadors of Jesus (Acts 16:17). In these cases one should understand that the unclean spirit rather than the one possessed shouts out. What they shout out is profoundly true. Jesus is indeed "Son of the Most High God." It is deeply ironic that demons can recognize what the disciples have yet to learn.

355

"What have you to do with me?" asks the demon. But perhaps at this point the voice of the man himself subtly joins that of the demon. Jesus does indeed have something to do not just with the unclean spirit but with the man, for his good. Jesus always has something to do with those gripped by evil. Ironically the demon, which is manifestly torturing the man, begs not to be tortured by Jesus. More irony: the word "beg" is often used in the language of prayer. Using a flashback technique, Luke tells the reader just what the spirit has done to the man. The man has been guarded and chained. Perhaps this should be understood as a futile attempt to keep him within the human community. The community often does not know what to do when faced by madness or evil. What the spirit does is a fraudulent imitation of liberation; it breaks the shackles and apparently frees the man from his restraints. But it also drives him away from community. Perhaps evil in our time also offers a counterfeit appearance of liberation that in the end makes human community impossible.

Jesus, by contrast, offers a genuine liberation. The signs of such a liberation fill the second half of the story. At this point, however, the story records a conversation with the demon. Jesus demands to know the name of the evil spirit. The name symbolizes the spirit's essence. That the spirit accedes to the demand is an acknowledgment of Jesus' power over it. The name "Legion" refers to a unit of five thousand or six thousand men in the Roman army. A contemporary equivalent of the name might be "Division." Perhaps in the tradition there was a subtle anti-Roman thrust in the use of this name. Luke himself, however, is not anti-Roman.

The demons beg not to be sent into the "abyss," the netherworld, surely their natural dwelling place. Rather, they ask to be sent into a herd of pigs, and Jesus accedes to the request. (Is this the first instance of deviled ham?) The trajectory toward death that is an inevitable consequence of evil, suggested earlier by the man's dwelling place among the tombs, is now confirmed by the destination of the pigs. They plunge to their death in the waters below. The waters, as in Genesis 1 and the story of Noah, symbolize chaos and disorder. Note that chaos and disorder is precisely what the spirits had inflicted on the man. On a symbolic level the punishment fits the crime. It is not clear, however, whether all this is at the will of Jesus or is a sign of the ultimately self-destructive nature of evil.

As a result of Jesus' action, the man is clothed and in his right mind. The disorder of evil is reversed. Even more significantly, he is "seated at Jesus' feet." That phrase reveals something more important than bodily position. Luke uses it elsewhere to describe one who learns from a rabbi. So, for example, the young Paul sat at the feet of Gamaliel (Acts 22:3), and Mary, sister of Martha, sat at the feet of Jesus (Luke 10:39). The one who had been possessed is now a disciple. The possibility of relationship which had been destroyed by evil is restored. Luke adds a key word that is obscured in many translations. In verse 36 we are told in the Greek not just that the man has been healed but that he has been "saved." This story is in part about what it means to be saved. To be saved means to have a right relationship with Jesus, with the self, and, insofar as possible, with others.

The reaction of "others" is complex, however. The story tells us that both those who have seen the saved man (v. 35) and all the people of the district (v. 37) are afraid. This is not entirely a surprising reaction. It happens frequently in the Gospel. The shepherds are sore afraid when the angel appears to them in the fields of Bethlehem. The disciples are afraid on the sea, not, it must be noted, when they are nearly swamped by the storm, but when Jesus saves them. And above all, the women are terrified in the empty tomb on Easter morning. We become used to an ordered life distant from a God we believe is confined to a few religious moments and ceremonies. It is a fearful thing when God steps into our ordered lives and shakes them up with the divine presence. Fear is neither a strange nor even a wrong response.

But what comes next is very wrong. They ask Jesus to leave the district. No reason for their request, other than their fear, is given in the story. But perhaps the parallel story in Luke-Acts, the exorcism of the slave girl in Acts 16, suggests another reason. There the anger of the girl's owners toward Paul and his companions is caused by their economic loss. They prefer swine to a savior. Possessions, even at the cost of possession, are more to be valued than a man. Perhaps we too ought to take warning here. The gospel and business as usual cannot coexist if business as usual depends on human misery.

This first venture into Gentile territory might, at first sight, be considered a failure, a strange result for the Evangelist who will later give us the book of Acts. But Jesus has left behind a disciple. That disciple begs — how much begging there is in this story! — to be taken along with Jesus, but instead Jesus gives him a task. "Return to your home, and declare how much God has done for you." The man receives the Gospel's first commission to proclaim what God has done through Christ. (The Twelve will not receive their commission until the next chapter [Luke 9:1].) The inhabitants of the city may drive out Jesus, but the witness to him remains. "So he went away, proclaiming throughout the city how much Jesus had done for him." Such a witness is not the prerogative of the Twelve nor of the clergy. It is the duty and also the delight of all those who have been touched by Jesus.

Stephen Farris

357

Last Sunday after the Epiphany (Transfiguration), Year C

First Lesson: Exodus 34:29-35
(Psalm 99)
Second Lesson: 2 Corinthians 3:12–4:2
Gospel Lesson: Luke 9:28-36, (37-43)

Luke follows the order common to the synoptic Gospels in the material leading up to the pericope. We read in all three Gospels of Peter's confession, of the first prediction of the passion, of the summons to pick up the cross and the enigmatic prediction, "But truly, I tell you, there are some standing here who will not see death before they see the kingdom of God." That prediction is answered by our pericope, in which at least a foretaste of the glory of the full kingdom is granted to three disciples. The story is heavily symbolic and is laden with allusions to and echoes of other stories both in the Old Testament and elsewhere in the Gospel of Luke. It must be read with a poet's eye and ear.

While Matthew and Mark specify that the transfiguration takes place on the "sixth day," Luke places the story eight days after the sayings recounted in the previous verses. Perhaps this is just a loose way of saying "about a week later," but there may be something more significant here. There may be a hint of the resurrection, which occurred on the "eighth day," that is, the day after the Sabbath. There are, as we shall see, certain resemblances between this story and Luke's account of the resurrection. It is also worthy of note that Christian worship likewise takes place on the eighth day. Hence there may be a suggestion that Christ's presence can be manifest to his followers in the church's worship. It is Luke, after all, who tells us in the story of the walk to Emmaus that the risen Christ makes hearts burn when the Scriptures are unfolded and is known in the breaking of bread, surely an allusion to Christian worship. Another significant alteration is that Luke alone specifies that the three disciples are taken with Jesus for the purpose of prayer. Particularly in the Gospel of Luke, Jesus is presented as one who prays. It is during prayer that Jesus is transfigured and the disciples are enabled to see him as he really is.

The three disciples Peter, John, and James (in that order in Luke) are already a privileged group. It is they who have witnessed Jesus' power over death in the healing of Jairus's daughter (Luke 8:51). Now their knowledge of Jesus will be increased further. Why only three disciples rather than the entire twelve are chosen to witness the transfiguration is a difficulty. But it is, in truth, always only a minority who gain a deeper and fuller sense of Jesus' glory. That too is a reality that is beyond complete explanation.

It is while Jesus is praying that the action of the story begins. The story as a whole has some of the features of an Old Testament epiphany, a manifestation of God's presence. There are particular echoes of the Sinai experience: a mountaintop, Jesus' dazzling clothes and face reminiscent of Moses, the mention of "glory" and a cloud indicating the divine presence. We might first think the text is naming Jesus as a second Moses. But "two men" appear to the disciples, perhaps an anticipation of the resurrection (Luke 24:4) and the ascension (Acts 1:10). Their names are given; Moses and Elijah appear in glory and speak with him. These two figures departed life mysteriously, according to the Scriptures, and are also featured in eschatological expectation. Some expected Elijah to return before the end (cf. Luke 9:19). Others expected a "prophet like Moses." But these figures converse with Jesus, so clearly he is neither. Moses and Elijah are also representative figures. Because of their presence the "law and the prophets" bear witness to Jesus, as on the Emmaus road.

Moses and Elijah speak with Jesus about his "departure, which he was about to accomplish at Jerusalem." The Greek word behind "departure" is "exodus," a word obviously replete with Old Testament connotations. The exodus is the saving act of God par excellence in the Old Testament. What Jesus will accomplish is as, or more, significant. If we remember that the first prediction of the passion appeared immediately before our pericope, there can be no confusion about the meaning of "exodus" here. It refers in the first instance to Jesus' death, or perhaps his death, resurrection, and ascension understood as a single event. Something more may be said, however. A unique feature of Luke's Gospel is the travel narrative that takes up the entire middle section of the Gospel. It begins at 9:51, almost immediately after our pericope, and does not conclude until the triumphal entry into Jerusalem at 19:28. A staple of sermons on this passage is to contrast this "mountaintop" experience with the suffering in the valley below (9:37-43). But perhaps the movement in Luke is wider than simply from mountaintop to valley. It is mountaintop to valley and on to Jerusalem. And from Jerusalem the movement is outward to all the nations (24:47). Who knows where disciples will go once they truly experience Jesus?

It is noteworthy that in this episode Peter and his companions are weighed down with sleep. This anticipates the scene in which Jesus prays in agony on the Mount of Olives (another mountain!) that the cup might be taken from him. There likewise the disciples are weighed down with sleep. (Luke, unlike the other synoptics, does not name Peter, James, and John in that scene, nor does he name the place Gethsemane.) Here, however, the disciples either stay awake despite their drowsiness or wake up. The Greek could be read either way. In this part of the Gospel there are a number of failures on the part of the disciples. The drowsiness signals yet another failure.

And failure does follow: Peter misunderstands what he has seen. His proposal to build three booths for Jesus, Moses, and Elijah implies that he considers them to be on a level. That this is an inadequate understanding of Jesus is demonstrated in a uniquely authoritative way. As on Mount Sinai, a cloud signifies the divine presence. The disciples are terrified; the presence of God is indeed a fearful thing. "They" enter the cloud — probably Jesus, Moses, and Elijah rather than the disciples. From the cloud a voice speaks. An encounter with God must always be described in anthropomorphic terms. How else can one communicate the reality and significance of what is said about God than in human terms?

As the voice speaks, we have reached the key event in the pericope. It is as if we, the readers of the Gospel, were sitting in the back row of a theater, and the director of the play has slipped up behind us and, to our surprise, taps us on the shoulder and whispers in our ears, "This is important. Listen to this." The story is about Jesus, not the disciples nor our religious experiences. Indeed, like so many pericopes in this part of the Gospel, it is about the identity of Jesus. The voice says, "This is my Son, my Chosen; listen to him!" Jesus is more than a lawgiver and more than a prophet. Even to call him Christ or Messiah is not enough if one does not recognize in that term a uniquely close relationship with God. Jesus is "Son." We have not yet reached the Council of Nicaea and its understanding of the meaning of the word "Son," but it is because of passages like this that the church did indeed eventually reach that point. He is the chosen one, the "elect" of God. What Israel has been as a whole, Jesus now is in his own person, the one through whom God's purposes for the world must be worked out. So, of course, "hear him!" And in the Bible the word "hear" always implies trust and obedience. Mystical mountaintop experiences are doubtless wonderful and exciting. But such experiences are, in truth, the province of only a few. But every Christian can, and must, hear, trust, and obey.

The lectionary offers the possibility of extending the reading for the day through the account of the healing of a boy possessed by an evil spirit. (The boy is surely an epileptic.) As mentioned earlier, this juxtaposition allows the preacher to contrast mystical experience and human need. We can't stay on the mountain because there is always trouble in the valley. The father plays a key role in the story, begging for Jesus' assistance and pointing out the disciples' failure. The failure of the disciples is indeed a persistent theme in this part of the Gospel. Note the argument later in the chapter over greatness and their complaint against an exorcist who is not one of them. The disciples don't "get it" any more than Peter does. But Luke does not devote as much attention as Mark does to the father of the boy. For example, the father's moving statement, "I believe; help my unbelief," is missing from Luke. This throws the rebuke to the disciples into greater prominence. But we ought also to observe the simple words with which Luke concludes the story. Jesus casts out the demon: "And all were astounded at the greatness of God." Not just a favored three but all around can see this miracle. And apparently you don't have to climb a mountain to witness in Jesus the greatness of God.

Stephen Farris

Sixth Sunday after Pentecost, Year C

First Lesson: 2 Kings 2:1-2, 6-14
(Psalm 77:1-2, 11-20)
Second Lesson: Galatians 5:1, 13-25
Gospel Lesson: Luke 9:51-62

A preacher preparing to communicate this text might take note of what the seating arrangement of the hearers is likely to be. Will they be hunkered down in hefty oak pews that are bolted to the floor? How about pew cushions — the velvety ones with little buttons? Are the worshipers apt to be squirming for a comfortable position in some old metal folding chairs? Are they happily situated on some tree stumps outside in the wilderness, gathered in a circle beneath some towering pines?

The vantage point from which one hears this passage in Luke makes a difference in how the text gets assimilated. This lesson opens the travel ministry of Jesus. Beginning here, and continuing through the next nine chapters in Luke's account, Jesus is on the move. Luke provides us with a whole series of glimpses of a very mobile Jesus. And the perspective of the hearers might well inform their receptivity to this roving teacher. Even the stability or comfort of the seats beneath those listening to a sermon may affect what words the preacher chooses to use for characterizing the nature of discipleship. Discipleship, we find out from Jesus, is a commitment that will always involve some shake-up of conventional and static ways of living.

Luke has crafted a text that is full of motion. We gain the most from it if we do not sit too still while reading or listening. Keeping track of all the movement language helps introduce us to Luke's picture of discipleship as a *journey*. Numerous references to the verb "go" highlight the opening verses: "while going," "they went," "as they were going," "wherever you go," "let me go," "go." Between verses 51 and 57, the word "journey" pops up four times. The passage concludes with a reference to the forward movement of a plow. These are not soothing verses for those disposed to motion sickness!

All this motion talk invites hearers to consider patterns for living that may be very different from those to which they're accustomed. Being stable citizens, hopelessly fixed to the safe environment of a comfortable home, does not prepare us adequately for discipleship. A willingness to move does. We encounter no standstill Jesus here, but rather one who seems open to whatever comes. We get several looks at his face — Luke mentions the face of Jesus three times here — or at least we're tipped off to where it is pointed: "He set his face to go to Jerusalem." The emphasis on direction is an expression of resolve, informed perhaps by the servant in Isaiah 50:7 ("I have set my face like flint, / and I know that I shall not be put to shame"). Jesus appears determined to warn others that the road of loyalty to God involves multiple bumps of rejection. The very mention of Jerusalem as a destination, the place where Jesus would eventually suffer and die, points to the close relationship between discipleship and rejection by others.

Two of the disciples, James and John, seem unfamiliar with how to handle rejection. In a reactive move against the opposing behavior of the Samaritans, these two pull a play out of the playbook of Elijah (2 Kings 1:10). "Lord, do you want us to command fire to come down from heaven and consume them?" Jesus will have nothing of such zealous punishment for those who may disagree. He summarily repudiates the disciples for their brash idea.

Luke may be opening up this lengthy travel section with a little visit into hostile Samaritan territory to try to awaken interested disciples with the knowledge that they would be following a rejected leader. The question lying just beneath the surface of Luke's narrative is, Do you know you are following a rejected leader? This is a question that the church in every age needs to address. Following Jesus in authentic ways is guaranteed to be a strenuous exercise. It is full of rigorous and consuming demands, not the least of which is the humility of being associated with one so thoroughly rejected by others. Given our general pursuit of successful and achieving leaders, we ought to ask one another whether we understand what we're saying when we speak of following Jesus. From the responses of the three individuals who form the "would-be" disciples in our text, it's not apparent that they understand the deep meaning of identifying with the rejected pieces of Jesus' life.

If the theme of journeying through inhospitable situations and communities of opposition punctuates Luke's definition of discipleship, it is underscored by the reality of Jesus' own homelessness. Luke depicts Jesus as without shelter, home, or family. Even the animals have it better than he does when it comes to earthly security. "Foxes have holes, and birds of the air have nests; but the Son of Man has nowhere to lay his head," says Jesus. Each of the three would-be followers in verses 57-62 has some reference to *home,* which contrasts with Jesus' homelessness. For the first one it is the comparison to birds having a roosting place. For the second it is the desire to go home and bury one's father. And for the third it is the expectation of going home to bid farewell to loved ones. Jesus, we find, has no security in earthly shelter or a family home. His security rests in God.

Would-be followers of Jesus is a suitable title for these three anonymous figures in our text. That's what they are. They are individuals who *wish to be* with Jesus or *intend to be* with him. Does this sound roughly familiar to your own circumstance? For all of our eagerness and interest in Jesus Christ, discipleship often looks most attractive when we set the terms. The figures who encounter Jesus on this road to Jerusalem haven't grasped his emphatic claim that even the best of human relationships must be subservient to following him. Even our deepest loves are subject to a higher allegiance owed God. We don't get the privilege of custom-designing the terms of our Christianity.

Each of the three would-be followers remains nameless. Their anonymity, along with their varied life and family obligations, gives this biblical vignette a timeless quality. We can envision ourselves in any one of their situations as we contemplate the ways in which we too bargain over the terms of discipleship.

The first individual to visit with Jesus along the road volunteers to be a follower of whatever path Jesus might take. This person is not recruited. He or she willingly offers up obedience. All we can detect is genuine spontaneity and exemplary desire. We naturally wonder whether or not this person comprehends the implications of following a rejected leader. Gethsemane and Golgotha, after all, are just around the corner.

One thing is clear. When Jesus offers up his sober reply about having nowhere to lay his head, we remember that the things we often consider necessary for everyday life are not at all essential for the journey with him. If anything, most material forms of security imperil our life of faith. When following Jesus becomes a priority, all other things fall by the wayside. We stop filling life up with misplaced goods and loves that inappropriately distract.

The second individual is recruited by Jesus for discipleship. This one responds to the invitation with a precondition. And a sensible one it appears to be! He begs for a waiting period so that he might go home and bury his dead father. Taken literally, it's a bit peculiar, as we wonder what he might be doing standing by the side of the road if his father is dead and awaiting burial someplace else. But that misses the point. Here is one who postpones his commitment to Jesus in order to take care of a reasonable duty, a traditional responsibility. Jesus' reply about the "dead burying their own dead" seems harsh and cruel at first glance. But if his goal is to remind us that sacrifice accompanies pursuit of the kingdom, he succeeds well in gaining our attention. Does Jesus' odd reply suggest that the "dead" who do the burying are really spiritually (and not physically) dead? Perhaps so. According to Rudolf Bultmann, "those who resist the call of Jesus are put on the same level as the dead."

The third individual is the sum of the previous two. Like the first, he volunteers to follow Jesus. Like the second, he has a precondition. Reminiscent of Elisha requesting a leave to bid farewell to his parents as a precondition for following Elijah (1 Kings 19:19-21), this individual proposes a delay as well. Jesus responds with a vivid image of a plowman who looks ahead. He thus lays bare his own idea of the stringent demands of the discipled life. It's a way of life that has a cost attached. It's one that is ill suited for those inclined to keep turning back in favor of family loyalties.

Whether recruited to follow Jesus or simply pursuing him of one's own accord, disciples are those who bring their undivided attention to the journey. They are unencumbered people, concerned only with what lies ahead, and not behind. Like the plow operator concentrating on guiding the plow blade ever so straight, the faithful follower of Jesus is the one with eyes fixed on the kingdom of God, the one willing to be rattled free from secure surroundings, the one open to rising from that wonderfully comfortable seat.

Peter W. Marty

Seventh Sunday after Pentecost, Year C

First Lesson: 2 Kings 5:1-14
(Psalm 30)
Second Lesson: Galatians 6:(1-6), 7-16
Gospel Lesson: Luke 10:1-11, 16-20

Luke loves writing about mission. Here, without a whiff of the missionary Spirit of Acts in the text, the focus is on the involvement of disciples in the mission of Jesus. In this respect this account of the sending of the seventy-two, found only in Luke, comes hot on the heels of the sending of the Twelve (9:1ff.) and the sending of "messengers" to go ahead of him (9:52ff.), both events containing some themes and phrases Luke uses again here. Unlike the case of the Twelve, there is no explicit giving of "power and authority" by Jesus to this group, and yet they go on mission as if these things have been given and return joyfully testifying to the fact. To be "sent" by Jesus is to trust and act on the assumption that what is required to achieve his desired purposes will be given. In a Gospel renowned for noting places and people, the lack of such in this passage is tantalizing. Is Luke permitting a universal application of the mission themes here?

The vagueness about accurate numbers — seventy-two or seventy — is not, of itself, something that warrants much pulpit time today. It is more important to note that whether seventy-two or seventy, the symbolic significance is missionary in nature. So in the Hebrew texts of Genesis 10 the nations of the world number seventy whereas in the Septuagint account they number seventy-two, which, according to legend, was the same number of elders of Israel commissioned to translate the Torah from Hebrew to Greek, Greek representing the "universal" language of the time. Whichever is the accurate number, Luke is presenting a mission which prefigures the mission "to the ends of the earth" he takes up in Acts.

But before such a universal mission can be undertaken, certain events must unfold: crucially, the death and resurrection of Christ. It's no mistake, then, that the seventy-two are sent out as Jesus sets out for Jerusalem (9:51), their saving missionary journey deliberately placed within his greater saving missionary journey. The message is clear: all Christian mission proceeds from and is based on what Jesus will achieve as a result of his grim journey to Jerusalem. Far from being abandoned as he turns to go to Jerusalem, Jesus' mission finds impetus through this greater number of messengers sent to prepare his way and declare the nearness of God's kingdom.

365

The journey to Jerusalem also signals the increasing rejection of and hostility toward Jesus and his ministry by his own people — another important mission theme. Besides accounting for some of the information given to the seventy-two (go in pairs, lambs among wolves, wipe the dust off your feet, etc.), this context of rejection provides the vehicle for an understanding of salvation much wider than that it "belongs to the Jews." The seventy-two represent Jesus (v. 16), and their ministry and message is an extension of his. To welcome the messengers is to welcome the message; to reject the messengers is to reject the message. In this way people judge themselves. Reception and acceptance bring salvation; rejection brings judgment. Consequently belonging to God's kingdom, being a member of the people of God, becomes not a matter of ethnic origin or religious observance but of receptivity to Jesus and his message. So wiping dust from the feet, usually an act of self-purification making the *traveler* clean, becomes a symbolic gesture that the *town* is unclean. The deliberate geographical vagueness of Luke's mission accounts makes it possible, at least theoretically, for a Jewish town to be declared unclean, outside the ranks of the people of God, while a Gentile village is declared clean and placed inside those ranks (cf. Matt. 10:5-6, which specifies mission only to the "lost sheep of Israel").

A sense of *urgency* pervades the narrative. The specter of cataclysmic events in Jerusalem, hostility, and a sense of the kingdom drawing near combine to bring an almost palpable tension into the text. The seventy-two are to prepare the way for the coming of Jesus, but the eschatological tone is such that Luke permits the speculation that it may be Jesus' parousia rather than his immediate arrival that his witnesses herald. "Greet no one on the way" (v. 4) is not an injunction to be deliberately rude, but probably equates to "don't dawdle about"! Similarly "The harvest is plentiful" (v. 2) implies "there's work to do, get on with it!" Harvests, by their nature, have to be harvested, and quickly — miss it and lose it. The notion of harvest as a mission field is not common in Scripture, but is clear enough here. A more common harvest image found in the Old Testament, relating to judgment and the final gathering of the people of God, rumbles in the background. Even the injunction to "go in pairs" may relate not only to protection and mutual support but also to the evangelistic value of hearing more than one testimony declaring the message. "Stay in that house . . ." (v. 7) warns against "doing the rounds" of hospitality, which takes up valuable time. They are to "eat what is set before them" (v. 8), which not only suggests a "put up with what you get" attitude but includes the possibility that the food offered may not pass the normal rigors of Jewish purity. The nature, importance, and exigency of the mission take precedence over such things. Traveling light — "no belt, bag or shoes" (v. 4) — is the order of the day.

"No belt, bag or shoes" also hints at another, related theme, that of dependence on God. They "go as they are," and in a spirit of trust. The "belt" they are not to take with them refers to a money belt and hints at a reliance on God for meeting their needs, seen here in the provision of hospitality. The risks involved require a profound trust in God and deep dedication to the task. Luke's use of "lambs" (rather than "sheep," as in Matthew) hints that their vulnerability is like that of Jesus — the Lamb of God. However, the Isaiah imagery of sheep and wolves, representing Israel among the nations — God's people among those who are not God's people — should not be ignored.

Alongside these allusions to the hostile environment into which the seventy-two are sent are significant, positive factors. It is assumed, for example, that houses and towns will be open rather than closed to the messengers. The text deals with those who "receive you" before moving on to those who "do not." "Children of peace" (v. 6), that is, those open and ready for the salvation coming into the world, are expected to be found, and in unlikely places. All this combines to produce a level of *expectancy* in the text. The missionaries can expect acceptance and reception as well as antagonism and rejection. So a generous and gracious approach is urged as the starting position, with appropriate responses to rejection as necessary, rather than vice versa. Such a mission strategy in a cultural climate that is both "hot and cold" to the gospel demands consideration, now as then.

This gracious approach is epitomized by the greeting "Peace be to this house" (v. 5), offered as the house is entered. Here as elsewhere in Luke-Acts, "peace" is a metonym for salvation rather than simply an everyday salutation. Rather than being a human wish or desire, this peace is a real entity, able to be given, received, accepted, or rejected. As such it is a gift of God freely offered, and so the messengers are not to be grudging about bestowing it. Nor are they to judge whether to give it or not. Like the message of the kingdom, it is to be declared to all; it will not remain where it is not wanted.

The "reporting back" of the seventy-two (vv. 16-20) reminds us just how little about the mission itself we actually know. How long was it? Where did it take place? Luke, unusually, leaves such holes unfilled. The report is upbeat and characterized by joy. Their use of "Lord" marks them as disciples of Jesus (a term not explicitly used of the seventy-two anywhere in this narrative). They have acted "in his name," and although not physically present with them, he has clearly been exalted in and through their lives (a common and humbling experience of Christians engaged in the work of the Lord).

Their triumph over the evil one is a particular cause for rejoicing, and as this ministry was not explicitly instructed to do so, it must be understood as a dimension of "healing the sick" (v. 9). Jesus' interpretation of this reportage is salutary and affirming, now as then. What may look like a few dozen mendicant preachers wandering around in a backwater is in fact a notable setback for Satan and a triumph for the kingdom of God! This very ordinary group exercise divine power. Yet to be carried away with either power or success is to miss the main point. Their role, like his, is to restore people to God and so bring them into the kingdom. That they share in the life of this kingdom is the greatest thing of all.

Martyn D. Atkins

Eighth Sunday after Pentecost, Year C

First Lesson: Amos 7:7-17
(Psalm 82)
Second Lesson: Colossians 1:1-14
Gospel Lesson: Luke 10:25-37

Jesus was traveling *to* Jerusalem with his disciples. Along the way he told a story about people who were traveling *from* Jerusalem. We have, therefore, a story told by Jesus on the road about people on the road. One cannot help wondering at the outset what these journeys may have to do with each other.

Jesus' journey is introduced by ominous signals. This is the journey Moses and Elijah had spoken about on the Mount of Transfiguration: "They appeared in glory and were speaking of his departure [lit. his *exodus*], which he was about to accomplish at Jerusalem" (9:31). Luke announces the beginning of the journey in words that only thinly disguise Jesus' earlier predictions of his suffering and death (9:21, 44): "When the days drew near for him to be taken up, he set his face to go to Jerusalem" (9:51). The Jerusalem destiny has collected these associations: exodus, suffering, rejection, death, betrayal, and being taken up. These clouds of suspense overshadow the beginning of Jesus' journey.

The first steps of the journey bring Samaria and Jerusalem together in a hostile relationship: "They [the Samaritans] did not receive him, because his face was set toward Jerusalem" (9:52-53). As if we needed another reminder, Luke serves notice that there was no love lost between Samaria and Judea. These ominous signs set the stage for the story Jesus will tell. Add to these references to Samaria and Jerusalem the tones of urgency and crisis that characterize Jesus' conversations from 9:51 through 10:24, and we are inclined to expect a story of conflict and judgment.

What we get instead is the beautiful, intriguing story of "the Good Samaritan" that is universally loved. It is the story of a man whom Charles Cousar calls "a secularized saint" (*Texts for Preaching — Year C* [Louisville: Westminster John Knox, 1994], p. 426). His name — though it does not appear in Jesus' story — has become familiar through "Good Samaritan laws" that protect roadside first-aiders from litigation and through generous churches and benevolent agencies that wear it without needing to explain it. The story is so well known and loved that even when reduced to a nickname for a campers' club (The Good Sams), it has power to warm the heart.

What is going on here? Does Jesus defuse all the tensions surrounding his journey with a story everyone can love? On the contrary, a careful rereading of the story will disclose a deep conflict that calls for decision and action yet today.

"Just then a lawyer stood up to test Jesus. 'Teacher,' he said, 'what must I do *(poiēsas)* to inherit eternal life?'" It is the ultimate question of life. Inheriting eternal life equals having a relationship with God that is good and right, and that transcends death. Do not dismiss the question by saying that inheriting eternal life is not the result of something *we* can *do*. It is better to notice that Jesus accepted the question as it was asked and even reinforced it in his response. When the lawyer summarized the law of love for God and neighbor, Jesus replied, "You have given the right answer; do *(poiei)* this, and you will live."

The emphasis on *doing* returns after Jesus told the story. Jesus then asked the lawyer, "Which of these three was a neighbor to the man who fell into the hands of the robbers?" Response: "The one who *did (poiēsas)* mercy." Jesus gave the bottom line: "Go and *do (poiei)* likewise." This emphasis on *doing* both by the lawyer and Jesus is like brackets placed before and after the story that reinforce the emphasis of Jesus on hearing and *doing* the will of God.

It would seem that the conversation could have ended after Jesus' words "Do this, and you will live" (v. 28). I can imagine the lawyer turning to leave, taking the first steps toward home, and then returning with his next question as an afterthought, "And who is my neighbor?"

That question was widely discussed among the rabbis. The commandment to love your neighbor as yourself was quoted from Leviticus 19:18. The "neighborhood" envisioned there was primarily the citizens of Israel; *primarily* because Leviticus 19:33-34 makes room for the resident alien in the neighborhood: "When an alien resides with you in your land, you shall not oppress the alien. The alien who resides with you shall be to you as the citizen among you; you shall love the alien as yourself, for you were aliens in the land of Egypt." The neighborhood in Leviticus includes citizens and resident aliens in Israel.

The history between Leviticus and Jesus had changed the neighborhood of the Israelites repeatedly. The question was always alive: Who is my neighbor in this time and place? Some drew a tight circle. Others were more expansive. Nearly everyone agreed, however, that it did not include Samaritans. That gives punch and power to the parable.

The question now takes on the same urgency as the first question. "What must I do to inherit eternal life?" and "Who is my neighbor?" are intimately related. The relationship is disclosed in the lawyer's motivation for asking: "But wanting to justify himself, he asked Jesus. . . ." The lawyer had no problem with the loving God part; loving his neighbor as himself was the difficult part. How could he inherit eternal life if he could not limit and control his neighborhood? His desire to justify himself becomes an important key to understanding the parable of Jesus. One unavoidable question the story puts to every preacher and listener is this: How big or small is the neighborhood?

"A (certain) man was going down from Jerusalem to Jericho, and fell into the hands of robbers, who stripped him, beat him, and went away, leaving him half dead" (v. 30). Not a Jewish man, a Gentile man, a Samaritan man, a rich man, a poor man, a good man, a bad man, a white man, a black man, or any other kind of man, but a "certain" *(tis)* man. The man is not characterized. The indefinite *tis* makes it emphatic. The same is true about the priest and the Samaritan in the parable. It was a *tis* man and a *tis* priest and a *tis* Samaritan. Wherever the adjective "good" to describe the Samaritan came from, it was not from Jesus. Neither the traveler nor the priest nor the Samaritan was characterized.

The traveler was "going down" the road from Jerusalem to Jericho. The descent was more than one-half mile; the distance was seventeen miles. The road was notorious as a high-crime district where travelers were warned to travel at their own risk. That day the road lived down to its reputation: the traveler was robbed, beaten, stripped, and left for dead. As the curtain falls on act one, the stage is set for the drama that follows.

A certain priest came down the road. Priests rode donkeys. They did not walk. (For this and what follows regarding the Levite and Samaritan, I am indebted to Kenneth E. Bailey, *Through Peasant Eyes* [Grand Rapids: Eerdmans, 1980], pp. 41ff., and Bernard Brandon Scott, *Hear Then the Parable* [Philadelphia: Fortress, 1989], pp. 198ff.) When he came to the place where the beaten traveler lay, the question of the lawyer became his: "What shall I do?" Whatever he did or whatever he left undone, the concern of the lawyer would also become his: "How can I justify myself?" The story itself leaves us without much help in answering these questions. But the lawyer's concern to justify himself on the basis of the law provides a clue. Keeping his distance, the priest would not know if the traveler was a Gentile or a corpse. The victim had no clothing or speech that could identify whether he was a neighbor. In the absence of these, the law regarding ritual impurity could justify his passing by on the other side.

Then the Levite came. He would be walking, not riding. Would he risk contaminating himself by touching a corpse or a Gentile? "What shall I do?" and "How can I justify myself?" would be his questions also.

The people who were listening to the story would expect that after the priest and the Levite, the next person down the road would be a Jewish layman who had been to the temple. Here the shock of the parable enters: a Samaritan, while traveling, came near him. He was moved with compassion. He was not under the laws governing the priest and the Levite. If he wondered, "What shall I do?" and "Is this my neighbor?," the law did not instruct or justify him. He was not detained by the lawyer's concerns about what to do or how to justify himself. With extravagant generosity and grace, he undid the violence of the robbers and the neglect of the priest and Levite. The Samaritan did not limit his neighborhood or his compassion on the basis of law. Nor did he desire to justify his extravagance. The despised Samaritan becomes a model of the compassion of Christ.

When the story was finished, Jesus asked a different question: "Which of these three, do you think, was a neighbor to the man who fell into the hands of the robbers?" The question is not "Who is my neighbor?" but "Who was a neighbor to the needy traveler?" The lawyer answered, but could not bring himself to say the "Samaritan" word.

The story of the Samaritan neighbor invites us to identify first with the priest and the Levite (and the lawyer himself) and confess that we cannot justify ourselves on the basis of a long list of laws or a short list of neighbors. Before God, no one can inherit eternal life or justify themselves that way. Second, identify with the wounded traveler. His only hope was the mercy of another who came with grace to heal and restore. Jesus put no prayer in the heart or on the lips of the unconscious victim, but if he had, it would have been that prayer for all seasons: "Lord, have mercy." Third, identify with the Samaritan and be a neighbor who shows the compassion of Christ. Jesus identified with the Samaritan on his journey to Jerusalem and the cross. The closing words of the story provide an open-ended adventure with a never ending calling: "Go and do likewise."

In another connection, Stephen Farris, deeply committed to the primacy of God's grace, wonders about the relationship between God's acceptance and God's demands. Noting that the Jerusalem journey is an exodus, he further observes: "Much of the exodus narrative in the Pentateuch answers the question, 'What does a life shaped by a covenant relationship with the God who rescued the people from Egypt look like?' Much of the travel narrative of the Gospel of Luke answers the question, 'What does a life shaped by grace look like?'" (Academy of Homiletics, *Papers of the Annual Meeting*, Thirty-fourth Meeting, pp. 1-3).

In this story, it looks like this: "A certain Samaritan while traveling came near him; and when he saw him he was moved with compassion."

Roger E. Van Harn

Ninth Sunday after Pentecost, Year C

First Lesson: Amos 8:1-12
(Psalm 52)
Second Lesson: Colossians 1:15-28
Gospel Lesson: Luke 10:38-42

The tensions and interpretive difficulties in this text are myriad. Although these two sisters appear in John 11:1-44; 12:1-11, the better-known scene is this one, unique to Luke. The most popular interpretation of Luke 10:38-42 is that Mary and Martha represent contemplation and action, respectively. They are said to exemplify the tension in the life of each disciple who tries to balance the two, and that one who serves actively can do so only after having listened to the word at the feet of Jesus. Although this is a true lesson for Christian life, one must ask why, if the ideal is to integrate contemplation and action, the two are cast dualistically in this text, with the one choice approved and the other denigrated.

A host of other questions arises: Why, in a Gospel where serving, *diakonein*, epitomizes the very mission of Jesus (22:27), does he reprimand Martha for doing such? Why is only hearing the word valued in this instance, when all through the Gospel there is a constant refrain that discipleship consists in both hearing and doing the word (e.g., 6:47; 8:15, 21; 11:28)?

To complicate matters, most women identify with Martha. Like her, they try to juggle all the household demands, usually in addition to working outside the home. There is no good news for them from a Jesus who reproaches one who pours out her life in such service. Interpretations abound that try to rescue the text, or rescue Jesus from being unfairly critical of hardworking women.

One such inadequate approach is that it is Martha's attitude, not her service, that is the problem. Some think Jesus disapproves of Martha's feeling burdened or distracted (v. 40) or anxious and worried (v. 41). (The variety of translations for *periespato* [v. 40] and *merimnas* and *thorybazē* in v. 41 is telling.) Others think Jesus' displeasure is caused by Martha's occupation with too many dishes for the meal and that Jesus wants only one simple dish so that Martha can also join in the theological discussions.

Another inadequate approach is to see Jesus as upholding theological education for women by approving Mary's abandonment of the traditional domestic roles. But exalting women's theological education in the character of Mary comes at the expense of Martha's service. The real crux of disagreement, both in the early church and today, is not whether women can study theology, but rather what ministries they may perform as a result of their theological education. It is around Martha that the controversies swirl, not Mary.

Key to the interpretation of this text is the meaning of *diakonia* and *diakonein* in verse 40. The verb *diakonein* refers to service of any sort on behalf of another and carries a wide variety of connotations. It denotes apostolic service (Acts 1:17, 25), financial ministry (Luke 8:3; Acts 11:29; Rom. 15:25), ministry of the word (Acts 6:4), and ministry of the table (Acts 6:2), which includes not only ordinary meals but eucharistic gatherings and all the ministries surrounding those, including presiding. It is not at all clear that a meal is involved in Luke 10:38-42. Translations which render *diakonia* in verse 40 as "details of hospitality" (1970 edition of NAB) or "her many tasks" (NRSV) and *diakonein* as "all the work" (NRSV) only exacerbate the problem.

Recently, Elisabeth Schüssler Fiorenza proposed that in Luke 10:38-42 we have a story that reflects a struggle in Luke's day over the proper ministerial roles for women, not one that records an incident from the life of Jesus. A clue to its setting in the life of the early church and not that of the earthly Jesus is the use of the title "Lord," *kyrie* and *kyrios*, in verses 40, 41, which reflects a postresurrection context.

The conflict represented in the story revolves around *diakonia*, ministerial service (v. 40), performed by women Christians. That there were women exercising a wide variety of ministries, including apostolic work, public proclamation, and leadership, is clear from a number of New Testament texts. Women like Phoebe, who led the church at Cenchreae, bore the title *diakonos* (Rom. 16:1). 1 Timothy 3:11 lists qualifications for women deacons. In Romans 16:7 Paul greets Junia, a prominent woman apostle. Others of his female coworkers include Mary (Rom. 16:6), Tryphaena, Tryphosa, Persis (Rom. 16:12), and Prisca (Rom. 16:3). Euodia and Syntyche struggled at Paul's side in promoting the gospel (Phil. 4:3).

It is also quite clear that the early church was not of one mind with regard to the propriety of such ministries being exercised by women. In the same letter in which Paul approves of both women and men praying and prophesying in the liturgical assembly (1 Cor. 11:4-5), a later copyist has inserted the admonition that women keep silent in the churches and "be subordinate, as even the law says" (1 Cor. 14:34). Women teachers such as Prisca were well known (Rom. 16:3-5; 1 Cor. 16:19; 2 Tim. 4:19) and applauded by Paul. However, the author of the Pastoral Letters, written later in the first century by a Christian using Paul's name, insists that women not "teach or have authority over a man" (1 Tim. 2:12). That there were similar divisions in Luke's churches over the exercise of ministry by women is evident in the Martha and Mary passage. The Third Evangelist resolves them by placing on the lips of Jesus his approval of the silent Mary (v. 42).

It is significant that the verb *hypedexato*, "welcomed him," is used in verse 38. It is a compound form of *dechomai*, "to receive," denoting hospitality, a crucial value everywhere in the ancient world. It takes on an even greater significance as a Christian ministry to those engaged in the apostolic work of traveling evangelists (Luke 9:5, 48; 10:8, 10; Acts 17:7). *Dechomai* is also used to speak of receiving the word (Luke 8:13; Acts 8:14; 11:1; 17:11), and the kingdom of God (Luke 18:17). Martha's welcoming of Jesus matches Mary's listening to him speak. In the first two verses, then, there is no opposition between the two sisters. Each receives Jesus and his word. The tension arises over how their acceptance of the word takes expression in ministry.

Read in light of the disputes in Luke's day over women's involvement in certain ministries, Martha's complaint to Jesus is not about having too much work to do, but rather that she is being denied her role in ministerial service. In the phrase *periespato peri pollēn diakonian* (v. 40), Martha is burdened *about* or *with reference to* her numerous ministerial works, not *by* or *with* them. Her distress *about* them is generated by the opposition of those who think she should be leaving them to men. Moreover, the primary definition of *periespaō* is "to be pulled or dragged away." The word alludes to Martha's being pulled away from her diaconal ministry by those who disapprove.

Furthermore, Martha bemoans the fact that her sister has been persuaded that silent listening is the proper role for women disciples, and has left her alone in the more visible ministries. In the ensuing verse, Luke portrays Jesus authoritatively siding against Martha in this dispute. It is the silent, passive Mary who has "chosen the better part."

That Martha's worry involves a more public matter is evident in the use of *thorybazō*, "be troubled" (v. 41). The cognates *thorybeō* and *thorybos* occur eleven times in the New Testament, always in the context of a disturbance made by a crowd. This suggests a conflict that has the whole community in an uproar.

A much different picture emerges from the way the Fourth Evangelist has shaped the traditions about these two sisters. In John 11–12 Martha plays a central role in the drama of the raising of Lazarus and makes a profession of faith in Jesus (11:25-27) that is equivalent to that made by Peter in the synoptic Gospels. The Fourth Gospel profiles strong women characters who engage in theological discussions with Jesus, profess their profound faith, and preach publicly and convincingly. Unlike the Gospel of Luke, it makes no attempt to silence women or to restrict them to quiet, behind-the-scenes, homebound ministries.

In proclaiming the story of Martha and Mary today, a preacher must be cognizant of the many difficulties the Lukan version presents. The temptation is very strong either to rescue Jesus or to redeem the text so as to blunt its absolute approval of Mary and reprimand of Martha. Our instincts are correct when they tell us that something is wrong with this picture; but to try to make it into something that it is not is equally problematic. The best approach is to recognize the historical situation reflected in this text and analyze both the similarities and differences from that of our day. It is important to know that the Lukan approval of silent, passive women is only one side of an early Christian debate. Contemporary preachers "choose the better part" when they speak of the rich diversity of gifts in the community that are to be used in service without regard to gender distinctions. They would do well to emphasize that both women and men are called to contemplative listening and both women and men are called to all forms of diaconal ministry.

Barbara E. Reid

Tenth Sunday after Pentecost, Year C

First Lesson: Hosea 1:2-10
(Psalm 85)
Second Lesson: Colossians 2:6-15, (16-19)
Gospel Lesson: Luke 11:1-13

On the final journey to Jerusalem and the climax of his earthly ministry, Jesus maintained his discipline of prayer. The disciples had observed the importance of prayer in the life of Jesus and asked him to teach them a prayer that would characterize their band of followers. The prayer recorded by Luke (and Matthew [6:9-13]) focuses on the realization of the kingdom of God that was central to his teachings. Stress is placed on relationships that will make the kingdom possible.

Jesus began by suggesting a form of address of God that implied a special relationship. "Abba" ("Father") (v. 2) was a warm term of endearment that stated a theology of familial relationship. Jesus' familiarity with God had infuriated his critics, and now he teaches the disciples to claim a closeness that makes the fulfillment of the rest of the prayer possible. God as parent precedes God as king. God is the loving parent who gives, nurtures, and sustains life.

Prayer for the establishment of the kingdom of God was common in the first century. Pious Jews prayed daily that the kingdom would be established in their lifetime. Of course, for a long time neither they nor the disciples understood what that meant. Jesus taught that the kingdom had begun with him, and that it was like a mustard seed that would grow and grow. The disciples were to pray for the reign of God over all creation. This would mean blessing for the poor and judgment for the unrighteous. To pray for the kingdom of God is to pray for the promised salvation made possible by the death and resurrection of Jesus. The point must not be lost that all personal desires and petitions should be subordinated to the will of God and God's kingdom.

The disciples were reminded that God cared for their personal needs. A form of Deism often creeps into the thought of Christians: the belief that God set in motion the flow of history and the mechanics of the universe but remains distant and aloof to individuals. Our confidence in the presence of God who is able to provide for our needs empowers us to resist the temptations to satisfy them in ways other than the way of Christ. Luke's account differs from Matthew's in using the present tense and adding "day by day" for emphasis. An appropriate paraphrase might be "keep on feeding us day after day." The manna in the wilderness could not be stored, and Jesus sent the apostles out with "no staff, nor bag, nor bread, nor money" (9:3). Implied in this petition is faith in God's willingness to provide our daily needs and be present daily for us.

Prayer should be linked to action in the same way our ethics reflects our true theology. What we believe about God is seen in the way we live as Christians in the world. Jesus presumed that his followers would forgive others:

> Forgive us our sins,
> for we ourselves forgive everyone who is indebted to us.

We forgive because we have been forgiven, and we dare to ask for forgiveness because we forgive. An early father of the church called this petition terrible because of the claim it makes on those who pray it. Forgiveness does not come easily for humans, and it was costly for God. Excuses abound for the failure of Christians and Christian nations to forgive, but the will of God in this matter is clear and the help of God is available.

Jesus taught the apostles to pray "give *us* . . . *our* daily bread . . . and forgive *us* . . . and bring *us* not into temptation." The disciples requested this teaching as a way of identifying their solidarity. The disciples were reminded that, their petty differences aside, their bond to Christ bound them together. Around the world in many languages this prayer is uttered every Sunday. The sincere praying of these words should contribute to the unity of the church.

The parable attached to this event is found only in Luke. Those present in Luke's account were Jesus' "friends," insiders who had a special responsibility. The scene Jesus depicted required no stretch of the imagination for first-century listeners. Travel was slow, hard, and often done late in the day to avoid the heat. Bread was typically prepared at home for the average family, and only enough for a single day was baked. Three loaves per person per meal was the usual serving. Sometimes, however, there were leftovers from that day. The bread is not the obstacle to assistance in this case.

In peasant households the family slept in rows across the floor of one-room houses with a parent at each end and the children in the middle. The whole household would have to be disturbed to accommodate the request. The beggar does not give up easily, and finally, because of his "persistence," gets what he "needs." The Greek word translated "persistence" literally means "shamelessness." The borrower does not give up easily, and the neighbor finally relents. Is the emphasis here on the persistence of the one in need or on the reluctant provider? Perhaps the key is in the following application and the "how much more" of verse 13.

Jesus urged the disciples to pray with confidence, but certain boundaries were implied: requests should be in keeping with necessities of life and the kingdom. Jesus went on to say that when you pray in this way, you can be confident that God will hear and respond. There is implied an understanding that disciples, then and now, will "ask" for and "search" for that which is within the will of the loving parent who is utterly trustworthy. The door at which we knock is the door to the kingdom. God wants God's people to ask and seek that which God wants to give, for it is best for us. This passage must be understood in the context of the whole gospel. We are to follow a different agenda and seek the things of the kingdom rather than those for which all the nations of the world seek (12:30-31). Those who suggest that this text encourages praying for wealth and comfort do violence to the Scriptures. Ask for what you really need, and God will provide it. The verb tense here is present, suggesting continuous action. Jesus says to "keep on asking, searching, knocking."

Luke draws on familiar images to make his point on parental care. There was an eel-like type of unclean fish in the Sea of Galilee. A loving parent would not give to a child anything that would be harmful to a child, even if it fit the category of the request. A baby cries for food, but some food is harmful. A scorpion may draw itself into a ball and assume the appearance of an egg. The eel or scorpion wrapped in a ball might appeal to a child, but the parent would exercise caution on behalf of the child. A parent must be wise enough not to be fooled, and our heavenly parent is wisdom itself. To interpret this passage as "just ask for whatever you want and an indulgent God will give it to you" is to miss the point altogether.

Luke states that God gives "the *Holy Spirit* to those who ask him." This is in keeping with the Lukan emphasis on the Holy Spirit and the new age inaugurated in Christ. The most important reason for praying is to receive the gift of Godself to those who ask. Jesus taught that we should pray "thy kingdom come," and he goes on to say that if we do, God can be trusted to "give the Holy Spirit to those who ask him." The promise of the Holy Spirit is the assurance of the abiding presence of God in every circumstance and trial.

The disciples wanted to pray like Jesus. They saw that there was a difference between the way he prayed and the popular exhibitions of prayer with which they were familiar. His response to their request to teach them to pray opened the door for them to experience a deeper and more vital relationship with God.

We need to pray, as did the disciples, to open the doors of our mind to the Holy Spirit. The primary purpose of prayer is not to tell God what we want, but to find out what God wants of us. Prayer is a means of receiving the will of God, the power of God, and the love of God. Effective prayer releases the will of God into the life of the believer and into the world. The greatest gift we have today is the gift of God's presence in the Holy Spirit. Prayer keeps us aware and in touch with that Spirit that guides us in every aspect of life. The Christian community in prayer for the full realization of the kingdom of God is more at one then than at any other time. Our unity rests not in theological propositions but in the relationship to God. This short and simple prayer is profound in its implications for the singular mission of the church to be of one mind with Christ. The question is not whether or not God is with us, but whether we are with God.

How we approach God in prayer reflects our understanding of who God is, what God wants to do for us, and what God wants us to do for God. We must not retreat in fear and bury our gift but move forward in the spirit of confident hope. Prayer is personal, but it is also universal.

Raymond Bailey

Eleventh Sunday after Pentecost, Year C

First Lesson: Hosea 11:1-11
(Psalm 107:1-9, 43)
Second Lesson: Colossians 3:1-11
Gospel Lesson: Luke 12:13-21

J esus told two parables against the rich: the story of the rich man and Lazarus is about the sinfulness of consuming wealth at the expense of the poor, while our present passage, the parable of the rich fool, is about the folly of accumulating wealth. The two parables, one in the prophetic tradition, the other in the wisdom tradition (cf. the rather close parallel in Sir. 11:14-19, and the similar teaching in James 4:13-16, which is also in wisdom style), illustrate the confluence of these two traditions of Jewish religious teaching in Jesus. Of course, in the wisdom tradition foolishness is not merely stupidity, but the obstinate disregard for God that is the opposite of the wisdom that flows from the fear of God.

In the introduction to the parable, Jesus is expected to behave as many a Jewish teacher of the law would, by settling a legal dispute over family inheritance. The father, following the old Israelite practice of family ownership, has left his farm as a unit to his two sons, but Jesus' questioner asserts his right to have the property divided. The implication is that the man's relationship with his brother has been ruptured by the desire for independent possession of his property. So Jesus responds with a wisdom saying (v. 15) that goes behind the question of legal rights to the motivation and misapprehension that drive the questioner. Insatiable greed for material possessions entails the illusion that the more we have, the better the quality of life. Though disproved even by empirical studies of levels of happiness among people of varying standards of living, this delusion rules contemporary life in the potent form of consumerism.

In Jesus' story an exceptionally good harvest makes a rich farmer even richer. His problem is not the most obvious one: what to do with his crops. It never occurs to him to do anything with them except keep them, and so his problem is simply *where* to keep them, and the solution is a major building program on the farm. In a soliloquy that betrays his self-isolation from anyone for whom he has real concern (compare the man in v. 13, who wants his property solely for himself), he anticipates the security he will enjoy, having all he needs for a good life for years to come.

But we already glimpse his foolishness if we recognize his self-injunction, "eat, drink, be merry," as a common saying deprived of its customary conclusion: "for tomorrow we die" (Isa. 22:13; 1 Cor. 15:32; there is a similarly ironic curtailment of the saying in Tob. 7:10, where the speaker knows full well that Tobias will die the next day; cf. also Eccles. 8:15; Sir. 11:19). (As well as its Jewish background, the sentiment expressed in this saying was attributed to the Epicurean philosophy, and the implicit critique was spelled out by Stoic and other philosophers in the New Testament period. For example, Seneca, in his epistle 101.4, writes: "How stupid to plan out the years ahead when you're not even master of tomorrow. What madness to start out with long-term hopes, thinking, 'I'll buy and sell and build, I'll lend money and take back more, and I'll gain positions of honour. And when I'm too old and tired, I'll retire.' Believe me when I tell you everything is unsure, even for the most fortunate" [translation by F. G. Downing].)

Up to verse 19 the story has only one character living in his own world, making plans and anticipating the future as though he were entirely in control of it. The abrupt divine intervention (v. 20) is the more arresting because this is the only Gospel parable in which God himself appears as a character and speaks. The significance of this emerges when we notice that this story is about a man who thinks he can write his own story. This is the value of his wealth for him: it gives him the control over the future that enables him to say his story is going to go on.

This control over his life is largely illusory, as we can see from the way he acquired his wealth: there just happened to be a good harvest. His wealth, in effect, was given to him. The same goes for all of us. To a limited extent we make our lives for ourselves, but only on the basis of or in conjunction with what is given to us: what we owe to family, friends, circumstances, occurrences which simply happen to us — good fortune, bad luck, or however we choose to interpret whatever we cannot engineer or control for ourselves. The writing of the stories of our lives is done only a little by ourselves, mostly by other people, by what happens *to* us, but ultimately by God. It is the affluent who most easily forget this. People living on the edge of destitution are naturally aware of how dependent they are on what happens to them. But the seduction of wealth is the illusion it gives us of control over our lives.

The shock of verse 20 for the rich man is in discovering that it is God who really writes his story. Not only his wealth but his very life have been given him and can therefore be taken back. The verb "required" suggests that the man's "soul" or "life" was given to him on loan by God, who can therefore require it back at any time. And the divine interruption has an apt sting in its tail: "the wealth you have stored up for the future — who will get it now?" (There may be an echo here of Ps. 49:10.) Whereas less selfish people might find some pleasure in passing on their wealth to their children or having it distributed to the poor, this man's wealth has no value for him except as his own wealth.

Another wisdom saying (v. 21) draws the moral explicitly. Accumulating wealth cannot give the security people expect from it, because it is impotent in the face of the most basic uncertainties of life, including the possibility of unexpected death. The parable suggests that, after all, it is really only sanctified common sense to trust *God* for the only kind of security we can have. It is only trusting in God that can overcome the primal human fear and insecurity that believes the false promises of mammon to provide security.

So true wealth — what really gives security — is being "rich toward God" (v. 21). This is the wealth we acquire when, trusting the future to God, we use what is given us unselfishly. The principle applies not only to material possessions, but ultimately to our lives and our selves. The parable points us back to that strange, provocative epigram that lies at the heart of Jesus' attitude to life: "Whoever wishes to preserve his life will lose it, but whoever loses his life for my sake will find it." In other words, if we direct our efforts to gaining for ourselves what we think will make life good and make sure of it, then security is bound to elude us. The way to real life is to give our lives away. If we expend ourselves and our possessions in the service of God and others, giving away what is given to us, then we find real life with God. Even in death, which is the ultimate disaster for the rich fool, we find life with God.

It hardly needs to be said that contemporary Western society is in the grip of the rich fool's delusion. That life consists in what we can get and keep and spend is probably the loudest of the confused voices of our mass culture, conveyed with seductive expertise in the advertising that forms our consciousness subliminally as well as overtly. Of course, we may soon discover that what we have acquired so far brings no real fulfillment in life, but the rich fool's philosophy encourages us to think that therefore we need more: a constant supply of new material possessions that cannot satisfy, new and expensive ways to take it easy, eat, drink, and enjoy ourselves. In simple cultures it does not take long to discover that material things cannot satisfy, but in affluent cultures, with their endless production of novelty and excitement, there are always other things we will soon be able to afford and to which we can attach our desires for fulfillment and security.

That this is "a striving after the wind" takes the hard-won wisdom of the Preacher in Ecclesiastes (2:11) to realize. For most of us fools in a foolish society, the awareness that security lies entirely beyond our reach in God can come only with the shock of divine intervention in our lives. When the parable works for us — and reminds us of all the stories it epitomizes — then it becomes itself that divine interruption of our lives. Through the parable we experience the rich fool's shock at second hand, and so what for him came too late reaches us before it is too late. The divine intervention which ended his story so unexpectedly can be for us an intervention which ends, not our story, but our attempt to write the story ourselves.

Richard Bauckham

Twelfth Sunday after Pentecost, Year C

First Lesson: Isaiah 1:1, 10-20
(Psalm 50:1-8, 22-23)
Second Lesson: Hebrews 11:1-3, 8-16
Gospel Lesson: Luke 12:32-40

The text for the day finds its place in the midst of a series of teachings of Jesus. The various individual sayings and parables in this chapter are so interwoven that any attempt to divide the material into liturgical readings is bound to be somewhat arbitrary. Though the verses selected by the lectionary authorities are inextricably bound with the surrounding material, they at least form a coherent unit of thought of manageable length. The verses chosen are a word to the early church: order your present attitudes and activities in light of the coming of Jesus, a coming that is certain with respect to its reality but uncertain with respect to time.

Earlier in the chapter we heard Jesus speak of fear. Christians are not to fear those who have power only over the body, but only the one who also has the authority to cast into hell (12:4-5). In our text Luke revisits the subject but with a very different tone. We now hear familiar words in the Gospel of Luke, "Fear not" (cf. 1:13, 30; 2:10; 5:10). Of these, the most interesting for our purposes is the word of the angel to the shepherds keeping watch over their flocks by night (2:10). Luke did not invent the phrase, however. The

383

words were already ancient and heavy with scriptural meaning long before Luke took pen in hand to write his Gospel. For that reason "Fear not!," with its echoes of the King James Version, is a more effective rendering than the newer "Do not be afraid." The words are an implicit reminder of a long history of salvation in which God has come to rescue the people. Behind the word "flock" is a reference to Israel (Ezek. 34:11-24) and a reminder that God is the shepherd of the faithful. The "little flock" in this case represents the disciples and through them the early Christian church. Though surrounded by troubles of every sort, the flock need not fear, for it is God's "good pleasure to give them the kingdom."

This part of the Gospel speaks very carefully of the coming of the kingdom. It may be and indeed must be striven for by humans (Luke 12:31). Lest we think, however, that the kingdom is a human achievement, we are reminded here that it is given by God as a result of God's good pleasure. The Greek word behind "good pleasure" is actually a verb. It is linguistically related to the noun behind "goodwill" in the angelic welcome to Jesus' birth (2:14). There the angels declare: "Peace on earth to those on whom God's favor rests." Parallels from Qumran show us that the word has to do with God's election of a people or group. The church may be small in numbers and experiencing persecution from what seems an irresistible and hostile world, but the followers of Christ may rest confident because God's choice rests unshakably on them. We may gain some sense of the significance of this promise if we remember that this verse became a key text for the Theological Declaration of Barmen of 1934. In this statement the Confessing Church of Germany, the little flock of Christians unalterably opposed to Hitler and to Nazism, declared their allegiance to God alone. It is God alone who can give the kingdom (*Reich* in German).

In light of the parables later in this chapter, it is apparent that the kingdom is here primarily an eschatological reality. It will not be built by humans, but will rather break in on them. The tense of the Greek verb, however, indicates that the divine choice that guarantees the coming of the kingdom has already been made.

The characteristic order of Scripture is observed here: divine grace, human response. Though the kingdom is given and not built, human action is required. The disciples are commanded to sell their possessions and give alms. But the word "command" is misleading. Verses 22-31 make it clear that the word is almost as much a matter of freedom as of demand. Because God's favor rests upon them, the disciples need not live with the fear that they will not have enough. Those who follow Jesus need not be, as so many are in our society, enslaved by their possessions. They need not frantically seek for a security they vainly hope will be found in the accumulation of things. "The one who dies with the most toys wins," says our society. No! Those who are free to give have won already. The "heart" is not the seat of feelings in the Bible. Rather, the word "heart" represents the fundamental orientation of the human person. Our treasure is an indicator of the direction of that fundamental orientation. It shows where the heart truly lies.

Jesus then commands the disciples to be dressed for action. The picture here is of servants who bind their long robes around the waist, "girding the loins," ready for active service. Moreover, the lamps are to be lit. There may be an echo here of Matthew's parable of the wise and foolish bridesmaids (Matt. 25:1-13). Luke's short parable contains several similar motifs, though used slightly differently, and makes a very similar point concerning readiness. In Luke servants are called to be prepared for the return of the master from a wedding banquet. As one might expect, readiness finds its reward: "Blessed are those slaves whom the master finds alert when he comes." This is, of course, the kind of moral point that preachers and congregations have come to expect in a sermon. At first sight there is no surprise here.

But if this parable were simply a first-century religious version of the Scouting motto, "Be prepared," it could end at this point. There is, however, a twist, and the heart of the parable is in the twist. Such a twist is common in Jesus' parables, particularly in Luke's Gospel. Samaritans don't write blank checks for wounded Jews. Shepherds don't leave ninety-nine sheep to seek one that is lost. And masters returning late at night do not tighten their belts and serve their slaves. Can we read these words and not think of John's story of Jesus washing the feet of the disciples? This is an unusual sort of master indeed, perhaps even the sort of master who might die for his servants. As so often in the parables, the expectations of the world are turned upside down. The expectations of preachers and listeners can be turned upside down also. We had been expecting from this text only moral exhortation, and suddenly we are hearing the gracious words of the gospel.

The time of the master's coming is uncertain. It might be the middle of the night or it might be near dawn. The servants and hence the church must be prepared to wait. It has been argued that the Gospel of Luke was written to deal with the problem of the delay of the parousia. Whether that is true for the Gospel as a whole, it is surely true of this parable. Perhaps the early Christians to whom Luke was writing were already tempted to abandon eschatological hope. Luke addresses that issue directly through these words. If the delay of the parousia was a problem in the first century, how much more is it a difficulty in the third millennium. The contemporary preacher

385

is well advised to imitate Luke's example and likewise address the difficulty directly.

Luke reminds us twice in a short span that the coming of the master is a blessing to those who are prepared. The Greek word behind "blessed" is the same as the one we find in the Beatitudes. But though the coming is a blessing, it is also a disruption. Luke introduces another image to describe the coming of the Lord, the sudden arrival of a thief. This striking image appears a number of times in the New Testament (cf. Matt. 24:43; 1 Thess. 5:2-4; 2 Pet. 3:10; and Rev. 16:15). The use of this image certainly reinforces the exhortation to readiness for the coming. But it also complicates our understanding of the nature of the coming. We are given in this reading two images, one positive and encouraging, the other threatening. Are Jesus' words a threat or a promise? The answer is "both." To those who claim Jesus as master and who by the orientation of their lives are prepared for his advent, the coming is indeed a blessing. But it is not so with those whose lives center on their possessions. It is no accident that the image of the thief appears in a chapter in which so many words are devoted to possessions. Repeatedly Jesus warns against centering our lives on our possessions. To those who fail to heed the warning and whose hearts are with their earthly treasures, the coming of Jesus will indeed be "as a thief in the night." "So you also must be ready."

Stephen Farris

Thirteenth Sunday after Pentecost, Year C

First Lesson: Isaiah 5:1-7
(Psalm 80:1-2, 8-19)
Second Lesson: Hebrews 11:29–12:2
Gospel Lesson: Luke 12:49-56

These words of Jesus are found in a discourse (Luke 12) characterized by a sense of urgent warning and encouragement for both "crowds" and "disciples," in view of the critical nature of the time. 12:1 indicates that though crowds were present, it was the disciples to whom the words were primarily addressed. This is reiterated in 12:22, but 12:54 (in the middle of the present passage) introduces a final section as spoken directly "to the crowds." This editorial framework suggests Luke's sense of the particular appropriateness of Jesus' words to "disciples" of Luke's own generation and milieu. Luke preserves the memory of the large hearing Jesus attracted, and his warnings to the populace at large — especially those who, to all outward appearance, were the guardians of its faith — but also the sense that it was a minority of his audience who took his words seriously and were thus constituted as his "little flock" (v. 32).

The section 12:49-56, then, divides into two: verses 49-53, which aim at correcting misconceptions among Jesus' fledgling group of followers about what can be expected from his ministry, and verses 54-56, which sharply condemn the blindness of those who fail to "interpret the time." Both sections challenge hearers to read the signs of the present correctly: the first in tones of urgent clarification for those whose hearts were fundamentally won, the second in tones of strident denunciation for those who refused to see and understand.

12:49-53 suggests that Jesus' ministry thus far had induced a certain euphoria in some who read the signs of his works and words as meaning that "peace on earth" (v. 51) was just around the corner (compare the elation of the disciples in returning from their mission in 10:17). No doubt it was peace in their own troubled part of the earth, then under foreign domination, which would be uppermost in such people's thoughts. Jesus' response is in the form of a threefold warning.

First, he reminds them that his mission is nothing less than "to cast fire upon the earth" (v. 49a). This image of purgation and judgment recalls the prophecy of John that the coming one would baptize "with the Holy Spirit and with fire" (3:16). The mighty works of Jesus were a sign and prelude of an awesome period of sifting for humanity. His followers should not so focus on the signs of God's power they were seeing in Jesus that they failed to realize the *meaning* of those signs. As for Jesus himself, he longed for the kindling of the fire (v. 49b) not, we may guess, out of zeal for destruction, but out of hunger for righteousness and yearning for the fulfillment of his mission. The "fire" itself would come in the Spirit's work of purifying God's people.

The second part of Jesus' warning hints at the cost to himself, the total investment of his life, that the whole process entails. The disciples should not imagine that Jesus' mighty works are the opening stages of a straightforward march to victory. He still has "a baptism to be baptized with"

(v. 50a). After the event, we can recognize this as a veiled reference to his suffering and death. The language is interesting, for it not only points ahead to the future symbolism of Christian baptism as dying and rising with Christ, but it points back to the baptism of John as the key to understanding the trauma to come. The baptism of John had required the self-humiliation of individuals as the gateway to renewal of their life as God's people. The "baptism" that Jesus was still to undergo was the real baptism to which John's pointed as sign and shadow. Entailing the humiliation of one individual in the shame and torture of public crucifixion, it accomplished that to which John's baptism could only look forward in hope. Only through the waters of death, experienced by this one man, would Israel and the world find their new life as the purifying fire of the Spirit descended. Sensing with foreboding what is yet to come, understandably Jesus is "constrained" (v. 50b), deeply preoccupied, until it is over.

It is significant not only that Jesus is recalled as having understood his forthcoming suffering in this way, but also that he is recalled as having shared the burden with his disciples. Here we see his very human longing that somehow they should bear the load with him, even if only by being aware of it. At least they should see that the remarkable healings and other signs of God's gracious rule taking place before their eyes were being wrought through the agency of a man in inner turmoil.

The third part of Jesus' warning to disciples directly confronts the misapprehension: "Do you think that I have come to give peace on earth?" (v. 51a). His answer was no doubt as troubling to his hearers as it is to us. His words and activity had initially been open to the interpretation that he was going to establish the peace for which Israel longed: security from fear of enemies, freedom to pursue devotion to Yahweh (cf. the hope expressed by John's father Zechariah in 1:74, 75). But here he warns of imminent division. "Henceforth" (v. 52) translates the same expression as "from now on" in Jesus' words to the Jewish council before his crucifixion (22:69): in both cases it speaks not only of chronology but also of the inauguration of a new epoch. The Son of Man will henceforth be seated at the right hand of the power of God, but his people will henceforth share in his sufferings, as he has shared in theirs.

The picture in verses 51b-53 of different members of a household being set against one another echoes the warning of Micah 7:6. It also seems to put "on hold" the hope of Malachi 4:6 (cited by Gabriel in Luke 1:16, in description of the future ministry of John) that the hearts of fathers and children will be turned toward each other. It starkly indicates the pain involved in the time of sifting which Jesus is ushering in: even those closest to one another will be divided — implicitly, on account of him. But the most powerful thrust of these words is surely against the comfortable assumption that the promised time of peace would involve perpetuation of the standard segregation of the world into the nation of Israel and "the nations," the Gentiles: the assumption that "peace" would involve victory of the former over the latter. Jesus challenges this assumption. Not only within the world at large, not only, indeed, within the nation of Israel, but even within the smallest social unit, the family, there will be division. The time for complacency about "being on the right side" because one belongs to a particular national or social grouping is over. But these solemn words possess — at least from our perspective — a penumbra of glorious hope. The *division* within families that Jesus set in train was the prelude to a new and thrilling *unity* transcending all the ancient barriers, even as his "baptism" of death is the prelude to life for the world.

Verses 54-56 speak "to the crowds." Jesus points to their ability to forecast imminent changes in the weather: a cloud in the west portends a shower, a south wind, scorching heat (vv. 54-55). This ability he contrasts with their impotence with regard to interpreting the "time" *(kairos)* — the present era of ultimate significance and opportunity (v. 56). When he calls them "hypocrites," the accusation seems to go further than this contrast between competence in a relatively trivial matter of discernment and incompetence in the supremely important ones. It is a general accusation of godlessness (this, rather than the frequently cited "playacting," is the probable connotation). In the present context it draws out the incongruity between the wisdom and folly that coexist side by side in the same people. A similar kind of incongruity — laughable if it were not tragic — is exposed by Jesus in other contexts where the word "hypocrite" is used: for example, Luke 6:42 (trying to remove a speck when blinded by a log) and 13:15 (caring for animals on the Sabbath but objecting to the healing of a woman).

This appeal to the wisdom they ought to have possessed is significant. It shows that, to Jesus' mind, misunderstanding of what was happening in his ministry was perversity, not to be excused on the grounds that the mystery of divine providence was nevertheless at work in their blindness (8:10).

Christian readers know that we are still in the "time" of ultimate decisions. Interpreting this "time" is the key to understanding the strange paradoxes disclosed by Jesus, for us as for his hearers. To reconcile the angels' song of peace (2:14) and Jesus' words about division (12:51-53) requires a sense of the time, of the progression in stages of God's purpose: division now, leading to true peace in the future.

Not only can we still expect division in our communities on account of Christ. We also share his prophetic ministry. We are called to expose the follies and incongruities of a generation which can (for instance) forecast the weather for days ahead through satellite technology; which sees and knows so much, yet still consistently fails to interpret the time; which fails to see in Jesus, in his followers, in the division he causes, and in all the signs of the Son of Man's rule in the world, God's summons to awake or die.

Stephen I. Wright

Third Sunday in Lent, Year C

First Lesson: Isaiah 55:1-9
(Psalm 63:1-8)
Second Lesson: 1 Corinthians 10:1-13
Gospel Lesson: Luke 13:1-9

This unsettling pericope, in which Jesus presents a stern and unsympathetic demeanor very far from sentimental depictions of "gentle Jesus, meek and mild," appears only in Luke's Gospel. It comes in the midst of varied material showing the recalcitrance of the Jews in the face of Jesus' stated mission, claims, and demands. This material also has a distinct eschatological tone: not only judgment, but final judgment, is coming. Jesus has just said, at the end of chapter 12, that he comes to cast fire on earth and will bring division, not peace; and that people should be able to read the signs of the times and should take swift action for reconciliation with opponents before it is too late. Immediately after this text come incidents showing the Jews' opposition to Jesus' acts of healing on the Sabbath, Jesus' warning that many will not in fact be able to enter the kingdom when they seek too late to do so, and his words of mourning over the Jerusalem that has over long centuries killed instead of welcomed the prophets that came to her. Given this context, it is important to acknowledge the political overtones of the pericope in its original setting, with the threat of devastating judgment hanging particularly over the nation of Israel insofar as it does not speedily repent and reform. But surely it would be rash to limit the threat to Israel alone and to presume that those later following in Israel's footsteps will escape a similar verdict.

It was while Jesus was speaking of the signs of the times (12:54-59) that the report came of Galileans killed by Pilate while they were offering sacrifices (presumably in Jerusalem: sacrifices were to be offered only in Jerusalem). It may be that a messenger had just arrived with the news, or perhaps the discussion of signs brought a recent incident to mind. What sort of sign was this terrible event? While our sympathies might immediately be aroused at this evidence of religious persecution and at the horrifying image of the blood of worshipers being mixed with that of the animals they had slain, Jesus' response reminds us that sympathy at such suffering was not in fact the first reaction of religious Jews of that day. Instead, Jews assumed that calamities and suffering evidenced God's judgment on sin (recall Job's friends, and the question of the disciples in John 9:2). Here (unlike John 9:3; cf. Job 42:7) Jesus neither challenges nor corrects this assumption, nor does he criticize Pilate. He moves immediately to remove his hearers from the safe position of bystanders and to extend the threat of imminent doom to them as well: "Do you think that because these Galileans suffered in this way they were worse sinners than all other Galileans? No, I tell you; but unless you repent, you will all perish as they did."

Nor is he content to let matters rest. From an act of persecution leading to death, he goes to a "natural" disaster, the fall of the tower of Siloam that killed eighteen "random" and "innocent" bystanders: that disaster, too, constitutes no more than just judgment of the sort awaiting all who do not repent. Then, upping the ante one more time, he tells of the barren fig tree that the owner will personally cut down if it fails to bear fruit. Not only is it unfruitful itself, but also it wastes good soil. Letting it remain is not neutral, as it may seem on the surface; it gets in the way of another tree that would produce fruit.

One recalls the sequence in Amos 5:19, where a man escaped from a lion only to be met by a bear, and when he escaped from the bear and thought himself safe in his own house, he was bitten by a scorpion. Here, if the hand of one's enemies and the hazards of the natural world leave one untouched, the judgment of God still awaits. God will give time, and may even extend the time: a fig tree that had not borne fruit in three years was mature and unlikely to bear later on, so granting the extra year was a particular act of grace. But he will not wait forever. Delay does not mean that judgment will not come; and it may come unexpectedly, at any time, as when a tower comes tumbling down. The whole of this pericope points to the urgency of repenting before it is too late — and the urgency of taking to heart the warning for oneself and of not assuming it applies only to other people.

Resistance to this text may arise from several underlying assumptions about ourselves and about God that are so prevalent as to be seldom stated out loud. The first simply has to do with the seriousness of sin, the ordinary sin of ordinary people: not many today readily believe that it is in fact deserving of death — indeed, of eternal death (reference to "perishing" in vv. 3 and 5 and to being "cut down" in v. 7 should be understood in this way). But everything Jesus says in these verses suggests that evils that befall one are no greater than one in any case deserves, unless one repents and bears the fruit of repentance. Such a word is almost unbearably harsh apart from an exceedingly robust view of sin and guilt.

Another assumption is that suffering is not in this life correlated one-to-one with guilt, a point that pastoral counselors have striven long and hard to impress upon the many who, as a kind of reflex, take every significant setback and especially every serious illness as evidence that God is punishing them for something. That assumption is surely right in an important sense, as even a text like 2 Timothy 3:12 says: those who seek to live a *godly* life will suffer persecution; trouble does not strike just because of unrighteous behaviors. We have already noted the examples of Job and the man born blind. Anyone can point to children born addicted to drugs through no fault of their own; the ravaging evils of our century, whether of natural or of human origin, have surely not distributed themselves equitably; and so on. It simply is not true that we bring every evil that befalls us upon ourselves, or that we ought to seek to retrieve a "God is going to zap you for that" mentality. Most emphatically — a point that cannot possibly be overemphasized — we have no justification for using a text like this one to free ourselves from anxiety about the fate of other people on the grounds that they are, after all, getting no more than they deserve. That would be to turn on its head what Jesus is doing here. What he is doing, though, is not very pleasant: he is telling those who are *not* at the moment suffering that they should not rest secure in their immediate comfort, for that comfort is not a sign of their positive moral deserts. The lack of a tidy and immediate correlation of sin and suffering goes both ways. Worse, he is charging them with guilt that requires a quick change of attitude: their hypothesis about the suffering of the *guilty* has led them into a false confidence in their own case. (Scripture does recognize a connection between sin and sickness or calamity, even if not a completely straightforward one. Among many texts one could cite in addition to this one, note in particular Exodus 15:26; Psalm 107:17; John 5:14; James 5:15-16.) Instead of resting secure, one should take grateful advantage of time given to repent, for it may be cut short at any moment.

A third prevalent assumption is the one that wholly dissociates God from any sort of nastiness committed by people or occurring in the natural order: these things "just happen"; God is with us in them, but he does not cause them. Well, no doubt God is with those who turn to him, and no doubt he does not "cause" these hurtful things in a scientific sense. However, Scripture does not hesitate to say that God can, say, arouse a heathen nation like the Chaldeans to wreak judgment on his people (Hab. 1:6). It is too low a view of God's providence that would suppose he cannot use even the sinful acts of people like Pilate (or Pharaoh or Judas), even the convulsions of the natural order (see the various apocalyptic portions of the Old and New Testaments) or its natural laws (the fall of a tower), to achieve his own ends. God may act directly (like an owner cutting down a fig tree), or he may allow his judgment to fall by other means. The danger here, of course, is speaking in such a way that God's character as wholly good is compromised; but those who see final judgment as inconsistent with God's character as loving and wholly good must contend with many biblical passages, not just this one.

For those who take texts like this one seriously, the real unkindness is not to set forward the reality of impending final judgment in all its uncompromising starkness. The real unkindness is failing to be as clear as Jesus was about the fatal consequences of failing to repent while there is yet time. The one who has heard this text as a message only to other people has not yet heard it.

Marguerite Shuster

Fourteenth Sunday after Pentecost, Year C

First Lesson: Jeremiah 1:4-10
(Psalm 71:1-6)
Second Lesson: Hebrews 12:18-29
Gospel Lesson: Luke 13:10-17

This episode is part of the great journey narrative (Luke 9:51–18:14) and is unique to Luke. It is the second of three Sabbath healings (6:6-11; 14:1-6) and weaves together a miracle story (vv. 10-13) with a controversy

393

story (vv. 14-17). The synagogue setting and Jesus' words about setting free a person who is bound evoke the episode that inaugurates Jesus' ministry in the synagogue at Nazareth (4:16-30), where he uses the words of the prophet Isaiah to describe his own mission. Just as those words provoked a divided response — first amazement at his gracious words (4:22), then fury and the attempt to hurl him over the cliff (4:28-29) — so this synagogue healing ends with a divided response (v. 17) and invites the hearer to choose Jesus' way.

In the first half (vv. 10-13) the woman is the center of the story. The seriousness of her disability is emphasized, which serves to highlight the potency of Jesus' healing power. She has been bent double for eighteen years, which would have been approximately half her life, given the short life span of people in the first century. Luke emphasizes not only the physical effects of her suffering, but the satanic forces to which the ancients attributed illness. The number of years of the woman's bondage recalls two lengthy periods of servitude in Israel's history. Israel was freed after eighteen years of bondage to Moab (Judg. 3:14) and after eighteen years of affliction from the Philistines and the Ammonites (Judg. 10:8). Likewise this healing story speaks of the freedom that is possible in the restored Israel within the Jesus tradition.

Despite the hardship her disability would pose for walking and for maneuvering in a crowd, the woman comes to the synagogue, presumably to pray. This text belies the common notion that women and men worshiped separately in the first century. There is no archaeological evidence for this; segregation of men and women in synagogue worship dates to a much later time. In fact, there is inscriptional evidence that women were not only present with men in early synagogues, but that they held important ministerial positions, including *archisynagōgos,* leader of the synagogue.

The text does not say that the woman came seeking healing from Jesus. He takes the initiative, sees her, calls her, lays hands on her, and declares that she is freed of her infirmity. The perfect passive form of the verb *apolelysai,* "you are freed," expresses that her freedom has already been accomplished by God before Jesus' intervention. This formulation is similar to Luke 5:20 and 7:47, where forgiveness on the lips of Jesus is articulated in the perfect passive tense. The effect in those instances, as here, is the assertion that it is God who frees the person. That this divine freeing power is understood to be mediated by Jesus becomes clear from the ensuing controversy.

The response of the woman is immediate: she stands upright and continues to glorify God. There are a number of instances (e.g., Pss. 144:14; 145:8; Jer. 40:2) in the Septuagint where the verb *anorthoō,* "to set up, make erect" (v. 13), refers to the restorative action of God. So, too, through Jesus' touch God restores this woman. The woman has come to worship God and continues to glorify God (the verb *edoxazen,* "glorified," in v. 13 carries the connotation of continued action). Moreover, the visible manifestation of God's power in her leads others to rejoice at such glorious deeds done by Jesus (v. 17).

The reaction of the synagogue official in the second part of the story stands in stark contrast to the woman's praise (v. 13) and the crowd's acclamation (v. 17). A play on the word *dei,* "it is necessary," in verses 14 and 16 underscores the conflict. The synagogue official argues from the necessity of working on the six other days (v. 14); Jesus insists on the necessity of God's saving plan being realized (v. 16). Jesus criticizes the hypocrisy of his opponents (as also 6:42; 12:1, 56), and argues from the lesser to the greater: if an ox or an ass, who is bound only a few hours, can be loosed on the Sabbath, how much more this daughter of Abraham and Sarah, fettered for eighteen years? Another wordplay strengthens the ironic contrast: one loosens *(lyein)* an ox or ass (v. 15); so must the woman be loosed *(lyein,* v. 16). A compound form of the same verb, *apolyein* (set free), introduced the wordplay in verse 12.

In the second half of the narrative the straightened woman recedes from the center as Jesus and his objectionable action becomes the focus. Whereas the freeing action had been attributed to God (v. 12), now the leader of the synagogue ascribes it to Jesus (v. 14). The identification of Jesus' works with God's is underscored by the use of the term *endoxois,* "mighty deeds," in verse 17. This same word is used in Deuteronomy 10:21 and Exodus 34:10 for what God has done for Israel.

This is a story that provides a vivid image of liberation for any who are weighed down with chronic illness or with oppressive burdens of any kind. It has provided a powerful image for women struggling to be freed from more than eighteen centuries of domination in patriarchal worlds. But there are also pitfalls in this narrative. With a Jewish religious leader cast as Jesus' opponent, a preacher will want to be wary of interpreting the story in a way that could foment anti-Judaism. It is important for the preacher to emphasize that Jesus was an observant Jew who did not arbitrarily disregard Sabbath observance, but interprets it differently from his adversaries. Jesus reasons from commonly accepted exemptions that some situations take precedence over others. The question is not whether to keep the Sabbath, but *how* to keep it. When the purpose of Sabbath rest is to be free to praise God, Jesus deems it necessary to free a bound woman so as to do precisely that. Just as Jesus challenges the synagogue leader to focus on the intent of the Law, it would be well for those Christians who tend toward legalistic interpretations of Scripture and tradition to hear a similar summons. A preacher might urge that instead of seeing a broken rule, we must see the broken person as of first importance.

Another danger in this story for a church and society that is struggling for gender equality is that it casts a woman in the role of victim and the male Jesus as the one who brings healing. If the hearer identifies with the male Jesus, then Christian identity is established as male and women believers are either left out or have to read as if they were male. If women identify with the woman as victim, the story can reinforce a dependency on males for well-being. Women who have suffered may also internalize the accusations of the synagogue leader. He blamed the woman for the broken Sabbath and interpreted her coming to the synagogue as deliberately looking for a cure that day (v. 14). In fact, the text does not say why the woman came. We have suggested that she came simply to praise God. It was Jesus who initiated the healing, not she (v. 12). For Christian men and women to work together to free the church and society from bonds of sexism, they must resist the temptation to blame the victim. Moreover, women must take an active part in the work of liberation. They cannot wait for men with power to notice their burden and lift it.

The preacher may want to emphasize that the text presents this healing as a matter of necessity in the present moment. The point at issue in the text is not the liberating of the woman, it is the timing. It is true that in terms of enduring her disability, the woman could have waited one more day. But Jesus is urgent that *now* is the time of salvation. Repeatedly in Luke there is a necessity about the present moment as the time to accept God's liberation (e.g., 4:21; 19:9; 23:43). Moreover, the ability of the whole people of God to be holy and glorify God is at stake. While there is any brokenness in the community, to that extent the entire people are in need of healing. This woman is a "daughter of Abraham" and Sarah, part of the people to whom God is bonded in covenant. "Daughter of Abraham" is a rare phrase. It occurs only here in the biblical tradition and rarely in rabbinic writings. In Luke 19:9 Jesus calls Zacchaeus a "son of Abraham" when he announces that salvation has come to him. In both that episode and this one Jesus initiated an encounter with a marginal member of the community and insisted that they belong now as fully integrated members. In our day many, like the woman bent double, have learned to live with the burdens of sexism, racism, economic inequity, etc. They have found a way to accommodate themselves to the system in such a way that they can still hobble their way in to give their praise to God. This Gospel can help believers realize the urgency of acting for liberation now. There will always be objections. Is there ever a convenient time for liberation?

Barbara E. Reid

Second Sunday in Lent, Year C

First Lesson: Genesis 15:1-12, 17-18
(Psalm 27)
Second Lesson: Philippians 3:17–4:1
Gospel Lesson: Luke 13:31-35

This section concludes and brings to a solemn climax a chapter of warnings to the nation of Israel. Jesus sees that Jerusalem is heading for the just fate of those who kill the messengers of God — among whom he himself is numbered. The passage falls into two parts: verses 31-33, in which Jesus responds to the cautionary warning of some Pharisees about his own safety, and verses 34-36, in which he utters a lament over Jerusalem.

The Pharisees of verse 31 are clearly sympathetic toward Jesus (like those of 7:36 and 14:1) and concerned for his safety. They report a threat of Herod (the ruler of Galilee, 3:1) against Jesus' life. The following Jesus was attracting no doubt made Herod wary of him as someone who could disturb the fragile peace it was Herod's job to guard in Galilee on Rome's behalf. (Luke's overall picture of Herod is one of ambivalence toward Jesus, as may be seen through comparing this verse with 23:8.) Jesus' response is to be understood in the larger context within which Luke sets these verses, the "travel narrative" of 9:51–19:27, which pictures Jesus on his way to Jerusalem. Jesus indicates that he is set on a course of action from which he will not be diverted; he is heading for a destination which cannot be avoided. Though he will indeed be leaving Herod's territory, he wants them to know that he is not running away from danger.

The tones of Jesus as they are recalled here are very different from the soft and serene voice which is often the caricature held by those who may revere him from afar but do not attend to or engage with the voice that actu-

397

ally comes through our Gospel texts. His words "go and tell . . ." are no doubt a rhetorical retort, with no expectation that these Pharisees will go and solemnly repeat what he says to Herod. He refers to Herod as a "fox" — hinting at his insignificance, deceitfulness, or maybe destructiveness — and resists the Pharisees' suggestion with an air of grim determination. The idiomatic turns of phrase — "today and tomorrow, and the third day" (v. 32), "today and tomorrow and the day following" (v. 33) — remind us of Jesus' rootedness in Jewish ways of thought and speech, and also suggest a strong sense of purpose. Verse 32 offers a succinct summary of Jesus' activity ("I cast out demons and perform cures"): he has work to do, and he will continue to do it until it is finished. In verse 33, instead of reassuring friendly observers that he will avoid the places of danger, he confirms their fears by insisting that as he carries on his work, he must "go on his way." He is conscious of a prophetic calling, and Jerusalem, the ancient heart of Israel, the place of greatest exposure and danger for him, is the place to which that calling unremittingly beckons. "It cannot be that a prophet should perish away from Jerusalem": to call this a "prediction of the passion" misses the form of the saying; it is rather a sidelong hint, a musing remark filled with irony and foreboding.

These two verses are heavy with the awareness of a divine purpose to which Jesus must submit. When he says "I finish my course" (v. 32), he hints at the completion of a task that has been given to him, not one he has given himself; the verb is that used in John 19:30 ("It is finished"), and also has overtones of priestly consecration. Within the "I must" and the "it cannot be" of verse 33 is the sense of a supreme, all-pervading will. Jesus is being drawn into the painful heart of the paradox, which onlookers and disciples will not be able to comprehend: that the God who has willed and commanded his work of healing and restoration somehow also wills him to the fate of a prophet. He saved others, but he cannot, indeed, save himself (Luke 23:35). Luke doubtless sees in Paul's later urge to go to Jerusalem, despite the danger, an echo of Jesus' lonely, misunderstood obedience (Acts 21:11-14).

In verses 34-35 Jesus turns from his own destiny to lament that of the city where it will be fulfilled. He sees in Jerusalem a seemingly inveterate tendency toward violent rejection of God's emissaries (v. 34a; cf. Neh. 9:26; Jer. 2:30). In a remarkable image, he speaks of his frequent yearning to protect and nurture Jerusalem's people, as a hen her brood, a yearning which they have spurned (v. 34b). There is similarity here with God's exposure of Israel's profoundly unnatural behavior in Isaiah 1:2, 3: they are rebellious children whose perversity is shown up as such when contrasted with the wise instincts of animals. There are also echoes of Old Testament language describing God's own tender care for his people (Deut. 32:11; Ps. 91:4; Isa. 31:5). Jesus' saying hints at a more extensive ministry in Jerusalem than is indicated by the general structure of the synoptic Gospels, where (unlike that of John) his controversial encounters with the Jewish teachers in the Holy City are concentrated in the final climactic week of his life.

The stark truth is told in verse 35a: Jerusalem's "house," the temple, the center of Judaism's life, the visible and focal point of her hopes in God, is "forsaken." Jeremiah had warned of the desolation of the "house" (here possibly the royal palace) if Israel did not heed God's words (Jer. 22:5). More vividly Ezekiel, in his exile in Babylon, before the First Temple's destruction, had visions of the abominations that were taking place there, and of the glory of Yahweh departing from his sanctuary (Ezek. 8–11). The fact of this departure was visible to the prophet's eye of faith before it was made plain in the destruction itself; so also Jesus sees that the second "house" is "forsaken" before the terrible events of 70 C.E. make it plain to all and sundry.

Verse 35b is rather obscure. On what seems a trivial level, Jesus' words are fulfilled in the story of his final approach to the city (19:38); he would then be saying here that his next visit will be at the time of the Passover, when the words of Psalm 118 were traditionally chanted. But the introductory "I tell you" — and of course the preceding verses — give a monitory tone to the promise, which makes one ask what ominous significance lies beneath the clauses "you will not see me" and "until you say." He seems to be implying that seeing him (and his mighty works — cf. v. 32) will give the people of Jerusalem their next — and perhaps last — opportunity to repent. If so far they have not responded to his pleadings during the periods when he has been present with them, what chance is there that they will do so in his absence? Clearly there is a sense of apprehension about the Passover feast that gives the hint of finality to this talk of "seeing" Jesus. Jesus must have been aware on a quite practical level that Passover was a time of both devotional fervor and political tension, which would make his presence in Jerusalem at that time particularly risky. If he did indeed get caught in the cross fire between a threatened Jewish leadership and Roman expediency, that could mean not only death for him but the end of Jerusalem's opportunity to avert disaster through repentance. Against this backcloth, Jesus' quotation of Psalm 118 has a wry sadness about it. The Jerusalemites will sing their Passover psalms; they will see Jesus; but will they recognize that he is no ordinary Passover pilgrim, but the one who "comes in the name of the Lord" par excellence?

These verses then show how, in Jesus' mind, Jerusalem's fate and his own are bound up together. He must go on his way, fulfilling his prophetic calling in works and words, and give Jerusalem her last chance. But he knows this is not the way of safety which some are counseling him to take; it is indeed the way of the prophet, going again to the people who reject both him and the one who sent him.

Jesus' perception of Jerusalem's rebelliousness stands as a perpetual question to all who think of themselves as "the people of God"; his lament stands as an appeal to all — whether they define themselves thus or not — who are rejecting God's purpose for their lives. His readiness to defy the cautionary warnings and head for the rebel city stands as a continual example to his followers, who must, like him, be prophets and be ready for the prophets' fate; not as mere gloomy fatalists, but as those who share their God's compassion for his intransigent people.

Stephen I. Wright

Fifteenth Sunday after Pentecost, Year C

First Lesson: Jeremiah 2:4-13
(Psalm 81:1, 10-16)
Second Lesson: Hebrews 13:1-8, 15-16
Gospel Lesson: Luke 14:1, 7-14

Luke sometimes provides a hermeneutical key to the reader by describing the audience present for Jesus' teaching. This is the case in chapter 14, as Luke tells us that Jesus went to eat "at the house of a ruler who belonged to the Pharisees" (v. 1) and addressed "lawyers and Pharisees" (v. 3). The parable (vv. 7-14) was for the benefit of the religious elite and social leaders of the day. A problem for the preacher is to get the contemporary Christian audience to identify with this group. The Pharisees were the good people of their day. They never missed a religious meeting, they studied the Scriptures, they tithed, and they set the moral standard for their cultures. Jesus did not choose the guests but accepted an invitation to join them. He was likely invited because "they were watching him." They thought he was being tested, but they were the ones who were having their values checked.

400

The Greek term "lawyer" appears six times in Luke, once in Matthew, and not at all in Mark or John. These were likely the same people referred to as scribes elsewhere. They were more like contemporary Bible scholars than modern attorneys. They interpreted the Scriptures and applied them to social and religious behavior (Pharisees did not distinguish between the two). Similarity to contemporary lawyers might be found in the use of their interpretations to support the interests of certain groups or individuals. Luke always uses the word in a negative way.

The occasion was a meal. Meals provided the setting for many encounters between Jesus and the various strata of society. Eastern culture had strict social rules about table fellowship. People then and now were highly selective about who they invited to their table and whose invitations they accepted. The religious laws regulating foods and ceremonial cleansing required care in table fellowship. One of the earliest attacks on Jesus was provoked by his eating with sinners and tax collectors (Mark 2:15-16). He was censured for his eating and drinking, labeled a "glutton and a drunkard" (Matt. 11:18-19). Jesus ate with all kinds of people, but no matter who was the host who arranged the meal, Jesus became the host, setting the agenda for all present. He often transformed ordinary meals into eschatological feasts using table situations as metaphors for comparing the present world to the kingdom to come. The Last Supper inaugurated one of the central and most universal Christian sacraments which serves a constant reminder of the universality of Jesus' invitation to fellowship with him and the heavenly banquet to come. Peter's reconciliation was linked to a sunrise breakfast, and Jesus was recognized by two followers after walking with them on the Emmaus road when "he was at table with them, he took the bread and blessed, and broke it, and gave it to them." The feeding of the multitudes is the only miracle recorded in all four Gospels. Bread was the symbol of life and sustenance, and meals were significant social events in the ancient Near East. It is somewhat ironic that social distinctions in the *agapē* meals in Corinth were a factor in division in that community. Jesus had a gift for making ordinary events into extraordinary revelatory moments. He took common objects and experiences and made them sacramental.

Americans make nearly every significant event, public and private, an occasion for a special meal. Birthdays, funerals, and anniversaries bring people together around a meal. Special menus are associated with Thanksgiving, Christmas, Easter, and the Fourth of July. Banquets are a favorite means of raising charitable funds and often feature celebrity guests. People donate large sums of money to political campaigns to get near public officials, and the biggest givers get the best seats. In addition to the ritual meal of the Eucharist, many churches have regular fellowship suppers. Religious and social identification of contemporaries with this parable should not be difficult.

Jesus offended his fellow guests by healing a man in the midst of their dinner party. It might have been considered just poor taste, but it was a Sabbath meal and therefore a violation of the law. The occasion was planned to provide the Pharisees an opportunity to observe Jesus, but he did some observing of his own. Jesus "marked how they chose the places of honor" and boldly — they might have thought rudely and arrogantly — began to instruct the leaders. He may have had in mind Proverbs 25:6-7 as he censured their self-promotion and warned them that their aggressiveness might result in humiliation. Have you ever seen a friend across a banquet hall and gone over to join her, only to be told that the table was reserved? The informality of American culture does not give the average citizen much occasion to learn or practice protocol, but appropriate ranking was important in the circle of the Pharisees and of the Jewish family. Those who rushed to the head table were asserting their own self-importance. Jesus told them that self-exaltation would result in embarrassment. True honor must be earned and can only be accorded by others. Jesus' words might have been understood as a practical lesson in social etiquette had he not turned to chide the host about the guest list for the party.

Human nature has really not changed much. The average person would have a hard time criticizing the host for inviting friends, social equals or superiors, and other interesting people. Party invitations to persons who are in a position to advance an individual's career or enhance his or her social standing are a common practice. As was so often the case in the stories Jesus told, there is a shocking reversal of what is a prevailing custom. Jesus said when you give a party — a "feast," not just a mission soup supper — "invite the poor, the maimed, the lame, the blind." The fact that this was a Sabbath meal added force to the impact of his words. Many of these people Jesus would have included on the guest list would not be allowed in synagogue or temple, and contact with them could result in ceremonial uncleanness. This typical Lukan social commentary (vv. 12-14) is found only in Luke. Luke portrays Jesus as one who believed that liberation comes to those who recognize that the poor should be included in any celebration. Jesus' purpose was not to condemn the guests or the host but to open them to true Sabbath joy in doing God's will. Blessing will result from caring for those who cannot care for themselves. Acts of inclusion and generosity are signs of true righteousness and "will be repaid at the resurrection." This is not a judgment parable, but one of revelation of the experience of grace. There will be a blessing that will go beyond any that might be gained in career advancement or social status in secular society. Such benefits as those would not last. Serving those who cannot do anything for you will reap the eternal reward of God for the "just." The challenge was to be just and wait for the final reward. The Pharisees taught that God would reward the righteous in the resurrection. The resurrection was one of the beliefs that distinguished the Pharisees. The just are those who fulfilled the Law or the will of God. Jesus reminded them that the care of the poor was a part of the will of God.

Jesus was himself a homeless person dependent upon others for shelter and food. He uses food as a symbol of universal need. Table fellowship was a demonstration of social structures and distinctions. Time and again Jesus challenged social hierarchies by welcoming outcasts to the table. Food is basic to human survival and remains a symbol of God's providence. The use and distribution of food remains a matter of justice.

Churches today are by and large homogeneous. Even when racial barriers are overcome, social ones continue. The dinner party is a teachable metaphor for examination of class distinctions. Luke offers a crib course for the final examination at the resurrection similar to that of Matthew 25. Perhaps God will ask, "Whom did you invite to your last dinner party?" Jesus watches us to see how often we dine with publicans and sinners, how often we seek places of honor or do only for those who can do for us.

Raymond Bailey

Sixteenth Sunday after Pentecost, Year C

First Lesson: Jeremiah 18:1-11
(Psalm 139:1-6, 13-18)
Second Lesson: Philemon 1-21
Gospel Lesson: Luke 14:25-33

While browsing in a bookstore one day, a friend ran across the F. F. Bruce book *The Hard Sayings of Jesus.* "I wasn't aware there were any *easy* ones," he wryly noted. True enough. Nevertheless, most preachers and parishioners recognize that some of Jesus' sayings are frankly harder than others. Luke 14:26 is one of them. "If anyone comes to me and does not hate his father and mother, his wife and children, his brothers and sisters . . . he cannot be my disciple." Here is a statement to widen the eyes. What can it possibly mean? During the 1990s American politicians repeatedly touted some version of "Judeo-Christian family values." Compared to that, Jesus' words in Luke 14 sound like the invitation to a cult!

Clearly this passage cries out for interpretation. However, although such exegesis may take a little of the bite out of these words, in what follows we should not lose sight of the radical nature of Luke 14. In the end, a stubbornly hard kernel of truth remains. Those who wispily bite into the gospel thinking it is so much sugar and meringue will crack a tooth on this particular gospel kernel.

To begin we need to recall the larger context of Luke 14. Starting in Luke 9:51 when Jesus resolutely set his face toward Jerusalem, Luke's Gospel has been tracking Jesus' relentless progress toward the cross. A cross is not a popular destination, however. So when Luke reports that "large crowds" were hounding Jesus, the discerning reader is alerted to something curious. If the place toward which Jesus is trekking is a location of abandonment and death — a place where crowds *scatter* — then there can be but one explanation for Jesus' current popularity: the crowds are reading Jesus wrong.

Perhaps they are pinning political hopes on Jesus, hoping he will soon take aim at Caesar and so restore the Holy Land to Israel. Perhaps they see him merely as a wonder-worker who can secure health and wealth for them on the spot. Whatever the conceptions of the crowds, Jesus senses they are *mis*conceptions and so begins to whittle down his followers by his shocking references to familial hatred and cross bearing. But what could such harsh words mean?

First, there is an important Old Testament background to the word "hate" (*miseō* in the Greek). In many passages the word is invoked to convey a lesser form of love. Some of the patriarchs were said to "love" one of their wives but "hated" all the others. Similarly God was once described as loving Jacob but "hating" Esau. These verses utilize hate not as some wild-eyed, loathing fury but as a lesser, secondary attachment. Matthew may have conveyed this nuance through his version of this saying: "Whoever loves his family *more* than me cannot be my disciple" (Matt. 10:37).

If this nuance of "hate" is correct, then it helps to explain how Jesus could say something about a disciple's family which is at variance with the law of God as well as with other sayings of Jesus himself. After all, in accordance with God's law (which Jesus came to fulfill, not abolish), Jesus frequently upheld the marriage relationship, reserving some of his strongest Gospel warnings for those guilty of adultery and divorce while also chiding those who showed a lack of respect for parents. Perhaps this is why the balance of the New Testament urges believers to have good family relationships. In 1 Timothy 5:8 Paul goes so far as to suggest that a man who fails to provide for family members has "denied the faith and is worse than an unbeliever" (F. F. Bruce, *The Hard Sayings of Jesus* [Downers Grove, Ill.: InterVarsity, 1983], pp. 119-21). Furthermore, since Jesus said the hallmark of discipleship is loving everyone, including even enemies and persecutors, it can hardly be the case that Jesus would literally call disciples to hate those closest to them. If you're supposed to love the one who whipped you, why not the one who nursed you?

So what do these words mean? Perhaps Jesus' words on bearing the cross can clarify this. The notion of cross bearing is one of the most commonly misapplied of all Jesus' sayings. In the popular imagination it is the stuff of pious platitudes such that a man may point to his arthritis or his wayward son or his less-than-fulfilling job or his cantankerous aunt Regina and then say, "Well, I guess that's my cross to bear in life." Unhappily, such a sentiment washes out the meaning of Jesus' image because then the cross becomes something that miserably happens *to* a person instead of being a lifestyle which is consciously chosen *by* a person. Jesus surely intends the latter — the cross we bear is the way we choose to look at all of life.

When Jesus first uttered his words about bearing a cross, everyone knew what he meant because in Jesus' day there was only one kind of person who walked around with a crossbar draped across his shoulders: a condemned man on his way to die. There is a totality to cross bearing. It's a putting to death of all that is sinful and worldly in favor of all that is sacrificial and God glorifying. Being under a death sentence affects everything — recall Samuel Johnson's famous saying that a death sentence has a marvelous ability to focus one's mind! So also the gospel involves a constant putting aside of self in favor of seeing all of life through the lens of service to God.

That's what being a follower of Jesus means, and it's well to know this up front. As Jesus scanned the large crowds attending him, he wanted to be honest in laying out the cost of discipleship. The two parables about counting the cost simply reinforced the point: a construction worker would not begin to build and a king would not launch a war without being well aware of what it would take to follow the undertaking through to completion. If taking inventory in advance is vital to construction and warfare, how much more vital would it be to setting the direction of one's entire life?

But we still have not fully answered this passage's most pressing question about family hatred. Perhaps on the simplest level this passage means that if it ever comes down to a choice between loyalty to family and loyalty to Jesus, Jesus must win. Of course, just such a choice is faced by many in our world. Families can be rough. Some believers face no more than needling jokes around the dinner table — snide comments by Uncle Ron about what a waste of time church is or self-satisfied rehashings of the latest scandal involving some famous minister (and the patently obvious conclusion that all Christians are hypocrites). Other believers face true life-and-death choices from families who will ostracize and sometimes murder those who convert to Christianity.

However, we should not slip into the trap of thinking that these words apply only to those with hostile relatives. What Luke 14 recommends is the cross-shaped life: a life with a thoroughgoing kingdom perspective. Clearly this applies to family relationships and the priorities we set within our homes. Nurturing kingdom perspectives in fellow family members, especially children, has perennially been an identifiable mark of the Christian home. But the accomplishment of this goal may come under cultural attack today in ways far more subtle than the obvious corrosives of pornography, violence, and drugs.

For instance, the drive to consumerism, the desire for success, and the attendant hectic pace of modern life have, in many quarters, eroded what was once known as "family time." That may itself be a moral issue, but one of the more insidious side effects has been that some families have cut back on church attendance in order to clear out Sunday as "family time." In some parts of the United States in recent years, youth soccer leagues have discovered that Sunday morning around ten o'clock is a very convenient time to schedule games. When pastors have complained to these organizations that this zaps church attendance, the pastors have been rebuffed with polite indifference. Worse, when pastors speak with parents about this, they discover that many refuse to interfere with their children's sports activities and so choose soccer over worship (and anyway, this promotes "family time" on Sunday mornings, and isn't that important in this age of family values?).

Perhaps Jesus' words in Luke 14 are more needed than we think. In the long run the paradox of the gospel applies to this passage as well: those who lose their lives for the gospel have those lives returned to them in abundance; so also those who "hate" their families in order to love Jesus end up loving their families in a deeper, more sacrificial sense. Luke 14 reminds readers, however, that the path to that deeper love leads through a cross. A hard saying indeed.

Scott Hoezee

Fourth Sunday in Lent, Year C

First Lesson: Joshua 5:9-12
(Psalm 32)
Second Lesson: 2 Corinthians 5:16-21
Gospel Lesson: Luke 15:1-3, 11b-32

When we approach this parable, the first order of the day is to rid ourselves of all the twelve or more titles that have been given to it. Most preachers will want to give a title to the sermon (although we may want to ask why), but the sermon title should not be given to the text. This parable cannot be contained in any one sermon. If every sermon should expose an intended meaning of a text, this parable has too many intended meanings to limit it to one title or sermon.

How refreshing, then, to come across Bernard Brandon Scott's title for this parable. In his book *Hear Then the Parable* (Minneapolis: Fortress, 1989), he has renamed all the parables the way the church has named most hymns: by words from their first lines. He has thereby neutralized the interpretative titles that have accrued to the parables. He calls this parable *A Man Had Two Sons*. That is an exegetically sound way to enter this parable. It leaves all the options open for discovering its teachings and for choosing the most edifying way to preach from it. From that opening line, a walk through the parable will yield a sermon appropriate for the present context.

"The younger of them said to his father, 'Father, give me the share of the property that will belong to me'" (v. 12). The request was insulting. There were laws providing for the possibility of the father distributing his property while he was alive. Under certain circumstances a son could be granted possession of his inheritance with the understanding that he would work the farm for the benefit of the family until his father died. But those conditions and assumptions were not at work here. The younger son wanted to possess his inheritance, convert it to cash, and leave the farm and family. His request was tantamount to saying to his father: "Drop dead."

What was happening in the request of the younger son? He wanted his rights without responsibility. Upon the father's death, the younger son would have a "right" to one-third of his father's estate, and the older son to two-thirds (Deut. 21:17). If the father chose, he could divide the inheritance while he was still alive, but if he did so, the heirs would also inherit the responsibility to care for the family until the father's death. But the younger son wanted his inheritance without the responsibility it would entail.

He also wanted freedom without relationships. Freedom without commitment to relationships is common today (see *Habits of the Heart* [New York: Harper and Row, 1986]), but it was unheard of in the world of the parable. Relationships with father, brother, family, and community were valued above individual freedom. The younger son's actions and attitudes were an offense to the values of the time and the standards of the village.

And he wanted his future without waiting. His inheritance belonged to the future; both would come to be his in due time. But he wanted it now without waiting in trust. He wanted tomorrow today. If a test of maturity is being willing to delay rewards, the younger son failed the test.

The insulting request of the younger son is met with an unexpected response: "So he divided his property between them" (v. 12). The parable thus begins with two shocking actions: the younger son's insulting request and the father's affirmative response. Some interpreters who are accustomed to calling this story "the prodigal" have stepped back from it to ask, "Who is the real prodigal here?" The father gambled his life *(ton bion)* by dividing it between his sons.

In his "prodigal" act of dividing his living between his sons, the father was reversing the actions of the younger son. First, if the younger son claimed his rights while surrendering responsibility, the father took responsibility for surrendering his rights. He had the right to retain the farm and property until he decided to turn it over or until he died. Second, if the younger son claimed his freedom at the expense of his relationships, the father risked his freedom because of his commitment to his sons. The father's commitment to his relationships was greater than his claim to the freedom to own and manage his property. Third, if the younger son wanted his future now without the need to wait in trust, the father risked his own future by trusting his sons today. By entrusting his living to his sons, his own future was placed in the hands of others.

Commentators have often noted that Luke's Gospel portrays the reversals in life that accompany the arrival of the kingdom of God. In this parable the father reverses the attitudes and actions of his son by setting aside his rights, giving up his freedom, and risking his future.

Then another reversal takes place in the younger son. He traveled to a far country — presumably to Gentile country — where he could exercise his rights, enjoy his freedom, and romp his way into his new future. But five rounds of tragedy conspired to rob him of all that he had bargained for. First, he wasted his "being" (*ousia*, translated "property," is from *eimi*, "to be." This is similar to his father dividing his *bion*, translated "property," meaning "life." The father divided his *life* between them; the son squandered his *being*). Second, he spent everything he owned; he was undoubtedly broke before he was poor. Third, a great famine left him destitute. Fourth, joining himself to a citizen (Gentile) and feeding swine (cf. Lev. 11:7 and Deut. 14:8) burned his last bridges back to his family and village; his break with his past was complete. Fifth, he asked for mercy, "and no one gave him anything" (v. 16). The younger son has lost his rights, his freedom, and his future.

His conversion (repentance) is somewhat ambiguous and invites speculation concerning his motive and goal for returning to his father. It is best to stay close to the language of the text. "When he came to himself" (v. 17) surely means that he faced the reality of where he had come from, where he was now, and how he came to be there. Remembering that his father's hired servants were well fed seemed like a promising prospect. His confession of sin, admission of unworthiness, and offer to hire on as a servant were crafted into a well-rehearsed speech. Rather than assign relative weights to his confession of sin and his offer to work, it may be more fruitful to wonder aloud if there can be any "pure repentance" among us. Is there any repentance so untouched with self-interest or bargaining that needs no grace to be acceptable?

And grace explodes in our face as we watch the meeting of the father and the son. It begins with the father running to meet him. "But while he was still far off, his father saw him and was filled with compassion; he ran and put his arms around him and kissed him" (v. 20). The father was watching, waiting. How long? We do not know, and it is best for us that no times are given. Kenneth Bailey supplies nuances of meaning and experience in the actions of the father. He knows that his son will be humiliated by the taunts of the villagers because of his conduct. To spare him that humiliation, the father humiliates himself by doing what no Oriental father would do: run in public to meet his son (*Poet and Peasant* [Grand Rapids: Eerdmans, 1976], p. 181). The embrace and the kiss are public signs of reconciliation before the son has the chance to deliver his prepared speech.

But the son speaks: "Father, I have sinned against heaven and before you; I am no longer worthy to be called your son" (v. 21). He does not get around to offering to be his father's hired servant. It makes no difference whether the son changed his mind about that part of his speech or that his father gave him no opportunity to say it. What matters is that the father had received his son back. It was the *relationship* of father and son that was restored by the grace of the father, not the bargaining of the son.

What follows are the signs of restoration. The best robe was the father's robe. The signet ring was a sign of restored authority and responsibility. The shoes were a sign that he was indeed a son, not a servant. The killing of the fatted calf was a sign that the whole community was invited to celebrate the restoration of the relationship. The unexpected, extravagant display of grace in restoring his son is accounted for by the father's own words: "Let us eat and celebrate; for this son of mine was dead and is alive again; he was lost and is found!" (vv. 23-24).

The parable has now come full circle. We are back to the beginning of the chapter: "Now all the tax collectors and sinners were coming near to listen to him. And the Pharisees and the scribes were grumbling and saying, 'This fellow welcomes sinners and eats with them'" (15:1-2). It has taken three stories to make one parable (v. 3). The three stories conspire to say that God in Christ loves a party that celebrates the restoration of life to the dead and of a relationship with the lost.

The shadow that approaches from the field is cast by the older brother. We have not heard of him since verse 12, "So he divided his property between them." With two-thirds of his father's property deeded to him, he has worked hard and been responsible. And as he approaches the house, hearing the music and dancing, he asks a child what is going on. Hearing that his brother has returned and that the party is in his honor, he is livid. He refuses to join the party. But the father remains in character. He had run out to meet his younger son, and now he comes out of the house to plead with his older son to join the party.

The same values that were at work in the younger son's departure come into play again in the older son's refusal to join the party. Did the younger claim his rights and surrender his responsibilities? Now the older son asks about his rights to which he is entitled because he had been "working like a slave" all these years. And he refuses to take responsibility for welcoming his brother home. Did the younger claim his freedom without commitment to family relationships? Now the older son wants freedom from any relationship with his brother: "This son of yours" (not "my brother") came home (v. 30). Did the younger reach for his future inheritance without waiting in trust? Now the older son can no longer trust a father who would welcome his wastrel son home and throw a party in his honor. His future was secure and well appointed until he heard the music and dancing.

The younger son sinned against his father and was welcomed home into a restored relationship with his father. The older son "slaved" for his father and sinned against him without leaving home. But the grace of the father is extended to both as he pleads with his son to join the party.

The story stops without being finished. When preachers move from the text to the sermon, they may want to invite the church to join the party and to finish the story. There is only one rule for finishing it: What would it be like for such grace to prevail?

Roger E. Van Harn

Seventeenth Sunday after Pentecost, Year C

First Lesson: Jeremiah 4:11-12, 22-28
(Psalm 14)
Second Lesson: 1 Timothy 1:12-17
Gospel Lesson: Luke 15:1-10

Persons familiar with this great chapter will be reluctant to stop with verse 10. Chapter 15 is clearly a single unit that includes three parables: the lost sheep, the lost coin, and the lost sons. Familiarity inclines many of us to treat the first two parables as preparation for and introduction to the third. The parable of the lost sons has range, depth, color, and immediacy that compel attention. Imagining the weight of a lost sheep draped over one's shoulders or the sparkle of a recovered coin cannot compete with the warmth of embracing a rebellious child who came home.

With attention drawn to the climactic third parable, the relationship of the chapter to the preceding context can easily be missed. Since announcing the beginning of the journey to Jerusalem in 9:51, Luke reports that the ministry of Jesus moved between teaching and growing opposition from the leaders. Furthermore, this teaching and conflict took place characteristically in the presence of "the crowd" (11:14, 27, 29; 12:1, 13, 54; 13:14, 17; 14:25). In 14:25 Jesus addressed the crowd in strong words about the qualifications for discipleship, concluding with: "Let anyone with ears to hear listen" (14:35). These are the same words with which Jesus concluded the parable of the sower: "Let anyone with ears to hear listen" (8:8).

Those words set the stage for the opening of chapter 15: "Now all the tax collectors and sinners were coming near to listen to him" (v. 1). Suddenly the situation has changed. In response to Jesus' "let anyone with ears to hear listen," tax collectors and sinners came near "to listen to him." Just as Jesus' disciples came asking him "what this parable meant" in response to the parable of the sower and the invitation to "listen," so now a new wave of would-be disciples drew near. Jesus' teaching and call to listen set the table for his table fellowship with tax collectors and sinners.

It was the reaction of the Pharisees and scribes against Jesus' behavior that became the occasion for the three parables. The parables would turn their words of complaint into a cause for celebration: "This fellow welcomes sinners and eats with them."

In our eagerness to identify with Jesus and the sinners he welcomed, we may miss the importance of identifying with the Pharisees and scribes. We do well to restrain our criticism long enough to listen to them. They loved God and lived in the hope of the coming of the Messiah to redeem Israel. Their role in that coming was to study, obey, interpret, and apply the law of Moses. Keeping the law would prepare the way for the coming redemption. The world could be divided into five or six groups ranking from the righteous (law-keepers) to sinners. Sinners were lawbreakers and those who worked at dishonorable occupations like tax collecting, shepherding, and leather tanning. Given the Pharisees' and scribes' love for God and law-shaped mission, Jesus' table fellowship with sinners was an offense and an obstacle to the coming redemption.

Jesus understood them. He identified with them as he told parables calculated to turn their complaint into celebration.

He began here: "Which one of you, having a hundred sheep and losing one of them. . . ." The parable opens with a powerful invitation for the leaders to identify with a *shepherd!* Shepherds belonged to the sinners — some of whom may have been seated at the table with Jesus. Jesus was at the table as a shepherd who was welcoming the lost, who identified with the lost, and who invited the religious leaders to identify with the lost by putting themselves in the sandals of a shepherd. The parable is already doing its work before the story line unfolds and the search gets under way.

The pinch of the first parable carries over to the second: "Or what woman . . . ?" The words of Jesus called them to imagine themselves as a woman to see what was happening in Jesus' table fellowship with tax collectors and sinners. Their daily prayer, "Thank you, Lord of the universe, that you did not make me a woman," distanced themselves from women. But Jesus closed the distance and called them to identify with a woman even before her actions were described. (For more on the significance of these addresses, see Kenneth E. Bailey, *Poet and Peasant* [Grand Rapids: Eerdmans, 1976], pp. 147, 158.)

But the parables are full of actions that interpret and illumine Jesus' behavior in his table fellowship. Both parables are about losing, searching, finding, restoring, and celebrating the return of what was lost. The parables turn the complaint of the Pharisees and scribes into a celebration: "This fellow welcomes sinners and eats with them." *Jesus was acting out God's gracious and determined search for the lost.* "Until he finds it" and "until she finds it" are expressions of hope that the search will be fruitful. There is no estimate of the value of the lost apart from the determined search itself. In a world where the value of persons is relativized and classified according to age, race, class, gender, wealth, power, and virtue, God's unrelenting search provides the true measure of a lost sinner's worth. Percentages are not factored into the intensity of the search (one of 100, one of ten); there is no acceptable margin of loss.

The parables disclose that in his table fellowship with sinners, *Jesus was already rejoicing in the restoration of the lost.* Joy dominates and climaxes both parables. In the first, the shepherd rejoices when he finds the sheep, and then carries it all the way home — in spite of the weight on his shoulders. Then the parties happen in which the whole community rejoices. The joy at the restoration of the lost reaches to heaven: "Just so, I tell you, there will be more joy in heaven over one sinner who repents than over ninety-nine righteous persons who need no repentance."

Heaven rejoices when a sinner repents; the shepherd and the woman rejoice when the lost is found. How are we to understand the relationship between repentance and being found? How are a found sheep and coin like the sinners who ate with Jesus at the table?

If we stay with this story as our primary resource for understanding what Jesus meant by repentance here, the clue is given at the outset. Jesus said for all to hear: "Let anyone with ears to hear listen." Then: "Now all the tax collectors and sinners were coming near to listen to him." That is the "repentance" that sets heaven rejoicing. Repentance is both the "coming near to listen" and the experience of being found by the one who calls. Repentance is not something we accomplish; repentance happens to us when we come close enough to listen.

How do the parables illumine the table fellowship? *Jesus was calling the Pharisees and scribes to identify with him in his search for the lost and in his joy at finding.* Jesus was not always this gentle with his judgments. His stories judged the Pharisees and scribes for their complaint, but the judgment was as gracious as the good news he brought. Who knows what would have happened if Jesus had repeated his first invitation *after* telling the parables and addressed them to the critics: "Let anyone with ears to hear listen."

Picture Jesus and his table guests in the middle of your church. People are coming and going. A steady stream of people from all nations, races, ages, and cultures make their way to the table. Sometimes there is a brief wait for a place to sit or stand around. No one seems hurried, yet no one is turned away. Quiet conversation can be heard around the table. Prayers intersperse the speaking and listening. Laughter and tears seem to take turns. Soup and bread are in steady supply. Songs seem spontaneous.

What would a church be like if it were shaped by Jesus' table fellowship with sinners?

First, it would be a safe place for people to come near to listen. What factors in the contemporary church seem threatening to persons who would otherwise come to listen? What barriers to listening are removable? How can we make the church a fellowship in which persons dare to come to listen? How can the church be a place where people feel free to wonder, to ask, and to listen?

Second, the church would be a place where people are nurtured for a seek-and-save mission in the world. The table talk would include encouragement to take the love and message of Jesus into the world. For people who are too afraid or angry to come to the table to listen, those who are there would be encouraged to bring the table fellowship to them. The table is not walled off from the world; the table is a sign of God's mission in and for the world. The church is a safe place for people to listen and the headquarters for bringing what is heard there to those who cannot yet come.

Third, the church would be a party house where celebrations happen. The rejoicing of the angels can be heard and sung in the songs. The church is a fellowship that reaches forward to the new heaven and the new earth and brings its joyful songs into the present. Jesus heard the songs of the angels at his table of fellowship with sinners. The church that is shaped by that table can do no less.

How can we get from where we are to the table fellowship in Luke 15 and back again? We can envision the church as a safe place for people to come near to listen, as a headquarters for our search-and-save mission in the world, and as a party house where seeking sinners echo the songs of the new heaven and earth where righteousness dwells.

Roger E. Van Harn

Eighteenth Sunday after Pentecost, Year C

First Lesson: Jeremiah 8:18–9:1
(Psalm 79:1-9)
Second Lesson: 1 Timothy 2:1-7
Gospel Lesson: Luke 16:1-13

Few texts have been more difficult for the church than the parable of the unjust steward. Part of the difficulty is two ways the church has interpreted the text that are revered and yet problematic. One is to take the characters of narratives as role models to emulate. The second is to take the words of the text, and particularly the words of Jesus, as expressions of universal principles. When this parable is appropriated through such lenses, readers supposedly should emulate the unjust steward in his cleverness in the belief that Jesus validates a principle of shrewdness when he says, "Make friends for yourselves by means of dishonest wealth so that when it is gone, they may welcome you into the eternal homes." But how could the parable be about emulating a shrewd manager who is characterized as deriving his behavior from injustice?

A brief word about interpreting parables is in order. I take parables to be vivid stories that seduce hearers (readers) to adopt an initial position that the parable then subverts. Like a movie with a surprise ending, the parable startles hearers so that they have to revise their thinking and view reality from a new perspective. Correspondingly, preachers might consider how to structure sermons so that they too have a subversive surprise that causes hearers to view reality in a different way.

Interpreters have often thought that Luke 16:1 shifts the context dramatically from the triad of parables about joy over finding what is lost in chapter 15. There are good reasons, however, to note strong continuity with the context. The father in the parable of the prodigal son pleads with the older brother to come inside and join the celebration over the return of his brother. He pleads with him like the gardener who cultivates a fig tree in Luke 13:6-9 so that it might bear fruit. The parable suspends without resolving whether the father convinces the older brother or not, and this leaves readers pondering which alternative he might take.

At this point Luke launches a new story about an unjust manager. Like the prodigal son, the steward misappropriates property acquired from someone else (the Greek verb is the same in both parables). In both instances the misappropriation creates a severe crisis. On the other hand, the

415

stories play out against two distinct social institutions. Whereas the matrix of the prodigal's story is the patriarchal family, the manager functions as a broker in a patron/client system.

Both stories also involve honor and shame codes in the culture of Mediterranean antiquity. Not only does the prodigal wind up feeding swine — an oxymoron for an Israelite — he also squanders the family inheritance. This was the ancestral heritage that the family traced back to Abrahamic promises through the distribution of the land after the conquest of Canaan. The prodigal thus doubly denies his Jewish identity, and the father thus willfully violates honor and shame codes by celebrating his return.

The situation is quite different for the manager. Jewish identity does not seem to be at stake. In fact, the characters need not even be Jewish. Rather, the issue is social acceptability. In the accepted system for exchanging goods, patrons and clients are socially unequal. To avoid dealing with one another directly, they work through a broker. The manager of the story is the broker between the rich man and the debtors. The issue of honor and shame for him is that without his position as broker, he will lose face: "I am ashamed to beg" (16:3).

Their differences notwithstanding, both the manager and the prodigal develop strategies for coping with their crises. The prodigal decides to return to his father as an indentured servant — to make himself indebted to his father. The manager resolves to make his master's clients indebted to him. His strategy is to make his master's clients complicitous in hoodwinking the patron — honor among thieves, so to speak.

Interpreters with the perspective of the dominant culture have usually taken the patron to be the wronged party. Recently some have suggested that peasants in Jesus' world would have sided rather with the broker and the clients. Patrons could be notorious for bilking peasant clients with excessive interest on loans, then grabbing their land if they were unable to repay the loan and interest. In this case the broker is like Jack in "Jack and the Beanstalk," who uses the system to best his more powerful competitor. Others have suggested that the manager merely deducts his own cut from the brokered transaction. But what is problematic for these interpretations is Jesus' characterization of the broker. English translations use an adjective to characterize the manager as "unjust" or "dishonest" (16:8). But Jesus characterizes him not with the adjective *adikos* in Greek ("unjust"), but with the noun *adikias*, which here is a genitive of origin. That is, Jesus characterizes him as one whose way of living derives from unrighteousness the way children's genes derive from their parents.

So we wind up with a story of a character who is called "the lord" (*kyrios*) praising the manager who derives his way of life from injustice. Further, there is some ambiguity as to whether the lord here is the patron or Jesus, who is relating the parable. Luther took it to be Jesus as Lord, and thus took the praise of the manager as Jesus' affirmation of shrewdness. More likely the lord in 16:8 is the rich man — "his master" in the NRSV.

But Jesus also lumps the broker in with a group he calls "children of this age" (16:8). The "children" of this age derive their living from a realm that is in conflict with God's realm, a corporate counterpart to the manager who derives his living from unrighteousness. The manager is one of the children of this age who is dealing with other children of this age, including the debtors and *the rich patron who praises him,* and Jesus plays *all of them* off against the children of light. In 16:9-13 Jesus reiterates the incompatibility of two realms. The realm of unrighteous mammon is irreconcilable with God's realm. Jesus insists that it is impossible to serve God and mammon. Therefore, it is impossible for the rich patron to serve God because he serves mammon. The criterion of serving mammon rather than God undermines the rich patron's praise of his manager as shrewd. The shrewdness of the manager, the complicitous debtors, and the rich man is the shrewdness of the children of this age in contrast to the children of light.

So how then are we to understand Jesus' apparent admonition to make friends by means of unrighteous mammon so that when it is gone, the friends will receive us into their eternal dwellings? Given the incompatibility of the two realms, Jesus' words of admonition are full of irony. In 10:21 Jesus inverts the wise and intelligent from whom truth is hidden with infants to whom truth is revealed. The shrewdness of the children of this age is that of the wise from whom truth is hidden. Further, the "eternal homes" are more literally "eternal tents," an oxymoron. There is nothing eternal about tents. Jesus' exhortation to make friends with unrighteous mammon means to test the strategy of children of this age. How eternal do you think such friends and their dwellings are? Such friends would ultimately be like those in the previous parable who would give the prodigal son nothing (15:16). Luke gives some further comments of Jesus in 16:10-13 that control the interpretation of the parable. "Whoever is dishonest in a very little is dishonest also in much. If then you have not been faithful with the dishonest wealth, who will entrust to you the true riches? And if you have not been faithful with what belongs to another, who will give you what is your own?" In light of these words, it is impossible to take the manager as an example for Luke's readers to imitate.

At the end of the parable some Pharisees ridicule Jesus as if to challenge his insistence that it is impossible to serve God and mammon (16:14-15).

These Pharisees are stereotypes. That is, they appear as one character. Many interpreters argue that Luke here uses the Pharisees as negative examples in a way that borders on anti-Judaism. Aside from the problem of taking characters as role models, one should note that even as stereotypes, they represent only some of the Pharisees. Further, rather than taking the Greek as characterizing all Pharisees as lovers of money, it is possible to take it as characterizing a group from among the Pharisees who were lovers of money: "Those Pharisees who were lovers of money." Is Jesus' encounter with them to be understood in the context of 13:6-9? Is Jesus like a gardener who cultivates an unfruitful fig tree so that it will bear fruit? At 16:15, are they like the older brother about whom the parable of the prodigal son leaves us in suspense, who may stay outside or come in and join the celebration?

Robert L. Brawley

Nineteenth Sunday after Pentecost, Year C

First Lesson: Jeremiah 32:1-3a, 6-15
(Psalm 91:1-6, 14-16)
Second Lesson: 1 Timothy 6:6-19
Gospel Lesson: Luke 16:19-31

The story generally known as the parable of the rich man and Lazarus takes up common Lukan themes such as the dangers of money, concern for the poor and disadvantaged, and the need for immediate conversion and repentance. To these themes are added the continuing validity of Old Testament teaching, the irrevocability of judgment upon death, and the inadequacy of miracles in themselves, no matter how great, to produce belief. If one fails to make right use of the opportunities available *now*, it will be, fatally and finally, too late.

This parable comes in the immediate context of teaching on the use of earthly possessions (16:1-15), verses containing sharp words on the impossibility of serving God and mammon and on how what humans prize is an abomination to God. Verses 16-17 vigorously affirm the ongoing authority of the law, despite the further revelation that has now come. Thus the story follows easily in the development of the chapter as a whole. (Verse 18, on divorce, seems like something of an intrusion. That divorce manifests or results from the kind of hardness of heart that the parable itself critiques is a possible but rather speculative connection.) The material following the parable (chap. 17) does not appear to connect to it closely. However, it is of great importance that, in the broader design of the Gospel, Jesus is here on his way to Jerusalem, to his own death and resurrection. One can hardly escape the reference to the fact that *Jesus'* resurrection will not prove enough to convince those who turn away now.

The basic form of the story, which involves reversals of fortune in the afterlife, is common in folklore and was popular among Jewish teachers (Caird). The story is unique among Jesus' parables, though, in that Lazarus has a name (a name with the underlying meaning "God has helped"). The rich man is not named; the common appellation Dives comes from the Latin word for "rich." His wealth is emphasized not only by his costly clothing and feasting, but even by the term for the entrance *(pylōna)* to his dwelling, which refers to a large gateway suitable to a grand house. Lazarus may have been not only poor and hungry but crippled (the passive of *ballein* may be used with that force); in any case, dogs licking his sores added to his degradation, since dogs were not well regarded in the culture. The rich man obviously claimed relationship to Abraham, calling out to him as "Father Abraham" (vv. 24, 27, 30; cf. Matt. 3:9 and Luke 3:8, where Jesus rebukes those seeking to justify themselves as being Abraham's children); Abraham did not deny the claim — he answered him as "child" — but it made no difference in the man's fate. But it was Lazarus, who is not represented as making any claims, who found himself with Abraham in paradise ("Abraham's bosom" was a common term for paradise), while the rich man suffered torment. Angels carried the poor man to heaven; no angels attended the rich man's death. The rich man had "his" good things on earth; the poor man had evil things, but evil things not designated as "his" (the possessive pronoun is lacking in the poor man's case). The contrasts build relentlessly and are finally established in their reversed form by the great, uncrossable chasm separating the two men in the afterlife. There will be no further changes in status.

The rich man's request that Abraham warn his still-living brothers by sending Lazarus to them suggests that he felt as if his failures were not entirely his fault: he had needed more information, more evidence, something a bit more convincing; had he only been given what he needed, he would have done differently himself. (One recalls Woody Allen's famous and only half-humorous plea that if God exists, he should provide a sign, like making a large deposit in his name in a Swiss bank.) Abraham's answer here — that Moses and the prophets are enough, and that those who do not heed them will not be responsive even to the most astonishing miracle — harmonizes with testimony elsewhere in the Gospels (e.g., Luke 11:9 par.; cf. John 7:17-19; note also that Jesus' own resurrection appearances would be not to unbelievers but only to his disciples): it is an evil and unbelieving generation that seeks signs, and the way to know the truth is to be obedient to God's revealed will. Wonders do not soften hard hearts. Punishment seldom softens them either, which reinforces the likelihood that we should read the rich man's request for a messenger to his brothers as self-justifying rather than compassionate. Even if compassion were the motive, however, it is too late.

Although the rich man's sin was one of omission rather than commission — he had not, apparently, actively mistreated Lazarus — it was not a sin committed in ignorance (see, similarly, Matt. 25:31-46). He knew Lazarus's name (v. 24). He recognized the man but had not recognized his own duty. Indeed, it may be that his desire even after death to use Lazarus as a sort of errand boy (vv. 24, 27) suggests his continuing utter inability to conceive of Lazarus as a person of like dignity to himself. And the fact that Lazarus died first means that the rich man lost his final opportunity to do good to him even before his own life ended. "Too late" can sneak up on us. God calls us to account not only for what we have done, but also for what we have left undone.

This story is often referred to in discussions of heaven, hell, and the intermediate state (the condition between an individual's death and the general resurrection and final judgment). One should be careful, though, about drawing firm conclusions from it because the "scenery" of the story is appropriated from developing ideas at the time; and the story itself is not designed to teach about the details of life after death, but rather about the essential character of acting aright now. Looking at this "scenery," we see depicted two regions of Hades (the equivalent of Sheol in Greek). Late in the Old Testament and in the intertestamental literature, Sheol was sometimes conceived not as the undifferentiated fate of all humans, all the dead being condemned to a shadowy existence there, but as allowing for separation of the righteous and unrighteous — a separation that developed into full-blown conceptions of heaven and hell. In this passage, it seems clear that one's destination is understood to be fixed at death; there is no thought of purgatory or of a "second chance" (see also Heb. 9:27). Old Testament worthies are assumed to be found in paradise (see also John 8:56; some have supposed that the alleged "harrowing of hell" of 1 Pet. 3:19, 20 relates specifically to these Old Testament saints, though how the work of Christ relates to God's covenant people who died before Christ's coming is not made specific; also, the "harrowing of hell" would be anachronistic here). Wealth in itself does not exclude one from paradise, for Abraham was rich; rather, one's disposition toward God and neighbor and one's use of wealth are key. The bodily form of Abraham, Lazarus, and the rich man cannot be used to establish our condition in the intermediate state — that is, it does not prove that bodily resurrection immediately follows death — because bodily form is required by the dynamics of the story. References to torment, fire, and agony (vv. 23-25) have often been read as confirming the traditional imagery of hell, though some have read them symbolically, as referring to insatiable desire and remorse (e.g., Plummer). Again, the details cannot be pressed with assurance. The reality of some sort of robust consequences in another life for one's behavior in this one, though, is essential to the story: were this life all there is, it might indeed make sense to eat, drink, and be merry, to take for oneself all the good things one can get and to take no thought for the poor at one's gate.

This life, however, is not all there is. And Luke warns us once again of the tendency of this world's blessings to make us self-consumed, self-important, self-satisfied, self-indulgent, and insensitive to others. When the fateful day comes, it will not be enough to say that we just did not pay attention, or that we had intended to help out tomorrow, or that we surely meant no harm to the helpless ones around us. Nor will it be enough to say that we lacked information about our obligations or that we needed more convincing evidence. The excuses themselves suggest the very hardness of heart that ensures that no further information and no miracle could make a difference. Excepting our greater knowledge of God through Christ and hence our greater responsibility, our situation does not differ greatly from that of the rich man: following the truth that he knew — that given by God's revelation of his will in the Mosaic law and the prophets — and making use of the opportunities he had would have made all the difference.

Marguerite Shuster

Twentieth Sunday after Pentecost, Year C

First Lesson: Lamentations 1:1-6
(Psalm 137)
Second Lesson: 2 Timothy 1:1-14
Gospel Lesson: Luke 17:5-10

The sayings of Jesus collected at the beginning of Luke 17 seem more loosely connected than many other sequences in Luke. Such a sequence should warn us against trying to force connections, as if Luke's narrative must be woven with equal tightness at all points, or as if there were not sayings of Jesus which were worth preserving even though they may not easily have "fitted" into the literary structure of the Gospel. Equally, however, we should not write such a collection down as merely miscellaneous just because the linkages do not seem obvious to us. Careful probing may lead to significant discoveries. At least we can expect to find a fundamental coherence in Jesus' sayings, and in their applicability within the early church.

We may therefore see the apostles' request to Jesus to "increase their faith" (v. 5) as linked in some way to the warning and exhortation of verses 1-4: they see more faith as a prerequisite for the kind of radical obedience which Jesus has called for in urging them to avoid leading others into sin (vv. 1-2) and to forgive one another indefinitely (vv. 3-4). Jesus' response is therefore an encouraging one: the demands he has made are not impossible. Implicitly he says faith is not something which needs to "increase"; it simply needs to exist. If it exists even in mustard-seed proportions, one would be able to command a "sycamine" tree — probably the proverbially deep-rooted fig-mulberry — to be rooted up and planted in the sea, and it would obey (v. 6). If we find ourselves wondering why anyone might want to issue such a command in the first place, we probably need to attune ourselves to the lightness of touch in Jesus' language. He uses an extraordinary example for effect. This does not mean, of course, that the statement is evacuated of its force. On the contrary, it makes its point about faith: if faith is there (as it is in the apostles, as they know and Jesus knows), one can do whatever is needed, whatever is commanded. The apostles should not be daunted — by the high demands of verses 3-4 or by any other requirements of their calling. They have faith; they can fulfill them!

This then helps us to see a closer connection with verses 7-10. The conclusion Jesus draws from the example of the slave waiting on his master

422

without expecting thanks is that when the disciples have done everything that has been commanded them, they should not think of themselves more highly than they ought, but simply as slaves who have done their duty (v. 10). A day is glimpsed when some (at least) of Jesus' flock have ceased to be stumbling blocks, have learned to forgive. They have fulfilled the commands — and done so, of course, by faith. That is the day when they need to remember that their faith was a gift — and not allocated to them by measure according to their worthiness. It is a very similar message to that contained in 10:19-20: the disciples can do many wonderful things (by faith), but it is not in these achievements, but in the gift of God, that they are to rejoice that their names are written in heaven. The simple gift of faith is always more important than what can be done with it.

Turning to the detail of the parable, we note first its similarity in form to 11:5-10 ("Which of you who has a friend will go to him at midnight . . ."), 11:11-13 ("What father among you, if his son asks for a fish . . ."), 15:3-7 ("What man of you, having a hundred sheep . . ."), and 15:8-10 ("What woman, having ten silver coins . . ."). Each of these short parables, not strictly narrative in form but encapsulating a situation in a vivid question, invites the hearers or readers to discern an everyday principle of wisdom or common sense. Jesus then applies this principle to an aspect of humans' relationship with God, an application characteristically introduced by the phrase "I tell you" (see 11:9; 15:7; 15:10). So it is here. Jesus presents an unlikely and then a likely scenario; everyday common sense suggests that it is the latter one which will occur. A master who has a slave will not normally invite the slave, at the end of his day's work, to eat first (a meal which in this case, presumably, would have to be prepared by the master, or more probably the mistress!) (v. 7). Rather, he will get the slave to prepare his master's meal (and, one surmises, that of the master's family too) and serve it before he can sit down to eat himself (v. 8). This is part of the slave's job; he does not think the master owes him any special favors for doing it (v. 9). We should avoid the language of "thanks" in our rendering of this verse; though the original could be translated "Does he thank the servant?" (RSV), "thanks" inevitably suggests modern social niceties, whereas here it is a matter of the basic mutual understanding of social roles. (See on this Kenneth Bailey, *Through Peasant Eyes* [Grand Rapids: Eerdmans, 1980], pp. 121-22; Joel B. Green, *The Gospel of Luke* [Grand Rapids: Eerdmans, 1997], p. 614.)

The vignette reflects, of course, the social realities of Jesus' world. This is a predominantly agrarian society (the slave is plowing or keeping sheep); it is also a slave-owning society. The social variety of Jesus' hearers is glimpsed through setting this story alongside that of the lost sheep in 15:4-

7. Some apparently owned at least one slave to work their farm ("Will any one of *you*, who has a slave . . . ," v. 7), though this by no means implies that they were rich. Others may have owned sheep, but had to undertake the despised task of shepherding themselves (15:4).

The implicit comparison of God with a slave owner (hinted at in the "divine passive" of "all that is commanded you," v. 10) raises questions for readers today about the extent to which even Jesus' picture of God was culture-bound. Four points may be made here.

First, these little question-parables are perhaps those where the classic analysis of Adolf Jülicher fits best. Jülicher argued that the parables are to be understood as straightforward similes making one main point; the comparison is not to be stretched. It should go without saying that Jesus did not intend his pictures to be accurate portrayals of God. They are, indeed, so homely as to ward off the literal minded; anyone attentive to the ancient revelation of Yahweh, the awesome and mysterious God who had spoken but was by no means to be imaged, cannot think that these word pictures of Jesus are to be taken as fixed doctrinal definitions. They are windows to truth.

Second, the master-slave relationship in antiquity was not necessarily cruel and oppressive. No doubt it was a symptom of a society rife with inequality, but a slave such as the one pictured in 17:7-10 was undoubtedly in a better situation than the beggar of 16:20-21, one of those driven off the land through the increasingly crushing burden of taxation, indebtedness, and expropriation of ancestral property under the Roman hegemony. The slave, at least, was of value to someone, and in that respect he or she had a measure of security, as well as daily provision.

Third, God had been described as Israel's master (Jer. 3:14; Mal. 1:6). As Israel's owner, he had authority over them but also protected and provided for them.

Fourth, in other places Jesus speaks of a remarkable role reversal in God's kingdom. In Luke 12:37 he promises that the "master" *will* wait on the faithful servants. In 22:26 and following he calls on his followers to imitate his own example "as one who serves." In 17:7-10 Jesus implicitly affirms the importance of continuing to think of God as master, but in his life he displays a new pattern for such "masterhood" which overturns the social expectations.

The picture, then, is not to be pressed into saying that God is ungrateful or into implying that he is the complaisant guarantor of a social order we now recognize as unjust. The clause translated "We are unworthy servants" (v. 10) sounds suspect to those who have seen the malign effect of some religious practices on human self-worth, but is more innocuous than that; it simply entails the recognition that no special favor is due. The culture of Jesus made the comparison a suitable one for stressing the simple point that discipleship is not about winning plaudits or doing favors, but about duty. Fulfilling the commands of God and of Jesus is possible through faith (v. 6) but never becomes cause for pride (vv. 7-10).

Can the preacher still use the image of the master and servant to make the point? Perhaps, with due explanation: to do so keeps us anchored in biblical revelation. But we must explore other possibilities for making this truth concrete today. This may be difficult, for in some cultures we say "thank you" very liberally, including, on many occasions, to those who *are* only doing their duty. But what man or woman of us will give a paid secretary a box of chocolates every time that secretary types a letter on our behalf?

Stephen I. Wright

Twenty-first Sunday after Pentecost, Year C

First Lesson: Jeremiah 29:1, 4-7
(Psalm 66:1-12)
Second Lesson: 2 Timothy 2:8-15
Gospel Lesson: Luke 17:11-19

Unlike many of the healing stories in the synoptic Gospels, the healing of the ten lepers in Luke 17 lacks any sign of physical contact between the hands of Jesus and those who suffer. There is no rubbing of spit onto eyelids or massaging of bumps on a crooked spine. The healing that occurs in Luke 17:11-19 comes through appeal and pronouncement and responsive faith. At first this absence of touch by Jesus seems inconsequential. But a closer look at this spatial gap between Jesus and those he heals reveals a larger design by Luke — one that shows Jesus erasing a host of boundary lines by merely speaking of God's purposes.

The story of the ten lepers is full of boundary lines drawn this way and that. Jerusalem would soon be known as the place where people would draw a line in the sand between those they considered acceptable and those they did not. Jesus moves closer to that city in this account, nearer to the verdict of being found unacceptable himself. On the way to Jerusalem he passes along between Samaria and Galilee. Luke's sense of Palestinian geography is a bit contorted here, as if his compass has failed. But geographical precision and cartographic accuracy are not the writer's special concern at the moment. Far more urgent is a display of the contrast between two very different regions and people. Samaria is the symbolic place of rejection, that community of foreigners who would not receive Jesus (9:51-56). Galilee is the home of Israelites, the starting point for Jesus' public life. It was in this region where his ministry acquired its early shape. Now Jesus walks the boundary line between these dissimilar communities, pressing to close the rift between disparate people.

His encounter with a group of lepers happened "as he entered" a village. Luke doesn't note the name of the village, if it was even known. The dwelling place of the lepers outside the city limits is what catches the reader's eye. There these sick individuals rest on the periphery, on the outside of acceptable life, in the land of repulsion. Ritual laws of impurity relegated them to such a place (Lev. 13:46), somewhere near where the town dump must have been situated. The easiest way to put people out of mind is to place them out of sight. Jewish regulations on impurity guaranteed that this could be accomplished.

Scholars continue the endless debate on what manner of skin disorder this leprosy might have been. Was it Hansen's disease or some milder blemish? Take your pick. Speculation about unsightly skin conditions in the first century will never be resolved! The plain and simple fact is that society had marginalized and ostracized these individuals. They suffered as much from a social disease as from a physical one. Their only home was apart from other people. Lepers dwelt in the land of isolation.

These particular lepers were much like those found outside the gates or walls of any other city. They could raise their voices and bellow out. Levitical law mandated that they announce their uncleanness to the world. One of the ways the world has always managed to keep marginalized people in their place is to have them acknowledge their own condition. For lepers this was accomplished when they lifted their voices to tell passersby, "Unclean, unclean" (Lev. 13:45). On this day, though, the cry of these ten was more than an announcement. It was a plea for mercy. And their plea opened with a summons to Jesus by name, referring to him specifically as "Master."

If this intimate form of address seems unusual, indeed it was. Where did these lepers learn a term — "master" — ordinarily employed only by the disciples? This we may never know. What is clear is their eagerness to receive something Jesus possessed but they did not. Perhaps he held the clue that could end their crippling social stigma. Luke indicates that even though they stood at a distance from Jesus, honoring a proper boundary, he nevertheless "was met" by them as he entered that village. Anticipation fueled their pleas for healing.

The instruction from Jesus that they go and show themselves to the priests is in line with what we might expect. Jesus knew Jewish law, and he knew the role of priests. When it came to leprosy, priests served as the purity inspectors. Their assignment wasn't all that different from modern-day customs officials, scrutinizing persons and their baggage for entrance into a different world. Priests alone had the authority to determine who was pure and who was not. Or so the law prescribed. They could alter the life of an individual with a simple and swift decision.

Surprisingly, it didn't matter if this group of lepers ever reached the holy checkpoint where priestly decisions were made. They were cleansed "as they went," Luke tells us. As they walked they were changed. Somewhere between their encounter with Jesus and some unnamed temple, they were cleansed. Was this a physical recovery? Or a cleansing brand of forgiveness? Or a restoration to the social fabric of the community? Whatever it was, it was a gift — a gift that had come from outside themselves. The boundary of uncleanness that had restricted their lives for so long was finally gone.

Were it not for the camera zooming in on one of the ten, we would never learn of yet another barrier that comes crashing down through the ministry of Jesus. We discover through this one individual that nationality and genealogy have no bearing on one's closeness to God. Physical ancestry does not make for faith. Nine of ten cleansed lepers may have made it to the temple. We don't know. But this tenth one never did. He was a Samaritan who lived with the double affliction of a dreadful disease and the wrong ethnic background. This ugly boundary of ethnicity is not an apparent theme early in the story. Not until verse 16b are we aware that this healing event is something other than routine. Suddenly the behavior of one, now identified as a Samaritan, forces a different look at what is happening through the beneficent work of Jesus.

The Samaritan *outcast,* underscored by the word "foreigner" in verse 18, responds to the cleansing experience in a dramatic way. Seeing that he has been healed, this outsider retraces his steps back to Jesus and spontaneously launches a three-part response. The first part is expected. Nothing would have been extraordinary about praising God for healed circumstances. The second and third parts come more unexpectedly. Falling at the feet of Jesus, this foreigner closes the spatial gap that customarily existed between Jews and Samaritans. He removes the usual distance of disease and social isolation. And in an act of reverent submission, he gives thanks to Jesus for the healing he has received. He has found the temple of praise, and it most certainly is not a building!

How often the stranger behaves more receptively than the insider! "He *saw* that he was healed." The Samaritan noticed his gift of new life and connected it with the Giver of that life. There is a self-awareness of blessing evident here — a perception that is presumably missing in the remaining nine. The eyes of faith on this lone outsider have been opened in such a way as to link the recognition of his own circumstances with a vivid desire to give thanks.

Jesus' comments on the other nine lepers have an indicting ring to them — at least on a first read. Strangely enough, these lepers were only doing as they were told. They were traveling to visit the priests. Obedience guided their footsteps. A second and closer read suggests that Jesus may not have intended words of reproach at all. He does not imply that obedient faith is lacking in these others. He merely intimates that faith is incomplete without some acknowledgment shown to the Giver of life. "Were not ten cleansed? Where are the other nine? Was no one found to return and give praise to God except this foreigner?" As we know from elsewhere in the Gospel, Jesus often used questions to help others look more imaginatively at faith. Perhaps that is what is happening here. Nine lepers have no problem recognizing that something in their lives has changed for the better. What they miss is the acknowledgment that this gift of healing has come from someone in particular.

Modern liturgies of the church weave together themes of mercy and thanksgiving in beautiful ways. Of course, ancient liturgies did the same thing (e.g., Ps. 30:10-12). Surely the most unique responsibility of the church in any age is to return thanks to the one who mercifully gifts us with new life over and over again. Giving credit where credit is due always deserves a deliberate act of thanksgiving from the faithful. But gratitude will always be in short supply whenever we become more interested in blessing than in the source of that blessing. Sometimes it takes a stranger from beyond our most familiar boundaries to heighten our perception of the richness and goodness of life. On this day we have a Samaritan who spontaneously shatters the disgrace of ingratitude, reminding us that who we are is God's gift to us, and what we do with our life becomes our gift to God.

Peter W. Marty

Twenty-second Sunday after Pentecost, Year C

First Lesson: Jeremiah 31:27-34
(Psalm 119:97-104)
Second Lesson: 2 Timothy 3:14–4:5
Gospel Lesson: Luke 18:1-8

Twice in chapter 18 (and nowhere else) Luke states the meaning of a parable before telling it. The lesson, Luke wrote, is that "they ought always to pray and not lose heart." Many rabbis taught that too much prayer annoyed God and that the set prayers prescribed for three hours of the day were sufficient. The disciples were not to lose heart if the kingdom did not come quickly or if their prayers were not immediately answered. The trials that Jesus had predicted they would face should not discourage them. They were soon to witness the injustice of Jesus' trial and execution, which would lead some to "lose heart." Through fire, famine, and injustice they were to continue to depend on God.

Judges, then as now, were persons with extraordinary power. In Israel the judge was the final arbiter. There was no jury, no court of appeal. The charge to judges was clear: "You must not be partial in judging: hear out the small and the great alike . . ." (Deut. 1:17). The judge was to administer justice according to the righteousness of God which could be found in the Law but which, like all written codes, was subject to interpretation and application. The judge in the parable is a law unto himself who has no sense of accountability to persons or God. He shirked his duty by not bothering to even hear the case. The poor of Israel, like the poor of all generations, had to contend with corrupt public officials. Implicit in this story is the promise of ultimate justice for those who persist in faith.

"Widow" — this one word spoke volumes as to the status of the plaintiff. The widow throughout the Bible, and especially in Luke and Acts, was a vulnerable victim. "Widow" was a symbol of helplessness. A widow could not inherit her husband's estate. Widows were dependent on the compassion of the community. Like Naomi in the book of Ruth, they were often homeless, left to live on what was left in the fields after harvest. God is the protector of widows and the judge of those who abuse them (Exod. 22:22-24; Deut. 27:19; Ps. 68:5; Isa. 10:1-2). Care of widows was recognized as a Christian responsibility in the early church and was given a special role in the community (1 Tim. 5:5; James 1:27). This characterization suggested the most vulnerable of adults. This widow's request, moreover, was only for justice.

429

No overloaded court docket delayed this hearing. The judge flouted judicial protocol and the Scriptures in refusing to hear her case. Isaiah 1:17 states that only the suit of an orphan should take precedence over that of a widow. The judge did not want to be inconvenienced by this case with no hope of a bribe and no fear of public pressure. Who was there to advocate for this welfare woman? Luke again magnified the grace of God and the responsibility of Christians by depicting a common injustice against the weak.

The judge finally did the right thing for the wrong reason. The woman had made a pest of herself. One might visualize her following him around in his daily pursuits, pleading that her case at least be heard. Some scholars suggest that he may finally have acted to avoid further embarrassment by this woman following him around. The word translated "bother" in our text literally means to punch someone in such a way as to blacken an eye. The image here is a blackened face equal to the Asian idea of "lost face." The judge feared being publicly disgraced. Jesus made clear that the judge's motive was not concern for the woman or regard for God. In response to the victim's persistence, the judge not only decided to hear her case but also to "grant her justice." The judge's thoughts confirm what was said of him in the beginning of the narrative. The surprise is that even a person of poor character may be persuaded by persistent pleading to act justly. The point here seems to be that those who pray to a just and loving God should never give up. If an unjust official could be persuaded to act justly, how much more could the righteous be trusted. A second-level meaning might be found in the importance of never giving up the cause of justice, no matter who has the power.

Luke does not portray Jesus as being at all subtle in this episode. He begins with a statement of the meaning of the story, tells the story, and restates the meaning. The rhetorical question states his case. God will be true to his nature and grant justice to those who plead "day and night." The granting of justice does not mean acquiescence to every human whim. God's justice is a higher standard than any legal code. God's righteousness in mercy will prevail. What was legal in Israel was not always morally right. This assurance is given to those who witnessed Jesus' austere lifestyle and experienced the Lord's demand for sacrifice. "Day and night" continues the Lukan emphasis on a life of prayer, continuing consciousness of the presence of God and the will of God. Luke records more prayers of Jesus than the other Gospels. Jesus was clearly a person of prayer who expected his followers to be people of prayer as well.

Waiting for God's answer was and is the hard part. The three days of Jesus' suffering and death surely seemed like a lifetime to his shocked followers. By the time of Luke's writing, many were becoming impatient at the delay in the Lord's coming. The disciples, like contemporary believers, lived in the meantime. The word was: "do not give up hope, keep on believing, praying, and expecting." God's granting of justice will come quickly and unexpectedly. Prayer is an act of faith and a theological statement. Christians pray to God, who cannot be seen or heard. Prayer bears witness to faith in the existence of God and to a belief that God is righteous, caring, and accessible.

When God's verdict is rendered and righteousness is established, will "widows" be still hanging on? The implication seems clear that Luke had observed some falling away and was concerned about despair among the people of the early church. The focus is shifted from the faithfulness of God to the potential loss of faith by some of the followers of Jesus. Prayer is a means of maintaining faith. When the time is right, God will act quickly to vindicate the faithful. Luke links the assurance of God's faithfulness to fears raised in chapter 17 that some will "lose heart and fall away." Luke, writing at a time of widespread disappointment in the delay of the Lord's return, voices a concern of Jesus as to whether any will persevere. "Son of Man" was a favorite self-designation of Jesus, appearing eighty-one times in the Gospels. Literally it simply means "the man" or "human being." Some suggest that its use identifies Jesus' humanity in the same way "Son of God" does his divinity. More likely its use is derived from Daniel 7:13 and is eschatological in nature. Daniel's vision was of one to whom was given "dominion and glory and kingdom" (7:14). This understanding best suits the context in Luke 17:18. It is important to keep in touch with the one who will bring the kingdom.

War movies often depict persons trapped behind enemy lines. The trapped live in fear that their situations are hopeless and they will be destroyed before friendly forces come to rescue them. The ability to maintain radio contact, to hear the voices of comrades, to be reassured that help is on the way gives them courage to keep up the fight and live in hope. The disciples were left behind enemy lines but were given a way of contact that would keep them moving toward their salvation.

Prayer is not the opposite of action. Critics of religion often suggest that activists serve the world better than spiritualists who spend their time in prayer. Those who think in this way do not understand Jesus, who found strength and direction for his actions in prayer. The parable in this week's material stresses action. The widow pursued the judge. She put feet to her words, as we should do.

A problem for modern readers of the Scriptures is often identifying too quickly with particular characters. The protagonist, the good character in this story, is evident. The judge is the obvious villain. All Christians immediately identify with the heroine of the story. From a socioeconomic perspective, Americans are more inclined to be like the judge than the widow. Most could obtain good legal advice, would not be in poverty, and have at least some power over others. Does the failure to pray reflect a disregard for God or a cocky self-reliance?

Raymond Bailey

Twenty-third Sunday after Pentecost, Year C

First Lesson: Joel 2:23-32
(Psalm 65)
Second Lesson: 2 Timothy 4:6-8, 16-18
Gospel Lesson: Luke 18:9-14

The parable recorded in 18:9-14 follows another in 18:1-8. The two parables share the common subject of prayer, but with different emphases for different audiences. As is often the case with Scripture, individuals and churches may need to hear the message of each at different points in their spiritual pilgrimage. The first is a word of encouragement to those who may find themselves in despair; the second is directed to those who err on the side of spiritual self-sufficiency. Whether or not Jesus actually told these parables together in a single setting is not important. Luke's placement and their order in the lectionary are helpful to identify the pitfalls at the opposite ends of the spiritual spectrum. Most congregations will include persons all along the spectrum who struggle with the efficacy of prayer and prayer as an instrument of transformation.

Luke introduced last week's pericope as one for those who might "lose heart." This week's passage is clearly labeled for "some who trusted in themselves that they were righteous and despised others." The latter audience is probably the toughest one preachers speak to, who feel that the biblical exhortations are for sinners "out there." The Pharisees certainly did not believe Jesus could teach them anything about prayer. The only prayers some Christians ever utter are the set ones of the liturgy.

Christians have a tendency to think of "us" and "them" and to always read Scripture from the vantage point of those who were objects of Jesus' compassion. Probably the majority of people in our middle-class churches are "elder brothers" (Luke 15), and the Christian is rare who does not in comparison to others feel righteous at some times. Few would confess to despising others, but a smug sense of moral superiority is hard to resist. To say that we have a lot of Pharisees in our churches or to be identified in that class is not necessarily a bad thing. Pharisees make good elders, stewards, or deacons. They are the ones who do the work of the church and provide the financial support necessary to support religious institutions. Pharisees were devoted to God and righteousness, and most of their faults were the result of overstriving for holiness. Their zeal was often misguided, but at least they had zeal in their desire to please God. In his harshest criticism of the Pharisees, Jesus did not condemn them completely: "For you tithe mint and rue and every herb, and neglect justice and the love of God; these you ought to have done, without neglecting the others" (11:42). Their fundamental problem was that religion became an end rather than a means. In modern terms we can become so busy playing church and being religious that we neglect being Christian in the world.

As in Luke 15, we have two men representing opposite attitudes and spiritual conditions. This is not a case of rich and poor, as both men were probably well-off. They function in different social circles, but neither could be cast as needy in a material sense. They go "up to the temple." Jerusalem is twenty-five hundred feet above sea level, requiring pilgrims to come "up" to the city, and the temple was the highest point in the city. The temple was a public forum always busy with the traffic of those bringing sacrifices, coming for Scripture study, teaching, or public or private prayer. There is no indication that this was one of the regular hours of prayer. The picture of just the two men in this particular time and place makes the contrast stark.

The self-righteous man "prayed with himself." The religious man thought he was talking to God but had become so preoccupied with himself that his prayer was in reality a soliloquy. The Pharisee "trusted in himself" and in reality prayed to himself. The self-sufficient do not need help from God. Luke marks the positions of the men as indicators of their respective attitudes. This man "stands," repudiating any act such as kneeling or falling prostrate that would suggest a need for humility. He came to praise himself rather than God.

Immediately following this parable is the episode of the blessing of the infants and the ruler who goes away sorrowing. This parable lays a foundation for Jesus' call for childlike dependence and humility. The conduct of the man in the parable is evidence for understanding why a suffering, sacrificial messiah would be rejected. This man's own conduct and life were in his mind worthy of the kingdom, and he had no need for a savior. He who had no sin did not need forgiveness.

His gratitude was genuine. He had much for which to be thankful. He was smug about those things that were not temptations for him. Here is a perfect example of the kind of person Jesus must have had in mind when he asked, "Why do you see the speck that is in your brother's eye, but do not notice the log that is in your own eye?" (6:41). Of course, the self-righteous sort in the parable would not want to claim a tax collector as a "brother." Focusing on the sins of others is a popular tactic for avoiding one's own faults.

Fasting was prescribed only on the Day of Atonement, but the most pious of the Pharisees fasted on Tuesdays and Thursdays every week. Tithes were required only on certain foods and animals, but this man tithed on all his income. His devotion is admirable. His sacrifices indirectly served others, as his gifts would go to the poor box as well as for the support of the temple. There is a temptation to condemn his acts and in the process excuse ourselves from similar practices of devotion. The problem was that the pious Pharisee was doing the right thing for the wrong reason. He did not honor God by his piety, but himself. He was obsessed with his own goodness. The sacrifices made were small in relationship to the ego satisfaction earned. The man who prayed "with himself" had become his own God. Spiritual pride is a great enemy of Christian living.

Jesus offered, in contrast to the perfect (in his own mind) Jew, one who belonged to a group that was almost universally despised. Every culture has its despised group. Egos thrive on finding others whose sins are greater or whose piety does not measure up. Jesus used Samaritans, women, and publicans frequently to make a point about God's universal mercy and love.

Tax officials are not popular in any culture, but Jews who made their living collecting taxes for the Romans were bitterly opposed by Jewish nationalists who viewed them as traitors. There were two kinds of collectors: those who sat at tollbooths and those, like Levi (5:27), who collected property taxes. The latter were probably the more detested, as they bought the collection rights from the Romans and then inflated the assessments, increasing their profit. They exploited their own people to serve the enemy who occupied their land and their own interests.

The Pharisee approached the altar and stood proudly for all, especially God, to admire. In sharp contrast the publican stood at some distance, refusing to look up. He had come to the place where he believed God could be found. Driven by a sense of sin, he came to throw himself on the mercy of God. His attitude would be the same later expressed by the apostle Paul when he wrote "that Christ Jesus came into the world to save sinners" and declared that he was the "foremost of sinners" (1 Tim. 1:15). With no pretense, no excuses, he pled for mercy. The lesson of this vignette is that such a plea will not be denied.

The despised tax collector went home, according to Jesus, "justified." The arrogant Pharisee felt no need for justification and received none. The sinner is made righteous; the self-righteous is exposed as a sinner. Often Jesus leaves parables open-ended; the responsibility for understanding and application was left to the hearer, but in this instance the teacher states the intended moral. The futility of self-exaltation and the potential embarrassment from such foolish acts is a recurring theme in Luke (see 14:1-14; 16:15). Jesus does not condemn all Pharisees or vindicate all publicans. The judgment is rendered according to individual behavior.

What is easily overlooked in this parable is that the protagonist is God. God will not be controlled by humans or human standards. The Pharisee's presumption was that God would automatically reward piety. The publican assumed condemnation, but God was merciful. Edward Schweizer applies the lesson to our contemporary situation as follows: "The parable sets us free from the notion of achievement, which revolves about what we have accomplished, and from that of incompetence which revolves about a lack of self-esteem, from the enthusiasm of success and the resignation of failure" (*The Good News according to Luke* [Atlanta: John Knox, 1984], pp. 283-84).

Raymond Bailey

Twenty-fourth Sunday after Pentecost, Year C

First Lesson: Habakkuk 1:1-4; 2:1-4
(Psalm 119:137-44)
Second Lesson: 2 Thessalonians 1:1-4, 11-12
Gospel Lesson: Luke 19:1-10

Jericho was one of the oldest biblical cities in Palestine, dating back to 3000 B.C.E. It was the city of palm trees (Deut. 34:3). Zacchaeus enjoyed a profitable franchise, as Jericho was on a primary trade route. It was a popular vacation spot in the first century because the Herods had built a winter palace with a theater, hippodrome, and beautiful gardens. A natural spring still active today makes it an oasis in the Judean wilderness. Under Palestinian governance, it remains a favorite tourist point today. Sycamore trees can still be found there. The sycamore tree has low, spreading branches which make it an ideal perch from which to watch a parade. A short man could climb into a sycamore tree with little strain.

Just outside the city Jesus had given sight to the blind beggar (18:35-43), and now he had entered the city where he would give spiritual sight to Zacchaeus and to those who understood the parable of grace acted out in this encounter. The action and words make a drama of forgiveness and repentance. Luke moves readers from the parable of grace for a tax collector (18:9-14) to an episode of the extension of grace to a living tax collector. Zacchaeus was a "chief tax collector," the only one designated in the Gospels. His authority was extensive and profitable. Zacchaeus was not only a tax collector; he was also rich. The rich do not fare well in the Gospel of Luke, but here Luke tells us that there is room for the wealthy among the followers of Christ. This is an interesting twist to the story of this last encounter between Jesus and an outsider before he enters Jerusalem. Luke's placement of this story after the story of the rich ruler and Jesus' dialogue with the disciples about the liability of riches intensifies its impact. The contrast between the response of the "ruler" in chapter 18, who turned away when Jesus told him that the peace he sought required surrendering his wealth, and Zacchaeus, who submits his riches without being asked, is emphasized by this juxtaposition.

Zacchaeus sought Jesus, as had the ruler and the blind man. As in the case of the blind man, the tax collector is hindered by the crowd. People are still sometimes shielded from Jesus by crowds, well meaning or otherwise. The disciples had tried to protect Jesus from the children, the multitude did not want the blind beggar to interrupt their parade, and the crowd wanted nothing to do with Zacchaeus and wanted the best places near Jesus (see 14:7-14).

The route of Jesus was probably not difficult to determine, being the main route through Jericho to Jerusalem. The little man ran ahead and found a viewing place in a tree. He must have been shocked when the teacher he had come to see and hear stopped, looked at him, and addressed him by name. Luke makes no comment to suggest that Jesus knew Zacchaeus's name through supernatural power. He may have seen the little man scramble up the tree and asked who he was. Those hostile to the publican may have warned the religious teacher to keep clear of this publican and told Jesus who he was. The meaning of the study may actually be enhanced if Jesus had to go to some trouble to find out who this little man shunned by the crowd was. On the journey to Jerusalem, Jesus may have physically sought the lost (v. 10).

Jesus does not rebuke this sinner, but invites himself to dinner at his home. Here is another addition to the list of homes Jesus visited. Jesus included sinners, publicans, males, females, Pharisees, the rich and the poor in the hospitality of grace. The house of the local rabbi or president of the synagogue would have been the logical choice for a place to dine and have conversation on religious matters.

Zacchaeus's response should be compared to that of the ruler in chapter 18. There is no hesitation, no questions; nothing is held back. He hurried down the tree and "joyfully" joined Jesus. Joy is a recurring theme in Luke's Gospel. Zechariah was told that John would bring joy to many (1:14), and Mary's visit to Elizabeth prompted John to jump for joy in the womb (1:44). The angels proclaimed great joy for all people when they appeared to the shepherds (2:10). Luke's Sermon on the Plain recorded Jesus telling the disciples that even rejection and suffering in God's service should invoke rejoicing (6:23). Joy is the refrain of those who hear and respond to Christ's good news (8:13; 10:17; 15:7, 10; 24:41, 52). The African American tradition more than most others has maintained a spirit of celebration of the hope embodied in Jesus even during periods of oppression. Some traditions have presented the gospel as a burden, bad news rather than good news. Preaching from Luke requires an emphasis on joy. Would thoughts of Jesus coming to one's home put one in a party spirit, or in a spirit of dread? If anyone had reason to dread the presence of a religious teacher who could be expected to roundly censure his profession and life, it was Zacchaeus, but something about Jesus set him at ease.

The reaction of the crowd was not unlike the reaction that some sinners could expect if they showed up at a Christian gathering. The mob is not of-fended by Zacchaeus's behavior as much as they are by Jesus'. They were shocked that Jesus would even speak to this Roman collaborator (who was probably hated all the more because his service to the Romans had made him rich), let alone walk with him through the town and be a guest in his house. They were appalled that Jesus was to be "guest of a man who is a sin-ner." The important thing about this statement is not what it says about Je-sus or Zacchaeus, but what it says about those who uttered it. These words echo the attitude of the Pharisee in the parable in last Sunday's Gospel les-son. These people do not consider themselves sinners, and such people can-not understand Jesus, the man or his message. There are few Christians to-day who would assert that they are not sinners, but there are many whose attitudes toward others indicate that they think they are not sinners, or at least not as bad as most.

The fact that this holy man had honored him by entering his house was not lost on Zacchaeus. He was transformed by Jesus' acceptance. With-out prompting he pledges half of his wealth to the poor. Immediately Zacchaeus demonstrates a changed lifestyle. He seemed to understand the claim of grace. The joy he experienced in being accepted spilled over to put joy into the lives of others. "Repentance" is a word rarely heard in some re-ligious quarters. Fear of legalism and works theology results in a failure to emphasize the transforming power of the grace of Christ. The word of grace and acceptance came first, invoking repentance. The tax collector meets the financial ethics of John the Baptist in the portion of his pledge; the one with two coats was to give one to a person with none (3:11-14). Zacchaeus repented of his former lifestyle and turned away from a history that may have included extortion and exploitation. In addition to his gifts of charity, he volunteered to repay fourfold any he had cheated. His volun-tary declaration commits him to the highest requirements of Old Testa-ment restitution (Lev. 6:5; Exod. 22:1, 4; 2 Sam. 12:6). It is assumed that all the publicans were dishonest; therefore, much of Zacchaeus's wealth was ill gotten. It should be noted, however, that he said, "if I have defrauded any one of anything." The "if" suggests that he may not have knowingly defrauded anyone. He is open to instruction. The laws and standards by which he had been operating were different from the rules of the Pharisees, but the standards of Jesus were superior to those of the Pharisees. There is a danger in stereotyping individuals. Many wealthy people amass fortunes without doing anything illegal, but also without awareness of the tran-scendent ethics of Jesus. There were undoubtedly in the crowd people who had strictly adhered to the law but who had neglected the poor. The example here should not be limited to rich crooks or even to those of great wealth.

Jesus declared that Zacchaeus was a true son of Abraham, a worthy heir of the covenant of faith. Zacchaeus, like Abraham, was the recipient of God's call and grace. Like Abraham, he had heard and accepted the invitation to a new life. He had received salvation not through the law, but by the gracious act of God in Christ. What did Jesus mean when he said, "Today salvation has come to your house?" The mercy and acceptance of Jesus delivered Zacchaeus immediately from estrangement from God. He was alienated from the family of Abraham but now was restored. "Today" there was a change in his spiritual status. There would still be those who would condemn him, and perhaps their number would grow because of his association with Jesus, but he had been set free from a personal sense of condemnation and delivered from a lifestyle that would lead to self-destruction. Jesus had set Zacchaeus on a new course, but there was still much to learn and do. The first encounter with Jesus may lead to conversion, but that conversion becomes an ongoing process.

The climax of this story focuses on Jesus. Jesus is the one who acts in this scene and who is the agent of salvation. Jesus sought Zacchaeus as much as Zacchaeus curiously sought Jesus. Zacchaeus may have sought Jesus only out of curiosity, but Jesus had a purpose in his seeking. Zacchaeus is the object of compassion, but he is even more the means of revelation. The scoffers had grumbled before about Jesus' indiscriminate contact with sinners (5:30), and he had said at that time, "I have not come to call the righteous, but sinners to repentance" (5:32). The grumblers were again disturbed by his attention to sinners, and he reminded them of his mission "to seek and to save the lost." Only when a person is lost and knows it will he seek direction. Inasmuch as Zacchaeus was a chief tax collector, we might speculate as to the effect of his transformation on those under his supervision. He was apparently in a position to have influence over other outsiders.

Raymond Bailey

Palm/Passion Sunday, Year C

First Lesson: Isaiah 50:4-9a
(Psalm 31:9-16)
Second Lesson: Philippians 2:5-11
Gospel Lesson: Luke 19:28-40

Luke's account of Jesus' approach to Jerusalem is linked closely to the parable of the pounds (19:11-27). According to Luke, Jesus told the parable "because he was near Jerusalem, and because they supposed that the kingdom of God was to appear immediately" (19:11). The parable counters this misapprehension, presumably, by its suggestion that there may be a considerable gap between a king being appointed and his actual taking of the reins of power; and that in that gap there is scope both for subjects to rebel and for loyal servants to take creative initiatives. Apparently this was not the first time Jesus had to counter premature euphoria among his followers (cf. 10:20).

So it is "after saying these things" — that is, telling the parable — that Jesus "went on ahead, going up to Jerusalem" (v. 28). What is the significance of this so-called "triumphal entry" in the light of the parable? We may answer this best in negative terms: What does it *not* mean?

First, we note that it does not symbolically signify that Jesus is now *being appointed* king. Jesus (like the nobleman in the parable when he departs "to receive a kingdom") is *already* king — like other ancient "triumphal entries," his presupposes "an already achieved victory" (Joel B. Green, *The Gospel of Luke* [Grand Rapids: Eerdmans, 1997], p. 683). Like that of Archelaus, to whom the parable may allude and who had journeyed to Rome in 4 B.C. to have his authority ratified, Jesus' succession to royal power is not in doubt.

But second, it does not signify the *entry of Jesus into his royal power.* If we read the event in the light of the parable, Jesus' approach to the Holy City is more akin to the *departure* of the nobleman to "receive a kingdom" (v. 12) than to his *return* to exercise his newly confirmed kingly authority (v. 15). Jerusalem is indeed where Jesus is to accomplish his "exodus" or departure (9:31). The ratification of his authority, taking place between "departure" and "return," will be strangely paradoxical; his proclamation as "king of the Jews" will take the form of an accusation nailed to a cross (23:38) and the witness of an empty tomb (24:3).

Third, we should note that 19:28-40 does not in fact record an entry into the city; in verse 41 Jesus is still "drawing near." It brings to completion, rather, the story of the journey which began at 9:51. In verse 28 Luke uses again his characteristic word for "go" (*eporeueto;* the nobleman in the parable also "went" — *eporeuthē,* v. 12) which he had used for Jesus' journeying (e.g., 9:51; 13:33). The story of his treatment by a Samaritan village in 9:52-56 — and the disciples' ill-judged vengefulness then — sets the tone for this final journey. It is not a clear march to victory, but a way marked by conflict and tension. During it Jesus faces rejection by some, and his disciples' understanding and commitment are tested: exactly the situation of the rebels and servants during the absence of the nobleman in the parable. For Luke, then, the entire journey, including the final approach to the city, is both a historical account and a dramatization of Jesus' own path as the suffering Messiah; but it is also the model of the situation in the time of the master's coming "absence" — during which rebels will continue to rise up and servants will continue to be tested.

It seems as if the arrangement of the colt as his mount for this final stage of the journey (vv. 29-34) was (as in the parable) intended to defuse false expectations of imminent messianic victory. This was not the warhorse of a conqueror, but a borrowed young ass which signified that its rider came in peace. The incident reveals Jesus' quiet authority over both people and animals. No doubt Luke intended us to meditate on the truth disclosed by certain details of the story. No one had yet sat on the colt (v. 30), just as no one had yet lain in Jesus' tomb (23:53): these were vessels set aside for holy use. The same word *(kyrios)* is used for the animal's "owners" (v. 33) and the "Lord" who needed it (vv. 31, 34): he is its true owner and master. He is also the prophet whose words come true (v. 32).

This attempt by Jesus to defuse euphoria, however, seems, according to Luke's account especially, to have misfired. The disciples who had fetched the colt threw their garments on it and "set Jesus upon it" (v. 35). Matthew and Mark both keep Jesus in control at this point, stating simply that Jesus sat; Luke implies that the disciples had an agenda. For the disciples, it seems, the very act of securing a beast to ride on may have suggested triumph — especially if reinforced by the memory of Zechariah's prophecy, cited by Matthew and John, that Zion's *king* would come to her riding on an ass (Zech. 9:9). The spreading of garments in the road (Luke 19:36) was a sign of homage for a king (cf. 2 Kings 9:13).

Matthew and Mark paint the subsequent scene as one in which Jesus simply becomes the focal point for the crowd's general enthusiasm as they chant the Passover psalms on the way to Jerusalem, in the highly charged atmosphere of first-century messianic expectation — no doubt having found a newly intense if vaguely understood hope that the great exodus events were in some way going to be repeated. Luke, however, says specifically that it was the "multitude of the disciples" who took the lead in the acclamations; they "began to rejoice and praise God with a loud voice for all the mighty works that they had seen" (v. 37). For Luke this is more than heightened Passover excitement; this is the praise of God by the new people of God for his mighty acts seen in Jesus. Such praise, with rejoicing, attended the births of John and Jesus (Luke 1:14, 46-55, 64, 67-79; 2:13-14, 28, 38) and would attend the birth of the new missionary movement at Pentecost (Acts 2:41). Luke pictures these disciples turning the spotlight of Psalm 118:26 directly on to Jesus, for here in verse 38 the words of the psalm ("Blessed is he . . .") have been altered to read "Blessed is *the King* who comes in the name of the Lord." The addition of "Peace in heaven" to "glory in the highest" again recalls the song of the angels at Jesus' birth (Luke 2:14), as well as hinting that "peace on earth," announced to the shepherds, is delayed in its outworking, though decided by God. The tableau has become for Luke another occasion in the drama of Jesus and his followers which bears strange witness to his glory. But it is a deeply ironic occasion for him. The parable of the pounds and the use of the colt — as well as what is shortly to happen — hint at the darker side of the event. The reader rightly asks about the depth of these disciples' understanding, and reflects that the specific limitation of the praise to the disciples means that there were others who stood by silent and suspicious.

The final two verses of the passage (vv. 39-40) introduce us to some such onlookers, who were in no doubt about the focus of the disciples' acclamations. The Pharisees — perhaps, like those of 13:31, wanting to save Jesus from enemies ready to misconstrue anything he did — warn him to rebuke his disciples for attaching such honor to him (v. 39). Jesus, however, would now rather accept this praise, even from those who might misunderstand the true nature and timing of his kingly power. The time was coming for the truth to be made fully open (cf. 22:70; 23:3), and praise would happen, even if it had to be called forth from the stones (v. 40).

The scene, then, is full of symbolic meaning, but of an ambiguous kind, different for different people. For Jesus, it seems, the procuring of the colt may have been intended not so much as a thinly veiled *assertion* of his messiahship as a *repudiation of wrong notions* of his messiahship. He accepted the ascription as king, at least indirectly (v. 40), but he wanted to say to the crowds, "I am not the kind of king you expect — though still a kind with which you ought to be familiar from the Scriptures." For the crowds at large, the occasion may have been little more than one of heightened Passover fervor, perhaps with little specific expectation surrounding Jesus himself. For the disciples the event was a further sign of Jesus' kingship, already glimpsed (9:20), and aroused excited praise and expectation. For the Pharisees it spelled a serious threat to order, probably both spiritual and political. Luke and his readers, knowing the sequel, can see the full irony of the story, but also the strange glory of this humble monarch.

We believe that the "nobleman" (19:12) has now, indeed, received his "kingdom," been confirmed in his authority. But since we still live in the time before his "return" to implement it in full, we are invited back to Bethphage and Bethany, to the descent of the Mount of Olives, to see where we find ourselves. Is it among the crowds, for whom Jesus may have been no more than a convenient focus for hopes of national liberation? Is it among the enthusiastic disciples who acclaimed Jesus as King but did not yet comprehend what his "departure" would entail, for him and for them? Among the Pharisees who wanted to silence them, for whom too much adulation of Jesus was bound to lead to trouble? Or among those ready to enter the city with their Master and face whatever he will face?

Stephen I. Wright

Twenty-fifth Sunday after Pentecost, Year C

First Lesson: Haggai 1:15b–2:9
(Psalm 145:1-5, 17-21)
Second Lesson: 2 Thessalonians 2:1-5, 13-17
Gospel Lesson: Luke 20:27-38

This passage is a difficult one, especially in our own day when it seems to be composed of arcane arguments over absurd points of laws that have long been ignored by Christians. It is almost too easy to be on Jesus' side, laughing with him at the Sadducees' lack of perception. Luke has set us up to enjoy Jesus' triumph over his challengers; verse 40 can be heard with relish. But if we move too quickly to agree with Jesus' response, if we think his answer is somehow obvious, we have missed the heart of the question and the good news at the heart of Jesus' answer.

Luke uses a double irony in this story, a technique familiar from Luke

443

7:36-39. On the one hand, he sets up the hostile questioners for a fall. On the other, he uses the question they ask, a throwaway for them, to make a very profound point. This latter point is the one of most use to contemporary preachers.

This passage comes late in Luke's Gospel, and late in the church year. Jesus has made the long journey to Jerusalem (9:51–19:28) and entered the city to the praises of the people. He had been teaching "day by day in the temple" so that "all the people" were captivated and their leaders, increasingly agitated (19:47). In 20:19-20 the frustration of the leaders is again described, as is their strategy for getting Jesus: "So they watched for their opportunity and sent agents in the guise of honest men to seize on some word of his that they could use as a pretext for handing him over to the authority and jurisdiction of the governor." When we come to our passage in 20:27, we are witnesses to the second attempt to find some objectionable word of Jesus. This pericope is presented as one more attempt to destroy Jesus by those who pretend to be honest or just (Gk. *dikaios*). The hearer is warned to hear the question of the Sadducees as self-conscious and malicious pretense.

At the beginning of the passage itself, Luke again warns that this question is a trick, both because it was posed by those who would bring Jesus down and because the Sadducees do not believe in the world about which they ask. They cannot possibly care about the resurrection life, Luke tells us, because they do not believe in a resurrection. In four verses of a carefully elaborated and highly unlikely scenario, the Sadducees imply that keeping what "Moses wrote" can be incompatible with resurrection life. How can Jesus answer without speaking against Moses or the resurrection? The question is posed within the passage by a pun on resurrection. In verse 27 *anastasis* (resurrection) is used to identify the Sadducees. It appears again in verse 28 as the duty of the brother (*exanastēsē*: raise up a child). In verse 33, at the *anastasis* (resurrection) is where these two cases of raising up come into conflict. The word appears also in verses 35 and 36. Clearly it is the focus of the passage.

The Sadducean query is based on Deuteronomy 25:6-10, where Levitical marriage is prescribed when a man dies childless. These verses enjoin a man to take his brother's widow in marriage and to beget a child with her. Verses 6, 7, and 8 each refer to the purpose of this injunction, to "perpetuate the dead brother's name in Israel." Death threatens the people, and these God-commanded marriages (with the begetting of children) are a way to thwart death. The command of the law has as its purpose the continuation of the brother's life among the people of God by the continuation of his name. But if the brothers all live a resurrected life after death and the woman with them, how is the marital arrangement managed?

In Luke 20:27-33 the repetitive mention of the brothers suggests an unrelenting battle with death in which death appears to win. One brother after another falls. One brother after another is unable to perpetuate his name in Israel. This tragedy for the family is precisely the one which the command to remarriage seeks to mitigate. Yet the remedy becomes absurd if there is a resurrection and no one will be blotted out of Israel in the afterlife. The Sadducees wonder why God would command such a remedy in the face of resurrection.

Jesus takes the question seriously, perhaps for the sake of his hearers and/or Luke's audience. (We include ourselves in the second group.) Jesus does not, however, try to prioritize or manage the intricate relationships of this complex resurrected family. He does not address the Deuteronomic law on its own terms. Rather than undercut or devalue either the law or Moses as a bona fide speaker of God's word, Jesus shifts the playing field. He contrasts the two ages, "this age" and its children in verse 34 and "that age" and those who are worthy of it in verse 35. He denies that God is a God of the dead, but insists that God is a God of the living (v. 38). What Moses has written for us has nothing to do with the relationships that will hold in resurrected life. Everything changes when we are no longer able to die.

This is his central point. Note that there are two uses of "for" (gar) in verse 36. With these words we get the reason for the distinctions in marriage practice between this age and the next (vv. 34-35). Verse 35 and verse 36 emphasize resurrection structurally: "Those considered worthy . . . of the resurrection of the dead . . . are children of God since they are children of the resurrection." In between we learn that such children of the resurrection do not participate in marriage because they are no longer able to die. They are equal to the angels and children of the resurrection. In other words, remarriage for the continuation of one's name is irrelevant when death is no longer a threat to one's life and participation with the covenant people of God.

For Jesus, Scripture proves the truth of his claim that because of resurrection the relationship of God and God's people continues after earthly death. He cites the present tense verb used by God in God's own self-identification as the God now of patriarchs long dead from an earthly point of view. God is the God of those who continue to live with God. That is, in fact, the next point. God is just that God with whom relationship (in v. 36 being a child of God) is for life. Of the many ways that God could have been identified, it is this particularly scriptural phrase with this particular interpretation that Jesus chooses. He thus uses Moses as his own authority, creating a community of interpretation with the Sadducees, and makes his own claim on the basis of Moses. God is a God of the living, even those who seem to us to be dead. There must be a resurrection, since God's self-definition is as one who continues in relationship. "*For* all live in God" (v. 38).

His interpretation is accepted and appreciated even by his enemies. There can be no refutation of such a powerful reading concerning God. "You have spoken well," some of the scribes say. Indeed, Jesus' argument was not only made on the basis of a source trusted by all the Jews, including the Sadducees, but it pushed them to think more deeply about their own tradition and about God. Who could ask for more than that in a theological argument? The answer to this question goes to the heart of what will happen to Jesus himself in the final chapters of the Gospel and to the heart of our own lives together as people of God.

Here in Luke's Gospel those who understand themselves as children of God, or yearn so to do, are pressed to question their own interpretations, even the best intentioned of them. A God of the living whose children we are is a lively God whose love is the basis for all of life (all live in him, v. 38). Given our human limitations, it is not possible for us to keep pace with the liveliness and great breadth of one who is God for all in this age and the next. Nonetheless, it is our calling. As Jesus describes this God who will not allow relationships to dissolve because of death, he uses Scripture and his own Spirit-led experience to challenge the limited thinking of the Sadducees.

Challenges to limited thinking, to time-honored traditions, even to our most loved and useful guiding tenets, are often not welcome. How easy for Christians to imagine that the role of Jesus was to challenge and reform the frustrating legalism of Jewish institutions and bring new Christian light and life to these stubborn and wrongheaded folks. Note well, however, that Luke's story shows us an argument *among* Jews about who God is and what we have most to hope for from God. Such arguing continues among Christians to this day. Indeed, it must, for we have a living God, an ancient Scripture, and many different Spirit-led experiences.

A preacher might well help us to imagine ourselves as the Sadducees, who for reasons of their own wanted to silence Jesus the rabble-rouser. Instead they got a profound confession about God's determination to be the God of the living even after we die. They heard Jesus insist that God is a determined lover who will not let the beloved go. This insistence, Jesus says, is at the heart of Scripture, and he quotes Exodus to prove it. Not only is this at the heart of Scripture, but the confession that God is a God of the living is of the utmost importance to everyone. To use our limited, even our best limited, concepts about our present lives to speculate about the future is a waste of time. God's measureless love that will not be broken by death will not be confounded by human interpretations and systems.

Sarah Henrich

Twenty-sixth Sunday after Pentecost, Year C

First Lesson: Isaiah 65:17-25
(Isaiah 12)
Second Lesson: 2 Thessalonians 3:6-13
Gospel Lesson: Luke 21:5-19

In spite of its dire warnings of cosmic, political, and personal distress, this lection does not invite end-time speculation. Indeed, the preacher who preaches this small piece of Jesus' much longer speech (Luke 21:3-36) should attend carefully to the brunt of what is said.

Chapters 20 and 21 in Luke's Gospel are full of examples of Jesus' teaching. Jesus had finally reached the end of his journey to Jerusalem in 19:28 (or 19:41, where he begins the long climb to the city). He drove the traders out of the temple and then spent his days teaching there. Luke tells us that the Jewish leaders were hostile and eager to bring about Jesus' death (20:19) while the people "hung on his words" (19:48). It was to Jesus' words that the leaders turned, hoping to find some evidence to hand him over to the authorities (20:20). In chapter 20 Jesus is publicly tested repeatedly and silences his opponents in public as well. In chapter 21 he turns to his disciples with words of prophecy about what is ahead and words to encourage their stalwart endurance.

Our section is at the beginning of Jesus' long speech to his disciples. It is a speech to insiders, to those who trust Jesus and seek to endure, to the church. By the time this Gospel was written, Luke's church knew, as do we, that many of these predictions had come true. Jerusalem had fallen, the temple had been destroyed, there had been earthquakes and famines. According to the Acts of the Apostles, also from Luke's hand, those who believed that Jesus was God's Messiah had indeed been handed over to kings and governors and had opportunity to testify. Some had been martyred. Verses 6, and 8 through 17, show us Jesus speaking the truth about what was to come. That Jesus is clearly correct about the things that have happened makes him all the more credible in regard to those things that have not yet come about (see esp. vv. 25-32).

It also makes him credible in regard to the instructions he gives the disciples. These instructions are central to the passage for Luke and certainly for contemporary preachers. The disciples ask for a sign. Why not? The temple was huge, beautiful, impressive, and backed by the might of Herod, who was backed by the might of Rome. For it to be so thoroughly destroyed that not one stone would be left on another meant the undoing of life as the disciples knew it. It would be good to be forewarned of such a change.

Jesus does not answer their question. Instead he almost teases them with the impossibility of answering. He lists a series of cataclysmic events, from wars and rebellions to plagues and portents. Then, just as he seems to get to the climax of his list, just as the end draws near, he backtracks and says, "But before all this happens. . . ." The list is no timetable. At best, it must be renumbered to accommodate another long list of difficulties that precedes it. Who can ascertain when all these things will happen? The refusal to set a timetable or even establish a clear sequence of events is repeated in Acts 1:6-7, where Jesus does answer the disciples' "time" question with a simple "It's not for you to know. . . ."

Not only does Jesus make it impossible to develop a timetable from his list of woes, but he also provides a much more important series of negative and positive instructions throughout chapter 21. In our section we get this list of negatives:

Do not be misled (v. 8).

Do not follow them (false claimants to messiahship, v. 8).

Do not panic (v. 9).

Do not prepare your defense beforehand (v. 14).

It is clear from this list that preoccupation with end-time scenarios is not appropriate for believers. The injunctions Jesus gives suggest that patience and discernment are the characteristics that Christian assemblies should cultivate. As he moves along further in this speech, Jesus says it will be impossible to miss the real events as they unfold. Some events will be opportunities for personal and corporate witness; others will simply call for long-suffering and hope. Just as believers cannot prepare a timetable and check off events and know when to anticipate the end, so they ought not spend time in anxiety about that future.

Luke's Jesus does offer constructive words to his disciples as well. These positive instructions and/or promises provide the core of this passage and of Luke's Gospel as a whole. This group includes:

This will be your opportunity to testify/witness (v. 13).
I myself will give you such words and wisdom which all those opposed to you cannot resist or refute (v. 15).
Not a hair of your head will be lost (v. 18).
By standing firm you will win yourselves life (v. 19).

Jesus puts a positive spin on the difficulties that may be encountered by believers by suggesting that these will be an opportunity to witness. These opportunities are abundantly illustrated in Acts in, for example, the stories of Stephen (Acts 7), Peter and Cornelius (Acts 10), Paul in Malta (Acts 28:1-10), to name only a few. Paul had already spoken in a similar way to the Philippians and had put a positive spin on his imprisonment as a chance to witness effectively to those around him (Phil. 1:12-14). The opportunity to witness fearlessly was a theme that significantly shaped the early church. Because this opportunity was likely to be given, Jesus' promise that he himself would provide the words of witness removed the focus from individual preparation.

Most important is the final verse in this passage. Again we see the emphasis; endurance or long-suffering *(hypomonē)* is placed in an emphatic position. By "hanging in there" you will gain your lives. (All the "you" words are plural in this passage.) Heroics are not called for, although patience itself can be heroic. It is significant that *hypomonē* appears in only one other location in Luke's Gospel, in 8:15. This verse is the climax of Luke's own version of the parable of the sower (Matt. 13:18-23; Mark 4:13-20). All three Evangelists close their interpretations with the need to bring forth good fruit, but only Luke speaks of "holding it [the word] fast" and bringing forth fruit "with patience." Likewise, only Luke changes Mark to suggest that a problem with the fruit, even for those who hear, is that it does not mature (8:14, *telesphoreō,* a word used only here in the New Testament).

These two words, *hypomonē* (endurance) and *telesphoreō* (coming to maturity), are worth mentioning. Luke alone of the Evangelists uses these terms, and, indeed, puts them into Jesus' own speech to his disciples near the beginning and end of his ministry. They delineate fruitful ways of being Christian for those who cannot know the end. Between 8:15 and 21:19 Luke has provided a story that gives both descriptions and examples of ways of being mature, patient, and fruitful. A preacher who reaches the end of a year

449

of preaching on Luke can call on many texts to develop these themes. One might consider the Sermon on the Plain, Jesus' command to have mercy in the parable of the Good Samaritan, the words about the children of light and darkness in the parable of the unjust steward, the call to perseverance in prayer, the way in which Zacchaeus chose to live, the challenge that Lazarus presented to the rich man and his brothers. These stories show us the hard work, the patience-demanding work, of living in the world with God's kingdom both around the corner and among us. This is where we are called to be fruitful. Our witness is our fruit and the words we are given to testify to the source of our life together. We have here Luke's challenge to the church, and it is of no mean proportion.

For Luke there are more important things for a Christian community to consider than end times. The "end" had been delayed past several points when it seems to have been anticipated. Luke's Gospel provides a way for the community to understand itself as earthbound for a longer haul. Jesus' instructions here and throughout the Gospel, as well as in the book of Acts, set some guidelines for Christian life together.

This passage, along with verses 34-36, shows us the heart of the church. We live by the promise that we will win life by trusting in the words of Jesus. This is the major theme of verses 5-19. All disciples have heard from Jesus that our "standing firm" includes the bearing of mature fruit. It is the vocation of the church to remind us of the promises, both of the winning of life and that God's kingdom will draw near (v. 31). It is also the church's vocation to hold before us those behaviors that we might call "mature fruit." It is the calling of the church and individual members thereof to keep alert for these fruits and glimpses of promise keeping in a world that has long preferred varieties of sedation except in moments of high drama. "Be on the alert, don't let yourself be dulled," for opportunities will come your way and you will win life, says Jesus. Alert for signs of the presence and the coming of the kingdom, yes. But alert also for opportunities to testify that the same Jesus who is Lord of life has commanded his disciples to "give food to the other servants at the right time. Blessed is that slave whom his Lord, when he comes, will find doing just that" (12:42-43). A sermon about the bearing of mature fruit and discerning opportunities for witness that come to us will be true to the intent of this chapter.

Sarah Henrich

First Sunday of Advent, Year C

First Lesson: Jeremiah 33:14-16
(Psalm 25:1-10)
Second Lesson: 1 Thessalonians 3:9-13
Gospel Lesson: Luke 21:25-36

This passage continues the apocalyptic discourse begun by Jesus at 21:5, but now he raises the stakes. Coming as they do directly upon the heels of his prediction of the fall of the temple and Jerusalem, the words communicate a time of great cataclysm, the dimensions of which are larger than the planet earth. The signs he identified before could have been local and regional in the form of earthquakes, famines, and floods (v. 11), even though they extended in a nonspecific way to include "great signs from heaven." Now the sun, the moon, and stars will demonstrate signs of this end time. Jesus clearly speaks of a cosmic event of universal significance. The signs are not something that can be restricted to this or that people or place, for they will come to all and cannot be escaped. They are experienced by entire nations that are in "anxiety" and "perplexity," particularly at what is happening with the sea because of its roaring and the sound of its surf. People will be so distressed they will faint with fear and will worry that even worse things will come upon them. Luke's version differs notably from Mark's in that it comes directly after the Lukan announcement that Jerusalem will fall and "will be trampled on by the Gentiles, until the times of the Gentiles are fulfilled" (v. 24). The word for Gentiles here is *ethnos*, the same word that most versions translate literally as nations in verse 25 in order to retain the universal status of the distress, but the prominence of the event for both Israel and the Gentiles is clear. The apocalyptic signs (vv. 25-26) are typical signs of the end times in the Old Testament (see Isa. 13:10; Joel 2:10; Zeph. 1:15), but they are not signs the Gentiles necessarily will recognize as predicted. Even "the powers of heaven will be shaken," a reference at minimum to those things people take for granted, perhaps the rhythm of night and day or the planets in their courses. Chaos will be manifest.

Perhaps a break should take place in the biblical text between verse 26 and verse 27, for at the end of 26 the tension that has been building since the beginning of verse 5 is the greatest. The people in the text and its readers are all wondering "what is coming upon the world" (v. 26). Luke builds an expectation that utter destruction will now be visited upon the world. The nations will be getting what they deserve, for what is coming is not a freak of nature but an intentional act of God, who is bringing forth "days of vengeance" (v. 22).

Verse 27 poses a surprise, however. Instead of destruction, the prophecy of Daniel 7:13-14 is fulfilled: the Son of Man approaches in a cloud with "power" and "great glory," key words that allude to divine power and the Messiah. Clearly this coming still marks "the end" spoken about in verse 9, presumably for all who are ashamed of Jesus Christ when the Son of Man comes (9:26), but the focus shifts away from the fate of these others to the hope that awaits those disciples who have been unwavering in their faith. What seemed like destruction is in fact "your redemption" drawing near (21:28).

The next sections, the parable of the fig tree and the warning for disciples to be attentive, come as a commentary on the preceding picture of the apocalypse. Just as the fig tree sprouts its leaves as an indication that summer is at hand (v. 30), so too these signs of the end times are evidence of the nearness of the kingdom of God. Concern over the reference to summer rather than harvest, which might make more sense, seems misguided. The point is simply that when the fig tree "and all the trees" sprout leaves, summer is at hand, and the signs of the end times will similarly mark unmistakably what is about to happen. Not only will the people "see" and "know" it, but "this generation will not pass away" (v. 32) before it happens.

Is "this generation" a reference to the people who will see these signs? Origen may have been wise in saying that not every biblical passage has a literal meaning: there is no fully satisfactory scholarly interpretation of this phrase although nearly every possibility has been ventured. Perhaps that ambiguity is part of the point (Matt. 24:36 and Mark 13:32 simply say, "But about that day . . . no one knows").

A word about "when" is in order. Jesus specifies in his complete discourse a precise sequence: the destruction of the temple, persecution, the fall of Jerusalem, the cosmic signs, continuing persecution (v. 36), and the coming of the Son of Man. Some scholars date Luke just before the fall of Jerusalem, and some shortly after, the latter arguing that he is the only synoptic writer to mention the fall and therefore must know of it. That dating can diminish the prophetic dimension of Jesus' words here (i.e., one might conclude that Luke put words in Jesus' mouth); alternatively, Luke's case for the nearness of the eschaton is strengthened by his ability to point to a material event already fulfilling one of Jesus' predicted signs. However the complex question of date is resolved, there is no mistaking the sense of the immediacy of the parousia, just as in Acts there is an effort to explain its delay.

Even the clearest of signs can be missed by those who are "weighed down with dissipation and drunkenness and the worries of this life" (v. 34). Jesus therefore exhorts his followers to be sober and alert, to pray for strength to withstand "these things," and to stand before the Son of Man. Jesus' words apparently had a powerful effect on those he taught in the temple, for their numbers increased daily (v. 38).

In the last few decades several global realities have been reminders of the possibility of end times. No sooner had the Cold War ended and the threat of nuclear holocaust been reduced (the famous countdown clock had its hands moved back a few minutes away from 12:00), than the press was filled with successive warnings about the ozone hole altering DNA in frogs and humans, global warming and the rising of the seas, the threat of oceans being contaminated by radioactivity from the rusting hulks of the abandoned Russian Bering Sea fleet, and NASA searching for rogue asteroids that could wipe out life as we know it on this planet. In moderation such warnings are valuable cautions, but they are easily abused by religious people as determinative of when the time will be. It can come at any time, and the church can learn from Luke some ways to frame the issue.

First, it is important to affirm that there will be an end time. Human life does have limitations set upon it, both in terms of individual actions and our time as a race upon this planet. Whether the end comes sooner or later, and whether it comes individually or collectively, an end will come. This can be a fearsome possibility, and yet, in the knowledge that we are God's creatures, we can discover the true freedom and grace of being God's creatures.

This biblical passage is not just a metaphor about death, individual or collective. It is talking about the eschaton, the reality of the end of time — but not the end of life with God. Our problem can be that we focus on the signs as though they have some independent significance. They derive all their significance from their author, and therefore in seeing them our focus is rightly on God and what God is doing. Our second learning therefore can be that God is in charge of this end time and all time. As humans we are not. Just as we know God who is revealed fully in Jesus Christ through the Holy Spirit, we are called to trust God in contemplating the future, for it is this same God who comes to us at the end of time. Time will end, but God's Word will not (v. 33).

Third, this God who created us at the beginning is worthy of all trust. God is not a spoiled child who is about to have a tantrum and destroy creation. Rather, the eschaton should be regarded as the time of fulfillment of all of God's promises. There is a sentence upon all who have failed to live according to God's law, and it is a good thing: just as God sets a limit on the

453

power evil can have over us, God sets a limit on all injustice and sin. It will not continue. Its days are numbered.

Fourth, this sentence is also passed upon each of us, for no one is capable of doing everything Jesus calls people to do in order to stand before the Son of Man. If we had been capable, Jesus need not have come the first time. Jesus instructs us not to wait until the end time to get our relationship right with God. In other words, what makes us right for meeting Christ at the end time is our relationship with him in the present that has already been defined by the cross, the resurrection, and the ascension. When we think of the future, the clearest sign of what to expect has been given in Christ and his ongoing presence in the church.

Finally, when we are preaching on the end times, we need not be caught up in the gloom of those who do not have faith and may be contemplating these issues. Certainly it would not seem right for us to be focused on the destruction of others, nor does Luke take that stance. When the Son of Man comes at the end of time, the fate of all nations will be up to him and not to us, so we rightly leave the judging to him (6:37). Rather, Luke focuses on the glory of the moment. Whether we contemplate the eschaton or just the end of our own personal days, we are wise to keep the wonderful message of Jesus in this text before us: when we think that the end is at hand, when we think we cannot cope any more, when all seems lost, when God seems to have forgotten about us, when the suffering of others continues unabated, we are not furthest from our salvation but closest to it. Christ may always be found in the midst of greatest need. Look up, not down, for your redemption is drawing near (21:28).

Paul Scott Wilson

Christ the King, Year C

First Lesson: Jeremiah 23:1-6
(Luke 1:68-79)
Second Lesson: Colossians 1:11-20
Gospel Lesson: Luke 23:33-43

L uke's account of the crucifixion of Jesus consists of a sequence of brief snapshots through which his readers can glimpse various dimensions of its meaning. Luke omits some of the detail of Matthew and Mark but adds unique material — Jesus' prayer in verse 34 and the exchange between the criminals and Jesus in verses 39-43 — which enables us to catch sight of Jesus continuing in these last moments what, according to Luke, has been the dominant activity of his ministry: mediating the forgiving love of God to sinful people.

The scene is set tersely in verse 33. Luke brings forward to this point the mention of the two criminals. This visualizing of the three crosses at the outset of the story emphasizes Jesus' identification with sinners that has been so evident through his ministry (cf. 3:21; 5:29; 7:36-50; 15:1-2; 19:5-6). The criminals are "evildoers" rather than the "robbers" of Matthew and Mark. For Luke, at some geographical as well as historical distance, the important thing is not what particular crimes these two were guilty of, but their general character. The identification of Jesus with sinners has indeed reached a climax at this point: we might say that throughout the Gospel the "sinners" have become worse — from the ordinary, undifferentiated "crowds" who went to the Jordan for baptism; through the tax collectors and those specifically designated "sinners," including a prostitute; to evildoers put to death for their wicked deeds. The picture builds to make the point powerfully: Jesus shared fellowship with, and therefore incurred shame with, "sinners" of all kinds, including the worst; and so he can save any and all.

Now that we can *see* the three crosses together, the rest of the story invites us especially to *hear.* Two sayings of Jesus (vv. 34, 43) frame a succession of remarks by others (vv. 35, 37, 39, 40-42). At the center stands a silent visual testimony, the inscription indicating the charge on which Jesus had been crucified (v. 38).

The sayings of Jesus reveal his personal concern not just for "sinners" in general but for the individuals around him: those whose task it was to hammer in the nails, those who shared his fate of crucifixion. The prayer to his

Father (v. 34), omitted in some of the oldest manuscripts, is surely at least true both to the spirit of Jesus' dealings with people and to the meaning of his death as the church came to discern it. In life and death Jesus intercedes with the Father for his fellow human beings who grope in the fog of ignorance about the enormity of their own deeds. Such "ignorance" in Scripture is not an attenuating circumstance which might cause God to relent, but a sinful condition from which God's forgiveness is the only release.

This prayer also enables us to see in perspective the sayings of others which follow. For Luke makes it quite clear that in these gruesome hours at the place of the Skull, the person with the clearest mind about what is happening is the one whose mind ought, one might think, to have been twisted out of shape by sheer torture, bewilderment, and shame. Jesus is in touch with the Father; he is lucid enough to recognize the ignorance of the soldiers; he knows where he and one of his neighbors are going (v. 43). The others who speak, however, demonstrate very clearly that indeed they know neither what they do nor what they say.

Since in Luke the "people," the faithful *laos,* say nothing, but only watch (v. 35) — unlike the "passersby" in Matthew and Mark — the first bystanders to speak are the "rulers" of Judaism who had finally engineered Jesus' death. Their tone is scoffing; they defy him to save himself as he "saved" others, if he is the Christ. Luke, and we, can see heavy irony here, on several levels.

First, we can see in the word "saved" a fullness of meaning quite unperceived by the scoffers, for whom it would have signified the outwardly manifest transformations wrought by Jesus. The Christian meaning of "salvation" includes these aspects but goes beyond them to embrace every dimension of life, including the conquest of death itself. Second, their words "he saved others" are presumably spoken in grudging recognition of Jesus' work but in complete blindness to the truth that work was meant to reveal. Third, Christians early on realized that it was precisely because Jesus did *not* save himself that he was able to "save" others in the larger personal and global sense that God purposed; the cross was in God's definite plan (Acts 2:23; 3:18). Fourth, we can see from our post-Easter perspective that as the "Chosen One" of God — a similar word is used by Luke at the transfiguration scene (9:35) — it was indeed Jesus' calling to "bring forth justice to the nations," but not through a show of assertive power (Isa. 42:1-4). It turned out to be in the very negation of power that his nature as the Chosen One, God's anointed King, was revealed.

The next group to comment are the soldiers. Luke thus presents representatives of the Gentile world as being on a level in their ignorant scorn with those of Judaism — just as, later, representatives of both are seen as drawn toward Jesus: the Roman centurion who recognizes that Jesus is "righteous" or "innocent" (23:47) and Joseph, the "good and righteous" Jew who had not consented to the plot to kill Jesus (23:50-51) and takes his body for burial (23:53-54). The soldiers' words in verse 37 are to be interpreted in the light of their attitude seen in verse 36 (cf. the attitude and words of the rulers in v. 35). To them the idea that Jesus is "King of the Jews" — the misunderstood claim on account of which the Jewish leaders brought him before the Roman governor (23:1-3) — is ludicrous. In the soldiers' mouths, the idea that Jesus might "save himself" has become a mere taunt; there is none of the rulers' smug and misguided sense of contrast between the power Jesus exercised for others and his total powerlessness on his own behalf. The offering of the vinegar (v. 36), like the casting of lots for garments (v. 34), is a vivid memory preserved by each Evangelist; both are scriptural allusions which show Jesus as epitomizing the tradition of the suffering of the righteous (cf. Pss. 22:18; 69:21). They remind us poignantly of what has been called "the banality of evil." For some, the crucifixion of Jesus was all in a day's work. Herein, for the Christian, lies part of its mysterious paradox.

After the silent glimpse of the inscription over Jesus (v. 38), mentioned by Luke here in connection with the soldiers' taunts and making us pause to see the words once again with characteristic double entendre — for us this *was* the King of the Jews, but not in a way understood by any at the time — attention shifts to the two criminals. The first comes out with a taunt similar to that of the rulers and soldiers, in his sarcasm calling on Jesus to save not only himself but also his fellow victims. "Save" for this man had a brutally physical sense; again we can see an ironic contrast between this desperate but unbelieving cry and the truth that "whoever calls on the name of the Lord [like the other criminal!] shall be saved" (Acts 2:21).

The second criminal sees that a right response to their situation is not sarcasm but the fear of God. His fellow wrongdoer is in no position to strike out verbally at Jesus, for he is being justly punished, whereas Jesus, who has been condemned along with him, has done nothing wrong (vv. 40, 41). In this response Luke dramatizes the implications of the contrast between the central figure and the outer two. The sight of the righteous man thus condemned should lead not to bitterness, but awe. It is so for us also, as in the two criminals we see ourselves under sentence of death on account of sin, and in Jesus the righteous one also condemned. Before there is any understanding of this mystery, any theory of atonement, there will be deep wonder and reverence before the ways of God.

In an extraordinary moment we then imagine the second criminal turning in his agony to Jesus as he utters the words "Jesus, remember me when you come into your kingdom" (v. 42). What could he have meant? Luke perhaps simply intends us to see here one who was able to penetrate through the fog of misunderstanding which concealed the true meaning of the title "King of the Jews" from almost everyone else on the scene. This man perceived, however dimly, something beyond the bitter irony of "failed" messianic pretensions. Something draws him to believe that, contrary to appearance, this is not failure; and that when Jesus receives his kingly power, he may be kindly disposed to such a supplicant. Many Jews believed in resurrection, especially in connection with martyrdom for faithfulness to Yahweh. This criminal apparently believes that though he is being justly punished, the faithful one beside him may nevertheless own him when he is raised to kingly power. He wants to make his peace with the coming King before he is enthroned.

Jesus' memorable answer makes a promise for a future much more immediate than the man seems to have envisaged (v. 43). Here is the last of Jesus' great "Today's" in Luke (cf. 4:21; 19:5, 9). Luke stresses the decisiveness of Jesus' time among us, the immediacy of God's gift. For the criminal there would be no long, anxious wait. That very day he would be with Jesus in "paradise," the park of rest and refreshment where the faithful dead await resurrection. Throughout his ministry Jesus had placed himself alongside sinful people, and in so doing brought liberation — physical, social, spiritual. In this moment of ultimate identification with sinners, the ultimate liberation is promised: release from death as bondage, as condemnation, as finality, into fellowship with Jesus in paradise. And such unrestricted fellowship with Jesus *is* paradise.

Stephen I. Wright

Resurrection of the Lord, Year C

First Lesson: Acts 10:34-43
(Psalm 118:1-2, 14-24)
Second Lesson: 1 Corinthians 15:19-26
Gospel Lesson: Luke 24:1-12

The women cannot complete their task of anointing Jesus' body until the first day of the week, when they approach the tomb at early dawn. These are the same women mentioned in 23:49 and 23:55 who had come with him from Galilee (8:1-3), had seen him crucified, and had seen him laid in the tomb. Luke wants no break in the story, even to tell their names, for he must establish that the women from Galilee who went away from the tomb to prepare the spices are the same women who return on Easter morning. They know Jesus and his teachings well. They are people of worthy character who come to the tomb in the expectation of finding his body. They have not mistaken his tomb for some other one. Their credentials are important if their witness is to be believed. Their actual names are withheld until the end of the story at verse 10, Mary Magdalene, Joanna, Mary the mother of James, and "the other women," as if to underline that there were more than the quorum of two required to verify witness under the law (Deut. 19:15).

The stone has already been rolled away from the entrance to the tomb by the time they arrive. As tombs generally were not spacious (see also Luke 24:12), we must assume that the five or more women were not in the tomb all at once and that the subsequent events take place outside it. Discovery that it is empty leaves the women "perplexed," the same word used to describe the anxiety of the nations at the raging of the seas (21:25). The empty tomb proves nothing in itself to the women (in contrast to Peter and the Beloved Apostle in John 20:8); they do not know what to think. While they are in this highly anxious state, two "men" stand beside them in clothing as bright as lightning. Their garments are like Jesus' own clothing in the transfiguration (Luke 9:29) and the garments of the two men mentioned at the ascension (Acts 1:10). The women are terrified and look to the ground (by contrast see Luke 21:28). The angels simply pronounce their message, omitting the words "Do not be afraid" that accompany each of the earlier angelic appearances to Zechariah (1:13), Mary (1:30), and the shepherds (2:10). Here the angels' words affirm the fact and reality of Jesus' resurrection: "Why do you look for the living among the dead?" As if to leave no doubt

459

about the import of their words, they add, "He is not here, but has risen." If they want to find their Lord, they are to look away from the empty tomb.

The angels do not try to prove the fact of the resurrection, but impress upon the women that the resurrection was foretold by Jesus in his own teaching. In other words, the resurrection is not a departure from what Jesus said and did in his earthly ministry but rather is its culmination and the fulfillment of God's purpose. The angels remind the women of Jesus' words (that are not specifically recorded earlier in Luke), "The Son of Man must be handed over to sinners, and be crucified, and on the third day rise again." The angels' action in illuminating Jesus' words for the women anticipates Jesus' own action of illuminating the Scriptures for the disciples on the road to Emmaus in the next scene (24:26-27). Both events point to the sufficiency of scriptural witness for belief in the resurrection. The effect of the angels' words on the women is that they do remember what Jesus said, and their anxiety is mentioned no further. They do not continue looking for his body, nor is any further conversation with the angels recorded. Instead, they return "to the eleven and to all the rest" to proclaim to them what they have witnessed. They believe because God has revealed God's truth to them.

In neither the case of the women nor of the disciples is there a predisposition to believe that Jesus is raised. This is not something they expect, secretly long to happen, or even conceive of. Rather, it is something they greet initially with anxiety and terror in one case and disbelief in the other. Their reluctance to believe can be interpreted as further evidence that their testimony is trustworthy. The men choose to think that what the women say in their grief is empty chatter ("an idle tale") rather than the most important news of their lives. Peter is at least open to the promise of the women's words and runs to the tomb to see for himself. In his case the testimony of the women, combined with the empty tomb and finding the linen cloths "by themselves," is enough to cause him to wonder or be "amazed at what had happened" (v. 12). He accepts the women's testimony and presumably believes that Christ is risen, but for the fullest expression of faith he must await his own experience (v. 34). The text gives no evidence of him going home immediately to testify, as the women had done.

As with so many biblical texts, the preacher can easily get swept away in the swirl of human activity and fail to give adequate focus to what God is doing in and behind this text. God has raised Jesus from the dead, and in so doing has authenticated all that Jesus did and said. What Jesus promised by way of salvation, God has fulfilled in raising him from the dead. What he promised by way of liberation for the sinners, the poor, and the outcast, God has demonstrated to be accomplished in breaking the bonds of death.

The kingdom of God that was present in Jesus' person and proclamation during his earthly ministry draws near to all people in his resurrection. Through Christ God reaches out to all the world in love and forgiveness, that looking on Christ we may "see" and "know" God (21:31) in the full sufficiency of God's grace.

Perhaps as evidence of the priority God places on the poor and oppressed, God chooses the women to be the first to know of the resurrection and to proclaim it. Seeing and knowing are important for Luke, who alone gives particular emphasis to the physical body of the resurrected Christ. The women believe on the basis of seeing the empty tomb and being encountered by the angelic messengers God sends to them. Peter and the disciples believe and proclaim when the risen Christ appears to them. Anytime any of us proclaims Jesus Christ to those who have not experienced him, our words are bound to sound like chatter or idle tales. But for Luke there is no need to minimize the importance of an encounter with the risen Christ for faith. People are entitled to see and thereby to know, for such experience is not trumped up; it is real, and God offers it to the faithful. Experience is important. As a church, we do not ask people to believe in something they cannot experience; rather, we offer them in word, sacrament, and other means an encounter with God, who comes to them not as information or abstract ideas but as an event that is both personal and Personal.

The angels give the women instruction in the continuity between what Jesus taught in his earthly ministry and his resurrection. This is important in helping to confirm that the Jesus who is raised from the dead is the same Jesus who died on the cross, not some other being. In the same manner God offers us knowledge of Christ through Scripture, that in knowing him there we may recognize him in our own daily lives in and through the power of the Holy Spirit.

Paul Scott Wilson

Third Sunday of Easter, Year A

First Lesson: Acts 2:14a, 36-41
(Psalm 116:1-4, 12-19)
Second Lesson: 1 Peter 1:17-23
Gospel Lesson: Luke 24:13-35

Two followers of Jesus are hiking out of Jerusalem on the first Easter morning. They are not among Jesus' central circle but are just ordinary disciples — this is the only time Cleopas is mentioned in the Bible. The other follower is not named. They have seen Jesus die and be buried, and now that the Sabbath is over they are journeying to Emmaus, "about seven miles from Jerusalem." As they walk a fellow traveler whom they do not recognize as Jesus ("their eyes were kept from recognizing him," v. 16) becomes involved in their discussion. They walk with him not just for company, one presumes, although hospitality in that culture was important, but for the added safety of traveling in numbers to discourage thieves.

The stranger does not seem to know anything about the events in Jerusalem. He simply asks them what they have been discussing, and the two disciples respond as though their topic of conversation should have been obvious, as though there could be none other: "Are you the only stranger in Jerusalem who does not know the things that have taken place there in these days?" (v. 18). They then instruct him about Jesus of Nazareth, who was "a prophet mighty in deed and word before God and all the people." They focus primarily on Jesus' death, placing responsibility on "our chief priests and leaders" (v. 20) for handing him over to the Roman authorities to be tried, condemned, and crucified. Their hope is expressed in the past tense — they "had hoped" he was the Messiah ("the one to redeem Israel") — the implication being that such hopes are abandoned now.

Verse 22 represents a break in their story between two days previous and the current day. The disciples do not seem heartened by the events of the morning; rather, they seem baffled, incapable of adding any interpretation as to the meaning of the events. They simply report what has transpired: Some of the women claimed to have been to the tomb, where they saw angels who told them that Jesus was alive. Other disciples went to the tomb (presumably after Peter in v. 12), and no one had seen Jesus.

At this point Jesus chastises them for being "foolish" and "slow of heart to believe." (This may be Luke's way of saying that here are the real "fools," not the women in verse 11.) Jesus teaches the two travelers extensively "the

462

things about himself in all the scriptures" (v. 27). The events they have described were all foretold by the prophets, including that "the Messiah should suffer these things and then enter into his glory" (v. 26). As he teaches them, they recall later, their hearts begin "burning within" them (v. 32). When they arrive at Emmaus, they invite Jesus to stay with them, and before the meal, "He took bread, blessed and broke it, and gave it to them." These are the same actions and words Jesus had said to and done with the twelve apostles three days before at the Last Supper (22:19). In the course of this meal "their eyes were opened, and they recognized him; and he vanished from their sight." Both in initially being prevented from recognizing Jesus and now in seeing who he is, the action of God is the determining factor. The identity of Jesus as the Messiah is a revelation from God.

Any lack of belief of Cleopas and his friend is now gone as they rush back to Jerusalem to tell the others what they have seen. The others are said to be "gathered together" (v. 33), a phrase that has liturgical implications, as have the words the others say: "The Lord has risen indeed, and he has appeared to Simon!" (v. 34). That these words are uttered before the two can tell their story is a way of claiming that the first appearance of Jesus was to Peter. The two then tell how they did not recognize Jesus until "the breaking of the bread" (v. 35), a phrase that later will become standard in the church for communion.

At the beginning of this story the resurrection is a problem for Cleopas and his friend. What is over is over. The alive are alive and the dead are dead. Some things are not possible. A dead person coming to life is one of those things that has the potential of upsetting all one's norms and expectations. If what the women said was true, that Jesus was alive, it was frightening — that the dead might come back to life. If it was not true, then other followers of Jesus in their grief were losing touch with reality — and that was also frightening. We have the expression that someone is a "doubting Thomas" from John 20:24-29, but we could equally have had the expression "doubting Cleopas" or "doubting whoever that other person was," putting in our own name. This was a specific event — it was not a general statement about what happens to everyone at death. It was a onetime thing, something that breaks all the rules of nature and does not make sense. If the resurrection ceases to be a problem at least some of the time, then perhaps we have lost sight of the tremendous and awe-inspiring miracle God has accomplished in Christ.

There are other times, however — one hopes they are in the majority — when the resurrection is not a problem but an answer. This happens when the resurrection helps account for what one has experienced. It is a conclusion that one arrives at because it is the only one that makes sense. It is a solution that helps explain what has been heard and seen and felt. What we see in this account from the road to Emmaus is the resurrection becoming an answer for Peter and for the two disciples as the most sensible way to explain events in their own lives. Even today the resurrection becomes an answer for us in the same way, when we meet Christ, or rather when Christ meets us, and God reveals to us who Christ is. The resurrection is not something we choose to believe against all evidence; it is something we conclude because of the evidence.

Jesus Christ continues to make his presence known. First, the resurrected Christ is revealed in and through the church, through disciples today who are "gathered together" in Christ's name. Second, even as Jesus led the disciples in a Bible study, we meet the resurrected Christ through Scripture in its interpretation and proclamation, as it is illuminated for us by the Holy Spirit. Third, the resurrected Jesus is known in prayer and in the breaking of the bread of the sacrament when we gather around his table. There are four basic actions of communion that Jesus instituted: we take the bread, bless it, break it, and give it in the name of Jesus, who still presides at the table. Fourth, our own witness becomes part of the ongoing witness of the church to the risen Christ, much as the witness of Cleopas and his friend has become part of the ongoing testimony of the church. Finally, the resurrected Jesus may appear to us revealed in strangers, particularly where crucifixion continues today, and in all who are in need and suffering. In short, the resurrection cannot be narrowly confined, for it pronounces through all the heavens one clear and simple message: God wins. The game is now fixed. God wins.

Paul Scott Wilson

Third Sunday of Easter, Year B

First Lesson: Acts 3:12-19
(Psalm 4)
Second Lesson: 1 John 3:1-7
Gospel Lesson: Luke 24:36b-48

Luke's third resurrection story falls on the Third Sunday of Easter. Jesus has appeared to individuals (Mary) and couples (going to Emmaus); now he appears to a larger group of disciples (the Eleven and those with them). This fearful, fragmented group is being reassembled in Jerusalem, not Galilee as Matthew and Mark have it, but Jerusalem, the essential location for the reception of God's Holy Spirit and the launchpad for the universal Christian mission Luke so vibrantly narrates in Acts. But before those heady, wonderful events can occur, these disciples have to embark on a steep spiritual learning curve. They have to come to believe that it *is* Jesus (vv. 36-43), and they have to apprehend who Jesus is (vv. 44-48). In a narrative containing several striking parallels to the preceding Emmaus story, true faith arises out of a combination of signs and Scripture. The disciples must accept the visible proofs and verbal assurances that it is Jesus *and* have the meaning of the Scriptures in relation to him opened up to them. In both cases Jesus is going to change "slowness of heart" and fearful misunderstanding into "opened minds" and joyful recognition.

Failure to recognize Jesus is a hallmark of his resurrection appearances, but it is especially acute here. Despite the accumulation of testimony to his resurrection (including that of Peter and the Emmaus travelers, all present in the room!), this group fails to make the connection between their own exclamation that "the Lord has risen" (v. 34) with the person standing in their midst. It appears it is one thing to accept something on someone else's sayso, and quite another to accept it for yourself — even when the evidence is right in front of you. So rather than Jesus they see a ghost, and rather than joy they experience fear. The Easter faith is currently disconnected from its source and is therefore empty and appears ridiculous.

Jesus sets about removing their nonapprehension and enabling belief in several ways. He speaks "peace" to them; always a metonym for salvation in Luke, it here hints at "Don't be afraid, it is I." He responds to their unspoken question about his identity by declaring, "It is I myself," inviting them to see and touch, and later eating food. Taken together, these elements produce what Raymond Brown describes as "the most materially realistic view of the body of the risen Jesus found in the New Testament." Luke wants his readers to understand (just as Jesus wants his disciples to understand): this *is Jesus,* not a ghost.

Despite this emphasis on the physical presence of Jesus, it is clear that the risen Jesus is not quite the same as before. Yes, it is Jesus. He has the flesh (the solidity) and bones (the rigid structure) of a normal human being. He eats and speaks. He has the marks of crucifixion. He is the living one who died, and not someone else. But he is not a resuscitated corpse. The disciples are startled because he suddenly appears in their midst, as if from nowhere. In resurrection narratives he is always coming and going, seemingly unconfined by some human limitations. "While I was still with you" (v. 44) suggests that although he is again present with them, it is not as it was — things have changed. Then there is their nonrecognition of him, a fact which, however reprehensible, Luke seems to understand and accept rather than criticize. This "same but not the same" theme is cleverly interwoven into Luke's text. Verse 36 illustrates this well. The term used for "stands" or "stood" can imply a normal human action. But it is also the term Luke uses to describe a visitation by a heavenly messenger, like the angel "standing" before the virgin Mary. This is the "normal-divine messenger" Jesus! His resurrection is neither completely corporeal nor totally ethereal, and by striking this balance Luke presents Jesus' resurrection in a way that rejects the main theories about the afterlife prevalent in the Hellenistic world at that time. Today, when so many "Christian" societies appear to favor various versions of reincarnation over resurrection faith, Luke's refusal to conform or reinterpret this key Christian belief is salutary.

In spite of the efforts Jesus makes to demonstrate his authentic presence to the disciples, Luke makes it clear that these are inadequate for producing the recognition required. The evidence needs interpreting. The illumination of Scripture is required in order that the material information is truly "seen." Only when these disciples take hold of Jesus' teachings and interpret his life, death, and resurrection in the light of the Scriptures will they really understand. So, from verse 44 onward, Luke moves to a favorite and recurrent theme — *the fulfillment of Scripture.* Scripture sets out God's purpose, which is brought to fulfillment in Jesus Christ. Joel Green suggests that this passage is the seam where the stories of Israel, Jesus, and the early Christian church are sewn together into one cloth.

The Emmaus travelers might well have commented, "I've heard this one," as Jesus begins to speak, so closely does it echo his exposition to them. The Scriptures bear testimony to Jesus. All of them! The reference to the Law, the Prophets, and the Psalms (unique in the New Testament) — the sections making up the Hebrew Bible — makes that clear. Consequently, although Jesus has hinted at his passion and resurrection many times, "my words which I spoke to you" probably refers to Scripture as a whole rather than any particular chapter and verse. To read the Scriptures through the lens of Jesus Christ, especially his death and resurrection, is to apprehend the quintessential truth about them — and him. But Scripture is not understood simply through hearing it. The message, after all, is not new; the disciples have heard it before but have not yet fully understood it (preachers will know that feeling all too well!). Understanding comes through revelation, through having the mind opened. This is a gift of the risen Jesus, which leads to the realization that Scripture is centered and focused in him. The repeated use of the first-person singular, "my words . . . I spoke . . . while I was still with you . . . about me . . . ," emphasizes this point and keeps alive the "it is I" theme that pervades the whole passage.

Scripture not only prophesies Jesus' death and resurrection, but also makes clear the missionary message of which the disciples are witnesses and heralds: repentance and forgiveness of sins is to be preached to all nations, in the name of Jesus. Not for the last time does the exposition of Scripture lead naturally to the commissioning of disciples. Repentance — *metanoia* — is much more than "turning round"; it connotes a complete reorientation of one's life, bringing it into line with God's purposes, moving to a Christian worldview. This is the appropriate and desired response to the gospel and results in the declaration of sins forgiven — a pattern repeatedly outlined in Acts from Peter's Pentecost sermon onward. "His name" is the authority for the message, which proceeds from who Jesus is and what he has done. As he is Lord of all, the gospel message can be proclaimed to all nations. Luke has always focused on Jesus' dealing with people on the margins of Jewish life, but rarely non-Jews explicitly. Now that "leap" is about to be made; the disciples will be his witnesses to all nations. The prophecy of Simeon that Jesus will be a light to the Gentiles, made at the beginning of the Gospel, is now about to be fulfilled at its end; he will preach through them. They must begin in Jerusalem, but not end there. This not only makes clear that repentance and forgiveness is directed first at Israel, but also hints at what becomes explicit in Acts, that the Christian mission will not conform to the traditional Jewish understanding of mission. The Jews had long worked with a centripetal model — the nations would come to Jerusalem — but Jesus' witnesses will engage in a centrifugal mission — going into "all the world." A witness not only experiences an event, but also willingly attests to it before others. These disciples are witnesses to the risen Lord himself, and his message, in his name: nothing more, nothing less, nothing else.

467

Some preachers will want to pick up and run with smaller portions of this rich text, so we will provide some starters. Verse 41, with its mixture of belief and doubt, is inviting. It appears the resurrection is considered just too good to be true, so it can't be! The disciples "disbelieve for joy," an emotion Luke contrasts with the "great joy" they experience when they see, recognize, and understand (v. 52). The bread of Emmaus and the fish here provide echoes of the feeding of the five thousand, an event which, at that time in that context, enabled the disciples to recognize Jesus' true identity — which is, of course, what is at stake here. The "things" of which the disciples are witnesses *(martyres)* include Jesus' passion, death, and resurrection. Their own experience, and that of many who will come after them, will be as his was: rejection, suffering, death — but also resurrection glory!

Martyn D. Atkins

Ascension of the Lord, Years A, B, C

First Lesson: Acts 1:1-11
(Psalm 47)
Second Lesson: Ephesians 1:15-23
Gospel Lesson: Luke 24:44-53

If we wonder when the period of Jesus' ministry ends and when the period of the church properly begins, the close of Luke's Gospel is the place to turn. Here at the end of the twenty-fourth chapter, Luke lays out Jesus' last words, his departure from earth, and his assignment for the disciples who are left behind. The narrative transition, moving from a time *with* Jesus to a new time *without* Jesus, is noticeably compact. Luke uses few words to spell out the shift. In a matter of no time at all after the resurrection, possibly as soon as Easter evening itself, Jesus is gone and a new era is under way.

Though we commonly speak of this text as an ascension text, Luke never actually says that Jesus "ascended." He speaks of Jesus being "carried up to heaven," similar to the appendix in Mark's Gospel where Jesus is purportedly "taken up into heaven." But the notion of ascension itself never enters the Christian tradition until Ephesians 4:8-10. Luke gives us premonitions of Jesus' ascension into heaven as early as his rejection in a Samaritan village (Luke 9:51) and as late as his address to the Sanhedrin council (22:69). But only here, and in Luke's other writing at the outset of Acts, does the New Testament give a specific time and place for this lifting up of Jesus.

What interests Luke is not what happens to Jesus in the act of being "carried up." His focus rests on the disciples left behind and what they will make of their lives. His emphasis on the physical removal of Jesus is slight compared to the attention he gives the ensuing ministry of the disciples. To set up their charge for ministry Jesus turns to — where else! — the Holy Scriptures. In a moment reminiscent of the roadside visit on the way to Emmaus earlier in the chapter (24:31-32), Jesus *opened* their minds to understand the Scriptures. How exactly this opening took place we cannot know. It did not happen by the Holy Spirit, whose power was yet to be delivered. Somehow Jesus' own gift of insight or proclamation or presence made the difference. He gives them the ability to understand the Scriptures, opening their minds to do so.

Clearly the ancient texts were on Jesus' mind at this last moment before his departure. As far as he was concerned, the truth to which all those Scriptures had pointed was now realized. With the light of the resurrection event so bright in the rearview mirror, the fulfillment of the Scriptures of old had the chance to be understood in a fresh way. Jesus references his place in the law of Moses, the Prophets, and, interestingly here, the Psalms (not paired up with Mosaic law anywhere else in the New Testament). It's possible that Luke makes note of the Psalms because of his own reliance on them for telling certain details of the passion account.

In any event, Jesus suggests to his followers that the Scriptures outline the content for their speaking role as witnesses. First, he says, the Messiah must suffer. Second, this Messiah will rise from the dead on the third day. And third, the task for witnesses of these important truths is to proclaim repentance for the forgiveness of sins, all in the name of Jesus. That's the substance of what the disciples are commissioned to communicate. But Jesus adds an interestingly little directive. The act of witnessing, he says, should begin from Jerusalem (and presumably emanate outward over time). Of this attention given Jerusalem, preachers should take special note.

Jerusalem had long been the focal point of religious activity for the people of Israel. But it was normally considered the center to which other nations would come. Jesus now reverses that role for Jerusalem, instead envisioning a sort of centrifugal mission extending out from the city. The great city on a hill had always been a destination point; now it was to be a starting

469

point. In his parting words Jesus says something further: "Behold, I am sending upon you what the Father promised; so stay here in the city until you have been clothed with power from on high." As Jesus' final words, or testament, his thoughts here carry a certain preeminence. What does he mean when he directs his followers to "stay in the city" until empowered by the Holy Spirit?

Is he trying to head off a splintering within the early church that is likely to erupt without his presence? Is Jesus giving the city of Jerusalem a special opportunity to find forgiveness for its role in crucifying the Messiah? Is the risen Lord simply asking that the city, with its many urgent and far-reaching needs, receive the first mission energies of the disciples? Any or all of these scenarios are plausible. The last possibility may draw the greatest interest among contemporary preachers. Certainly "the city" has always been a place of need. Modern urban crises only magnify the desperation. Perhaps Jesus was interested in consolidating the witness of the church to address the urban issues first. One might think of it as a first-century version of fighting suburban flight, only with a missiological purpose at heart! As it turned out, the first place the disciples headed after Jesus disappeared into heaven was Jerusalem. And they headed there together.

In order for Scripture to be completely fulfilled, these companions of Jesus who had seen his death and knew the truth of his resurrection would need to get the word out. They would need to attest publicly to the power of the events they had experienced firsthand. So Jesus appoints his followers to be "witnesses" or testifiers to the truth. Sharing personal opinion with others would not suffice. Dispensing tidbits of worldly wisdom was not their task. This was to be a mission guided by God, not one where they would proceed on their own terms. They were to be clothed with power from on high.

Surprisingly, there is no actual mention of the Spirit in this text. It is only implied in the language of being "clothed with power." And not until the opening chapters of Acts does Luke give a full-bored treatment of the necessity of the Spirit. The church is powerless on its own without the Spirit. Anyone serving in Jesus' name would need to be guided by the strength of the Spirit. And this strength or power would be the basis for the confidence of the church (see, e.g., Peter's bold speech in Acts 2).

Of the New Testament writers who expend great quantities of ink on the Spirit, John, Paul, and Luke stand above their peers. John speaks of the Spirit primarily in the language of guidance, defense, consolation, and continued presence. Paul likes to think of the Spirit as the one who inspires the Christian life through the granting of special gifts. And it is Luke who considers the role of the Spirit to be one which empowers the church.

What we referred to at the outset as the emerging "period of the church" springs to life with the departure of Jesus and the coming of the Spirit. Luke draws a close connection between the ascension of the Lord and the outpouring of the Spirit. The ministry of Jesus feeds directly into the mission of the early church, as only the Spirit can make possible.

The actual ascension event in Luke's Gospel is more a theological image than a lesson in aeronautics. We're told that Jesus led his followers to a place called Bethany, the same place where he had known triumph just days earlier (19:19-40). Now he would bless them and withdraw. Some have questioned Luke's accuracy of the timing of this departure. If Luke makes note elsewhere, as he does in Acts 1:3, of a forty-day period of resurrection appearances prior to the ascension of Jesus, why doesn't he do the same here? Depending on how one reads the passage, and what Luke's specific motives were, we don't have to assume that he meant to construe the "lifting up" event as occurring late on Easter Day. For all we know, he intentionally collapsed time to surface a more fervent interest in what the disciples would make of their new responsibility.

The disciples took the word and the blessing of Jesus to heart. Two things distinguished their earliest moments of togetherness: worship and joy. There is no sadness in their new condition. In fact, if they even pulled out a single tissue with which to pat their eyes, it certainly isn't evident to the reader. The dumbfounded stupor of the *left-behinds* in Acts 1 is completely absent here. We see no dazed look into the distant sky, no trauma of some depressing good-bye, no fear of being orphaned. Jesus has left his disciples with too much work to do. And of the optional responses available, self-pity would not figure in. No, it was joy that would mark the first steps of these disciples — great joy! It would be joy of the exhilarating and contagious variety (see 2:10). And this joy would lead the church into the work of love and service that never ends.

Peter W. Marty

Second Sunday after Christmas, Years A, B, C

First Lesson: Jeremiah 31:7-14
(Psalm 147:12-20)
Second Lesson: Ephesians 1:3-14
Gospel Lesson: John 1:(1-9), 10-18

Christmas is dominated by readings about the baby Jesus, angels, shepherds, infancy stories, and perhaps even an early wise man or two already arriving. It is all marvelous stuff — but what does it actually mean? Today the opening of John's Gospel explains it — one of the most magnificent pieces of religious literature written. Often called "the prologue," it is more like an overture, for it introduces some key themes and words which the writer will use over and over in his Gospel. Yet, like many overtures, it also stands alone in its own right, and is heard on many different occasions. The preacher may therefore expound it as the meaning of Christmas and the incarnation, or as an introduction to the theology of Saint John, or just by itself as one of the best-known and most loved Bible passages. For this Sunday the lectionary makes the first nine verses optional, but since they are necessary to understand the second half, we shall include them — and they are so wonderful that to omit them seems almost a sacrilege!

Mark starts with Jesus being baptized and Matthew begins with Jesus' birth, while Luke goes back to the birth of John the Baptist — and their opening chapters provide many Christmas readings. But John is traditionally symbolized by an eagle — and he certainly takes the high-flying perspective here! Jesus cannot be introduced in terms of time and place and human ancestry: he existed "in the beginning" (1:1). This phrase reminds us immediately of the opening words of the Bible, "in the beginning" (Gen. 1:1). Indeed, while "Genesis" is Greek for "beginning," the Jews called it by its opening Hebrew words, "in the beginning." Yet John goes even further, for Genesis starts with the creation of everything *at* the beginning and John takes us back *before* then, when only God existed.

John does not name Jesus until the end (1:17). Instead, he calls him "the Word." The Jews thought that God's word was alive and active (Isa. 55:11) from the creation, when God had only to say "let there be . . ." for things to come into being (Gen. 1:3, 6, 9), to God's word coming through all the prophets. In Greek philosophy the "word," *logos,* was used for the logical rationality behind the universe. In later Jewish beliefs this masculine principle was complemented by the feminine figure of Lady Wisdom, who was present with God at the creation (Prov. 8:22-31).

But it is John who pulls these threads together with the amazing idea that the Word was not only preexistent with God but also personal. In 1:1-2 he states that "the Word was with [the] God," including the definite article "the" to stress how the Word existed with the creator Father God of Jewish monotheism — for there is no other god. Furthermore, "the Word was God" without any article. It is not "the Word was *a* god" with the indefinite article, implying that Jesus was some lesser divinity, as some groups who have split away from orthodox Christianity believe. Nor does he say, "the Word was *the* God," for that would imply that Jesus was all there is to God. No, he carefully writes, "the Word was God," divine, personal, and existing in the unity of the Godhead and yet somehow distinct — for "the Word became flesh and dwelt among us" (1:14).

Greek philosophy and many Eastern religions had an essential "dualism," a separation between our material world and the spiritual realm where God exists. Human beings were seen in a similar dualistic fashion: the physical body is sinful flesh or meaningless matter, inhabited by the soul which strives to return to the divine light. Thus ancient philosophy sought "enlightenment" or "knowledge" to set the soul free into the bright intellectual realms, while many Eastern religions offered "salvation" through initiation into mysteries to enable the soul to leave the body after death and ascend back to the divine.

Similarly, John depicts the Word preexisting with God in glorious light but descending into our world of darkness to bring salvation, before returning to the Father. However, John has been nourished in the Jewish biblical tradition that the world is the creation of a loving God: "The earth is the Lord's and all it contains" (Ps. 24). Thus he affirms the world's goodness and the Word's involvement in creation in a way abhorrent to any dualist. First, "all things came into being" through the Word, and nothing exists without him (1:3). At a stroke the Evangelist inspires the great Christian involvement in both the arts and the sciences. Scientific inquiry is possible if the world is not some malicious fantasy but the result of a creator's love — to study the laws of physics is to search out the mind of God. Equally, rather than trying to escape the material body, our humanity can be explored in sculpture and paint, poetry and prose, dance and drama, music and song — because "in him was life" (1:4).

Suddenly two fanfares burst out of John's overture to announce his major themes of light and life, words he uses twice as often as the other Gospels together. All "life" is found in the Word, which life is also "the light of all

473

people" (1:4). John uses light and darkness as a contrasting pair throughout the Gospel. Now "the light shines in the darkness, and the darkness cannot master it" (1:5). The English "master" reflects the double meaning of the Greek, both to "understand" and to "overcome" or "extinguish." For John the coming of light into darkness inevitably creates shadows, so there will be conflict and judgment.

Unlike the dualists' god, who has no contact with the world, John stresses that the nature of God is to "send"; first, John the Baptist was "sent from God" (1:6), then Jesus, who will eventually send us also into the world (20:21). John is sent as a "witness to the light" (1:7). The Greek word *martyr-* gives us the English "martyr" for a witness even to death. The theme of witness is another key idea in this Gospel. John the Baptist had many followers, but "he himself was not the light," but came as a "witness to the light, so that all might believe through him" (1:7-8).

In contrast, the Word is "the true light" (1:9). Another key motif, the words "true" and "truth," is featured nearly fifty times in this Gospel, three times the total in the other Gospels. Here too John turns the dualists' ideas around; Greek philosophy stressed how true reality was only in the realm above and everything in our world was merely pale shadows and reflections. So for John, Jesus is "the truth," foreshadowed by the prophets' beliefs and ideas of God's light coming in glory (Isa. 9:2; 42:6; 60:1). That light, says John, is personal, as he breaks grammar from the neuter "light" to the pronoun "he," and "coming into the world." We do not leave the world to find enlightenment; he "enlightens everyone." The scale of John's insight is staggering; what is true and good in all philosophies and religions, thought and culture, arts and science — all of it comes from the enlightenment of the Word.

John's stupendous claim, which no dualist would contemplate, is that the divine Word, the true light, has come "into the world" (1:9). To them "the world" was negative and evil. John is more subtle: the world is positive, the good creation of the loving God, but it becomes negative when the world rejects Jesus: "He was in the world, and the world was made through him, yet the world did not know him" (1:10).

The Word, the true light, came into the world "to his own," a neuter phrase for his own possession or home. The Old Testament proclaims that while "the whole world" belongs to God, Israel is his "special possession" (Exod. 19:5) and the Jews "his people" (Deut. 7:6; 14:2). But John moves from the neuter to the personal pronoun to say that "his own people did not accept him." So 1:11 is a summary of the first half of this Gospel, as Jesus comes to his own people, but many of them, especially the religious leaders, do not accept him. But alongside that rejection is the counterpoint of "all who received him, who believed in his name." Thus 1:12 is the summary of the second half of the Gospel. Although "his own people" did not accept him, Jesus called together a group who "believed in him." To these he gives "the authority to become children of God," who are born not by natural means but by a spiritual rebirth "of God" (1:13).

In the first part of his overture, John set his composition against a cosmic backdrop of the divine light above and our dark world below; then his middle section challenged this dualistic system as the Word enters into our world. In the final movement he brings themes from the Old Testament to a final climax which confronts Greek philosophy and Jewish beliefs alike.

"The Word became flesh" (1:14) would make any dualists listening jump! The Word "coming into the world" was bad enough, but for the divine to enter something as physical and sinful as human flesh and blood was outrageous. Even some early Christians (called the Docetics) had problems with this, believing that Jesus only "seemed" (dokein in Greek) to be human. While John has the clearest emphasis of all the Gospels on the divinity of Jesus, here he stresses Jesus' humanity in this ringing declaration of the incarnation. If this idea was difficult for Greeks, the next phrase would have startled Jews. "He lived (eskēnōsen) among us" means "dwelt in a tent," like the tabernacle (skēnē) where God resided during the desert wanderings (Exod. 25:8-9). The prophets longed for God to "pitch his tent" among his people again (Ezek. 37:27; Joel 3:17; Zech. 2:10). This, declares John, is what has happened in Jesus.

Furthermore, the shekinah, the glorious cloud of God's presence on Mount Sinai, filled the tent and later the temple (Exod. 24:16; 40:34-35; 1 Kings 8:10-11). So John says, "We have seen his glory." The other Gospels depict the glory of God coming upon Jesus at the transfiguration. John does not relate this, for he sees the glory of God in all Jesus says and does; supremely the hour for Jesus to be glorified is the crucifixion (12:23; 13:32; 17:1). Jesus shares God's glory as an only son resembles his father. This is John's favorite description for the relationship of Jesus and God. In the Old Testament God is always "abounding in steadfast love and faithfulness" (Exod. 34:6). Here John translates this into Jesus being "full of grace and truth." Thus 1:14 is an astounding verse. In one sentence John breaches the dualistic divide of Greek philosophy, counters early Christian heresy about Jesus' humanity and divinity, and gathers together Jewish ideas of the presence, glory, mercy, and love of God — all of this, he says, can now be seen among us in Jesus!

Next John the Baptist again bears "witness" to Jesus (1:15). Many

475

thought the Baptist was bringing all Jewish hopes to their consummation — but he witnesses that it is Jesus who does this, not he. Jesus has given us "fullness" and "grace" (1:16). We saw above that "grace" represents the "steadfast love of the LORD" in the Old Testament. Now John notes that "the law was given through Moses, but grace and truth came through Jesus Christ" (1:17). No one has ever seen God (1:18). Even Moses was not allowed to see God's face (Exod. 33:18-23). But Jesus, the Word, who was with God in the beginning, the only Son who exists "in the Father's heart" — he has revealed him and "made him known."

And so the prologue has come full circle, the overture has developed all John's themes and climaxes with a loud cry that Jesus is nothing less than God come among us. This is the true meaning of Christmas, the truth which we are to preach at this time of year — and always.

Richard A. Burridge

Nativity of the Lord (Christmas Day), Years A, B, C

First Lesson: Isaiah 52:7-10
(Psalm 98)
Second Lesson: Hebrews 1:1-4, (5-12)
Gospel Lesson: John 1:1-14

The Johannine prologue divides into two principal themes. The first concerns creation and receives its primary expression in the first five verses. The second concerns covenant and receives its primary expression in the last five verses (vv. 14-18). The intervening verses (vv. 6-13) form an overview of the Gospel narrative itself, beginning with John the Baptizer (vv. 6-8), continuing with Jesus' ministry and fate (vv. 10-11), and concluding with those who believe in Jesus (vv. 12-13). To understand the prologue it is necessary to appreciate the point the author is trying to make about creation and covenant and how each is realized in the coming of God's Son.

The opening words of John 1:1, "In the beginning was the Word," offer an unmistakable echo of the opening words of Genesis 1:1, "In the beginning God created. . . ." John 1:3 goes on to declare that through the Word "all things came into being," thus tying the Johannine prologue quite closely to the creation account of Genesis. Moreover, John's statement that it was the Word that was with God probably reflects an Aramaic interpretive tendency in the synagogue of late antiquity, as is now attested in the *Neofiti Targum*, which in Genesis 1:1 reads: "From the beginning with wisdom the Word of the Lord created. . . ."

The affirmation that it was through an agent that God created is part of Israel's wisdom tradition. In an intertestamental text personified Wisdom (*sophia* in the Greek; *ḥokmah* in the Hebrew) boasts that she came forth from God's mouth (Sir. 24:3), she whose origins were "from eternity, in the beginning" (24:9). In saying this she implies that she is God's spoken word. Wisdom also claims that she was commanded to pitch her "tent" in Israel (24:8), and there "in the holy tabernacle" she ministered before God (24:10). The idea of Wisdom as a personification is found in the Hebrew Scriptures themselves (e.g., Prov. 8–9). It was not too difficult to apply this concept to God's Word (*dabar* in Hebrew or *me'mar* in Aramaic).

The Johannine Evangelist has adopted Jewish wisdom ideas for his Christology. As he understands it, the wisdom of God that came to earth, that "became flesh" and pitched a "tent among us," was none other than God's Word *(logos)* embodied in the person of Jesus of Nazareth. In the Word there was life and light, which again alludes to the Genesis creation account (cf. Gen. 1:3, "Let there be light"; 1:20, 24, "Let the waters bring forth swarms of living creatures. . . . Let the earth bring forth living creatures"). The Johannine prologue also declares that the "darkness has not overcome" the light (John 1:5). This is an allusion to later interpretive tradition that understood light and darkness as opposing powers that struggled for dominion (cf. Philo, *De opificio mundi* 33). Light overcame the darkness, both at the time of creation and later in the giving of the covenant.

Thus far everything that the Evangelist has said about the Word, about its presence at creation, its light and life-giving power, its victory over darkness, and its presence before God (v. 1 literally reads: "and the Word was facing [*pros*] God") is unremarkable. Few Jewish persons of late antiquity would have found anything objectionable in the first five verses. Philo the Jewish theologian and philosopher of Alexandria, Egypt, had said similar things a generation earlier. He spoke of God's Word as a "second God" of sorts, through whom God created (cf. *Quaestiones in Genesim* 2.62). Even earlier still, the sage Jesus ben Sira, whose work was cited above, also spoke of personified Wisdom who existed with God from eternity and was active in creation.

It is not until the Evangelist declares that the Word "became flesh" has something been said that would have raised the eyebrows of the faithful in the synagogue. This declaration is unparalleled. Nowhere in Jewish exegesis and tradition do we hear of God's Word, Wisdom, or Spirit becoming *flesh*. Indeed, the antithesis between spirit and flesh is attested in the Jewish Scriptures (e.g., Gen. 6:3, "Then the LORD said, 'My spirit shall not abide in man for ever, for he is flesh'"; cf. Isa. 31:3). Philo comes close when he says God's Word is "the human being [made] after his image" (*De confusione linguarum* 146), but he is really making a different point. And elsewhere he seems to regard Moses as in some sense a second God who shared in the divine nature (*De vita Mosis* 1.155-58; *De posteritati Caini* 28; *Quaestiones in Exodum* 2.29). But again, Philo's highly symbolic interpretation cautions against the conclusion that he is actually thinking in terms that approximate the incarnational ideas of the Johannine prologue.

Not only does the Johannine prologue declare that the Word became flesh, it says the Word "dwelt among us, and we beheld its glory." These words allude to the descent of God's glory into the tabernacle, described in Exodus 40. "Dwelt" (*skēnoun*) in John 1:14 literally means to dwell in a tent or tabernacle. Taking up residence in a tent and revealing glory is what happened after the giving of the covenant at Sinai and the completion of the tabernacle: "and the glory of the LORD filled the tabernacle" (Exod. 40:34), which took place "in the sight of all the house of Israel" (40:38). This time, however, the Word of the Lord has taken up residence in a tent of flesh, a human being, and like the time in the wilderness, the glory of the Lord is once again seen.

The incarnate Word is said to be "full of grace and truth" (*plērēs charitos kai alētheias*), which is the Greek equivalent of the Hebrew phrase "abounding in steadfast love and faithfulness" (*rab ḥesed we-'emet*). This important phrase takes the attentive reader back to Exodus 34:6, where a compassionate God is willing to forgive sinful Israel and restore the broken covenant. In the aftermath of the golden calf (Exod. 32), it was necessary to renew the covenant. Moses cuts two more tablets of stone and then requests that he might see God's glory (Exod. 33:18). God, however, tells the great lawgiver: "You cannot see my face; for man shall not see me and live" (33:20). Therefore it is necessary for Moses to be hidden behind a rock. When God passed before him, Moses was able only to catch a fleeting glimpse of God's retreating back (33:21-23). As he passed by, God declared: "The LORD, the LORD, a God merciful and gracious, slow to anger, and abounding in steadfast love and faithfulness" (34:6).

It is to this awesome moment in Israel's redemptive history that the

Johannine prologue alludes. "The law was given through Moses," but the "grace and truth" (John 1:17) of which God spoke in Exodus 34:6 was given through Jesus Christ. This then explains what is meant by the phrase "grace in place of [*anti*] grace" in John 1:16. The new covenant grace of Jesus Christ has taken the place of the old covenant grace that Moses brokered for Israel long ago. The giving of the second covenant was foreshadowed in Exodus 34 and was fulfilled in the second filling of the tabernacle with the glory of God, a glory that "we beheld." In contrast to Moses, who caught only a fleeting glimpse of God's retreating back, Jesus, the "only Son," the incarnate Word of God, "who is in the bosom of the Father," has beheld the front side of God from the very beginning of creation. He is therefore a greater lawgiver and covenant maker than Moses. Through the Word made flesh, "grace and truth" have been fully experienced. It is for this reason that the prologue declares that the only Son is he who has made the Father known (1:18).

Accordingly, then, those who receive the Word made flesh will "become children of God," birthed not by human bloodlines or by a human capacity, but by the will of God (1:13). Those who receive God's Word enter the new covenant, the covenant that is "full of grace and truth."

Craig A. Evans

Third Sunday of Advent, Year B

First Lesson: Isaiah 61:1-4, 8-11
(Psalm 126)
Second Lesson: 1 Thessalonians 5:16-24
Gospel Lesson: John 1:6-8, 19-28

The opening sentences about "John" are revealing in many respects. Foremost, perhaps, is that they are in ordinary prose, while language about Jesus is poetry. The prologue to the narrative speaks of the "Word" that was with God and that is God, through which all things were made, a Word that is light and life. We learn later in the poetic introduction that this "Word" becomes flesh in Jesus. Throughout the Gospel Jesus is identified

479

by metaphors ("living water," "light of the world," "bread from heaven," "vine"). What Jesus is and means cannot be captured in ordinary language. That is not true of John. Though he is someone of enormous importance — important enough to interrupt the poetic introduction to the Gospel — ordinary language is sufficient.

The way John is introduced likewise indicates that readers are expected to know a good bit about him. His name is simply "John." Crucial is that he is sent from God and that he "baptizes," though we are not told what the practice means and how it is related to other religious practices. Since his ministry requires water, it is not surprising that he works along the Jordan — though we are not told what it may mean that he works along the river in the very south (Bethany [1:28]) and also farther north (Aenon near Salim [3:23]). Though there is a clear indication that John is headed for trouble ("Now John had not yet been put in prison" [3:24]), there is no indication of who imprisons John or why, and there is no account of his death. For such information we depend on the synoptic Gospels. Luke in particular provides an introduction to John's ministry by narrating the circumstances of his birth to an old priest and his wife who is related to Mary, Jesus' mother. The other Gospels likewise tell us why John was so important and how he got into trouble with Herod in a fashion that cost him his life. That such information is not provided in the Fourth Gospel suggests that readers are expected to know John's story — and that John's significance has less to do with the particulars of his own ministry than with his relationship to Jesus.

What is important is not so much John's political as his religious significance — or rather his lack of significance. What is denied John is extraordinary: He was not the light (1:8); he is not the Christ, nor Elijah, nor the prophet (1:20-25; 3:28). He is unworthy to untie the sandal of the one coming after him (1:27). While he baptizes with water, the one coming after him will baptize with the Holy Spirit (1:33). He is not the bridegroom (3:29). "He must increase, but I must decrease" (3:30). The explicit denials and the repeated subordination of John to Jesus suggest that getting the relationship of the two straight is an important feature of the story. That in turn presumes that, for some, John was not simply a figure of secondary importance but the one expected from God. That the Fourth Gospel must restate the case indicates that John's influence did not cease with his death. That the Jewish historian Josephus regards John the Baptizer as a far more significant figure than Jesus suggests that it was not obvious to Jesus' contemporaries that he was "the one to come" and John merely a forerunner. The book of Acts tells of Paul's discovery of a group of "disciples" in Ephesus who were baptized not in Jesus' name but "into John's baptism" (Acts 19:2-

6). Understanding that John's ministry is only a preliminary to the main act suggests that what holds promise and what does not are not always obvious.

Significant is the role accorded John: he is a witness; he comes to bear testimony. "Witness" and "testimony" translate the same Greek root that has its place in the law court. Even a cursory reading through the Gospel will show how frequently the language of witness occurs. The noun occurs fifteen times, the verb over thirty times. John is the first to bear testimony. Witnesses include Jesus' signs, the Father, the Spirit, and the one responsible for the story ("He who saw it has borne witness" [19:35]). It is not surprising that the climax of the story is a trial at which Jesus is brought before Pilate, testimony is offered, and Jesus is condemned and executed as "the King of the Jews."

The trial image is even more basic to the story. It is not only Jesus who is on trial. It is the world, focused in the Jewish and Roman leaders. They are entrusted with the authority to judge for the well-being of the world. Like the authorities in the story of the man born blind whom Jesus healed (chap. 9), they gather testimony and must eventually offer a ruling. In so doing, however, they pronounce judgment on themselves. Jesus does not come for judgment (3:17) — but those who do not come to the light are judged already. Employing an image from Isaiah, the Fourth Gospel tells the story of Jesus' coming as a great trial. Testimony is offered. Even Moses bears witness — not on behalf of Israel, however, but on Jesus' behalf: "Do not think that I will accuse you before the Father; your accuser is Moses, on whom you have set your hope" (5:45).

Jesus' coming demands a decision. His "signs" are too powerful to ignore. There is real risk, since Jesus seems to be careless about the Sabbath (9:16-17). He is either a prophet — or a false prophet who must die. He claims authority that belongs to God alone. Such claims constitute blasphemy and merit death (19:7). The testimony is persistent and requires a verdict. And in pronouncing judgment on Jesus, "the world" is judged.

The story calls attention to an important feature of "testimony." In our context "testifying to one's faith" is often used with little sense of its legal connotations. The setting of the court may still be an appropriate image to characterize public truth-speaking. Offering testimony to the gospel has public consequences. It is like shining a light into the darkness. It reveals things. The reaction to the light includes both welcome and avoidance (3:19-21). Testimony is not a neutral thing; it forces choices that have enormous consequences. It changes the world. Those who wish to confine religion to the realm of the private sense this is true. The story John tells is of a God who is bound to speak, a God who is Word. Once the Word becomes flesh, it cannot remain a private matter. The Word is for the world, and the world will have to judge. John the Baptist is the first to offer testimony to Jesus that will provoke "the world" to act. The intrusion of the Light into a world of darkness will not leave things as they are. The story argues that judgments will have to be made once the testimony is offered — judgments about God that will reveal the world to be a place of unbelief. Why this should be the case and what God will do in response are what make for the drama in which we have everything at stake.

Donald Juel

Second Sunday after the Epiphany, Year A

First Lesson: Isaiah 49:1-7
(Psalm 40:1-11)
Second Lesson: 1 Corinthians 1:1-9
Gospel Lesson: John 1:29-42

The text for this Sunday follows Matthew's story of Jesus' baptism, which is the lection for the preceding Sunday. The movement from the baptismal story in Matthew to John 1:29-42 is interesting. Both texts clearly have elements of epiphanies; in both something about the identity of Jesus is revealed, which is appropriate for the Sundays following Epiphany. In John's text, however, there is no voice from heaven announcing to the crowds, "This is my Son, the Beloved, in whom I am well pleased" (Matt. 3:17). Rather we have a series of human actions. The revelation of Jesus' identity depends not on a voice from heaven, but on the testimony of John and the discipleship of those who follow Jesus. Rather than a direct revelation from heaven, the emphasis shifts to the human testimony, faith, and discipleship through which the identity of Jesus Christ is embodied and made known in the world.

The text opens with the testimony of John. At this point there seems to be nothing really special about Jesus: "The next day [John] saw Jesus coming toward him." Jesus is apparently just a guy walking around Bethany — no great credentials, no "signs and wonders," nothing to make him stand out from the crowd. But then John begins to testify to what he has seen and heard. Everything here depends on the witness. As Walter Brueggemann has put it, the new reality is not really available until it is uttered ("Testimony as a Decentered Mode of Preaching," in *Cadences of Home: Preaching among Exiles* [Louisville: Westminster John Knox, 1997], p. 44). Jesus' identity is spoken into the world through the testimony of John.

And what a testimony it is. John piles up image upon image, title upon title, mystery upon mystery, as if he can't fully capture what he has to say in words: "Here is the Lamb of God who takes away the sin of the world! This is he of whom I said, 'After me comes a man who ranks ahead of me because he was before me.'" Here is the one on whom I saw the Spirit descend like a dove. Here is the one who will baptize with the Holy Spirit. "And I myself have seen and testified that this is the Son of God." It is difficult to capture the richness of John's testimony. Jesus draws to himself the most central and powerful imagery and titles in Scripture: Jesus is the Passover lamb of the exodus as well as the eschatological "lamb who was slain" (Rev. 5); he is the Word who was with God and was God "in the beginning," long before John arrived on the scene (John 1:1); he is the one on whom the Holy Spirit of God — the Spirit of the prophets and the new creation — descends and remains, the one who embodies that new creation and breathes that Spirit on others (John 20:22); he is, indeed, the very Son of God. John testifies that Jesus not only embodies and continues the story of Israel, but in fact is the Alpha and the Omega, the one who was with God at the beginning and will be with God at the end.

Everything swirls around the identity of Jesus. But at this point the revelation of that identity relies not on a definitive voice from heaven, but on John's fragile and vulnerable testimony. That's the way of testimony. It is always a risky venture, which can offer no "proofs" beyond what the witness has seen and heard. The witness always testifies before a "jury" judging his or her words. All the witness can do is invite others to accept or reject the testimony based on the integrity and faithfulness of the witness's words and life. (I am indebted to my colleagues, Walter Brueggemann and Anna Carter Florence, for these insights into the character of testimony. See, e.g., Brueggemann, pp. 38-56.) Not surprisingly, John's own disciples, those who know him and trust him, are the first ones to follow Jesus.

The initial encounter between these disciples and Jesus keeps the issue of Jesus' identity at the forefront and introduces the role of discipleship. When Jesus notices these disciples following him, he speaks his first words in the Gospel of John — a question posed not only to the characters in the story but to all of us who would follow him: "What are you looking for?" Or better, "What are you seeking?" At first glance the disciples' response seems strange: "Where are you staying?" Asked a momentous, life-challenging question by the one proclaimed as the Son of God, the followers reply by asking for Jesus' address. One might have expected a more profound response: "I'm seeking the meaning of life" or "Why is there so much suffering in the world?" Those would seem to be worthy responses to Jesus' question. Instead, the "seekers" simply reply, "Where are you staying?"

As strange as it may seem, however, the question is the right one. John's former disciples are not seeking answers to abstract questions or theoretical speculations. Rather, they are seeking Jesus — to be with him, to know him, and to follow him. So they must know where he is staying; that is the most important thing. Their simple question challenges the church today to examine what we are seeking — Jesus or something else.

Jesus' reply to the disciples' request is an excellent example of the Gospel of John's multilayered meanings. At one level Jesus' reply, "Come and see," may simply invite the followers to come with him and see where he is staying. At a deeper level, however, these words are a call to discipleship. "Come and see" is the Gospel of John's equivalent to Jesus' invitation in the synoptic Gospels: "Follow me." And what is most interesting about this particular invitation — "Come and see" — is the *order* of the words. When many of us think of discipleship, we often think that we must believe in Jesus and know who he is ("see") before we can follow ("come"). But here the order is reversed. First we follow Jesus along the path of discipleship, and then along the way we come more fully to believe and understand who he is.

Certainly this will be the case in the Gospel of John. At this point all the disciples have is a set of titles and images, given them by John, which define Jesus' identity. As the story progresses, however, Jesus will himself flesh out the meaning of these titles and images, as well as redefine them and add to them; Jesus himself will provide the content for any titles or images he assumes. Only along the path of discipleship can the followers of Jesus come fully to believe in him and understand who he is. (The same thing is true in the synoptic Gospels. Jesus first calls the disciples to follow him. They can come to know Jesus and believe in him only along the path of discipleship.)

So the disciples do as Jesus says. They go to where Jesus is staying, and they remain with him. And they discover that Jesus' words — "Come and see" — are not just an invitation but a promise. While the disciples are with Jesus, something happens to them; they do indeed begin to "see." And the next thing we know, these new disciples have themselves become bold witnesses. They take the place of John, who disappears after giving his testimony. Now these disciples are the ones testifying to Jesus. "Come and see," they tell everyone they know. "Come and see. We have found the Messiah" (yet another title that Jesus will fill with content as the story progresses). The story moves forward through the pattern of testimony, discipleship, and further testimony.

And that is the way the story continues through the life and witness of the church today. The church is the community of disciples that bears witness to Jesus. The church is now the community that is called to follow Jesus and invite others to "come and see." God depends on the church to make Jesus known in the world through its life and witness. We're not given any ways to prove who Jesus is — no voices from heaven. Rather, just as God depended on John to speak the reality of Jesus into the world, so God depends on the church to make Jesus known. In the power of the Spirit, which Jesus has breathed upon us, we offer our fragile and vulnerable testimony to Jesus, backed up by the faithfulness and integrity of our life together.

At a time when the church is tempted to become just another appealing commodity for middle-class consumers, the text from John poses a significant challenge to our communities of faith: Do our words and deeds bear witness to Jesus? And when we invite people to "come," will they be able to "see" Jesus in our congregations? Will they be able to say, "Yes, Jesus stays here; yes, the Spirit that rested on Jesus is at work here"?

Charles L. Campbell

Second Sunday after the Epiphany, Year B

First Lesson: 1 Samuel 3:1-10, (11-20)
(Psalm 139:1-6, 13-18)
Second Lesson: 1 Corinthians 6:12-20
Gospel Lesson: John 1:43-51

The liturgical placement of this reading in the Revised Common Lectionary is chronologically and theologically significant. It comes the week after the Baptism of the Lord in the church year. It matches liturgically the quick move that all the Gospels make from the baptism of Jesus to his ministry and to the calling of the disciples. Even though the Fourth Gospel does not actually report the baptism, Jesus' ministry begins at the Jordan in conjunction with his journey to the exaltation of the cross. He puts in place a group of leaders corresponding in role and number to the sons of Israel, the patriarchs of the twelve tribes. The calling of the Twelve is vital to Jesus' messianic mission both in its symbolism and in their later function as witnesses to the resurrection.

There are numerous similarities in outline to the early events of Jesus' ministry in the synoptics, but John, as ever, brings a unique witness and provides a rich interpretive context. It is still only chapter 1 when we read this story of the calling of Philip and Nathanael, but there is a great deal that precedes it. There is the prologue with its profound theology and its clear distinction between the ministries of John the Baptist and Jesus. After the close of the prologue, this distinction is underlined by John, who "did not deny it, but confessed, 'I am not the Messiah,'" when confronted on the issue by the clergy from Jerusalem. It is only "the next day" when he sees Jesus and proclaims him "the Lamb of God who takes away the sin of the world." On "the next day" he reiterates this confession, and Jesus calls away two of John's disciples, Andrew and Simon, who gets (at a different place and much earlier than in Matthew) his nickname, Cephas.

The events of today's Gospel occur on yet "the next day" as Jesus prepares to leave the lower Jordan Valley for Galilee. Philip and Nathanael are called. (Nathanael is not named in the other Gospels. From ancient times commentators have speculated that he is the same as Bartholomew, but there is no way to know, and he might not even be one of the Twelve.) Obviously, the sequence and the priorities are different for the Fourth Gospel, and the Evangelist never will give us a full list of twelve disciples. But he plainly gives great importance to their call and their role. The next event will be the first miracle, changing water into wine at the wedding at Cana in Galilee.

The theological assertions of the opening of the Fourth Gospel are similar to those of the synoptics. Jesus, the Son of God, is affirmed by John the Baptist and shortly thereafter assembles his core (or should it be corps?) of followers. He reveals himself in miracles. He manifests his identity by prophetic actions. (In John the next event after the first miracle is the expulsion of the money changers.) He shows himself to be the Son of God in his teaching, and in John he reveals himself as Word, Truth, and Light. (So the next event after the cleansing of the temple is his instruction of Nicodemus by night.)

John, like the other Gospels, intends simply to tell us who and what Jesus is. The Evangelist moves in quick, orderly fashion to do so. The pericope under discussion is one building block of that argument. Jesus calls two disciples, but this is no mere neutral report of an interesting factoid. In this account several important revelations about him are made, and they are all consistent. He is identified in verse 45 as the one about whom Moses and the prophets wrote. His divine insight is shown in his knowledge of Nathanael before their introduction. Nathanael acknowledges him as a teacher ("Rabbi") and as the Son of God and King of Israel. Jesus predicts his glory in the final verse, verse 51: "You will see heaven opened and the angels of God ascending and descending upon the Son of Man." All of this is very particularly Johannine, and yet it resonates with the good news reported in the other Gospels. It is really quite similar to the tight opening of Mark and its declaration of Jesus Christ, the Son of God. The unique witness of the Fourth Gospel is consistent with the rest of the canon and with the other Gospels, even though there are unique angles and arguments.

As ever, those unique angles and arguments show up in many ways, subtle and obvious.

Nathanael is an Israelite in whom there is no guile. This seemingly off-hand remark identifies the fulfillment that will come about in the church. Israel needs renewal; the name, after all, is that given by God to Jacob, the guileful patriarch. In this Israelite Jesus, in the renewed Israel, such guile will be transcended. Somewhat obscurely, these words of Jesus echo the prophetic hope that God's people will in time live in that innocence appropriate to those whom God has given his Torah and his promises.

The origins of historic Israel form the story in another way. When Jesus promises Philip and Nathanael a fuller vision, "greater things than these," he alludes to Jacob/Israel's dream of the angels ascending and descending the stairway to heaven. The original event guarantees the unworthy Jacob's place in the life of Israel and in the ancestry of Jesus. And as that place became holy, Bethel (which means "house of God"), so Jesus himself is now the dwelling place of God. The angels will ascend and descend upon him as they did upon Bethel. The reference is subtle but not obscure; for Christianity Jesus is the holy place. As God dwelt at Bethel and ultimately in the temple at Jerusalem, so he dwells in the Word made flesh and wherever the Spirit makes Christ present in the church.

This same verse also has an apocalyptic aspect. The heavens are opened and Jesus is identified by the apocalyptic messianic title "Son of Man." Modern commentators have often suggested that John is so "spiritual" that it is free of apocalyptic traits and expectations, but that is at best an overstatement, at worst an outright distortion. The language and approach are different, but the Fourth Gospel looks to the last judgment and the kingdom of God. Here already in the first chapter we are reminded, and there will be eleven more "Son of Man" passages in John. (Note also that two verses earlier Nathanael identifies him as the King of Israel, the Davidic Messiah of synoptic apocalyptic.) With additional titles and from new angles, this pericope continues the naming and identification of Jesus so critical to the beginnings of all the Gospels, from the terse announcement of Mark to the nativity stories of Luke to John 1.

Proclamation should keep in mind the basic function of this text. First, the simple story of the selection of two disciples is full of signs identifying Jesus and his ministry. Second, the naming of apostles is critical in identifying Jesus and in grounding our hope in their witness and proclamation. The church is not incidentally apostolic. It is genetically apostolic. The Word of God does not come to expression in a vacuum. Neither does it leave one. It creates a community in which it is proclaimed, believed, and lived, and that community is necessarily apostolic because the apostles are our direct link to Jesus. We need Philip and Nathanael. We need Andrew and Peter.

Keeping in mind the function of the apostles, we can avoid a common error in preaching texts like this and this Sunday's Old Testament counterpart, the call of Samuel. That error is to use the call of the apostles and the prophets as the template for our vocation as Christian disciples. I do not mean to deny any relevance, but in the first instance the calls that occur in the Bible are not — this should be obvious — about us. They are about what God has done in and for his people to preserve his Word and revelation. The call of Philip and Nathanael is about Jesus and who he is. It is about God and how he provides for his people. In precisely this sense it is gospel. It is good news that God thus provides for his people.

We should not turn a deaf ear to God's call, but it will not usually come to us as it came to the disciples and the prophets. Nor should we expect it to. It comes to us through stories such as these. God has built his church on the foundation of the apostles and the prophets. Thus grounded, we may imitate them in service, witness, faithfulness, and devotion. We should not, however, confuse God's call to us with the unique historical moments represented by the call of the apostles and prophets, even though they may genuinely help us reflect on our own calling. The good news in this pericope is, first and foremost, that God has cared for his people and made faith possible for us by providing prophets and apostles.

Leonard R. Klein

Second Sunday after the Epiphany, Year C

First Lesson: Isaiah 62:1-5
(Psalm 36:5-10)
Second Lesson: 1 Corinthians 12:1-11
Gospel Lesson: John 2:1-11

John makes much of the fact that this was the first of Jesus' miracles (v. 11), which (unlike the synoptics) he regularly calls "signs." The term indicates that they are not mere supernatural feats, but significant acts. They draw attention to Jesus because they are astounding acts of divine power. But for those who have eyes to see their real meaning, they also highlight the significance of Jesus as Savior and the nature of the salvation he brings. As John says (v. 11), they reveal his glory and evoke belief.

One contrast between John's Gospel and the other three is that John is highly selective in the narratives about Jesus he chooses to include. He narrates only seven miracle stories, far fewer than in any of the synoptics. So his selection of this story as the very first significant thing Jesus does when embarking on his ministry suggests that it should carry considerable significance. But the significance is not obvious to most readers. Up to a point the story conforms to the general pattern of the Gospel miracles: Jesus meets a human need with miraculous divine provision. But the need in this case is that the hosts at a party have run out of wine. Compared with the needs of the desperately sick or seriously disabled that Jesus usually healed, or even with the hunger of the crowds he fed, more wine for a party seems more like a luxury than a need. Certainly it would be a serious social disgrace to run out of wine on such an occasion. But the family is evidently not poor: they have servants (v. 5) and expensive stone jars (v. 6). Could they not send out to buy more wine? It seems we must recognize that Jesus does not so much meet a need as supply an extravagance. The huge quantity of wine which is his contribution to the party (v. 6) is far more than the party could have drunk, even though wedding celebrations traditionally continued for a week. Moreover, the wine was of much better quality than they would normally have expected to be drinking. "Luxury" and "extravagance" are the words we have to use of this miracle, and so it may be that precisely this extravagant quality, unusual among Jesus' miracles, is essential to the greater significance John wants us to discern.

Most of the signs later in John's Gospel have an explicit interpretation attached to them, but this one does not. This must be because the story itself makes its significance clear enough. It need not make the significance obvious, because John likes to puzzle, to tease, and to provoke his readers into thinking about what he writes. He does not spell everything out and leave us no readerly work to do for ourselves. But the significance of this story must be clear enough for some reflection to uncover it. In our search of its meaning, the story's own dynamics lead us to the end (v. 10). This is a story with a punch line, somewhat resembling the so-called "pronounce-ment stories" in the synoptic Gospels, where the point is to be found in a significant saying of Jesus to which the story leads up. But in this case it is not Jesus but the headwaiter who has the punch line (v. 10).

John frequently has his characters say more than they realize, and read-ers are invited to understand what the characters themselves do not under-stand. (The best-known example is 11:50.) In this story the headwaiter's comment, at the purely literal level, is a joke at the host's expense. Usually people serve the best wine first because, once drunk, the guests will not no-tice the quality of the wine. The waiter points out how silly the host is to leave the best wine till last. However, the waiter does not know that the wine is a miraculous divine provision. For readers, who do know this, the waiter's words mean: God has done a very surprising thing. He has saved up till last his very best gift to Israel and the world. His best gift was not in Israel's past, when he gave Moses the law and Israel the land. He has kept the best wine until the coming of Jesus. Thus, appropriately for the first of Jesus' signs, the story relates the coming of Jesus to the history of Israel and identifies it as a surpassing climax to God's history with his people.

Commentators frequently suppose that Jesus' transformation of water, said in verse 6 to be for use in the Jewish purification rites, into wine indi-cates that the salvation Jesus brings supersedes the old dispensation of Ju-daism. But this understanding of the water as symbolic of the Mosaic reve-lation is at odds with the story's punch line (v. 10), which is the real key to the significance of the miracle. According to that saying, the best wine fol-lows, not water, but inferior *wine*. God's provision of salvation for his people before the coming of Jesus was, in the symbolism implied here, wine, not water. This is consistent with the prologue to the Gospel, where the salva-tion Jesus makes available is called "grace in addition to grace" (1:16), mean-ing that the Mosaic law (1:17) was already divine grace, while the salvation brought by Jesus was the fullness of grace, the real thing ("truth"; 1:17) to which previous grace was leading ("grace and truth"). The reason why the story of the wedding at Cana refers to the six stone water jars used for ritual ablutions (2:6) is that the story must both indicate what a vast quantity of wine Jesus produced and how it was that the water was available. (Stone jars were used by Jews who could afford them because they did not transmit impurity as vessels made of other substances did.) Such a factual detail is part of the genre of John's miracle stories (see also 5:5; 6:13; 9:1; 11:17, 39). There need be no more allegorical significance here than in the thirty-eight years for which the sick man had been ill (5:5). We should resist the temptation to find symbolism in every detail of John's narratives. These often have an overall figurative meaning, but the details are usually of a matter-of-fact nature, required for narrative reasons and/or to locate the story of Jesus in real time and space. This is why in our story John makes clear its location in Cana, which was a village near Nazareth and thus explains the presence of Jesus and his mother at the wedding celebration.

We return to the significance of the headwaiter's joke. The eccentric and surprising nature of the host's behavior, in serving the best wine last, applies also at the level of interpretation, in which it stands for God's act in the coming of Jesus. People in the ancient world commonly thought oldest was best. Ancient wisdom was the truest, the golden age was in the past. From that perspective the surpassing significance here given to God's most recent activity is surprising. But there was one tradition of thought in which it would not be surprising: the Jewish eschatological tradition of expectation of the messianic age of salvation at the end of history. Two images, well known in this tradition, for the extravagant joy of the messianic age were the wedding banquet (Isa. 61:10; 62:5; Jer. 33:10-11; Matt. 25:1-13; Rev. 19:6-9) and abundance of wine (Joel 3:18; Amos 9:13; Isa. 25:6; Luke 22:18; for wine producing joy, see Ps. 4:7; Eccles. 9:7). It would naturally be the very best wine that God will serve at the messianic feast (Isa. 25:6). As often in John, readers who do not know the Jewish background of the imagery can grasp the main thrust of the meaning, but knowing the specifically Jewish religious connotations of a universal image such as wine gives fuller insight into John's use of it.

Thus the extravagance of Jesus' gift of wine is integral to the story's significance. Jesus is introducing into the ordinary life of people like those of Cana that messianic enhancement of life that the prophets predicted. He enacts in the miracle what he later in this Gospel says: "I am come that they might have life, and have it abundantly" (10:10). When John's Gospel speaks of salvation as life, the meaning is not mere life, but life in its maximal sense: life invigorated and intensified. That temporary enlivening of life which wine effects on a superficial level symbolizes aptly the profound and permanent enhancement of life that is salvation. When Jesus tells his mother that his "hour has not yet come" (2:4), the immediate meaning is that he will not perform when his mother asks but only when God requires it. But the further significance, in the light of later occurrences of the phrase

(7:6, 8, 30; 8:20; 12:27; 13:1), is that the time of Jesus' glorification in cross and resurrection has not yet come. This makes the sign, which reveals Jesus' glory (2:11), an anticipation of the climax of all the signs: Jesus' death and exaltation. It is through the latter that Jesus really bestows the eternal life that wine at Cana symbolizes.

Jesus gives life by connecting people with the divine springs of life from which the vitality of life is constantly sustained and replenished. The church has not always conveyed well the impression that salvation is not only redemption and healing but also the fullness of life, given not sparingly but extravagantly by God. A preacher could well reflect on Kierkegaard's comment: "Christ turned water into wine, but the church has succeeded in doing something even more difficult: it has turned wine into water."

Richard Bauckham

Third Sunday in Lent, Year B

First Lesson: Exodus 20:1-17
(Psalm 19)
Second Lesson: 1 Corinthians 1:18-25
Gospel Lesson: John 2:13-22

The narrative of Jesus cleansing the temple is one of the rare stories that can be found in all four of the Gospels. For a preacher interpreting the Johannine version, the existence of parallel accounts raises an important question in regard to the chronology of Jesus' ministry. Matthew, Mark, and Luke place the story in the context of Jesus' triumphant arrival in Jerusalem just prior to the passion (his first and only trip to the Holy City, according to the synoptics). In these accounts the event functions as a major motivating factor prompting the chief priests and scribes to seek Jesus' execution. Jesus simply cannot be allowed to live after interfering with the economy of the temple market and threatening the very institution of the temple itself (e.g., Luke 19:47). In fact, in two of the Gospels his words on this occasion are used (misquoted actually) at his trial by "witnesses" to this scene (Matt.

26:61; Mark 14:58). By contrast, the event in John that finally prompts the religious authorities to press for Jesus' death is the raising of Lazarus (John 11:53), while the story of the cleansing of the temple is placed early in the literary scheme of the Fourth Gospel. Set at the beginning of his ministry, what is the theological import of the story of Jesus driving the money changers and animal sellers from the temple?

At the start of this passage readers are told that Jesus has traveled to Jerusalem in order to be there for the celebration of Passover. This is the first of three Passover observances marked by John. As noted on the eve of John's "third" Passover (11:55), it was common for Jews to journey to the temple in Jerusalem to engage in purification rituals as preparation for the festival. Perhaps journeying to participate in such "cleansing" practices, Jesus is passing through the outer courtyard of the temple when he comes upon merchants selling animals and changing coins. Both pursuits were necessary to the daily functioning of the temple. Animal vendors sold the various creatures that were to be sacrificed. Money changers enabled worshipers to change some of their everyday money into Jewish currency to pay the half-shekel temple tax. This essential service came about because the use of Roman or Greek coins with their blasphemous imagery and captions (some Roman coins declared Caesar to be divine) was prohibited in the temple. Was Jesus inherently antagonistic to these vendors and their wares? While there are passages in the Gospels that suggest that Jesus was opposed to animal sacrifice (e.g., Matt. 12:7), Jesus' words in this text do not focus on the activities of these vendors but on their problematic location within the temple complex. "Take these things out of here!" (John 2:16).

Traditionally, the various stalls selling animals and changing money had been located nearby in the Kidron Valley or on the slopes of the Mount of Olives. Evidence in the Mishnah suggests that it was Caiaphas himself who allowed merchants to set up shop *within* the confines of the temple. So it is possible that the vendors' occupancy of the temple grounds was a fairly recent development. It was not, however, unprecedented in the history of the people of Israel. In fact, the book of Zechariah envisions a future in which there would "no longer be traders in the house of the LORD" (Zech. 14:21). In line with these prophetic sentiments, Jesus fashions a whip, overturns the vendors' tables, and makes the powerful claim that this space is "his Father's house" and not the "house of the market" *(oikon emporiou)*. The repeated use of "house" *(oikos)* in this passage provides an interesting trajectory for a sermon, giving preachers the opportunity to explore together Jesus' use of "house" and our ongoing appropriation of the term to describe contemporary places of worship.

As Jesus evicts the merchants from the temple grounds, the disciples recall a verse from one of the psalms, "Zeal for your house will consume me" (John 2:17). Taken from Psalm 69, this verse belongs to a lament uttered by someone whose passion for God has resulted in separation from both kindred and community. The psalmist describes a life lived faithfully, but replete with shame, dishonor, and insult. Indeed, the character of this psalm is so stark that the Fourth Gospel will again allude to its imagery in describing the final living moments of the crucified Jesus (19:28-29). In quoting this psalm in chapter 2, John provides readers with an important interpretive clue to the story of the purification of the temple. The ministry of this Jesus is going to be rooted in zeal for his Father's house, and this fervor is going to lead to alienation.

The first hints of this can be discerned immediately. John tells us that "the Jews" requested a sign that would authorize Jesus' bold actions in the temple — behavior reminiscent of the prophets of old or perhaps even heralding the Messiah. Notice that John speaks of "the Jews" here, whereas the synoptics refer to the "the chief priests, the scribes, and the elders" (e.g., Mark 11:27). Where Matthew, Mark, and Luke make distinctions, John clusters these specific groups together and provides them with a more expansive identity — an ethnic one. In using this ethnic title, John implies that Jesus' actions do not risk alienation and reproach from a few select leaders, but from his entire people. This very factor has led some to see John's Gospel as anti-Semitic in character, but others have pointed out that the kind of ministry that would place a prophet at odds with his people is congruent with many of the prophetic portraits given to us by Old Testament witnesses (e.g., Jer. 20:7).

Instead of providing his questioners with a sign that will authorize his messianic actions, Jesus answers them with something that sounds like a challenge: "Destroy this temple, and in three days I will raise it up again" (John 2:19). Implicit in this comment is the notion that the temple is already being destroyed by those who would cede ownership to the marketplace for this holy house. This comment also resonates with older witnesses, especially Jeremiah, who spoke of the people's disobedience and corruption as leading to the destruction of the temple (Jer. 7:13-14). Jesus promises, however, that he will raise up the destroyed temple in three days. This claim strikes those in attendance as ludicrous given the fact that the current temple had been under construction for forty-six years (John 2:20). Yet Jesus' claim would also have had a strong messianic undertone for later readers who believed that the coming of the Messiah would bring about the reconstruction of the temple.

John, however, seeks to prevent a literal stone-on-stone understanding of verse 19 by telling us that Jesus was "speaking of the temple of his body" (2:21). Continuing in this line, the Fourth Gospel looks ahead to the resurrection, and envisages the disciples remembering this moment and interpreting Jesus' remarks about the temple as referring to Jesus' body being "raised from the dead" (2:22). In a sense this verse provides a response to those who requested an authoritative sign to support Jesus' actions. Jesus has authority in this house because he is the resurrected one. In effect, to the many other "I am" statements that populate John's Gospel (e.g., "I am the . . . light, way, truth, bread of life, living water, resurrection . . ."), readers can add, "I am the destroyed and rebuilt temple." Certainly one could also use the imagery of Jesus' body as temple as grist for a sermon, and along the way draw intriguing parallels to Paul's assertion that the church is the body of Christ.

Scott Black Johnston

Second Sunday in Lent, Year A

First Lesson: Genesis 12:1-4a
(Psalm 121)
Second Lesson: Romans 4:1-5, 13-17
Gospel Lesson: John 3:1-17

Trinity Sunday, Year B

First Lesson: Isaiah 6:1-8
(Psalm 29)
Second Lesson: Romans 8:12-17
Gospel Lesson: John 3:1-17

As John's third chapter gets under way, a man named Nicodemus arrives at an undisclosed place in Jerusalem. He has come to check out the new rabbi in town — a maverick teacher who literally *whipped* this year's Passover festivities into a frenzy by driving the money changers from the temple (2:13-22). Nicodemus sports an impressive pedigree. He is a Pharisee — a person of rigorous piety. He is a leader of the Jews, perhaps occupying a seat on the council of elders — the Sanhedrin. Despite these credentials, however, Nicodemus arrives *at night,* under the cover of darkness, to conduct his investigation after the public eye has shut. Why is Nicodemus interested in secrecy? Has he come out of personal curiosity and is afraid to let other Pharisees know of his interest? Perhaps. But Nicodemus's words to Jesus suggest otherwise. "We," he says, as in "we" the folks who run the show around here. "Rabbi, *we* know that you are a teacher who has come from God." It sounds like a compliment, or at least a recognition of the legitimacy of Jesus' ministry. After all, chapter 2 does conclude with testimony to signs and miracles, things that cannot be done without the presence of God (2:23-25). Maybe Nicodemus is a representative of those who have come to believe during the Passover celebration? Yet it is only while the masses lie fast asleep that the Pharisee risks his off-the-record remark, "We know you have come from God." Having said that, Nicodemus waits, carefully watching to see how Jesus will respond. Will the new rabbi fit in with the rest of the teachers, elders, and priests — the religious establishment in Jerusalem? Or was that stunt at the temple evidence of a lone ranger intent on bucking the system?

Jesus' response is one of the most familiar in all of Scripture: "Very truly, I tell you, no one can see the kingdom of God without being born from above" (3:3). The possibility of rebirth provided by Jesus has a captivating allure — hinting at the possibility of new life. It is not surprising that Christian movements like American revivalism have latched onto this compelling image as a central expression of a person's commitment to a fresh start in faith. But to Nicodemus it sounds like a bad riddle. How can anyone be born after growing old? Reentering the womb is a physical impossibility. But even as the Pharisee protests, Jesus persists, "Very truly, I tell you, no one can enter the kingdom of God without being born of water and Spirit. What is born of the flesh is flesh, and what is born of the Spirit is spirit. Do not be astonished that I said to you, 'You must be born from above.'" The crucial Greek word here is *anōthen*. You must be born *anōthen*. It means either "from above" or "again." The ambiguity seems deliberate. For when Nicodemus obsesses over the physical impossibility of this event, Jesus is provided an opportunity to push the envelope even further. "Listen closely," says Jesus. "Yes, born *again*." But this is not a physical rebirth, not a second trip through life. I am talking about being born from *above* — born of the Spirit. Faced with a concept so scandalous, Nicodemus sputters, "How can these things be?" (3:9). What began as a clandestine attempt to check out

496

the new guy in town has evolved into a challenging theological lesson that shakes the spiritual world of the Pharisee.

In preaching on this passage, we should attend to the fact that being "born again/from above" is an image that suggests that we have little choice in the matter. It is ironic that many Christians treat the question, "Are you born again?" as if it involves making a decision for God. Yet babies do not *decide* to be born. Indeed, the central feature of this textual image seems to preclude our active role in the process. Instead, God is the primary player in this passage. With this in mind, more than a few interpreters have argued that this chapter provides readers with John's equivalent to a birth narrative. Unlike the stories found in Matthew and Luke that focus on the events leading up to the birth of Jesus, John focuses on the spiritual birth of the Christian. What does that look like? How can we detect the presence of the Spirit in someone's life? That seems to be a difficult question to answer. It is an elusive thing, Jesus tells Nicodemus, for like the wind in the treetops, you cannot see the gusts of air themselves but only hear the results of their passing presence (v. 8). Perhaps then, being born from above is something that can only be discerned over time. One trajectory for a sermon along these lines could trace the life of Nicodemus as it plays out in John. The next time he appears in John's Gospel (7:50-52) the chief priests and Pharisees are trying to get Jesus arrested. As the temple authorities chastise the police, first for not nabbing Jesus and second for not knowing the law, Nicodemus speaks up to defend Jesus with his knowledge of the law. The final time Nicodemus shows up in John's Gospel, we watch as the Pharisee assists Joseph of Arimathea in embalming the body of Jesus after it is removed from the cross (19:39-42). Clearly, something has happened in the life of this Pharisee, and heeding Jesus' comments about the Spirit, we might conclude that the skeptical Nicodemus provides us with an example of new birth.

This text is suggested as one of the lessons for Trinity Sunday. Often Trinity Sunday is referred to as an "idea feast" in recognition of the fact that instead of a concrete event in the life of Christ (e.g., Good Friday), this particular day has its roots in a complex set of doctrinal formulations. Often sermons on this day fail because they set as their admirable, but unreachable, goal the exposition of the "idea" of the Trinity in twenty minutes. This text frees preachers from that approach to Trinity Sunday, for instead of an idea we encounter the Trinity in this text through a series of divine actions. In fact, all three persons of the Trinity are at work here. The Holy Spirit birthing God's children; the Father begetting and sending the Son; and the Son testifying to the Father and the Spirit. In this text the actions of the triune God are focused on God's desire to be near to us, engaging us and shaping us to be a holy people. This brings us to verse 16 and what Martin Luther called "The Gospel in Brief." The impetus behind God's desire to see us born of the Spirit is love. God's love is portrayed by Jesus in a sweeping manner — God loves (*agapē*) all of creation, the *cosmos*. Out of this expansive love, God sent the Son into the world to bring eternal life (v. 16) and salvation for all. This reflects one of the most interesting aspects of trinitarian study. The bond which unites the persons of the triune God is also the bond extended to us — love.

Scott Black Johnston

Fourth Sunday in Lent, Year B

First Lesson: Numbers 21:4-9
(Psalm 107:1-3, 17-22)
Second Lesson: Ephesians 2:1-10
Gospel Lesson: John 3:14-21

This passage sets a feast before a preacher, containing at its heart probably the most famous verse in the Bible: "For God so loved the world that he gave his only begotten Son, that whoever believes in him should not perish but have eternal life" (John 3:16). One problem with being so well known is that this passage is often reprinted everywhere — from T-shirts to bumper stickers — completely removed from its setting here. Yet while this verse may be at the heart of the feast, a well-balanced diet requires the rest of the meal — what accompanies it, and what goes before or comes afterward.

This reading comes quite early in the narrative of the Fourth Gospel. After the sublime heights of the prologue, describing how Jesus has come from being with God "in the beginning" to dwell among us as a human being (1:1-18), the story began with the witness of John the Baptist to Jesus and the call of the first disciples (1:19-51). Jesus starts his ministry by bringing the new wine of the kingdom of God into a wedding at Cana and the new life of his coming death and resurrection into the worship at the temple at Jerusalem (2:1-22). And yet, Jesus did not "trust" himself to people who "trusted" in him just because of his signs (2:23-24).

In the following chapters, many people will come to Jesus because of his signs — the Samaritan woman (4:29), the official whose son is healed (4:47), the paralytic (5:9), the crowd who were fed (6:14), the blind man (9:25) — all of whom need to move on from signs to faith in Jesus himself. Nicodemus is first a Pharisee and "a ruler of the Jews," a member of the Sanhedrin, the Jewish council (3:1). He is a man of influence and wealth (he buys spices in 19:39) whom Jesus calls "a teacher of Israel." He comes "by night," perhaps out of fear, or because he wants to talk to Jesus undisturbed (3:2). In due course he will come out into the open to speak for Jesus (7:50) and to bury him (19:39); for the moment he conducts a private dialogue with Jesus about how one may enter the kingdom of God, be born again, and receive new life in the Spirit (3:3-13).

Yet something strange happens to the conversation as Nicodemus disappears from view. In verse 11 "truly I tell you" is singular, addressing Nicodemus, but after that Jesus uses plural pronouns, "we" and "you" plural. Furthermore, it is not clear when Jesus' speech ends. Since ancient manuscripts had no punctuation, modern editors have to work out where to put quotation marks around someone's speech. Usually it is clear where someone stops speaking and the narrator restarts — but not in John. Some translations end the quotation in 3:15 while others run it through to 3:21, since both the narrative and Jesus' speech use the same style and words. It is as though the quiet nighttime conversation between Jesus and Nicodemus is replaced by Jesus speaking through the Evangelist to the rest of the Jews and on to the whole human race, asking them to "receive our testimony" (3:11).

The lectionary gives us verses 14-21 as a single reading — but what a reading! In the end, *who* says these words is less important than *what* they say, for this is one of this Gospel's supreme passages, full of John's favorite vocabulary and themes. John is fond of balancing opposites such as above and below, life and death, truth and falsehood. Such pairings are also found in Greek philosophy and in the Dead Sea Scrolls found at Qumran. In using these pairs, John explains the gospel in words and ideas accessible to his own day, but which also have had a profound influence upon human history ever since.

The passage begins with the story of Numbers 21:4-9, where the Israelites grumble against Moses and God and are punished by a plague of poisonous snakes. As a remedy God told Moses to make a bronze snake and to display it "lifted up" on a pole — and anyone who looked at it was healed. The bronze snake was eventually smashed by Hezekiah because people were treating it like an idol (2 Kings 18:4). However, the book of Wisdom, written in intertestamental times and now in the Apocrypha, describes it as a "symbol of salvation" (Wis. 16:6). John uses it similarly here as he seizes on the verb *hypsoun,* to "lift up," which is capable of several levels of meaning. Its positive meaning is to raise or exalt, but when Jesus talks here (and in 8:28 and 12:32-34) of the Son of Man being "lifted up," we know that it will be on a cross. Like the dying Israelites looking to the snake "lifted up" for healing, we are to see in Jesus' broken body "lifted up" on an instrument of torture our healing and the source of eternal life (3:14-15).

With this story as our "first course," John sets up his first balancing pair — life or death: to die of the serpent's bite or to look to God's healing remedy, to have eternal life or to perish. John's contrasting of the heavenly realm with the earthly could lead to accusations of dualism, seeing everything as either positive or negative. Certainly Greek philosophy tended to value the heavenly above the earthly, seeing the physical, material world as something from which to escape — and John sometimes uses "the world" in a negative sense for those opposed to God, especially in the Last Supper discourses. But "for God so loved the world" tells us that it is the *world,* for all its sin and shortcomings, which is the object of God's love. Sometimes Christians, in their neglect of the world, act as if John 3:16 read "For God so loved the *church* that he gave. . . ." Yet this Gospel makes it abundantly clear that God cares for the whole world in sending his "only Son." This phrase recalls another Old Testament story, where Abraham is to take "your son, your only son, Isaac whom you love" up the mountain for sacrifice (Gen. 22:2, 12). While Abraham was spared this ultimate sacrifice, God did not spare his Son, Jesus, but gave him so that the world should not perish. For this is the ultimate choice John puts before his readers: to perish apart from God, or to receive his gift of eternal life in his Son. There is no other option — and for this reason "God sent his Son into the world."

The image of God "sending" Jesus is one of John's most frequent, occurring over fifty times. But he is also clear why God sent the Son — not to condemn the world but to save it (3:17). The Greek verb *krinein* means to judge, and gives us the English words "crisis" and "critic." The coming of Jesus provokes a crisis both for the world and for all people, a "critical moment" of judgment and decision. Jesus does not come to condemn the world, for those who do not believe are already lost in their darkness and evil deeds (3:17-19). Instead he comes to save, that they might receive eternal life. Judgment is often thought to happen at the end of everything on Judgment Day. But John is clear that this deciding, this judgment, is already happening in every "critical moment" here and now. For John "eschatology" (things to do with the end, *eschaton* in Greek) is made real in the present, as Jesus comes into the world to save us.

The coming of light into darkness creates shadows, and this is the crisis, the judgment, because some prefer to remain in the shadows (3:19). Here is another contrast, between those who practice what is true, who come to the light, and those who do evil, who hide in darkness (3:20-21). But since Jesus comes not to condemn the world but to save it, not only those who do truth may come forward. Those who stumble in the darkness may also come to the light, as Nicodemus does by night, and find love. Later, as Nicodemus comes more out into the open, Judas will leave Jesus to go out into the darkness of the night (13:30). The options, the opposing contrasts, are always before us at each critical moment, which is why God sent his Son into the world, that we should not perish but have eternal life.

A preacher faced with this passage at this point in Lent will naturally focus on penitence and judgment, and there is much here about those Lenten themes. And yet at the same time, we must begin to look ahead to Holy Week and the passion — when the Son of Man will be "lifted up so that whoever believes in him may have eternal life" (3:14-15). This is a good opportunity to check our use of John 3:16. Is it just a slogan to put on our notice boards or to hit people with as a bumper sticker — or is it a real program for the church? If "God so loved the world" that he gave the ultimate sacrifice of his only Son, we dare not stay safely in our warm fellowships. We too must shine the light in all the dark places and encourage every man, woman, and child to come to the light and find eternal life.

Richard A. Burridge

Third Sunday in Lent, Year A

First Lesson: Exodus 17:1-7
(Psalm 95)
Second Lesson: Romans 5:1-11
Gospel Lesson: John 4:5-42

The narratives of Nicodemus and the Samaritan woman constitute a diptych of contrasting models of disciples in the early chapters of the Book of Signs (3:1–4:42). Contrast is an effective strategy for enlivening imaginations and inviting new insights. Major differences occur in setting, character development, plot, and climax to indicate how Jesus and an individual relate, communicate, and change.

The settings establish the basis for the drama of encounter: night (3:2) in Jerusalem (implied) and noon (4:6) in Sychar (4:5). An initial statement about the characters identifies religious/social locations. "Pharisee . . . a leader of the Jews . . . a teacher of Israel" (3:1, 10, NRSV) describe prominent status, while the proper name "Nicodemus" may designate a specific tradition. In contrast, the "woman" is mentioned four times according to her regional status "Samaritan" (4:7-10). The narrator's editorial note reminds the reader of her unacceptable status: "Jews do not share things in common with Samaritans" (4:9). Her present situation of having no husband compared to five previous ones indicates her conspicuous but lovely status (4:17-18).

A hint of reversals, however, occurs in the introductions to the dialogues. The time of Nicodemus's encounter with Jesus is "by night" (3:2). Since the symbolic dark/light dichotomy identifies the world/Jesus (1:9-11) and nonbelievers/disciples, Nicodemus represents a group who does not readily accept Jesus. Nonetheless, as a prominent teacher, Nicodemus takes the initiative with Jesus by recognizing his credentials (3:2). The Samaritan woman, however, recalls the hostile tradition between Jews and Samaritans. As teacher, she questions his demand: "How is it that you, a Jew, ask a drink of me, a woman of Samaria?" (4:9).

When Jesus replies to Nicodemus, he declares the necessity of being "born from above" in order to "see the kingdom of God" (3:3). Nicodemus misunderstands Jesus and considers his words literally when he conjures up the image of returning to a mother's womb as an old man. The play on the word *anōthen*, "from above" or "again," did not occur to him (3:4). Jesus develops his statement by equating "water" and "Spirit" with "born from above" (3:5-8). When Nicodemus asks how it will happen, Jesus responds rhetorically, "Are you a teacher of Israel, and yet you do not understand these things?" (3:9-10).

When Nicodemus appears a second time, the Pharisees are arguing about arresting Jesus. Nicodemus asks if it would be a proper procedure since their law doesn't condemn persons "without first giving them a hearing to find out what they are doing, does it?" (7:50-51). The Pharisees respond by taunting him: "Surely you are not also from Galilee, are you?" (7:52). Nicodemus's status suffers. In his final appearance, Nicodemus assists Joseph of Arimathea with Jesus' burial. He brings "a mixture of myrrh and aloes, weighing about a hundred pounds" (19:38-42).

Nicodemus's portrayal is consistent. The introductory phrase "came to Jesus" (3:2) is repeated in other appearances (7:50; 19:39). His silence after Jesus' monologue (3:11-21) is repeated when the Pharisees taunt him (7:52) and when he does not join Joseph in speaking about securing Jesus' body from the authorities. He is silent while preparing Jesus' body for burial. A clue to his behavior is his association with Joseph, "a disciple of Jesus, though a secret one because of his fear of the Jews" (19:38).

Jesus' first dialogue with the Samaritan woman, however, is lively! His statement challenges her imagination: "If you knew the gift of God, and who it is that is saying to you, 'Give me a drink,' you would have asked him, and he would have given you living water" (4:10). Instead of simply questioning Jesus as Nicodemus did, the woman discloses her own logic. How will Jesus produce the "flowing water" since there is no visible bucket to draw from the deep well (v. 11)?

Again, as teacher, she recalls her own history about Jacob and the well. Ironically she dismisses Jesus' greater claims with another question (4:11-12). Jesus replies by declaring that his gift of water will satiate persons' thirst definitively. How? It will become "in them a spring of water gushing up to eternal life" (4:14). The woman does not resist Jesus now. Not to be thirsty and no more daily trips to draw water from the well are wonderful possibilities in her life. "Sir, give me this water," she exclaims (4:15).

When we return to the second half of the Nicodemus narrative (3:11-21), monologue replaces dialogue. The speaker insists that testimony is based on knowing and seeing. If Nicodemus neither accepts nor believes statements about "earthly things," how can he believe "heavenly things" (3:11-12)? In the introductory verses Nicodemus's inability to grasp testimony links the monologue with the preceding dialogue (3:4, 9, 10). The monologue describes how an individual is "born of the Spirit," to clarify Jesus' enigmatic statements (3:5-8). Jesus as God's "only Son" was sent into the world to save it by being "lifted up" (crucified and risen). Consequently, believers "may not perish but may have eternal life" (3:14-16). God did not send his Son to condemn the world. Self-condemnation occurs when an individual refuses to believe in Jesus. Practicing evil (deeds) corresponds to the refusal to believe (3:17-20). By believing in Jesus an individual avoids condemnation.

Unlike Nicodemus, who replies to neither Jesus' statement (3:10) nor the monologue (3:11-21), the Samaritan woman responds to Jesus, who replies in the next section of the dialogue (4:16-26). Again Jesus begins the dialogue with a command to call her husband and return to him (4:16; cf. v. 7). The woman's reply, however, is a subtle change from the first scene where she was instructing Jesus with well-known tradition. Here she speaks the truth of her present situation: "I have no husband" (v. 17). By acknowledging her past and present situation, Jesus enables the woman to create his new identity. She calls him a "prophet" and refers to the tradition of different locales of worship for Samaritans and Judeans (4:19-22).

Similar to the change of speaker in the Nicodemian monologue (3:11-21), Jesus begins as the speaker but shifts to "we" statements (4:21-22) when he addresses the Samaritan woman. True worship is not defined by Mount Gerizim (an ancient holy place for the Samaritans) or Jerusalem. Rather, "in spirit and truth" describes authentic worshipers (4:21-24). While the monologue addressed the question of how believers would have access to the Spirit, Jesus' response to the woman describes one ability that the Spirit gives to believers.

The woman's understanding of "prophet" is an inclusion device for Jesus' instruction on worship. While she had identified Jesus as a prophet (4:19), now she connects the function of prophet to the coming Messiah (4:25). Again Jesus acknowledges the truth of her statement: "I am he, the one who is speaking to you" (4:26). Jesus' self-identification recalls to readers the divine name revealed to Moses on Mount Sinai (Exod. 3:14). Suddenly the disciples arrive, and their ability to ask Jesus about the situation precludes dialogue. Unlike Nicodemus, however, the woman leaves Jesus to acknowledge her experience to the townspeople. She considers the possibility of Jesus as the Messiah (4:28-29). The effect of her witness prompts them to come to Jesus (4:30).

The split scene whereby the disciples are silent before Jesus while the woman witnesses to him before the Samaritans (4:27-30) shifts to a dialogue between Jesus and the disciples (4:31-38). Again, the Johannine device of misunderstanding followed by Jesus' monologue is functional and draws attention to the first scene between Jesus and the woman. The interlude provides another contrast between their understanding of Jesus and the insight of a new disciple, the Samaritan woman.

Finally the scene shifts to the townspeople. They are believers in Jesus through the catalyst of the woman's proclamation. After asking Jesus to spend time with them, their belief deepens through Jesus' word. By hearing for themselves, they identify Jesus more extensively than the woman: "We know that this is truly the Savior of the world" (4:39-42).

Although the Samaritan woman appears only once, her importance is evident in her continuity with other characters. Some examples are: She led the townspeople to Jesus like the Baptist led two of his disciples to follow him (1:35-38). Her identification of Jesus as "prophet" is repeated by a Galilean and Judean crowd who were fed on the hillside (6:1-14). Unlike the disciples, she was not afraid to ask Jesus questions (4:4-42).

However, the woman symbolizes more. Her marginal status compared with Judeans, Galileans, and even her own townspeople is transformed because of her deep commitment as a disciple to Jesus. She represents the invitation of Jesus to each person regardless of status. Nicodemus, her foil, had a secure status yet lacked the imagination and daring to reconsider traditional viewpoints.

Breaking through the barrier of silence (forbidden by tradition in Jewish and Samaritan as well as male/female relationships outside the home) was the woman's first step toward liberation. Keeping silence, not expected by tradition, was the rabbi's first step toward stagnation. Inviting persons to freedom by contrasting relationships with Jesus in the Gospel is one challenge for preachers.

Mary Margaret Pazdan

Tenth Sunday after Pentecost, Year B

First Lesson: 2 Samuel 11:1-15
(Psalm 14)
Second Lesson: Ephesians 3:14-21
Gospel Lesson: John 6:1-21

This passage from John's Gospel covers two miracle stories: the feeding of the five thousand and Jesus walking on the water. Only the former is paralleled in all three synoptics. (In addition, Matthew and Mark have a story about a feeding of four thousand.) The story of Jesus walking on the water follows the story of the feeding of the five thousand in Mark and Matthew (but is not present in Luke). These were stories of obvious importance to the early church, and though we tend to read them separately, they clearly belong together — especially in John's Gospel, where the account of Jesus walking on the water is followed by Jesus' efforts to explain the miracle of the bread and the fish.

John uses these two stories to invite us into relationship with the living Christ. The true miracle is not the multiplication of loaves and fish, but the multiplication of God's grace — not that Jesus walks on water, but that he comes to us and takes hold of us. The God who is the source of all life offers us the possibility of participating in the divine life, of discovering a "true" life and "eternal" life in God that is stronger than evil and death, stronger than all our desperate efforts to multiply life for ourselves or to go it alone across the rough seas of life.

While questions of historicity (did these things really happen?) are inevitable, they will offer us little help in delving into the deeper meaning of these two stories. John himself writes that those who sought Jesus because they were impressed with the miraculous feeding did not really see the "sign" (6:26). They were looking for the wrong kind of bread. These two stories are more than journalistic accounts for the morning newspaper; they are rich theological constructions that draw on larger biblical themes.

Even a cursory examination of the story of the feeding of the five thousand reveals numerous Old Testament allusions. The feeding occurs near the time of the Passover (v. 4). Jesus' question to Philip, "Where are we to buy bread for these people to eat?" (v. 5), is reminiscent of Moses' dilemma in the wilderness, "Where am I to get meat to give to all this people?" (Num. 11:13). (The miraculous feeding of the people of Israel with manna, bread from heaven, is also suggested, and the analogy is made explicit later in the chapter [vv. 30-35].) Jesus multiplies loaves of barley bread, just as Elijah once ensured that the jar of meal and the jug of oil would not fail the widow of Zarephath (1 Kings 17:8-16) and Elisha once multiplied a widow's oil (2 Kings 4:1-7).

Even closer is the parallel to 2 Kings 4:42-44, where Elisha tells his servant to feed a hundred people with the twenty loaves of barley and fresh ears of grain in his sack. Elisha's servant protests that the few loaves will not suffice, like Philip, who in the feeding of the five thousand declares that "six months' wages would not buy enough bread for each of them to get a little" (v. 7); both stories end with food left over.

These Old Testament allusions point us to the past, to the key acts of divine salvation manifested in the time of the exodus and the prophets. Other allusions point us to the future, to the culmination of God's saving purposes, as anticipated by synagogue and church. Some scholars have suggested that the feeding of the five thousand with fish is an allusion to Old Testament and intertestamental depictions of the Leviathan, who will be slaughtered and consumed at the eschatological banquet (see Isa. 51:9; 4 Ezra 6:52; 2 Bar. 29:3-8). Jesus feeds the five thousand up on a "mountain"

(v. 3), just as Isaiah once prophesied that "on this mountain the LORD of hosts will make for all peoples / a feast of rich food" (25:6). When the people see Jesus perform the miracle, they call him "the prophet who is to come into the world" (v. 14), a reference to Deuteronomy 18:15, which anticipates the anointed one whom God will raise up at the end of time. The people's desire to take Jesus by force and make him king (v. 15) also reflects their hope in a messianic figure whom God will send to save the nation.

Intrascriptural allusions are less obvious in the story of Jesus walking on the water, but its theological import is no less clear. Both Moses and Elijah experienced theophanies that terrified them. Yet God spoke to Moses out of the burning bush and commissioned him to lead the people of Israel out of Egypt (Exod. 3:1-11); God spoke to Elijah in the still, small voice and girded him to return to the valley (1 Kings 19:1-18). The God whom the disciples meet in the breaking of the bread on the hillside is also the God who will meet them on the rough seas, in their times of deepest doubt, and will strengthen them again to serve him.

Exodus and eschaton came together for the early church in Jesus. Jesus (like a new Moses) offers liberation from every force of evil and oppression, and Jesus (in fulfillment of Old Testament prophecy) brings the kingdom of God near. Jesus initiates a new order in which enduring, flourishing communion between humans and humans, between humans and God, and between humans and the rest of creation becomes a real, even if elusive, possibility. To meet Christ is to be seized by fear and trembling, even doubt and confusion, for it is to come into the presence of the almighty God. Yet Christ also comforts, strengthens, and commissions us to follow him again.

These themes of communion and commissioning, fulfillment of the past and anticipation of the future, echo in one other biblical allusion that runs throughout our passage: Psalm 23. The feeding of the five thousand takes place beside the Sea of Galilee ("still waters"). The people are like sheep on a grassy hillside ("green pastures"), and Jesus has compassion on them ("the LORD is my shepherd"). When he feeds them, they are satisfied ("I shall not want"). He will lead them "in paths of righteousness" and will protect them in times of trouble ("I will fear no evil, for thou art with me").

In the early church Psalm 23 was sung during the paschal night as the newly baptized processed through the church to take their first communion. The psalm's images of a set table and an overflowing cup were easily related to participation in the holy meal; green pastures, to the catechesis or kerygma that nourishes the soul to receive the Eucharist. Eucharistic overtones are also apparent in John 6. Jesus takes the loaves, gives thanks, and distributes them; so also the fish (v. 11). There is enough for all; everyone is satisfied. Afterward the fragments are gathered up so that nothing might be lost (v. 12).

These allusions to Eucharist further unlock the significance of this passage for the church then and now. Week after week — century after century — Jesus' followers have discovered that Eucharist brings together these themes of exodus and eschaton, and of communion and commissioning. John, who does not have a Last Supper account (instead, he has Jesus washing the feet of his disciples), seems to use the feeding of the five thousand as his Eucharist story. (The eucharistic flavor of the story is further strengthened by the rest of the chapter, as Jesus declares that his flesh is true food and his blood is true drink [v. 55].)

The feeding of the five thousand and the walking on the water lead to a confrontation. Jesus turns to the crowd and asks whether they know the bread that is from heaven or only the bread that fills their stomachs (vv. 26-27). He poses the same question to us. Do we truly know Christ, or do we simply use him — or any other wonder-worker we can find — to fill our self-defined "needs." Casinos are built apace; investors pour money into an "irrationally exuberant" stock market; new technologies (the Internet, email, voice mail, cell phones) promise us greater productivity and ever expanding possibilities to be "in touch" with each other. It turns out that a secular age is the most superstitious of all, with no end in sight to our desperate efforts to multiply ourselves and our well-being — if possible by luck, or if need be by technique (diet, drugs, fertilization, even cloning!). Too often the sacrament itself becomes fast food, just another ploy to create a superficial sense of "community."

John's sacramental words tell us that we cannot know ourselves until we know the one before whom we stand. The homiletical task — indeed, the challenge to every part of our worship — is to offer people Christ. We are to preach eucharistically — by preparing people for the table, but by using our words as a means of grace by which people might encounter the presence and reality of Christ. John's preaching of Scripture challenges us to offer people nourishment, communion. We are called to preach exodus and eschaton, communion and commissioning, so that people may feed on the text — in the assurance that they will be fed Christ as well.

John P. Burgess

Eleventh Sunday after Pentecost, Year B

First Lesson: 2 Samuel 11:26–12:13a
(Psalm 51:1-12)
Second Lesson: Ephesians 4:1-16
Gospel Lesson: John 6:24-35

The lectionary focuses on John 6 for this Sunday and the next three. Needless to say, the chapter is rich. One difficulty is that breaking it up misses the coherence that only a reading of the whole brings to light. Those who preach on any of the four lessons would do well to read the entire chapter in worship at least once to allow the congregation to experience the whole. The "meaning" of the passage cannot be abstracted from the movement of the story; even the repetition is an important component in its impact.

Notice that the chapter follows Jesus' statement about Moses and his writings "bearing witness to me." Jesus' great sign — feeding five thousand people with five loaves and two fish — cannot be understood apart from the scriptural antecedents. A similar story is told about Elisha the prophet in 2 Kings 4:42-44, and the narrator expects readers to know what it means that Jesus' sign occurs when "the Passover, the feast of the Jews, was at hand." Traditions about the miraculous provision of food in the wilderness for the escaped slaves form the backdrop for the account of Jesus' miracle and for the discourse that follows.

The interaction between Jesus and the crowd is the more striking in view of what has just occurred. Those who ate the bread were so impressed at Jesus' miracle that they confessed, "This is indeed the prophet who is to come into the world" (6:14), and were apparently ready to make Jesus king "by force" (6:15). Jesus' initial response to the crowd is thus unexpected: you seek me not because you saw signs but because you ate your fill. Appreciating Jesus' multiplication of the loaves as something that has deeper significance is apparently what it means to "see signs." While the crowd has eyes, we soon learn they cannot see. The story reveals the truth of what Jesus says.

The conversation between Jesus and the crowd begins as earlier conversations, with misunderstanding. Jesus tells the crowd that they are to "labor for the food that does not perish but endures to eternal life." The crowd has little sense of what he is talking about. Their response, "What work must we do to be doing the work of God?" elicits from Jesus a statement about faith: the "work" of God is to have faith in the one God sent. The crowd's response confirms Jesus' earlier statement: "What sign do you do?" The crowd has of course just witnessed Jesus' sign — but they have apparently not understood it as a sign. They understand on one level but, like Nicodemus, do not perceive the deeper (or higher) meaning.

Again returning to the theme of Moses' writings, the crowd challenges Jesus with a quotation from the Scriptures. Those who look up the citation will discover that it is not exactly like any verse in the Old Testament, though it is close to Exodus 16:14; Nehemiah 9:15; Psalm 78:24; and Psalm 105:40. Important in the challenge from the crowd is that the verse presumably speaks of Moses as the subject, the verb refers to a past event, and "bread from heaven" refers to the manna. Jesus proposes a new reading of the same verse: the subject "he" refers not to Moses but to God; the verb is not past tense but present; and "bread from heaven" refers not to manna but to something in the present (Jesus will soon refer the image to himself). The only difficulty in the Greek text of the Fourth Gospel (and the English translation) is that it is not clear how Jesus can declare a past tense in the biblical verse a present tense. If the reader knows that the crowd quotes a text in Hebrew, the comment makes perfect sense. The same three Hebrew letters in the verb "to give" can be read as a past or a present tense — depending on the vowels. Without vowels, as the Hebrew text in the first century was written, interpreters could supply the vowels for a different word. Much in the style of Jewish preachers, Jesus begins his discourse with a novel interpretation of a biblical text: don't read "He [Moses] gave [past tense] bread from heaven [manna] to eat," but read "He [God — my Father] gives [present tense] the true bread from heaven [referent to be supplied]." Jesus then goes on to explain what this "true bread" is.

While this explanation of the passage is hypothetical (particularly since there is no real evidence of a Semitic "original" of the Gospel), it does explain Jesus' comment and makes good sense of the whole passage. And it indicates a problem the passage explores, with the rest of the Gospel: "having eyes, they do not see." The crowd cannot even read the Scriptures properly. They see the words, but they do not know what they mean. Understanding the testimony of Moses will require something more than an understanding of the words. People must discover that Israel's Scriptures point to Jesus — and that insight is a matter requiring more than eyes and ears. One must be "born from above."

Jesus' description of the "bread from heaven" in verse 33 can be translated in two ways. The Greek can mean "the one who" comes down from heaven or "that which" comes down from heaven. The NRSV has chosen to translate as the crowd hears: "For the bread of God is *that which* comes down from heaven and gives life to the world." The crowd certainly understands

Jesus to be speaking about some supernatural bread, like manna. Jesus' explanation begins to make things clearer: he is speaking about himself. The bread "that comes down from heaven" is the "one who" has come. One could thus translate the Greek from the reader's perspective as "For the bread of God is the *one who* comes down from heaven." Important here is that, as readers, we understand throughout what the crowd cannot. That awareness is one of the things the story depends on.

Metaphorical use of "bread" to speak of what God gives to sustain life occurs already in the Scriptures, particularly in Proverbs where Dame Wisdom speaks of herself in such terms:

> "You that are simple, turn in here!"
>   To those without sense she says,
> "Come, eat of my bread
>   and drink of the wine I have mixed."   (Prov. 9:4-5)

Partaking of wisdom is described in terms of eating and drinking in a long poem in which Dame Wisdom again speaks in Jesus ben Sirach 24:19-21:

> Come to me, you who desire me,
>   and eat your fill of my fruits.
> For the memory of me is sweeter than honey,
>   and the possession of me sweeter than the honeycomb.
> Those who eat of me will hunger for more,
>   and those who drink of me will thirst for more.

Unique here in John is that God's wisdom that comes down from heaven is embodied in Jesus; he is the "Word" that proceeded from God's mouth, that served as God's agent in creating the world, and that now comes to give life.

The more we learn about the passage, the most striking is the claim. Jesus insists that the God who gives life is known in the particular — and that he is the embodiment of that life. Everything comes to focus on him. He is the source of life over which death has no power; if there is a "Wisdom of God," it will be known only in him and through him. The reality of God is not distant or abstract; it is concrete and present. The statement is both promising and disconcerting. The crowd will become increasingly uncomfortable with Jesus' insistence that he is that "bread" of which the Scriptures speak.

511

While the issue is appropriate to this and the following three lessons from chapter 6, preachers might focus on the "argument" these opening verses seek to make. The point is not simply that Jesus is the source of life. It is that the crowd does not understand in what sense that is true. They look at Jesus and have no idea what they are seeing. They look at the words of Scripture and have no idea what they mean. While in Mark's Gospel Jesus' identity is a mystery that he seeks to conceal at least for a time, in John's Gospel Jesus' identity is a mystery even though he speaks about it constantly. That sight and insight are gifts of God is repeated throughout the Gospel. Here the message is embodied in the story as it unfolds. How that is true in Christian experience is a topic worth developing.

Donald Juel

Twelfth Sunday after Pentecost, Year B

First Lesson: 2 Samuel 18:5-9, 15, 31-33
(Psalm 130)
Second Lesson: Ephesians 4:25–5:2
Gospel Lesson: John 6:35, 41-51

Perhaps the first thing to say is that verses 35-51 should be read without omitting 36-40, as the lectionary proposes. Those who listen to the passage will be struck by the redundancy: Jesus repeats himself. Twice in the omitted verses Jesus speaks of "raising them up at the last day" (vv. 39 and 40). The words are echoed in 44, 47, 50, and 51. If the purpose of stories were only to convey information, the omission of the verses would make sense. They provide no new information. The function of the story is not only to convey information, however; it is to make an impression. Saying the same things over and over makes all the more remarkable the crowd's inability to hear what Jesus says.

I don't recall ever having been as impressed by the effect of repetition as when I read Marilyn French's book *The Women's Room*. The book is lengthy — over five hundred pages. Any effort to abridge the work, however, destroys the effect of the argument. The thesis — that a woman must choose between living with a man and surrendering her freedom, or being free but living alone — becomes convincing as the narrative follows the stories of so many women, all very different, whose diverse experience inevitably confronts them with the same stark alternative. The drastic abridgments required to make a movie based on the novel utterly destroyed the impact on the audience.

Far from being marks of combined sources or a lack of artistry, repetition in Jesus' discourse contributes to the "mystery" surrounding his identity. More accurately, it contributes to an experience of the "mystery." While in Mark the "messianic secret" involves Jesus' purposeful concealment of his identity, in the Fourth Gospel the mystery involves Jesus' repeated reference to his identity and the crowd's inability to understand and believe. Repetition not only emphasizes a point (i.e., that Jesus will raise the faithful at the last day); it also brings the issue of communication to the forefront. Why can't people hear and understand what is made so obvious to readers? How many times does Jesus need to say something for it to be understood?

The same is true of Jesus' reference to the work of "the Father." Twice in the omitted verses Jesus speaks of God's work of "giving" people to Jesus: "All that the Father gives me will come to me" (v. 37); "And this is the will of him who sent me, that I should lose nothing of all that he has given me" (v. 39). The activity is further defined in the verses that follow: "No one can come to me unless drawn by the Father who sent me" (v. 44); "It is written in the prophets, 'And they shall all be taught by God.' Everyone who has heard and learned from the Father comes to me" (v. 45).

The point is repeated often enough finally to make its impact. It is possible, of course, that contemporary hearers may react like the crowds and the disciples in the story. That we understand Jesus' words does not necessarily mean that we will agree. The notion that communication, understanding, and faith are made possible by the actions of God is a prominent theme in the Gospel. In later chapters Jesus will speak of the Spirit in just this way. "I still have many things to say to you, but you cannot bear them now. When the Spirit of truth comes, he will guide you into all the truth; for he will not speak on his own, but will speak whatever he hears, and he will declare to you the things that are to come. He will glorify me, because he will take what is mine and declare it to you. All that the Father has is mine. For this reason I said that he will take what is mine and declare it to you" (16:12-15).

That understanding requires the action of God may prove a difficult idea for many who imagine that such matters belong in the realm of human choice and freedom. It is difficult to avoid the impression, however, that something blocks access to understanding. John's Gospel does not argue that those who do not believe lack the intelligence to understand. The problem is more like bondage ("slaves to sin" in chap. 8) or blindness (chap. 9). Those who are enslaved to sin cannot simply be told to stop sinning; they must be freed. The blind will not be helped by assigning blame ("Who sinned, this man or his parents, that he was born blind?" [9:2]) or by giving advice about how to see; they will have to be healed. In the absence of liberation and healing, the response of the crowd is predictable. No matter how many times Jesus testifies to the truth, they cannot and will not hear. It is likewise the case that his words are not neutral. The promises they make also offend, even today. That we must trust God to open eyes and ears is a topic that generates uneasiness and even anger. The alternatives available to Jesus' audience were to believe his words or to silence him.

"I'm not comfortable with a God like this," a student said in class recently. The assumption was that he should find God comfortable. That he did not was a sign he was beginning to understand — and that the discomfort could be caused by a simple story from the Bible is testimony to the power of the Word of God. Preaching on this passage can be a useful test of the preacher's faith. Can God be trusted with the task of creating and sustaining faith? If so, the discomfort of a congregation may be an indication that God is at work; the discomfort is only the reverse side of faith that can rely on nothing but God's promise to free bound imaginations and open eyes.

We cannot forget that what animates the crowd — and present readers — is simply a promise that God has come near so as to give the gift of life.

Donald Juel

Thirteenth Sunday after Pentecost, Year B

First Lesson: 1 Kings 2:10-12; 3:3-14
(Psalm 111)
Second Lesson: Ephesians 5:15-20
Gospel Lesson: John 6:51-58

These remarkable sentences mark the climax of Jesus' discourse. Hearing them is apparently confirmation for the crowd that while Jesus may have been able to provide bread for them, his teaching is utterly unpalatable. Even his disciples find the words distasteful: "This is a hard saying. Who can listen to it?" And they leave.

It's not difficult to understand why Jesus' words offend. The notion of eating flesh is abhorrent. And if eating flesh isn't offensive enough, Jesus speaks of drinking blood — an action expressly forbidden not only for Jews but for all included in the covenant God makes with Noah (Gen. 9:1-6). Jesus' words place him outside the bounds of civilized society in the world God created and is invested in through the law.

Jesus' words are offensive not only to an ancient audience. It is remarkable that any readers find these words palatable. Most will find some way to make the sentences respectable by reading them as symbolic: Jesus couldn't have meant his flesh and blood but was referring to something else. While some sort of symbolic reading seems inevitable, it is striking that Jesus does nothing to nudge his audience in this direction. His use of another Greek word for "eat" ("Those who eat [*trōgein*] my flesh" [6:54, 56, 58]) — a verb used among other things to speak of animal eating (much like the German *fressen*) — only makes it harder for his audience. English translators have obviously sought to make the statements more respectable by sanitizing the translation.

What can these strange words of Jesus mean? Contemporary readers can have no doubt that Jesus was pointing ahead to the Lord's Supper where, in the synoptic Gospels, Jesus' offering of bread and wine to his disciples is accompanied by the words "This is my body . . . this is my blood." So accustomed have some readers become to the language of the liturgy, in fact, that there is little shock in what Jesus says. But do Jesus' words point to the Lord's Supper? This interpretation has been disputed. The greatest difficulty in reading the words as presuming the Last Supper is that in the Fourth Gospel the account of Jesus' last meal includes no such words. The meal, described in John 13, features an account of Jesus' washing the disciples' feet, a prediction of his betrayal, and a lengthy farewell discourse that extends to the end of chapter 17. The dramatic difference between John and the synoptics at this point, which includes even the dating of the Last Supper, raises all sorts of interesting questions about the history of the traditions behind the Gospels and their relationship to one another. The likelihood that the language is used in light of its place in Christian worship makes most sense if the author of the Fourth Gospel knows something of the traditions on which Matthew, Mark, and Luke drew. An interpretation of Jesus' words cannot await a solution to such questions, however.

Nor will the problem be solved through source criticism. Some scholars, following Rudolf Bultmann, discount the "eucharistic" interpretation of John 6 by arguing that verses 51-58 are a later addition to an "original" Gospel of John. The solution is unconvincing. While it may be that the Gospel gives evidence of various stages in the history of composition, the church's Bible includes a Fourth Gospel with verses 51-58 in chapter 6. We cannot do better, perhaps, than to note that the church has made sense of these words in the Fourth Gospel by understanding them in light of the Lord's Supper. If the author of the Fourth Gospel had something else in mind, we have no access to it.

Even if the language is understood as a reference to the Lord's Supper, the matter of its offense is not solved. Preachers may wish to explore in more depth the use of language about eating the flesh and drinking the blood of Jesus. While the Fourth Gospel regularly uses metaphors like "water" and "bread" for which there is precedent in the wisdom tradition, there is something about the use here that is startlingly tangible. The "religious" nature of the symbolism which can keep it at a safe distance breaks down here. The "real" Jesus gets too close for comfort. Yet that is precisely what the church has found promising. There is finally no distance between the Lord and the faithful. The reality of Jesus — the reality of God — can be held in the hand and eaten and digested. While theologians have sought to make sense of the metaphor in terms of prevailing metaphysics, the language of these verses breaks through layers of respectability and the reality of Jesus comes near. Perhaps that is precisely the promise of the passage.

If that is true, all the more striking is the movement of the whole passage. What begins as a conversation in which a crowd, fed with real bread by Jesus, comes seeking more, ends with the crowd thoroughly scandalized. What finally drives them off are the words of Jesus — his testimony to the truth. Preliminary misunderstanding turns to grumbling and finally to utter disgust. The more Jesus speaks, the further the crowds are distanced from the life-giving truth, until they leave. The movement is the opposite for those who are "inside." Imagery that begins in the more abstract becomes more and more concrete, until Jesus speaks about eating his body and drinking his blood. A more intimate image by which to speak of how Jesus is life for those who believe is hardly conceivable. The language of the Lord's Supper, strangest from the perspective of the world, is closest to the heart of the gospel truth.

It may be enough in a sermon to celebrate the tangible gift of the one who does not withhold himself from the faithful, who gives himself — his flesh and blood — to give life. A sermon may also provide an opportunity to think in broader terms about what the passage means. The movement of the passage plays out a major theme from the prologue: he came to his own, and his own people did not receive him. Again the light shines in the darkness, and the darkness does not grasp it. The light shines, and those who do evil run for the shadows. Important to note is that what drives people from the light is not a series of oppressive demands but Jesus' promises. What people find impossible to believe is that the reality of God should come so close and that it should be embodied in one like Jesus. Neighbors know his mother and father (6:42). Despite the presence of food that endures to eternal life, they cannot eat. They prove unable to swallow what will guarantee eternal life. The problem is not that Jesus is unclear and confusing. It is that people do not have an appetite for what Jesus offers; they do not have the eyes to see and the ears to hear.

Such passages are difficult for those who imagine that problems of unbelief are matters resolvable at the level of human choice. The history of discussion within the Christian tradition that includes such figures as Augustine, Pelagius, Luther, Calvin, and Erasmus is significant because it is not about theoretical but real issues. What happens when people are offended by the promises of God? What does it mean that the same words can encourage and sustain the faithful and turn others off — or even make them angry? Insisting that people are responsible for their reactions and that they can simply will to change them is untrue to actual human experience. At this point in John's Gospel, at least, readers are left at the mercy of a God whose Spirit blows where it wills. The question is whether or not we are able to trust such a God — and if not, what God will do about it. Trusting God will mean, at the very least, that preachers do not need to be unsettled when people are troubled by the promises of the gospel — and they can be patient, leaving to God the task of opening people to discover that they can taste and see that the Lord is good.

Donald Juel

517

Fourteenth Sunday after Pentecost, Year B

First Lesson: 1 Kings 8:(1, 6, 10-11), 22-30, 41-43
(Psalm 84)
Second Lesson: Ephesians 6:10-20
Gospel Lesson: John 6:56-69

The conclusion of the discourse is anticlimactic: "He said these things while he was teaching in the synagogue at Capernaum." The action of the crowd is no longer important. They have no rebuttal. They will have an opportunity to speak later.

The scandal of Jesus' discourse is not reserved for the crowd. The majority of his "disciples" also find his words difficult. Jesus' comments about "returning to where he came from" as an even greater offense are related to his repeated reference to his having "come down from heaven" earlier in the chapter. The offense is not simply a mistake, the result of some misunderstanding. It has to do with Jesus' identity as the one who has come from the Father and will return to where he was.

The words about "spirit" and "flesh" have had a long history in Christian theological conversation. They served Zwingli as ammunition for his symbolic interpretation of the Lord's Supper, a fiercely debated topic that has proved church-dividing. The term "flesh" is rare in John, with three of the five occurrences within a few verses here in Jesus' discourse. While he speaks of the necessity of eating his "flesh," here he tells the disciples, "It is the Spirit [spirit?] that gives life; the flesh is useless. The words that I have spoken to you are spirit [Spirit?] and life." Zwingli's argument was that it was not actually the "flesh" of Jesus in the Lord's Supper that was the life-giving element but the "Spirit," by which he meant a symbolic interpretation of the earthly elements. It is Jesus' words, after all, that are "Spirit and life" (6:63).

While such a reading is not impossible, it does not fit well with the statement in the prologue that the Word "became flesh," and it would seem to contradict directly Jesus' explicit statements about the necessity of eating his flesh. The exegetical problem is not a small one. Major interpreters, from Bultmann to Bornkamm to Brown, have argued that the interpretive problems are related to the "insertion" of verses 51-58 into the context of a coherent discourse. It is certainly the case that Jesus' statement about flesh, Spirit, and his words is more easily understood against the background of 35-50. Jesus' reference to his ascending ties to comments about his having come down from heaven (6:33, 38, 50, 51) at which the crowd is offended. The comments about flesh and Spirit are related to the comments about being "drawn by God" (6:44) and "taught by God" (6:45). While there may be evidence that the Fourth Gospel has undergone successive stages in its editing, such theories are not necessary for interpretation. Even in the context of the Gospel as we know it, we can understand "the flesh" in 6:63 not as a reference to "my flesh" but to "flesh" in contrast to "Spirit," as in Jesus' comment to Nicodemus: "What is born of the flesh is flesh, and what is born of the Spirit is spirit" (3:6), and in light of Jesus' promise of the Spirit later in the Gospel.

That the disciples cannot understand his words and find them an offense is an indication that they have not been "born of God" or "from above" (1:13; 3:3). Without the Spirit they cannot understand. Jesus' words promise life — but a large group of disciples, with the crowd, cannot believe. They are among those who have not been "taught by God."

By the end of the chapter it is only the Twelve who remain. Jesus' question to them is the occasion for Peter's "confession." Speaking for the Twelve, Peter acknowledges that Jesus "has the words of eternal life." They have heard and understood: "We have come to believe and know that you are the Holy One of God" (6:69). While not as full a confession as John the Baptist's or Mary's or Martha's, Peter's statement says all that is necessary. "We have come to believe. . . ." While the disciples do not understand fully and even perform badly when the crisis comes, there is something that sets them apart from others. The author of the Fourth Gospel writes, confident that others will come to believe (20:30-31).

There is an exception even here: Jesus' innermost circle contains a traitor. The omission of the last few verses of the chapter from the lection is without justification. Jesus' response to Peter — and his last words in the chapter — change the tone of the lesson considerably. "Did I not choose you twelve, and one of you is a devil?" Even the circle of the Twelve will not remain intact. Somehow Judas never understands.

The last lines are a striking conclusion to a chapter that begins with more than five thousand people and ends with eleven! Jesus' teaching has not resulted in mass conversions. "He came to his own, and his own people did not receive him." "The light shines in the darkness, and the darkness does not grasp it." If Peter and the little band around Jesus see and understand, if they recognize in Jesus' words the promise of life, it has little to do with their virtues or intelligence or performance. "The Spirit blows where it wills."

Those who know the rest of the story will point out, of course, that the

Spirit has not yet been given. It is not until he departs, Jesus tells his disciples, that he will send the Spirit:

> But the Advocate, the Holy Spirit, whom the Father will send in my name, will teach you everything, and remind you of all that I have said to you. (14:26)

> Nevertheless I tell you the truth: it is to your advantage that I go away, for if I do not go away, the Advocate will not come to you; but if I go, I will send him to you. And when he comes, he will prove the world wrong about sin and righteousness and judgment: about sin, because they do not believe in me; about righteousness, because I am going to the Father and you will see me no longer; about judgment, because the ruler of this world has been condemned. I still have many things to say to you, but you cannot bear them now. When the Spirit of truth comes, he will guide you into all the truth; for he will not speak on his own, but will speak whatever he hears, and he will declare to you the things that are to come. (16:7-13)

There is a sense in which the crowd cannot be expected to comprehend fully what Jesus says. Even the disciples do not understand much of what Jesus says until after he is raised from the dead (2:22). It is thus among present readers that Jesus' words do their most important work. They are "Spirit and life"; they promise insight into the heart of God which only the one who comes from the Father can provide. The words are embodied in "visible words," as Augustine described the sacraments. And while the words still have the power to offend, preachers must also trust that they can give life.

Donald Juel

Fourth Sunday in Lent, Year A

First Lesson: 1 Samuel 16:1-13
(Psalm 23)
Second Lesson: Ephesians 5:8-14
Gospel Lesson: John 9:1-41

L ike many healing stories, the narrative in John 9 centers on a blind man
who, upon recovering his sight, immediately begins to walk around like
a typical sighted person. However, as neurologists like Oliver Sacks point
out, if it really happened this way, then this once-blind man was the recipient of a double miracle: not only had Jesus fixed his optic hardware but he
must also have installed the necessary mental software which allowed the
man to make sense of the information coming through his eyes. Although
we do not realize it most of the time, the ability to see is one part physical
phenomenon and another part mental exercise. Functioning as a sighted
person requires having access to a long backlog of visual *experience*.

For this reason blind people who surgically receive the ability to see cannot instantly begin to act like all other seeing persons. Without having had
any prior experience with things like depth perception, the formerly blind
find themselves reaching for objects that are actually well out of reach even
as they may knock over a glass of water which is closer than they thought.
Likewise, the once-blind misjudge steps and bump into walls because they
have not yet acquired the knack for interpreting visual data. Some even continue to use their white canes for a while so that they can slowly begin to
connect how the world has always *felt* through the tip of the cane with how
it now *looks* through their eyeballs. It also takes time to learn how to recognize objects which previously had been known only by their shape and tex-
ture. The once-blind may know what a telephone receiver feels like, but may
have to be told "That's a phone" the first time they *see* one.

As it turns out, this matter of sight is a bit more complex than we might
think. But then John 9 bears witness to this same fact, albeit in the spiritual
realm. As is the case in many classical Greek dramas, so in John 9 irony is
created through the fact that the man who had been blind turns out to have
a sharper spiritual vision than people who never had any optic difficulties.
Conversely the Pharisees, who believe their vision can penetrate spiritual
matters with laserlike precision, turn out to be the truly blind ones.

Homiletically this lection is rich with possibilities. The option of an em-
bellished retelling is certainly a strong one, particularly with some of this

story's built-in humor and irony. There is even an element of mystery as Jesus disappears after verse 7, reappearing only at the very end of the story (though even then Jesus is a mystery figure since the once-blind man has quite literally never laid eyes on Jesus and so does not recognize him at first). There is also the humor of the healed man's becoming ever more impatient with the silly interrogation by the Pharisees.

However, since this passage is assigned as a Lenten reading, perhaps a more apropos approach would be to trace through its obvious motif of sin. Lent is a season which calls believers to be serious about sin. Yet, in an ironic way this story provides a Lenten caution not to say more about sin than is prudent.

Like the disciples at the outset of this story, so many people look for connections between sins and circumstances in a simple cause and effect schema. For instance, some years ago parts of California experienced a particularly devastating earthquake resulting in significant damage and loss of life. Desperate to make sense of this tragedy — and perhaps also eager to score some points for God — one southern California congregation invited Richard Mouw to come the week following the quake to help them discern what God was saying to the folks in that sometimes-secularized part of the country. Mouw, however, was not interested in playing into any naive equating of this event with God's wrath, and so chose as his sermon text for that Sunday the portion of the Elijah story which says, "But God was not in the earthquake"!

There are, of course, places in the Bible where God himself makes clear that sometimes there is a correlation between a tragic event and God's punishment of sin. When God himself reveals such a judgment, it can be taken as reliable. However, even in the Bible, when human beings try to make such connections on their own, they nearly always get it wrong. The disciples in John 9 do, too. They see a man born blind and assume someone must have sinned.

In John 9:3, however, Jesus provides the Bible's single most striking counterargument against the simple equating of bad things with specific sins. The blind man's unhappy situation may ultimately be a tragic fallout of a world that had fallen into sin, but it was not the result of any proximate sin. In other words, sometimes a little holy agnosticism is called for when it comes to talking too glibly about other people's sins.

The Pharisees possess no such pious caution. They start by once again lobbing the sobriquet "sinner" toward Jesus himself. Since Jesus had, by their definition, broken the Sabbath, he could not be some God-sent prophet. On the other hand, however, the Pharisees could not deny the punch behind the argument that a miracle as grand as healing a man born blind could not have been performed by anyone *other* than a heaven-sent servant of God. Hence the Pharisees launch plan B, which is to impugn the miracle itself lest Jesus get credit for something which, undeniably, would bolster his divine credentials.

Alas, plan B does not work either, as it soon becomes clear that the healed man is no fake — he's too well known as the town's blind beggar. So the Pharisees fall back, regroup, and return to plan A; namely, calling Jesus a sinner. But this tack works no better on the second go-round, as this time it is the healed man himself who provides the same counterargument: no mere sinner could have the kind of pull with God that Jesus clearly has. Frustrated, fed up, and frankly also defeated, the Pharisees dispense with the man by returning to the same idea which the disciples had when the story began: namely, it is *this* man who was steeped in sin at birth (which is why he was born blind in the first place), and so he is not a credible witness.

Hilariously, by calling this man a sinner on account of his having been born blind, the Pharisees now tacitly acknowledge the miracle, thereby playing into the logic of Jesus' divine character after all! Thus Jesus, having begun the story by repudiating the disciples' cozy assumptions about sin, concludes by targeting the genuine sin of the Pharisees. If the Pharisees really were ignorant (or spiritually blind) as to the logic which properly equates the ability to heal with being divine, then they would not be guilty of sin. But Jesus knew (as did the Pharisees deep down) that they both saw and understood the implications of this healing. Their spiritual eyesight was just fine. Their stubborn rejection of Jesus came not from blind ignorance but sin.

John 9 counsels caution to those who, out of a sincere but misguided desire to show pious seriousness, say more about the sins of others than they know. By way of counterexample the Pharisees, through their convenient dismissal of both Jesus and the healed man as lousy sinners, remind us that it is possible for the devout to use the sin label as a way to avoid those who, if only we would listen, have something important to teach us. More chilling still is the end of this story, which contains more than a hint that sometimes the very people who talk the most about sin (*other people's* sin) are themselves the most blind, sinful folks of all.

Perhaps it seems odd to encounter such a text halfway through Lent. In some ways John 9 could make us wary to talk too much about sin in the center of a season which centers on confession of sin! But perhaps this lection calls for us to import into our doctrine of sin a slogan of the ecological movement: Think Globally, Act Locally. The global sin of the world is a matter of great seriousness — it explains why the Son of God came to die. But too much focus on all the sin that is "out there" in the wider world can quickly transmogrify into a self-righteous smugness. This can then make us so blind to our own need for grace that we become stingy in doling out this same grace to those around us who are desperate to hear the good news that the light of the world has come in Christ Jesus — a gracious light of mercy and forgiveness in whose ambient glow all people can see the glory of God.

Scott Hoezee

Fourth Sunday of Easter, Year A

First Lesson: Acts 2:42-47
(Psalm 23)
Second Lesson: 1 Peter 2:19-25
Gospel Lesson: John 10:1-10

Jesus has a lot to say about sheep and shepherds in this chapter. In fact, he stretches this pastoral metaphor to cover such an expanse of territory that many interpreters will become frustrated. Who exactly is Jesus supposed to be in relation to the sheep? Is he "the gatekeeper," "the gate," or "the shepherd"? How should a preacher approach these transposing images? Over time some have treated this chapter as a series of shifting allegories that can be decoded in a this-equals-that manner (e.g., "bandit" = "Pharisee"). Although tempting, this tactic misses the profundity of the Fourth Gospel's rhetoric. As with other prominent images in John (bread, water, light, etc.), the linguistic pictures found in chapter 10 have a depth that transcends the narrow interpretive dimensions of allegory. As these images overlap and transform, they explore a central theme in John's Gospel — the theological relationship between Jesus and those under his care.

Before examining the evolving play of images in this text, we should consider questions of audience. Who is listening as Jesus speaks? At the close of the previous chapter, 9:40-41, Jesus is chastising the Pharisees. Perhaps Jesus is continuing his criticism of these religious leaders in 10:1 when he describes a trespasser in the sheepfold as a "thief" or a "bandit." Yet by the time we get to 10:6, we are told that those listening "did not understand" Jesus' remarks about the gatekeeper and the sheep. Usually the role of misunderstanding in John is reserved for the disciples. So perhaps Jesus has switched locales and is speaking exclusively to his followers. While these explanations provide a plausible audience for Jesus, they may be trying to unmask an intentional ambiguity. In other words, perhaps John did *not* make a fledgling author's mistake and forget to identify the listeners in 10:1. Instead, John purposefully left the identity of the hearers unclear. By allowing the identity of Jesus' listeners to become murky at various points in the Gospel, John resists grounding Jesus' words in a specific historical moment and allows his speech to establish a unique connection with readers. In this case the statements this text makes about false leaders and true callings are not simply a commentary on the poor leadership of the Pharisees, but extend beyond first-century Palestine to describe the world of the reader. As such, this text beckons today's preachers to think about contemporary leaders who are both bad and good.

With this in mind, the parable told by Jesus appears relatively straightforward. There is a faithful way to enter the sheepfold, and an unfaithful way. Thieves and bandits leap over the wall — their disreputable intentions revealed by their choice of entrance. The shepherd, on the other hand, enters via the *thyra* (gate or door). As sheep, we are able to discern between the shepherd and the thief because the shepherd alone conforms to an established protocol (arrival via the gate) in approaching the flock. But what is the significance of this protocol? What does the gate used by the shepherd symbolize? Perhaps it refers to the law (i.e., the shepherd approaches the flock in a manner consistent with God's command). Or perhaps the gate reflects the expectations that the people have about the Messiah (i.e., Jesus approaches as one who has the recognizable traits of God's Anointed). As we ponder these possibilities, we may want to glance ahead to 10:7 where Jesus declares, "I am the gate." The shift marked by this verse makes the passage seem rather circular. In verse 2 we were told that the "gate" assists the sheep to distinguish who is and who is not the shepherd. Then, after listeners profess an inability in verse 6 to interpret this "figure of speech," Jesus claims to be the gate. How can Jesus be both the shepherd and the gate? To maneuver around this paradox, some argue that Jesus has changed topics and is speaking a new parable with a new central image. While this approach seeks to explain Jesus' shift in language, the claim that these are discrete parables misses something that John consistently conveys about Jesus. Simply put, the manner in which Jesus approaches the flock (through the gate) is not established by some external source (i.e., "This is what the Messiah will be like . . ."), but by Jesus himself. He is both the shepherd who approaches the sheep in a proper manner and the gate that defines a proper approach. He is both the Messiah and the criteria that establish who the Messiah is and what the Messiah does. Preachers who wish to explore this trajectory in their sermons may want to discuss how our expectations for God are skewed if they are not grounded in the person of Christ. In other words, if we desire Christ to be our shepherd, we cannot take it upon ourselves to define the gate that he must enter through. God's Son approaches us on his own terms. He is the shepherd and the gate.

If Jesus is both the shepherd and the gate, how then does one recognize him? Curiously, Jesus implies that his followers know him instinctively. Evidently the sheep's ability to identify their shepherd extends beyond spot checks that monitor how different folks are entering the fold. The shepherd calls his own sheep by name (10:3). As a result, the sheep hear *(akouō)* the shepherd's voice, and they follow that voice and not the voice of a stranger. The notion that Jesus' followers (as opposed to the nonattentive "world") instinctively recognize the summons of God can be found throughout John's Gospel — perhaps most poignantly in 14:17. Are we to interpret this intuitive "knowing" as an internal confidence that steadfastly directs a believer's attention toward Jesus? Perhaps. Yet even the disciples, who are repeatedly told that they "know" Jesus, appear befuddled from time to time (e.g., 10:6 and 14:7-9) and seem not to know or hear, and hence lose the ability to follow God's voice. So, at a deep level, the sheep know the particular cadence of the voice of truth, and yet they occasionally manage to forget what that voice sounds like. Preachers might find this an engaging tributary for a sermon. What distinguishes the shepherd's call from the voice of strangers — the voice that causes the sheep to run? At root this is an ethical question for contemporary Christians whose attention and devotion is being clamored for by so many competing voices.

Finally, the central aspect of this passage lies in the great concern that Jesus manifests toward his followers. He is the gate that provides salvation for the sheep (10:10), and the shepherd who comes that the sheep may have life, and have it abundantly (10:11). Even as Jesus shifts his posture from shepherd to gate and back to shepherd again, we get a clear sense that the focus of his energies (whether as gate or shepherd) is bent on providing generously for the well-being of his flock. Once again this beneficent approach is contrasted with the intent of the thief in 10:10, who comes to take life away. Thus this passage closes with a warning and a promise. The sheep are cautioned lest they fall prey to a leader who approaches in a suspicious manner and whose desire for them is destruction. The sheep are directed toward a shepherd whose voice they already know, whose desire for them is abundant life, and whose vocation is to care for them. The precise shape that this "care" will take is addressed by the next portion of chapter 10.

Scott Black Johnston

Fourth Sunday of Easter, Year B

First Lesson: Acts 4:5-12
(Psalm 23)
Second Lesson: 1 John 3:16-24
Gospel Lesson: John 10:11-18

The images of sheep and shepherds found in this chapter draw upon and interact with other "sheep" stories and psalms found elsewhere in the canon. The manner in which these images interpret each other provides the preacher of John 10 with some fascinating opportunities.

To start, consider the initial image in this passage — the good shepherd. Why does Jesus refer to himself as the "good" shepherd? Clearly this metaphor is infused with Old Testament imagery. So, why doesn't Jesus mirror these well-known texts by simply saying (as God does in Psalm 23 and Ezekiel 34) that he is the people's shepherd? The adjective "good" (*kalos;* also: right, proper, honorable, and beautiful) adds a new layer of meaning. To an established metaphor for leadership and for God, Jesus contributes an explicit distinction, a contrast between good and bad. Are there "bad" shepherds? The Bible is actually replete with images of shepherds who were less than good. In Isaiah 56:10-12 God describes the rulers of the people as shepherds who care only about themselves, and who get drunk when they should be watching their flock. In Jeremiah 10:21 God refers to Judah's leadership as "stupid" shepherds who have allowed the sheep to become scattered. In Ezekiel 34 we find God's most extensive denunciation of bad shepherds. The "shepherds" of Israel are accused of feeding themselves and not the sheep. These shepherds do not bind up the injured creature's

527

wounds nor care for the sick. They do not love the sheep; instead they rule over them with harshness and violence. Bad shepherds, indeed!

Informing us that he is not one of those bad shepherds, Jesus gives content to the claim that he is the "good" shepherd. He explains that the good shepherd lays down his life for the sheep. Jesus contrasts this perilous approach to that taken by the hired hand. The hired hand does not own the sheep, and hence flees at the first sign of danger. As preachers, we should not belittle the logic embodied by the hired hand. It makes good sense. The hired hand knows that her life is of more value than a mere sheep, and since the hired hand does not even have property at stake (she does not actually own the sheep), she flees to tend sheep another day. Of course, from the sheep's perspective the hired hand's actions have disastrous results. When the shepherd flees, the wolf comes in to snatch a meal and scatter the remainder of the flock. At this point, it may be that readers are supposed to recall an alternative, model shepherd, the young David (destined to be king) who defended his flock by slaying a lion and a bear (1 Sam. 17:34-37). Is Jesus the "good" shepherd as David was a good shepherd? In Jesus, do we find a leader who will place his own life at risk to protect us — a ferocious defender who will fight and not run? It is tempting to head down this path in order to frame a sermon, but before doing so we need to look carefully at what John's Gospel does *not* say. However much we may desire an aggressive response to the wolf, Jesus does not say he will fight the beast, beating it off with stones, keeping the sheep safe and secure. Instead, Jesus simply and repeatedly tells us that he will lay down his life. This may lead the preacher to explore a sticky but interesting question: Is the leadership provided by this shepherd any better than that offered by the hired hand?

In this passage Jesus claims to know his sheep, and furthermore, he states that his sheep know him. Moreover, the manner in which Jesus claims to know his own (and in which his own know him) is compared to the way the Father knows the Son and the Son knows the Father. This is an important and powerful comparison, given the exceedingly close connection that John's Gospel draws between the Father and the Son. We need only read a bit further in the chapter (10:38) to find a crystalline example of how well the Father and the Son know each other, when Jesus states that "the Father is in me and I am in the Father." Returning to verses 14-15, we are told that the same kind of intimate connection that exists between Jesus and the Father inheres between Jesus and his followers. What does this have to say about the relationship between the shepherd and the sheep? Throughout the Bible one finds frequent affirmation that God knows God's people. In Nahum 1:7 we are told that God knows (*yada'*) them that seek refuge in the

528

Lord. In 1 Corinthians 8:3 Paul states that "anyone who loves God is known by him." John's Gospel contributes extensively to the biblical testimony that God "knows" us. Starting with the surprising assertion that the divine *logos* became flesh and dwelt among us, John proclaims that God has inhabited the world in the person of Jesus in a unique way. God knows the people from up close. God does not know as the hired hand knows (i.e., as an appropriate calculation in which one weighs one's own life against the value of a lesser being); God the shepherd (the Word become flesh) knows from an intimate perspective. In fact, one might go so far as to say that this is a shepherd who knows exactly what it is like to be a sheep, and by extension, what it is like to be snatched by the wolf. A sermon following this interpretive trajectory may want to point out that John's account of the passion places Jesus in the role of the Passover lamb (the crucifixion happens even as the ritual lambs are being slaughtered at the temple [19:14]), or that the book of Revelation uses Lamb of God imagery to refer to Jesus.

Jesus has the power to lay down his life and to take it up again. This language supplies a subtle contrast to the usual manner in which the New Testament speaks of Christ's resurrection. Commonly the New Testament writers make Jesus the object of God's resurrecting power (e.g., Acts 2:24: "God raised him up"). At this point, however, John's Gospel once again emphasizes the similarity between the Father and the Son by asserting that they share in the divine power that brings about the resurrection. Even so, John maintains the crucial distinction that has been forged throughout this Gospel showing Christ to be in a posture of obedience toward the Father even as he wields this power. Jesus lays down and takes up his life according to the loving commandment of the Father (10:18).

Those interested in pursuing the question of the "other sheep" may find themselves speculating about the mission of the early church to the Gentiles. The chances are good that Jesus is in fact speaking of ministry to those who are non-Jews, but the preacher should also note the heavy emphasis Jesus places on unity in verse 16. Ultimately, despite the differences between the flocks, the shepherd brings about oneness amongst the sheep.

Scott Black Johnston

Fourth Sunday of Easter, Year C

First Lesson: Acts 9:36-43
(Psalm 23)
Second Lesson: Revelation 7:9-17
Gospel Lesson: John 10:22-30

John's readers are probably to understand that Jesus has stayed three months in Jerusalem, from the Feast of Booths (7:2) until the Feast of the Dedication (Hanukkah). This latter was the Jewish festival most recently instituted and the only one not prescribed in the Hebrew Bible. But it commemorated an event of potent significance in Jewish memory: the cleansing and rededication of the temple by Judas Maccabeus in 164 B.C.E., following its pagan desecration by Antiochus Epiphanes and Judas's successful military campaign to liberate it (1 Macc. 4:46-59; 2 Macc. 10:1-8). In the time of Jesus the major temple festivals had acquired eschatological significance, associated in popular celebration with the hope of deliverance from Israel's pagan oppressors and the blessings of the messianic age to come. This makes it particularly apt for John's Gospel to depict Jesus' appropriating the symbolism and significance of these festivals with reference to himself, as he does especially in chapters 6–8. It is not so much, as commentators tend to say, that Jesus supersedes these festivals or the temple itself to which they were attached, but that they find their true, eschatological meaning and fulfillment in Jesus and the salvation he brings.

When John specifies the particular festival in question (contrast 5:1, where the feast is left unspecified), he does so because it is significant for what Jesus says and does at that time. This must also be the case with the Feast of the Dedication, and is clearest in 10:36, where Jesus himself is said to have been "consecrated" (dedicated, like the temple) by the Father. This picks up a major christological theme of the Gospel, that Jesus himself is the new temple, the eschatological presence of God with his people. The Feast of the Dedication surely evoked for many who attended the hope of another great deliverance of Israel from the pagans who desecrated the Holy Land, like the great victory of Judas Maccabeus. The holiness of the temple, as the place of God's presence with Israel, was always central to Jewish eschatological expectation. Since the dedication was a festival about the temple itself, it is appropriate that in John's Gospel it is the last festival Jesus attends before his final Passover. It gathers up the associations between Jesus and the temple which the Gospel has made from the prologue (1:14) onward, and portrays Jesus as himself the new "place" of God's presence. Like the temple in the Maccabean period, Jesus is about to suffer desecration by pagans, aided and abetted by Jewish apostates, as Antiochus Epiphanes also was. Whether the theme of the dedication significantly informs John's narrative before it reaches (beyond our passage) 10:36 is not certain. But it could be seen in verse 30: because Jesus and his Father are one, God is present in him as in the temple. Less probably, "the Jews" who do not believe in him (vv. 25-26) and later attempt to destroy him (vv. 31, 39) correspond to the Jewish apostates who connived at Antiochus's desecration of the temple.

"The Jews" in this passage are not the Jewish people in general, but the Jewish leaders in Jerusalem, as is clear from the fact that throughout chapters 7–10 this term, "the Jews," alternates with the terms "the chief priests and the Pharisees" (7:32, 45) or just "the Pharisees" (7:32; 8:13, 22; 9:40). (The Pharisees in question are those few Pharisees of aristocratic families who belonged to the Jewish governing body, the high priest's council.) It is these who, alarmed by the popular idea that he might be the Messiah (7:25-31; 9:22), have since chapter 7 been debating his claims with him. Some of them have been inclined to believe him (8:31; 10:19-21; 12:42). As in the synoptic Gospels, Jesus in John's Gospel has never directly claimed the title Messiah for himself, but has spoken of himself and his mission in a whole variety of ways that take up but also go far beyond common Jewish notions of the Messiah. Most recently he has used the image of the good shepherd (10:1-18), to which he reverts here in verses 26-27. For the full significance of verses 26-28, one must appreciate how they allude briefly to the picture painted especially in verses 3-4, 12-15.

Before reflecting on the theological and pastoral significance of verses 26-30, it is worth noticing how remarkable it is that Jesus speaks of the true Israel as "my flock" and, addressing some of the official leaders of the Jewish theocracy, denies that they belong to it. Throughout the Old Testament Israel is depicted as God's flock. Like some other Jewish teachers and leaders of his time (probably the bandits and thieves of v. 8), Jesus speaks of a remnant, the true Israel, to which not all who claim descent from Abraham belong. This true Israel are the sheep who recognize *Jesus* as their shepherd, hearing *his* voice (i.e., recognizing it; cf. vv. 3, 8) and following *him*. Thus the imagery of shepherd and sheep as Jesus here uses it already prepares for the climactic statement about Jesus' relation to his Father in verse 30.

So "the Jews" show, by not believing in Jesus, by not recognizing who he is in spite of the miracles which show his Father's authorization of him, that they do not belong to his flock. Verses 25-29 are one of several passages in

John which speak of God's election or enabling as the prior condition for belief (cf. 6:36-40, 44), a theme which is also, as here in verses 28-29, linked with that of the security of believers who cannot be taken out of Jesus' or God's safekeeping (6:39-40; 17:6-12). Of course, these passages have been the object of doctrinal debate about the meaning of election in the New Testament and the relationship between divine sovereignty and human responsibility. Some points are worth bearing in mind: (1) Jesus' declaration in verse 26 does not prevent him from continuing to challenge "the Jews" to believe in verses 37-38. (2) The main concern in verses 26-27 is to present believing recognition of Jesus as what marks out his sheep, that is, the true Israel, from others. (3) The main point of verses 28-29 is to assure those who do believe in Jesus that they are in no danger from the thieves or the wolf (vv. 10, 12). The main pastoral application of verses 28-29 will surely be to assure believers that God's hold on them is much more reliable than their hold on God.

Verses 28-29, while still echoing, in the word "snatch," the imagery of the shepherd and the flock (cf. v. 12), take a step further than what had been said up to verse 18. There the good shepherd, Jesus, is distinguished from the hired hand by the fact that the sheep are his own, and so he cares so much for them as to lay down his life for them. What is not said there is that he has the power infallibly to protect his flock from being snatched by wolves or thieves. This is what is emphatically stated in verse 28, and which requires a further explication with reference to the Father in verse 29. That *no one* can snatch believers from Jesus' hand can only be true if his hand is the unchallengeable and indefeasible power of God. In this, as in all things, Jesus acts with the unique authority of his Father, such that his own hand (v. 28) is equivalent to the Father's hand (v. 29). There is a difficult textual problem in verse 29a, where purely text-critical considerations would favor, as the harder reading: "What my Father has given me is greater than all else" (NRSV). However, the train of thought we have just explained favors, as more coherent with its context, the reading: "My Father who has given them to me is greater than all" (NRSV margin). It makes little sense to say that the flock is "greater than all," but that God is "greater than all" is fundamental to the biblical and Jewish understanding of God, and is the presupposition for believing that no one can snatch believers from God's hand.

As often in John, a soteriological argument leads to a christological claim: "The Father and I are one" (v. 30). Since the Greek for "one" is neuter, not masculine, this is not a claim that Jesus and the Father are identically the same person. This point was important in the role this verse, with some other key Johannine texts on the relation of the Father and the Son, played in the trinitarian controversies of the fourth century and the resultant definition of Nicene trinitarian orthodoxy. (To put it in a modern paraphrase: Father, Son, and Holy Spirit are *who* God is, but the one divine being is *what* God is and *what* Father, Son, and Holy Spirit are.) Modern commentators tend to distinguish the text from this patristic use of it by claiming it refers to the unity of purpose and function of Father and Son, not to any "metaphysical" unity of substance. But when the "function" in question is, as it is here, the uniquely all-powerful sovereignty of God over all things, it is a mistake to suppose that even in first-century Jewish thought this could be understood as *merely* functional, as though it could be delegated to someone who is not God. It belongs to God's very identity as God, and so the claim in verse 30 does include Jesus within the unique divine identity. It is not surprising that it provokes "the Jews" (here again, appropriately to their action, the Jewish *authorities*) to prepare to stone him for blasphemy (v. 31).

Richard Bauckham

Fifth Sunday in Lent, Year A

First Lesson: Ezekiel 37:1-14
(Psalm 130)
Second Lesson: Romans 8:6-11
Gospel Lesson: John 11:1-45

We remember that on the Third Sunday in Lent, Year A, the narrative of the Samaritan woman invited us to consider how Jesus is living water for our lives (John 4). On the Fourth Sunday the narrative of the man born blind described how Jesus is light for our lives (John 9). On this Sunday we hear that the raising of Lazarus embraces the claim: Jesus is the life whom we are seeking (John 11).

In this seventh sign *(sēmeion)*, Lazarus's illness is inextricably connected with a manifestation of God's glory: God's power shines through Jesus' sign (v. 4). According to the narrator, Jesus' hour of glorification begins proleptically since the raising of Lazarus is the catalyst for plotting Jesus' death (11:45-53). This narrative also draws hearers to the drama that precipitates Jesus' passion and death. The basic struggle between life and death is ours as preachers as we proclaim John 11 and its challenge.

In earlier narratives of healing and feeding in the Book of Signs, Jesus performs a *sēmeion* and speaks about its significance afterward (cf. 5:1-47; 6:1-59; 9:1-41). The literary structure is reversed in the raising of Lazarus, where dialogue is prominent in relation to Lazarus's situation and Jesus' self-identification. There is no indication of a miracle until Jesus' command: "Lazarus, come out!" (v. 43).

The characters *(dramatis personae)* who appear in chapter 11 symbolically constitute a full range of responses to Jesus. There are opportunities to identify with one or several characters as the plot unfolds. The unnamed disciples who accompany Jesus play a minor role by misunderstanding what Lazarus's death implies. They can only hear and interpret Jesus' statement literally: "Lord, if he has fallen asleep, he will be all right" (v. 12). Jesus' correction, "Lazarus is dead. . . . let us go to him" (vv. 14-15), prompts the only named disciple, Thomas, to comment, "Let us also go, that we may die with him" (v. 16). How the disciples accompanied Jesus in the raising of Lazarus and afterward is left to our imaginations.

Martha's believing in Jesus constitutes a contrast to the disciples. She sends a message (with her sister Mary): "Lord, he whom you love is ill" (v. 3). She relies on Jesus, her friend, in this dire situation. Immediately we are confronted by Jesus' reception of her message: "This illness does not lead to death; rather it is for God's glory, so that the Son of God may be glorified through it" (v. 4). The narrator's comment that affirms Jesus' love for Martha, her sister, and Lazarus appears puzzling when we learn that Jesus "stayed two days longer in the place where he was" (v. 6).

Next, Martha meets Jesus on the road before he even reaches Bethany (vv. 17-20). She wastes no time in greeting her friend. She berates him for his absence; yet she also expresses confidence in his presence: "But even now I know that God will give you whatever you ask of him" (v. 22). Jesus' reply, "I am the resurrection and the life" (v. 25a), prompts Martha to respond with an extraordinary confession: "Yes, Lord, I believe that you are the Messiah, the Son of God, the one coming into the world" (v. 27).

Martha's proclamation parallels Nathanael's: "Rabbi, you are the Son of God! You are the King of Israel!" (1:49). Her statement is a variation of the Petrine confession at Caesarea Philippi (Matt. 16:16 par.). It also supersedes the Galilean official's. His belief in Jesus' word was followed by the confirming sign that restored life to his son (4:46-53). Martha's belief precedes Jesus' sign and enables her to witness his glory (11:40). Her response is a contrast to the disciples at Cana, who saw the sign and then believed in Jesus (2:11).

Martha's final appearance is at the tomb. Here she protests Jesus' request to take away the stone: "Lord, already there is a stench because he has been dead for four days" (v. 39). Some scribes believed that the soul hovered around the dead person's body for three days. After four days there was no hope. Now Jesus recalls an earlier conversation with Martha: "Did I not tell you that if you believed, you would see the glory of God?" (v. 40; cf. vv. 4, 23, 25).

When we contrast her to Martha, Mary is a secondary, two-dimensional character (cf. Luke 10:38-42). She does not advance the drama either by her actions or her speech, which are stylized to repeat Martha's character and draw attention to her significance (cf. vv. 20 and 29, 31; 21 and 32). Nonetheless, when Jesus saw Mary weeping, "he was greatly disturbed in spirit and deeply moved" (v. 33). The narrator repeats his agitation as Jesus approaches the tomb (v. 38). Here it is essential to differentiate a cultural code of the first century with a postmodern understanding of Jesus' emotional involvement. By using a cultural anthropological model, interpreters emphasize that Jesus was "disturbed" because Mary had challenged him publicly. He had to respond to protect his honor.

Lazarus, their brother, is the only voiceless character in the narrative. His restoration to life essentially links him with Jesus to the extent that the chief priests also plot his death (12:10-11). In chapter 12 his home is the place of hospitality for Jesus. It is where Martha takes on a characteristic role of serving while Mary anoints Jesus' feet (vv. 2-3).

The "Jews" also have roles in the narrative. They are generally described in a positive light: consoling Martha and Mary (v. 19), staying with Mary in the house and accompanying her to the grave (v. 31), showing Jesus Lazarus's tomb (v. 34), and acknowledging Jesus' love for Lazarus (v. 36). After the disagreement over Jesus (vv. 36-37) develops, we notice some changes in the Jews.

The raising of Lazarus elicits faith from one group who was present at the tomb (11:34; 12:11). They witness to Jesus because of his sign (12:17). The tense of the verb *(emartyrei)* suggests that their faith in Jesus prompts a continuous witness. Some of those present at the tomb, however, report Jesus' action to the authorities (11:46). His sign does not lead to belief. A third group, "a great crowd," appears in chapter 12. Since they are in Jerusalem for the Passover, they are drawn to Jesus because they heard about Lazarus (12:12, 18). Although they greet him enthusiastically with palm branches and acclamation (12:13), there is no indication of subsequent belief.

The officials are another group in the narrative (11:46; 12:10, 19). They are generally unnamed, like the various groups of the Jews. The chief priests and Pharisees realize that Jesus' signs are dangerously persuasive: "Everyone will believe in him" (11:47-48; cf. 12:11, 19). Caiaphas, the high priest, criticizes and offers them a plan: "You know nothing at all! You do not understand that it is better for you to have one man die for the people than to have the whole nation destroyed" (vv. 49b-50). His prophecy rallies the officials to plot Jesus' death (v. 53).

How can we evaluate the characters? Lazarus and Martha are the only ones Jesus addresses directly. While Lazarus's response to Jesus' command is not recorded, Martha's response is a confession, an appropriate genre of revelation. Jesus identifies himself: "I am *(egō eimi)* the resurrection and the life" (v. 25a). He is the life for those "who believe in me, even though they die, . . . and everyone who lives and believes in me will never die" (vv. 25b-26).

Earlier the narrator notes that believing in Jesus promises that death is not the ultimate condition: "Whoever believes in him should not perish but have eternal life" (3:16b). The death implied in "perish" is clarified in 11:25-26, where physical death is not denied; rather, the assurance of everlasting life beyond the grave is emphasized.

Whether or not the noun "life" *(zōē)* is qualified by the adjective "eternal" *(aiōnios)* is not significant since whenever "life" appears in any verse of the Gospel, it signifies the life of the Father and Son that is shared by the believer. Participation in divine life is a present reality for the believer.

Believers possess resources that are needed to face experiences that threaten life. First, Jesus provides nourishment: "I am the bread of life; whoever comes to me shall not hunger, and whoever believes in me will never thirst" (6:35). Jesus' teaching (6:35-50) and his body and blood (6:51-58) also sustain and satisfy.

Second, to free individuals from final condemnation, Jesus cancels the judgment (3:18). Judgment occurs during an individual's life. Believing in Jesus means participating now in eternal life; conversely, those who do not believe condemn themselves as long as their failure to believe persists.

Third, to dispel the darkness experienced in life, Jesus offers himself as the source of light: "Whoever believes in me may not remain in darkness" (8:12; 9:5, 39).

The gospel does not deny life and its limitations. Rather, it identifies the life of the Father and Son as what sustains the believer now and after death.

Mary Margaret Pazdan

Fifth Sunday in Lent, Year C

First Lesson: Isaiah 43:16-21
(Psalm 126)
Second Lesson: Philippians 3:4b-14
Gospel Lesson: John 12:1-8

Today, the Fifth Sunday in Lent, is the start of the last full week of Lent, which will be followed by Palm Sunday and Holy Week when we remember Jesus' entry into Jerusalem leading to his passion and death. It is therefore a turning point when we can look both backward and forward, back across our Lenten journey of penitence and discipline and forward to the climax of Good Friday and Easter.

This reading is also a turning point. John's Gospel is structured in two main parts — Jesus' ministry of teaching and healing (1:19–10:42), and the last few days of his ministry and his death and resurrection (chaps. 12–20). The prologue (1:1-18) and the epilogue (chap. 21) balance each other, while at the heart of the Gospel comes an interlude of events at Bethany (chaps. 11–12).

Chapter 11 tells the story of the illness and death of Lazarus, whom Jesus restores to life; this theme of life and death recurs at the end of the chapter with the Sanhedrin deciding to kill Jesus the life giver (11:51-53, 57). After today's passage chapter 12 continues with Jesus' entry into Jerusalem and the various reactions from the Pharisees, some Greeks, and the crowds of people, before John goes on to his second part with the Last Supper in chapters 13–17.

The first verses of this passage about "dinner with Lazarus" also reflect this turning point: verse 1 reminds us that Jesus had raised Lazarus from the dead in the previous chapter, while the use of the word *deipnon* for "supper" is used only here in verse 2 and in 13:2, where it refers to the "last supper." This is the time for eating together, for the Passover is at hand, and people have come from all over Israel and the ancient Mediterranean to Jerusalem to prepare themselves for this important religious festival (11:55). It is six days before the feast when Jesus arrives for dinner at Bethany, which makes this Saturday evening, the end of the Sabbath at the start of this holy week leading to Passover, a week which will be Jesus' last. Lazarus may have been raised by Jesus from the dead, but Jesus, the giver of life, is setting out on the journey to his own death and burial. The conversation at the table between the one who had come out of the tomb and the other on his way to the tomb must have been interesting!

Lazarus is the Greek version of the Hebrew "Eleazar," meaning "God is my help" (the name of a son of Aaron; see Exod. 6:23-25), while Bethany means "house of affliction." In Jesus, God came to help this household when they were in great affliction over Lazarus's fatal illness. Then his two sisters, Mary and Martha, met Jesus in different ways. Martha, the great activist, came out to confront him with accusations and warnings about the smell in the tomb (11:20-27, 39). Mary remained quietly sitting in the house, and then fell at Jesus' feet weeping (11:20, 33). Their very different personalities are also reflected in the story of Mary sitting with the male disciples listening at Jesus' feet while Martha was distracted "with much serving" in Luke 10:38-42. Exactly the same characteristics are manifested here. As a man, Lazarus reclines at table with Jesus, while Martha is once again busy "serving" (*diakonein* in John 12:2, the same word as in Luke 10:40, and from which our word "deacon" comes). Mary, however, again heads for Jesus' feet, which she had clasped outside her brother's tomb, not with tears this time but with ointment. Once more there are hints of Jesus' coming death: at the end of this week his crucified body will be anointed (19:39). To prepare for and balance that event, John begins with Jesus being anointed by Mary at this supper in Bethany.

Before we study the story in detail, it is helpful to note the accounts of Jesus being anointed in the other Gospels. Mark 14:3-9 and Matthew 26:6-13 describe Jesus being anointed on his head in Bethany two days before Passover at the house of Simon the leper by an unnamed woman; in Luke 7:36-38 he is anointed on his feet earlier in Galilee in the house of Simon the Pharisee by a sinful woman who wipes his feet with her hair. In both cases this leads to angry protests and debate about what the woman has done. Whether these accounts describe two different events or two versions of the same anointing is much debated by scholars. John's story includes elements from both, while at the same time setting the scene beautifully for his account of the passion. However, in the early church people's imagination linked Luke's sinful woman and John's Mary of Bethany to produce the story of Jesus being anointed by Mary Magdalene, who was then seen as a "sinner"! It is important, therefore, when preaching on this passage to study what John actually says very carefully — and expound that, rather than the popular amalgam.

Mary has some "perfume of pure nard," *myrou nardou pistikēs,* an exact phrase shared with Mark (John 12:3; cp. Mark 14:3). The word "pure," *pistikos,* occurs only here and may be connected with *pisteuō,* to believe or have faith, which has recurred throughout recent chapters of this Gospel; if so, it means "faithful" or "genuine" in quality, reflecting Mary's genuine faith and love for Jesus. "Nard" is an oil derived from the root and spike of the nard plant, and the best examples were imported from as far east as India, hence its extreme expense. A "pound" (or "litre," from the Greek word here, *litra*) is an extraordinarily extravagant amount, recalling the vast quantity of wine created in Jesus' first sign at another dinner party at the wedding in Cana (2:6). Yet Mary pours this fragrant ointment not on Jesus' *head*, where people wore perfume at dinner parties and kings were anointed at their coronations, but on his *feet*, where the preparation of a corpse for burial would start. Once again Jesus' coming death is foreshadowed, as the "ointment" here, *myrou*, recalls the use of myrrh for the dead. Given the amount and quality of the ointment, it is no wonder the whole "house was filled with the fragrance." Is it too fanciful to be reminded of Paul's words that we are the "fragrance of Christ" spreading through the whole world, bringing life among those who are dying for lack of the gospel (2 Cor. 2:14-16)? Finally, Mary undoes her hair to wipe Jesus' feet. Jewish women kept their hair tied up in public, and only let it loose when undressing for a husband or as a sign of distraction in mourning. Mary would have had her hair loose when she fell at Jesus' feet in her grief over Lazarus (11:32); now she does so again, in her unabashed love for him — but the hints of burial and the grief to come are impossible to ignore.

Judas Iscariot, however, has other thoughts (12:4-5). He protests at the waste: so much good perfume might have realized "three hundred denarii"; if a denarius was a worker's daily wage, this is a year's salary, even more than the cost of bread for the five thousand (see John 6:7). He claims to want to give it to the poor, perhaps in the Passover almsgiving as the group's treasurer. He has already been identified as the betrayer (6:70-71), and now he is called a "thief," because he used to "carry" the group's purse; the verb *bastazō*, "to carry," could also be a euphemism for "steal," like the English "lift" (12:6). The "thief comes only to steal and destroy" and is recognized by the good shepherd (10:10), who now rebukes him and protects his sheep: "leave her alone," *aphes*, is the same word as "forgive" in the Lord's Prayer — but it was also used by Jesus when he told people to untie Lazarus's bandages and "let him go" (John 12:7; cp. Matt. 6:12 and John 11:44). Once again we pick up hints of the burial ritual in what Mary has done, and it reminds us of Jesus' coming death. Of course, Passover is a good time to remember that "the poor are always with you" and to obey Scripture's instructions to be generous, to "open your hand to the poor and needy" (Deut. 15:11). But it is also the beginning of the week when "you will not always have me," as Jesus heads resolutely toward his own death (12:8).

Toward the end of Lent is also a good time to check on the relationship of our devotion to Jesus with serving the poor, who are still "always with us." On the one hand we have the ministry of a Martha, serving like a "deacon," trying to feed all the hungry mouths around. But there is also a time to be like Mary, to fall at Jesus' feet, to listen to his teaching, to weep for our part in his death and to express our love for him flagrantly and fragrantly. Both of course are needed — and this passage offers a preacher the opportunity to invite people to meditate upon them. Are we like Lazarus sitting at table with Jesus, or perhaps going around serving like Martha? Do we show our love for Jesus by kneeling with Mary at his feet, or are we complaining along with Judas? And what might Jesus have to say to each of us? Perhaps there is some diaconal service we should be doing for the poor during Lent — but also we must start to prepare for Christ's coming passion and death.

Richard A. Burridge

Fifth Sunday in Lent, Year B

First Lesson: Jeremiah 31:31-34
(Psalm 51:1-12)
Second Lesson: Hebrews 5:5-10
Gospel Lesson: John 12:20-33

Today, the Fifth Sunday in Lent, is the start of the last full week of Lent, to be followed by Palm Sunday and Holy Week when we remember Jesus' entry into Jerusalem, his passion and death. It is therefore a turning point when we can look both backward and forward, back across our Lenten journey of penitence and discipline and forward to the climax of Good Friday and Easter.

This reading is also a turning point for John. The Gospel is structured in two main parts — Jesus' ministry of teaching and healing (1:19–10:42), and the last few days of his ministry and his death and resurrection (chaps. 12–20). The prologue (1:1-18) and the epilogue (chap. 21) balance each other, while in the middle comes an interlude of events around Bethany (chaps. 11–12).

Chapter 11 describes the illness and death of Lazarus, whom Jesus restores to life; this theme of life and death recurs as the Sanhedrin decides to kill Jesus the life giver (11:51-53, 57). After Mary anoints Jesus at Bethany (12:1-8), Jesus enters Jerusalem (12:12-19). Today's passage concerns the reactions from some Greeks and the crowds of people, before John goes on to his second part with the Last Supper in chapters 13–17. In John's account of Jesus being welcomed into Jerusalem by the crowd, Jesus rejects the hints of violent revolution in the crowd's acclamation of him as "king of Israel" by riding in humility on a young donkey. This causes the Pharisees to despair that "all the world has gone after him" (12:19). Both these themes of universalism and humble suffering are developed further in today's Gospel.

First, among the crowd which came to Jerusalem for the Passover "were some Greeks" (12:20). Many Greek-speaking Jews would return to Jerusalem from all over the Mediterranean for festivals, but these are usually called "Hellenists" (e.g., Acts 6:1). Thus these "Greeks" are not Jews; they might be proselytes, non-Jews interested in the Jewish faith, but they may just be visitors. The Greeks were renowned for their inquisitive nature, traveling around the ancient world in search of something new. At Jerusalem they would have been allowed into the Court of the Gentiles in the temple. Here they are part of "the world" which has gone after Jesus (12:19). As they watch this procession welcoming Jesus, the Greeks too want to see Jesus. They find Philip, a disciple with a Greek name (meaning "horse lover") from a mixed Greek-Jewish town, Bethsaida (see 1:43-44). Philip goes to find Andrew, who also has a Greek name and comes from the same town, and together they go to Jesus, as they did with the little boy with the loaves and fishes (12:22; see 1:40-42; 6:5-8). If Philip and Andrew's behavior provides a pattern for all who wish to bring others to Jesus, the Greeks' request is the classic text for all who speak, teach, preach, or listen: "We want to see Jesus" (12:21). It is so easy to be seduced by our own eloquence or communication skills, but the message is more important than the messenger, and the one spoken about is greater than the speaker. The preacher's task is to communicate such that people see Jesus.

The fact that Gentiles want "to see Jesus" helps Jesus realize that the crucial moment has finally arrived. After his ministry in Galilee, Judea, Samaria, and Jerusalem, now "the world" is seeking him. He told his mother and the Samaritan woman that his "hour is not yet" (2:4; 4:21-23), and he has evaded capture because "his hour had not yet come" (7:30; 8:20). But now "the hour has come for the Son of Man to be glorified" (12:23). The whole story has been leading toward this — and we might expect it to be glorious.

However, as he tried to show the welcoming crowd, Jesus' glory is not in human triumph. He uses the image of the grain of wheat in a way reminiscent of the other Gospels' seed parables. A grain of wheat must fall into earth and be buried; its external husk has to be broken open for the life within to come out. Only if it "dies" will it bear "much fruit" (12:24). So too Jesus sees his own forthcoming death. It would be so easy to avoid it, to choose the path of human glory and follow the crowd to revolution. But if the seed is not placed in the earth, "it remains alone." If one seed reproduces itself fortyfold in the ear of corn which grows from it, and these are all replanted, and so on each year, it would only take just over six years before that one seed results in as many seeds as there are human beings on this planet — all from one seed buried in the ground. Jesus' path to glory will also put him in the ground before he can bring his fruit to his Father.

As far too many human conflicts show, those who fight to preserve their lives end up losing them. Jesus teaches that those who sacrifice their lives in this world will find eternal life (12:25). The paradox is that in such self-denial we find that we are with Jesus, being honored by his Father (12:26). Although this is all expressed in John's distinctive language, it is exactly the same message found at the heart of the other Gospels (see Mark 8:34-35; Matt. 10:38-40; Luke 17:33). Jesus taught consistently and repeatedly that the way to life is through self-sacrifice and the path of glory found only in crucifixion. Greeks coming "to see Jesus" means that now is the "hour to be glorified," the time to put the words into action.

Yet no one can face imminent death without some pause. Jesus may have been the Son of God, but he was also incarnate fully as a human being, and here John gives a brief insight into Jesus' human emotions: "Now is my soul troubled" (12:27). The word "troubled" is *tarassō*, also used to describe his feelings at Lazarus's grave (11:33). Jesus' prayer reflects how the psalmist often describes his inner turmoil (e.g., Pss. 42:6; 55:4). In the other Gospels such agony in prayer happens in the Garden of Gethsemane before Jesus' arrest. John, however, has no agonized prayer at that point, when Jesus is in control and heading for his destiny. In many ways, then, this passage serves as the Gethsemane experience for John. As in Gethsemane, Jesus' first thought is to pray for God's deliverance: "Father, save me from this hour." Yet after so many times when the "hour was not yet," how can he avoid its final arrival? He has come for this hour, and the whole story has led to this point (12:27). He must remain true to his purpose: "Father, glorify your name" (12:28).

In response to Jesus' decision to put the glory of God ahead of his own apprehension comes "a voice from heaven." Not only does John not describe Gethsemane, he also has no account of the transfiguration. He prefers to show how Jesus reflects and shares God's glory not just on one occasion, but always. Here we get a voice from heaven as in the other Gospels' accounts of the transfiguration, as God confirms that he is being glorified in Jesus. The crowd is divided, as some think it is merely "thunder" while others assume it is an "angel" (12:29). In C. S. Lewis's stories about Narnia, the voice of Aslan, the great lion, seems a terrifying roar only to those who oppose him, but gentle words and strength to the children who love him. So now, Jesus says the voice is not for his benefit but for the bystanders'; whether they understand it or not, it is a sign to them that God is with him (12:30).

This moment is also "the judgment of this world" (12:31). John describes the devil, or Satan, as the "ruler of this world" (see also 14:30; 16:11). It has been the "rulers" in this world, Caiaphas, the priests and Pharisees, who have been opposing Jesus, to keep their power here and now. But behind them is the "ruler of this world" who will now be "cast out" (12:31). However, as Satan is cast down and out, so Jesus is "lifted up" (12:32). This word, *hypsoun,* was also featured in last week's Gospel with its double meaning of to "exalt" and to be "lifted up"; as Moses lifted up the serpent, so Jesus will be (see 3:14). Now its use for death by crucifixion is made explicit (12:33), while the universal implications of the Greeks coming to see Jesus are brought out. Jesus' death on the cross will be how he will "draw all people" to himself (12:32).

At this turning point in Lent we are reminded of the universal implications of Jesus' coming death and resurrection. He did not live and die just for one group of people, but to be "lifted up" to draw all men and women to himself. How can we ensure in our preaching that everyone can "see Jesus," and not just admire our cleverness? Perhaps the answer can only be found in following Jesus' own example of humility and being prepared to be the grain which falls into the earth and dies, dies to our own vanity and pretensions, to be willing to suffer and to lose our life for his sake — so that these buried seeds may multiply and bring forth fruit to the glory of the Father throughout the whole world.

Richard A. Burridge

543

Fifth Sunday of Easter, Year C

First Lesson: Acts 11:1-18
(Psalm 148)
Second Lesson: Revelation 21:1-6
Gospel Lesson: John 13:31-35

Today's Gospel is taken from the discourses set at the Last Supper in John 13–17. In the context of the narrative flow of the Gospel, Jesus is preparing his disciples at this point for the fact that he will shortly be taken from them when he is betrayed and crucified. And yet, while his words are spoken to the frightened disciples just before his death, their import is directed at the wider church growing after the resurrection. This is one reason why they make excellent readings for the Easter season leading up to the ascension. For while the earthly Jesus is reassuring his apprehensive followers before he is taken from them, at the same time our risen Lord addresses the concerns of all Christians about how we should live once he has returned to his Father's side.

John 13 begins with Jesus and his disciples at supper together before the Passover — and Jesus realizes that his time has come to "depart out of this world" (13:1). Such is his love for this motley crew of followers that he removes his garments, picks up a bowl and a towel, and washes their feet. Walking in open sandals on unsurfaced roads that were dusty or, in wet weather, muddy made everyone's feet dirty. Water would be provided for new arrivals to wash their feet, and if they were lucky, a servant to do it. However, so menial a task could not be required of a Jewish male servant, only from women, children, or non-Jews. But in Jesus the usual order is reversed. Jesus does for us what none of us are prepared to do for each other. Like someone nursing a dying spouse for whom even the most menial tasks are an act of love, so Jesus kneels at his disciples' feet (13:5).

Having begun with this "visual aid" of his love, he begins to teach them to follow his example in their care for one another (13:16). However, as he looks around them at their supper together, he sees Peter, who will deny him, and Judas, who will betray him — and so he warns them of this coming betrayal. After Jesus shares his bread with him, Judas "immediately went out — and it was night"; the time of darkness has arrived (13:30).

Because Judas's exit begins the events which will lead to Jesus' death, Jesus starts explaining things to his disciples. Today's Gospel passage introduces several themes which will recur through the great farewell discourse

544

of chapters 14–17. There is no clear structure to these chapters, but the themes are mixed together, returning and repeating as the conversation progresses. It is more like a symphony, weaving several motifs together, than a logical sequence. So it is better understood through prayerful meditation than by analysis. However, the main point is crystal clear: Jesus is going away, and he wants to comfort and prepare the disciples, reassuring them that everything will be all right in the plan of God. These verses act like an overture setting up the key themes for the coming main piece — the themes of glory and love seen in the context of Jesus' departure.

Now that Judas has gone out, it is "night," but the hour of darkness is paradoxically also the hour of glorification. Jesus begins with how he and God are glorified in each other (13:31). He refers to himself for the last time in this Gospel by the teasing phrase, the "Son of Man." This Aramaic expression is a way of referring to "oneself" in the third person, particularly in contexts of humbling or exaltation. In the first half of John's Gospel, Jesus uses it eleven times, often bringing together both abasement and being raised up through sayings about the Son of Man being "lifted up," which link being lifted up on a cross with being exalted (see 3:14; 8:28; 12:34). It is hard to imagine a more graphic image of how the hour of darkness can be the time when God's glory is revealed than that a horrible death on a cross is also the means for the salvation of the world. Throughout the Gospel Jesus' signs and words have revealed God's glory (see 1:14; 8:54; 11:4, 40). John has used the phrase "to be glorified" to refer to Jesus' passion and his return through death to his Father (see 7:39; 12:16, 23). Now that the hour has finally come for Jesus the Son of Man to be glorified, it is also when God will be glorified in him (13:31). So if God has been glorified like this in Jesus, then, in response, Jesus will be glorified in God himself (13:32). Jesus knows that his coming departure and death will be a great shock to his disciples, but he stresses right at the start that he is on his way to glory. This motif of glory will be developed further in his prayer at the end of the Last Supper discourses in chapter 17.

After this reminder of glory, Jesus breaks the news gently to his "little children"; this phrase occurs only here in the Gospel, but it is a favorite way that John addresses his readers in his first letter, appearing seven times in a few chapters (see 1 John 2:1; 2:12; etc.). It is common in the Bible for people about to depart or to die to give a "farewell speech," looking ahead to what will happen when they have gone, with their hopes for the future, warnings about betrayals or fighting, and prayers for their friends without their leader (see the farewells of Jacob in Gen. 49; Moses, Deut. 31; Joshua, Josh. 23–24; David, 1 Kings 2). So now Jesus announces the grave news: "I will be with you only a little longer" (13:33). They will look for him, but as he told "the Jews," now he tells the disciples that they cannot come with him. "The Jews" is a phrase John uses for the authorities of the time, rather than Jews in general — after all, Jesus and all the disciples are Jewish themselves. This comment refers to two earlier instances when the authorities were seeking to catch Jesus, and he warned them that he would be here only "a little longer" but would "go away" soon (7:33-36; 8:21-22). The "Jews" did not understand what he meant then, nor will the disciples now, so Jesus tries to explain that they cannot come where he is going.

If these first two themes reveal that Jesus' way to glory involves going away, then thirdly the disciples need a new way of living without him physically present, to love each other "as I have loved you" (13:34). We began with Jesus demonstrating his love for his disciples by washing their feet (13:1-5); now he repeats his command that they should love one another in the same way. In one sense this is not "a new commandment" at all. The heart of the Jewish law is to "love your neighbor as yourself" (Lev. 19:18), and it forms part of most moral codes. On the other hand, it is also a universal human experience that it is not so easy to put this into practice, such is our selfishness. What is "new" is that Jesus gives us a new motive and power. We do not love others simply to fulfill an ethical demand, but in response to Jesus, "as I have loved you." "God so loved the world that he gave his only Son," and he loved the disciples to the extreme of washing their feet and going to die for them.

Jerome preserves a story about Saint John in his old age reduced to simply repeating "my little children, love one another" (*Ad Galatianos* 3.6.10). Yet this is the heart of the gospel — so simple, and yet so difficult to do. Such extreme love is the mark of the Christian life, the way by which others will know "you are my disciples" (13:35). In the centuries of poverty and persecution which followed, this was one characteristic which the world could not ignore as they opened up their homes to the poor and needy: "see how these Christians love one another," says Tertullian (*Apology* 39.7). Today, when we truly follow Jesus' example of self-sacrificial love, people will say the same. Unfortunately, these words are all too often hurled as a sarcastic taunt at churches when we fight among ourselves and put other concerns before this central imperative! No wonder Jesus gave the disciples this example and this new commandment at the start of his farewell address, which he then stresses and replays in the following chapters.

We are not in the darkness of the night like those first frightened disciples. We live in the light of Easter and in the glory of the risen Christ. And yet, in this Easter season, we are preparing for the ascension, for Jesus' final "going away," back to the Father who sent him to give himself for us and for the whole world. As we wait for his "coming again in glory," we are still challenged by this simple yet all-demanding "new commandment," to love one another as he loved us. What might such a church look like in the third millennium? Sometimes it does feel like night, like it is dark outside — and it is hard to see where the glory has gone. At other times, perhaps when something has gone particularly well, life will feel glorious. Whatever the personal situation of the preacher, or the context of the preacher's church or audience, the challenge remains the same: "Love one another as I have loved you." In doing that, and that alone, will we find how self-sacrifice finally leads to glory.

Richard A. Burridge

Fifth Sunday of Easter, Year A

First Lesson: Acts 7:55-60
(Psalm 31:1-5, 15-16)
Second Lesson: 1 Peter 2:2-10
Gospel Lesson: John 14:1-14

Theological exegesis that serves the church's preaching and teaching takes into account both the person in the *pew* and the community of *scholarship*. It also explores a text's *meaning* in relation to perennial Christian doctrine and to its *significance* for a particular time and place. This passage is especially well suited for exposing the workings of such a full-orbed inquiry, one attentive to these four dimensions. With some similarities to the ancient construal of Scripture in a multiple sense — literal, tropological, allegorical, and anagogical — the four can be described as the common, critical, canonical, and contextual perspectives on a lection (developed in the writer's *The Christian Story*, vol. 2, *Scripture in the Church for the World* [Grand Rapids: Eerdmans, 1987]).

A *"common* sense" approach to John 14:1-14 through the careful eye of a person in the pew (the "perspicuity" of Scripture) will find it to be part of an unfolding supper conversation between Jesus and his disciples. After a foot washing and exchange with his betrayer, Jesus speaks about his imminent departure, prompting an anxious inquiry from Peter (chap. 13). Our own passage begins with Jesus assuring the disciples not to be "troubled" (14:1), for the "Father's house" with its many rooms is ready for occupancy, his and theirs (14:2). But Thomas is puzzled about how to get there (14:5). The answer is: "I am the way, and the truth, and the life. No one comes to the Father except through me" (14:6). The disciples remain confused, and Philip pleads, "Lord, show us the Father" (14:8). Jesus replies: Don't you get it? If you've seen me, you have "seen the Father. . . . I am in the Father and the Father is in me" (14:9, 10, 11). Look at the manifestations of God's own power, in me and my name (14:12-14).

The pivot of the passage is the word "way." The disciples want to know the route to the Father's house. Jesus declares that the path to the place is "me"; Jesus and the Father are inseparable. And what goes with that one way home is "truth" and "life." These refrains concerning "the scandal of particularity" in way, truth, and life — *reconciliation, revelation,* and *redemption* — continue throughout John. Many are the allusions to Jesus' unity with the Father, and many are Jesus' "I am" assertions concerning his singular deed, disclosure, and deliverance.

Critical tools from the academy join the foregoing *sensus literalis,* opening up new aspects of the passage. We learn that it is situated in a "book of signs" that runs from 1:19 through 12:50, succeeded by a "book of glory" from chapter 13 through 20:29, featuring rich symbols and a rearrangement of chronology to fit a theological intent. This core is surrounded by a prologue in 1:1-18, concluding remarks in 20:30-31, and an epilogue in chapter 21 that are probably from a canonical hand shaping the book toward future audiences. Further, the "only way" motif is to be read in relation to Isaiah 40:3 — preparing "the way of the Lord, / [making] straight in the desert a highway for our God" — and parallel references to the path from and to God in the prologue and epilogue of John. So understood, the *hodos* in 14:6 is the singular *path* God takes into the world in Jesus, and thus the inseparability of Son and Father. "Truth" and "life," therefore, are epexegetical, for the one way brings with it true believing and living (20:31). The *egō eimi* refrain throughout John echoes the particularity of the path, and the unity of the Father and Son, dramatically so when seen in conjunction with the divine "I am who I am" of Exodus 3:14. At the same time, in the Gospel as a whole a note of universality appears alongside its particularity, albeit one grounded in Christ, as in the declaration that "I have other sheep that do not belong to this fold" (10:16).

Critical light is also shed by the scholarly thesis that the book's decided particularism reflects a Johannine community faced in the eighties by the *birkat ha-minim*. The ban meant that Jews who held Jesus to be the Messiah were expelled from the synagogue. The self-definition process within Judaism produced a responsive self-affirmation in kind.

A *critical consciousness* alert to language usage can discern female imagery throughout. The organic "in me" and "life" suggest womb analogies. When associated with the separation theme of the passage, the cutting of the umbilical cord comes quickly to mind. As such, "father" language is theologically deconstructed, anticipating the seventh-century Council of Toledo's allusion to "the womb of the Father" and Barth's later counsel to read Scripture's paternal figures by the analogy of faith. The Father of John's Gospel is not the extrapolation of human experience; it is to be defined by the biblical story, not confined by cultural patriarchies. The "Jesus as mother" tradition of medieval piety strikes a similar note.

A *canonical* reading of John 14:1-14 appropriates the common and critical senses of the passage and interprets them in the framework of the full Scripture and the canonical story witnessed to in the church's tradition. When so lodged in this encompassing setting, the particularist "way" and its derivative "truth" and "life" are reinforced and refined. At the same time, the hint of universality in John's "other sheep" on the circumference around this core is repeated and clarified.

Jesus as the unique enlightening and saving Way God makes into the world is echoed throughout the New Testament in its rich variety of images and titles: Messiah, Lord, Savior, Word, Redeemer, Son of God, Son of Man, Master, Servant, Lamb of God. . . . In all cases he is the one who brings revelation and salvation, truth and life. The church has sifted and sorted the images and their import into ecumenical affirmations prompted by questions and controversies over the centuries. Thus the *being* of the Way is testified to in the description of Christ as one person in both divine and human natures. And his *doing* is formulated as a threefold work of prophetic, priestly, and royal ministry. These two dimensions are developed in the classical doctrines of incarnation and atonement. In them the *truth* that overcomes ignorance and error is given by the prophetic seer of the Light, and eternal *life* comes from the priest who saves from sin and the king who overcomes suffering and death. These victories are accomplished only when God makes the divine *way* into the world as the Word enfleshed.

How far is the range of this one way? Here is a road that wound through a wilderness lighted by a night's pillar of fire (Exod. 13:21), a route traced back to Israel's journey and forward to Christ's person and work. And further yet the way wends, for there are spurs out from Easter to a wider world. The same Word made flesh in Jesus is at work universally to give whatever "light" and "life" are needed by "all people" (John 1:4) to keep the story going forward to its center and end. In its earliest centuries the church recognized the journey of the indwelling Logos, Jesus Christ *(logos endiathetos)*, through his outgoing *(logos prophorikos)* in a seminal work *(logos spermatikos)* that gives what light and life are required by a fallen world to see and make a livable way ahead to its goal in the embodiment of that Word *(logos ensarkos)*.

Contextual interpretation of the scandal of particularity in John 14 will speak to the issues posed by the parishioner's experience of twenty-first-century religious pluralism. How can Christians assert that Christ is the only way, truth, and life when surrounded by the evidence of the holy, good, and true in the other faiths? Preaching that deals with this question should be familiar with the variety of current theological views on this agitated question. We review a spectrum of them.

A cluster of views is *pluralist,* seeking accommodation to the new context. One is "modern" in its rejection of particularity and welcome of every religion that serves enlightened moral ends, interpreting John's threefold claim as the poetry of personal commitment, one that does not preclude a believer in another faith from using its own love language for its own way, truth, and life. Another is "postmodern," skeptical of any access to the holy, but allowing for talk of Jesus as one's way, truth, and life if it "works *for me*" in making sense of the world. Another view shares the latter postmodern relativism but stresses the corporate nature of belief, requiring the rigorous norms of one's community, a Christ who is true *for us,* not just "for me," though making no claim that he is true *for all.* Another view looks toward the time of a global religion in which the best from each faith is appropriated, with Christians merging their perspective on reconciliation, revelation, and redemption with other religions' contributions. Another pluralist view maintains that all religions have their own valid ways, truths, and lives, but like Everest on its mountain chain, the highest peak is Jesus, a difference in degree but not kind.

A second range of views is *particularist,* for all declare for Christ as *the* way that God makes into the world to turn it from alienation to reconciliation. Yet the issues of religious pluralism are addressed in one way or another. The first view holds that while the singular way is known only to Christians, Christ is mysteriously at work in all high religions and people of goodwill, offering eternal life when received by sincere response to the truth so given, making the respondent an "anonymous Christian." Another view holds to the absolute particularity of Christ's truth as well as his way, yet the decisiveness of this divine action makes all human beings "virtual" brothers and sisters in Christ, though what happens de jure on Calvary must be yet determined de facto by the sovereign God, universal salvation being an article of hope, not an article of faith. Another view asserts the scandal of particularity in redemption as well as reconciliation and revelation, yet the mystery and generosity of God are such that other kinds of "religious ends" may be achieved by other faiths, though lesser than the salvation wrought in Christ. Another view declares all the foregoing to be compromises of Johannine teaching, truth being found only in the church's Christ and eternal life granted only to those who accept him here and now.

Is there an alternative to the foregoing options? Such would make these points:

1. The biblical story turns on the chapter on Christ, here asserted as the *way* God makes into the world to move it from alienation to reconciliation, disclosing the *truth* of the same and offering *life* for those with ears to hear, the unambiguous particularity of 14:6.

2. This central chapter is preceded by a preparatory one, the "covenant with Noah" (Gen. 9:8-16). (The important place of the special "covenant with Israel" is presupposed here as discussed in the exegesis of Acts 3:12-19.) A fallen world is granted enough light and life to move its story forward, disclosures and deliverances that sustain the world and allow the drama to unfold. That God has not left it "without a witness in doing good" (Acts 14:17) is a necessary canonical background in universality to the particularity of John 14:6. World religions are a medium for these charisms of "common grace." All such truth and life, having their source in the one way to and from the triune God, are gifts of Christ.

3. The unique way of Christ cannot be closed off by the doors of death. Those who have not come in hailing distance of it in their earthly journey will not be denied Word of it. About such "other sheep," Christ says, "I must bring them also, and they will listen to my voice" (John 10:16). So the canon's cryptic references to the Christ who proclaims the gospel "even to the dead" (1 Pet. 4:6 and 3:19), echoed in the Apostles' Creed citation of his "descent to the dead" and the widespread preaching of that conviction in early Christian centuries.

Preaching on John 14:1-14 will be to ears attuned to the challenging questions of religious pluralism. We need here, as elsewhere, to attend to the richness of Scripture's senses, and to listen for the plenitude of its wisdom.

Gabriel Fackre

Day of Pentecost, Year C

First Lesson: Acts 2:1-21
(Psalm 104:24-34, 35b)
Second Lesson: Romans 8:14-17
Gospel Lesson: John 14:8-17, (25-27)

G reat stories often reach an ending with a glorious climax, but whatever happens then not only concludes the story but also opens the door to another story. Thus in the two huge epics of Homer, the *Iliad* and the *Odyssey*, particular stories come to a conclusion — and yet their ending leads into the next phase. The same happens in the individual books which make up Tolkien's *Lord of the Rings* and George Lucas's *Star Wars* movies.

Pentecost feels rather like this. This is the great climax of the whole story of Jesus, stretching back to when he left his Father's side to dwell among us as a human being. His birth and life, his preaching and healing, his arrest and death, his resurrection and his appearances have all led up to his ascension, taking our humanity to be in the presence of God the Father for all eternity. From on high he pours out upon his followers the "farewell gift" he had promised — the Holy Spirit at Pentecost. And yet that climax of the story of Jesus is only the beginning of the story of the church as he continues to inspire his people through the Holy Spirit toward the final consummation of the whole universe with God the Father.

Both the church's year and the lectionary present the preacher with this sense of climax and new beginning at Pentecost — the climax of the sequence from Christmas, through Epiphany-tide and Lent, to Holy Week and the passion, culminating in Easter and the ascension. But it is also the birthday of the church, and ahead stretch the Sundays after Pentecost and Trinity. The lectionary reflects this with the Gospel reading from Jesus' farewell. In the narrative flow of John's Gospel, it takes place at the Last Supper as Jesus warns his disciples that he will be taken from them and tries to comfort them. Yet as we read and preach it today, we hear the risen Christ assuring his people that although he has ascended to his Father, he is still with us now through the Holy Spirit.

The Last Supper begins with Jesus washing the disciples' feet as a sign of how they are to love one another and Judas going out to betray him (13:1-30). Then Jesus starts to explain that he is going away; Peter and Thomas do not understand and ask him where he is going. Jesus' replies take us deeper into the relationship between himself and his Father; to know Jesus is to know the Father (13:31–14:7). Now it is Philip's turn to ask the silly question! One of the first disciples, he brought others like Nathanael and some Greeks to Jesus (1:43-48; 12:21-22). He looks at the physical level, as in his pessimism that feeding the five thousand would cost over half a year's wages (6:7). To such a literal thinker Jesus' comment that "you know and have seen the Father" (14:7) would seem odd. If only Jesus would "show us the Father," then we would all be satisfied and life would be clearer (14:8).

The desire to see God is a basic instinct. Moses asked to see his glory, but had to be content with a view of his back (Exod. 33:18-23). The psalmist longs to behold the face of God (e.g., Pss. 13:1; 27:8; 42:1-2). However, as John says, "No one has ever seen God" (John 1:18). Philip's request is so simple yet so profound — but it also reveals how little he has understood. There is resigned sadness in Jesus' reply that even one of the first he called still does not see, as he addresses Philip directly: "Have I been with you all [plural] so long, Philip, and yet you [singular] still do not know me?" (14:9). "How can *you* say . . . ?" and "do *you* not believe?" continue as "you" singular. It is incredible that Philip, who brought others to Jesus, can still not realize that "whoever has seen me has seen the Father. . . . I am in the Father and the Father is in me" (14:9-10).

Jesus says the Father "dwells" in him, just as there are many "dwelling places" in his Father's house (using same stem *men-* in 14:2 and v. 10). It is the Father who "does his works in me." To see Jesus heal the paralyzed and blind men and to raise Lazarus was to see God at work; to watch Jesus turn water into wine and feed the crowd was to marvel at the abundance of God; to hear Jesus speak was to see God pleading with his people. So Jesus changes back to the "you" plural and appeals to them all: "Believe me that I am in the Father and the Father is in me" (14:11). And if that is too hard, they should believe "because of the works themselves" as "signs" that Jesus has come "from God." John calls Jesus' miracles "signs" because they point people toward God, who sent him (see 3:2; 9:33; 10:31-38).

The discourse at the Last Supper is like a farewell speech, where the person about to leave looks ahead to what will happen after he or she has gone. Jesus lifts his horizon beyond Philip's lack of insight to describe what those "who believe in me" will do in the future. Not only will they "do the works that I do," but they will also do "greater works" (14:12). There is debate about what these "greater works" mean (see also 5:20). The early church did many miracles, as seen in Acts and the lists of spiritual gifts (e.g., 1 Cor. 12:7-10). All great spiritual reawakenings, from the founding of monasteries to the revivals of John Wesley, have been accompanied by such "works." In recent years a renewed expectation that God is active through his Holy

Spirit has brought a resurgence of miracles, and some seek to do "greater works" than Jesus. Whenever someone is healed or prayers are answered, we should rejoice, but this verse does not mean that we should "outperform" Jesus.

The "greater works" are "because I am going to the Father." From his Father Jesus poured out his Holy Spirit on the Day of Pentecost to send the church out in mission. In the incarnation Jesus was limited by his human form; he could only travel within one locality and touch so many people. Since the ascension and his return to the Father, he has sent disciples across the whole world, to touch millions. These are the prayers he longs to answer when we "ask in my name" (14:13). The "whatever" and the "anything" (14:13-14) are sometimes understood that all our prayers can be answered. Yet they have to be "in my name." This is not a magic formula tacked on to the end of any outrageous request. Jesus could do nothing "on my own," but only because the Father was dwelling in him (14:10). Similarly, we pray in his name only when we so dwell in Jesus that through the answer to our prayers, "the Father may be glorified in the Son" (14:13). Then not only will we, and Philip, see the Father, but so will all the world, and "be satisfied."

Jesus moves from believers' prayers to how we keep his commandments (14:15). The word for "keep," *tērēsete,* could be a command, "if you love me, keep," suggesting that we should show our love by striving to obey him; however, it can also be a future tense, "if you love me, you will keep my commandments," so that obedience flows naturally out of our love for him — and that is a consequence of his gift of the Spirit, a new theme introduced into the discourse at this point.

Jesus says he will ask the Father to give us "another Paraclete" (14:16). The word *Paraclete* means "someone called alongside" to help. Its Latin translation gives us the word "advocate." In law courts it means someone "called in" to speak for someone, either as a defending counsel or to intercede with the judge on that person's behalf. Thus two possible English translations are "Counselor" and "Intercessor," which are found in some Bibles. The second idea of interceding can be seen in 1 John 2:1, where Jesus is our "advocate *(paraklētos)* with the Father." Another greatly loved translation is "Comforter." This suggests someone "called in" to console those in need or grief; but the original meaning of "comfort" through the Latin is to give strength or courage *(fort-).* The Bayeux Tapestry has "Bishop Odo comforteth his men," where the good bishop is encouraging them by prodding them with a spear from behind! Thus the Paraclete is our counselor, advocate, intercessor, comforter, strengthener — an all around helper.

He is further identified as "another Paraclete," where the word "another," *allos,* is another of the same sort, like the last one, rather than "another, different one." The Paraclete is "another Jesus" to be with the disciples as Jesus goes away. Then he is finally identified as "the Spirit of truth" (14:17). As Jesus has taught them the "truth," so the Spirit will continue Jesus' work when he is taken away. The "world cannot receive" him; that which is opposed to God cannot see or know him. But if we know him, we will find that he "abides" in us, again using the word *men-,* linking back to 14:2 and 10.

The lectionary concludes this Gospel reading with the option of 14:25-27, which summarizes Jesus' description of the Holy Spirit as the Paraclete, coming in his name to teach the disciples everything. Through this Pentecostal gift of the Spirit Jesus' promise of "peace," *shalom,* is fulfilled. These verses were also in the Gospel for two weeks ago, the Sixth Sunday of Easter, Year C, and more detailed comment can be found there.

Whether or not the preacher includes this addition, the use of this Gospel at Pentecost offers a wonderful opportunity to enable the people of God to celebrate the birthday of the church — to look back at the whole story from Christmas to the ascension and then forward to the challenge which lies before us. What might it mean to build a church where the Holy Spirit is truly "another Paraclete" called alongside us, where the words and works of the Father seen in Jesus are demonstrated among us so that the world may believe?

Richard A. Burridge

Sixth Sunday of Easter, Year A

First Lesson: Acts 17:22-31
(Psalm 66:8-20)
Second Lesson: 1 Peter 3:13-22
Gospel Lesson: John 14:15-21

As we come to the Sixth Sunday of Easter, the joy and excitement of the Easter season builds almost to its climax. Over these past weeks we have been celebrating the joy of the resurrection and the presence of the risen Christ appearing to his first disciples and being among us still. And yet on Thursday it will be Ascension Day, when we remember Jesus' departure from his disciples and his return to be with his heavenly Father for all eternity. Liturgically, therefore, we are approaching a turning point.

The lectionary cleverly reflects this by the use of the farewell discourses from John's Gospel, for they also have this ambivalence. In the narrative context of the flow of John's story, they are delivered by Jesus to his disciples over supper together on the night before he was crucified. In these chapters, 14–17, he tries to prepare his apprehensive followers for the shock when he is taken away from them and his coming death; he wants to reassure them of his continuing love and presence with them afterwards. Yet, of course, John's audience, the readers of this Gospel and all of us who study it or preach it today, can never get back behind Easter. We hear Jesus' reassurances to his disciples in the light of our Easter experience, knowing that he rose again from death to be with them and with us. So his warnings of being taken from them and the coming of the Holy Spirit now resonate in our experience as we look toward Ascension Day on Thursday and Pentecost soon to come.

In the first part of John 14, which was last week's Gospel, Jesus is concerned to reassure his disciples, "let not your hearts be troubled," as he warns them that he is going away (14:1-4). Thomas says we do not know the way and asks where he is going, which produces the glorious saying that Jesus is "the way, the truth and the life" (14:5-6). Philip has a simple yet extraordinary request: "Lord, show us the Father" (14:8)! Jesus responds by explaining more of his relationship with the Father (14:9-14). Because of the love of the Father and the Son, not only will we see God, but he will dwell with us. This is all made possible through the coming of the Holy Spirit, a new theme now introduced in today's Gospel reading, then repeated and developed in the following chapters of John.

First, Jesus talks about how we keep his commandments (14:15). The word for "keep" in Greek, *tērēsete,* could be a command, "if you love me, keep my commandments." This would mean that we are to show our love for Jesus by striving to obey him. But this can quickly become legalistic, with the implication that if we do not keep all the commandments, we do not love God — and he may not love us. However, the verb can also be a future tense, "if you love me, you will keep my commandments." In this case obedience is not human effort but flows naturally out of our love for him. Either way, the connection of loving Jesus and doing what he says is clear — and a sensitive preacher may apply it differently in different contexts, depending on his or her knowledge of the congregation.

Next Jesus says he will ask the Father to give us "another Paraclete"

(14:16). This is the first use of an important term in these discourses. The word *Paraclete* means "someone called alongside" to help or assist. Its direct translation into Latin gives us the word "advocate." It is often used in the law courts to mean someone who is "called in" to speak for someone on trial, either as that person's defending counsel or to intercede with the judge on his or her behalf. Thus two possible English translations are "Counselor" and "Intercessor," both of which can be found in some Bibles. The second idea of interceding can be seen in 1 John 2:1, where Jesus is our "advocate (*paraklētos*) with the Father."

Another greatly loved translation is "Comforter." In America a "comforter" — called a "dummy" in Britain — is something given to soothe a crying child. It is something for a child to suck on to be reassured. The image of Linus in the *Peanuts* cartoon with his "comfort blanket" immediately comes to mind! Certainly the word can convey the image of someone "called in" to console those in need or grief, as indeed the disciples are here. But the original meaning of "comfort" through the Latin is to give strength (*fort-*) or courage. Thus the Paraclete is our counselor, advocate, intercessor, comforter, strengthener — an all around helper.

He is further identified as "*another* Paraclete." In English the phrase "Would you like another drink?" could mean "Would you like something different?" in the case where you did not like the one you just had, or if you enjoyed it and finished it, "Would you like another one of the same sort?" Here the word "another" is *allos* in Greek, another of the same kind, like the last one, rather than *heteros*, "another, different one." Since everything said about the Paraclete is also said of Jesus elsewhere in this Gospel, he is "another of the same sort," "another Jesus" to be with the disciples as Jesus goes away. In seeking to determine whether something or someone is inspired by the Holy Spirit, the ultimate test is whether the consequence is something Jesus would have said or done. The Christlike nature of the Holy Spirit is because he is "another Paraclete."

Finally, he is further identified as "the Spirit of truth" (14:17). "Truth" is a key theme throughout John's Gospel, and this description of the Holy Spirit as both "Paraclete" and "Spirit of truth" will be developed later in the discourses (14:26; 15:26; 16:7, 13). At this point he is stressing that the Spirit is coming for the disciples, to replace Jesus when he is taken from them. The "world cannot receive" the Spirit; that which is opposed to God cannot recognize him, cannot see or know him. But if we know him, we will find that he "abides" in us; the word *menō*, "to dwell," is used, which picks up the "many abodes" or "many rooms in my Father's house" used by Jesus to comfort the disciples at the beginning in 14:2.

557

Thus Jesus will be with those first disciples and all who love him and keep his commandments through the Holy Spirit, the Paraclete. Even though he is going away, he can give us the marvelous promise, "I will not leave you desolate; I am coming to you" (14:18). The word here is literally "orphans" and was used of children without parents or of pupils without a master, such as the followers of Socrates when he was executed. This text is sometimes given to Christians, especially those new in the faith, as a "personal promise." But it is important to note that while this promise is to each individual Christian, the pronoun for "you" is plural. It is in our relationship all together that we find Jesus coming to us. In "a little while" the world will see him no longer; but we will see him: "Because I live, you also will live" (14:19). Jesus answered Philip's desire to see the Father by reassuring him that "the Father is in me and I in the Father" (14:10-11). Through the Holy Spirit, Jesus will also be one with those who love him: "you in me and I in you," and so we are caught up into the very life of the Godhead (14:20). Thus are those who keep Jesus' words loved not only by him but by his Father also, and through this he is able to reveal himself to them, even when he has physically departed from them (14:21).

Therefore, at this liturgical turning point at the end of the Easter season and looking ahead to the ascension, this Gospel passage gives us the opportunity to apply the Last Supper discourse to people's lives today. It is right that we celebrate the joy and enthusiasm of Eastertide and the presence of the risen Christ in his church. At the same time, as we open our hearts to him, so he promises us the gift of the Holy Spirit. A church full of "Easter people" will be a place where grieving or searching souls can be comforted, encouraged, and strengthened — a community where the risen and ascended Christ and his heavenly Father are made known through our life together in the Spirit, and from which we are sent out with good news for all the world.

Richard A. Burridge

Sixth Sunday of Easter, Year C

First Lesson: Acts 16:9-15
(Psalm 67)
Second Lesson: Revelation 21:10; 21:22–22:5
Gospel Lesson: John 14:23-29

As we come to the Sixth Sunday of Easter, the excitement of the Easter season builds almost to its climax. Over these past weeks we have been celebrating the joy of the resurrection and the presence of the risen Christ appearing to his first disciples and being among us still. And yet on Thursday it will be Ascension Day, when we remember Jesus' departure from his disciples and his return to be with his heavenly Father for all eternity. Liturgically, therefore, we are approaching a turning point.

The lectionary cleverly reflects this by using the Last Supper conversations from John's Gospel for this pivot. In the first few Sundays of Easter in Year C, the Gospel reading is taken from John's account of the resurrection in chapters 20–21. However, last week's and today's readings are from the start of the farewell discourses. In the narrative context of the flow of John's story, this is delivered by Jesus to his disciples over supper together on the night before he was crucified. In chapters 14–17 he tries to prepare his apprehensive followers for the shock when he is taken away from them and his coming death; he wants to reassure them of his continuing love and presence with them afterward. Yet, of course, John's audience, the readers of this Gospel and all of us who study it or preach it today, can never get back behind Easter. We hear Jesus' reassurances to his disciples in the light of our Easter experience, knowing that he rose again from death to be with them and with us. So his warnings of being taken from them and the coming of the Holy Spirit now resonate in our experience as we look toward Ascension Day on Thursday and Pentecost soon to come.

In last week's Gospel we saw how Jesus washed his disciples' feet as a visual aid of how Christians are to "love one another as I have loved you" (13:1-15, 31-35). However, Judas's exit into the night to betray Jesus also led to Jesus telling his disciples that he was going to be taken from them. He is concerned to reassure them, "let not your hearts be troubled," as he warns them of his departure (14:1-4). Each time he talks of going away, one of the disciples asks a question about what is happening — Peter, Thomas, Philip (13:36; 14:5, 8). Each question elicits from Jesus a further clarification about where he is going, how he will return, and his relationship with God his heavenly Father (14:1-14). Gradually he develops the idea that because of the love of the Father and the Son, not only will we see God, but he will dwell with us. This is all made possible through the coming of the Holy Spirit, whom Jesus will send to be with them (14:15-21).

Now it is the turn of Judas to ask a question; he is identified as "not Iscariot," not the betrayer, who has gone out into the night. We know nothing else about him, although Luke also mentions a "Judas, son of James" different from Iscariot (Luke 6:16; Acts 1:13). This Judas asks why Jesus will reveal himself to the disciples but not to the world (John 14:22). Jesus' reply recalls his previous words about loving him and keeping his commandments (14:15). Only those who love him and keep his word, which is not his anyway, but "from the Father who sent me," can accept his revelation; those who do not love or obey him will not recognize him, or his Father (14:23-24). Yet to those who do love him, not only will Jesus reveal himself, but he and his Father will come and "dwell" with them. Jesus and his Father will "make our home with them"; the word *menō* is used for "home," like the many "dwelling places" in the Father's house (14:2). Not only does Jesus prepare a place for us in God, but he also makes a place for God in us.

This mutual indwelling of God in us and we in God is wonderful, but not easy to grasp. So Jesus reminds the disciples that he says all this to explain it to them "while I am still with you," before he goes away (14:25). This theme is repeated frequently in the chapters which follow (15:11; 16:1, 4, 6, 25, 33). But Jesus does not expect them to comprehend it all now. It is the task of the Paraclete, the Holy Spirit, to teach it to them. The word *Paraclete* means "someone called alongside" to help or assist. Its direct translation into Latin gives us the word "advocate." It is often used in the law courts to mean someone who is "called in" to speak for someone on trial, either as that person's defending counsel or to intercede with the judge on his or her behalf. Thus two possible English translations are "Counselor" and "Intercessor," both of which can be found in some Bibles. The second idea of interceding can be seen in 1 John 2:1, where Jesus is our "advocate *(paraklētos)* with the Father." For more on *paraklētos* as "Comforter," see my comments on pages 554 and 557.

Thus the word "Paraclete" can be translated as counselor, advocate, intercessor, comforter, strengthener — an all-round helper. Here, however, his task is a particular one: the Holy Spirit will be sent by the Father to "teach you everything, and remind you of all that I have said to you" (14:26). "Disciples" means learners, and they have called Jesus their rabbi, or teacher. Now that Jesus will be taken from the disciples, the Holy Spirit will be their rabbi, "another Paraclete" (see 14:16), teaching them as Jesus taught them.

Christians need to be "lifelong learners" as we grow in our faith and discipleship. But the teaching we learn from the Spirit cannot be different from Jesus' words. The Spirit comes from the Father "in my name," as we respond also "in my name" in prayer to the Father (see 14:13). This is the test when someone claims a new revelation or some teaching from the Spirit: Is it consistent with Jesus' words and example, and can it be done in his name?

Jesus returns to his central theme of reassurance as he gives them his parting gift of peace (14:27). It is customary during a farewell speech to bequeath those listening something "to remember me by," like an inheritance in a will. Jesus' bequest is the gift of peace, but "not as the world gives," where peace is merely the absence of conflict. The Hebrew concept of "shalom" includes peace, health, and well-being. It is a regular greeting and leave-taking: live long and prosper. The "shalom" of God is often promised in the Old Testament as a mark of God's coming in his glorious kingdom. Such a leaving gift of peace from Jesus is the reason the disciples must not let their "hearts be troubled," as this phrase picks up the beginning of the chapter (14:1).

Why would they still be troubled? Jesus suggests that it is because they heard him repeat several times "I am going away" (14:28). The grief this saying causes them shows that their love is actually possessive, only concerned for themselves. If they really understood and loved Jesus, they would rejoice because "I am going to the Father." While they may be sad for their sake, they should be pleased for Jesus' sake as he returns to God. Since "the Father is greater than I," Jesus can leave in perfect trust that God knows what he is doing. In the christological controversies which followed in the first centuries of the church, some people, particularly those who followed the heretic Arius, argued that this phrase implied that Jesus is less than God. But the whole point of the conversation so far is that to have seen Jesus is to have seen the Father, as he replied to Philip (14:9). This verse must be seen in the context of the whole discourse.

Furthermore, the Father's greatness is what Jesus is returning to, and the reason why he seeks to reassure them again: "I have told you this before it happens" (14:29). This is to build up their faith, so that his death is not a destructive disaster but helps them believe because Jesus has warned them about it. Once again we see the double level of time going on in John's narrative. At the level of the narrative, the warnings about Jesus' departure refer to his coming death the next day. But all the phrases about "going to the Father" look beyond the crucifixion to the ascension, which we will celebrate later this coming week.

Thus those who preach at this time of the liturgical year are faced with

the same challenge as the Evangelist was: to take the story of the first frightened disciples being reassured by Jesus and to apply it to our audience who
have to live the Christian life without the physical presence of Jesus alongside. John's answer was to remind his readers of the love and mutual indwelling of the Father and the Son in the Holy Spirit — and it is the task of
that same Spirit to teach us these things. So too as we move from Eastertide
toward Ascension and Pentecost, we now invite him to be our paraclete, to
come alongside us, to teach us all this and to bring us Jesus' farewell gift of
peace.

Richard A. Burridge

Fifth Sunday of Easter, Year B

First Lesson: Acts 8:26-40
(Psalm 22:25-31)
Second Lesson: 1 John 4:7-21
Gospel Lesson: John 15:1-8

In her liturgies of Holy Week and the Easter season, the church offers
readings from John 13–17 to comfort and challenge worshipers. Christians whose imagination is fed with sophisticated and disturbing multime-
dia may be puzzled about how the Spirit speaks to the church today in these
chapters. Is the language of a sectarian group of first-century believers accessible and meaningful to contemporary disciples of Jesus? As preachers,
how can we enter into Jesus' activity and instruction?

Jesus' parable *(mashal)* of the vine and the branches (15:1-8) and its explanations (15:9-17) are embedded in the larger narrative unit of the last
discourses material (13:1–17:24). This section is distinctive in its imagery
and lack of dialogue. Structurally, it is the central icon (C) of the last discourses. It is framed twice. The inner frame (B, B') is the announcements of
Jesus' imminent departure, persecutions, and the promise of the Paraclete
(14:1-31; 15:18–16:33). The outer frame (A, A') describes Jesus' betrayal, the
foot washing, and Jesus' prayer (13:1-38; 17:1-24).

A sequential review of A and B provides a context for chapter 15. The narrator surprises us with unexpected details about Jesus' meal with the disciples (John 13). We listen for directions about preparations of the meal. There are none. We anticipate a description of food and the ritual blessing of bread and wine to which Jesus adds new significance and instruction. They are omitted.

What details does the narrator offer us about the Last Supper? Jesus takes the initiative in speaking and acting on behalf of his disciples. He speaks about his imminent betrayal (13:10-11, 18-19, 21, 26-27, 37) that begins his return to the Father (13:1, 3). Jesus freely participates in his betrayal, suffering, and death to continue his love for his own to the end (13:1). The one who betrays him is the one who receives the morsel of friendship from Jesus (13:26). When Judas goes out into the night to betray him (13:30), he rejects the light of the world (8:12).

Peter, another one of the Twelve, will also betray Jesus (18:17, 25-27). In this scene he is unwilling to have Jesus wash his feet. However, Jesus challenges him: "Unless I wash you, you have no share with me" (13:6-8, NRSV). Peter does not understand that the washing is a symbolic, prophetic ritual that foreshadows Jesus' suffering and death. If he is to share in Jesus' hour, he needs to submit to the washing. Peter complies with his head and hands and feet (13:9).

The foreboding announcements about betrayal and the foot washing anticipate Jesus' declaration of his imminent departure (13:33). He offers them one challenge: "I give you a new commandment, that you love one another. Just as I have loved you, you also should love one another. By this everyone will know that you are my disciples, if you have love for one another" (13:34-35).

Imagine with the first disciples how Jesus' departure and return to the Father affects the present and future of all who believe in him. It is Jesus' relationship to the Father, "the only Son, who is close to the Father's heart" (1:18b), that impels him to leave the disciples (13:1; 16:28). Jesus goes to prepare a "dwelling place" for his own (14:2). The separation, however, is only temporary.

We listen as Jesus promises his disciples: "I will come again and will take you to myself, so that where I am, there you may be also" (14:3). Jesus' one desire is that believers may permanently abide with him by sharing in the intimate life that he enjoys with the Father. Jesus' departure and return, then, is part of the inner frame that surrounds his instruction to the disciples (14:2-3; 16:22). He concludes with an extraordinary promise: "I will see you again, and your hearts will rejoice, and no one will take your joy from you" (16:22).

After Jesus announces his departure and return (14:2-3), he encourages the disciples: "And you know the way to the place where I am going" (14:4). How will the disciples know that they are on the way to Jesus and the Father? Jesus promises them another Advocate, the Spirit of truth, to be with them and within them (14:16-18, 26). Also, Jesus and the Father will make their "dwelling place" with the disciples, an experience of eternal life now (14:23-27).

Next, Jesus uses vine imagery to recall a favorite memory. God chose Israel, planted and cultivated her to bear abundant fruit. Yet the prophets described her as unfruitful (e.g., Isa. 5:1-7; Jer. 2:21; Ezek. 19:10-14). However, the *mashal* proclaims something radically new: "I am the true *(alēthinē)* vine, and my Father is the vinegrower" (John 15:1). Jesus, as God's beloved Son, is the authentic vine who shares extraordinary mutual life with the vinegrower and the branches: "Abide in me as I abide in you" (v. 4).

The reality of mutual abiding echoes earlier moments in the Gospel: "My flesh is true *(alēthēs)* food and my blood is true *(alēthēs)* drink. Those who eat my flesh and drink my blood abide in me, and I in them" (6:55-56). Jesus' freely laying down his life to take it up again (10:18) provides the disciples with mutual abiding, the fundamental relationship with Jesus and the Father. Without this relationship the disciples can do nothing (15:4b).

The mystical union of mutual abiding does not exist for itself. Rather, disciples abide in Jesus to bear lasting fruit (15:5-8). As the vinegrower, the Father, too, prunes the branches to be fruitful (15:2b). What is the fruit of mutual abiding? Disciples witness to their experience of shared life with Jesus and the Father by loving one another in the community. Bearing much fruit (v. 8) is also going outside the community to continue Jesus' word and works in the world. The gift of Jesus after his resurrection enables the disciples' mission: "'As the Father has sent me, so I send you.' . . . he breathed on them and said to them, 'Receive the Holy Spirit'" (20:21-22).

Then Jesus teaches about mutual loving. The greatest love between friends is to lay down one's life for the other. Jesus' decision to lay down his life freely is the ultimate model for the disciples' mutual loving (15:12-14). As a friend, Jesus makes known to them everything he hears from the Father (15:15). Friends resemble one another in their thinking, speaking, and acting.

A sequential review of A′ and B′ completes the inner and outer frames of 15:1-17. What will motivate the disciples to live in mutual love and be servants of all? Will they be able to withstand the hatred and persecution of nonbelievers? Jesus' departure will benefit them because he will send the Advocate, the Spirit of truth, who will guide them (16:5-7, 13).

564

John 17 is the prayer of Jesus' heart. Although the disciples had heard fragments of his prayer, and he had instructed them about praying to the Father, they had never heard such intimate praise and petition. Listening to Jesus' prayer happens when we rest on the breast of Jesus as beloved disciples (13:23). Then we pray with the beloved Son.

"Father, the hour has come; glorify your Son so that the Son may glorify you" (17:1b). Jesus recalls the glory he shared with the Father before his earthly sojourn. He has been faithful to teaching his Father's revelation and continuing his work. As Son, Jesus freely and lovingly embraces his imminent "hour," that is, his suffering, dying, rising, to return to the Father. However, Jesus acknowledges that he can do nothing by himself: "Father, glorify me" (17:1, 5).

Next Jesus remembers how he gave the Father's words to the disciples; and they believed in him. Now it is the Father's turn to protect and guard the disciples from the evil one (17:11-12, 15). Jesus' confidence is rooted in the intimate mutual life that he shares with the Father and desires for the disciples: "so that they may be one, as we are one" (17:11).

Jesus does not ask the Father anything for the disciples that he has not experienced. When he prays, "Sanctify them in truth; your word is truth" (17:17), he is aware of its personal cost. Jesus will lay down his life "so that they also may be sanctified in truth" (17:19). Again, as the Father sent Jesus into the world (1:10-12), so he sent the disciples into the world (17:18; cf. 20:21-22).

Finally, Jesus prays for those who will believe in him through the disciples' word and witness (17:20). The mutual abiding of Jesus, the Father, and the disciples is an unambiguous sign that draws others to believe in Jesus and to know that they are loved even as the Father has loved Jesus (17:21, 23). As preachers, we proclaim Jesus' word and invite our congregations to believe in the promise of the *mashal*: mutual abiding with Jesus, the Father, and one another.

Mary Margaret Pazdan

Sixth Sunday of Easter, Year B

First Lesson: Acts 10:44-48
(Psalm 98)
Second Lesson: 1 John 5:1-6
Gospel Lesson: John 15:9-17

As we come to the Sixth Sunday of Easter, the excitement of the Easter season builds almost to its climax. Over these past weeks we have been celebrating the joy of the resurrection and the presence of the risen Christ appearing to his first disciples and being among us still. And yet on Thursday it will be Ascension Day, when we remember Jesus' departure from his disciples and his return to be with his heavenly Father for all eternity. Liturgically, therefore, we are approaching a turning point.

The lectionary cleverly reflects this by using the Last Supper discourses from John's Gospel for this fulcrum. The first few Sundays of Easter in Year B have the appearances of the risen Christ for the Gospel readings. However, last week's and today's Gospels come from the heart of the farewell discourses. In the narrative context of the flow of John's story, they are delivered by Jesus to his disciples over supper together on the night before he was crucified. In these chapters, 14–17, he tries to prepare his apprehensive followers for the shock when he is taken away from them and his coming death; he wants to reassure them of his continuing love and presence with them afterward, and give them instructions for how the church should live. Yet, of course, John's audience, the readers of this Gospel and all of us who study it or preach it today, can never get back behind Easter. We hear Jesus' reassurances to his disciples in the light of our Easter experience, knowing that he rose again from death to be with them and with us. So his warnings of his departure and the coming of the Holy Spirit to guide the life of the church now resonate in our experience as we look toward Ascension Day on Thursday and Pentecost soon to come.

The first part of the farewell discourse over supper concerns Jesus' imminent departure, as his disciples ask where he is going. His reassurances to them are based on the relationship he has with God his heavenly Father, and the way the Holy Spirit will enable the disciples to share in that relationship (13:31–14:31). In chapter 15 Jesus uses a new image, the vine, to describe his relationship with his disciples, even when he is physically absent: "I am the true [or 'real'] vine" (15:1-8). This is the last of the seven great "I am" sayings in John's Gospel, where Jesus claims to be the bread of life; the light of the world; the door to the sheepfold; the good shepherd; the resurrection and the life; the way, truth, and life; and now the true vine (6:35, 41, 51; 8:12; 9:5; 10:7, 9; 10:11, 14; 11:25; 14:6; 15:1, 5). Not only do these hint at the divine name "I am," but the descriptions are all central images of the Jewish faith and Law now fulfilled in Jesus. Because he is the culmination of these hopes, Jesus' physical departure from us changes nothing: we can "remain" in him and he in us, as he is the vine and we are the branches. We must remain in the vine to bear fruit, and thus prove to be his disciples (15:8).

This fruit is the fruit of love, which is one of the key themes in both the farewell discourse and in John's Gospel as a whole. All through the Gospel Jesus has been dependent upon his Father in everything. Now he shows that the Father is the source of all love: "As the Father has loved me, so I have loved you" (15:9). The Greek tense of these verbs is aorist, depicting definite and concrete events in the past, which affect us now. Jesus was so secure in his Father's love that he could even show his love for his disciples by washing their feet to give them an example or visual aid of real love (13:1-5, 15).

Throughout this discourse Jesus uses the verbs and nouns from the Greek stem *men-* for to "remain" or "dwell" in him and in his Father, whose house has many "dwelling places" (e.g., 14:2, 17, 23). Now Jesus tells us to "abide" in his love, just as he "abides" in his Father's love (15:9). We do this by keeping his commandments, as he has kept his Father's commandments (15:10). This theme of remaining in love through obedience also ran through the previous chapter (see 14:15, 21, 23-24), but now it is linked to joy. Jesus is explaining all this so that "my joy may be in you" and our joy might be "fully complete" (15:11). He has already told the disciples that they should rejoice at his going to the Father (14:28), and this theme of joy will be developed later (16:20-33). Since the fruit of the vine is wine, which brings joy to "gladden our hearts" (Ps. 104:15), we may have here a hint of the institution of communion, which is described in the other Gospels at the Last Supper, but not in John.

As the Father has loved Jesus and Jesus has loved us, so in turn we are to abide in his love and to love one another in the same way (15:9). Thus the church is to be a community of love where the new commandment is lived out. Jesus reminds the disciples of the foot washing: "This is my commandment, that you love one another as I have loved you" (15:12, picking up 13:34). Jesus' specific act of love is his self-sacrifice, to lay down his life "for his friends" (15:13). This was foreshadowed in the good shepherd laying down his life for the sheep (10:11), and now he prepares them for his sacrificial death. The word "for," *hyper*, means "on behalf of," that his death is for our benefit. The same word comes in the institution of the communion, "This is my body, given *for* you" (Luke 22:19-20; 1 Cor. 11:24), so here we have another hint of the Eucharist. If we are to love each other as Jesus has loved us, then we must be ready to pay the ultimate sacrifice. Earlier in the meal Peter offered to lay down his life, and although only Jesus is to die now, we know that Peter's time will also come (13:37; 21:19).

Talking of laying down his life "for his friends" moves Jesus to call his disciples not "servants" but "friends," *philoi,* which comes from the verb "to love" and indicates "dear ones," "beloved." We show that we are his "beloved" by our love for him in keeping his commandment, as mentioned earlier (15:14, 10). There is, of course, nothing wrong in being "God's servant." Many Old Testament prophets, priests, and kings were glad to be called this, including Joshua and David (Josh. 24:29; Ps. 89:20). Jesus himself took the servant's role when he washed their feet but, as their master, accepted them as his servants (13:13-16). But now he calls them his "loved ones," as Moses was the "friend" of God (Exod. 33:11). The Roman emperor's inner circle of "friends," *amici,* were his principal advisers. So Jesus wants to "make known" everything to his friends, his beloved disciples (15:15). Christians are often so busy being God's servants, "working for Jesus," that we forget he wants us to be his friends, to love him and be loved by him.

Rabbis did not usually look for disciples. Young people seeking a teacher would "shop around," visit several rabbis, and choose the one they wanted. But not Jesus, who reminds his disciples that he chose them, and did so for a purpose, that they should "go and bear fruit" (15:16). This fruit is to "last," "abide" (using *menō* again), and it results in the Father answering their prayers (compare 14:13 and 15:7). Then he repeats his final command, "Love one another" (15:17). Farewells typically include some last words or instructions, and we take them very seriously and try to do them. Thus Jesus' disciples are his "beloved," loved by him as he is by his Father, and he wants them to be a community of love, loving each other, even to the ultimate limit of self-sacrifice.

This means that we cannot just stay with the risen Christ in the fervent joy of Eastertide. Yes, he loves us so much that not even death can take him from us — but he returns to give us his love. But this is not in order for us to be an introverted, cozy, warm church where we are all having a wonderful time. Jesus has also ascended to his Father, from where he pours out the Spirit of Pentecost so that we might "go and bear fruit that will last" as we reach out in love to the world around us. Thus, as the lectionary marks this time of year with this Gospel reading, so preachers must not only reassure congregations of their place "abiding" in the risen Christ's love. We must also follow his example of love in practical ways in our church and out in our community, laying down our lives so that the vine may produce much fruit for the vinedresser, even God our Father.

Richard A. Burridge

Day of Pentecost, Year B

First Lesson: Acts 2:1-21
(Psalm 104:24-34, 35b)
Second Lesson: Romans 8:22-27
Gospel Lesson: John 15:26-27; 16:4b-15

Many great stories reach their climax with the departure or even death of the hero, but the last scene is taken up with who will be the hero's successor and how things might continue after the hero has gone. Modern examples include the hand-over from Obi-Wan Kenobi to Luke Skywalker in the original *Star Wars* movie of George Lucas, or from Bilbo Baggins to Frodo the Hobbit at the start of Tolkien's *Lord of the Rings*. Yet this motif goes back to ancient epics like Homer, or the stories in the Hebrew Scriptures. Sometimes the end of one story becomes the beginning of another. Thus the hand-over from Elijah to Elisha may be the end of Elijah's story but is only the beginning of the second book of Kings as Elisha picks up Elijah's "cloak" from where it had fallen as his master was taken away into heaven (2 Kings 2:1-15). We even use the old English translation when someone takes over the "mantle" of a great predecessor.

Pentecost feels rather like this. This is the climax of the whole story of Jesus, stretching back to when he left his Father's side to dwell among us as a human being. His birth and life, his preaching and healing, his arrest and death, his resurrection and his appearances have all led up to his ascension, taking our humanity to be in the presence of God the Father for all eternity. From on high he pours out on his followers the "farewell gift" of his "successor" — the Holy Spirit at Pentecost. And so the climax of the story of Jesus becomes the beginning of the story of the church as the Holy Spirit guides his people toward the final consummation of the whole universe with God the Father.

Both the church's year and the lectionary present the preacher with this sense of climax and new beginning at Pentecost — the climax of the sequence from Christmas, through Epiphany-tide and Lent, to Holy Week and the passion, culminating in Easter and Ascension. But it is also the birthday of the church, and ahead stretch the Sundays after Pentecost and Trinity. The lectionary reflects this with the Gospel reading from Jesus' farewell. In the narrative flow of John's Gospel, it takes place at the Last Supper, as Jesus warns his disciples that he will be taken from them and tries to comfort them. Yet as we read and preach it today, we hear the risen Christ assuring his people that although he has ascended to his Father, he is still with us now through the Holy Spirit, the one who will continue his work.

Jesus has been warning his disciples of his imminent departure and trying to answer their questions about where he is going (John 13:31–14:31). At the same time, he has used the image of the vine and the branches to explain how they will still be united with him, as we saw in the Gospel reading two weeks ago on the Sixth Sunday of Easter (15:1-17). This identification of his followers with Jesus is particularly important because the world will persecute them as it did him (15:18-25).

This context of opposition leads Jesus to describe the Holy Spirit as the "Paraclete." This Greek word means "someone called alongside" to help. A greatly loved translation is "Comforter," suggesting someone "called in" to console those in need or grief, or to give them new strength (*fort-* in Latin). However, the direct translation of "paraclete" into Latin gives us the word "advocate." It is a legal term for someone "called in" to speak for those on trial, either as their defending counsel or to intercede with the judge on their behalf. Thus two translations found in some Bibles are "Counselor" and "Intercessor." When Jesus first mentioned the "paraclete," he called him "the Spirit of truth" (14:16-17). In a situation of accusation, defense, and witness, one who can speak the truth is vital. So now Jesus says that he is sending the Spirit of truth to "testify on my behalf" (15:26).

The Spirit is described here as one who comes "from the Father," yet also one "whom I will send to you." This verse caused endless debates in the early church which continue today between the Eastern Orthodox and the Western churches about whether the Nicene Creed should say that the Holy Spirit "proceeds from the Father" or "from the Father and the Son." However, John was thinking more of the mission and witness of the church than of eternal relationships within the Trinity! Not only will the Spirit witness to Jesus, but as the encouraging Comforter he will stir up the disciples to testify what they have seen, having been "with me from the beginning" (15:27). There is always the temptation at Pentecost to expound the nature and theology of the Spirit — and that is very important. But this Gospel reading reminds us that the Spirit's task is to send us in witness and mission to the world.

The reading continues as Jesus reminds them that he is returning to "the one who sent me" (16:5). They are so sunk in their concern that no disciple asks, "Where are you going?" as Peter and Thomas did earlier (13:36; 14:5). Their lack of questioning shows how they are too wrapped up in grief to ask Jesus about his joy at returning to his Father. Despite his repeated stress that their hearts should "not be troubled" (14:1), "sorrow has filled" them now (16:6). Jesus tries to enable them to understand: "It is to your advantage that I go away." Jesus' departure means that he will be able to send them his successor, the Paraclete. If Jesus does not face death and "go away," the Spirit cannot come (16:7; see also 7:39). Jesus is limited in space and time by his physical body, but when he has returned to his Father he will send the Spirit, "another helper" to be alongside them, just as he was, but one not so limited. This is indeed to their advantage, but the disciples are too absorbed to realize it.

So Jesus explains the Spirit's particular task when he comes into the world. If the Spirit is "another Paraclete" like Jesus (14:16), he will do what Jesus did, just as Elisha inherited Elijah's mantle. Jesus came into the world to save it, not condemn it; but when the light came into the darkness, some preferred to stay in the shadows lest their evil deeds be "exposed" (3:16-20). Now the Spirit's task is the same: he will "convict" the world (16:8). In both verses the word is *elenchō*. As "paraclete" is used for a legal counsel, so *elenchō* means to "prove wrong," "convict," "reprove," in cross-examination in a trial. The three things the Spirit will "convince" the world of are also legal words meaning "crime," "justice," and "verdict." Yet, as so often with John, if we look closer, we will see that they have a spiritual meaning also.

The first word, *hamartia*, can mean "mistake," or "crime," which at the spiritual level means "sin." In the cross-examination of Jesus after those who were going to stone the woman taken in adultery went away aware of their own sin, Jesus asked, "Which of you convicts *(elencho)* me of sin *(hamartia)*?" (8:46). At his coming trial they will "convict" him and sentence him to death. It is the task of the Spirit to "convince" the world that this was wrong; instead, they are guilty of the most basic sin, that God has come among them and they "do not believe" in him (16:9). It is still the first work of the Spirit to convince men and women of their sin and lack of faith in Jesus.

Secondly, he will "convict" them of "justice," or "righteousness," *dikaiosynē*. This is the only time this favorite word of Paul appears in John. The Spirit will convince the world that Jesus' death was not a "just" condemnation of a criminal. But what was a human injustice, God has made his "righteousness"; through it Jesus has returned to his Father, and his presence with God now is the final proof (16:10).

Finally, the Spirit will "expose" the "verdict," *krisis*. At the cross, it looks as though evil has triumphed and Jesus has been condemned. In fact, the coming of Jesus brought the "critical moment," the "judgment" that people loved darkness rather than light (3:19). So the third task of the Spirit is to convince the world that Jesus' death on the cross is actually the "judgment" when the "ruler of this world" is condemned (16:11; see 12:31).

If the Paraclete comes as a cross-examining counsel to convince the world, so he comes also to the disciples to "guide you into all truth" (16:13). As Jesus was their teacher, so now the Spirit will be also. But what he teaches will not be his own teaching; instead he will continue Jesus' teaching. Jesus still has "many things to say" to the disciples which they are not ready for yet (16:12). We must always beware of thinking that we know it all. Christian discipleship is a journey of lifelong learning in the guidance of the Spirit of truth. It is his task to speak "whatever he hears" from Jesus and the Father, to "declare what is to come" (16:13). As Jesus glorified the Father by doing the will of the one who sent him, so the Spirit will glorify Jesus by taking "what is mine" and declaring it to us (16:14). And because of the unity of love within the Holy Trinity, "what is mine" is actually "all that the Father has" (16:15). The Paraclete invites us to share and abide in the unity of love between the Father, the Son, and the Spirit.

Like Elijah, Jesus has ascended into heaven — but his mantle falls not on just one successor. The gift of the Holy Spirit is poured out at Pentecost upon all people. The climax of the story of Jesus is the start of the continuing saga of the comforting and convicting work of the Spirit in and through us all until the whole world is convinced of the truth and love of God. The use of this Gospel reading at Pentecost gives a preacher the opportunity to invite his congregation not just to receive the Spirit for themselves — but to join in the Spirit's task for the sake of the whole creation.

Richard A. Burridge

Trinity Sunday, Year C

First Lesson: Proverbs 8:1-4, 22-31
(Psalm 8)
Second Lesson: Romans 5:1-5
Gospel Lesson: John 16:12-15

In the midst of his farewell discourse, Jesus hints that there are things that he has not yet revealed to his disciples (16:12). This pronouncement seems to stand in stark contrast to Jesus' remarks elsewhere in John. Indeed, earlier in this section of the Gospel Jesus professes a sort of "full disclosure" to his followers, telling them that "I have called you friends, because I have made known to you everything that I have heard from my Father" (15:15). This apparent contradiction presents interpreters with an interesting theological question for Trinity Sunday: Do Christians have the full revelation of God in Christ in hand, or is it ongoing? The answer, in this particular case, lies in grappling with what Jesus means when he says there are things that the disciples "cannot bear" now (16:12). To what does this refer? Some have argued that this statement hints at the chronology of the passion and points to the fact that there are aspects of who Christ is that can be understood (and indeed "shouldered") by the disciples only in the aftermath of the resurrection. Others suggest a more expansive chronology that reaches beyond the lives of those closest to Jesus to the Johannine community and beyond, arguing that God's revelation is an ongoing happening in the life of the church as it inclines its ear toward the utterances of the Holy Spirit.

As described in this text, the role of the Holy Spirit assists us in sorting through these revelatory options. First, we are told that when the "Spirit of truth" (*alētheia*) comes, it will guide people "in the fullness of the truth" (16:13). What is the nature of this truth? In John, of course, the answer leads us directly back to Jesus himself. In fact, just two chapters earlier Jesus used "the truth" (*alētheia*) as one in a series of powerful self-designations (14:6). Accordingly, readers are to understand that the revelation spoken by the Spirit is none other than the central affirmation of John's Gospel, namely, that Jesus is the Word become flesh, the only-begotten Son of the Father, who has come out of love that people might believe and have life. So, in an important way, this passage suggests that the revealing activity of the Spirit will not unveil something that the disciples have yet to hear, a secret word that God is going to dispense later in time. For, in fact, the Spirit will witness to the very same truth that has been the centerpiece of Jesus' ministry.

We will be reminded of this in chapter 18 when, in the trial before Pilate, Jesus states, "For this I was born, and for this I came into the world, to testify to the truth (*alētheia*)" (18:37). John's Gospel clearly emphasizes that the Spirit and the Son together witness to an identical *alētheia*.

Still, the disciples are promised that this Spirit "will declare things that are to come" (16:13). Does this phrase suggest that the Paraclete will prophetically reveal previously unheralded things to Jesus' followers? Crucial to understanding this entire passage is the word *anangellein*, frequently translated here as simply "will declare." Three times in this short passage we find the Spirit coupled with the verb *anangellein*. On one hand this word could be translated as simply the future tense of "to preach," "to report," or "to announce." Yet a number of interpreters have pointed out that the use of the Greek prefix *an* here is akin to placing the English prefix "re-" in front of a word. Simply put, *anangellein* might be best translated "will redeclare" or "will preach again." Hence, even the vocabulary of the Gospel works to suggest that the pronouncements of the Spirit are continuous with the efforts of Jesus — "reproclaiming" the truth of Christ, taking the gospel the Father gave to the Son and persistently preaching it to the glorification of Jesus (16:14-15).

The strong emphasis in this passage on the continuity between the proclamation of Jesus and the declarations of the Spirit may lead us to discount any interpretation of verse 12 that suggests that the Spirit has things to say to the church that have not been heard previously. Yet, while the proclamation of the Spirit is in effect a repreaching of the gospel of Jesus the Christ, this reproclamation happens in ever changing times and circumstances. In other words, there are things in Christ's own proclamation that the disciples "cannot bear" precisely because of where they stand in the flow of human history (16:12). As history unfolds, the disciples will experience various events (John places particular emphasis on the crucifixion and the resurrection of Jesus — e.g., 2:22) that will alter their perspective and change their capacity to be grasped by the truth of Christ. This is not to say that the Spirit will enable us to master the truth of Christ with time. Such an attitude would certainly be arrogant in the face of the mysterious truth of God. Yet this passage does remind us that the Spirit of truth is ever at work, tirelessly proclaiming the gospel so that people will come to believe, and in believing will encounter Christ anew in the concrete moments of history.

The text provides preachers with a number of promising trajectories for a Trinity Sunday sermon. One route to a sermon might trace the interconnected roles and relationships that inhere between the Father, the Son, and the Spirit as they bear witness to the truth on our behalf. Another sermon might examine the continuity that this text depicts between the mission of Jesus and the work of the Spirit. A third approach could explore the affirmation that through the Spirit, God continues to speak the gospel of Christ to an ever changing world. All these possible routes to a sermon touch on the connections that reside between the various persons of the Trinity (a.k.a. the "immanent" Trinity), but do not remain there. Instead, this text also pushes preachers to speak of the encounter between contemporary believers and the triune God (a.k.a. the "economic" Trinity) — the divine three-in-one who dwells among us and continually proclaims the good news.

Scott Black Johnston

Seventh Sunday of Easter, Year A

First Lesson: Acts 1:6-14
(Psalm 68:1-10, 32-35)
Second Lesson: 1 Peter 4:12-14; 5:6-11
Gospel Lesson: John 17:1-11

John 17:1-26 presents the last scene in Jesus' farewell meal with his disciples (which has included the foot-washing scene in 13:1-3 and the farewell discourse in 14:1–16:33). With an elegance surpassed in John only by its prologue (1:1-18), the chapter's theological power is expressed in the repetition and expansion of a few key words and phrases. Often called the "high priestly prayer," it depicts Jesus' deeply personal prayer to his Father before his arrest (in 18:1-12). Identified with Moses' farewell speeches at the end of Deuteronomy (31:30–32:47; 33:1-29), the prayer follows the standard conventions of the "farewell prayer," a genre well documented in ancient Mediterranean religious literature. Yet this prayer is more than simply the utterance of a dying man. In fact, it can be contrasted with Mark's depiction of Jesus' prayer in Gethsemane just before he was taken prisoner. Instead of a "grieved" Jesus who asks the Father to "remove this cup from me" (see Mark 14:34-36), the Jesus in John 17 has shared the Father's glory "before the world existed" and is now asking the Father to glorify him with that very glory (vv. 1-5). Further, the glorification he asks for is defined by what he asks for "on behalf" of his disciples and not himself (vv. 9, 20). But, although the prayer is *about* the disciples, we will see that its theological import for them — and by implication for us — lies in the deeply personal encounter it depicts between the Father and Son.

The prayer itself begins when Jesus looks up to heaven in verse 1. He is not addressing the disciples anymore (as he had in John 14–16), but is now addressing the "Father." The first thing he tells the Father is that his "hour" has come — a time that is at once imminent (vv. 1, 5), has already begun (vv. 11-13), and yet by implication is also eternal (vv. 5, 24). What Jesus wants the Father to do is "glorify" him (v. 1). As we shall see, all that happens in this prayer between the Father and Son is an expansion of this request, which is repeated in verse 5 (see also v. 24).

A kind of reciprocity is implied in verses 1-5. Not only *will* the Son glorify the Father and *has* he already done so (cf. vv. 1c and 4), but he has already *had* the very glory he is asking for "before the world existed" (v. 5). This last phrase echoes the prologue (1:1-3), which in turn echoes Jewish understandings of the Wisdom existing "before the beginning of the earth" (though in John it is clear that the "Word was God" and not simply the personified Wisdom "created" by the Lord; see Prov. 8:22-23). Yet another analogue is the hymn in Philippians 2:6-11, which speaks of Christ Jesus as one who, though "in the form of God," nonetheless "emptied himself." But there is a difference. In John what is stressed is not "emptying" but the incarnation — becoming "flesh and [living] among us." The Son's and the Father's glory are directly linked with Jesus' humanity (1:14). The reason Jesus should be glorified is given in verses 2 and 4. He should be glorified because he has glorified the Father by "finishing" what the Father gave him "authority over all people" to do: to give eternal life to those the Father has given him. Although Jesus recognizes the significance of what he has done, he also recognizes that those who benefit from his work — and prayers (vv. 9, 20) — are gifts from the Father, a point reiterated throughout the chapter (vv. 2, 6-8, 9, 24). Verse 3 is usually interpreted as a parenthetical comment inserted to clarify what "eternal life" means. Like 3:16-21, this verse makes a theological point: eternal life entails "knowing" the "only true God" — that is, the Father who sends Jesus Christ — and the Jesus Christ he sends.

Verses 6-8 define more specifically what Jesus has accomplished for the Father. These verses spell out what was alluded to in verse 4. First, Jesus has made the Father's "name known" (v. 6) by way of the "words" the Father has given him (v. 8). "Name" here refers to God's character and identity (cf. Ps. 22:22; Isa. 52:6). Like the prophet Moses who speaks God's "words" (Deut.

18:18), Jesus reveals God's character and identity by speaking God's "words" (John 17:6, 8; cf. 1:18). But the disciples given to Jesus already keep the Father's "word" (v. 6b); they already live in ways that are consistent with that word. What is new is their response to Jesus' activity, a response that defines what it means to "know" him. To know Jesus is to know that everything he has is from God (v. 7). To know him is to "receive" the words the Father has given him and to "know in truth" (i.e., "believe") that he has been sent by the Father (vv. 8b and c).

The phrase "I am asking on their behalf" introduces a shift in the prayer. Jesus is now explicitly praying on behalf of the disciples, the ones the Father has given him. He makes clear that he is not praying "on behalf of the world" but only on behalf of those the Father has given him (v. 9). A sharp dualism is expressed in this prayer, as it is throughout John (1:10-11; 7:7; 12:31; 15:18-19; 16:8-11). Of course, John also depicts Jesus as the one in whom the world was created (1:3). Jesus has authority "over all people" (17:2); and the disciples themselves are from the world (v. 6) and are sent back into the world (v. 18). Indeed, Jesus was sent into the world precisely because God loved it so much (3:16). Nonetheless, eternal life is given only to those the Father has given Jesus from out of the world. In this context (17:9-16), the "world" is defined very specifically as the place Jesus has left to be with the Father but where the disciples remain. Jesus expresses a harsh realism about this time and place — this eschatological interim. Like Jesus, the disciples do not belong to the world; indeed, the world "hates" them and does not know the Father (v. 14). But Jesus does not want to take the disciples out of the world. In fact, he will send them into the world, just as he was sent into it. Rather, what he prays for is their "protection" precisely as they are in the world.

And here we arrive at the climax of this lection. Jesus asks the Father to protect the disciples so that "they may be one, as we are one." This request is repeated four times in the prayer (vv. 11, 21-23). The phrase "as we are one" (in vv. 11, 22) is expanded by "as you, Father, are in me and I am in you" (v. 21) and "I in them and you in me" (v. 23). Given this repetition and expansion, we might say that this request is key to the chapter, and to what it means for the Father to glorify the Son. Why does Jesus want the Father to protect the disciples? So that they might share with each other the intimacy and reciprocity he shares with the Father.

What does this poetic — and theologically dense — prayer have to say to us today? Like the disciples, we too find ourselves in a world that is hostile to the "one true God." We too are in need of the protection Jesus prays for on our behalf. But we must not miss the larger perspective the prayer offers. All that is said in the prayer simply expands upon what it means for the Father and Son to "glorify" each other. Their mutual "glory" consists not only of the intimacy and reciprocity they have shared from the beginning, but in our being able to participate in that glory by "knowing" Jesus and the Father as well. Such "knowing" entails the ancient Jewish sense of knowing someone in a deeply intimate and personal way. And it entails not only knowing the Father and Son and their full mutuality, but knowing one another in this way as well. What the prayer tells us is that we are embedded in a reality, a "world" if you will, defined by relationship. Such relationship does not efface personal identity. Rather, the Father and Son are who they are, in distinction from each other, precisely in their relationship to each other.

Indeed, the point of the prayer is expressed not only by its content but also by its form: the fact that we are overhearing a deeply intimate conversation between Jesus and his Father. And what do we overhear in this conversation? We hear that we are protected from the evil one and the world's hatred — and, we might add, our own fears that lead us to hate God and one another (cf. 1 John 4:18) — by the very intimacy, the very reciprocity, Jesus shares with the Father (see, e.g., vv. 11, 21-23). We can face "the world" without fear precisely because we "indwell" this reality, the world of the Father's and Son's intimacy and reciprocity, a mutuality we share with them and with one another as well.

Lois Malcolm

Seventh Sunday of Easter, Year B

First Lesson: Acts 1:15-17, 21-26
(Psalm 1)
Second Lesson: 1 John 5:9-13
Gospel Lesson: John 17:6-19

As noted in the lection for John 17:1-11, chapter 17 has been called the high priestly prayer. This prayer serves as the climactic scene of Jesus' last meal with his disciples (John 13–16) before his crucifixion. It follows a set genre in ancient Mediterranean religious literature — that of a farewell speech before one's death (see, e.g., Moses' speeches in Deut. 31–33).

Nonetheless, its use of tenses depicts the unique character of its subject. The prayer is uttered by one who not only was "before the world existed" (v. 5) but has already left the world (v. 11) even as he anticipates his physical death. Although the heart of this lection is Jesus' prayer "on behalf" of his disciples (vv. 9-16), we can only understand the full implications of what he prays on their — and, by implication, our — behalf if we understand the broader context of the history and character of his relationship to the Father. The setting for the verses that make up this lection (vv. 6-19) is established in verse 1 where Jesus looks up to heaven and tells the Father that the "hour" has come for the Father to "glorify" him. What the lection will describe is the full complexity of what this "hour" entails — this hour when Jesus goes to the Father and leaves the disciples in the world, this hour depicted by such an unusual use of tenses.

The section introducing this lection (vv. 6-8) describes how Jesus has "glorified" the Father by "finishing the work" the Father has given him to do (v. 4). Jesus has made the Father's "name known" to the disciples, those the Father has given him from the world (v. 6). He has done so by giving the disciples the "words" the Father has given him. What does it mean to make the Father's "name known"? In the Old Testament, to make God's name known is to reveal God's character and identity. Such revelation always entails a way of life, a life of keeping God's "words" — God's commandments. Since the disciples already are God's — indeed, they are gifts to Jesus (v. 6b) — what is new in their response to this revelation is not their obedience to God, but the fact that they "know" that everything Jesus has is from God, and thus receive his words and believe that he was sent by God (v. 8b, c). The Jewish concept of "knowing" here entails not only intellectual assent but also the deeply personal sense of knowing another person in an intimate way.

Given this backdrop, the heart of this lection (in vv. 9-16) is Jesus' prayer "on behalf" of the disciples (v. 9). Jesus' statement "I am asking on their behalf" indicates a shift in the topic of his prayer, a shift linked with the sharp distinction he draws between the disciples and the "world." In John "the world" is the sphere of enmity with God, although, we should note, for John Jesus is also the one in whom "the world" was created (1:3), and "the world" is the place God loved so much that he sent Jesus into it (3:16), and later the disciples (17:18). Nonetheless, in this context the world is what Jesus is leaving, and where the disciples are still left. This "world" hates them (v. 14) because they do not belong to it. As a place where the evil one resides (v. 15), it is a place in which the disciples need protection (vv. 11,

12, 15). This "world," therefore, is contrasted with "those" the Father has given Jesus, the ones who already belong to the Father but who — because of the profound reciprocity shared between Jesus and the Father — have been given to Jesus. Jesus is glorified "in" these disciples precisely because it is "in" them that he glorifies the Father by doing what the Father has given him to do (v. 4) — give eternal life to them. In turn, and here we come full circle, it is precisely in the disciples' response to him — in their receiving him — that Jesus is glorified.

We now arrive at Jesus' depiction of this unique eschatological interim, this "hour" when he returns to the Father and yet is leaving the disciples in the world (v. 11). It is precisely in this period that the disciples need protection. This protection will entail their sharing in the reciprocity and intimacy the Father and Son have shared with each other (v. 11, a theme repeated later on in the chapter; see vv. 20-22). Indeed, we might note that the Christian community is founded precisely on the relationship between the Father and the Son. When Jesus was with the disciples, he had protected those the Father had given him (v. 12). He had "guarded" them so carefully that only one of them, Judas, was lost (a theme developed earlier in chap. 13). But now Jesus is coming to the Father and he wants the Father to protect them so that their joy may be made "complete in themselves" (v. 13).

But the world hates the disciples. It hates them the same way it hated Jesus. They do not belong to the world in the same way that Jesus did not belong to it (vv. 14, 15). Yet Jesus is not asking that the Father take them out of the world. This request that their joy be made complete is simply linked with the request that they be "protected." Jesus' intent, then, in praying for them is not that they be taken out of the world. His purpose is simply that they have complete joy — a joy they can have even in this world.

So how do they receive this joy? How are they "protected" even if they are in this world? They receive this joy and are protected precisely by living in the truth. And here we come to the culminating section of this lection: Jesus' request for the disciples' consecration or "sanctification" (in vv. 17-19). In verse 17 Jesus asks the Father to sanctify the disciples "in the truth," the "truth" being the Father's "word" (vv. 6, 8, 14, 17). Here we have an echo of an Old Testament theme whereby the "sanctification" (or consecration) of priests is directly linked with keeping the commandments. In verse 18 Jesus speaks about "sending," which he has already spoken of as the Father's work, but now we find a reciprocity between what the Father does and what Jesus does. In the same way that the Father has sent Jesus into the world, so Jesus sends the disciples into the world. In verse 19 we return to the theme of "sanctification." But now the focus is on Jesus himself. Jesus has sanctified himself — note that he and not the Father now is the agent — precisely so that the disciples might be sanctified. Is this reference to Jesus' sanctification a reference to his death, that is, to his high priestly role as both the one who sacrifices and the one who is sacrificed (cf. Hebrews)? Whether or not his death is implied here, the whole mission of his life, which culminates in death, is an act of obedience to the Father, and thus an act of consecration. The point in this verse is that there is an intrinsic connection between the disciples' consecration and Jesus' own self-consecration, a consecration defined by his obedience to the Father's mission for him. We have an echo here of a central New Testament theme, a theme depicted, for example, in the foot-washing scene of John 13. Jesus' self-giving for the disciples is something they too — precisely because of Jesus' own self-giving — are enabled to enact.

Like the disciples, we too live in that in-between time when Jesus has returned to the Father yet has left us here in the world. It is significant that Jesus does not request that the Father take us out of the world, although he recognizes that the world may be a very dangerous place for us to be in. Instead, what he prays for is our protection and joy. But that protection and joy is finally defined in terms of our consecration, our being "sanctified in truth." So what does it mean to be "sanctified in truth"? To understand this we need to take seriously the context of the whole prayer itself — the fact that Jesus is praying to the Father on our behalf. It is the intimacy he shares with the Father, which in turn they share with us, that grounds the "truth" defining our lives. Their mutuality — which is intrinsically linked with the mutuality we share with one another as Christians — is the source of our joy and protection even in the face of the world's dangers. Thus, although the world has its dangers — and Jesus does not mince any words describing the harsh reality of this world — we can nonetheless be assured of complete joy and full protection even as we await the time when we, like Jesus, can return to the Father.

Lois Malcolm

Seventh Sunday of Easter, Year C

First Lesson: Acts 16:16-34
(Psalm 97)
Second Lesson: Revelation 22:12-14, 16-17, 20-21
Gospel Lesson: John 17:20-26

This passage is about unity, the unity of Christians with one another and with Christ. But the precise character of this unity is defined in rather specific terms: the mutual indwelling of the Father and Son. And the intimacy shared between the Father and Son is also defined in very specific ways in John 17: the Father's sending the Son into the world and the Son's fulfilling what the Father sent him into the world to do (vv. 1-8). Further, the very genre of this chapter — that it is Jesus' final prayer addressed to the Father before his death — is important to note because the form of the prayer itself enacts the very intimacy and trust that characterize this relationship. Throughout the prayer Jesus directly addresses the Father; we the readers are merely overhearing their deeply intimate conversation. On the one hand, the disciples and their followers are the ostensible topic of this conversation. Jesus is talking about the disciples to the Father, and those who will believe in him "through their word" (v. 20). But what Jesus is praying for is precisely that these disciples and their followers might have — with one another and with him — the mutuality he shares with the Father, a mutuality expressed in the very tenor of the prayer itself. Thus the two specific requests of this lection — (1) "that they may all be one" (v. 21; cf. v. 22) and (2) "that those also . . . may be with me" (v. 24) — can only be understood against the backdrop of the relationship between the Father and Son and the deep drama of their intimacy and mutuality.

The lection has been preceded by Jesus' request that the Father glorify him (vv. 1-8) and his request for the disciples' protection and sanctification as they remain in the world (vv. 9-19). We know that a shift has occurred in the prayer at verse 20 because, following the same pattern he used in verse 9 ("I ask . . . on behalf"), Jesus now prays not only on behalf of the disciples but "on behalf of those who will believe in me through their word" (v. 20). Thus, although this passage speaks of a profound intimacy between believers and Jesus, this intimacy is a mediated one. The disciples' followers believe in Jesus because they have heard the "word" of his disciples (v. 20), just as the disciples initially believed in Jesus because he gave them the "word" that the Father gave him (vv. 6, 8, 14, 18). In contrast to a gnostic pattern of knowing that transcends all forms of mediation, the mutual indwelling and interpersonal knowing that this lection speaks of is not one that does away with the mediation of a distinct "word," a distinct "name" (vv. 6, 11, 12, 26), a distinct "truth" (vv. 17-19), and a distinctive way of living (e.g., v. 6: "they have kept your word").

A central climax in the prayer is reached in verse 21 where Jesus prays "that they may all be one." This request has already been made (in v. 11), but here it is explicitly linked not only with the Father's and Son's intimacy with each other ("as we are one," vv. 11, 22; see also 21) but with the believers' intimacy with the Father and Son ("may they also be in us," v. 21, and "I in them and you in me," v. 23). There is a clear sense in this prayer that the reciprocity the Father and Son share with each other is to be shared among the disciples. The Son has given the disciples the very glory the Father has given him (v. 22; cf. vv. 1, 5). In the same way that the sharing of this glory demonstrated the Father's and Son's reciprocity with each other, so now it demonstrates the believers' reciprocity with one another. Moreover, this reciprocity is not simply a self-enclosed mutuality. In the same way that the Father's and Son's mutuality was linked with the Son's mission into the world (vv. 1-9), so now the mutuality among believers is linked with their mission into the world. The whole purpose of the believers' unity with one another — and with the Father and Son — is so that the world may know that the Father has sent Jesus (vv. 21, 22).

The last section of this passage is introduced by another request: Jesus' desire that the believers be with him where he is. Again we see a stress on being mutually present, but now the focus is on believers being with Jesus at the place where he "sees" the glory he has shared with the Father even "before the foundation of the world" (v. 24; cf. v. 5). In other words, Jesus simply wants his disciples to be with him, and he wants to share with them what he shares with the Father: the glory of God. In verse 25 reference is made to the sharp dualism between the "world" (which does not know the Father and Jesus) and the disciples (who know the Father and that Jesus has been sent by him). Jesus has made the Father's "name known" to the disciples — that is, he has revealed to them the character and identity of God. The kind of "knowing" implied here is not merely intellectual assent but an intimate personal knowing. This is made clear in the last part of verse 26 where Jesus explicitly identifies the purpose for such knowing: that the love the Father has had for him may be "in" the believers. And it is not only love that is to indwell the believers but Jesus himself — in the same way that Jesus is "in" the Father and the Father in him (cf. vv. 21, 23).

This passage is often used to buttress ecumenical efforts. It does. But it is important that we not miss the rich theological complexity of this prayer. It is clear in this passage that church unity resides not in a particular church structure or program — a particular hierarchy, set of beliefs, or even set of practices or experiences. Rather, it resides in the love and mutuality the Father and Son share with each other and us (as, e.g., in the phrases "as you, Father, are in me and I am in you," v. 21, and "I in them and you in me," v. 23). The mutuality shared among believers can only be understood in relation to the larger drama of the Father's mission for the Son and the Son's obedience.

Not only have we been given access to the intimacy the Father and Son share with each other, but by way of our participation in their intimacy we are enabled to be intimate and reciprocal with one another. The link between the Father's and Son's mutuality and our mutuality with one another and them — especially when it relates to the sharing of divine "glory" (v. 24) — has profound implications for how we actually participate in the divine life. In the first place, it is clear from this passage that we do not participate in it as individuals but as a community of believers who share in the Father's and Son's communion with each other.

Further — and this point is often lost in discussions of communion and intimacy — the whole purpose for this mutual indwelling is so that the world might know that the Father has sent the Son. In other words, this mutuality has an end, a mission, and this mission is defined in rather specific terms: enabling the world to know the Father and the Son he has sent. On the one hand, we cannot truly preach Jesus if we ourselves are not united with one another and with the Father. On the other hand, the purpose of our unity is so that the world might know the Father and Jesus, whom he has sent. In the same way that the Son goes into the world to enable us to know him and the Father, so we too are sent into the world to enable others to share in that intimacy.

And if unity and mission mutually implicate each other in this passage, then knowledge and love cannot be separated from each other either. Jesus' intent is that the "world" might know the Father and the fact that the Father has sent him. But such knowing is a deep interpersonal knowing; it is a "knowing" that enables the disciples to experience the love the Father has given the Son (v. 26); it is a knowing that leads them to share in the sweet intimacy the Father and Son have with each other. Moreover, this knowing entails not merely a private truth, even though it is a deeply personal and interpersonal truth. It is linked, rather, with the truth of the cosmos, the very truth that undergirds the "foundation of the world" (v. 24; cf. v. 5 and 1:1-5) — and therefore lies at the heart of reality. In sum, even as we live in the "world" — with all its dangers (vv. 9-16) — we participate in yet a more powerful reality, the love between the Father and Son and, because of that love, the very tangible presence of Jesus in our lives (v. 26). This is the ultimate truth that governs our lives, and as we participate in that truth in community with one another, we enable others to participate in that truth as well.

Lois Malcolm

Christel the King, Year B

First Lesson: 2 Samuel 23:1-7
(Psalm 132:1-12, [13-18])
Second Lesson: Revelation 1:4b-8
Gospel Lesson: John 18:33-37

This passage provides one of the occasions when preachers are going to want to argue with the limits defined by the Revised Common Lectionary, and rightly so. It is impossible to get the full sense of these five verses without looking at the dialogue that eventuates in Pilate asking Jesus if he is "the King of the Jews." It is also irresponsible for an interpreter of these verses not to follow this narrative to its conclusion as both Pilate and the crowd respond to Jesus. On the other hand, the framers of the lectionary did choose a fascinating passage for Christ the King Sunday. For in many ways this passage assists preachers to examine what Christians mean when we speak of the kingly role of Christ.

Chapter 18 traces the arrest and trial of Jesus (first before Annas, then before Caiaphas, and finally before Pilate). This progression suggests that Pilate was the figure in first-century Jerusalem who had final civil authority over Jewish requests for executions. Indeed, when Pilate asks the Jews to take Jesus and judge him according to their own laws, the Jews reply that they are "not permitted to put anyone to death" (18:31). Yet, there is some dispute as to whether this is a historically accurate statement. Some claim that religious officials could sentence someone to death for blasphemy and carry out the punishment (e.g., Stephen in Acts 7:58-60) without the blessing of the Roman authorities. Others argue that such episodes happened

585

with official sanction and suggest that events like Stephen's death were the result of mob violence. In any case, this text conveys that the crowd is seeking the death penalty for Jesus, and they act and speak as if the Roman official is the only one who can authorize such a punishment.

Throughout the scenes of this trial, Pilate is depicted as an official who wants to do what is right. Of course, his understanding of "right" is almost exclusively based on the needs and dictates of the political state that he represents. Nevertheless, the Pilate we encounter in John's Gospel is a reluctant figure — a governor who is not convinced that the man on trial presents any risk to the state. The narrative describes Pilate shuttling back and forth between his inner chambers where Jesus is held and the outer courtyard where the crowd waits. Each time Pilate emerges to speak to the crowd, he seeks an option that will allow him to avoid an execution.

Pilate begins his interrogation of Jesus by asking, "Are you the King (*basileus*) of the Jews?" (18:33), a question that implies a political understanding of kingship. Pilate's opening question carries with it a host of political queries: Are you the king of a people whose country is occupied by its enemies and governed according to foreign rule? Are you going to stir up trouble, gather an army, seek revolt, or in any way attempt to usurp the power that belongs to the Roman emperor? As such, Pilate's initial question discloses the governor's fundamental concern: Does this man constitute a threat to the state? If not, then Jesus, whatever his purported crimes, is a problem that should pass to someone else's jurisdiction.

Jesus' "answer" to Pilate comes in the form of a question. In effect, 18:34 could be put this way: "Are you really concerned that I am a threat to Rome, or has someone else put you up to this?" Jesus suggests that Pilate is being manipulated into investigating a charge for which he has no evidence. The fact that Jesus, the accused, puts a question to Pilate, the man who reportedly has power over Jesus' life, is not insignificant. Throughout the passion John wants us to see Jesus as submitting to the will of the Father, not as one who blithely follows a fated course but as an agent who is actively choosing to follow this difficult path. In other words, while to the world this looks to be a situation in which Pilate holds all the cards, the careful reader of John will recognize that Jesus is not a pawn in these circumstances, and that his choices are the ones which will carry the day. John's Gospel echoes this particular theme throughout, but nowhere more explicitly than in 10:17-18. "For this reason the Father loves me, because I lay down my life in order to take it up again. No one takes it from me, but I lay it down of my own accord. I have power to lay it down, and I have power to take it up again. I have received this command from my Father." As the events of the trial play out, this realization even seems to dawn on Pilate (see 19:9-10).

Pilate answers Jesus' question by uttering the obvious: "I am not a Jew, am I?" — a statement that both hints at the procurator's confusion regarding the ways of the indigenous people and reminds the accused that he is dealing with an individual of unique power and privilege. Having reestablished that he is there to represent Rome, the governor admits that he does not have his own body of evidence, but is nonetheless concerned with the crowd's complaint. "It is your own people who have handed you over to me. . . . What have you done?" (18:35). Jesus responds, again not by answering Pilate's original question (Are you a king?), but by speaking of his kingdom (basileia). The kingdom of which Jesus speaks is "not of this world." To explain, Jesus points to events that Pilate might expect to see if Jesus was a typical worldly ruler. In effect, Jesus explains, "If I were the kind of king that you have in mind, my followers would be revolting in the land and trying to effect my release" (18:36). When he hears the word "kingdom," Pilate's political antennae perk up. "So you are a king?" Still bent on discovering the potential threat this guy might pose to the state, the governor misses the fact that Jesus is bent on redefining the very notion of "king" and "kingdom."

Again Jesus reminds Pilate that his understanding of "king" may be inadequate to the task. "*You* say that I am a king" (18:37). This response provides preachers with a promising trajectory for a sermon. When we say that Christ is king, what do we mean? The ever present danger in answering such a question is that we will allow our notion of what a king is to define who Christ is. Reversing this logic, verse 37 helps us approach this question from a theologically more adequate angle as Christ defines "king." Jesus accomplishes this by defining his kingdom. This ruler is the sovereign not of a certain parcel of land or a particular race of people, but of truth! This truth is not simply a proposition to which one can give assent, but the very gospel to which Christ's life bears witness — a truth to which people belong (18:37).

Is Rome threatened by this kind of kingdom? Should the state concern itself with a doomed convict who makes mystical claims about a transcendent kingdom? On one hand, the real threat here seems to be one that menaces the religious establishment. After all, they are the folk who lay claim to the "truth," and they are the ones petitioning the government for Jesus' death. On the other hand, the state is being asked to participate in this event, and this particular state will eventually give in to the cries of a mob. This is where following John's Gospel further is crucial. Two events in chapter 19 shed light on this passage. The first is the crowd's assertion that "we have no king but the emperor" (19:15). This statement finally pushes the politically minded Pilate to hand Jesus over to be crucified. In the end, the procurator's hand is forced both by those who clamor at his gates and by the flogged prisoner who quietly answers his questions. He who appeared to be in control was not. The second event that assists preachers to think through this passage for Christ the King Sunday comes almost a chapter later. There, following Jesus' journey to Golgotha, Pilate surfaces to author the inscription that hangs above the crucified Christ, "Jesus of Nazareth, the King of the Jews" (19:19). Irony pervades both of these pronouncements. First, the people declare the emperor to be their king — a blasphemous statement, for God alone is king, and God's anointed. Second, Pilate the Roman procurator answers his original question (18:33) by declaring the crucified Jesus to be king — identifying the suffering, dying one as royalty, and, as such, proclaiming the truth of the gospel.

Scott Black Johnston

Resurrection of the Lord, Years A, B, C

First Lesson: Acts 10:34-43
(Psalm 118:1-2, 14-24)
Second Lesson: Colossians 3:1-4 (A); 1 Corinthians 15:1-11 (B); 1 Corinthians 15:19-25 (C)
Gospel Lesson: John 20:1-18

The first postresurrection narrative in John 20 is the proclamation of the church to celebrate Easter Sunday for all three years of the lectionary. The pericope functions as the denouement to the passion narrative that is proclaimed on Good Friday. Why is the Johannine witness significant for the passion and resurrection accounts of Jesus? In particular, how can the encounter of Jesus and Mary Magdalene embrace the mystery of Easter for preachers? Can the importance of John 20:1-18 be utilized as the basis for other reflections during the six Sundays of Easter that present additional Johannine traditions?

All four Gospels mention Mary Magdalene in scenes before and after Jesus' resurrection. Only the Fourth Gospel highlights her as the one woman at the tomb. The synoptic Gospels have postresurrection scenes similar in setting and instructions to that of John 20:1-18. However, the distinctiveness of the Johannine tradition is evident from the inclusion of one female (Mary Magdalene) and one male character (Jesus) who speak with different emphases (cf. Matt. 28:1-8; Mark 16:1-8; Luke 24:1-10).

Now, let us draw near to the garden where Jesus was buried. Notice that in 20:1-18 there are two distinctive scenes that are dependent on each other (vv. 1-10, 11-18). In the first scene Mary Magdalene, who had stood near the cross of Jesus (19:25), comes to the tomb and sees that the stone was rolled back (v. 1). Immediately she runs to Simon Peter and the Beloved Disciple and reports her loss: "They have taken the Lord out of the tomb, and we do not know where they have laid him" (v. 2, NRSV). It is not clear if she expects them to assist her in the search to find Jesus' body.

Mary Magdalene disappears, and the reader can focus full attention on Simon Peter and the Beloved Disciple, who are principal characters in the scene. Both run toward the tomb, but the Beloved Disciple arrives first and peers into the tomb. However, he waits to enter until after Simon Peter arrives and enters. There they find the linen cloths and the head napkin lying in separate places (vv. 3-7). While neither disciple speaks, the Beloved Disciple "saw and believed" (v. 8). The narrator comments: "For as yet they did not understand the scripture, that he must rise from the dead" (v. 9). When the disciples return home, there are no characters in the garden area (v. 10).

The second scene confirms Mary Magdalene's earlier discovery (vv. 11-18). Does it present anything new for us? It depends on the reader's understanding of what the Beloved Disciple "saw and believed" (v. 8) as well as the narrator's comment (v. 9). The Beloved Disciple is an intuitive, close friend of Jesus. Remember how he rested on Jesus' chest at the Last Supper? He dared to ask about the identity of the betrayer (13:23-25). At the foot of the cross Jesus gave him and Jesus' mother new, mutual relationships (19:26-27). Here, however, if the Beloved Disciple grasped the mystery of Jesus' resurrection, would the disciples return to their homes? The accounts in the synoptic Gospels do not suggest indifference to Jesus' resurrection. Rather, the disciples leave the tomb and go out to witness to others (Matt. 28:8; Luke 24:10). The Beloved Disciple's "seeing and believing" is not a confessional genre. It is limited to noticing the empty tomb and the burial clothes in different places. (For expansion of this position, see Paul Minear, "'We Don't Know Where . . .' John 20:2," *Interpretation* 30 [1976]: 125-39.)

In addition, when we look for the characterization of call and response, we find that it is missing. Simon Peter had denied Jesus' call and had not responded to him after he denied him three times in the courtyard (18:15-17, 25-27). Although the Beloved Disciple had stood faithfully at the cross (19:25-27), he had not heard the voice of the risen Jesus. There can be no response without a prior call.

Mary Magdalene reenters to resume the plot. While she is weeping, she stands outside the tomb and then peers inside it (v. 11). Two angels are seated where the body of Jesus was. The reader is surprised, too, since the disciples found only burial wrappings in the same place. By describing the precise position of the angels, the narrator emphasizes why Mary is searching. When the angels ask her why she is weeping, she repeats the same statement she gave to the disciples (vv. 12-13).

Turning around, she sees Jesus but does not recognize him. After echoing the angels' question, Jesus adds his own: "Woman, why are you weeping? Whom are you looking for?" Assuming that he is the gardener, she speaks about her search again: "Sir, if you have carried him away, tell me where you have laid him, and I will take him away" (vv. 14-15).

Mary Magdalene engages in three conversations while she is trying to find Jesus' body. Her weeping and the loss of Jesus' body are consistent elements in her announcements to the disciples, angels, and Jesus (vv. 13-15). Since she misunderstands his identity, Jesus takes the initiative to end her search. He calls her by name: "Mary," and she recognizes him as her teacher, "Rabbouni" (v. 16; cf. 10:4). In knowing both Jesus' absence (vv. 2, 13, 15) and his presence, Mary clings to him (v. 17). If the scene concluded here, there would be a clear pattern of call and response. The scene would mirror two other encounters where Jesus addresses the same question to two followers of the Baptizer and the crowd in the garden: "What (or Whom) are you looking for?" (1:38; 18:4). One group responded by following Jesus, while the other group seized him for crucifixion.

Although there is a climax of mutual recognition between Jesus and the woman, what follows surpasses any expectations of Mary Magdalene and the reader. Jesus commands her: "Do not hold on to me, because I have not yet ascended to the Father. But go to my brothers [and sisters] and say to them, 'I am ascending to my Father and your Father, to my God and your God'" (v. 17). By connecting his resurrection to the ascension, Jesus indicates that his relationship to Mary Magdalene (and all believers) will be different. His return to the Father, to be where he dwells, is another moment of the hour in which he is glorified. The theological rather than the chronological and spatial intention of verse 17 also indicates a new relationship which the disciples will enjoy with the risen Jesus and the Father. Jesus' hour of glorification enables the disciples to be children of the Father and brothers and sisters of Jesus.

The familial language of "children," "brothers," and "sisters" does not designate persons who are under parental care as dependents. Rather, the terms identify adult believers who belong to the household of God. Jesus, the beloved Son, is the epitome of what it means to be a son or daughter of God and in relationship with others. Jesus enjoys dynamic living with the Father that is characterized as mutual knowing, loving, and abiding. Being a disciple of Jesus invites persons to that dynamic living. The last discourses of Jesus (13:1–17:24) that are proclaimed during the Easter season unfold the themes of mutual knowing, loving, and abiding with Jesus, the Father, and other disciples.

When we analyze the final verses of this scene (vv. 17-18), we notice a parallel to the witness of the resurrection in the synoptic Gospels (Matt. 28:7-8; Luke 24:6-9; cf. Mark 16:8). However, there are two differences in the Johannine account. First, the message of Jesus is about resurrection-ascension and new relationships (v. 17). Second, Mary Magdalene is the sole witness to the apostles: "Mary Magdalene went and announced to the disciples, 'I have seen the Lord'; and she told them that he had said these things to her" (v. 18).

The dynamic of Jesus and Mary Magdalene is a clear illustration of call and response in climactic sequence. First, Jesus addresses her as "woman" (v. 13), a courteous greeting (cf. 2:4; 19:26). Next, he calls her by name, "Mary," which enables her to recognize him personally. Finally, he claims her as his "sister" in the family of God, whom he addresses intimately as "Father." The narrator identifies Mary Magdalene as an "apostle" according to Pauline criteria: an experience of the risen Jesus and a commission to preach the good news (1 Cor. 15:3-11). As the first witness of the resurrection, Mary Magdalene responds to Jesus' new calling. She fulfills her commission by identifying Jesus for the disciples with new understanding.

Similarly, Mary Magdalene calls Jesus by different names. First, she addresses him as "Sir," a respectful greeting (v. 15). Next, she identifies him as "Rabbouni" (v. 16), a name with which the disciples address Jesus (1:38, 49; 4:31; 9:2; 11:8). Finally, she names him "Lord" (v. 18), which is similar to Thomas's recognition: "My Lord and my God" (20:28).

One possibility for preachers is to identify Mary Magdalene as the Beloved Disciple to open up possibilities for the gospel.

Mary Margaret Pazdan

Day of Pentecost, Year A

First Lesson: Acts 2:1-21
(Psalm 104:24-34, 35b)
Second Lesson: 1 Corinthians 12:3b-13
Gospel Lesson: John 20:19-23

An Easter Day resurrection account on the Day of Pentecost? Have the compilers of the lectionary got it right? John would say so. The sharp distinction between Jesus' resurrection and the arrival of the Spirit (signaled, e.g., in Luke's Gospel and Acts) is not found here. For John the death and resurrection of Jesus Christ, and his giving the Holy Spirit to his disciples, belong together. They are of a piece, the unfolding nature of God's salvation plan. The church lectionary rightly follows Lukan chronology: Easter to Ascension, forty days; Easter to Pentecost, fifty days. This gives the Christian community time to taste and digest a rich diet. After all, God only invented time so that everything doesn't happen all at once! But today's lection lives with John's chronology, not Luke's. It is, by implication, Easter evening, and the risen Jesus gifts the Holy Spirit to his disciples as soon as it is possible for him to do so. He has told them he must go away before the Comforter can come, and we witness the process of transference. An apt Pentecost passage? Absolutely!

The immediate context is a room (often regarded an "upper" room, though that isn't explicit in the text) in which are an unspecified number of unnamed disciples. Some suggest this vagueness is deliberate, implying that the features of this event — encounter with the risen Christ, reception of peace, commission for mission, reception of the Spirit — are offered as a pattern for *all* Christian disciples, in every time and place. These disciples are fearful of "the Jews," a term commonly employed by John to identify those opposed to Jesus and his ministry. The doors are "shut" or "closed" rather than locked, and it is worth speculating whether or not this hints at the spiritual condition of the disciples — not locked away as much as closed up. If so, the joy of Christ and the release of the Spirit are required rather than simply desired.

Into this closed and apprehensive atmosphere comes Jesus with his proclamation of peace. The manner of his arrival is not specified (through the door? simply materializing in the room?), but it clearly signals his superiority over human circumstances and limitations; Jesus' gift of peace is going to overcome their understandable fear. "Peace be with you" was, of course, a common Jewish greeting, yet in the circumstances this cannot be regarded as a conventional salutation, but rather one heavily laden with significance. The disciples are in a state of bewilderment and confusion. Mary has told them she has seen the Lord (v. 18), and they don't know what to make of it. It is even conceivable that some of them are fearful that the Lord *will* appear. After denials, failures, and shortcomings, encountering him again may be regarded only marginally better than meeting the Jews! And suddenly he is there, and they wince, and hold their breath, and wonder what's coming next. He opens his mouth and says, "Peace be with you" — with no hint of sarcasm. Astonishing! Perhaps the only sound in the room at that point was a group of disciples breathing a huge, collective sigh of relief.

As is the case in Matthew 28:17, doubt is present in the midst of reverence. Is this really Jesus? It is a feature of resurrection appearances that seeing is rarely believing. Here as elsewhere, evidence for the resurrection is insufficient to remove fear and unbelief. With typical grace and understanding, as if recognizing their need for reassurance, Jesus shows them his hands and side. This is a very anti-Docetic piece of gospel, for it is clear this is no ghost. Nowhere in the New Testament, and certainly not here, is the resurrection of Jesus portrayed as simple death reversal. He is not "as good as new." The risen Jesus bears the scars of crucifixion. Some writers, especially those focusing on theologies of disability, point out that the "scars of imperfection" in the risen Jesus are highly significant and deeply moving. Jesus' scars also serve to hold together his death and resurrection as a single theme. He is the living one who died. Even in resurrection glory the signs of crucifixion are evident, and the meaning of both is more fully apprehended through the lens of the other.

The recognition of Jesus by the disciples brings joy into a narrative which, up to this point, has been somewhat somber in tone. F. F. Bruce used to note that — postresurrection — there is not a note of hopeless sorrow in the New Testament. These disciples experience what so many have experienced down the centuries, even today: the arrival of Jesus, even in the midst of strain, turmoil, and uncertainty, brings the possibility of receiving joy.

A second "peace be with you" moves us into what many regard as the "great commission" in John. The repetition may simply be for emphasis, or may hint at a peace that saves — the peace of reconciliation with God resulting from Christ's death and resurrection. What is clear is that this peace is closely connected with the commission Jesus gives to the disciples: "As the Father has sent me, I also send you." "Sentness" is a key theme in John's Gospel. The sending of the disciples has its origin in the missionary nature of God. The Father sends the Son, and the Spirit, and the Son sends the disciples, equipped and filled with the Spirit. As is so often the case in the New Testament, so here, the role of the Spirit is essentially missionary. The disciples are sent "as," that is, in the same manner as the Father has sent the Son. Their mission proceeds from his and is modeled on his. "Sentness" is therefore at the heart of Christian discipleship.

Jesus' breathing over them, linked to the reception of the Holy Spirit, has obvious connotations with Genesis 2 where the breath of God created a living soul from dry dust. This graphic allusion to new life and a new beginning would not be missed on those who knew their Jewish Scriptures, and should not be lost to preachers on this, the "birthday" of the church. The powerful image was certainly not lost to C. S. Lewis, who, in the Narnia Chronicles, has Aslan the Christ lion breathing over the petrified and so restoring them to life. It is the reception of the Holy Spirit that makes the seemingly impossible commission possible. The disciples are, in effect, to "be Jesus" in the world. This is impossible without the Spirit's equipping and enabling, so the Spirit is given. It should be noted that some manuscripts leave out "on them," having simply "Jesus breathed, and said," leading to the consideration that the Holy Spirit is not so much a specific gift given to a variety of individuals as a collective gift given to "disciples" — all disciples.

The gift of the Spirit is here closely connected to forgiveness and judgment. It appears that the Spirit brings not only joy and peace but also authority and responsibility. To suggest that the disciples can now arbitrarily dispense or withhold forgiveness on the basis of personal whims — "I like your necktie, you're forgiven; I don't like your hair, you're not forgiven" — is to misunderstand what is going on here. To be about the business of forgiveness and judgment emerges naturally out of being sent by Christ, filled with the Holy Spirit, into the world. Throughout John's Gospel, people encounter Jesus; it is a Gospel full of encounters. Just *how* people respond to Jesus relates closely to judgment and forgiveness. If they believe him and receive him, they are forgiven; if they reject him, then they judge *themselves* by the very act of rejection. So in the same way, as people encounter Jesus' Spirit-filled disciples, forgiveness and judgment occur. To respond to the freely declared message of forgiveness is to receive it; to reject the offer of grace is not to receive it. It is important to remember that this matter of forgiveness and judgment occurs within moments of the disciples themselves being forgiven rather than judged by Jesus' word of peace. Those forgiven by Christ are told to proclaim his forgiveness. Then, as now, if Christ's disciples follow his example, they will come to realize how best to exercise this gospel ministry.

In conclusion of this point, it is worth noting that the text does not permit a starkly individual application of the principle; "sins of any" and "their sins" imply whatever *people* more than whatever *person*. On the other hand, what applies to groups clearly affects individuals.

John's Easter and post-Easter narratives illustrate an unfolding progression toward faith on the part of the disciples. In John's complete postresurrection narrative, and the pericopes that combine to make it up (of which this is one), disciples move from fear, incredulity, and unbelief to conditional faith, to unconditional acceptance of Jesus as risen Lord. The suggestion that the progression of all Christian disciples is reflected in the experiences of these disciples has much to commend it.

Martyn D. Atkins

Second Sunday of Easter, Years A, B, C

First Lesson: Acts 2:14a, 22-32 (A); Acts 4:32-35 (B); Acts 5:27-32 (C)
(Psalm 16 [A]; Psalm 133 [B]; Psalm 118:14-29 [C])
Second Lesson: 1 Peter 1:3-9 (A); 1 John 1:1–2:2 (B); Revelation 1:4-8 (C)
Gospel Lesson: John 20:19-31

This reading from John's Gospel is located within a series of three postresurrection stories. The first of these (20:1-18) is the Easter morning narrative, in which the risen Jesus appears to Mary Magdalene, concluding with her recognition of who he is (20:16). That story is now behind us. It is the Gospel for Easter Day for all three years (A, B, and C), although alternative readings are possible.

The next two postresurrection stories take place on two different occasions, and they make up the reading for the Second Sunday of Easter. The first (20:19-25) takes place on the evening of Easter Day, an appearance of Jesus to his disciples, when Thomas is absent. The second (20:26-31) narrates an appearance of Jesus to his disciples a week later, when Thomas is present.

The opening verse (20:19) provides the setting. We are to assume that the house in which the disciples are gathered is in or near Jerusalem, since the previous material in the chapter has that location. The reason the disciples met behind locked doors was fear, but the effect upon us as we hear the story is that we anticipate a miracle. And we are not disappointed. The resurrected Jesus appears miraculously.

The reason for the meeting of the disciples is not given. But in the previous verse (20:18) the Evangelist says Mary Magdalene had reported the news of Jesus' resurrection to the disciples. Both Peter and the Beloved Disciple had come to the tomb in the morning, but only the Beloved Disciple had actually come to believe in Jesus' resurrection (20:8). Peter had not yet come to believe, nor had the other disciples. Then in the sequel, related in 20:11-18, the risen Jesus appears to Mary Magdalene and she recognizes who he is. It is she who tells the other disciples that she has seen the risen Lord.

The story unfolds in 20:19b-23 with (1) an appearance of the risen Christ to his disciples, (2) a commission, (3) the giving of the Spirit, and (4) a promise. It is only at the end of this series of events that we are told that Thomas was not present with the others (20:24-25). Comments follow concerning each of the four events.

1. Jesus appears in the midst of the disciples and gives them the common Jewish greeting: "Peace" ("Shalom"). He goes on to identify himself, proving himself to be the crucified Jesus, by showing his hands and side. The reaction of the disciples is one of rejoicing, as in the NRSV (the RSV is too bland when it says that they "were glad"), and that fulfills the words of Jesus in 16:20, where he says to his disciples that, when he returns to the Father, they will have pain, but that their pain will turn into joy.

2. A commissioning follows (20:21). Jesus says, first of all, that he had been sent by the Father. That is a common affirmation in the Gospel of John, showing up some forty-one times. It is a prominent ingredient in Johannine Christology: Jesus has been sent into the world to reveal the Father, to teach, and to gather disciples. And he has said already, back in 17:18, in his high priestly prayer, that one of his purposes of being sent into the world is to send his disciples to continue his ministry, once he has returned to the Father. Now that is being fulfilled in the text before us. He commissions his disciples to be in the world to continue his ministry.

3. The "Johannine Pentecost" follows in 20:22. According to the Fourth Evangelist, the gift of the Spirit was bestowed on the evening of Easter Day itself, not on Pentecost some seven weeks later, as Luke has it. The disciples are immediately commissioned and given the Spirit as a power that will enable them to witness to Christ.

4. The authorization to forgive sins completes the series of events on Easter Day (20:23). The passage is similar to those in Matthew 16:19 and

18:18. In any case, the disciples — therefore members of the church — are given authority to forgive and retain sins.

Important as the foregoing scene is, the interest of the preacher and the congregation will focus primarily on the second of the two scenes in our reading, which takes place a week later (20:26-29).

The opening verse (20:26) is virtually a repetition of 20:19, except that Thomas is now present. Jesus invites Thomas to touch his wounds and to believe. We are not told that Thomas actually does so, but he makes a confession of faith: "My Lord and my God!" In making that confession, it is not likely that (the Johannine) Thomas is expressing a full-blown ontological Christology, as presented in the creeds and christological formulas of the fourth and fifth centuries. What he says, in effect, is that he has encountered the presence of God in the risen Jesus.

The final verse of the scene (20:29) is a bit tricky. One could take it as a rebuke of Thomas, whose faith is dependent on seeing Jesus, in contrast to those who believe without seeing him. The popular designation of Thomas as "doubting Thomas" is based on such a reading. But that reading of the story is not necessary. The faith of Thomas, and his coming to faith through seeing, are not discredited. After all, the basis for his faith is no different from that of the others, for they too believe only on the basis of the appearance of Christ to them. It is better to discern a different contrast altogether, one between two ways of coming to faith. The one is through seeing; the other is through a means apart from seeing. And that is through believing the gospel proclaimed by Jesus' witnesses.

Jesus speaks a beatitude: "Blessed are those who have not seen and yet have come to believe." That puts all Christians of all times and places on the same level before God as the original disciples. The original circle of disciples, to whom the risen Jesus appeared, is bound by time and place in first-century Jerusalem. But others will come to believe far and wide without their originating experience. The beatitude is addressed at the literary level to the reader or hearer of the Gospel of John. We who have come to faith are declared blessed as we hear the Gospel being read.

The most obvious reason for assigning this reading to the Second Sunday of Easter is that the Thomas story falls chronologically on the Sunday after Easter. But there is another reason for using it as a basis for preaching, and that is to emphasize its two ways of coming to faith: (1) faith through an encounter with the risen Jesus, who appears, and (2) faith that comes through hearing the witness of those who have gone before us and have testified to him as the Living One who grants forgiveness of sins and new and eternal life.

On Easter we celebrated the resurrection. But now we reflect more deeply on the meaning of the resurrection for ourselves, who have not experienced an appearance of the risen Jesus.

What does it take for a person to be a believer? God works in two ways — first through the early disciples, and then through them and countless others throughout history, persons who have caught a glimpse of the eternal and the divine in the story of Jesus.

The preacher should be aware that it is impossible to establish the facticity of the resurrection to the satisfaction of everyone. As with the affirmation that God created the world, so too the affirmation that God raised Jesus from death to life goes beyond the usual rules of evidence. The experience of Thomas (as related by the Fourth Evangelist), who saw the pierced hands and side of the risen Jesus, is not repeatable — at least not until the world to come.

But what is clear is that the twin claims that God created the world and that God raised Jesus from the dead are consistent. They are consistent with one another (both speak of creation out of nothing), and they are consistent with the kind of God who is revealed in the Scriptures.

The doubts Thomas expressed initially (20:25) should be neither denigrated nor celebrated. But Thomas's problem and Jesus' beatitude together provide instruction in the meaning of faith for Christians after the first generation. Faith is not a certainty based on physical perception, but is trust grounded in insight into the reality of God, what God is capable of doing, and how Jesus fits into the larger drama.

Arland J. Hultgren

Third Sunday of Easter, Year C

First Lesson: Acts 9:1-6, (7-20)
(Psalm 30)
Second Lesson: Revelation 5:11-14
Gospel Lesson: John 21:1-19

Although the resurrection accounts of the four Evangelists differ from one another on various details, the one thing all four writers share in common is a fine knack for dramatic understatement. These days, however, Easter Sunday has become the day for churches to be anything *but* understated. Instead we pull out all the stops in order to be as noisy, flashy, dramatic, and scintillating as possible.

Some years ago one church conveyed the power of Easter with a service that began a bit sedately, only to have two women suddenly burst through the back doors of the sanctuary, flailing their way down the aisle even as they screamed, "He's alive!" This, then, was the cue for the choir to jump to its feet in a rousing anthem, accompanied by all the brass the church could muster. Still other churches now make much use of drama — in one such drama I saw the corpse of Jesus' body in a tomb. As the congregation watched, suddenly little Christmas tree lights began to blink up and down along the length of the body. Then a trap door opened and the body of Jesus disappeared. The actor who portrayed Jesus then reappeared high above the stage surrounded by wisps of clouds with a slide of a sunny blue sky projected onto a screen behind him. The congregation rose to its feet and cheered even as the choir hit a jazzed-up version of Handel's "Hallelujah Chorus."

How very different are the Gospel accounts of Easter! As Frederick Buechner once said, the Evangelists get to the climax of their stories only to whisper. Mark famously ends in a lurch with silent, terrified women fleeing the tomb. The other Gospels say a bit more, but even so, the stories are so common and mundane. A stranger walks up from behind and casually inquires, "What's up?" A man mistaken for a gardener shuffles up behind Mary to ask, "Why are you crying?" In John 21 a stranger appears along the crescent of a lake's shoreline, cupping his hands around his mouth as he shouts, "Catch anything?" In these stories there are no bright lights, no angel bands, no brass, no cheering throngs.

Instead Jesus is recognized when he does or says something the disciples had seen before. The way he broke the bread gave him away in Emmaus.

The tone of his voice when he said simply, "Mary," is what caused Mary to whirl around in astonished recognition. His ability to turn the disciples from perennially bad fishermen into successful anglers after all is what catches the attention of John, and then Peter, in John 21.

But once the disciples get to the shore, there are still no trumpets. Instead it's a vaguely awkward scene. Peter looks ridiculous, having mindlessly put his clothes back *on* before jumping into the water. No one knows quite what to say. It's Jesus all right, but with a difference. "None of the disciples dared to ask, 'Who are you?' because they knew it was the Lord." The resurrection was a shocking event which shattered cosmic reality. Those closest to the epicenter of this shattering were as numb as they were happy. (As theologian Michael Welker likes to say, after the resurrection you don't find anyone casually clapping Jesus on the shoulders and saying with a grin, "We're so glad you're back, Jesus!")

Indeed, John 21 opens after Jesus had already appeared to the disciples twice. Yet the disciples seem still lost. They've gone back to the fishing business. They don't know what to do with themselves, having not yet received any new marching orders. In a sense it could legitimately be said that the resurrection event on which the entire church is founded got off to a slow start!

But partly this was because Jesus had to take care of some old business before things could move forward. There was, for instance, the matter of Peter's denial to deal with. Peter needed a word of forgiveness and restoration, but really Peter is no different from anyone. We've all got "old business" which only the hope and grace of Jesus' resurrection can address.

Ernest Hemingway once related an anecdote through which he wanted to show the extreme popularity of the Spanish name "Paco." One day, Hemingway claimed, an ad appeared in the classifieds of a Spanish newspaper: "Paco, meet me at the Hotel Montana at noon Wednesday. All is forgiven. Love, Papa." That Wednesday the authorities had to muster a whole squad of police to contain the crowd of eight hundred Pacos who had shown up at the Hotel Montana!

Even more than revealing how popular the name Paco is, this story underscores the common human need for restoration, forgiveness, and fresh starts. At any given moment throngs of people yearn to hear a word of graced forgiveness. Peter is Everyman. He had betrayed his Lord, failed to live up to his finest claims for himself. He was in no position to ask for forgiveness, nor does he do so in John 21. But the forgiveness comes anyway.

The verbal exchange between Jesus and Peter in verses 15-17 is the stuff of great lexical debate. The controversy centers on the alternation of the

Greek words *phileō* and *agapaō*. Jesus twice asks if he has Peter's *agapē,* and Peter twice answers that Jesus most certainly does have Peter's *philos.* Finally, the third time Jesus switches verbiage to ask if he has Peter's *philos,* and John tells us that Peter was sad because Jesus had asked for *philos.*

But some scholars claim the Greek language was in flux at the time John was written, with the word *agapē* overtaking the word *philos* as the standard Greek word for "love" (even as *philos* was slowly sliding into a word meaning "kiss"). If so, it would not be the case that *agapē* referred to any higher, more sacrificial level of love (vis-à-vis *philos,* which was perhaps a more common love of friendship). Hence, some claim, the alternation in John 21 represents no more than literary variety — a mere exchange of synonyms.

Others (including this author) find it difficult to resist the idea that this alternation, taking place as it does in the tight space of this brief conversation, does represent something. Perhaps it shows Peter's wariness, not wanting to claim *too* much for his love. Considering how dismally he had only recently failed to live up to his own hype, perhaps Peter now hedges a bit. In the end it looks like Jesus is coming down to Peter's level, maybe giving up on him a bit (which is what makes Peter sad).

But Jesus is not giving up on Peter. Rather, Jesus expresses a gracious willingness to give Peter time to grow in grace and spiritual maturity. After all, despite Peter's past failure, despite what may be his cautious hedging in this exchange, nevertheless Jesus puts Peter in charge of the flock, asking him to tend, feed, and keep the sheep of Jesus' pasture.

Peter was restored. Though perhaps an understated story lacking in blaring brass, this quiet acceptance of Peter just as he is — and Jesus' simultaneous giving to Peter the greatest of all tasks — represents what the resurrection is all about. Like this story in John 21, so in our lives: the power of Jesus is not stunning as the world recognizes the spectacular. It is not about razzle or dazzle, glitz or eye-popping special effects. Instead it's about the quiet way of Jesus with his people, forgiving their failures, recognizing their limitations, but in grace setting them to work anyway.

In Flannery O'Connor's short story "Wise Blood," a man is encouraged to shape up because, as someone says to him, "Jesus died for your sins." To this the unhappy young man replies, "I never ast him to!" The truth is that none of us ever asked Jesus to die for our sins — certainly Peter did not. Peter had even tried to *stop* Jesus' death! But it does not matter: grace cannot be held back!

This lection concludes with a curious reference to Peter's death. One day Peter would die for his Lord. Before he did, however, he sent out one last epistle, the very last sentence of which has Peter encouraging his readers to "grow in the grace and knowledge of our Lord Jesus Christ" (2 Pet. 3:18). Such growth in grace is something Peter knew well.

So should we all. For though we sometimes fall back in failure, Jesus keeps accepting us where we are even as he gently calls us to grow more and come farther along on the journey of discipleship. Perhaps that is why this story ends at the beginning as Jesus returns Peter to square one, saying to him the same thing Jesus said when he first encountered each disciple, "Follow me!" Grace means new beginnings, setting us all back on square one (again and again and again, if need be) so that we can every day pick ourselves up to continue our growth in grace in the resurrection life which Jesus alone gives.

Scott Hoezee

Augustinian Preaching and the Nurture of Christians

C. CLIFTON BLACK

I. Confessions of a Parish Priest

Saint Augustine of Hippo (A.D. 354-430) seems an unlikely subject to accompany a volume on preaching from the Gospels. If remembered at all, he is typically associated with original sin, predestination, and other ideas consigned by many Christians to a theological flea market.

While we do well to engage all our ancestors' writings before dismissing their views as antiquated or pernicious, I do not aim to act as apologist for Augustine's thought, much less to attempt his rehabilitation among present-day skeptics. (Those wanting orientation to Augustine's mature thought might begin with *The Augustine Catechism: The Enchiridion on Faith, Hope, and Love,* ed. John E. Rotelle, trans. Bruce Harbert, Augustine Series [Hyde Park, N.Y.: New City, 1999]. For a sympathetic presentation of Augustinian theology, William Mallard, *Language and Love: Introducing Augustine's Religious Thought through the Confessions Story* [University Park: Pennsylvania State University Press, 1994], is highly recommended.) This is a book for preachers, and whatever else he was, Augustine was a preacher. That fact is sometimes forgotten, even by those who endorse Augustinian theology. Though he was astonishingly prolific, Augustine enjoyed no ivory tower. His pivotal masterpieces — *Confessions, The Trinity, The City of God,* to name but three — were written on the margins of his life as a diligent bishop in Hippo Regius, a scruffy African harbor town. In those days a bishop was not the diocesan administrator that some contemporary denominations elect. Essentially, Augustine served as priest of a large parish comprising mostly poor, largely illiterate, brutally hot-tempered, thoroughly superstitious Christians. His days were consumed by pastoral care, case arbitration in municipal court, humanization of Rome's penal machinery, and trawling a bottomless river of correspondence. His prayer life suffered; he complained of being sucked into useless, time-wasting duties that he nevertheless discharged with scrupulous care (see his *Letters to Eudoxius* [48.1] and *To Marcellinus* [133], in *Letters of St. Augustine*, Nicene and Post-Nicene Fathers, ser. 1, vol. 1 [1886; reprint, Peabody, Mass.: Hendrickson, 1994], pp. 294-95, 470-71).

Among Augustine's daily responsibilities, no activity outstripped preaching. "Here," as Pamela Bright notes, "is his home and place, his preferred environment" (*Augustine and the Bible*, ed. and trans. Pamela Bright [Notre Dame: University of Notre Dame Press, 1999], p. xv. Nevertheless, scholarly treatments of Augustine the preacher are scarce. Still useful are older assessments by A. D. R. Polmann, *The Word of God according to St. Augustine* [Grand Rapids: Eerdmans, 1961], pp. 123-76, and F. van der Meer, *Augustine the Bishop: The Life and Work of a Father of the Church*, trans. Brian Battershaw and G. R. Lamb [London and New York: Sheed & Ward, 1961], pp. 405-67. More recently, consult George Lawless, "Augustine of Hippo as Preacher," in *Saint Augustine as Bishop: A Book of Essays*, ed. Fannie LeMoine and Christopher Kleinhenz [New York and London: Garland, 1994], pp. 13-37; William Harmless, *Augustine and the Catechumenate*, Pueblo Book [Collegeville, Minn.: Liturgical Press, 1995], pp. 156-93; and *Augustine and the Bible*, pp. 243-315. For specimens of Augustine's own Sunday sermons on the Gospels, see *Augustine on the Sunday Gospel*, ed. John E. Rotelle [Villanova, Pa.: Augustinian Press, 1998]). He preached *ex cathedra*, from an elevated chair, almost every day and occasionally more than once a day. Depending on the liturgical circumstances, his sermons ranged in length from ten minutes to two hours before a standing congregation, without pews. Those of his sermons that have survived were transcribed on the spot by *notarii*, much like our court stenographers, while the bishop preached extemporaneously, without manuscript or notes, reading then laying aside a biblical book. Whatever their degree of material accuracy, these transcriptions no more convey his verbal firepower than a newspaper report could possibly capture the experience of "I Have a Dream," delivered from the steps of the Lincoln Memorial by Martin Luther King, Jr. Like King, Augustine was a natural stem-winder. His listeners clapped and shouted, at times to the preacher's dismay: "What have I said? Why are you applauding? We're still battling the problem, and you've already started cheering" (*Sermon on Mark* 8:34, translation adapted from *Sermons [94A-147A] on the New Testament,* ed. John E. Rotelle, trans. Edmund Hill, Works of Saint Augustine 3/4 [Brooklyn, N.Y.: New City, 1992], p. 32). "[T]he Lord's trumpet blows through Augustine's mouth," marveled Paulinus of Nola *(Letter to Romanianus).* Even theological opponents conceded his power as a preacher: alleging his inability "to discern a Christian in [Augustine]," Secundinus the Manichee found him "on all occasions a born orator, a veritable god of eloquence" (quotations of Secundinus and Paulinus from van der Meer, p. 412).

A professional rhetorician before his conversion to Christianity (*Confessions* 4.2), Augustine carried every homiletical arrow in his quiver. As a preacher, what did he think he was accomplishing? On the anniversary of his ordination, he tells us: "To rebuke those who stir up strife, to cheer up the faint-hearted, to support the weak, to refute the gospel's opponents, to be wary in sidestepping their traps, to teach the unlearned, to shake the lazy awake, to discourage those consumed by buying and selling, to put the proud in their place, to hold the quarrelsome in check, to help the needy, to liberate the oppressed, to encourage the good, to endure the evil, to love all people" (*Sermon* 340.3, translation adapted from *Sermons [306-340A] on the Saints,* ed. John E. Rotelle, trans. Edmund Hill, Works of Saint Augustine 3/9 [Hyde Park, N.Y.: New City, 1994], p. 293). Augustine yearned for escape from the rat race. "And yet," he confessed,

> it's the gospel itself that scares me [away from that softer way of life]. Sure, I could say: What business is it of mine to bore people? To reprove the wicked by telling them, "Quit acting wickedly. Act like this. Stop doing that"? What do I get out of burdening people? . . . Just let me sign for what *I've* received. Why should I give an account for others? Because of the gospel. It's terrifying. Nobody could outdo me in enjoying anxiety-free leisure. There's nothing better, nothing more pleasant than rummaging through [Scripture's] divine treasure chest, with nobody making a commotion. It's sweet. It's good. But to preach, to refute, to correct, to build up, to manage for everybody — that's a great burden, a great weight, a great labor. Who wouldn't run away from such a job? It's the gospel that reigns me in. (*Sermon* 339.4, translation adapted from *Sermons [306-340A] on the Saints,* p. 282)

II. Nothing but Charity

Saint Augustine is responsible for the first and most influential handbook for preachers in the Western Church: *De doctrina christiana* (begun 396; completed 426). (A fresh, inexpensive translation is available: *Teaching Christianity: "De Doctrina Christiana,"* ed. John E. Rotelle, trans. Edmund Hill, Works of Saint Augustine I/11 [Hyde Park, N.Y.: New City, 1996]. On the influence of this Christian classic across the Middle Ages to the Renaissance, see Edward E. English, ed., *Reading and Wisdom: The "De Doctrina Christiana" of Augustine in the Middle Ages* [Notre Dame and London: University of Notre Dame Press, 1995].) A mature work containing almost all the bishop ever wrote on the art of preaching, *Teaching Christianity* commends a preacher's entrée to the interpretive process through a door very different from that emphasized by most theological curricula in twenty-first-century North America. Unlike readers who "objectively" ground exegesis in the historical or literary particulars of pericopes, and at odds with self-styled ideological critics who "subjectively" locate interpretation within their subcultures' particularist experiences, Augustine begins with an unshakable theological conviction so outré that its *kairos* may have arrived: "Scripture commands nothing but charity" (*Teaching Christianity* 3.10.36).

Caritas, for Augustine, is a love properly ordered and conformed to the way things really are: love for the triune God, in whom alone genuine fulfillment is found; love for the neighbor, with whom this love for God is shared in common (1.22.2–1.35.39). That indivisibly double love is *the* epistemological principle of all exegesis and preaching that are set to rights. Hence, Augustine's audacious claim: "Some may think they have understood scripture, but if their views fail to build up this double love of God and neighbor, they have not yet succeeded in understanding" (1.36.40). Conversely, those whose views edify that double love will escape serious interpretive error, even if they mistake what the biblical authors actually had in mind. (For much in this paragraph, I am indebted to William S. Babcock, "*Caritas* and Signification in *De Doctrina Christiana* 1-3," in *"De Doctrina Christiana": A Classic of Western Culture,* ed. Duane W. H. Arnold and Pamela Bright [Notre Dame and London: University of Notre Dame Press, 1995], pp. 145-63.) "Therefore, a person strengthened by faith, hope, and love, and who steadfastly holds on to them, has no need of the scriptures except to instruct others" (1.39.43, trans. R. P. H. Green in *Augustine: "De Doctrina Christiana"* [Oxford: Clarendon, 1995], p. 53). Augustine's relentless concentration on this twin love of God and neighbor probably accounts for the remarkable lack of interest in technique in *Teaching Christianity*. Its "strategies for preaching" can be summed up in a few pieces of practical advice: Know your listeners. Expound the Scriptures. People must understand, so be clear. Pray for clarity. If good preaching is beyond your ability, don't worry: it is better to say wisely what you cannot say well than to say well what you cannot say wisely (4.4.6–4.5.7; 4.8.22–4.10.25). Most important of all: "Abundantly eloquent is the preacher whose life can speak" (4.27.59).

Moreover, for Augustine Christian doctrine frames the context within which Scripture should be interpreted and preached. "So when, on closer inspection, you see that it is still uncertain how something is to be punctuated or pronounced, you should refer it to the rule of faith [*regulam fidei*], which you have received through the plainer passages of scriptures and the authority of the church [*ecclesiae auctoritate*]" (3.2.2). There, in a single sentence, is just about everything historical criticism was designed to combat: an interpretive magisterium and a foisting of dogma upon the biblical word. In fairness, let the church confess and repent of the dangerously excessive influence over biblical interpretation that its hierarchy has sometimes wielded. Lately, however, our homiletical sins run along a different line. Whether sipping or guzzling from the wells of critical theory and pop psychotherapy, preachers who would never dream of warning their listeners away from the Seven Deadly Sins will, without a moment's hesitation, trumpet a sermon series on the Seven Habits of Highly Effective Churches (see Marsha G. Witten, *All Is Forgiven: The Secular Message in American Protestantism* [Princeton: Princeton University Press, 1993], for a sobering account of the tension that stretches contemporary Christian preaching between traditional piety and secularity's individualism and ideological relativism). Nor have theologians exhibited thumping success in disentangling from the biblical witness one intellectual construct — the rule of faith — without implanting listless, secularized alternatives in its place. (Perhaps the tide is beginning to turn. One sees hopeful signs in David S. Yeago, "The New Testament and the Nicene Dogma: A Contribution to the Recovery of Theological Exegesis," in *The Theological Interpretation of Scripture: Classic and Contemporary Texts*, ed. Stephen E. Fowl [Malden, Mass., and Oxford: Blackwell, 1997], pp. 87-100; Geoffrey Wainwright, "Towards an Ecumenical Hermeneutic: How Can All Christians Read the Scriptures Together?" *Gregorianum* 76 [1995]: 639-62; and Carl E. Braaten, "Scripture, Church, and Dogma," *Interpretation* 50 [1996]: 142-55.) At risk is a generation of sadly backward Anselmians whose understanding desperately seeks faith. Augustine offers us preachers an alternative: to lead our listeners back into the depths of the triune God, into whose merciful likeness we are being transformed.

III. Faithful Preaching as Christian Nurture

Each of the church's doctors has endowed us with peculiar gifts for Scripture's interpretation: Origen (ca. 185–ca. 254), the beginnings of a theology of exegesis; Theodore of Mopsuestia (ca. 350-428), respect for the Bible's historical particularities; Jerome (ca. 346-420), mastery of ancient languages and their translation (consult "The Bible in the Early Church," in *The Cambridge History of the Bible*, vol. 1, *From the Beginnings to Jerome*, ed. P. R. Ackroyd and C. F. Evans [Cambridge: Cambridge University Press, 1970], pp. 412-586). From Augustine we receive an inestimable legacy of scriptural interpretation in the service of nurturing Christians. Not merely does he set forth a program of catechesis, for which biblical study provides raw material. Augustine catechizes *through* exegesis, showing us how biblical preaching itself *functions as* Christian nurture. Augustine boldly proposes that, when we approach the Bible as Scripture — when we inquire after God through assiduous study of the biblical text — it is there that we encounter the God who is relentlessly inquiring after us.

Were we to accept his challenge, what might Saint Augustine teach us about the interpretation of Scripture for preaching in our day?

Who Is Interpreting Whom?

Augustine refuses to support us in the illusion that scriptural interpretation, properly understood, is an end in itself. He would surely have been bored — if not appalled — by philological, philosophical, historical, traditional, or literary studies of the Bible undertaken for their own sake, divorced from humanity's restless quest for God: the God to whom the biblical witness points, the God who uses many media — the sacraments and their observance, prayer and its practice, Scripture and its exegesis — to graciously conform our wills to God's own.

Biblical study as an end in itself — or as a mere instrument for such derivative objectives as fulfilling requirements for a degree or eliciting a facile answer to some burning question of our day — would be, to Augustine's thinking, nothing more than a practical expression of that idolatry summed up by Paul in Romans 1:25: humanity's radically confused worship and service of the creature rather than of the Creator. "Suppose," Augustine muses,

> a man should make for his betrothed a ring, and she should prefer the ring given her to the betrothed who made it for her. Would not her heart be

convicted of infidelity in respect of the very gift of her betrothed, though what she loved were what he gave. Certainly let her love his gift; but if she should say, "The ring is enough, I don't want to see his face again," what would we say of her? . . . Yet surely the pledge is given by the betrothed, just that in his pledge he himself may be loved. Just so, God has given you all these things: therefore, love him who made them. There is more that [God] would give you — even himself, their Maker. (*On John's First Epistle* 2.11, from *Augustine: Later Works,* trans. John Burnaby, Library of Christian Classics [Philadelphia: Westminster, 1955], pp. 275-76, slightly modified)

As Augustine notes elsewhere (*On the Catechizing of the Uninstructed* 4.8; 10.15–15.23), education is anchored in love. The ultimate aim of education is the discovery and arousal of our love for God. Though we may think we have begun to search for God through scriptural interpretation, in Augustinian perspective the truth is actually the reverse. *It is we who are interpreted by Scripture, which reveals the God who is searching after us.* Nor is that inquiry ours to begin: if we turn to the Bible as a means of grace, it is only because God has bestirred us in that divinely appointed direction. The only fountain that can slake humanity's deepest thirst is the Holy Spirit, and "God's Spirit calls you to drink of himself" (*On John's First Epistle* 7.6).

Who Is God for Us?

For Augustine, 1 John 4 crystallizes what human beings can know of God: "If nothing else were said in praise of love in all the pages of this epistle, nothing else whatever in all other pages of scripture, and this were the only thing we heard from the voice of God's Spirit — 'For God is love' — we should ask for nothing more" (*On John's First Epistle* 7.4). "Eternal Truth, true Love, beloved Eternity — all this, my God, you are": so confesses Augustine (*Confessions* 7.10). Likewise, "the plenitude and end of the law and of all the sacred scriptures is the love of a Being who is to be enjoyed and of a Being who can share that enjoyment with us" (*Teaching Christianity* 1.35.39). With God, as with Scripture, the touchstone is *caritas,* a love that *heals.* This insight provides a key to his characterization of Christ: Jesus is preeminently the physician, who heals those incapable of healing themselves (Matt. 9:12; Mark 2:17a; Luke 5:31).

Consider the manner of Christ's own love . . . : "Father," he says, "forgive them, for they know not what they do" [Luke 23:34]. The will for their pardoning was a will for their transformation: in willing that they should be transformed, he deigned to make brothers out of enemies; and so in very truth, he did. . . . Think of the physician's love for the sick: he does not love them *as* sick people. If he did, he would want them always to be sick. He loves the sick, not so that they may remain sick people, but so that they may become healthy instead of sick. And how much he may have to suffer from them in their delirium — abuse, not seldom blows! . . . The physician takes away the thing that shows hostility to him, in order that the patient may live to give him thanks. So it is with you. (*On John's First Epistle* 8.10-11)

If in our exegesis for preaching we took Augustine seriously, we would realize that, through Scripture as through the incarnation — "The Lord Jesus Christ has come in the flesh for no reason other . . . than to vivify, save, liberate, redeem, and illuminate those who formerly were in death, weakness, slavery, prison, and under the shadow of sins" (*On Merits and Remission of Sins* 1.26.39) — *God's sole intention is to restore all human beings to their proper dignity, to that perfection of love indigenous to their creation in God's own image.* In an age like ours, tempted by a Nietzschean "hermeneutics of suspicion" whose goal is the subversion of biblical texts assumed to be potentially, pervasively "dangerous to your health and survival" (Elisabeth Schüssler Fiorenza, "The Will to Choose or to Reject: Continuing Our Critical Work," in *Feminist Interpretation of the Bible,* ed. Letty M. Russell [Philadelphia: Westminster, 1985], pp. 125-36, here 130 [italicized in the original]), Augustine may offer us the most cogent, powerful justification for our adoption of a "hermeneutics of trust" (Richard B. Hays, "Salvation by Trust? Reading the Bible Faithfully," *Christian Century* [February 26, 1997]: 218-23). While Schüssler Fiorenza acknowledges that "women in all walks of life testify to a different, inspiring, challenging, and liberating experience with the Bible" (p. 130), her interpretive model "locates revelation not in biblical texts but in the experience of women struggling for liberation from patriarchy" (p. 136). It is no authorization of oppressive structures, patriarchal or otherwise, to observe that such a norm is, formally, narrowly experiential rather than expansively scriptural and, materially, gynocentric rather than theocentric. In my view Hays correctly advocates a critical approach to the Bible that welcomes the liberationist refusal to accept everything in the text at face value while rejecting the liberationist preoccupation with ideological exposé whose primary norm — a particular experience of oppression — is unduly credulous. However, Hays's alternative — "that we take our cue from the Reformation and return to scripture itself" (p. 219) — does not go far enough in answering the liberationist challenge. Unless something like Augustine's attitude toward Scripture is claimed — that Scripture is intended by a loving God to heal us, not to make us sicker — then neither Schüssler Fiorenza nor Hays nor anyone else would have good reason to entrust oneself to the Bible. Indeed, if his appraisal is accepted, we have a reason par excellence to entrust ourselves to the God who meets us on Scripture's pages, a reason articulated by Augustine in the language of maternal nurturance: "[I]t is to you [my God] that I sigh by night and day. . . . I realized that I was far away from you. It was as though I were in a land where all is different from your own and I heard your voice calling from on high, saying, 'I am the food of full-grown adults. Grow and you shall feed on me. But you shall not change me into your own substance, as you do with the food of your body. Instead you shall be changed into me'" (*Confessions* 7.10, from *Saint Augustine: Confessions*, trans. R. S. Pine-Coffin [London: Penguin Books, 1961], p. 147, with modifications).

Transformation, Not Information

As a serious partner in our conversation between exegesis and preaching, Augustine reminds us of *God's power to transform us, through Scripture, as interpreters of love in deed and in truth*. We begin to comprehend that the discovery of "authorial intention" in Scripture is practically impossible unless our own "lectorial intention" is in proper alignment with the grace and love of God revealed by Scripture. "Open your heart's ear!" cries Augustine to his church (*On John's First Epistle* 6.12). One who approaches the text from a posture of hostility or fear will be inevitably deaf to Scripture's resonance, and blind in guiding others into Scripture's deepest mysteries — no matter how superficially intriguing, clever, or persuasive that reader's interpretations may be. For this reason "purity in heart" — a soul continuously aspiring in love for God, that *caritas* which is the only basis for proper love of oneself (*On the Morals of the Catholic Church* 1.26.48) — is for Augustine a *sine qua non* for the biblical interpreter. Bluntly put, there is more penetrating scriptural exegesis in the steady recitation of the Psalms by an unschooled grandmother to children of wandering minds and runny noses than in a thousand sermons delivered by a preacher whose sights are set no higher than the tallest steeple. The one nurtures *caritas;* the other engorges pride.

If we took as seriously as did Augustine Scripture's transformative power, what might this mean for the ways in which we view ourselves, our neighbors, and our benevolent projects? First, we would see ourselves as Christ sees us: "Like trees from the wood, we have been looked upon by the

Carpenter, and his thought turns to the building he will make of us, not to the timber that we were" (*On John's First Epistle* 8.10). Second, we would comprehend the inseparable entwinement of our love for God and our love for neighbor. In a given moment one of these two may receive greater emphasis, but each necessarily implies the other (9.10). From this it follows that there's no material distinction between what we sometimes contrast as "theology" and "praxis," or, as Augustine prefers, the contemplative life and the active life. Love for the neighbor is actually a form of contemplation in the midst of action. As far as I am aware, Augustine nowhere suggests that love for the neighbor is exclusively coterminous with the active life, or that love for God is a province exclusively defined as the contemplative life. Any detachment of spirituality from social witness can only corrupt them both. Jesus is honored by *both* Mary at his feet *and* Martha in her kitchen (*Sermons on Luke* 10:38-42 and *On Philippians* 3:3-16).

Guided by Augustine in the interpretation of Scripture for preaching, we would recognize humility as the proper sense of self for those claimed by the Messiah who gave himself up for our healing. "God has humbled himself — and still man is proud!" (*Sermon on 1 Corinthians* 12:31–13:13). Let us be clear that Augustine never confused humility with self-contempt, as have too many Christians after him. Created in the image of God with a capacity for elevation to the God who desires us, human beings possess extraordinary dignity in Augustinian thought (*The Trinity* 14.4.6; 14.8.11; 14.14.18; 14.16.22; 15.8.4; *City of God* 12.1.3). This Augustine dared to believe amidst a civilization collapsing around him, a blood-drenched society in which "a real man" or "a real woman" would demand a vendetta when injured (*On John's First Epistle* 7.3). Yet Augustine reminded his congregation of the gospel's utterly countercultural strategy, predicated not on "nature red in tooth and claw" (Tennyson, *In Memoriam* 55.4) but on God's subversive love, which enkindles that God-given nobility within ourselves from which we have gotten so far out of touch. To understand Scripture is to *stand under* its paradoxical yet invincible convictions that humanity's future lies not in revenge but in reconciliation; that only under Christ's discipline can his disciples know healthy freedom; that the needy whom we benefit are every bit as much our benefactors, through whom God re-forms us in Christ.

Where We Meet Molds Where We Live

Finally, if we apprenticed ourselves to Augustine, we would learn afresh that *Scripture's native habitat is the church catholic,* which is neither interchangeable with nor reducible to any party, sect, or denomination — much less some wing of the academy that feeds parasitically on religious organizations. A child of monastic spirituality, Augustine could appreciate more easily than we that Scripture is as much *a network of formative understanding* as of sheer information. Traditionally, the church has not simply "applied" hermeneutics to the Bible, as a diner slathers mustard on pumpernickel. By confessing the Bible to be Scripture ("inspired") and canon ("regulative") for that family of God into which they have been baptized, Christians have found *in* Scripture their hermeneutic (their framework for understanding) and in the Holy Spirit their epistemic instrument (the means by which they are able to understand). Across history, however, Scripture has not been the church's solitary canon, as William J. Abraham has astutely demonstrated (*Canon and Criterion in Christian Theology: From the Fathers to Feminism* [Oxford: Clarendon, 1998]). In most congregations Scripture continues to be read within the authoritative context of the church's prayers, liturgies, creeds, disciplines, and practices. Such was certainly the case for Augustine, who loved Christ's church as "the mother of us all" (*Confessions* 1.11) and who came to accept that it is, indeed, the walls of the church that make the Christian (*Confessions* 8.2; *On the Usefulness of Belief* 14.31).

Investigating Scripture's role in early Christian monasticism, Douglas Burton-Christie has suggested that the desert mothers and fathers "saw the sacred texts as projecting worlds of possible meaning that they were called upon to enter" (*The Word in the Desert: Scripture and the Quest for Holiness in Early Christian Monasticism* [New York and Oxford: Oxford University Press, 1993], p. 299). With differences of emphasis yet equal cogency, David Dawson and Frances Young have argued that patristic typologists and allegorists did not so much assimilate Scripture to their ambient culture as they profoundly Christianized its dominant worldview (David Dawson, *Allegorical Readers and Cultural Revision in Ancient Alexandria* [Berkeley: University of California Press, 1992]; Frances M. Young, *Biblical Exegesis and the Formation of Christian Culture* [Cambridge: Cambridge University Press, 1997]). Say what we may about the follies of monasticism, and the record goes unchanged: by their preaching the monks educated God's children to entrust themselves to those radically new possibilities of sacred imagination and holy conduct that God, true Love and beloved Eternity, still offers through Scripture. By nurturing their communities with the preached word, embraced by the church's prayers and praise, they kept Christian faith alive. Will our children's grandchildren be able to say the same of us?

IV. Serving the Food of Full-Grown Adults

Again we undertake a biblical exegesis for Sunday's sermon. Don't just do something. Stand there. Take your place beside Saint Augustine and shiver: "Wondrous is the profundity of your utterances. We see their surface before us, enticing us as children. But wondrous is their profundity — my God, wondrous their profundity! To look into them is to experience a shudder, the shudder of awe and the trembling of love" (*Confessions* 12.14.17, translated by Thomas Finan in Finan, "St. Augustine on the 'Mira Profunditas' of Scripture: Texts and Contexts," in *Scriptural Interpretation in the Fathers: Letter and Spirit,* ed. Thomas Finan and Vincent Twomey [Dublin: Four Courts, 1995], pp. 163-99, quotation on 173).

> So shall my word be that goes out of my mouth —
>> It shall not return to me barren,
> Without having done the thing that I pleased,
>> And accomplishing the purpose for which I sent it.   (Isa. 55:11)

The Word of the Lord is not rhetoric pragmatically invoked for a church's consolation and consolidation. Nor is it an arrogant harangue of this world's ignorance, lovelessness, and abuse of power. The Word released in the preached word, the Word conveyed through the sacrament, really changes us, our listeners, and our world — sometimes patently, often secretly, but always actually, blessedly, stunningly. Revealed by our Lord Jesus Christ is the God of healing eloquence, the very Word made flesh, whose sweetness is creating within us a new character: one nurtured by the Spirit, stamped with faith and hope and *caritas.*

The nourishment for which we are most famished lies, not in ourselves, but in the Scripture that nurtures. Directing our most careful study is that conviction which keeps every preacher honest, as Saint Augustine candidly admitted to his church and we rightly confess to ours: "What I serve you isn't mine. What you eat, I eat. What you live on, I live on. We have in heaven a common pantry. That, you see, is where the Word of God comes from" (*Sermon on Mark* 8:1-9, translation adapted from *Sermons [94A-147A] on the New Testament,* p. 24).

Contributors

William J. Abraham
Perkins School of Theology
Dallas, Texas

Elizabeth Achtemeier
Union Theological Seminary
Richmond, Virginia

Ronald J. Allen
Christian Theological Seminary
Indianapolis, Indiana

Dale C. Allison
Pittsburgh Theological Seminary
Pittsburgh, Pennsylvania

Gary A. Anderson
Harvard Divinity School
Cambridge, Massachusetts

Martyn D. Atkins
Cliff College
North Sheffield, England

Raymond Bailey, Pastor
Seventh and James Baptist Church
Waco, Texas

Andrew Bandstra
Calvin Theological Seminary
Grand Rapids, Michigan

Andrew H. Bartelt
Concordia Seminary
St. Louis, Missouri

Charles L. Bartow
Princeton Theological Seminary
Princeton, New Jersey

Richard Bauckham
University of St. Andrews
St. Andrews, Scotland

C. Clifton Black
Princeton Theological Seminary
Princeton, New Jersey

Robert L. Brawley
McCormick Theological Seminary
Chicago, Illinois

Annette G. Brownlee
Ascension Episcopal Church
Pueblo, Colorado

615

CONTRIBUTORS

John P. Burgess
Pittsburgh Theological Seminary
Pittsburgh, Pennsylvania

Richard A. Burridge, Dean
King's College
London, England

Charles L. Campbell
Columbia Theological Seminary
Decatur, Georgia

Lewis R. Donelson
Austin Presbyterian Theological Seminary
Austin, Texas

Patricia Dutcher-Walls
Knox College
Toronto, Ontario

Craig A. Evans
Trinity Western University
Langley, British Columbia

Gabriel Fackre
Andover Newton Theological School
Boston, Massachusetts

Lawrence W. Farris, Pastor
Presbyterian Church (USA)
Three Rivers, Michigan

Stephen Farris
Knox College
Toronto, Ontario

Robert A. J. Gagnon
Pittsburgh Theological Seminary
Pittsburgh, Pennsylvania

Thomas W. Gillespie, President
Princeton Theological Seminary
Princeton, New Jersey

John Goldingay
Fuller Theological Seminary
Pasadena, California

Colin J. D. Greene
British and Foreign Bible Society
Swindon, England

Sidney Greidanus
Calvin Theological Seminary
Grand Rapids, Michigan

Colin E. Gunton
King's College
London, England

Sarah Henrich
Luther Seminary
St. Paul, Minnesota

Scott Hoezee, Pastor
Calvin Christian Reformed Church
Grand Rapids, Michigan

John C. Holbert
Perkins School of Theology
Dallas, Texas

David E. Holwerda
Calvin Theological Seminary
Grand Rapids, Michigan

Leslie J. Hoppe
Catholic Theological Union
Chicago, Illinois

Arland J. Hultgren
Luther Seminary
St. Paul, Minnesota

George Hunsinger
Princeton Theological Seminary
Princeton, New Jersey

Robert W. Jenson
Center of Theological Inquiry
Princeton, New Jersey

Robert Jewett
Garrett-Evangelical Theological Seminary
Evanston, Illinois

Karen Jobes
Westmont College
Santa Barbara, California

Scott Black Johnston
Austin Presbyterian Theological Seminary
Austin, Texas

Donald Juel
Princeton Theological Seminary
Princeton, New Jersey

James F. Kay
Princeton Theological Seminary
Princeton, New Jersey

Craig S. Keener
Eastern Seminary
St. David's, Pennsylvania

Leonard R. Klein, Pastor
Christ Lutheran Church
York, Pennsylvania

Joel E. Kok, Pastor
Trinity Christian Reformed Church
Broomall, Pennsylvania

James Limburg
Luther Seminary
St. Paul, Minnesota

Tremper Longman III
Westmont College
Santa Barbara, California

F. Dean Lueking, Pastor
Grace Lutheran Church
River Forest, Illinois

Lois Malcolm
Luther Seminary
St. Paul, Minnesota

Martin E. Marty
The Fairfax M. Cone Distinguished
  Service Professor
The University of Chicago
Chicago, Illinois

Peter W. Marty, Pastor
St. Paul Lutheran Church
Davenport, Iowa

J. Clinton McCann, Jr.
Eden Theological Seminary
St. Louis, Missouri

Douglas Moo
Wheaton Graduate School
Wheaton, Illinois

Thorsten Moritz
Cheltenham and Gloucester College
  of Higher Education
Cheltenham, England

Roland E. Murphy, O. Carm.
George Washington University
Washington, D.C.

Hughes Oliphant Old
Research Theologian
Trenton, New Jersey

Dennis T. Olson
Princeton Theological Seminary
Princeton, New Jersey

Earl F. Palmer, Pastor
University Presbyterian Church
Seattle, Washington

Steven D. Paulson
Luther Seminary
St. Paul, Minnesota

Mary Margaret Pazdan, O.P.
Aquinas Institute of Theology
St. Louis, Missouri

CONTRIBUTORS

Christine E. Pilkington
Christ Church University College
Canterbury, England

Daniel J. Price, Pastor
First Presbyterian Church
Eureka, California

Paul R. Raabe
Concordia Seminary
St. Louis, Missouri

Ephraim Radner, Rector
Ascension Episcopal Church
Pueblo, Colorado

Stephen W. Ramp, Pastor
First Trinity Presbyterian Church
Laurel, Mississippi

Barbara E. Reid
Catholic Theological Union
Chicago, Illinois

Stephen Breck Reid
Austin Presbyterian Theological Seminary
Austin, Texas

André Resner, Jr., Pastor
Lamington Presbyterian Church
Bedminster, New Jersey

Michael Rogness
Luther Seminary
St. Paul, Minnesota

John M. Rottman
Emmanuel College
Toronto, Ontario

The Reverend Fleming Rutledge
Priest of the Episcopal Church
Diocese of New York

Timothy E. Saleska
Concordia Seminary
St. Louis, Missouri

Marguerite Shuster
Fuller Theological Seminary
Pasadena, California

Graydon F. Snyder
Chicago Theological Seminary
Chicago, Illinois

Frank Anthony Spina
Seattle Pacific University
Seattle, Washington

Brent A. Strawn
Candler School of Theology
Atlanta, Georgia

Roger E. Van Harn, Pastor
Christian Reformed Church
Grand Rapids, Michigan

Robert W. Wall
Seattle Pacific University
Seattle, Washington

William H. Willimon, Dean of the Chapel
Duke University
Durham, North Carolina

Paul Scott Wilson
Emmanuel College
Toronto, Ontario

Stephen I. Wright, Director
College of Preachers
London, England

Index of Authors

619

Index of Readings for Years A, B, and C

YEAR A

First Sunday of Advent
Isaiah 2:1-5 I:295
(Psalm 122)
Romans 13:11-14 II:128
Matthew 24:36-44 III:140

Second Sunday of Advent
Isaiah 11:1-10 I:320
(Psalm 72:1-7, 18-19)
Romans 15:4-13 II:137
Matthew 3:1-12 III:12

Third Sunday of Advent
Isaiah 35:1-10 I:324
(Psalm 146:5-10 or Luke 1:47-55)
James 5:7-10 II:535
Matthew 11:2-11 III:64

Fourth Sunday of Advent
Isaiah 7:10-16 I:310
(Psalm 80:1-7, 17-19)
Romans 1:1-7 II:10
Matthew 1:18-25 III:1

Nativity of the Lord (Christmas Day)
Isaiah 9:2-7 I:316
(Psalm 96)
Titus 2:11-14 III:456
Luke 2:1-14 (15-20) III:294

OR

Isaiah 62:6-12 I:388
(Psalm 97)
Titus 3:4-7 II:460
Luke 2:(1-7), 8-20 III:297

OR

Isaiah 52:7-10 I:360
(Psalm 98)
Hebrews 1:1-4, (5-12) II:468
John 1:1-14 III:476

First Sunday after Christmas Day
Isaiah 63:7-9 I:392
(Psalm 148)
Hebrews 2:10-18 II:475
Matthew 2:13-23 III:8

YEAR B

YEAR C